A Comprehensive Guide

for
Integrated
Treatment

of People with
Co-Occurring Disorders

A Comprehensive Guide

for

Integrated Treatment

of People with
Co-Occurring Disorders

Edited by
Diane Doyle Pita
LeRoy Spaniol

Center for Psychiatric Rehabilitation
Sargent College of Health and Rehabilitation Sciences
Boston University

Published by:

Center for Psychiatric Rehabilitation
Sargent College of Health and Rehabilitation Sciences
Boston University
940 Commonwealth Avenue West
Boston, MA 02215
http://www.bu.edu/cpr/

The Center for Psychiatric Rehabilitation is partially funded by the National Institute on Disability and Rehabilitation Research and the Center for Mental Health Services, Substance Abuse and Mental Health Services Administration.

Printed in the United States of America

Cover and text design by Linda Getgen

Library of Congress Control Number: 2002108128
ISBN 1-878512-12-9

To Max Schneier (1916–2002)
"He made a difference"

The publication of this book was supported by The Elizabeth Whitney Post Fund, Sargent College of Health and Rehabilitation Sciences, Boston University.

All proceeds from the sale of this book are used to further the work of the Center for Psychiatric Rehabilitation. No royalties are paid to the editors or authors.

Chapter Three: **Treatment**

Chapter Four: Cognitive-Behavioral Approaches

Chapter Eight: Legal System Involvement

Foreword

In the mid 1970s I was asked by Fordham University to speak to a group of social work students. At that time I was President of the Federation of Parents Organizations for the New York State Mental Institutions. The textbook used at that time at Fordham University had nothing in it about the holistic special issues surrounding people with dual diagnosis of mental illnesses and substance abuse, or as it has come to be called, co-occurring disorders. The times are changing, and how fortunate we now are to have this textbook. It is must reading for anyone studying or working in the fields of severe mental illnesses or substance abuse.

I have been involved in the field of severe mental illnesses and substance abuse in a variety of capacities, and rarely have I seen a book of this importance. Approximately 25 years ago I founded three major psychosocial rehabilitation programs. I have served on the SAMHSA (Substance Abuse and Mental Health Services Administration) National Advisory Council for two terms, during which time I chaired the Subcommittee on Services Integration. In that capacity I convened a panel of more than 100 experts in the field of co-occurring disorders; the recommendations of that distinguished group included strong support for the concept of integrated treatment. Based on research and accumulated knowledge in the field, these experts concluded that both disorders should be treated simultaneously; in one setting, using cross-trained staff that would provide medical or service treatment by a single clinician or teams of clinicians, supervised by a psychiatrist. Cost effective integrated services with integrated treatment was bringing about the clinical, functional, and quality of life outcomes desired by all people, including people with co-occurring disorders. *A Comprehensive Guide for Integrated Treatment of People with Co-Occurring Disorders* is the critical resource for training professionals in the field.

Using the 2001 Census and recent studies as the basis for their estimates, experts have conservatively estimated that 14 to 16 million Americans experience a co-occurring disorder. People with co-occurring disorders are more apt to seek treatment than those individuals who have only one of these disorders. As a result, a clear majority of people in treatment for substance abuse problems also have a mental disorder; community-based mental health treatment settings often estimate the rate of co-occurrence at 70 to 80 percent. A book such as this that examines the range of issues in co-occurring disorders is obviously needed.

The field of such co-occurring disorders must also be understood in the political and legislative context. While the National Institute of Mental Health has understood and supported the importance of cost-effective, integrated treatment based on their research, Congress has not been able to enact legislation that would facilitate and encourage integrated treatment. Rather, current legislation authorizing SAMHSA, the federal agency charged with administering service programs for people with mental illnesses and people with addictive disorders, does not attempt to co-finance cost-effective integrated treatment programs. Such "blended funding" for the treatment of people with dual disorders is contrary to the existing administrative structure, in which funding for mental illnesses and substance abuse are the responsibility and under the supervision of SAMHSA's administrator, Charles B. Currie, D.S.W.

Let us be clear about what is preventing the use of SAMHSA funds for cost-effective, integrated treatment or services. It is not lack of knowledge, which this book clearly shows not to be true. Instead, it is professional rivalries and jealousies, and a desire to keep one's power base at the expense of the people who need holistic integrated services. As a result, professionals have not been sufficiently and properly cross-trained; for the most part, most of them prefer to do what most have learned, i.e., work only with persons with the one disorder for which they are trained.

In 1992 Congress mandated that the National Institutes of Health (NIH) and its three institutes for mental health, alcoholism, and drug abuse conduct services research, with the results to be turned over to SAMHSA for national dissemination. There can be no question that Congress's intent was for SAMHSA to formulate service policies for mental health, alcoholism, and drug abuse, as well as co-occurring disorders that were based on the services research of the three institutes, i. e., NIMH, NIDA and NIAAA. In correspondence with me, NIH has stated that, based on available research, an integrated treatment model is the best approach in treating co-occurring disorders. *A Comprehensive Guide for Integrated Treatment of People with Co-Occurring Disorders* impressively organizes this material for students, professional, advocates, and administrators. These individuals have to familiarize themselves with this up-to-date material and educate others about the facts of co-occurring disorders. It is extremely difficult for me to envision how Congress can continue with the dual status quo of parallel and sequential treatment, which has not been proven through research. In fact, research supported by the federal government shows that, in most cases, parallel and sequential treatment of both disorders has failed. The NIH and the officials of two of its Institutes have reported that existing dual diagnosis treatment has failed. Research personnel from both of these Institutes have found that the treatment of co-occurring disorders does not meet acceptable standards for treating the medical as well as the mental disorders.

Those who fail to act on this knowledge will have to bear on their collective consciences the fact that they extended the aforementioned status quo, thus preventing over 16 million Americans with co-occurring disorders from receiving holistic medical treatment and services that would help them recover.

Let us not succumb to the pressures of some of the alcohol and substance abuse national organizations. Let us persevere, armed with the knowledge that will change our existing, out-of-date efforts. The researchers and scholars in this book have written eloquently about the medical and service issues in the co-occurring disorders field. Now is the time to get this holistic information into the mainstream of academia, practice, administration, and legislation. Let us make wise use of the knowledge that is so well presented in *A Comprehensive Guide for Integrated Treatment of People with Co-Occurring Disorders.*

MAX SCHNEIER, J.D.

Preface

The concept of dual disorders has been around for over 20 years and is currently recognized as one of the most significant problems facing mental health systems. About 30 percent of people with a substance use disorder (SUD) also have a mental health disorder, and about 50 percent of people with severe mental illnesses (SMI) have a substance use disorder. Clearly there is a need for an effective response to this problem. There is less of a consensus on what is the most effective and efficient way to provide the person with a dual disorder with dual treatment. In many states, treatment programs are combining mental health and substance abuse interventions in what are called integrated treatment programs. Research on these integrated treatments is very promising.

Kenneth Minkoff, M.D., often cited as the nation's leading expert on dual disorders, has developed an integrated treatment model, the Comprehensive, Continuous, Integrated Systems of Care (CCISC). In helping states to implement this model, Minkoff argues that integrated treatment doesn't require all treatment dollars to be merged into one funding stream, however, it does necessitate an integrated approach to system planning. Programs do not have to change dramatically in order for them to serve people with dual disorders. Clinicians trained in either mental health or substance abuse treatment don't have to become experts in both specialties in order to serve the person with a dual disorder. They do need to acquire a basic level of competency in the field in which they were not originally trained.

Substance abuse is common and the consequences severe. Everyone touched by the problem—from program administrators and clinicians in mental health, substance abuse, and rehabilitation programs to those who struggle with recovery from dual disorders and their family members—need to be educated in the latest developments. The purpose of this book is to provide that information in a manageable format. This book was developed during an experience of the authors as coteachers of a course on dual disorders—with Dr. Doyle Pita approaching dual disorders primarily as a substance dependence expert and Dr. Spaniol as an expert in severe mental illnesses. The intended use of this book is as a text in an academic course or for in-service training, with the instructors or trainers offering context through their own experience working in the field. The articles reprinted here were selected for inclusion from a broad review of articles. Articles dealing with the most salient concepts and critical issues were selected.

The articles are grouped into eight chapters (parameters and course of disorders, assessment, treatment, cognitive-behavioral approaches, clinical issues, role recovery, family and self-help support, and legal system involvement). The parameters and course of disorders chapter includes five articles. The first four define and describe the course of dual disorders. Setting forth the parameters of dual disorders is essential. The literature at times defines a dual disorder as including only a severe mental illness, and at other times, as any mental illness. Including all mental illnesses increases the difficulty of providing valid prevalence estimates, assessment tools, and effective treatment plans because so many more variables are introduced. This book defines dual disorders as a co-occurring severe mental illness (SMI) and a substance use disorder (SUD)—not all mental illnesses and not all substance uses. Understanding the variable course of dual disorders is essential given the patterns of relapse and recovery throughout the lifetime of an individual. A person abstinent at intake may have relapsed at the second interview—the sobriety status impacts all aspect of functioning. An additional aspect of dual disorders introduced in this section is the relationship between substance use and psychosis. Our ability to determine how the two disorders are related affects treatment. For instance, if a psychosis preceded substance dependence then the person may need medication for the psychosis. However, the psychosis may, in fact, be a result of substance dependence. In the latter case, the person does not necessarily need medication. The fifth article (Malloy) is a personal account of the impact of a dual disorder on a family, with particular focus on the difficulty of access to effective treatment and, yet, despite all the chaos and barriers, the hope of recovery.

Chapter 2 includes three articles on assessment. Effective treatment is dependent upon valid and reliable assessment. Despite the high base rates, a substance use disorder is often undetected. Two articles (Carey & Correia; Rosenberg et al.) present the many factors that contribute to the problem of a valid and reliable assessment, along with possible solutions. Christie Cline, M.D, as medical director of the New

Mexico Department of Health's Behavioral Services Division, discovered that by introducing a more valid assessment tool (in this case, part of Minkoff's CCISC model) they were able to increase identification of people with dual disorders from 8 to 20 percent. The third article (Barry et al.) presents an assessment tool developed for detection of a substance use disorder in people with a severe mental illness.

The treatment chapter contains ten articles outlining effective treatment strategies that clinicians can utilize in treating people with dual disorders. The consensus is that individuals with dual disorders require interventions that simultaneously address both mental health and substance use disorders, i. e., integrated treatment. The first article (Minkoff) reviews a four-step intervention strategy for engagement of people in the treatment and recovery process. The second article (Drake & Mueser) provides an overview of research on the epidemiology, adverse consequences, and phenomenology of dual diagnosis, followed by a more extensive review of approaches to services, assessment, and treatment. The third article (Mueser et al.) provides a brief summary of problems related to traditional treatment approaches for people with dual disorders. Integrated dual-disorders treatment is described including common components of these programs, e.g., assertive outreach, comprehensiveness, long-term perspective, shared decision-making, stage-wise treatment, and pharmacotherapy. The authors also discuss the stages of treatment. The fourth article (Bellack & DiClemente) discusses assumptions about treatment of substance abuse and reviews the features of a transtheoretical model of change based on the view that behavior change is a longitudinal process consisting of several stages. The fifth article (Mueser & Noordsy) describes what is considered a core component of integrated treatment program, i.e., group-based interventions. The sixth article (Weiss, et al.) describes a 20-session relapse prevention group therapy approach for people with coexisting bipolar disorder and substance use disorder. The treatment uses an integrated approach, discussing topics relevant to both disorders and highlighting common aspects of recovery from, and relapse to, each disorder. The seventh article (Mueser et al.) assesses the lifetime prevalence of traumatic events and current posttraumatic stress disorder in patients with severe mental illnesses. Their findings suggest that PTSD is a common comorbid disorder in people with severe mental illnesses and that it is frequently overlooked in mental health settings. The eighth article

(Moggi et al.) study examines a model of treatment for patients with substance use disorders and concomitant psychiatric disorders. The model describes five interrelated sets of variables (social background, intake functioning, dual diagnosis treatment orientation, patients' change on proximal outcomes, and aftercare participation) that are hypothesized to affect people with dual diagnoses with 1-year of post-treatment outcomes. The ninth article (Humphreys & Weisner) evaluates the use of exclusion criteria in alcohol treatment outcome research and the effect of use of exclusion criteria on the comparability of research subjects with real-world individuals seeking alcohol treatment. The final article (Fleshner) is a first person account of the "terror and hell" experienced by a person with schizophrenia and depression.

Chapter 4 is comprised of three articles examining specific treatment components and strategies within the cognitive-behavioral arena. Treatment and recovery for alcohol and drug addiction usually includes both addiction treatment and participation in Alcoholics Anonymous (AA). This first article (Steigerwald & Stone) examines the 12-Step process from the perspective of cognitive restructuring. The second article (Finney et al.) evaluates substance abuse treatment process models and outcome during 12-Step and cognitive-behavioral treatment. The final article (Triffleman et al.) presents an integrated cognitive-behavioral approach to co-occurring substance dependence and PTSD.

Clinical issues are addressed in chapter 5. The first article (Minkoff) discusses common dilemmas faced by clinicians and then describes seven principles that can guide treatment interventions. Consistently recognized within the field of dual disorders is the need for a collaborative relationship between client and therapist. The second article (Fisher & Goldsmith) presents guiding principles of the relationship between staff members and people with mental illnesses. The third article (Connors et al.) explores factors predicting therapeutic alliance in alcoholism treatment. They found the strongest relationship between clients' motivational readiness to change and their ratings of the therapeutic alliance. A second issue crucial to recovery is medication. The fourth article (Laudet et al.) presents interview data from people with dual diagnoses in self-help groups concerning the challenges confronting them in their recovery. Their findings indicate that people struggle with emotional and socioeconomic issues, which bear significantly on their ability to handle adequately other aspects of their recovery. The last two articles (Wilkins; Fenton et al.) address factors impacting use of medication. The issue of medication is especially complex given that the person with a dual disorder is recovering from the abuse of drugs and, yet, needs to learn how to take prescribed medications responsibly.

Chapter 6 includes five articles on role recovery. To be sustained, recovery needs to include more than abstinence from alcohol and drugs and symptom management. Recovery involves obtaining meaningful roles. In order for clinicians to help people attain these life goals, clinicians need data clarifying the barriers to role attainment and retention, and these data come from outcome studies. And, yet, outcome studies can lack model fidelity, which leads to false conclusions regarding the efficacy of program components. For instance, assertive community treatment is the most widely tested model of community care for people with severe mental illnesses and, yet, only recently has program fidelity been an issue.

The first article (Anthony) describes the importance of recovery as a vision for mental health systems. He describes how recovery needs to become embedded at all levels of the system. The second article (McHugo et al.) points up the importance of program fidelity showing that faithful implementation of, and adherence to, the assertive community treatment model for people with dual disorders was associated with superior outcomes in the area of substance use. The third article (Osher & Dixon) discusses housing barriers and suggests housing, treatment, and support services to overcome these barriers. The fourth article (Anthony et al.) overviews the people served, outcomes, and types of interventions that characterize the field of psychiatric rehabilitation. It also discusses current and future research issues. The fifth article (Shern et al.) is a study that tested a psychiatric rehabilitation approach for organizing and delivering services to street-dwelling persons with severe mental illnesses. It found that with an appropriate service model, it is possible to engage people who are disaffiliated, expand their use of human services, and improve their housing conditions, quality of life, and mental health status.

Seven articles comprise the section on family and self-help support. Without the support of family and self-help, the likelihood of sustained recovery drops. As discussed in the first article (Clark), families are critically important sources of housing, financial support, and direct care. Substance abuse appears to play a primary role in families pulling back their support from people with dual disorders. Poor family support and substance abuse are both associated with homelessness. The second article (Dixon et al.) found that substance abuse is associated with low levels of satisfaction with family relationships among persons with severe mental illnesses. Family interventions need to meet the stated needs of people with mental illnesses and a comorbid substance use disorder and this might help to engage people with co-occurring disorders and their family members in treatment. The third article (Noordsy et al.) indicates that support also comes in the form of self-help groups such as AA and Double Trouble, developed specifically for those with dual disorders. However, clinicians often do not know how to determine if a client is benefiting from attendance at self-help meetings. The fourth article (Laudet, et al.) provides further evidence of the importance of support, finding that people with higher levels of support and greater participation in dual recovery reported less substance use and mental health. The fifth article (Vogel) describes a self-help approach for people with co-occurring disorders. The last article, a first person account, is written by the parents of a child who is diagnosed with schizophrenia and abusing substances. They recount the pain in dealing with their son's chronic relapses.

Chapter 8 contains four articles that focus on the legal aspects of co-occurring disorders. Legal system involvement is discussed through four articles. The first article (Swartz et al.) examines the combined impact of substance abuse and medication noncompliance on the risk of serious violence among people with severe mental illnesses. The combination of medication noncompliance and abusing alcohol or substances was significantly associated with serious violent acts in the community. Reduction of such risk requires carefully targeted community interventions, including integrated mental health and substance abuse treatment. In the second article (Clark et al.), people with co-occurring severe mental illnesses and substance use disorders were studied to understand how they are involved with the legal system and to identify factors associated with different kinds of legal system involvement. The third article (Goodman et al.) reviews the research literature on the prevalence, symptomatic and behavioral correlates, and treatment of abuse among women, particularly women with schizophrenia. Within each topic, the authors discuss relevant research findings, limitations of available studies, and key questions that remain unanswered. They also discuss mechanisms that may underlie the relationship between trauma and schizophrenia spectrum disorders. The authors conclude by outlining directions for future research in this area. The last article (Soyka) evaluated the literature to assess whether people with schizophrenia who use substances have an increased risk for violence and disturbed behaviour. They found that male gender, more severe psychopathology, a primary antisocial personality, repeated intoxications, and non-adherence with treatment are important confounding variables. Abusing substances has been shown to be a significant risk factor for violence and disturbed behavior.

The articles in the eight sections clearly show that there is significant support for an integrated approach to treatment. Integration can occur on many levels, from cross-training clinical staff to systemic integration. Clearly, reducing substance abuse in people with serious mental illnesses reduces negative consequences associated with such use such as from victimization to hospitalizations. It is not clear how widespread integration at any level is today. Anecdotal evidence presents itself to us on a weekly basis. Ten or fifteen years ago, people on psychiatric medications were told at AA meetings that they are "chewing their booze." Today, there is more acceptance of medication. Ten or fifteen years ago substance abuse program managers were reluctant to accept into treatment people with serious mental illnesses. Today, they are more likely to accept them into treatment. However, they do lack knowledge around best treatment practices once they are admitted. Case managers in substance abuse settings are more likely to accept people with dual diagnoses and refer them out for mental health treatment than in the past. Substance abuse counseling is provided in-house, and mental health counseling at a local outpatient setting. Even "old timers" are able to see that advice such as "go to a meeting," has its limitations. Treatment must be individualized.

Recently, Dr. Doyle Pita had the opportunity to treat a person who had relapsed many times, was referred by a recovery home, and who for the first time in his life agreed to take an anti-depressant. From an attitude of apathy, "I don't care if I drink," to a strong motivation for recovery miraculously occurred within one month. This person is now in sustained full remission from alcohol and drugs. On the mental health side, we have witnessed an increase in requests for trainings in substance abuse treatment, and we see more offerings of dual disorder trainings.

Progress in the field is slow, but it is happening. Hopefully, this book, through its compassionate and dedicated readers, will create further impetus for change.

DIANE DOYLE PITA, PH.D.
LEROY SPANIOL, PH.D.

Chapter One: **Parameters and Course of Disorders**

Definition and Prevalence of Severe and Persistent Mental Illness

Mirella Ruggeri, Morven Leese, Graham Thornicroft, Giulia Bisoffi &
Michele Tansella

This article originally appeared in the *British Journal of Psychiatry,* 177(August), 2000, 149–155, and is reprinted with permission.

Mirella Ruggeri, Ph.D., Dipartimento di Medicina e Sanità Pubblica, Sezione di Psichiatria, Università di Verona, Ospedale Policlinico, Verona, Italy; Morven Leese, Ph.D., Graham Thornicroft, Ph.D., Section of Community Psychiatry (PRiSM), Institute of Psychiatry, London; Giulia Bisoffi, Dr. Stat, & Michele Tansella, M.D., Dipartimento di Medicina e Sanità Pubblica, Sezione di Psichiatria, Università di Verona, Ospedale Policlinico, Verona, Italy.

Funding was provided by the University of Verona and the Bethlem and Maudsley NHS Trust.

There is little consistency in how severe mental illness (SMI) is defined in practice, and no operational definitions. The aim of this study was to test two operationalised definitions, based on the National Institute of Mental Health (1987) definition: the first uses three criteria (diagnosis of psychosis; duration of service contact ≥ 2 years; GAF score ≤ 50), the second only the last two. Annual prevalence rates of SMI in two European catchment areas for each criterion and the criteria combined were calculated. The first definition produced rates of 2.55 and 1.34/1000 in London and Verona, respectively; the second permitted an additional 0.98/1000 nonpsychotic disorders to be included in Verona. The three-dimensional definition selects a small group of patients with SMI who have psychotic disorders. The two-dimensional approach allows estimates of SMI prevalence rates that include all forms of mental disorder.

In recent years a consensus has emerged in many areas, including the UK, that mental health services should be especially targeted at those suffering from severe mental illness (SMI). Several reports on mental health services have indicated deficiencies in this respect (House of Commons Health Select Committee, 1994). In other countries, such as Italy, there is no clear guidance on targeting specific groups among those with mental illness; nevertheless there is an increasing awareness that those with SMI should be given higher priority. However, there is no internationally agreed definition of SMI. Three key issues emerge: how should SMI be defined; what is the prevalence of such morbidity; how can this information best be used for service planning and provision?

A widespread survey in England (Slade et al., 1996) found little consistency in how SMI is defined in practice. The most complete review of the subject is that of Schinnar et al. (1990), who compared 17 definitions of severe and persistent mental illness used in the USA between 1972 and 1987. They found wide inconsistencies in these definitions: when applied to 222 adult inpatients in Philadelphia, between 4% and 88% of patients qualified as having SMI, depending upon the definition selected. The authors concluded that the definition with the widest measure of consensus, and most representative of the middle range of prevalence, was that of the National Institute of Mental Health (NIMH) (1987). This definition categorized individuals as having SMI if they met three criteria: a diagnosis of non-organic psychosis or personality disorder; duration characterized as involving "prolonged illness and long-term treatment" and operationalised as a 2-year or longer history of mental illness or treatment; and disability, which was described as including at least three of the eight specified criteria (NIMH, 1987).

The present study is an extension of the work of Schinnar et al. (1990), and its aims are to calculate prevalence rates of SMI according to narrow (three-dimensional) and broad (two-dimensional) operationalised definitions of SMI, both derived from the NIMH (1987) definition, and to provide population-based prevalence rates of SMI, defined according to both definitions, in two catchment areas in Europe (South London and South Verona).

Method

The London data are drawn from the baseline assessment of a prospective controlled trial of community mental health services (CMHS) for people with psychotic disorders in an epidemiologically defined area of South London (the PRiSM study) that took place between 1991 and 1992 (Thornicroft et al., 1998). Verona data are drawn from an outcome study conducted in 1994 (the South Verona Outcome Project; Ruggeri et al., 1998a,b) of patients living in an epidemiologically defined area and attending the South Verona CMHS.

Operationalised Definitions of SMI

The narrow definition that we test in this paper (the "three-dimensional definition") is that a patient has severe mental illness when he or she has the following: a diagnosis of any non-organic psychosis; a duration of treatment of 2 years or more; dysfunction, as measured by the

Global Assessment of Functioning (GAF) scale (American Psychiatric Association, 1987). Specifically, the two levels of dysfunction defined by cut-off points of the GAF are tested: moderate or severe dysfunction (a GAF score of 70 or less, indicating mild symptoms or some difficulty in social, occupation or school functioning); or only severe dysfunction (a GAF score of 50 or less, indicating severe symptoms or severe difficulty in social, occupational or school functioning). The broad definition (the "two-dimensional definition") is based on the fulfillment of the latter two criteria only.

These definitions differ from the one operationalised by Schinnar et al. (1990) in the following respects: psychoses are included, but personality disorders are excluded; the criterion of duration has been simplified, with the exclusion of duration of illness and the inclusion of duration of treatment; a simple operationalisation of the disability criterion was made by using the concept of dysfunction as defined by the GAF.

The reasons for these changes are the following: the diagnosis of personality disorders has low interrater reliability (Zimmermann, 1994); the duration of treatment can be assessed much more precisely than duration of illness (Schinnar et al., 1990); insufficient information is given on how to operationalise the disability criterion in both the original NIMH (1987) definition and the further work of Schinnar et al. We chose the GAF, despite some limitation in its specificity in measuring disability (Roy-Byrne et al., 1996), because of its simplicity, reliability and widespread use as a proxy measure of disability (Jones et al., 1995).

Characteristics of the Catchment Areas

The Nunhead and Norwood sectors (geographical catchment areas) of South London are severely socially deprived areas (see Thornicroft et al., 1998 for more details). The South Verona area of northeast Italy is relatively affluent and predominantly middle class. In 1994 the population aged over 18 was 62,240. The South Verona CMHS is a public service established in 1978 within the newly organised Italian National Health Service, and is the main psychiatric service providing care to South Verona residents (see Tansella et al., 1998 for more details).

Patient Inclusion Criteria

Psychotic diagnoses. This study includes all people with functional psychosis aged over 18 who had an ICD-10 diagnosis of an affective or nonaffective functional psychotic disorder (codes F20–F22, F24, F25, F28–F31, F32.3, F33.3) (World Health Organization, 1992a). Patients with organic psychotic disorders were excluded from the study, as they do not usually use adult mental health services and are cared for by specialist geriatric services.

Non-psychotic diagnoses. This study includes all South Verona patients aged over 18 with an ICD-10 diagnosis of mental disorder other than functional psychosis.

Assessments

Diagnosis. In South London, as part of the PRiSM psychosis study, identification of cases of functional psychotic disorders for the index year (1991–1992) was carried out according to the procedure described in Thornicroft et al. (1998). Briefly, those who had a clinical diagnosis at any time in their lives of any psychotic disorder were identified. Diagnoses were made from case notes by researchers (under the supervision of a psychiatrist) using the Operational Criteria Checklist (McGuffin et al., 1991; OPCRIT, version 3.2) to produce ICD-10 diagnoses. About half were randomly re-assessed using Schedules for Clinical Assessment in Neuropsychiatry (SCAN; World Health Organization, 1992b) interviews conducted by trained psychiatrists. The reliability of this procedure has been demonstrated in another study (McGuffin et al., 1991). In the current study, regular interrater reliability checks were made for both procedures. Of the 566 cases originally identified in the first phase, 514 were considered as "prevalent" cases in these terms; of these, 511 met the age criterion for the comparison reported here.

In South Verona, diagnosis was established by using the local psychiatric case register (PCR) (Tansella et al., 1998). Diagnoses were made by senior professionals using ICD-10 criteria, and all were reviewed by the director of the PCR. The reliability of this diagnostic procedure is known to be satisfactory (Balestrieri et al., 1997; Systema et al., 1989).

Service utilisation. Information was collected from clinical case records in London and the PCR in Verona. Duration of service contact was operationalised as the time elapsed from the date of first contact with any psychiatric service until the start of the respective study period, and dichotomised as either less than 2 years, or 2 years or longer.

Global functioning. In South London, functioning according to the GAF was rated by trained research staff on the basis of information gathered from patients' case notes (using sources in mental health and primary health care services) and from social services records, while in Verona the GAF was completed by the patients' key professionals (psychiatrists or psychologists), who had received appropriate training. In both sites GAF assessments referred to the previous month. All assessors attended a 3-hour session that provided a description of the scale and instruction on its use. The good interrater reliability of the GAF when used under routine clinical conditions by members of a community mental health team has been demonstrated in previous studies (Jones et al., 1995). In this study, two interrater reliability exercises were conducted at the end of the training session; interrater reliability was always over 0.90 (intraclass correlation coefficient).

Statistical Methods

Data were analysed using SPSS version 7.0 (SPSS, 1996). Missing values, which were usually a result of sparse information in case notes, were assumed to be missing at random. Annual prevalence rates were then calculated for each combination of criteria for the two- and three-dimensional definitions, on the basis of the proportions of patients with valid data having the required characteristics, assuming independence of categories within each site.

All data for London relate to a 1-year period prevalence, whereas Verona used data for dysfunction from patients observed over 3 months; for this reason, the 3-month annual period prevalence rates for Verona were further adjusted by a factor equal to the total number of patients registered in the PCR in the index year divided by the total over 3 months. We computed 95% confidence intervals (CIs) for prevalence rates on the basis of the raw unadjusted frequencies, and then applied the appropriate factors.

Table I

Socio-demographic and service utilisation characteristics of patients with psychosis aged over 18 from Nunhead and Norwood (London) and South Verona

Characteristic	London (n = 511)[1]		South Verona (n = 212)[1]		p[2]
Age (years)					
Mean	42.2		47.5		
95% CI	40.8–43.6		45.5–49.6		<0.001
Median	39		46		
Gender					
Male	251	(49%)	98	(46%)	0.419
Female	260	(51%)	114	(54%)	
Ethnic group					
White	315	(63%)	212	(100%)	
Non-White	187	(37%)	0		<0.001
Missing data	9		0		
Living situation					
Alone	185	(40%)	43	(21%)	
With family	200	(43%)	153	(73%)	<0.001
Sheltered accommodation	51	(11%)	13	(6%)	
Other	25	(5%)	0		
Missing data	50		3		
Employment					
Employed	79	(19%)	62	(29%)	
Not employed	340	(81%)	149	(71%)	0.003
Missing data	98		1		
Duration of contacts					
<2 years	58	(12%)	30	(15%)	
≥2 years	430	(88%)	173	(85%)	0.299
Missing data	23		9		
In-patient admission in previous year					
None	329	(65%)	156	(74%)	
At least one	181	(35%)	56	(26%)	0.018
Missing data	1		0		
Out-patient attendances in previous year					
None	130	(27%)	46	(21.7%)	
At least one	356	(73%)	166	(78.3%)	0.158
Missing data	25		0		
Compulsory admission					
None	157	(37%)	163	(77%)	
At least one	265	(63%)	49	(23%)	<0.001
Missing data	89		0		

1. Number of patients identified in 1 year.
2. Chi-squared, Fisher's exact test or t-test

Results

Prevalence of Psychosis and Other Mental Illness

Table 1 shows the socio-demographic and service use characteristics of the London and Verona patients. Five hundred and eleven cases of psychosis were identified in a 1-year period in London and 212 in Verona, with annual prevalences per thousand inhabitants of 7.84 (95% CI 7.16–8.52) and 3.41 (95% CI 2.79–4.02), respectively. Among patients with psychosis in London and Verona, there were 67% and 74% with schizophrenia, 6% and 26% with affective disorder, and 27% and 1% with an ICD-10 diagnosis of other non-organic psychotic syndrome (F28) or unspecified non-organic psychosis (F29), respectively. The higher number of unspecified diagnoses in London was due to a greater proportion of case notes with incomplete clinical information. This problem did not exist in Verona because diagnoses were made for all patients as part of routine clinical practice.

In South Verona, 711 patients with a diagnosis of mental disorder other than psychosis were identified by the PCR in the index year, with an annual period prevalence per thousand inhabitants of 11.42 (95% CI 10.58–12.26). Fifteen percent of these patients had an ICD-10 diagnosis of personality disorder, 20% of neurotic somatoform disorder, and 39% of neurotic depression, while 17% had other diagnoses (including F10 alcoholism and F11–19, F55 drug misuse), and 8.5% had missing data.

Assessment of Duration and Dysfunction

All identified cases of psychosis in the index year in London underwent the social functioning assessment. Assessments of duration and dysfunction were missing in 23 and 108 cases, respectively, usually because of very brief case records. Possible bias due to the large proportion of missing values was investigated by comparing those with and without case-note GAF scores using the GAF from an interview approximately 1 year later (available from the main PRiSM study) for a randomly chosen subsample. Those with and without missing case-note GAF scores had very similar mean interview GAF scores (59.2 compared with 63.9, $P=0.12$).

In Verona only the patients of the catchment area attending the South Verona CMHS ($n=542$) underwent the social functioning assessment. In this group most missing data resulted from the study design, which is based on routine clinical assessments made by the key professionals and not by researchers. Global Assessment of Functioning assessments were missing in 187 patients: in 49 cases GAF assessments were missing because the patients, although in contact with other professionals such as nurses or social workers, had not been seen by a doctor or psychologist in the 3-month index period; in the remaining 138 cases assessments were missing because, owing to lack of time, the key professionals could not complete the GAF assessment after their visit. Patients with missing assessments had had significantly fewer contacts with the service in the previous year ($P<0.01$), but did not differ from the patients assessed for any other sociodemographic or service utilisation characteristic.

Criteria Based on Duration and Dysfunction

Table 2 shows the application of the operationalised criteria based on duration and dysfunction, both individually and combined, to all patients with psychotic and non-psychotic disorders identified in the index period in London and Verona. Despite the overall differences in prevalence, the data for psychosis show that the relative proportions of patients with SMI for each criterion of the operationalised definition were very similar between the two sites, although there is some weak evidence for a higher proportion of patients with severe dysfunction in Verona (44% v. 35%, $P=0.08$). Log-linear analysis confirmed this finding, but showed no evidence of association between duration and dysfunction at either site.

Among the patients with non-psychotic disorders, those with an ICD-10 diagnosis of personality disorder or alcohol and drug misuse had a significantly higher percentage of SMI than patients with neurotic disorders; specifically, a longer duration of treatment (over 70% with duration of over 2 years in patients with personality disorder and other diagnoses v. 60% in patients with a neurotic disorder) and more severe dysfunction (around 35% v. less than 10%) were found. Owing to the small number of cases in each category, the possible combination of criteria was not assessed for these separate diagnostic categories.

Table 2

Annual period prevalence rates of severe and persistent mental illness in Nunhead and Norwood (London) and South Verona using operationalised criteria applied to patients with and without psychotic disorders

Operationalised Criteria	London (65,150 inhabitants over 18)[1] With psychosis (n=511)[1]			South Verona (62,240 inhabitants over 18)[2] With psychosis (n=212)[2]			Without psychosis (n=711)[3]		
	Rate per 1000	95% CI	Estimated % of patients	Rate per 1000	95% CI	Estimated % of patients	Rate per 1000	95% CI	Estimated %
Dysfunction									
GAF ≤ 70	6.31	5.62–6.99	80%	2.85	2.29–3.42	84%	7.70	6.50–0.89	67%
GAF ≤ 50	2.76	2.31–3.22	35%	1.51	1.10–1.93	44%	1.60	1.05–2.14	14%
Duration ≥ 2 years	6.91	6.26–7.56	88%	3.01	2.53–3.49	88%	6.99	6.07–7.92	62%
Dysfunction/duration									
GAF ≤ 70, ≥ 2 years	5.67	4.95–6.35	72%	2.45	1.92–2.98	72%	4.32	3.48–5.16	38%
GAF ≤ 50, ≥ 2 years	2.55	2.11–3.00	32%	1.34	0.95–1.73	40%	0.98	0.58–1.39	9%

GAF:scores on the Global Assessment of Functioning scale.

1. PRiSM study, case identification over 1 year. Basis for estimation of annual rates: 403 valid cases for dysfunction, 488 for duration and 390 for both diagnosis and duration.

2. Registered (psychiatric case register) in 1 year: 177 registered in 3 months. Basis for estimation of 3-month rates: 117 valid cases for dysfunction, 171 for duration, 113 for both duration and dysfunction. Rates adjusted to 1 year.

3. Registered (psychiatric case register) in 1 year: 401 registered in 3 months. Basis for estimation of 3-month rates: 236 valid cases for dysfunction, 361 for duration, 228 for both duration and dysfunction. Rates adjusted to 1 year.

Table 3
Annual period prevalence rates of severe and persistent mental illness in South Verona using operationalised criteria applied to all patients

Operationalised Criteria			South Verona (62,240 inhabitants over 18) (n=933)[1]		
			Rate per 1000	95% CI	Estimated % of all cases
One-dimensional definitions					
Diagnosis of			3.41	2.79–4.02	23%
Psychosis	Dysfunction				
	GAF ≤ 70		10.54	9.22–11.86	70%
	GAF ≤ 50		3.11	2.43–3.79	21%
		Duration			
		≥ 2 years	10.00	8.96–11.04	67%
Two-dimensional definitions					
	Dysfunction				
Diagnosis of	GAF ≤ 70		2.85	2.29–3.42	19%
Psychosis	GAF ≤ 50		1.51	1.10–1.93	10%
Diagnosis of		Duration			
Psychosis		≥ 2 years	3.01	2.53–3.49	20%
	Dysfunction	Duration			
	GAF ≤ 70	≥ 2 years	6.77	5.78–7.77	45%
	GAF ≤ 50	≥ 2 years	2.33	1.77–2.89	16%
Three-dimensional definition					
	Dysfunction	Duration			
Diagnosis of	GAF ≤ 70	≥ 2 years	2.45	1.92–2.98	16%
Psychosis	GAF ≤ 50	≥ 2 years	1.34	0.95–1.73	9%

GAF: scores on the Global Assessment of Functioning scale.

1. 933 patients registered in 1 year: 578 in 3 months. Basis for estimation of 3-month rates: 353 valid cases for dysfunction, 532 for duration, 341 for both duration and dysfunction. Rates adjusted to 1 year.

Application of Combined Criteria

Table 3 shows the application of both two- and three-dimensional definitions in all patients with a diagnosis of mental disorder identified in the index period in the South Verona area. Prevalence rates of SMI vary widely depending on the criteria applied, with low discrimination by the separate criteria of moderate dysfunction and long duration (taken individually or combined) and higher discrimination by the criteria of diagnosis and severe dysfunction. Application of the two-dimensional definition criteria based on severe dysfunction and duration gives a total prevalence rate of SMI of 2.33 per thousand for all disorders; it is noteworthy that of these only 58% are cases of psychosis.

Discussion

This is the first epidemiologically based study in Europe to operationalise and apply the NIMH (1987) criteria for SMI. The advantages of the current study over previous work are that the definition used is fully operationalised for each criterion, and so the study can be easily replicated and prevalence rates in other settings calculated, and that the type of operationalisation proposed is based on easily obtainable data, and so can be of widespread use.

Prevalence of SMI Among Patients with Psychosis

The annual period prevalence of psychosis in South Verona (3.41 per thousand inhabitants) is similar to that found in previous studies in the rest of Italy (Balestrieri et al., 1992) and other European countries and the USA (Robins & Regier, 1991). The higher rate in South London (7.84 per thousand inhabitants) found in this study is in agreement with other findings for inner London (Johnson et al., 1997) and is consistent with a recent psychiatric morbidity survey which found annual period prevalence rates of between 2.0 and 9.0 per thousand inhabitants in the population throughout Britain (Meltzer et al., 1996). These higher rates are partly due to the higher proportion of ethnic minorities, who more frequently suffer from schizophrenia (McCreadie, 1982).

When the three-dimensional definition (functional psychosis, duration of treatment longer than 2 years, and a severe dysfunction lasting for at least 1 month) is applied, prevalence rates of SMI among patients with psychosis are higher in south London than in south Verona (2.55 v. 1.34 per thousand inhabitants). The difference in prevalence of SMI in the two areas matches in general terms the difference in prevalence of psychosis noted above. However, the relative proportion of SMI among those with psychosis is somewhat lower in London than in Verona (31% v. 40%).

The results show that in patients with psychosis, the more restrictive criterion for severity of illness is the high severity of dysfunction (a GAF score of 50 or less), since the majority of patients with psychosis had a long duration (88% in both areas) and at least a moderate (a GAF score of 70 or less) level of dysfunction (80% and 84% in London and Verona, respectively).

Prevalence of SMI Among Patients with Non-Psychotic Disorders

In South Verona the total prevalence of non-psychotic disorders treated by psychiatric services was 11.42 per thousand inhabitants. When the full set of two-dimensional definitions has to be fulfilled, the prevalence of SMI among patients with non-psychotic disorders is 0.98 per thousand inhabitants (9%). The criteria of duration and dysfunction both play an important role in the selection of patients.

Prevalence of SMI Among Patients with Any Mental Disorder Attending Adult Services

The total population-based annual prevalence of SMI patients in South Verona is 1.34 per thousand when we apply all criteria of the three-dimensional definition and 2.33 per thousand when all criteria of the two-dimensional definition are applied. The former definition is therefore more powerful in selecting a smaller subgroup of patients with SMI from among all patients with any mental disorder.

According to the two-dimensional definition, in Verona 40% of all patients with psychosis and 9% those without have SMI. When considering all patients with a diagnosis of mental disorder, the SMI group according to the two-dimensional definition is composed of 58% with psychosis and 42% with non-psychotic disorders. Is it legitimate not to consider such a large proportion of patients (people with non-psychotic disorders) when planning services dedicated to SMI?

Limitations of the Study

This study has a number of limitations. The annual total prevalence rates were accurately estimated, albeit with a possible slight underestimation in London, but there were some missing values for the definitions based on dysfunction. Although there was no evidence that this caused major problems, it would be preferable to minimize bias when using the operationalised criteria to assess prevalence, and this study suggests some improvements that could be made.

For interview data, one improvement would be to make a GAF assessment for a known proportion of all types of patients, including those who would not normally be seen frequently. Weighted methods of analysis can then be used to combine their results with those of routine attenders (see, for example, Dunn et al., 1999). With regard to case-note data, the London results suggest that case-note assessments are acceptable where patients are not seen in person, and that missing data do not lead to major bias. However, further research is needed to eliminate specific bias in GAF assessments based on case notes rather than interviews. Another limitation is that the reliability of GAF assessment, as well as that of the ICD-10 diagnostic coding, is based on previous work done by our group and other groups, but has not been assessed within this study.

A further possibility of bias (overestimation) in SMI, resulting from dysfunction being measured cross-sectionally, might have occurred. This was also the case for duration, since cross-sectional samples are more likely to sample long-duration than short-duration illnesses. However, the much higher degree of feasibility of a cross-sectional assessment compared with a longitudinal one suggests that this procedure is to be preferred despite its limitations.

This study did not consider the whole range of mental illnesses in both areas, since in London only cases of functional psychosis were included in the study. Moreover, the fact that in London some of the diagnoses were made from clinical records may have caused an increase in the number of unspecified cases of psychosis; it has been estimated that there was a 3% underestimation of prevalence as a result of cases having neither adequate case notes nor later interview.

In the group of patients with psychosis a refined diagnostic breakdown was not possible, hence the relative contribution of schizophrenia and affective psychosis in this group has not been explored. Diagnostic breakdown was also not possible in the group of patients with non-psychotic disorders in Verona, owing to the smaller number of cases in several categories. An exploratory analysis showed that patients with a diagnosis of personality disorder, alcoholism or drug misuse may suffer from SMI more frequently than the other diagnostic groups. This deserves further investigation.

Another limitation of this study is that two different methods of case identification were employed at the two sites—a population-based method in London and a case register method in Verona. Data in South London reflect the general population prevalence, while data in South Verona are representative of the treated prevalence in specialist services only (all hospitals, both public and private, as well as community psychiatric services). It is well known that treated cases are a selection of community cases, but we also know that severity of illness is the main selective factor in passing from having a mental disorder to searching for specialist treatment for that disorder. According to Olfson & Klerman (1992), "mental health care utilisation is a reasonable proxy for psychiatric distress and is therefore an acceptable criterion for validating the presence of psychiatric disorder." Moreover, in Italy the vast majority of patients with a diagnosis of psychosis are treated in public psychiatric services or in private hospitals (Balestrieri et al., 1994). All these institutions report to the South Verona PCR, so PCR estimates of prevalence of psychosis may be considered reasonably accurate; hence the comparison with London prevalence rates is appropriate. For people with nonpsychotic disorders, PCR prevalence rates are certainly an underestimation of the true prevalence; even so, we consider that the vast majority of the more severely ill people with non-psychotic disorders are included in the estimates.

Finally, some significant differences between the English and Italian samples were found for age, ethnicity, living situation and service utilisation. These differences derive both from the different sociocultural contexts and from the different models of psychiatric care applied in the two settings; however, they did not relate to the percentages of SMI in the two areas.

Implications of the Study

This study has several implications. On a practical level it has shown the feasibility of applying simple definitions of SMI in two different situations, neither of which was originally designed for prevalence estimation, namely a population-based research project and a case-register project. Annual period prevalence rates of SMI using the three-dimensional model have been compared in two areas in Europe that differ both in the social context and in the type of psychiatric care provided. Despite the limitations of the study mentioned above, these data could provide the first step toward extrapolation to national estimates of SMI throughout Great Britain and Italy and comparison with prevalence of SMI in other countries. In spite of the difference in the annual prevalence rates of SMI, the proportions of SMI among cases with psychosis are similar. This finding, if confirmed in other areas, suggests that there is a type of cross-cultural stability in the proportion of functional psychosis patients who have SMI, which is independent of local prevalence rates of mental illness and could be used for planning.

Epidemiological data collected in one of the sites (Verona) suggest that the use of the two-dimensional definition, with a combination of the criteria of duration of treatment and severe dysfunction, is preferable to the three-dimensional version. This is because the two-dimensional definition does not discriminate against patients with severe non-functional psychotic disorders, and because it allows further research to explore the burden placed on services and carers by patients with severe and enduring non-psychotic mental illnesses.

Future research priorities include testing the validity of these definitions and checking whether those patients who are identified as having SMI at a baseline point are those who suffer more and will cause more burden subsequently, and whether there are differences in the burden and disability profiles between SMI patients with and without psychosis.

References

American Psychiatric Association (1987). *Diagnostic and statistical manual of mental Disorders (3rd edition, revised) (DSM-III-R)*. Washington, DC: APA.

Balestrieri, M., Micciolo, R., De Salvia, D., et al. (1992). Confronti e prospettive nella utilizzazione dei Registri Psichiatrici dei Casi. *Epidemiologia e Psichiatria Sociale, 1,* 133–148.

Balestrieri, M., Bon, M. G., Rodriguez-Sacristan, A., et al. (1994). Pathways to psychiatric care in South Verona, Italy. *Psychological Medicine, 24,* 641–649.

Balestrieri, M., Rucci, P. & Nicolau, S. (1997). Gender-specific decline and seasonality of births in operationally defined schizophrenics in Italy. *Schizophrenia Research, 27,* 73–81.

Dunn, G., Pickles, A., Tansella, M., et al. (1999). Two-phase epidemiological surveys in psychiatric research. *British Journal of Psychiatry, 174,* 95–100.

House of Commons Health Select Committee (1994). *First report of the Health Committee: Better off in the community? The care of people who are seriously mentally ill.* London: HMSO.

Johnson, S., Brooks, L. & Thornicroft, G. (1997). *London's Mental Health.* London: King's Fund.

Jones, S. H., Thornicroft, G., Coffey, M., et al. (1995). A brief mental health outcome scale. Reliability and validity of the Global Assessment of Functioning (GAF). *British Journal of Psychiatry, 166,* 654–659.

McCreadie, R. (1982). The Nithsdale schizophrenia survey: I. Psychiatric and social handicaps. *British Journal of Psychiatry, 140,* 582–586.

McGuffin, P., Farmer, A. & Harvey, I. (1991). A polydiagnostic application of operational criteria in studies of psychotic illness. Development and reliability of the OPCRIT system. *Archives of General Psychiatry, 48,* 764–770.

Meltzer, H., Gill, B., Petticrew, M., et al. (1996). *OPCS surveys of psychiatric morbidity in Great Britain.* London: HMSO.

National Institute of Mental Health (1987). *Towards a model for a comprehensive community-based mental health system.* Washington, DC: NIMH.

Olfson, M. & Klerman, G. L. (1992). Depressive symptoms and mental health service utilization in a community sample. *Social Psychiatry and Psychiatric Epidemiology, 27,* 161–167.

Robins, L. N. & Regier, D. A. (eds.) (1991). *Psychiatric disorders in America: The Epidemiologic Catchment Area Study.* New York: Free Press.

Roy-Byrne, P., Dagadakis, C., Unutzer, J., et al. (1996). Evidence for limited validity of the revised Global Assessment of Functioning Scale. *Psychiatric Services, 47,* 864–866.

Ruggeri, M., Biggeri, A., Rucci, P., et al. (1998a). Multivariate analysis of outcome of mental health care using graphical chain models. The South Verona Outcome Project I. *Psychological Medicine, 28,* 1421–1431.

Ruggeri, M., Riani, M., Rucci, P., et al. (1998b). Multidimensional assessment of outcome in psychiatry: the use of graphical displays. The South Verona Outcome Project 2. *International Journal of Methods in Psychiatric Research, 7,* 186–198.

Schinnar, A. P., Rothbard, A. B., Kanter, R., et al. (1990). An empirical literature review of definitions of severe and persistent mental illness. *American Journal of Psychiatry, 147,* 1602–1608.

Slade, M., Powell, R. & Strathdee, G. (1996). Current approaches to identifying the severely mentally ill. *Social Psychiatry and Psychiatric Epidemiology, 32,* 177–184.

SPSS (1996). *SPSS for Windows: Base system user's guide. Release 7.0.* Chicago, IL: SPSS Inc.

Systema, S., Giel, R., Ten Horn, G. H., et al. (1989). The reliability of diagnostic coding in psychiatric case registers. *Psychological Medicine, 9,* 999–1006.

Tansella, M., Amaddeo, F., Burti, L., et al. (1998). Community-based mental health care in Verona, Italy. In D. Goldberg & G. Thornicroft (eds.), *Mental health in our future cities.* London: Erlbaum (UK), Taylor & Francis (Psychology Press), pp. 239–262.

Thornicraft, G., Strathdee, G., Phelan, M., et al. (1998). Rationale and design. PRiSM Psychosis Study 1. *British Journal of Psychiatry, 173,* 363–370.

World Health Organization (1992a). *The tenth revision of the International Classification of Diseases and Related Health Problems (ICD-10).* Geneva: WHO.

World Health Organization (1992b). *Schedules for clinical assessment in neuropsychiatry.* Geneva: WHO.

Zimmermann, M. (1994). Diagnosing personality disorders: a review of issues and research methods. *Archives of General Psychiatry, 51,* 225–245.

Patterns of Current and Lifetime Substance Use in Schizophrenia

Ian L. Fowler, Vaughan J. Carr, Natalia T. Carter & Terry J. Lewin

This article originally appeared in *Schizophrenia Bulletin*, 24(3), 1998, 443–455, and is reprinted with permission.

Ian L. Fowler, M.B. B.S., F.R.A.N.Z.C.P., is a psychiatrist in private practice. Vaughan J. Carr, M.D., F.R.C.P.C., F.R.A.N.Z.C.P., is Professor of Psychiatry and Director of Hunter Mental Health Services. Natalia T. Carter, B.Sc. Hons, is a Research Assistant and Medical Student. Terry J. Lewin, B.Com (Psych) Hons, is a Professional Officer. All four authors are affiliated with the Discipline of Psychiatry, Faculty of Medicine and Health Sciences, University of Newcastle, New South Wales, Australia.

A structured interview and standardized rating scales were used to assess a sample of 194 outpatients with schizophrenia in a regional Australian mental health service for substance use, abuse, and dependence. Case manager assessments and urine drug screens were also used to determine substance use. Additional measurements included demographic information, history of criminal charges, symptom self-reports, personal hopefulness, and social support. The sample was predominantly male and showed relative instability in accommodations, and almost half had a history of criminal offenses, most frequently drug or alcohol related. The 6-month and lifetime prevalence of substance abuse or dependence was 26.8 and 59.8%, respectively, with alcohol, cannabis, and amphetamines being the most commonly abused substances. Current users of alcohol comprised 77.3% and current users of other nonprescribed substances (excluding tobacco and caffeine) comprised 29.9% of the sample. Rates of tobacco and caffeine consumption were high. There was a moderate degree of concordance between case manager determinations of a substance-use problem and research diagnoses. Subjects with current or lifetime diagnoses of substance abuse/dependence were predominantly young, single males with higher rates of criminal charges; however, there was no evidence of increased rates of suicide attempts, hospital admissions, or daily doses of antipsychotic drugs in these groups compared with subjects with no past or current diagnosis of substance abuse or dependence. Subjects with a current diagnosis of substance use were younger at first treatment and currently more symptomatic than those with no past or current substance use diagnosis. The picture emerging from this study replicates the high rate of substance abuse in persons with schizophrenia reported in North American studies but differs from the latter in finding a slightly different pattern of substances abused (i.e., absence of cocaine), reflecting relative differences in the availability of certain drugs.

The problem of schizophrenia and substance abuse comorbidity has attracted considerable attention in recent years (Mueser et al., 1992a; Selzer & Lieberman, 1993; Smith & Hucker, 1994; Westermeyer, 1992). In an epidemiological study of the community prevalence of mental disorders, the rate of substance abuse or dependence comorbidity among patients with schizophrenia was estimated at 47% (Regier et al., 1990). However, most estimates of the nature and extent of substance abuse in association with schizophrenia are based on clinical populations of patients.

A literature search using the selection criteria of Mueser et al. (1990)—a minimum sample size of 15, subjects not selected on the basis of a history of substance abuse, specification of the class of substance used—was undertaken to identify all studies that have examined the prevalence of substance use in schizophrenia. Among the 32 studies identified, findings varied widely. Lifetime rates of abuse and/or dependence varied between 12.3 and 50% for alcohol (Alterman et al., 1981; Drake et al., 1990), 12.5 and 35.8% for cannabis (Barbee et al., 1989; Cohen & Klein, 1970), 11.3 and 31% for stimulants (Barbee et al., 1989; Mueser et al., 1992b), 5.7 and 15.2% for hallucinogens (Barbee et al., 1989; Breakey et al., 1974), 2 and 9% for opiates (Mueser et al. 1992b; Siris et al., 1988), and 3.5 and 11.3% for sedatives (Barbee et al. 1989; McLellan & Druley, 1977). Although difficult to interpret because of variations in sample size, subject selection, diagnostic criteria, and definitions of abuse and dependence, there was some suggestion of changes in the patterns of substance use over time. For instance, estimates of lifetime alcohol abuse and dependence appear to have increased from 14 to 22% in the 1960s and 1970s (McLellan & Druley, 1977; Parker et al., 1960; Pokorny, 1965) to 25 to 50% in the 1990s (Dixon et al., 1991; Drake et al., 1990; Mueser et al., 1992b), as have those of stimulant abuse or dependence, which moved from 11 to 15% in the 1970s (Breakey et al., 1974; McLellan & Druley, 1977) to 17 to 31% in the 1990s (Dixon et al., 1991; Mueser et al., 1992b). However, estimates of lifetime hallucinogen abuse and dependence appear to have declined from 9.9 to 15.2% in the 1970s (Breakey et al., 1974; McLellan & Druley, 1977) to 6 to 8% in the 1990s (Dixon et al., 1991; Mueser et al., 1992b), while comparable estimates for cannabis have shown little change over time. Although the data are too sparse to form opinions on changes in lifetime opiate or sedative abuse and dependence, there is little indication of change.

Substance Abuse and the Course of Schizophrenia

Several investigators have found associations between the course of schizophrenia and substance abuse, although the direction of influence is unclear. Schizophrenia with substance abuse has been associated with: younger males (DeQuardo et al., 1994; Mueser et al., 1990); poor treatment compliance (Drake & Wallach, 1989; Pristach & Smith, 1990); increased rates of hospital admissions, depressive symptoms (Brady et al., 1990; Drake et al., 1990; Zisook et al., 1992), suicide (Rich et al., 1988), and assaultive behavior (Swanson et al., 1990; Test et al., 1989); instability in accommodations and homelessness (Belcher, 1989; Drake et al., 1989b, 1990); and increased risk of HIV infection (Hanson et al., 1992; Seeman et al., 1990). Alcohol abuse in particular has been associated with more hospital admissions, greater severity of positive symptoms, increased rates of tardive dyskinesia (Dixon et al., 1992; Duke et al., 1994; Olivera et al., 1990), decreased serum fluphenazine levels (Soni & Brownlee, 1991; Soni et al., 1991), and "relative neuroleptic refractoriness" (Bowers et al., 1990). Other studies have found that alcohol-abusing schizophrenia patients are disruptive and disinhibited, but not necessarily more acutely psychotic (Drake et al., 1990). Likewise, no differences in antipsychotic dose have been found between substance abusing and non-substance-abusing patients with schizophrenia (Duke et al., 1994; Miller & Tanenbaum, 1989).

Cannabis abuse has been associated with the exacerbation of psychotic symptoms, increased hospital admissions (Linszen et al., 1994; Martinez-Arevalo et al., 1994; Safer, 1987) and increased tardive dyskinesia (Zaretsky et al., 1993). Unexpectedly, Mueser et al. (1990) found that cannabis-abusing patients with schizophrenia had fewer hospitalizations. They also found that recent cannabis use was not associated with increased psychotic symptoms. Cocaine has emerged as a particular problem in the United States, where it has been found to be associated with increased risk of depression (Brady et al., 1990; Weiss et al.,

1988), less severe negative symptoms (Lysaker et al., 1994), and increased hospital readmission (Brady et al., 1990), yet in a large inpatient study, Mueser et al. (1990) found no effects of stimulant abuse on psychotic symptoms or other clinical variables.

Methodological Issues

Interpreting findings in relation to prevalence and clinical consequences involves a number of problems, not the least of which is their limited generalizability. Most of the studies are North American, where the patterns of drug availability and health care provision are extremely varied and tend to differ from those of other countries (Drake et al., 1991; Johnson & Muffler, 1997). There is clearly a need for local surveys to gauge the nature and extent of local problems and how best to deal with them.

Several methodological problems have hampered research in this field, among them reduced reliability of the diagnosis of schizophrenia in the presence of concurrent substance abuse (Bryant et al., 1992; Corty et al., 1993); lack of specification of diagnostic criteria (Richard et al., 1985; Rockwell & Ostwald, 1988); nonuse of structured clinical interviews (Alterman et al., 1981; Drake et al., 1989a; O'Farrell et al., 1983; Pristach & Smith, 1990; Seibyl et al., 1993; Shaner et al., 1993); and uncertainty as to the relative contributions of schizophrenia and substance use to impaired functioning (Skinner & Sheu, 1982). Also, severe problems associated with substance use may still be found even when DSM-IV criteria (American Psychiatric Association, 1994) for substance abuse or dependence are not met (Dixon et al., 1993; Helzer et al., 1978), prevalence rates based on self-report questionnaires are consistently higher than those based on interviews (Turner et al., 1992), and there appears to be a differential willingness to report past use over current use (McNagny & Parker, 1992).

The population from which a sample is drawn can give inflated prevalence figures for substance abuse. For example, in a sample of outpatients with schizophrenia, Drake et al. (1990) found the current rate of alcohol abuse/dependence to be 25%, whereas in a sample of acute inpatients with schizophrenia, Shaner et al. (1993) found a rate of 45%. Berkson (1946) suggested that as a result of the additive effects of seeking treatment for each individual disorder, comorbidity will always be higher in clinical samples than in representative community samples. Dufort et al. (1993) have further suggested that treatment-seeking is a function of both the number and type of disorders. Substance-use disorders are associated with a low probability of seeking treatment, but this probability increases in the presence of other disorders.

Many of the aforementioned difficulties could be reduced if a longitudinal view of the subject is obtained from multiple sources such as families, case managers, hospital and community files, structured interviews, and drug urine screens (Drake et al., 1990; McKenna & Ross, 1994).

The Current Study

This study is the first detailed investigation of schizophrenia and substance abuse comorbidity in Australia. The sample size is substantial and comprised entirely of patients living in the community. Some of the methodological shortcomings of earlier studies were overcome by adhering to operational criteria for diagnosing both schizophrenia and substance abuse, by using a structured clinical interview for diagnosis, by considering a wide variety of substances with abuse potential and quantifying their consumption, by using multiple sources of information (patient, case manager, urine samples), and by focusing only on patients receiving treatment in the community. This article reports the prevalence rates for all substances assessed in the study and examines the characteristics of subjects with different histories of substance abuse or dependence.

Methods

Subject Selection

Through the community mental health clinics of the Hunter Area Health Service, we sought to contact all patients of the public mental health services who had a clinical diagnosis of schizophrenia. To be eligible for screening, before entry into the study, potential subjects identified by clinic staff were required to meet the following criteria: probable clinical diagnosis of schizophrenia; absence of mental retardation, major mood disorder, organic brain disease or injury, and acute psychotic symptoms; age between 18 and 60 years; and likely ability to tolerate an extended interview.

Procedures

Case managers were asked to identify potential subjects. They were requested not to approach only those whom they believed to have a substance-abuse problem but to attempt to recruit all patients with schizophrenia on their caseloads who met the above criteria. Patients who agreed to be interviewed by a member of the research team were then introduced to the interviewer who explained the nature of the research project and sought their informed consent. Patients who were not well enough to participate in the study (e.g., exhibiting acute exacerbation of psychotic symptoms) were approached again in 3 to 6 months' time, if their clinical condition permitted, and asked to participate. Each interview took between 30 and 170 minutes to complete (mean time: 67 minutes). When subjects found the interview process too tiring and requested to terminate the interview before its completion, the interview was suspended but completed within 48 hours. At the end of the interview, each subject was asked to give a urine sample for drug analysis; 98% (191/194) agreed.

Researcher Training

Interviews were performed by a graduate research assistant (N.T.C.) who was trained in how to conduct the interview by the first author (I.L.F.). Training initially focused on the Structured Clinical Interview for *DSM-III-R* (SCID-R; Spitzer et al., 1987). During the training phase, the Psychotic Disorders and Substance Use Disorders sections of the SCID-R were used to interview inpatients in an acute psychiatric hospital who had a clinical diagnosis of psychosis who were about to be discharged. The first 10 interviews were performed by both researchers, with consensual diagnoses being determined. The next 18 were performed by each researcher alternatively, with one conducting the interview and both independently scoring the responses. The latter interviews were used to calculate interrater agreement coefficients based on assignments to the three categories: no abuse or dependence, abuse only, and dependence. Across the range of substances assessed in this study, the overall agreement between the raters was 99% (unweighted kappa = 0.95).

Instruments

The structured interview used in the study collected demographic data, including frequency of changes in accommodations and history of criminal charges, and clinical information (e.g., duration of illness, frequency of hospitalizations, current psychotropic medications, and number of suicide attempts). Diagnoses of schizophrenia and substance abuse or dependence were made using the relevant sections of the SCID-

R. Six-month and lifetime diagnoses of substance abuse and dependence were determined. Nonalcoholic substances that were considered were illicit drugs (cannabis, amphetamines, hallucinogens, heroin, cocaine), caffeine, tobacco, solvents and aerosols, and prescription drugs (benzodiazepines, anticholinergics, antihistamines, barbiturates, opiates, appetite suppressants). Current psychiatric symptoms were assessed using the Symptom Checklist-90-Revised (SCL-90-R; Derogatis, 1977). A measure of global personal hopefulness (GPH; Nunn et al., 1996) was included, as well as an estimate of the subject's current social support (Tucker, 1982). It should be noted that all of the self-report instruments were administered verbally, within the interview format. Four global ratings comprising estimates of each subject's usage of alcohol and other substances both during their lifetime and during the prior 6 months, were also obtained from case managers. Following Drake et al. (1990), anchored 5-point severity ratings were used, with point labels based on *DSM-III-R* criteria (American Psychiatric Association, 1987) for abuse and dependence. The utility of clinicians' ratings of substance abuse among psychiatric outpatients has been demonstrated by Drake et al. (1990) and, more recently, by Carey et al. (1996).

Pilot Phase

A pilot study using 38 male, consecutive outpatient attenders with schizophrenia was completed in late 1992. Shortcomings identified in the pilot study led to modifications in the protocol for the main study, specifically the addition of measures of caffeine and tobacco consumption, an assessment of GPH (Nunn et al., 1996), global case manager ratings, and a more thorough drug urine screening (e.g., including antihistamines, anticholinergics, and barbiturates). The questions on caffeine consumption asked about use of coffee, tea, chocolate, and cola and were used to generate an index of caffeine intake per day (in milligrams).

Urine Analysis

In the main study, comprehensive urine analyses were performed by the laboratories of the Royal North Shore Toxicology Unit (Sydney) according to the following protocol. Each specimen was subjected to EMIT (enzyme multiplied immunoassay technique) for opiates, cannabinoids, benzodiazepines, amphetamine types, and cocaine. Enzyme dehydrogenase procedures were used to test for alcohol and confirmed by gas chromatography. In addition, all samples were sub-

jected to high-performance thin-layer chromatography after betaglu-
curonidase incubation and liquid-liquid extraction. This technique identified a wide range of additional substances, both therapeutic and illicit,
including nicotine, anticholinergics, antipsychotics, antihistamines,
antiepileptics, antiarrhythmics, antidepressants, and other sympath-
omimetics. Finally, samples were analyzed by gas chromatography mass
spectroscopy for caffeine and all other presumptive positives.

Data Analysis

Analysis was performed using data from the pilot phase and the
main study, since the methods in each case were sufficiently similar. Data
analysis was undertaken using BMDP (Biomedical Data Package) statistical software (Dixon et al., 1988) on the mainframe computer at the
University of Newcastle.

Results

Sample Characteristics

Of the 312 outpatients contacted, 214 (69%) agreed to take part in
the study. Of these potential subjects, 20 met exclusion criteria and were
rejected from the study; 194 (62%) completed the interview. Only nine
of these subjects (4.6%) were employed, with most of the remainder
drawing sickness benefits or a pension (88.7%). The characteristics of
the sample are shown in table 1. The prototypical subject was an unmarried 36-year-old male, who had completed 10 years of education or less,
and who lived alone in rented accommodations or at home with his parents. There was a high rate of change in accommodations, with 47.4%
changing their place of residence at least once in the preceding 2 years.
Approximately one-half of the sample admitted to having been charged
with a criminal offense. The most common offenses were either drug or
alcohol related or else were minor property offenses; however, 1 in 14
subjects (7.2%) had been charged with major assault.

Patterns of Substance Use

The 6-month and lifetime prevalence of substance-use disorders is
shown in table 2. Overall, approximately 1 in 4 subjects (26.8%) was
found to have been diagnosed with substance-use disorder in the preceding 6 months, with 60.3% using but not reaching diagnostic criteria
for a substance-use disorder. Almost three in five patients (59.8%) had a
lifetime diagnosis of substance abuse or dependence. Nearly half of the

Table 1
Sample Characteristics (*n* = 194)

Characteristic	
Mean age (years)	36.3
Gender, %	
Female	27.3
Male	72.7
Marital status, %	
Never married	67.5
Married or de facto	13.9
Separated or divorced	18.5
Highest education level, %	
10 years schooling or less	59.2
Completed secondary education	13.4
Technical qualification	21.1
University qualification	6.2
Area of residence, %	
Urban	72.3
Rural or semirural	26.3
Accommodation type, %	
Rented home or unit	41.7
Parent's home	27.8
Own home or unit	11.9
Boardinghouse	7.7
Other	10.8
Persons with whom they live, %	
Alone	35.6
With parents	31.4
With partner and/or other family	20.1
With friends	6.7
Other	6.2
Mean changes in accommodation during previous 2 years	1.2 (range 0-10)
Criminal charges, %	
Any charge	47.9
Property damage	9.8
Breaking and entering	13.9
Driving while intoxicated	17.5
Minor assault	7.7
Major assault	7.2
Drug possession	11.3
Other	16.0

subjects were found to have a lifetime diagnosis of alcohol abuse/dependence (48.4%), over one-third a lifetime diagnosis of cannabis abuse/dependence (36.0%), and almost one in eight a lifetime diagnosis of prescribed substance abuse/dependence (11.3%). Of the substances listed in table 2, alcohol, cannabis, and amphetamines were clearly the most commonly used. Although opiates, hallucinogens, and solvents/aerosols were currently being used by a small minority, these substances had been more extensively used in the past. In contrast to the U.S. experience (Elangavan et al., 1993; Mueser et al., 1992b; Shaner et al., 1993), cocaine was rarely used in this sample. Prescribed drugs, most commonly benzodiazepines, anticholinergics, and opiates, were infrequently abused relative to illicit substances.

The mean daily caffeine intake for the sample was 404.7 mg (range: 0–2,914 mg), with 17.3% of subjects consuming more than 600 mg of caffeine daily (mean = 938.2 mg per day). Tobacco smokers comprised 74.2% of the sample: 30.4% smoked 20 to 40 cigarettes per day and 39.7% smoked more than this amount.

Reasons for Use

Subjects were asked open-ended questions about their "reasons for use" for each category of substance they had used during the preceding 6 months; they could nominate up to three reasons for use, and these were subsequently grouped into four main categories:

- *drug intoxication effects* (e.g., to get "a lift," get "stoned," "high," a "buzz," a "rev," "to feel good," "get the adrenalin going," "get drunk," to "enhance things");

- *dysphoria relief* (e.g., "to relax," "feel happier," "stop the depression," "feel less anxious," "relieve tension," "be calm," "take bad feelings away");

- *social effects* (e.g., "be sociable," "be part of a group," "something to do with friends," "beats the boredom," "to face people better," "fit in with the crowd"); and

- *illness and medication-related effects* (e.g., "to get away from the thoughts," "help forget the...hallucinations," "get away from voices," "relieve the feeling of ill health").

Table 2

Current usage (previous 6 months) and lifetime usage of nonprescribed and prescribed substances (n = 194)

Substance	Current usage (previous 6 months) (%)				Lifetime usage (%)			
	No use	Some use	Abuse	Dependence	No use	Some use	Abuse	Dependence
Alcohol	22.7	59.3	2.1	16.0	1.0	50.5	1.5	46.9
Nonprescribed								
Cannabis	70.1	17.0	4.1	8.8	34.0	29.9	7.7	28.3
Hallucinogens	96.9	3.1	0.0	0.0	62.9	29.9	3.1	4.1
Amphetamines	90.2	7.7	1.0	1.0	66.0	20.6	4.1	9.3
Solvents and aerosols	98.5	1.5	0.0	0.0	81.4	14.4	0.5	3.6
Cocaine	100.0	0.0	0.0	0.0	84.5	13.9	0.0	1.5
Opiates	97.4	2.1	0.5	0.0	88.7	8.2	0.5	2.6
Any nonprescribed	70.1	17.0	3.6	9.3	32.5	30.9	6.2	30.4
Prescribed								
Anticholinergics	62.9	35.1	1.0	1.0	27.3	68.0	1.0	3.6
Benzodiazepines	92.3	4.6	1.5	1.5	35.6	57.2	1.0	6.2
Antihistamines	99.5	0.5	0.0	0.0	71.1	26.8	0.0	2.1
Opiates	94.8	3.6	0.0	1.5	77.8	20.1	0.0	2.1
Appetite suppressants	99.5	0.0	0.0	0.5	91.8	7.2	0.0	1.0
Barbiturates	100.0	0.0	0.0	0.0	95.9	3.6	0.5	0.0
Any prescribed	56.7	38.1	2.1	3.1	13.9	74.7	1.0	10.3
Any substance	12.9	60.3	3.1	23.7	0.0	40.2	4.6	55.2

Table 3

Characteristics of subjects with different histories of substance abuse or dependence ($n = 194$)

Variable	History of substance abuse or dependence			Pattern of significant differences[1]
	(N) No abuse or dependence	(P) Past abuse or significant dependence	(C) Current abuse or dependence	
Sample size	78	64	52	
Mean age (years), %	40.81	34.55	31.83	$F = 17.58$[2] N > P, C
Female	48.7	12.5	13.5	$\chi^2 = 30.10$[2] N > P, C
Never married	52.6	76.6	78.8	$\chi^2 = 13.58$[3] N < P, C
10 years' schooling or less	56.4	62.5	59.6	$\chi^2 = 0.54$
Urban area	67.9	78.1	75.0	$\chi^2 = 1.97$
Mean social support	2.45	2.66	2.21	$F = 1.71$
Mean changes in accommodations (previous 2 years)	0.82	1.34	1.82	$F = 4.61$[3] N < C
Any criminal charge, %	21.8	56.3	76.9	$\chi^2 = 17.84$[2] N < P < C
Mean age at first treatment	25.56	23.14	21.42	$F = 6.32$[3] N > C
Mean number of admissions	5.86	4.95	6.60	$F = 0.75$
Mean # of suicide attempts	0.78	1.16	1.51	$F = 1.73$
Mean antipsychotic drug dose (chlorpromazine equivalents)	435.37	521.27	539.51	$F = 1.06$
Mean caffeine intake (mg/day)	356.33	383.28	525.80	$F = 3.14$[4] N < C
Currently smoking tobacco, %	57.7	78.1	94.2	$\chi^2 = 22.53$[2] N < P < C

(continued)

Table 3 *(continued)*

Characteristics of subjects with different histories of substance abuse or dependence ($n = 194$)

Variable	History of substance abuse or dependence			Pattern of significant differences[1]
	(N) No abuse or dependence	(P) Past abuse or significant dependence	(C) Current abuse or dependence	
Mean global personal hopefulness	28.65	33.0	32.80	$F = 1.88$
Mean SCL-90-R scores:				
Interpersonal sensitivity	0.81	1.14	1.36	$F = 6.96^3$ N < C
Depression	0.88	1.18	1.37	$F = 5.74^3$ N < C
Anxiety	0.51	0.95	1.13	$F = 11.49^2$ N < P, C
Hostility	0.32	0.61	0.84	$F = 8.68^2$ N < C
Paranoid ideation	0.67	1.03	1.38	$F = 9.97^2$ N < C
Psychoticism	0.59	0.91	1.24	$F = 11.00^2$ N < C
Global severity index	0.63	0.96	1.18	$F = 11.90^2$ N < P, C

Note. SCL-90-R = Symptom Checklist-90-Revised. (Derogatis 1977).

1. The statistics reported are either overall χ^2 (categorical variables) or F-ratios from one-way analyses of variance (continuous variables). The letters following these statistics indicate the pattern of significant differences among the three subgroups using appropriate follow-up tests (e.g., N<C: subjects with no history (N) of abuse or dependence were significantly lower than those with current (C) abuse or dependence problems).

2. $p < 0.001$.
3. $p < 0.01$.
4. $p < 0.05$.

Most caffeine users (78%) and amphetamine users (79%) nominated drug intoxication effects, as described in terms similar to the above, as one of their reasons for use. Half of the users of these drugs (52% and 47%, respectively) also nominated dysphoria relief among their reasons. Tobacco was used both to relieve dysphoria (69%) and for its intoxication effects (62%), and a similar profile emerged for cannabis, with corresponding values of 62 and 41%. Alcohol was equally likely to be used for dysphoria relief and for social reasons (58%). Illness-related reasons, including the relief of antipsychotic drug side effects, were nominated by 0 to 9% of users across the drug classes that were examined.

Overall, there were minimal differences between substance "users" and substance "abusers" in their stated reasons for using alcohol, cannabis, and amphetamines. However, abusers of alcohol during the preceding 6 months were more likely than users to nominate illness and medication-related reasons for substance use (14.3% vs. 2.6%, $\chi^2 = 7.25$, $p < 0.01$). Likewise, cannabis abusers were more likely than users to nominate illness and medication-related reasons for substance use (16.0% vs. 0%, $\chi^2 = 5.51$, $p < 0.05$).

Characteristics of Subjects with Different Substance Use Histories

On the basis of their history of substance abuse or dependence, subjects were allocated to one of three groups: those with no current or past history of abuse or dependence ($n = 78$, 40%); those reporting a history but no current abuse or dependence ($n = 64$, 33%); and those with current (i.e., 6-month) abuse or dependence ($n = 52$, 27%). Table 3 summarizes the analyses that were undertaken to assess differences in the characteristics of these three groups. Only two of the variables in table 3 differentiated significantly between subjects with current substance abuse or dependence and those with a history of abuse or dependence, namely criminal charges (76.9% vs. 56.3%) and current tobacco consumption (94.2% vs. 78.1%). Subjects with a history of substance abuse or dependence were significantly different from the "no abuse or dependence" group on seven of the variables assessed in table 3. The former were younger, more likely to be male, less likely to have been married, more likely to have been charged with a criminal offense, more likely to be smokers, and likely to have reported a higher level of anxiety symptoms and higher global severity index (GSI) scores on the SCL–90–R.

Subjects with a current history of substance abuse or dependence were significantly different from those with no history of abuse or dependence on each of the seven variables described above. In addition, they were more likely to have changed accommodations during the preceding 2 years, likely to have been first treated for schizophrenia at a younger age, likely to have a higher daily intake of caffeine, and likely to have higher symptom scores on all of the SCL–90–R subscales reported in table 3. There were no significant differences between the three groups in terms of education, area of residence, social support, rates of psychiatric hospitalization, number of suicide attempts, antipsychotic drug dose, or levels of personal hopefulness. Overall, the subjects in this study reported very low levels of personal hopefulness, with a grand mean of 31.05, which is two standard deviations (*SDs*) below the normative population data reported by Nunn et al. (1996) (mean=56.07, *SD*=12.53).

Review of Diagnostic Assessments

Global case manager ratings were not used during the pilot phase, and in the main study the "Unknown" option was chosen 23% of the time (i.e., "Case Manager does not know person OR does not know about client's use of alcohol or other substances"). Furthermore, case managers were more prepared to make ratings for the preceding 6 months than for lifetime usage (alcohol: 87% vs. 76%, $\chi^2 = 6.05$, $p<0.05$; other substances: 80% vs. 67%, $\chi^2 = 5.95$, $p< 0.05$). On the basis of the cases that were rated, there was a moderate level of agreement between the case managers' ratings and SCID–R-based diagnoses of substance abuse or dependence. For example, collapsing the case managers' ratings into two categories, "no substance abuse problems or mild problems" versus "moderate or severe problems" ("related to...recurrent dangerous use"), and the interview-based assessments into two categories, "no use or some use" versus "abuse or dependence," there was 83% agreement about alcohol-use disorders during the preceding 6 months (kappa = 0.33) and 70% agreement for lifetime alcohol-use disorders (kappa = 0.39). The corresponding values for nonalcohol-related substance-use disorders were 78% for the preceding 6 months (kappa = 0.27) and 76% for lifetime problems (kappa = 0.49). Classification mismatches were evenly distributed for alcohol-use disorders during the preceding 6 months and for lifetime abuse of other substances. By comparison, lifetime alcohol problems were noted by case managers in 36% of subjects, compared with 47% identified during the interview, whereas the reverse was true for abuse of other substances during the prior 6 months (case managers: 24%; interview: 13%).

Urine screening tests for substances assessed in both the pilot phase and the main study (e.g., cannabis) were based on 176 samples, while those assessed only in the main study (e.g., antihistamines) were based on 139 samples. The percentages of urine samples that were "positive" for the substances under investigation were (in descending order) caffeine (71.2%, 99/139), nicotine (64.7%, 90/139), cannabis (10.2%, 18/176), benzodiazepines (6.3%, 11/176), alcohol (4.5%, 8/176), antihistamines (4.3%, 6/139), anticholinergics (3.6%, 5/139), opiates (2.8%, 5/176), and amphetamines (2.3%, 4/176). Recent alcohol consumption aside, these rates are generally consistent with the "current usage" profiles in tables 2 and 3.

Overall, for the seven substances listed above and in table 2 (excluding caffeine and nicotine), 27.8% of the subjects (49/176) had at least one positive drug urine test. However, only 5% of the 1,158 urine screening tests were positive, of which two-thirds (or 3.4% overall) were from subjects who had acknowledged recent use, whereas the remaining one-third (or 1.6% overall) were from subjects who had not reported using that drug during the preceding 6 months. In practice, this amounted to only 18 screening tests (from 18 separate subjects) that might have led to a reclassification of recent usage from nonuser to user: they involved benzodiazepines (6), antihistamines (6), alcohol (2), opiates (2), cannabis (1), and amphetamines (1).

Discussion

The prevalence of substance abuse and dependence found in the present study is comparable to the results of most other studies. Our estimate of lifetime alcohol abuse/dependence (48.4%) was at the upper end of the range reported in recent studies (Dixon et al., 1991; Drake et al., 1990; Mueser et al., 1992b), as was that for cannabis (36.0%) (Barbee et al., 1989; DeQuardo et al., 1994; Dixon et al., 1989, 1991), whereas that for amphetamines (13.4%) was at the lower end of the range reported by most North American studies (Barbee et al., 1989; DeQuardo et al., 1994; Dixon et al., 1989, 1991; Khalsa et al., 1991; Mueser et al., 1990, 1992b). The only marked difference from North American studies was the low lifetime rate of cocaine abuse/dependence (1.5%) and the complete absence of current cocaine abuse/dependence in our sample, compared with U.S. data (Elangavan et al., 1993; Shaner et al., 1993). The latter finding is likely to reflect the relatively low level of cocaine availability in this country. The extent of tobacco use found in the present study is similar to that reported by others and indicates that this group of patients is at high risk for smoking-related diseases. Likewise, the level of caffeine consumption in a substantial minority would suggest a significant risk of caffeinism, which may adversely affect the patient's clinical condition.

This is the first large-scale study to estimate the rates of abuse of prescribed substances or over-the-counter preparations such as antihistamines. High rates of abuse of these substances relative to nonprescribed substances were not found, the most frequent being benzodiazepines at 3.0% (current), which is several times the community prevalence estimates of 0.2 to 0.5% (Heather et al., 1989). However, since the rate of positive urine screens for benzodiazepines and antihistamines exceeded the self-report rates, there is evidently some under-reporting of actual use of these substances. The rates of anticholinergic drug abuse/dependence were not high (2.0% current and 4.6% lifetime) relative to the abuse of other substances although this phenomenon has been reported elsewhere (Marken et al., 1996).

The reasons for substance use stated by our subjects run counter to the self-medication hypothesis, except perhaps for those with a pattern of recent alcohol or cannabis abuse who cited illness-related reasons for their heavy use. However, the latter may represent merely a post hoc justification. Overall, these findings are similar to earlier studies in which substance use is described as relieving anxiety, dysphoria, and difficulty socializing (Dixon et al., 1990; Noordsy et al., 1991; Test et al., 1989). The bulk of our data suggests that patients with schizophrenia use/abuse drugs for essentially the same reasons as young people in the general population do, namely to enjoy the experience of intoxication, to escape from emotional distress, or to take part in a social activity.

The fact that almost one-quarter (23%) of the case managers approached were unwilling to rate their clients' substance abuse histories may be an isolated finding, reflecting the local restructuring of community health services that occurred during the course of the present study. Nevertheless, although there was reasonable agreement between case managers' assessments and the research diagnoses, it did not reach the levels found in other studies (Carey et al., 1996; Drake et al., 1990), possibly because in the current study the case managers were untrained. Thus, efforts to train case managers and to heighten their awareness of substance-use problems in their patients may be timely.

The clinical and demographic differences between the subjects with current (6-month) or lifetime abuse/dependence disorders and those with no current or past substance-use disorders suggest that the former are predominantly single, young males with unstable accommodations, high rates of criminal behavior, and high levels of symptomatology. The earlier age at first treatment for schizophrenia in the current abuse/dependence group may reflect the possibility that early substance abuse brought forward the onset of schizophrenia or exacerbated preexisting symptoms to a level that rendered the individual sufficiently conspicuous as to make treatment imperative. However, the present study cannot confirm this, and the failure to find a similarly early age of illness onset in those with past substance abuse/dependence only does not support this conclusion.

Some studies have suggested that substance abuse is associated with an increased number of hospital admissions (Brady et al., 1990; Drake et al., 1989a, 1990; Duke et al., 1994; Safer, 1987), although others have not found such an association (Mueser et al., 1990). The failure to find such an association in the present study may be due to the fact that the area in which this study was conducted had extended-hours mobile community teams, which treat most acute psychoses in the patient's home, thereby avoiding hospitalizations that might otherwise have been necessary. Alternative explanations may lie with a public sector selection bias toward more disabled patients overall or the inherent limitations of cross-sectional, retrospective studies compared with longitudinal studies in assessing service utilization. Similarly, the failure to find an association between substance abuse and either higher doses of antipsychotic drugs or increased rates of suicide attempts conflicts with some previous research (Bowers et al., 1990; Duke et al., 1994; Miller & Tanenbaum, 1989; Rich et al., 1988; Satel et al., 1991), but not others (Bartels et al., 1992; Drake et al., 1984; Siris et al., 1993). However, a nonsignificant trend in the direction of more suicide attempts in the substance-abusing groups should be noted (see table 3).

An important factor that may modify the course of schizophrenia with substance abuse is the community setting. In Australia, there is a system of universal health care and income security, including free hospital and community care, subsidized medications, public housing, and pensions for the chronically ill.

Limitations of the Study

Among the limitations of the present study, three issues stand out: the nonrepresentativeness of the sample, the reliance on a single assessment occasion, and the lack of relevant comparison data. Given the 3:1 male: female ratio and the fact that the sample was recruited from public community mental health services, it is clear that this sample was not representative of all persons with schizophrenia in the population. Excluded were patients being treated in the private sector, either by specialists or family physicians, those not in treatment at all, and patients under inpatient care, either short- or long-term. The former two groups, which would be more likely to comprise better functioning individuals, could be expected to have lower rates of substance-use disorders, while acute inpatients would be more likely to have higher rates, judging by previous findings reported for this group (e.g., Mueser et al., 1990). However, the 69% response rate for all potential subjects located in the community clinics, the gender ratio, marital status, education level, and accommodations situation all suggest that the sample is likely to be representative of the relatively poor-prognosis patients with schizophrenia who attend public mental health services in the community. If anything, the rates of substance abuse/dependence found in this sample are likely to be underestimates if a significant proportion of those who declined to participate did so for reasons of wanting to conceal their substance-use problems. Given the relative reluctance of individuals to report current use patterns accurately as compared to past use, the rates of current abuse/dependence may also have been underestimated. The finding that 60.3% of the sample was currently using substances below the threshold for a diagnosis of abuse or dependence may similarly reflect this reporting bias, or may be due to the relative insensitivity of the diagnostic instrument used.

Although the reliability of determining lifetime substance-use disorders can be questioned, the finding of a more than twofold difference between 6-month and lifetime estimates of prevalence, if taken at the face value, suggests that substance-use disorders are not static in this group, as indeed they are not in the general population, but instead represent a temporary stage in the course of schizophrenia for which risk factors such as age, gender, marital status, and criminal behavior may be as important as they are in the general population. However, only longitudinal studies can confirm whether this is indeed the case and whether substance abuse is largely a problem in younger male patients that remits, at least temporarily, in at least 50% of cases. Longitudinal studies may also enable the predictors of continued abuse versus recurrent abuse versus abstinence or controlled use to be determined so that improved intervention techniques can be devised and more effectively administered.

There have been no Australian epidemiological studies of substance abuse/dependence using a methodology similar to ours with which to directly compare our results. However, national survey data on lifetime use of illicit drugs does provide a useful guide against which to evaluate the overall level of drug use by our subjects. For example, in the 1991 national survey, 38% of males reported ever using marijuana (Commonwealth Department of Health, Housing and Community Services, 1992), compared with 66% of our sample. This pattern was similar for most illicit substances, with the lifetime usage rates in the current study typically being two to three times those reported by males in the general population. Further evidence of a marked difference in substance-use patterns can be found in the urine screen results, which revealed a 10.2% rate of cannabis use in the current sample, more than seven times the rate found previously in the Newcastle population (Hancock et al., 1991). To some extent, comparisons with normal populations are misleading since the demographic characteristics of the present sample of patients with schizophrenia in treatment differ substantially from population norms. A relevant comparison group would probably consist of young to middle-aged, predominantly male, single, unemployed persons. Nevertheless, the available figures strongly suggest that the prevalence of substance abuse/dependence in the sample of patients with schizophrenia is substantially higher than in the general community.

Conclusions

A high level of substance use and abuse similar to that in North American studies (except for the pattern of substance use) was found. Substance abusers with schizophrenia in this sample tended to be young males with high rates of criminal offenses. The reasons for substance use were similar to those found in other studies. We saw little evidence that substance abuse adversely affects the course of schizophrenia in this sample, in that there was no increase in hospital admissions, suicide attempts, or prescribed doses of antipsychotic drugs in those with concurrent abuse/dependence. This study highlights the need for local epidemiological and clinical studies of substance abuse in schizophrenia, to help ensure that therapeutic interventions are targeted more effectively.

References

Alterman, A. I., Erdlen, F. R., & Murphy, E. (1981). Alcohol abuse in the psychiatric hospital population. *Addictive Behavior, 6,* 69–73.

American Psychiatric Association. (1987). *DSM-III-R: Diagnostic and Statistical Manual of Mental Disorders. 3rd ed.,* revised. Washington, DC: Author.

American Psychiatric Association. (1994). *DSM-IV: Diagnostic and Statistical Manual of Mental Disorders. 4th ed.* Washington, DC: Author.

Barbee, J. G., Clark, P. D., Crapanzo, M. S., Heintz, G. C., & Kehoe, C. E. (1989). Alcohol and substance abuse among schizophrenic patients presenting to an emergency psychiatry service. *Journal of Nervous and Mental Disease, 177,* 400–477.

Bartels, S. J., Drake, R. E., & McHugo, G. J. (1992). Alcohol abuse, depression and suicidal behavior in schizophrenia. *American Journal of Psychiatry, 149,* 394–395.

Belcher, J. R. (1989). On becoming homeless: A study of chronically mentally ill persons. *Journal of Community Psychology, 17,* 173–185.

Berkson, J. (1946). Limitations of the application of fourfold table analysis to hospital data. *Biometrics, 2,* 47–53.

Bowers, M. B., Jr., Mazure, C. M., Nelson, J. C., & Jatlow, P. I. (1990). Psychotogenic drug use and neuroleptic response. *Schizophrenia Bulletin, 16*(1), 81–85.

Brady, K., Anton, R., Ballenger, J. C., Lydiard, B., Adinoff, B., & Selander, J. (1990). Cocaine abuse among schizophrenic patients. *American Journal of Psychiatry, 147,* 1164–1167.

Breakey, W. R., Goodell, H., Lorenz, P. C., & McHugh, P. R. (1974). Hallucinogenic drugs as precipitants of schizophrenia. *Psychological Medicine, 4,* 255–261.

Bryant, K. J., Rounsaville, B., Spitzer, R. L., & Williams, J. B. W. (1992). Reliability of dual diagnosis: Substance dependence and psychiatric disorders. *Journal of Nervous and Mental Disease, 180,* 251–257.

Carey, K. B., Cocco, K. M., & Simons, J. S. (1996). Concurrent validity of clinicians' ratings of substance abuse among psychiatric outpatients. *Psychiatric Services, 47,* 842–847.

Cohen, M., and Klein, D. F. (1970). Drug abuse in a young psychiatric population. *American Journal of Orthopsychiatry, 40,* 448–455.

Commonwealth Department of Health, Housing and Community Services (1992). *Statistics on drug abuse in Australia.* Canberra, Australia: Australian Government Printing Service.

Corty, E., Lehman, A.F., & Myers, C. P. (1993). Influence of psychoactive substance use on the reliability of psychiatric diagnosis. *Journal of Consulting and Clinical Psychology, 61,* 165–170.

DeQuardo, J. R., Carpenter, C. F., & Tandon, R. (1994). Patterns of substance abuse in schizophrenia: Nature and significance. *Journal of Psychiatric Research, 28,* 267–275.

Derogatis, L. (1977). SCL–90–R *Version: Manual 1.* Baltimore, MD: Johns Hopkins University Press.

Dixon, L., Dibietz, E., Myers, P., Conley, R., Medoff, D., & Lehman, A. F. (1993). Comparison of *DSM-III-R* diagnoses and a brief interview for substance use among state hospital patients. *Hospital and Community Psychiatry, 44,* 748–752.

Dixon, L., Haas, G., Dulit, R., Weiden, P., Sweeney, J., & Hien, D. (1989). Schizophrenia and substance abuse: Preferences, predictors, and psychopathology. [Abstract] *Schizophrenia Research, 2,* 6.

Dixon, L., Haas, G., Weiden, P., Sweeney, J., & Frances, A. (1990). Acute effects of drug abuse in schizophrenic patients: Clinical observations and patients' self-reports. *Schizophrenia Bulletin, 16*(1), 69–79.

Dixon, L., Haas, G., Weiden, P. J., Sweeney, J., & Frances, A. J. (1991). Drug abuse in schizophrenic patients: Clinical correlates and reasons for use. *American Journal of Psychiatry, 148,* 224–230.

Dixon, L., Weiden, P. J., Haas, G., Sweeney, J., & Frances, A. J. (1992). Increased tardive dyskinesia in alcohol-abusing schizophrenic patients. *Comprehensive Psychiatry, 33,* 121–122.

Dixon, W. J., Brown, M. B., Engelman, L., Hill, M. A., & Jennrich, R. I., (eds.). (1988). *BMDP Statistical Software Manual. Vols. 1 and 2.* Los Angeles, CA: University of California Press.

Drake, R. E., Antosca, L. M., Noordsy, D. L., Bartels, S. J., & Osher, F. C. (1991). New Hampshire's specialized services for the dually diagnosed. *New Directions for Mental Health Services, 50,* 57–67.

Drake, R. E., Gates, C., Cotton, P. G., & Whitaker, A. (1984). Suicide among schizophrenics: Who is at risk? *Journal of Nervous and Mental Disease, 172,* 613–617.

Drake, R. E., Osher, F. C., Noordsy, D. L., Hurlbut, S. C., Teague, G. B., & Beaudett, M. S. (1990). Diagnosis of alcohol use disorders in schizophrenia. *Schizophrenia Bulletin, 16*(1), 57–67.

Drake, R. E., Osher, F. C., & Wallach, M. A. (1989a). Alcohol use and abuse in schizophrenia: A prospective community study. *Journal of Nervous and Mental Disease, 17,* 408–414.

Drake, R. E., & Wallach, M. A. (1989). Substance abuse among the chronic mentally ill. *Hospital and Community Psychiatry, 40,* 1041–1045.

Drake, R. E., Wallach, M. A., & Hoffman, J. S. (1989b). Housing instability and homelessness among aftercare patients of an urban state hospital. *Hospital and Community Psychiatry, 40,* 46–51.

Dufort, G. G., Newman, S. C., & Bland, R. C. (1993). Psychiatric comorbidity and treatment seeking: Sources of selection bias in the study of clinical populations. *Journal of Nervous and Mental Disease, 181,* 467–474.

Duke, P. J., Pantelis, C., & Barnes, T. R. E. (1994). South Westminster schizophrenia survey: Alcohol use and its relationship to symptoms, tardive dyskinesia and illness onset. *British Journal of Psychiatry, 164,* 630–636.

Elangavan, N., Berman, S., Meinzer, A., Gianelli, P., Miller, H., & Longmore, W. (1993). Substance abuse among patients presenting at an inner-city psychiatric emergency room. *Hospital and Community Psychiatry, 44,* 782–784.

Hancock, L., Hennrikus, D., Henry, D. A., Sanson-Fisher, R., Walsh, R., & Lewis, J. H. (1991). Agreement between two measures of drug use in a low-prevalence population. *Addictive Behaviours, 16,* 507–516.

Hanson, M., Kramer, T. H., Gross, W., Quintana, J., Li, P. W., & Asher, R. (1992). AIDS awareness and risk behaviours among dually disordered adults. *AIDS Education and Prevention, 4,* 41–51.

Heather, N., Batey, R., Saunders, J. B., & Wodak, A. D. (1989). The effectiveness of treatment for drug and alcohol problems: An overview. *National Campaign Against Drug Abuse. Monograph Series, No. 11.* Canberra, Australia: Australian Government Publishing Service.

Helzer, J. E., Clayton, P. J., Pambakion, R., & Woodruff, R. A. (1978). Concurrent diagnostic validity of a structured psychiatric interview. *Archives of General Psychiatry, 35,* 849–853.

Johnson, B. D., & Muffler, J. Sociocultural determinants and perpetuators of substance abuse. In: Lowinson, J. H., Ruiz, P., Millman, R. B., & Langrod, J. G., (eds.). *Substance abuse: A comprehensive textbook, 3rd ed.* Baltimore, MD: Williams & Wilkins Company, 1997. pp. 107–117.

Khalsa, H. K., Shaner, A., Anglin, M. D., & Wang, J. (1991). Prevalence of substance abuse in a psychiatric evaluation unit. *Drug and Alcohol Dependence, 28,* 215–223.

Linszen, D. H., Dingemans, P. M., & Lentor, M. E. (1994). Cannabis abuse and the course of recent-onset schizophrenic disorders. *Archives of General Psychiatry, 51,* 273–279.

Lysaker, P., Bell, M., Beam-Goulet, J., & Milstein, R. (1994). Relationship of positive and negative symptoms to cocaine abuse in schizophrenia. *Journal of Nervous and Mental Disease, 182,* 109–112.

Marken, P. A., Stoner, S. C., & Bunker, M. T. (1996). Anticholinergic drug abuse and misuse—epidemiology and therapeutic implications. *CNS Drugs, 5,* 190–199.

Martinez-Arevalo, M. J., Calcedo-Ordonez, A., & Varo-Prieto, J. R. (1994). Cannabis consumption as a prognostic factor in schizophrenia. *British Journal of Psychiatry, 164,* 679–681.

McKenna, C., & Ross, C. R. (1994). Diagnostic conundrums in substance abusers with psychiatric symptoms: Variables suggestive of dual diagnosis. *American Journal of Drug and Alcohol Abuse, 20,* 397–412.

McLellan, A. T., & Druley, K. A. (1977). Non-random relation between drugs of abuse and psychiatric diagnosis. *Psychiatric Research, 13,* 179–184.

McNagny, S. E., & Parker, R. M. (1992). High prevalence of recent cocaine use and the unreliability of patient self-report in an inner-city walk-in clinic. *Journal of the American Medical Association, 267,* 1106-1108.

Miller, F. T., & Tanenbaum, J. H. (1989). Drug abuse in schizophrenia. *Hospital and Community Psychiatry, 40,* 847–849.

Mueser, K. T., Bellack, A. S., & Blanchard, J. J. (1992a). Comorbidity of schizophrenia and substance abuse: Implications for treatment. *Journal of Consulting and Clinical Psychology, 60,* 845–856.

Mueser, K. T., Yarnold, P. R., & Bellack, A. S. (1992b). Diagnostic and demographic correlates of substance abuse in schizophrenia and major affective disorder. *Acta Psychiatrica Scandinavica, 85,* 48–55.

Mueser, K. T., Yarnold, P. R., Levinson, D. F., Singh, H., Bellack, A. S., Kee, K., Morrison, R. L., & Yadalam, K. G. (1990). Prevalence of substance abuse in schizophrenia: Demographic and clinical correlates. *Schizophrenia Bulletin, 16*(1), 31–56.

Noordsy, D. L., Drake, R. E., Teague, G. B., Osher, F. C., Hurlbut, S. C., Beaudett, M. S., & Paskus, T. S. (1991). Subjective experiences related to alcohol use among schizophrenics. *Journal of Nervous and Mental Disease, 179,* 410–414.

Nunn, K. P., Lewin, T. J., Walton, J. M., & Carr, V. J. (1996). The construction and characteristics of an instrument to measure personal hopefulness. *Psychological Medicine, 26,* 531–545.

O'Farrell, T. J., Connors, G. J., & Upper, D. (1983). Addictive behaviors among hospitalized psychiatric patients. *Addictive Behaviors, 8,* 329–333.

Olivera, A. A., Keifer, M. W., & Manley, N. K. (1990). Tardive dyskinesia in psychiatric patients with substance use disorders. *American Journal of Drug and Alcohol Abuse, 16,* 57–66.

Parker, J. B., Meiller, R. M., & Andrews, G. W. (1960). Major psychiatric disorders masquerading as alcoholism. *Southern Medical Journal, 53,* 560–564.

Pokorny, A. D. (1965). The multiple readmission psychiatric patient. *Psychiatric Quarterly, 39,* 70–78.

Pristach, C. A., & Smith, C. M. (1990). Medication compliance and substance abuse among schizophrenic patients. *Hospital and Community Psychiatry, 41,* 1345–1348.

Regier, D. A., Farmer, M. E., Rae, D. S., Locke, B. Z., Keith, S. J., Judd, L. L., & Goodwin, F. K. (1990). Comorbidity of mental disorders with alcohol and other drug abuse. *Journal of the American Medical Association, 264,* 2511–2518.

Rich, C. L., Motooka, M. S., Fowler, R. C., & Young, D. (1988). Suicide by psychotics. *Biological Psychiatry, 23,* 595–601.

Richard, M. L., Liskow, B. I., & Perry, P. J. (1985). Recent psychostimulant use in hospitalized schizophrenics. *Journal of Clinical Psychiatry, 46,* 79–83.

Rockwell, D. A., & Ostwald, P. (1988). Amphetamine use and abuse in psychiatric patients. *Archives of General Psychiatry, 45,* 1023–1031.

Safer, D. (1987). Substance abuse by young adult chronic patients. *Hospital and Community Psychiatry, 38,* 511–514.

Satel, S. L., Seibyl, J. P., & Charney, D. S. (1991). Prolonged cocaine psychosis implies underlying major psychopathology. *Journal of Clinical Psychiatry, 52,* 349–350.

Seeman, M. V., Lang, M., & Rector, N. (1990). Chronic schizophrenia: A risk factor for HIV? *Canadian Journal of Psychiatry, 35,* 765–768.

Seibyl, J. P., Satel, S. L., Anthony, D., Southwick, S. M., Krystal, J. H., & Charney, D. S. (1993). Effects of cocaine on hospital course in schizophrenia. *Journal of Nervous and Mental Disease, 181,* 31–37.

Selzer, J. A., & Lieberman, J. A. (1993). Schizophrenia and substance abuse. *Psychiatric Clinics of North America, 16,* 401–412.

Shaner, A., Khalsa, M. A., Roberts, L., Wilkins, J., Anglin D., & Hsieh, S. C. (1993). Unrecognized cocaine use among schizophrenic patients. *American Journal of Psychiatry, 150,* 758–762.

Siris, S. G., Kane, J. M., Frechen, K., Sellow, A. P., Mandeli, J., & Fasano-Dube, B. (1988). Histories of substance abuse in patients with post-psychotic depressions. *Comprehensive Psychiatry, 29,* 550–557.

Siris, S. G., Mason, S. E., & Shuwall, M. A. (1993). Histories of substance abuse, panic, and suicidal ideation in schizophrenia patients with histories of postpsychotic depressions. *Progress in Neuropsychopharmacology and Biological Psychiatry, 17,* 609–617.

Skinner, M. A., & Sheu, W. J. (1982). Reliability of alcohol use indices: Lifetime drinking history and the MAST. *Journal of Studies on Alcohol, 42,* 1157–1170.

Smith, J., & Hucker, S. (1994). Schizophrenia and substance abuse. *British Journal of Psychiatry, 165,* 13–21.

Soni, S. D., Bamrah, J. S., & Krska, J. (1991). Effects of alcohol on serum fluphenazine levels in stable chronic schizophrenics. *Human Psychopharmacology, 6,* 301–306.

Soni, S. D., & Brownlee, M. (1991). Alcohol abuse in chronic schizophrenics: Implications for management in the community. *Acta Psychiatrica Scandinavia, 84,* 272–276.

Spitzer, R. L., Williams, J. B. W., & Gibbon, M. (1987). *Structured Clinical Interview for DSM-III-R (SCID-R).* New York, NY: New York State Psychiatric Institute, Biometrics Research.

Swanson, J. W., Holzer, C. E., Ganju, V. K., & Jono, R. T. (1990). Violence and psychiatric disorder in the community: Evidence from the Epidemiologic Catchment Area surveys. *Hospital and Community Psychiatry, 41,* 761–770.

Test, M. A., Wallisch, L. S., Allness, D. J., & Ripp, K. (1989). Substance use in young adults with schizophrenic disorders. *Schizophrenia Bulletin, 15*(3), 465–476.

Tucker, M. B. (1982). Social support and coping: Applications for the study of female drug abuse. *Journal of Social Issues, 38,* 117–137.

Turner, C., Lessler, J., & Devore, J. (1992). Effects of mode of administration and wording on reporting of drug use. In: Turner, C. F., Lessler, J. T., and Gfroerer, J. C., (eds.) *Survey Measurement of Drug Use: Methodological Studies.* Washington, DC: U.S. Government Printing Office, DHHS Publication No. (ADM) 92–1929, pp. 177–220.

Weiss, R. D., Mirin, S. M., Griffin, M. L., & Michael, J. L. (1988). Psychopathology in cocaine abusers: Changing trends. *Journal of Nervous and Mental Disease, 176,* 719–725.

Westermeyer, J. Schizophrenia and substance abuse. (1992). In: Tasman, A., & Riba, M. B., (eds.). *Review of Psychiatry. Vol. 11.* Washington, DC: American Psychiatric Press, pp. 379–401.

Zaretsky, A., Rector, N. A., Seeman, M. V., & Fornazzari, X. (1993). Current cannabis use and tardive dyskinesia. *Schizophrenia Research, 11,* 3–8.

Zisook, S., Heaton, R., Moranville, J., Kuck, J., Jernigan, T., & Braff, D. (1992). Past substance abuse and clinical course of schizophrenia. *American Journal of Psychiatry, 149,* 552–553.

Remission of Substance Use Disorder Among Psychiatric Inpatients with Mental Illness

Lisa Dixon, Scot McNary & Anthony F. Lehman

This article originally appeared in the *American Journal of Psychiatry*, 155, 2, February 1998, 239–243, and is reprinted with permission.

Lisa Dixon, M.D., M.P.H., Scot McNary, M.A., and Anthony F. Lehman, M.D., M.S.P.H.

Dr. Dixon is at the Department of Psychiatry, University of Maryland, Baltimore, Maryland.

Supported by National Institute of Drug Abuse grant DA-05114 and NIMH grant MH-01250

Objective: The authors assessed the nature and stability of remission of substance use disorder among persons with severe mental illness at index hospitalization and at 1-year follow-up. Method: Consecutively admitted inpatients with severe mental illness completed the Structured Clinical Interview for DSM-III-R, Quality of Life Interview, and Addiction Severity Index at admission and 1 year later. Of the 268 patients, 70 were classified as past substance abusers in remission at baseline. Baseline characteristics and 1-year outcomes of this group were compared with those of the 109 current substance abusers and the 89 patients who were not substance abusers. Results: The past abusers were significantly more likely to be women, and they consistently differed significantly from the current abusers in variables involving frequency of drug and alcohol use at baseline. During the follow-up period, the patients with current abuse at baseline were significantly more likely to have recurrences of substance use disorders and to use substance abuse services, and they had significantly more months of alcohol use and alcohol use to excess during follow-up than did the past abusers. Conclusions: Baseline and follow-up assessments suggested that a substantial proportion of severely mentally ill patients with past substance use disorders are in stable remission.

Little is known about the course of substance use disorders when they occur with mental illness (Bartels, Drake, & Wallach, 1995). In a recent review of the literature on course and outcome of substance use in severely mentally ill adults, Drake et al. (Drake et al., 1992) concluded that the rate of remission of substance use disorder for persons with severe mental illness is broadly similar to that for the general population, i.e., only a few patients achieve stable remission. A 7-year naturalistic study of 148 persons with severe mental illness (Bartels, Drake, & Wallach, 1995) showed that the prevalence of active substance use disorders changed little from baseline to follow-up and that individuals with baseline diagnoses of abuse rather than dependence were more likely to have achieved remission after 7 years. Treatment studies have yielded inconsistent results, but the authors of a review of 13 studies of treatment for dually diagnosed patients concluded that overall substance abuse was only minimally reduced (Mercer-McFadden & Drake, 1995).

Related to the course of substance abuse in dually diagnosed individuals is the extent to which the adverse consequences of substance use can be reversed with sobriety. Ries et al. (Ries, Mullen, & Cox, 1994) compared current substance abusers, past abusers, and nonabusers among 104 hospitalized patients. They found a continuum of symptoms and resource use; patients with current substance use disorders had the most severe symptoms and used the most treatment resources, patients with past substance use disorders were in the middle, and patients without substance use disorders had the least severe symptoms and least resource use. Kovasznay (Kovasznay, 1991) compared similar groups of patients and found that the mean number of hospitalizations differed significantly between patients with current substance abuse and nonabusers; patients with past substance abuse fell in between. Other investigators (Cleghorn et al., 1991; Zisook et al., 1992) have found few clinical differences between past substance abusers and nonabusers.

These studies suggest that remission of substance abuse does occur in persons with serious mental illness and that the adverse consequences of substance abuse may attenuate over time. However, these conclusions are speculative in the absence of prospective studies of persons with mental illness and substance use disorders that evaluate diverse outcomes. In this study we took advantage of a database of consecutively admitted psychiatric inpatients with severe mental illness who were systematically evaluated at admission and 1-year follow-up. We compared the nature of substance use patterns and remission in persons with current substance use disorders and those with past substance use disorders. We also compared these groups on clinical and demographic characteristics and assessed the association of substance abuse status (none versus current versus past) with functioning, quality of life, and service utilization at baseline and follow-up.

Method

Procedure

All patients admitted to two inner-city psychiatric hospitals, one state operated and the other university operated, were screened between May 1988 and November 1990. These two hospitals are the principal psychiatric facilities serving an urban catchment area of approximately 160,000. The inclusion criteria for all the subjects in the study were as follows: age 18 to 65 years, current residence in the catchment area, ability to speak English, not currently being a ward of the criminal justice system, and competency to give informed consent. All patients were screened within 1 week after admission. After complete description of the study, all subjects provided written informed consent. Information was protected by a Federal Certificate of Confidentiality.

A total of 435 patients admitted to the two psychiatric hospitals during the 30-month recruitment period entered the study. The overall consent rate was 71%. The participants did not differ from the nonparticipants on gender, race, and age; however, the nonparticipants had higher rates of schizophrenia and other psychoses than did the participants. The subjects were contacted again 1 year after their baseline interviews.

Measures

The Structured Clinical Interview for *DSM-III-R*—Patient Version (SCID-P) (Spitzer, Williams, & Gibbon, 1987) was used to assess current and lifetime *DSM-III-R* axis I diagnoses. The interrater reliability (kappa) for the SCID-P principal diagnosis was 0.81. The SCID-P also provided information on the percentage of time over the last 5 years for which the patients reported symptoms of substance use disorder. As discussed extensively elsewhere (Lehman et al., 1993), the SCID-P was modified in this study to distinguish patients thought to have an independent mental disorder not due to substance abuse from those with a mental disorder due to substance abuse. This study included only the individuals with current mental disorders that were definitely not due to current substance use disorders.

The Addiction Severity Index (McLellan et al., 1980) is a structured interview assessing the severity of problems related to alcohol and/or drug abuse in seven areas. It also yields detailed information on the course of substance use during the last 30 days. The reliabilities (intraclass correlations) for the Addiction Severity Index composite scores ranged from 0.87 to 0.99.

The Quality of Life Interview (Lehman, 1988) is a 45-minute structured patient interview assessing the quality of life in eight areas: living situation, family relations, social relations, leisure activities, work, finances, safety and legal problems, and health. Interrater reliabilities for the life satisfaction domains ranged from 0.67 to 0.95. The Quality of Life Interview also provided information about the use of specific psychiatric, alcohol, and drug treatment services during the follow-up period.

After the baseline hospitalization, a record review form was used to review each patient's medical records to abstract data on a wide variety of clinical and treatment variables, including the results of urine toxicology screens done at admission.

Data Analysis

Chi-square tests of association were conducted to assess group differences among the patients with current substance use disorders, those with past substance use disorders, and those with no substance use disorders in categorical demographic, clinical, and service use variables. Analysis of variance (ANOVA) was used to assess group differences among the patients with current, past, and no substance use disorders in continuous clinical status variables. Results for overall ANOVAs and all other tests were considered to be significant for p values of less than 0.01. The ANOVAs were followed by Tukey's honestly significant difference adjustment for multiple comparisons. Kruskal-Wallis tests were used to assess differences between the substance-abusing groups in numbers of days, months, and years of substance use before the assessments and in number of previous treatments. A nonparametric test was used because of positively skewed data. All tests were two-tailed.

Attrition

Approximately 66% of the patients were reinterviewed. The proportions of patients lost to follow-up were similar across substance use groups: current, 35%; past, 33%; none, 34%. Follow-up assessments were completed for 71 patients with current substance use disorder at baseline, 47 patients with past substance use disorder, and 59 patients without substance use disorder. The patients lost to follow-up did not differ from those who completed the second interview in demographic characteristics or in baseline clinical status. The results of the analyses of baseline data did not differ when the patients lost to follow-up were excluded.

Table I

Characteristics of hospitalized patients with severe mental illness and current substance abuse, past substance abuse, or no substance abuse

Variable	Current Substance Use Disorder $(N = 109)^a$		Past Substance Use Disorder $(N = 70)^a$		No Substance Use Disorder $(N = 89)^a$		Total $(N = 268)^a$	
	Mean	SD	Mean	SD	Mean	SD	Mean	SD
Age (years)	33.7	9.3	34.1	9.8	34.0	10.7	33.9	9.8
	N	%	N	%	N	%	N	%
Male	71	65[b]	29	43	35	42	135	52
African American	60	58	39	57	54	67	153	60
Never married	63	58	38	57	50	59	151	58
High school graduate	47	44	43	63	36	44	126	49
Schizophrenia	42	39	31	44	33	37	106	40
Alcohol use disorder without other substance abuse	34	31	27	39				

a. Total number of subjects varies because of missing data.
b. $\chi^2 = 13.13, df = 2, p = 0.001$.

Results

Study Group

A total of 268 patients with primary *DSM-III-R* axis I diagnoses other than substance use disorder were classified into three groups. There were 109 individuals diagnosed with current comorbid substance use disorders, 70 individuals with past comorbid substance use disorders, and 89 individuals with no substance use diagnosis. Toxicology screens performed for 46 past abusers showed only two patients (4%) with positive tests, one for marijuana and another for cocaine. The past abusers were more likely to be women (table 1).

Baseline

The baseline assessments (table 2) showed that during the past month the patients with current substance use disorders had used the following substances on more days than had the patients with past substance use disorders: alcohol, alcohol to excess, heroin, cocaine, cannabis, and multiple substances. The patients with current substance abuse had higher scores on the Addiction Severity Index measures of alcohol and drug problems than did the past abusers and nonabusers (table 2).

The patients with current substance use disorders were significantly *more* likely to report having experienced alcohol or drug disorder symptoms more than 50% of the time during the 5 years before the baseline assessment, and they were *less* likely to report having had alcohol or drug disorder symptoms 0% of the time (table 2). The current abusers reported significantly more lifetime total years of alcohol use and of alcohol use to intoxication (table 2). The current abusers had also received significantly more treatments for alcohol use than had the past abusers (table 2).

With regard to measures other than those directly involving substance abuse, the patients with past substance use disorders had greater severity of family problems, as shown by the Addiction Severity Index, than did the nonabusers (past abusers: mean score = 0.33, SD = 0.25; nonabusers: mean = 0.16, SD = 0.21) (t = 3.39, df = 89, $p<0.01$). The current substance abusers had significantly greater severity of legal problems, as shown by scores on the Addiction Severity Index (mean = 0.11, SD = 0.20), than did the past abusers (mean = 0.02, SD = 0.06) or the nonabusers (mean = 0.02, SD = 0.07) (current versus past: t = 3.42, df = 106, $p<0.005$; current versus none: t = 3.61, df = 116, $p<0.005$).

Follow-Up

During the follow-up period the patients with current substance abuse at baseline were significantly more likely to experience a recurrence of substance use disorder, were more likely to use a substance abuse service, and had more months of alcohol use and alcohol use to excess than past substance abusers (table 3). There were no significant differences in the use of psychiatric services. The current abusers also had significantly greater severity of alcohol problems than the nonabusers at follow-up (table 3). When baseline status was controlled for, no differences emerged in the drug and alcohol composite scores from the Addiction Severity Index. No significant differences among the groups were found at follow-up in measures other than substance abuse.

Discussion

This naturalistic study suggests that a substantial proportion of patients with severe mental illness and past substance use disorders have stable remissions of their substance use disorders. Evidence from patient self-report, toxicology screens, and clinical records at baseline and from 1-year follow-up patient interviews suggests that as many as 75% of patients whose self-reports are consistent with past diagnoses of substance use disorders may in fact be experiencing stable remission or recovery. If it is assumed that all of the patients who were lost to follow-up had suffered recurrences of their substance use disorders, a more conservative estimate of stable recovery from this study would be 50%, still impressive given the unfortunate vulnerability of these individuals to substance abuse. The lower rate of substance abuse during follow-up reported by persons in remission at baseline was accompanied by a lower rate of use of treatment services for substance abuse.

Men were more likely to be classified as current users than women. It is possible that women are more likely to achieve recovery than men. It is also possible that this observation is an artifact of the study setting; men with current substance use disorders may be more likely to develop substance-induced behavioral problems resulting in hospitalization. This finding may also be related to the possibility that women with substance use disorders are underrepresented in substance abuse treatment (Center for Substance Abuse Treatment, 1994).

The lack of differences in non-substance-abuse outcomes observed between nonabusers and both current and past abusers is surprising. It might be due to the fact that the inpatient sampling procedure resulted in selection of patients with a restricted range of functioning and high levels of symptoms and acute problems, obscuring any differences due to substance abuse. Also, the subjects in the study group tended to suffer from poverty and a host of other social problems, factors that may diminish the marginal effects of substance abuse on overall outcome.

This study has several important limitations. First, the study group was representative of an urban catchment area and may not resemble other groups of dually diagnosed patients in substance disorder symptoms or course. The patients reinterviewed at 1-year follow-up may not be representative of dually diagnosed patients, who are difficult to engage in assessment and treatment (Drake et al., 1992). Finally, although collected by way of structured clinical interviews and review of medical charts, the data were largely gathered through self-report and were susceptible to selective responses by the patients. In spite of these limitations, we think these findings provide reason for some optimism regarding remission of substance abuse among persons with mental illness, even those who experience major problems with their mental illness leading to inpatient hospitalization.

Table 2

Significant differences at baseline among hospitalized patients with severe mental illness and current substance abuse, past substance abuse, or no substance abuse

Baseline Variable	Current Substance Use Disorder (N = 109)		Past Substance Use Disorder (N = 70)		No Substance Use Disorder (N = 89)		Analysis		
	Mean	SD	Mean	SD	Mean	SD	χ^2	df	p
Days of substance use in past month									
Alcohol	8.91	10.64	1.96	5.33	—	—	16.78	1	<0.001
Alcohol to excess	6.22	9.33	0.21	0.75	—	—	21.75	1	<0.001
Heroin	2.97	8.56	0.00	0.00	—	—	10.70	1	<0.005
Cocaine	3.91	9.23	0.04	0.29	—	—	19.30	1	<0.001
Cannabis	3.30	8.02	0.08	0.35	—	—	11.71	1	<0.001
Multiple substances	3.77	8.22	0.17	1.17	—	—	17.02	1	<0.001
Past years of alcohol use									
Alcohol	12.39	10.17	5.02	7.81	—	—	16.75	1	<0.001
Alcohol to excess	7.43	8.72	3.40	7.00	—	—	11.73	1	<0.001
Number of previous treatments for alcohol disorders	1.91	3.99	0.34	0.92	—	—	11.21	1	<0.001

(continued)

Table 2 (continued)

Significant differences at baseline among hospitalized patients with severe mental illness and current substance abuse, past substance abuse, or no substance abuse

Baseline Variable	Current Substance Use Disorder (N = 109)		Past Substance Use Disorder (N = 70)		No Substance Use Disorder (N = 89)		Analysis		
	Mean	SD	Mean	SD	Mean	SD	χ^2	df	p
Addiction Severity Index severity scores									
Alcohol	0.24	0.26	0.04	0.07	0.02	0.04			
Current versus past abusers							5.82	88	<0.001
Current versus nonabusers							6.65	96	<0.001
Drugs	0.11	0.14	0.01	0.02	0.00	0.01			
Current versus past abusers							5.39	88	<0.001
Current versus nonabusers							6.07	97	<0.001
	N	%	N	%	N	%	χ^2	df	p
Proportion of time in last 5 years in which substance abuse symptoms were present[a]									
More than 50% of time									
Alcohol[b]	47	59	8	23			12.57	1	<0.001
Drugs[c]	39	50	8	20			9.93	1	<0.005
0% of time									
Alcohol[b]	5	6	18	51			31.06	1	<0.001
Drugs[c]	12	15	19	48			14.08	1	<0.01

a. Recorded on the SCID-P for each patient who received a diagnosis of drug or alcohol dependence.

b. Current abusers, N = 80; past abusers, N = 35.

c. Current abusers, N = 78; past abusers, N = 40.

Table 3

Significant differences at follow-up among hospitalized patients with severe mental illness and current substance abuse, past substance abuse, or no substance abuse at baseline

Follow-Up Variable	Current Substance Use Disorder (N = 71)		Past Substance Use Disorder (N = 47)		No Substance Use Disorder (N = 59)		Analysis		
	N	%	N	%	N	%	χ^2	df	p
Recurrence of substance use disorder[a]	41	59	10	22			22.64	1	<0.001
Treatment for substance abuse	30	42	9	19			6.82	1	<0.01
	Mean	SD	Mean	SD	Mean	SD	t	df	p
Addiction Severity Index severity score for alcohol	0.13	0.20	0.06	0.11	0.03	0.12	3.16[b]	96	<0.01
	Mean	SD	Mean	SD	Mean	SD	χ^2	df	p
Months of alcohol use in past year									
Alcohol	6.43	5.86	3.36	5.56	—	—	9.55	1	<0.01
Alcohol to excess	4.21	5.62	2.15	5.13	—	—	9.83	1	<0.005

a. Current abusers, N = 70; past abusers, N = 46.
b. Current abusers versus nonabusers.

References

Bartels, S. J., Drake, R. E., & Wallach, M. A. (1995). Long-term course of substance use disorders among patients with severe mental illness. *Psychiatric Services, 46,* 248-251.

Center for Substance Abuse Treatment. (1994). *Practical approaches in the treatment of women who abuse alcohol and other drugs.* Rockville, MD: Center for Substance Abuse Treatment.

Cleghorn, J. M., Kaplan, R. D., Szechtman, B., Szechtman, H., Brown, G. R., & Franco, S. (1991). Substance abuse and schizophrenia: Effect on symptoms but not on neurocognitive function. *Journal of Clinical Psychiatry, 52,* 26-30.

Drake, R. E., Mueser, K. T., Clark, R. E., & Wallach, M. A. (1996). The course, treatment, and outcome of substance disorder in persons with severe mental illness. *American Journal of Orthopsychiatry, 66,* 42-51.

Kovasznay, B. (1991). Substance abuse among veterans with a diagnosis of schizophrenia. *Hospital and Community Psychiatry, 42,* 948-949.

Lehman, A. F. (1988). A quality of life interview for the chronically mentally ill. *Evaluation and Program Planning, 11,* 51-62.

Lehman, A. F., Myers, C. P., Thompson, J. W., & Corty, E. (1993). Implications of mental and substance use disorders: A comparison of single and dual diagnosis patients. *Journal of Nervous and Mental Disease, 181,* 365-370.

McLellan, A. T., Luborsky, L., Woody, G. E., & O'Brien, C. P. (1980). An improved diagnostic evaluation instrument for substance abuse patients: The Addiction Severity Index. *Journal of Nervous and Mental Disease, 168,* 26-33.

Mercer-McFadden, C., & Drake, R. E. (1995). *A review of 13 NIMH demonstration projects for young adults with severe mental illness and substance abuse problems.* Rockville, MD: US Department of Health and Human Services, Center for Mental Health Services, Community Support Program.

Ries, R., Mullen, M., & Cox, G. (1994). Symptom severity and utilization of treatment resources among dually diagnosed inpatients. *Hospital and Community Psychiatry, 45,* 562-567.

Spitzer, R. L., Williams, J. B. W., & Gibbon, M. (1987). *Structured clinical interview for DSM-III-R-Patient Version (SCID-P).* New York, NY: State Psychiatric Institute, Biometrics Research.

Zisook, S., Heaton, R., Moranville, J., Kuck, J., Jernigan, T., & Braff, D. (1992). Past substance abuse and clinical course of schizophrenia. *American Journal of Psychiatry, 149,* 552-553.

Effect of Substance Misuse in Early Psychosis

Jean Addington & Donald Addington

This article originally appeared in *The British Journal of Psychiatry*, 172, (supplement 33), 134–136, 1998, and is reprinted with permission.

Jean Addington, Ph.D., Donald Addington, FRCPC, Department of Psychiatry, University of Calgary, Alberta, Canada.

Background: Studies examining the temporal relationship between substance use and the onset of psychotic symptoms in schizophrenia are inconclusive. Method: Three groups of outpatients with schizophrenia were compared on onset of illness, symptoms and quality of life. Fifty-one subjects had no past or present history of substance misuse, 29 subjects had a history of past substance misuse occurring around the onset of their illness, and 33 subjects were currently misusing substances. Results: Current substance misusers had poorer quality of life scores and less negative symptoms than the non-users. Those who had a past history of substance misuse had a significantly earlier age of onset than those with no substance use. Conclusions: Attention should be paid to substance misuse present at the first episode. Treatment for schizophrenia should begin even though a diagnosis of drug-induced psychosis cannot be ruled out.

Studies examining the temporal relationship between substance use and the onset of psychotic symptoms in schizophrenia are inconclusive. From the literature there appears to be a high incidence of substance misuse in first-episode samples (Hambrecht & Hafner, 1996). Several reasons for this have been proposed. Substance use may precede the onset of the illness and thus be considered a precipitant or cause. For example, there is evidence to suggest that certain drugs, such as stimulants, can precipitate onset at an earlier age in biologically vulnerable people (Breakey et al., 1974; Richard et al., 1985; Tsuang et al., 1982). Although it is unclear how this may happen it has been suggested that repeated stimulant misuse may alter the dopamine system (Mueser et al., 1992). Substance misuse may follow the onset of the illness and may be seen as an attempt to self-medicate (Dixon et al., 1991; Schneier & Siris, 1987). Thus, in the case of people with first-episode psychosis, early symptom onset may be a risk factor for substance misuse. Substance misuse may accompany the schizophrenia disorder independently, that is in the absence of a causal relationship. This is probably the least likely since the incidence of substance misuse has consistently been reported to be higher in people with schizophrenia compared with control groups (Mueser et al., 1992).

Thus, no studies are conclusive with respect to the relationship between substance use and the onset of psychotic symptoms (Turner & Tsuang, 1990). However a recent study attempts to clarify the position (Hambrecht & Hafner, 1998). In this study the onset and course of schizophrenia and substance misuse were retrospectively assessed in 232 people with first-episode schizophrenia. Alcohol misuse more often followed than preceded the first symptom of schizophrenia. Drug misuse preceded the first symptom in 27.5 % of the cases, followed it in 37.9%, and emerged within the same month in 34.6% of the cases. The mean age at onset of schizophrenia as well as the age at first admission was lower in people who had misused drugs than those without a history of substance misuse.

The incidence of substance misuse in these young people with first episodes generally raises clinical concern. Our attention was further drawn to this issue when two observations were made about data from earlier studies. First, in a sample of 33 individuals diagnosed with schizophrenia and substance misuse (Addington & Addington, 1997) it was noted that approximately 50% had received at least one diagnosis of drug-induced psychosis in the early course of their illness. This fitted with our clinical experience that many young people with schizophrenia first present with what may appear to be a substance-induced psychosis. As a result they may not be offered treatment for schizophrenia until a later admission. This is of concern given recent evidence that suggests a delay in treatment may have an impact on later recovery. Duration of illness before neuroleptic treatment has been found to be significantly associated with time to remission and with level of remission (Loebel et al., 1992; Szymanski et al., 1996; Wyatt, 1991).

The second observation was in a sample of 80 stable outpatients with schizophrenia who were recruited for a social and cognitive functioning study (Addington & Addington, 1998). This sample was representative of an outpatient clinic in a department of psychiatry in a general hospital. Substance misuse in the past year was an exclusion criterion for this study. However, 29 (36%) of the subjects had a past history of substance misuse or dependence. For all of these people the misuse had either occurred up to three years prior to the onset of the schizophrenia or at the most three years after first admission. This suggests that the substance misuse is associated with the onset of schizophrenia.

Most studies examining correlates or predictors of substance misuse in schizophrenia tend to compare people with schizophrenia who misuse substances with people with schizophrenia with no history of substance misuse. We were concerned about people with first episodes and we wanted to see if there were differences between people with schizophrenia with no history of substance misuse with those whose problems with substances occurred in the period immediately before the onset of their illness and immediately after. In particular we were interested in differences in age at onset, age at first admission and outcome in terms of symptoms and level of functioning.

Method

Subjects

Eighty outpatients (54 males, 26 females) with schizophrenia were identified from an outpatient clinic in a general hospital department of psychiatry and a community mental health clinic. They were recruited for a larger study that was examining the relationship between social and cognitive functioning in schizophrenia. These people were divided into two groups. One group consisted of 51 people who had no past or current history of substance misuse or dependence. The other consisted of 29 people who had no current substance misuse or dependence but retrospectively met *DSM-III-R* criteria (American Psychiatric Association, 1987) for substance misuse or dependence sometime in the three years before or the five years after the onset of their illness. Onset of illness was determined as the time that psychotic symptoms were first apparent. This information was obtained by using the Structured Clinical Interview for *DSM-III-R* (SCID; Spitzer et al., 1990) and chart review.

A third group of 33 outpatients (29 males, 4 females) with schizophrenia who met criteria for substance misuse or dependence were identified from an outpatient clinic in a general hospital department of psychiatry and a community mental health clinic and were recruited for the present study. The substance misuse group met criteria for dependence of at least one substance. This group was further divided into the following subgroups: (a) alcohol dependence (12 people); (b) cannabis dependence (five people); (c) alcohol dependence or misuse plus cannabis dependence or misuse (12 people); and (d) other criteria (four people, one with alcohol dependence plus past "crack" cocaine dependence, one with codeine dependence, one with codeine (in the form of a systemic cough and decongestant preparation) dependence, and one with alcohol and barbiturate dependence). All of the people in the substance misuse group had at one time or other been referred to a substance or dual-diagnosis program for treatment. The implication is that either caregivers or significant others had perceived these individuals to have a problem with substances. The majority of the subjects were single, lived alone and received governmental financial support.

Diagnoses of schizophrenia and substance misuse or dependence according to *DSM-III-R* criteria (American Psychiatric Association, 1987) were made, using the SCID interview. Diagnoses were made by D.A. and J.A. Interrater reliability was determined in a separate sample of 10 people by 100% agreement on the diagnosis and at least 80% agreement for symptom presence. All the individuals met criteria for schizophrenia. However, they were excluded if they had: (a) evidence of an organic central nervous system disorder (e.g. epilepsy, traumatic brain injury, infectious or toxic cerebrovascular disease); (b) learning disability; (c) under 18 or over 65 years of age. The study was described verbally and in writing to each participant. Written informed consent was obtained from each person.

Measures

The Positive and Negative Syndrome Scale (PANSS; Kay et al., 1987) was used to obtain ratings for positive and negative symptoms. The PANSS was administered by J.A. and a clinical research nurse. Interrater reliability was determined in a separate sample of five people to at least 85% reliability on the syndrome scores and no more than one point difference on any individual symptom items.

The Quality of Life Scale (QLS; Heinrichs et al., 1984) is a 21-item interviewer rating scale, providing information on functioning during the preceding four weeks. Each item is rated on a seven-point scale and in all but two cases requires a judgement by the clinician. It measures adjustment on four sub-scales: interpersonal relations, instrumental role functioning, intrapsychic foundations (e.g. motivation), and common objects and activities (owning a car, reading a book). The QLS was administered by a clinical research nurse.

Effect of Substance Misuse in Early Psychosis

Table I
Differences among groups in study

	No Substance Misuse Group (n = 51)		Past Substance Misuse Group (n = 29)		Current Substance Misuse Group (n = 33)		F	d.f. (110,2)
	mean	(SD)	mean	(SD)	mean	(SD)		
Gender (male:female)	31:20		23:6		29:4			
Age	38.1	(9.6)¹	31.2	(7.7)¹	34.3	(7.7)	6.2**	
Age at onset	24.7	(7.3)¹	20.4	(4.5)¹	23.0	(7.02)	4.1*	
Age at first admission	26.0	(7.8)	22.4	(8.6)	24.2	(6.6)	NS	
PANSS (positive)	13.6	(5.6)	13.8	(5.5)	15.3	(5.5)	NS	
PANSS (negative)	17.1	(6.7)¹	16.1	(5.4)	14.0	(4.0)¹	2.9*	
PANSS (GPS)	26.5	(7.3)	28.4	(8.0)	28.0	(6.1)	NS	
Quality of life	76.3	(16.9)	75.0	(17.7)	59.8	(20.6)²	8.9***	

PANSS. Positive and Negative Syndrome Scale: GPS, General Psychopathology Scale.
1. Significantly different from each other.
2. Significantly different from the other two groups.
*$P<0.05$, **$P < 0.01$. ***$P <0.001$.

Results

Seven one-way ANOVAs were conducted to compare the three groups on age, age at first admission, age at onset, symptoms, and quality of life total scores. The significant results were that people with past substance misuse were significantly younger at age of onset than those with no history of substance misuse. Those who were currently misusing substances had poorer quality of life scores than the other two groups and less negative symptoms than the non-misuser group. Results are presented in table 1.

In the group of current misusers, of the four people in the subgroup "other criteria," none of the PANSS or QLS scores were more than two SDs above or below the means for the substance-misusing group as a whole.

Discussion

Results of this study suggest that individuals with schizophrenia and substance misuse function at a lower level than their peers in the non-misusing group with schizophrenia in areas of interpersonal relationships, motivation, role functioning, activities and ownership of possessions. They also have lower levels of negative symptoms. However, the most notable difference among the three groups is that the people with past substance misuse had a significantly younger age of onset than those people in the non-misuser group. This was not accounted for by gender differences. It is possible that for the past misuse group the first psychotic episode was exacerbated by the use of drugs and/or alcohol or that early onset symptoms are a risk factor for using substances. Although not significant the past misuse group had a younger age of onset than the people in the current misuse group.

Retrospectively, people who would have been diagnosed with substance misuse in the early stages of the schizophrenic illness fall into two groups in the later stages of the illness. First, those who continue to use substances and second, those whose substance misuse occurred immediately prior to and/or immediately after the onset of schizophrenia. For the latter group there are several possibilities. It may be that drug and alcohol misuse is part of the poor premorbid history that is evident in many individuals with schizophrenia. However, substance misuse is not uncommon and for those with a vulnerability to schizophrenia the substance misuse may act as a trigger to the onset of the illness. Third, the substance misuse may occur in either the prodromal stage or with the onset of psychotic symptoms as a means to either cope with the illness or to self-medicate the symptoms. The substance misuse may then ameliorate once the illness is stabilized. Finally, those individuals who have an early onset of symptoms could be more vulnerable to substance misuse.

This study clearly has limitations. Diagnoses of past substance misuse were done retrospectively. The age of onset was determined by interviewing the individuals and chart review. There is a greater risk of inaccuracy in determining the time of onset if the individual is using substances. Although only seven ANOVAs were conducted there are dangers in carrying out multiple analyses in this way. Despite these tentative results, there are some implications for clinical management. Regardless of the potentially different reasons for misusing substances in people with first-episode psychosis substance use should be routinely assessed and treatment should be immediately available if required. This also raises the possibility that prophylactic pharmacotherapy may have the potential to reduce relapse rates even though drug-induced psychosis cannot initially be ruled out.

References

Addington, J., & Addington, D. (1997). Cognitive and social functioning in schizophrenia out-patients who abuse substances. *Journal of Psychiatry and Neuroscience, 22,* 99–104.

Addington, J., & Addington, D. (1998). Neurocognitive and social functioning in schizophrenia. *Schizophrenic Bulletin,* in press.

American Psychiatric Association (1987). *Diagnostic and Statistical Manual for Mental Disorders (3rd ed., revised) (DSM-III-R).* Washington, DC: APA.

Breakey, W. R., Goodell, H., Lorenz, P. C., et al. (1974). Hallucinogenic drugs as precipitants of schizophrenia. *Psychological Medicine, 4,* 255–261.

Dixon, L., Haas, G., Weiden, P., et al. (1991). Drug abuse in schizophrenic patients: clinical correlates and reasons for use. *American Journal of Psychiatry, 148,* 224–230.

Hambrecht, M. & Hafner, H. (1996). Substance abuse and the onset of schizophrenia. *Biological Psychiatry, 39,* 1–9.

Heinrichs, D. W., Hanlon, T. E., & Carpenter, W. T. (1984). The Quality of Life Scale: an instrument for rating the schizophrenic deficit syndrome. *Schizophrenic Bulletin, 10,* 388–398.

Kay, S. R., Fiszbein, A., & Opler, L. A. (1987). The positive and negative syndrome Scale PANSS for Schizophrenia. *Schizophrenia Bulletin, 13,* 261–276.

Loebel, A. D., Lieberman, J. A., Alvir, J. M. J., et al. (1992). Duration of psychosis and outcome in first-episode schizophrenia. *American Journal of Psychiatry, 149,* 1183–1188.

Mueser, K. T., Bellack, A. S., & Blanchard, J. J. (1992). Comorbidity of schizophrenia and substance abuse: implications for treatment. *Journal of Clinical and Consulting Psychology, 60,* 845–856.

Richard, M. L., Liskow, B. I., & Perry, P. J. (1985). Recent psychostimulant use in hospitalized schizophrenics. *Journal of Clinical Psychiatry, 46,* 79–83.

Schneier, F. R., & Siris, S. G. (1987). A review of psychoactive substance use and abuse in schizophrenia. *Journal of Nervous and Mental Disease, 175,* 641–652.

Spitzer, R. L., Williams, J. B., Gibbon, M., et al. (1990). *User's guide for the Structured Clinical Interview for DSM-III-R SCID.* Washington, DC: American Psychiatric Press.

Szymanski, S. R., Cannon, T. D., Gallacher, F., et al. (1996). Course of treatment response in first-episode and chronic schizophrenia. *American Journal of Psychiatry, 153,* 519–525.

Tsuang, M. T., Simpson, J. C., & Kronfol, Z. (1982). Subtypes of drug abuse with psychosis: demographic characteristics, clinical features and family history. *Archives of General Psychiatry , 39,* 141–147.

Turner, W. M., & Tsuang, M. T. (1990). Impact of substance abuse on the course and outcome of schizophrenia. *Schizophrenia Bulletin, 16,* 87–95.

Wyatt, R. J. (1991). Neuroleptics and the natural course of schizophrenia. *Schizophrenia Bulletin, 17,* 325–351.

First Person Account: My Voyage Through Turbulence

Ruth Malloy

This article originally appeared in the *Schizophrenia Bulletin*, 1998, 24(3), 495–497.

Ruth Malloy is a naturalized Canadian who was born in the United States. She received primary and secondary school education in the United States and has a BA and an MA from the University of Toronto. She retired in 1994 from a position as teacher of English as a Second Language and Literacy at Queen Street Mental Health Centre in Toronto, and is involved in voluntary advocacy and support work for persons with schizophrenia and their families. Ms. Malloy is past president of the Schizophrenia Society of Ontario, East York chapter.

In young adulthood I watched a generous, brilliant, and respected father lose everything as a result of an undiagnosed and untreated mental disorder. He had several implausible stories he liked to tell about how he had outwitted people who were plotting against him. Could his mysterious breakdown have been due to a mild schizophrenia spectrum disorder? Perhaps!

When I married and had children, I tried to compensate with good parenting skills for any predisposition toward mental illness they might have inherited from their grandfather. Ironically, we also found mental illness in my husband's family later on. Moreover, childhood emotional trauma or skewed family relationships do not cause schizophrenia. When three of our eight children developed schizophrenia, it was probably inevitable.

Sylvia Geist, presently president of the Schizophrenia Society of Canada, in her doctoral thesis, called coping with schizophrenia a voyage through turbulence. Our voyage through turbulence began around our son's 18th birthday. We noticed an odd change in his facial expression. It might have been due to the abnormal eye tracking movements sometimes seen in people with schizophrenia. He started to come home from work rather late that summer and changed schools in the fall. His sister found a starter pistol in the trunk of his car. He started listening to the police band on a scanner. These incidents seemed more significant afterward than at the time.

Finally, he came to me with a story about a gang he was afraid might try to hurt his family. He had waited till late to sneak into the apartment after work. He changed schools to get away from them and had bought a gun to scare them. He could hear them plotting against him on the scanner. I began to suspect that he might be mentally ill, but his father believed the story. I went to the principal of his old school to check it out. The principal suggested seeing the board psychiatrist, but I knew from our previous experience with my father that persuading a loved one to consent to psychiatric assessment and treatment is one of the toughest challenges anyone could ever face. I decided to wait.

In January, after our son had a few beers alone at a local beer parlor, he smashed up some dishes and furniture and dumped the dining room table onto his brother's lap. Then, his face smeared with blood, he left the apartment and disappeared into the darkness. We reported the incident to the police and walked around the neighborhood trying to find him. We found drops of blood on the subway platform, so we concluded that he was on the subway and went home. His brother found him in the apartment house lobby at 6 o'clock the next morning. Soon after he fell asleep.

While our son was asleep, my husband and I talked. My husband told me to take him to a psychiatrist. That evening I was still not at all sure I could persuade him to go to the hospital. I went into his room, leaned over his bed, took a long deep breath, and said, "You've handled this alone long enough. You need help. Let's go to the hospital." Miraculously, he went with me.

He was not admitted to the hospital. They talked to him for a while and gave him an outpatient appointment. The doctor at the follow-up appointment referred him to a youth agency for counseling. This referral fizzled. After he answered a series of bizarre questions, the counselor suggested that he go back to outpatients. The next week a teacher at his school noticed that he was seriously disoriented and arranged for him to go to the hospital by taxi at school board expense. This time he was admitted.

Looking back on this admission, I realize that he received excellent care even though it was not at all what I expected. Ours was a functional family, but we were hardly the Waltons. I naively assumed at first that he was having a reactive psychosis brought on by skewed family dynamics. I also didn't like the drugs they were giving him. When he said that he liked the drugs, that really unsettled me. I was afraid he might become addicted. After discharge he attended day treatment for several months, then was referred to the weekly medication clinic, and after a while entered a group home.

Our son's first suicide attempt took place while he was in the group home. I had started playing Scrabble with him after his first hospitalization. We both loved the game. It did wonders for his self-esteem to beat his mother, and I am convinced it helped him regain some of his cognitive functioning. He won consistently except when he was decompensating. If I began to win, I knew he was due for a relapse. One evening we played Scrabble, then he went downstairs, swallowed a handful of pills, and waited to die. When nothing happened, he went to the hospital, hoping to talk to somebody. The pills hit him while he was waiting to be seen. He narrowly missed dying that evening, but I was not informed until he phoned me himself several days later.

I went on an 18-year suicide watch after that, and I slept with my clothes on for the next 10 years. There have been two more attempts since. He is not suicidal on his present medication, but I still keep enough gas in the family car to get to Emergency if the need should arise.

When our voyage through turbulence began, my husband and I were in our child-launching years. Now we are in young old age, but we still have a sweet and gentle but spirited 4-foot-11-inch daughter to launch. Her illness began at about age 14 with truancy and running away. She would suddenly disappear for several days. If you asked her where she had been, she would just say, "I don't know." I was so concerned for her safety that I sent her for martial arts classes, hoping she would learn to defend herself if she ran into trouble. It once took three men to restrain her in Emergency.

Finally, she went for help on her own. She spent her 16th birthday in a psychiatric unit, terrified of aliens from outer space who she thought were trying to abduct her. This hospital kept her for 5 days, then discharged her with no further treatment and a referral to a community-based youth counseling agency because she was too young for an adult unit and all the adolescent beds in our city were filled.

That evening, we tried taking her to a local children's hospital whose motto is"No child shall knock in vain." They gave her a complete physical, told me they had no beds, and said to phone for an appointment for an assessment in the morning. They added that the earliest she could be seen would be in 3 weeks. Dumbfounded, I protested vehemently, but I finally had to take her home.

We improvised at home for the next 7 weeks. When she finally got a bed, the accommodations and treatment were markedly inferior to the treatment her brother had had. Adding insult to injury, her therapist put her on token economy and refused to allow her family, which had been holding her together for the past 7 weeks, to visit her. She screamed for days. That unit has been upgraded since, but the supply of adolescent beds in our city is still desperately inadequate.

The effects of this admission were long lasting. Her trust in the system was gone. Over the next 10 years she was in and out of 10 hospitals, and on and off a half dozen antipsychotic medications. She rejected the help of untold community outreach workers and spent two more birthdays in psychiatric units. A major break came when she was accepted into the Community Integration Program at the Clarke Institute of Psychiatry. This program exercised a multidisciplinary treatment team approach. Each patient had a case manager and was assigned to a multidisciplinary team. I most sincerely hope the model will be widely duplicated now that the Clarke has proven its efficacy.

Our oldest child, now age 44, was the third of our children to get schizophrenia. Her official diagnosis is actually schizoaffective disorder. Her main symptom was hearing voices telling her to kill the kitties and to jump in front of subway trains. She was first diagnosed in her late thirties. She thought she was past the age of greatest risk, but schizophrenia can happen at any age. Fortunately, she has been compliant from the beginning and has a good understanding of the illness. She had been quite hostile toward her younger sister, but that changed when she developed schizophrenia herself—they have become quite close.

Things are much better now. All three children are stabilized on appropriate medication. Like many other people with schizophrenia, their vocational and social functioning is impaired because of negative symptoms, but we have had only one very short crisis admission this year. At this point, I would like to switch from our personal story to some of my favorite opinions and observations.

I feel strongly that people with schizophrenia should stay on their medication. If legal ways were implemented to force people to stay on their medication, fewer would get into trouble in the community. Moreover, the cost of restabilizing patients who repeatedly go off their medication is an expense that is becoming harder and harder to justify.

The following examples will illustrate what happens when people with severe schizophrenia stop taking their medication. My son decided to go off his medication to lose weight. After a couple of months, his symptoms suddenly started to come back. He got lost trying to get to Emergency. By the time he found his way again, he was in an acutely psychotic state. He was standing on his seat on the bus shouting obscenities at the other passengers. He was thrown off the bus and had to walk the rest of the way. One time our daughter decided to try faith healing. Some days we hardly saw her. Her brother noticed one day that we had not seen her for 3 days. He went to investigate and found her in bed, very thirsty and very hungry. She told him the "aliens" had placed force fields around her ankles and her wrists and would not allow her to get out of bed. We gave her something to eat and started her back on her medication. Next morning we had to call an ambulance because we couldn't get her out of bed to take her to the hospital.

I also strongly believe that families need more education about the negative symptoms of schizophrenia. These can be very frustrating. If people with schizophrenia and their families were better informed about these negative symptoms, they would be less likely to blame the medication for the frustrating behavior and more realistic in their expectations.

I also have strong feelings about shock treatment. When my son told me he was going to have shock treatment, I was absolutely terrified, then simply amazed by the result. He was ready to come home a week later. Electroshock, as it is administered today, is altogether different from the old insulin shock. It is safe, effective, humane, and a highly sanctionable treatment. I firmly believe that the permanent memory loss formerly thought to be linked to shock treatment is actually a negative symptom of the schizophrenia. My son, who has had two courses of electroshock, has a far better memory today than his sister, who has never had shock treatment at all.

Finally, a word about family blaming theories, which have now fortunately become outdated. People with schizophrenia and their families need support. Family blaming was vicious and counterproductive and undermined their natural instinct to support one another and led them to place blame instead.

One more thing I believe with all my heart? Stress does not cause schizophrenia. Stress may exacerbate the symptoms, but it is not the underlying cause. Our voyage through turbulence was highly stressful.

If stress caused schizophrenia, I and all of my family should be basket cases, and we are not! We may not be the Waltons, but we are a good strong family.

Chapter Two: **Assessment**

Severe Mental Illness and Addictions: Assessment Considerations

Kate B. Carey & Christopher J. Correia

This article originally appeared in *Addictive Behaviors*, 1998, 23(6), 735–748, and is reprinted with permission.

This article provides a selective overview of the empirical literature on substance use assessment for persons with severe mental illness. We organize the review around key questions related to three assessment goals. With regard to screening, we address what screening tools are appropriate for use in psychiatric settings, and what methodological concerns arise regarding their use in these contexts. With regard to diagnosis, we discuss why diagnosing comorbid disorders is difficult and how clinicians can enhance the reliability and validity of their diagnoses. With regard to the related goals of treatment planning and outcome evaluation, we consider what are appropriate outcome measures, and how assessment information can assist in treatment planning. Finally, we outline three promising directions for future research: (a) evaluating the psychometric properties of established substance-related measures in persons with severe mental illness, (b) identifying the conditions under which self-report information is more or less accurate, and (c) improving the population relevance of substance assessment instruments.

Substance use disorders co-occur with severe mental disorders at elevated rates relative to the general population. According to the Epidemiological Catchment Area Study (ECA; Regier et al., 1990), the prevalence of substance abuse and dependence in the U.S. population is 16%; however, 29% of persons with a mental disorder were comorbid for substance use disorder. Persons with severe mental illness (SMI) are at the most risk—47% of persons with schizophrenia and 56% of persons with bipolar disorder have lifetime diagnoses of substance abuse or dependence. The base rates of alcohol and drug problems indicate the importance of systematic assessment for substance use disorders (SUD).

Despite the high base rates, SUD are often overlooked and under-diagnosed in mental health treatment settings (Ananth et al., 1989;

Shaner et al., 1993). Several factors contribute to the underdetection of substance use problems among persons with SMI. First, abuse of alcohol and other drugs occurs in the context of multiple psychosocial dysfunction due to SMI; hence the negative consequences of substance abuse may not be as salient as they would be in persons without comorbid SMI. Second, the cognitive and emotional effects of substance abuse can include depression, anxiety, confusion, hallucinations and delusions; hence they may be misattributed to psychiatric conditions (e.g., Schuckit, 1983). Third, mental health staff may lack the training or expertise to make informed decisions regarding appropriate methods of detecting SUDs. Perhaps the most significant obstacle to the detection of SUDs remains the lack of substance-specific assessment in mental health treatment settings. Inadequate assessment is likely to lead to inappropriate treatment; failure to take SUD into account in treatment planning is likely to lead to poor outcomes, such as relapse, readmission, and substantial psychological and economic costs (Bartels et al., 1993; Safer, 1987, Shaner et al., 1995).

Given the prevalence of SUD among psychiatric patients, mental health professionals must attend to the assessment of alcohol and drug use and related problems. Toward that end, it is useful to keep in mind that assessment serves multiple purposes, including screening, diagnosis, and treatment planning/outcome assessment (K. B. Carey & Teitelbaum, 1996). Screening involves the identification of persons who are likely to have a SUD, and can take place in acute settings (emergency rooms and psychiatric admissions facilities) or in ongoing psychiatric treatment. Screening often involves brief assessment tools that are evaluated in terms of their sensitivity (ability to detect a SUD if it is there) and specificity (ability to accurately identify persons who do not have a SUD). Diagnosis involves obtaining a more detailed evaluation of substance use and consequences. This assessment helps to determine whether the problem behavior meets formal diagnostic criteria for a SUD, which substances are involved, and whether the SUD is current or in remission. The most common methods of diagnosing SUDs involve structured or semi-structured interviews, using criteria from the *Diagnostic and Statistical Manual for Mental Disorders (DSM-IV*; American Psychiatric Association, 1994). Treatment planning and outcome assessment constitute a heterogeneous set of goals, related by their relevance to designing appropriate treatments and evaluating their effectiveness. Relevant assessment information includes consumption patterns, substance-related life problems, expectancies and motives for use, and situational contexts for use.

The purpose of this article is to provide an overview of the empirical literature on substance use assessment for persons with SMI. For each of the three goals of assessment, key methodological questions are posed, the literature selectively reviewed, and assessment recommendations offered. We conclude with directions for future research and practice recommendations.

Screening

As summarized by K. B. Carey and Teitelbaum (1996), assessment modalities for screening include observational strategies, collateral information, biochemical tests, and self-report measures. Each modality has advantages and disadvantages with SMI patients (Drake, Alterman, & Rosenberg, 1993). Hence, the following questions can be posed regarding screening for SUDs. What screening tools are appropriate for use with SMI patients? What are the methodological concerns regarding their use in mental health contexts?

What are Appropriate Screening Tools?

Observational screening methods such as physical exams tend to be relatively insensitive screening tools among persons who have not yet developed observable physical harm due to their substance abuse (Bohn, Babor, & Kranzler, 1995). On the other hand, collateral information sources have long been found to be useful in substance abuse treatment settings (Maisto & Connors, 1992). Collateral information sources include friends and family, other treatment providers, official records, and reports from legal or other agencies. The value of collateral informants increases with the extent of their direct contact with or awareness of the substance use behaviors of the client (Wilson & Grube, 1994). Collaterals' ratings of their confidence in the information they provide correlated positively with the level of agreement between collaterals and subjects regarding substance use (Sobell, Agrawal, & Sobell, 1997). Thus, collaterals may vary in their usefulness depending on the degree of contact and confidence, two dimensions that are relatively easily assessed. However, some persons with SMI may not have reliable collateral informants, perhaps due to social isolation, estrangement from family, and/or involvement in social networks with other patients. In addition, preliminary evidence suggests that collaterals underreport substance use relative to self-reports by stable psychiatric outpatients (K. B. Carey, 1997a).

One promising source of collateral information consists of case managers or treatment personnel who know the client. Two 5-point clinician-rating scales, one for alcohol use and one for other drug use, have been developed to classify persons with SMI into categories corresponding to increasing severity of substance use. The clinician uses all available information accumulated over a period of up to 6 months to make the ratings. The Alcohol Use Scale (AUS) and Drug Use Scale (DUS; Drake, Mueser, & McHugo, 1996) can be completed reliably and correspond with more intensive interview-based methods of establishing SUD diagnoses. These rating scales can be useful for patients who have a recent history of contact with case managers or other treatment personnel.

Biochemical methods of detecting SUDs include analysis of blood, breath, or urine samples for direct metabolites of abused substances, or indirect evidence of biological changes often related to prolonged substance abuse such as elevated liver enzymes or changes in blood chemistry (Gold & Dackis, 1986). When used alone, these markers are imperfect screens for SUDs. Metabolites remain in a person's system for a limited time after substance use (often 1–3 days; Hawks & Chiang, 1986); thus, they are relatively insensitive indices of patterns of abuse, and may result in false negatives if there is substantial delay between last use and testing. Repeated positive findings on biochemical tests can help to establish abuse patterns. The value of indirect biological markers is limited if the abuse patterns have not been prolonged or intense enough to produce such changes, and they are nonspecific with regard to substance abuse.

Although biochemical tests alone are inadequate screening tools, these screening methods can play a role in a more comprehensive assessment approach. Systematic use of urine screens in acute care psychiatric settings does increase the identification of substance use. For example, Galletly, Field, and Prior (1993) reported that urinalysis detected alcohol or psychoactive drugs in 17% of a sample of persons admitted to a public psychiatric hospital. All of the patients who tested positive for alcohol had reported recent alcohol use, but none of the 14 patients testing positive for drugs had reported using them. Similarly, studies of both inpatients and outpatients with schizophrenia document substantial underreporting of cocaine use, revealed only when self-reports were compared to urine drug screens (Shaner et al., 1993; Stone, Greenstein, Gamble, & McLellan, 1993). Furthermore, the availability of urinalysis data leads to an increase in alcohol and drug use disorder diagnoses upon discharge from a psychiatric hospital (Appleby, Luchins, & Dyson, 1995). Hence, urine screens help to identify some patients who have not reported substance use and serve to sensitize mental health staff to the possibility of SUDs. The incremental effect of urine screens may be greater for identifying drug abusers than alcohol abusers.

Self-report methods of screening for SUDs remain a flexible and noninvasive option. Although patients tend to underrepresent their substance use in acute crisis, such as in the emergency room and upon admission to a psychiatric hospital, a different picture has emerged from studies evaluating self-report screens in outpatient samples. Weiss et al. (1998) found self-reported use to be consistent with urine screen results 95% of the time in a sample of dually diagnosed patients in treatment. When the two sources of information did not agree, 89% of the time it was because subjects reported more substance use than was detected by the urine screens. Evidence supports the internal consistency and test-retest reliability of the DAST (Cocco & Carey, in press), MAST, and CAGE (Teitelbaum, 1998) with psychiatric outpatients; these instruments have also shown adequate criterion validity when used to predict relevant SUD diagnoses. Teitelbaum and Carey (1996) summarized additional information on the criterion validity of alcohol screening tools.

Recently a new screening tool has been developed specifically for the identification of SUDs in persons with SMI (Rosenberg et al., 1998). The Dartmouth Assessment of Lifestyle Instrument (DALI) consists of 18 interviewer-administered items derived from several existing screening tools; items were selected to maximize prediction of SUD diagnoses. Eight items predict drug use disorders and nine items (with two overlapping items) predict alcohol use disorders. The preliminary report indicates that it is reliable over time and across interviewers, and more sensitive and specific than the MAST, TWEAK, CAGE, or DAST. To date, the DALI is the only screening instrument specifically designed to identify SUDs among patients hospitalized for psychiatric illness.

What Methodological Concerns Arise Regarding Screening?

This question has been addressed in part by the preceding review. First, the utility of collateral reports for confirming self-reported substance use and problems remains understudied in this context. Although collateral information may identify unreported substance use in a few cases, the methods for obtaining reliable collateral reports from non-treatment personnel warrant further study. Second, little attention has been devoted to considerations regarding interpretation of biochemical markers for alcohol and drug abuse. For example, we do not know if the sensitivity or specificity of urine or blood tests used to identify recent substance use is altered in persons with SMI, given their frequent use of psychotropic medications. Also, biological markers may be less sensitive screens in this population, given the lower levels of use characteristic of substance abusing SMI patients (Drake & Wallach, 1989).

Third, the use of self-report information continues to raise methodological concerns. For example, although reliable and valid in some contexts, self-reports cannot be trusted in other contexts. Existing data suggest that stable outpatients can give quite reliable, and apparently valid, self-reports of their drinking behavior. On the other hand, patients admitted to acute psychiatric settings often underreport their recent drug use. If these assessment situations represent the two ends of the continuum, much remains to be learned about self-report accuracy in a variety of psychiatric treatment settings and with a wide range of patients. Furthermore, when self-report screening tools are used, such as the DALI or MAST, they are usually interviewer-administered rather than self-administered. Thus, several investigators have changed the mode of administration to account for literacy and/or attentional difficulties characteristic of persons with SMI. We do not know whether these procedural changes affect the ability of these tools to identify persons with SUDs.

We recommend combining self-report screening tools with other sources of available information. This convergent validity approach (Sobell & Sobell, 1980) promises to improve detection over single assessment methods especially for suspected drug (vs. alcohol) abusers, and also in settings where patients are experiencing acute psychiatric distress. Screening tools are not designed to provide sufficient information for diagnosing SUDs; thus they should be considered the first step to a more comprehensive assessment. With this in mind, treatment sites can decide whether they prefer maximizing the sensitivity versus the specificity of screening procedures.

Diagnosis

A positive screen is generally followed by a diagnostic assessment. A SUD diagnosis signifies that a client has developed maladaptive patterns of substance use that result in clinically significant physical, psychological, or social impairment (American Psychiatric Association, 1994). Accurate diagnosis requires a more extensive evaluation of substance use and related problems over time, and differentiation between substance abuse and substance dependence. As noted by Shaner et al. (in press), misdiagnosis can be costly. Identifying a primary psychotic disorder in a client who actually has substance induced psychosis could lead to inappropriately prolonged use of antipsychotic medications. Furthermore, diagnostic inaccuracy can exclude a person from appropriate treatment programs. With regard to establishing a SUD diagnosis in a person with SMI, two questions emerge: Why is diagnosing comorbid disorders so difficult? How can diagnosticians ensure that they arrive at reliable and accurate diagnoses?

Why Is Diagnosing Comorbid Disorders So Difficult?

Ample evidence points to the conclusion that diagnoses are less reliable when comorbid disorders are present. With regard to test-retest reliability, current substance abusers give less reliable reports of past or current psychiatric disorders than nondrug-abusing individuals (Bryant, Rounsaville, Spitzer, & Williams, 1992; Corty, Lehman. & Myers, 1993). Symptoms that are caused by substance use can mimic symptoms of other disorders. Common examples include depressive episodes caused by cocaine withdrawal, and amphetamine-induced psychosis. Thus, interactions between abused substances and psychiatric syndromes make it difficult to determine reliably the primary cause for presenting symptoms.

Drake et al. (1990) suggested that relying on a single interview to assess alcohol use could misclassify a significant proportion of individuals with schizophrenia and drinking problems as nonproblematic drinkers. Denial or minimization of substance use can result from psychological defenses, neuropsychological impairments, lack of insight into connections between drinking and symptoms, and/or tendency to provide socially desirable responses. The timing of a diagnostic interview may affect the reliability and validity of the results, and diagnoses made early in treatment may need to be revised as more information becomes available over time (Ananth et al., 1989).

A recent study directly addressed the possible causes of unreliability in diagnosing comorbid disorders. Shaner et al. (in press) documented sources of diagnostic uncertainty in a sample of 160 inpatients with chronic psychosis and active cocaine abuse. The diagnostic assessment consisted of the Structured Clinical Interview for *DSM-III-R* (SCID; Spitzer, Williams, Gibbon, & First, 1990), urine screens, review of hospital records, and collateral interviews. Modifications to the SCID allowed interviewers to rate diagnostic criteria as either met or uncertain, and any sources of uncertainty were recorded. Initial assessment produced a definitive diagnosis in only 18% of the cases. In the remaining cases, a definitive diagnosis could not be reached because of one or more sources of uncertainty, including insufficient abstinence to rule out substance-induced symptoms (78%), poor memory (24%), or inconsistent reporting (20%). Uncertainty remained in 75% of the cases after a reassessment at 18 months. These results highlight the potential problems of basing diagnostic decisions on a single interview. The persistence or remission of psychotic symptoms during periods of abstinence may clarify the diagnosis. Thus, the ability to observe patients under conditions of prolonged abstinence facilitates determination of diagnoses. However, consensus has yet to be achieved regarding the length of abstinence required.

How Can Diagnosticians Make Reliable and Accurate Diagnoses?

Diagnosing comorbid disorders presents a unique set of challenges. Diagnoses tend to be less reliable when comorbid disorders are present, and a single interview may misattribute the cause of symptoms and/or underestimate the prevalence of comorbid disorders. These challenges notwithstanding, we offer several suggestions.

The recommended procedure for diagnosing SUDs consists of structured and semi-structured interviews, designed to enhance the reliability of the diagnostic process (e.g., the Structured Clinical Interview for *DSM-IV* [SCID-IV]; First, Spitzer, Gibbon, & Williams, 1995). Both types of interviews provide data on the severity of substance use problems and information relevant to differential diagnosis. However, research suggests that they may need to be supplemented with other sources of information.

Because uncertainty can remain after a single diagnostic interview, a number of authors (e.g., Drake & Wallach, 1989; Safer, 1987) have advocated the use of longitudinal behavioral observations and collateral information to assess SUDs in psychiatric patients. For example, Drake et al. (1990) suggest that clinicians who work closely with psychotic patients over time can identify problematic drinking that is denied by patients themselves. Longitudinal observations would also increase the possibility of observing the client under conditions of abstinence. Continuing psychiatric symptoms during periods of abstinence help to establish the *DSM-IV* criterion of "not due to substance use." Alternatively, resolution of some (or all) of the psychiatric symptoms during periods of little or no use is consistent with a substance-induced disorder.

An example of an integrative approach to diagnosing comorbid disorders is the Longitudinal Expert All Data Procedure (LEAD; Kranzler, Kadden, Babor, & Rounsaville, 1994). The LEAD procedure consists of repeated assessments conducted by clinicians experienced with both psychiatric and SUDs. Diagnosticians integrate patient observations over time with information from family members, significant others, ward personnel, therapists, laboratory tests, and case records. The length of the assessment period may be brief or may be years, depending on the complexity of the case and the opportunity to observe sufficient periods of abstinence. When compared to a single interview, the LEAD procedure increases the likelihood of detecting SUDS. The advantage of the LEAD approach appears to be specific to certain types of disorders, as it did not increase the reliability of comorbid mood or anxiety disorder diagnoses.

A similar approach has been described for diagnosing SUDs in persons with schizophrenia (Drake et al., 1990). The consensus approach combines self-report and interview data with longitudinal and collateral information provided by case managers. The consensus diagnoses proved to be more sensitive and specific than single methods of diagnosing SUDs. Given the shortcomings of the single interview, more studies utilizing variants of the LEAD approach are warranted. Improvements to the quality of the diagnostic process may ultimately lead to more informed treatment decisions.

Treatment Planning and Outcome Evaluation

These two assessment goals are considered together because much of the information needed for developing individualized treatment plans is also suitable for monitoring treatment outcomes, such as an assessment of substance use patterns and related life problems. Additional variables that can inform the treatment planning process include substance-related expectancies, motives for use, antecedents and consequences of use, adaptive skills, and motivations for change. Because very little has been published about treatment planning for dual disorders, the empirical literature provides little guidance on the treatment validity of any assessment procedure. Thus, relevant questions include the following: What constitute minimum, appropriate outcome measures for substance use problems? How can assessment information assist in treatment planning? To answer these questions, we highlight assessment tools that have undergone psychometric evaluation with SMI patients.

What Are Appropriate Outcome Measures?

Documentation of use patterns is used to evaluate the scope and severity of current behaviors and to monitor changes over time. Common markers of improvement include reduction in use frequency and/or average quantity, reductions in heavy or high-risk use patterns, and increases in the number of abstinent days over a given outcome interval. The Timeline Followback is one instrument that allows for flexibility in calculating these outcome variables (Sobell & Sobell, 1996). The TLFB records daily drinking patterns over periods ranging from 30–365 days, using a calendar as a visual recall prompt; specified interview strategies help to identify salient events and patterns of use that facilitate recall. The TLFB has sound psychometric properties among patients in alcohol treatment, community residents, and college students (Sobell & Sobell, 1996). Among the SMI, frequency and quantity measures from the 30-day TLFB were temporally stable (K. B. Carey, 1997b; Teitelbaum, 1998) and significantly associated with independent measures of drinking frequency and problems (K. B. Carey, 1997b; K. B. Carey, Cocco, & Simons, 1996). Experience with SMI participants suggests that drug use days can be effectively integrated into the TLFB procedure (M. P. Carey, Weinhardt, Carey, Maisto, & Gordon, 1998). With patients who are less reliable historians, repeated assessments with relatively short time frames (e.g., 1–4 weeks) can be used to establish a representative baseline of use patterns.

SUDs are defined in terms of their consequences for adaptive functioning rather than in terms of specific amounts of use (American Psychiatric Association, 1994). Hence, outcome measures should include indices of adaptive function and life problems. More intense involvement with substances tends to be associated with problems in areas such as finances, housing, employment, social relationships, medication and other treatment compliance, and legal complications (e.g., Drake, Osher, & Wallach, 1989). Few suitable measures have been systematically evaluated. The MAST and a variant on the DAST have been used to quantify alcohol- and drug-related problems among persons with schizophrenia (Mueser, Nishith, Tracy, DeGirolamo, & Molinaro, 1995). The AUS and DUS (Drake et al., 1996) can provide global indices of the severity of problems. However, because problem severity is rated on a single 5-point scale these may be less helpful in tracking the resolution of specific psychosocial problems.

How Can Assessment Information Assist in Treatment Planning?

Treatment planning involves identification of the specific problem areas that need changing and the intervention strategies that are best suited to a given individual. Although little has been published about ways to link assessment to treatment for substance abuse among the SMI, several recent studies have reported relevant data.

The first set of studies addressed whether assessing motives for substance use and substance-related expectancies can be informative in the SMI. Unstructured motives assessments indicated that the reasons reported by the SMI for using alcohol and other drugs resemble those reported by other populations (e.g., Dixon, Haas, Weiden, Sweeney, & Francis, 1991); these include interpersonal (e.g., social facilitation) and intrapersonal (e.g., relief of dysphoria) motivations. Using an internally consistent motives measure, K. B. Carey and Carey (1995) found that both negative reinforcement and positive reinforcement motives differentiated current drinkers from current non-drinkers, and both motives correlated significantly with maximum quantity consumed in the last year. Participants who had been treated for alcohol or drug problems endorsed higher negative reinforcement motives than nontreated participants; the presence of a treated SUD did not result in differential scores for positive reinforcement motives. Mueser et al. (1995) provided additional evidence for the validity of motives assessments. Motives for both drug and alcohol use were associated in a non-specific way with SUDs and substance-related problems. However, data regarding expectancies revealed a much more specific set of associations. Alcohol expectancies were higher in patients with documented alcohol use disorders, whereas drug expectancies were higher in patients with drug use disorders. These studies suggest that treatment approaches that invoke motivational and cognitive expectancy constructs could be extended to persons with both psychiatric and substance use disorders.

Stasiewicz, Carey, Bradizza, and Maisto (1996) illustrate a method of linking assessment to treatment planning and outcome evaluation. They conducted a thorough behavioral assessment (cf. Sobell, Toneatto, & Sobell, 1994) with a man with a history of major depression with psychotic features, alcohol and cannabis dependence. Antecedents were initially identified with the Inventory of Drinking Situations (Annis & Davis, 1988) and the Inventory of Drug-Taking Situations (Annis & Martin, 1985). These instruments produce a profile of situations associated with heavy drinking or drug use. After identifying specific examples of common high-risk situations, behavior chains were constructed to include the following components: situational context, thought, feeling, behavior (substance use), and consequences. Consideration of both positive and negative as well as immediate and delayed consequences of drug and alcohol use helps to establish the functional role of substance use in different contexts. This analysis of antecedents and consequences helps to organize the initial treatment plan. Consistent with social learning and relapse prevention models of substance abuse treatment (Marlatt & Gordon, 1985), identification of situational, emotional, and cognitive triggers can suggest strategies for avoiding or changing high-risk situations. These strategies may include stimulus control, mood management skills, or cognitive restructuring. In addition, better appreciation of the functional role of substance use can suggest more adaptive behavioral alternatives to substance use; appropriate responses may involve skills training, or involvement in alternate pleasurable activities. The idiographic nature of behavioral assessment lends itself to demonstrating functional relationships between psychiatric symptoms and substance use (Stasiewicz et al., 1996).

An additional consideration for treatment planning consists of a motivational assessment. According to the transtheoretical model of change (Prochaska, DiClemente, & Norcross, 1992), the person in the action stage of change will be more receptive to behavioral change strategies. Intervention strategies such as consciousness raising via assessment feedback may be better suited for persons with lower readiness to change. Using a stage-based classification strategy, Ziedonis and Trudeau (1997) demonstrated that dually diagnosed outpatients endorsed a wide range of readiness to change. Fully 51% of the marijuana abusers and 48% of the alcohol abusers were determined to be in precontemplation or contemplation stages of change. However, stage of change was not related to involvement in substance abuse or dual diagnosis treatment. Readiness to change warrants further attention in this population.

The Substance Abuse Treatment Scale (SATS; McHugo, Drake, Burton, & Ackerson, 1995) represents a different motivational assessment approach. The SATS was developed to describe psychiatric patients in terms of their involvement in substance abuse treatment and recovery. Consistent with the Osher and Kofoed (1989) four-stage model of dual diagnosis treatment, the SATS specifies eight treatment stages: pre-engagement, engagement, early persuasion, late persuasion, early active treatment, late active treatment, relapse prevention, remission or recovery. Clinicians select a stage reflecting patients' treatment involvement during the last 6 months. The SATS is reliable across raters and reflects change over time, as fewer participants in dual diagnosis treatment remained in early stages of change and greater numbers of participants moved to later stages of change.

Self-report measures of readiness to change are available (e.g., the SOCRATES, Miller & Tonigan, 1996; or the URICA, McConnaughy, Prochaska, & Velicer, 1983), but these instruments have not yet been evaluated for their application to substance abusers with SMI. Motivational assessments have also included decisional balance exercises (e.g., Miller & Rollnick, 1991), consisting of a systematic consideration of the pros and cons of continuing to use substances and of quitting. Preliminary qualitative evidence suggests that participants with schizophrenia can engage in decisional balance activities (K. B. Carey, Purnine, Maisto, Carey, & Barnes, 1998).

We recommend that substance abuse be integrated with other problem areas addressed in psychiatric treatment. This strategy requires recognition of the relationships among substance use, psychiatric functioning, and other psychosocial problems. Behavioral assessment strategies that explore the functional role of substance use may lead to ideas for helpful interventions. Enhancement of motivation for treatment constitutes an appropriate treatment goal. A rudimentary outcome evaluation would require first the identification of key markers of psychiatric status and adaptive function, and then a plan for tracking these markers and substance use patterns over time.

Future Directions

Despite the substantial progress made in the last decade regarding the assessment of substance use and related problems in the SMI, many promising directions for future research remain. These include: (a) investigating the adequacy of existing assessment options; (b) identifying the conditions under which self-reports are more or less accurate; and (c) enhancing the population appropriateness of assessment tools.

First, we need additional psychometric evaluation of established assessment instruments. Even instruments with well-established psychometric properties may not be effectively used in populations other than those for which they were developed. For example, the Addiction Severity Index (ASI; McLellan et al., 1992) is commonly used in substance abuse treatment settings to quantify problem severity on multiple dimensions. However, recent research raises questions about the psychometric qualities of the ASI when used with the SMI, because reliability and validity coefficients for many of the summary variables produced by the ASI do not meet acceptable thresholds (K. B. Carey, Cocco, & Correia, 1997). Similarly, a recent review concluded that other well-established scales could not identify persons with alcohol problems at rates exceeding chance, given the presence of an SMI (Teitelbaum & Carey, 1996). On the other hand, some measures developed in other contexts have proven to be psychometrically sound, such as the DAST (Cocco & Carey, in press) and the alcohol, marijuana, and cocaine expectancy measures used by Mueser et al. (1995). When instruments are exported for use with the SMI, psychometric evaluation is indicated. In addition, the generalizability of measures newly developed for this population (e.g., the DALI and the SATS) also needs to be established.

Second, conditions that maximize the accuracy of self-report information deserve greater attention. Self-report remains an essential tool, and the best way to gain access to private information. Despite the historical suspicion of substance abusers' self-reports, empirical evidence now supports their reliability and validity in community and substance abuse treatment populations, when certain procedures are followed (e.g., Skinner, 1984). Concerns about the accuracy of self-reports from substance abusers with SMI might best be addressed by considering the respondent and situational variables that influence the accuracy of self-report information (see Babor, Brown, & DelBoca, 1990, for a more complete discussion). However, few investigations of substance assessment with the SMI have incorporated these methodological suggestions. These include (but are not limited to) the following.

1. *Sobriety:* Intoxication at the time of assessment is associated with unreliable and invalid self-reports (e.g., Brown, Kranzler, & DelBoca, 1992). Thus, ensuring sobriety through the use of breath or urine screening can enhance the accuracy of assessment data (Skinner, 1984).

2. *Acute distress:* Assessment should take place at a point when the individual is not in acute psychiatric crisis, as underreporting of recent substance use is likely in acute admissions settings (e.g., Shaner et al., 1993). In contrast, high reliability and validity coefficients are found when stable outpatients give self-report data on standard measures (e.g., Cocco & Carey, in press; Teitelbaum, 1998).

3. *Cognitive impairment:* It is likely that some persons with SMI experience cognitive deficits sufficient to impair their ability to provide accurate self-reports. There is evidence that cognitive impairment correlates with underreporting of recent drinking by patients relative to collaterals (Miller & Barasch, 1985). With the exception of the findings regarding acute psychiatric distress, direct evidence for this hypothesis has not yet been reported with the SMI. In fact, a recently completed study found that neither memory performance nor psychological symptoms were related to the reliability of the MAST (Teitelbaum, 1998). Additional study is needed to determine the role of cognitive dysfunction in self-report accuracy.

4. *Motivated deception:* Concerns about confidentiality can reduce self-report accuracy, especially when negative consequences (e.g., legal or housing) are contingent upon admitting to using substances. In general, research interviews that are able to provide assurances of confidentiality elicit more information about substance use and related life events in psychiatric settings (e.g., Ananth et al., 1989). Persons responsible for alcohol assessment should carefully consider patients' confidentiality concerns and program requirements regarding confidentiality. Additional motivational factors include obvious contingencies for over reporting (e.g., access to treatment, self-handicapping) or underreporting (e.g., access to job training, maintaining privileges). Patients have articulated concerns regarding potentially judgmental attitudes or other threats to self-esteem. In sum, clinicians and researchers working with dually diagnosed individuals are best served by considering the kinds of respondent and situational variables that may influence their confidence in self-report data.

Third, attention to the population appropriateness of assessments is needed. Both the structure and content of assessment tools must be considered. Persons in acute care settings find extensive interviews difficult to complete (Barbee, Clark, Crapanzano, Heintz, & Kehoe, 1989), raising the issue of respondent burden among severely disabled persons. Instruments that are often self-administered in other populations may need to be administered by trained interviewers with the SMI. Also, simplification of sentence structure, vocabulary, and response options can help persons with SMI to participate more meaningfully in the assessment process.

Some investigators have suggested that the content of assessment measures may need to be tailored to the SMI. Drake et al. (1990) observed that "typical alcohol-related problems for schizophrenic patients include increased symptoms, disruptive behavior, housing instability, and treatment non-compliance...rather than the familial and vocational problems typical of nonschizophrenic alcoholics" (p. 64). Corse, Hirschinger, and Zanis (1995) also noted that interviews developed for nonpsychiatric substance abusers are likely to be insensitive to the severity of psychiatric, employment, and financial problems experienced by persons with SMI. Furthermore, evaluations of social functioning that emphasize conflicts within established relationships do not capture social problems associated with isolation or estrangement (Corse et al., 1995). Thus, measures of negative consequences commonly experienced by persons with SMI would be helpful, as would markers of adaptive function that are sensitive both to a wide range of social competencies and to the effects of substance use on a baseline of impaired function. New measures may supplement established measures to ensure that substance abuse assessment is sensitive to the psychosocial context of substance use by the SMI.

References

American Psychiatric Association. (1994). *Diagnostic and statistical manual of mental disorders (4th ed.).* Washington, DC: Author.

Ananth, J., Vandewater, S., Kamal, M., Brodsky, A., Gamal, R. & Miller, M. (1989). Missed diagnosis of substance abuse in psychiatric patients. *Hospital and Community Psychiatry, 40,* 297–299.

Annis, H. M., & Davis, C. S. (1988). Assessment of expectations. In G. Marlatt & D. Donovan (Eds.), *Assessment of addictive behaviors.* New York: Guilford.

Annis, H. M., & Martin, G. (1985). *Inventory of Drug-Taking Situations.* Toronto: Addiction Research Foundation of Ontario.

Appleby, L., Luchins, D. J., & Dyson. V. (1995). Effects of mandatory drug screens on substance use diagnoses in a mental hospital population. *Journal of Nervous and Mental Disease, 183,* 183–184.

Babor, T. F., Brown, J., & DelBoca, F. K. (1990). Validity of self-reports in applied research on addictive behaviors: Fact or fiction? *Behavioral Assessment, 12,* 5–31.

Barbee, J. G., Clark, P. D., Crapanzano, M. S., Heintz, G. C., & Kehoe, C. E. (1989). Alcohol and substance abuse among schizophrenic patients presenting to an emergency psychiatric service. *Journal of Nervous and Mental Disease, 177,* 400–407.

Bartels, S. J., Teague, G. B., Drake, R. E., Clark, R. E., Bush, P. W., & Noordsy, D. L. (1993). Substance abuse in schizophrenia: Service utilization and costs. *Journal of Nervous and Mental Disease, 181,* 227–232.

Bohn, M. J., Babor, T. F., & Kranzler, H. R. (1995). The Alcohol Use Disorders Identification Test (AUDIT): Validation of a screening instrument for use in medical settings. *Journal of Studies on Alcohol, 56,* 423–432.

Brown, J., Kranzler, H. R., & DelBoca, F. K. (1992). Self-reports by alcohol and drug abuse inpatients: Factors affecting reliability and validity. *British Journal of Addiction, 87,* 1013–1024.

Bryant, K. J., Rounsaville, B., Spitzer, R. L., & Williams, J. B. W. (1992). Reliability of dual diagnosis: Substance dependence and psychiatric disorders. *Journal of Nervous and Mental Disorders, 180,* 251–257.

Carey, K. B. (1997a). Challenges in assessing substance use patterns in persons with comorbid mental and addictive disorders. In L. Onken, J. D. Blaine, S. Genser, & A. M. Horton (Eds.), *Treatment of drug-dependent individuals with comorbid mental disorders* (NIDA Research Monograph 172, NIH Publication No. 97-4172, pp. 16–32). Washington, DC: Superintendent of Documents, U.S. Government Printing Office.

Carey, K. B. (1997b). Reliability and validity of the Timeline Follow-Back Interview among psychiatric outpatients: A preliminary report. *Psychology of Addictive Behaviors, 11,* 26–33.

Carey, K. B., & Carey, M. P. (1995). Reasons for drinking among psychiatric outpatients: Relationship to drinking patterns. *Psychology of Addictive Behaviors, 9,* 251–257.

Carey, K. B., Cocco, K. M., & Correia, C. J. (1997). Reliability and validity of the Addiction Severity Index among outpatients with severe mental illness. *Psychological Assessment, 9,* 422–428.

Carey, K. B., Cocco, K. M., & Simons, J. S. (1996). Concurrent validity of substance abuse ratings by outpatient clinicians. *Psychiatric Services, 47,* 842–847.

Carey, K. B., Purnine, D. M., Maisto, S. A., Carey, M. P., & Barnes, K. L. (1998). *Decisional balance regarding substance use among persons with schizophrenia.* Manuscript submitted for publication.

Carey, K. B., & Teitelbaum, L. M. (1996). Goals and methods of alcohol assessment. *Professional Psychology: Research and Practice, 27,* 460–466.

Carey, M. P., Weinhardt, L. S., Carey, K. B., Maisto, S. A., & Gordon, C. M. (1998, April). *Development of the Super Timeline Followback Interview for the comprehensive evaluation of sexual behavior and substance use.* Paper presented at the National Institute of Mental Health, Bethesda, MD.

Cocco, K. M., & Carey, K. B. (in press). Psychometric properties of the Drug Abuse Screening Test in psychiatric outpatients. *Psychological Assessment.*

Corse, S. J., Hirschinger, N. B., & Zanis, D. (1995). The use of the Addiction Severity Index with people with severe mental illness. *Psychiatric Rehabilitation Journal, 19,* 9–18.

Corty, E., Lehman, A. F., & Myers, C. F. (1993). Influence of psychoactive substance use on the reliability of psychiatric diagnosis. *Journal of Consulting and Clinical Psychology, 61,* 165–170.

Dixon, L., Haas, G., Weiden, P. J., Sweeney, J., & Francis, A. J. (1991). Drug abuse in schizophrenic patients: Clinical correlates and reasons for use. *American Journal of Psychiatry, 148,* 224–230.

Drake, R. E., Alterman, A. I., & Rosenberg, S. R. (1993). Detection of substance use disorders in severely mentally ill patients. *Community Mental Health Journal, 29,* 175–192.

Drake, R. E., Mueser, K. T., & McHugo, G. J. (1996). Clinical rating scales: Alcohol Use Scale (AUS), Drug Use Scale (DUS), and Substance Abuse Treatment Scale (SATS). In L. I. Sederer & B. Dickey (Eds.). *Outcomes assessment in clinical practice* (pp. 113–116). Baltimore: Williams & Wilkins.

Drake, R. E., Osher, F. C., Noordsy, D. L., Hurlbut, S. C., Teague, G. B., & Beaudett, M. S. (1990). Diagnosis of alcohol use disorders in schizophrenia. *Schizophrenia Bulletin, 16,* 57–67.

Drake. R. E., Osher, F. C., & Wallach, M. A. (1989). Alcohol use and abuse in schizophrenia: A prospective community study. *Journal of Nervous and Mental Disease, 177,* 408–414.

Drake, R. E., & Wallach. M. A. (1989). Substance abuse among the chronically mentally ill. *Hospital and Community Psychiatry, 40,* 1041–1046.

First, M. B., Spitzer, R. L., Gibbon, M., & Williams, J. B. W. (1995). *Structured Clinical Interview for DSM-IV Axis I Disorders—Patient Edition.* New York: Biometrics Research Department, New York State Psychiatric Institute.

Galletly, C. A., Field, C. D., & Prior, M. (1993). Urine drug screening of patients admitted to a state psychiatric hospital. *Hospital and Community Psychiatry, 44,* 587–589.

Gold, M. S., & Dackis, C. A. (1986). The role of the laboratory in evaluation of suspected drug abusers. *Journal of Clinical Psychiatry, 47,* 17–23.

Hawks, R. L., & Chiang, C. N. (Eds.). (1986). *Urine-testing for drugs of abuse* (DHHS Publication No. ADM 87-1481). Washington, DC: U.S. Government Printing Office.

Kranzler, H. R., Kadden, R. M., Babor, T. F., & Rounsaville, B. J. (1994). Longitudinal, expert, all data procedure for psychiatric diagnosis in patients with psychoactive substance use disorders. *Journal of Nervous and Mental Disorders, 182,* 277–283.

Maisto, S. A., & Connors, G. J. (1992). Using subject and collateral reports to measure alcohol consumption. In R. Z. Litten & J. P. Allen (Eds.), *Measuring alcohol consumption: Psychosocial and biological methods* (pp. 73–96). Totowa, NJ: Humana.

Marlatt, G. A., & Gordon, J. R. (1985). *Relapse prevention: Maintenance strategies in the treatment of addictive behaviors.* New York: Guilford.

McConnaughy, E. A., Prochaska, J. O., & Velicer, W. F. (1983). Stages of change in psychotherapy: Measurement and sample profiles. *Psychotherapy: Theory, Research and Practice, 20,* 368–375.

McHugo, G. J., Drake, R. E., Burton, H. L., & Ackerson, T. H. (1995). A scale for assessing the stage of substance abuse treatment in persons with severe mental illness. *Journal of Nervous and Mental Disease, 183,* 762–767.

McLellan, A. T., Kushner, H., Metzger, D., Peters, R., Smith, I., Grissom, G., & Pettinati, H. (1992). The fifth edition of the Addiction Severity Index: Historical critique and normative data. *Journal of Substance Abuse Treatment, 9,* 199–213.

Miller, F., & Barasch, A. (1985). The under-reporting of alcohol use: The role of organic mental syndromes. *Drug and Alcohol Dependence, 15,* 347–351.

Miller, W. R., & Rollnick, S. (1991). *Motivational interviewing: Preparing people to change addictive behavior.* New York: Guilford.

Miller, W. R., & Tonigan, J. S. (1996). Assessing drinkers' motivation for change: The Stages of Change Readiness and Treatment Eagerness Scale (SOCRATES). *Psychology of Addictive Behaviors, 10,* 81–89.

Mueser, K. T., Nishith, P., Tracy. J. I., DeGirolamo, J., & Molinaro, M. (1995). Expectations and motives for substance use in schizophrenia. *Schizophrenia Bulletin, 21,* 367–378.

Osher, F. C., & Kofoed, L. L. (1989). Treatment of patients with psychiatric and psychoactive substance abuse disorders. *Hospital and Community Psychiatry, 40,* 1025–1030.

Prochaska, J. O., DiClemente, C. C., & Norcross, J. C. (1992). In search of how people change: Applications to addictive behaviors. *American Psychologist, 47,* 1102–1114.

Regier, D. A., Farmer, M. E., Rae, D. S., Locke, B. Z., Keith, S. J., Judd, L. L., & Goodwin, F. K. (1990). Comorbidity of mental disorders with alcohol and other drug abuse: Results from the Epidemiological Catchment Area (ECA) Study. *Journal of the American Medical Association, 21,* 2511–2518.

Rosenberg, S. D., Drake, R. E., Wolford, G. L., Mueser, K. T., Oxman, T. E., Vidaver, R. M., Carrieri, K. L., & Luckoor, R. (1998). Dartmouth Assessment of Lifestyle Instrument (DALI): A substance use disorder screen for people with severe mental illness. *American Journal of Psychiatry, 155,* 232–238.

Safer, D. J. (1987). Substance abuse by young adult chronic patients. *Hospital and Community Psychiatry, 38,* 511–514.

Schuckit, M. A. (1983). Alcoholism and other psychiatric disorders. *Hospital and Community Psychiatry, 34,* 1022–1026.

Shaner, A., Eckman, T. A., Roberts, L. J., Wilkins, J. N., Tucker, D. E., Tsuang, J. W., & Mintz, J. (1995). Disability income, cocaine use, and repeated hospitalization among schizophrenic cocaine abusers. *New England Journal of Medicine, 333,* 777–783.

Shaner, A., Khalsa, M., Roberts, L., Wilkins, J., Anglin, D., & Hsieh, S. (1993). Unrecognized cocaine use among schizophrenic patients. *American Journal of Psychiatry, 150,* 758–762.

Shaner, A., Roberts, L. J., Racenstein, J. M., Eckman, T. A., Tucker, D. E., & Tsuang, J. W. (in press). Sources of diagnostic uncertainty among chronically psychotic cocaine abusers. *Psychiatric Services.*

Skinner, H. A. (1984). Assessing alcohol use by patients in treatment. In R. G. Smart, H. Cappell, F. Glazer, Y. Israel, H. Kalant, R. E. Popham, W. Schmidt, & E. M. Sellers (Eds.), *Research advances in alcohol and drug problems* (Vol. 8, pp. 183–207). New York: Plenum.

Sobell, L. C., Agrawal, S., & Sobell, M. B. (1997). Factors affecting agreement between alcohol abusers' and their collaterals' reports. *Journal of Studies on Alcohol, 58,* 405–413.

Sobell, L. C., & Sobell, M. B. (1980). Convergent validity: An approach to increasing confidence in treatment outcome conclusions with alcohol and drug abusers. In L. C. Sobell, M. B. Sobell, & E. Ward (Eds.), *Evaluating alcohol and drug abuse treatment effectiveness: Recent advances* (pp. 177–183). New York: Pergamon.

Sobell, L. C., & Sobell, M. B. (1996). *Timeline FollowBack user's guide: A calendar method for assessing alcohol and drug use.* Toronto: Addiction Research Foundation.

Sobell, L. C., Toneatto, T., & Sobell, M. B. (1994). Behavioral assessment and treatment planning for alcohol, tobacco, and other drug problems: Current status with an emphasis on clinical applications. *Behavior Therapy, 25,* 533–580.

Spitzer, R. L., Williams, J. B., Gibbon, M., & First, M. B. (1990). *Structured Clinical Interview for DSM-III-R: Patient edition.* Washington, DC: American Psychiatric Press.

Stasiewicz, P. R., Carey, K. B., Bradizza, C. M., & Maisto, S. A. (1996). Behavioral assessment of substance abuse with co-occurring psychiatric disorder. *Cognitive and Behavioral Practice, 3,* 91–105.

Stone, A. M., Greenstein. R. A., Gamble, G., & McLellan, A. T. (1993). Cocaine use by schizophrenic outpatients who receive depot neuroleptic medication. *Hospital and Community Psychiatry, 44,* 176–177.

Teitelbaum, L. M. (1998). *Reliability of self-reported alcohol use in psychiatric settings.* Unpublished doctoral dissertation, Syracuse University, Syracuse, NY.

Teitelbaum, L. M., & Carey, K. B. (1996). Alcohol assessment in psychiatric patients: A critical review of the literature. *Clinical Psychology: Science and Practice, 3,* 323–338.

Weiss, R. D., Najavits, L. M., Greenfield, S. F., Soto, J. A., Shaw, S. R., & Wyner, D. (1998). Validity of substance use self-reports in dually diagnosed outpatients. *American Journal of Psychiatry, 155,* 127–128.

Wilson, D. K., & Grube, J. (1994). Role of psychosocial factors in obtaining self-reports of alcohol use in a DUI population. *Psychology of Addictive Behaviors, 8,* 139–151.

Ziedonis, D. M., & Trudeau, K. (1997). Motivation to quit using substances among individuals with schizophrenia: Implications for a motivation-based treatment model. *Schizophrenia Bulletin, 23,* 229–238.

Dartmouth Assessment of Lifestyle Instrument (DALI): A Substance Use Disorder Screen for People with Severe Mental Illness

Stanley D. Rosenberg, Robert E. Drake, George L. Wolford, Kim T. Mueser, Thomas E. Oxman, Robert M. Vidaver, Karen L. Carrieri, & Ravindra Luckoor

This article originally appeared in *American Journal of Psychiatry,* 1998,155(2), 232–238, and is reprinted with permission.

Presented at the 30th annual meeting of the Association for the Advancement of Behavior Therapy, New York, Nov. 21–24, 1996. From the Department of Psychiatry, Dartmouth Medical School, and Department of Psychology, Dartmouth College, Hanover, N.H.; the New Hampshire-Dartmouth Psychiatric Research Center, Concord and Lebanon, N.H.; and the New Hampshire Hospital, Concord, N.H.

Supported by NIMH grants MH-50094 and MH-00839.

Objective: Despite high rates of co-occurring substance use disorder in people with severe mental illness, substance use disorder is often undetected in acute-care psychiatric settings. Because underdetection is related to the failure of traditional screening instruments with this population, the authors developed a new screen for detection of substance use disorder in people with severe mental illness. Method: On the basis of criterion ("gold standard") diagnoses of substance use disorder for 247 patients admitted to a state hospital, the authors used logistic regression to select the best items from 10 current screening instruments and constructed a new instrument. They then tested the validity of the new instrument, compared with other screens, on an independent group of 73 admitted patients. Results: The new screening instrument, the Dartmouth Assessment of Lifestyle Instrument (DALI), is brief, is easy to use, and exhibits high classification accuracy for both alcohol and drug (cannabis and cocaine) use disorders. Receiver operating characteristic curves showed that the DALI functioned significantly better than traditional instruments for both alcohol and drug use disorders. Conclusions: Initial findings suggest the DALI may be useful for detecting substance use disorder in acutely ill psychiatric patients. Further research is needed to validate the DALI in other settings and with other groups of psychiatric patients.

Almost 20% of people in the U.S. population have a substance use disorder at some point in their lives, yet one-half or more of the cases of current substance use disorders go undetected by medical providers (Coulehan et al., 1987). Detection of substance use disorder in psychiatric patients is even more critical because of the high rate of comorbidity (approximately 50%) in people with severe disorders, such as schizophrenia or bipolar disorder (Barry et al., 1995; Drake et al., 1990; Lehman et al., 1996; Mueser et al., 1990; Regier et al., 1990), and because of the negative consequences of substance abuse in this population (Cournos et al., 1991; Drake, Osher, & Wallach, 1989; Haywood et al., 1995; Linszen, Dingemans, & Lenoir, 1994; Shaner et al., 1993). Nevertheless, substance use disorders frequently go undetected in psychiatric care settings (Ananth et al., 1989; Galletley, Field, & Prior, 1993; Shaner et al., 1993; Stone et al., 1993).

One reason for the frequent underdetection of these disorders in the psychiatric population is the limitations of available approaches. Acutely ill psychiatric patients are frequently unable to complete lengthy structured interviews (Barbee et al., 1989). Many psychiatric patients deny, minimize, or fail to perceive the consequences of substance abuse when responding to interviews (Test et al., 1989). For example, Goldfinger et al. (1996) found that the substance use disorder section of the Structured Clinical Interview for *DSM-III-R* had only 24% sensitivity with a group of homeless mentally ill patients. Medical examinations also have poor detection rates with psychiatric patients, possibly because psychiatric patients who abuse substances often do not have the long histories of heavy drinking that produce medical sequelae (Wolford et al., 1996). The picture with laboratory tests is more mixed. Although these tests yield many false negatives and are ineffective when there are delays between drug use and testing, they often detect current use that is denied by patients (Galletley, Field, & Prior, 1993; Shaner et al., 1993; Stone et al., 1993).

The most common approach to screening for substance use disorder has been the use of brief self-report or interview instruments. A number of these tests have been developed, but they often have poor classification accuracy for specific groups other than the ones with which they have been developed, and few have been carefully tested with psychiatric patients. For example, the Michigan Alcoholism Screening Test (MAST) (Selzer, 1971), which is reliable and valid as a screening tool for persons with primary alcoholism, has been tested several times with psychiatric patients and found to have poor specificity (36%–89%) (Hedlund & Vieweg, 1984). Many of the MAST items are irrelevant or confusing for people with severe mental illness (Searles, Alterman, & Purtill, 1990).

Thus, previous work strongly supports the need for a brief screen for substance use disorder that is specifically tailored for psychiatric patients in acute-care settings. In this paper we describe the development and initial testing of a new screen for the detection of substance use disorder in people with severe mental illness, the Dartmouth Assessment of Lifestyle Instrument (DALI). The DALI focuses on alcohol, cannabis, and cocaine use disorders, which are by far the most common substance use disorders among psychiatric patients (Barry et al., 1995; Lehman et al., 1996; Mueser et al., 1990; Mueser, Yarnold, & Bellack, 1992; Teague et al., 1994; Toner et al., 1992).

Method

Overview

We established criterion diagnoses of substance use disorder for patients entering a state hospital by using a structured clinical interview and clinician ratings from the community. The patients were then evaluated by using 10 current screening instruments, and an optimal set of items for detecting alcohol use disorder and drug use disorder was selected by means of logistic regression. The DALI was then validated in a second group of admissions by using receiver operating characteristic curves to compare its classification accuracy with that of other screening instruments.

Study Groups

We evaluated all eligible admissions to New Hampshire Hospital over 2 years between 1994 and 1996. As the only public psychiatric hospital in the state, New Hampshire Hospital receives admissions from all regions of New Hampshire. The eligibility criteria for the study included a diagnosis of severe and persistent mental illness (e.g., schizophrenia, schizoaffective disorder, bipolar disorder, major depression) according to the Structured Clinical Interview for *DSM-III-R* (SCID) (Spitzer et al, 1988), no organic mental syndrome or disorder, and a 6-month connection with a clinician in the New Hampshire mental health system.

The selection procedure for study inclusion was blind to the clients' substance abuse status. A prior connection in the New Hampshire mental health system was necessary to obtain the clinician ratings of substance use disorder used in establishing the criterion diagnosis (to be described). Each patient was enrolled in the study only once, regardless of the number of admissions to New Hampshire Hospital over the course of the study. During the 2-year period, 352 patients met these eligibility criteria, and 320 (90.9%) of the eligible patients provided written informed consent to participate in the study. The first 247 patients admitted became the index study group, and the next 73 patients formed the validation study group.

The index study group of 247 patients had an average age of 38.03 years ($SD=8.82$); 52.2% were female ($N=129$), 1.6% were non-Caucasian (four of 246), 84.6% were not married ($N=209$), and 73.9% had graduated from high school or had equivalent education (176 of 238). Primary psychiatric diagnoses were available for 245 patients; most patients had primary diagnoses of schizophrenia (19.2%, $N=47$), schizoaffective disorder (24.9%, $N=61$), bipolar disorder (19.2%, $N=47$), or major depression (12.7%, $N=31$); 24.1% of the patients ($N=59$) had other diagnoses. A group of 73 patients consecutively admitted after the index group constituted the validation study group. These patients were similar to the index group on all demographic and clinical characteristics. Both groups were similar to all patients admitted to this hospital during this period on age, education, ethnicity, and marital status. Approximately one-third of all admitted patients were not eligible for the study because their diagnoses did not qualify as severe mental illness (e.g., personality disorders, adjustment disorder, or acute stress disorder).

Measures

Criterion diagnosis. The criterion, or "gold standard," diagnosis was based on clinician ratings on the Clinician Rating Scale (Drake et al., 1990) and an independent diagnosis for current (last 6 months) substance use disorder according to the SCID. Our criterion for alcohol or drug use disorder was a finding of active abuse or dependence in the past 6 months according to either the Clinician Rating Scale or the SCID.

The Clinician Rating Scale addresses the problem of diagnostic sensitivity by reducing the rater's reliance on disclosure through either self-report or interview procedures. Trained clinicians make ratings on this scale on the basis of self-reports, interviews, longitudinal behavioral observations, collateral reports, and all clinical records, including results from medical examinations, psychiatric evaluations, and laboratory tests, over the past 6 months. Separate ratings are made for alcohol and other drugs on 5-point scales: 1=abstinence; 2=use without impairment; 3=abuse (*DSM-III-R* criteria); 4=dependence (*DSM-III-R* criteria); and 5=severe dependence (*DSM-III-R* criteria for dependence plus a recurrent need for institutionalization due to substance use disorder). For the purpose of examining screening devices, we collapsed the five Clinician Rating Scale ratings into two levels: ratings of 1 and 2 indicated nonabuse, and ratings of 3–5 denoted substance use disorder. Clinicians made separate ratings for alcohol, cannabis, and cocaine.

The Clinician Rating Scale is reliable, sensitive, and specific when used by case managers who follow their mentally ill patients over time in the community (Carey, Cocco, & Simons, 1996; Drake et al., 1990; Drake, Osher, & Wallach, 1989; Drake et al., in press; Irvin et al., 1995; Mueser et al., 1995). Analyses of interrater reliability, comparing ratings of trained clinical case managers and team psychiatrists, have yielded kappa coefficients between 0.80 and 0.95 for current use disorder (Drake et al., 1990; Drake, Osher, & Wallach, 1989). Clinician Rating Scale ratings have been validated with psychiatric patients by using other substance abuse measures (Carey, Cocco, & Simons, 1996; Drake et al., 1990; Irvin et al., 1995) and measures of motives and expectations for substance abuse (Mueser et al., 1995). Other researchers (Barry et al., 1995; Comtois, Reis, & Armstrong, 1994; Goldfinger et al., 1996; Test et al., 1989) have also shown that clinician ratings are better for detecting substance use disorder than is self-report.

The SCID (Spitzer et al., 1988) is a structured interview that entails specific questions for *DSM-III-R* criteria. The substance use disorder section addresses alcohol and other drugs separately. For the purpose of this study, interviewers focused the alcohol and drug questions on the 6 months preceding hospitalization so that the time interval coincided with that represented by the Clinician Rating Scale ratings.

Substance use disorder among psychiatric patients is often detected with one mode of assessment but not another, and the discrepancy between any two measures is typically due to nondisclosure on one measure rather than to a false positive on the other (Drake et al., 1990; Drake et al., 1997; Goldfinger et al., 1996; Shaner et al., 1993). For this reason, our criterion diagnosis was defined as the presence of substance use disorder according to either the Clinician Rating Scale or the SCID. Among the total of 118 patients with an alcohol use disorder according to either the Clinician Rating Scale (scores of 3–5) or the SCID, 46 patients (39.0%) were identified by both the Clinician Rating Scale and SCID, 47 patients (39.8%) were identified by only the Clinician Rating Scale, and 25 patients (21.2%) were identified by only the SCID. Among the 69 patients with drug use disorder, 26 (37.7%) were identified by both the Clinician Rating Scale and SCID, 26 (37.7%) were identified by only the Clinician Rating Scale, and 17 (24.6%) were identified by only the SCID. The SCID-only diagnoses were taken as face valid, as already described, but the diagnoses determined by only the Clinician Rating Scale were confirmed by a check of all community records on 15 randomly selected patients. These records contained strong confirmatory evidence. For example, one patient had been hospitalized five times because of alcohol abuse during the 6-month interval but was not given a diagnosis of substance use disorder with the SCID because he denied any use.

Substance use disorder screening instruments. The following widely used screens were administered in their entirety to all participants as part of a comprehensive battery: MAST (Selzer, 1971), CAGE (Mayfield, McLeod, & Hall, 1974), T-ACE (Sokol, Martier, & Ager, 1989), NET (Bottoms, Martier, & Sokol, 1989), TWEAK (Russell et al., 1994), Drug Abuse Screening Test (Skinner, 1982), and Reasons for Drug Use Screening Test (Grant, Hasin, & Harford, 1988). These scales vary in length from three to 31 items, and all have shown good reliability and validity with nonpsychiatric populations. Although these screens are often self-administered, in this study trained interviewers administered the entire battery. This procedure has been recommended by both researchers and clinicians assessing acutely and severely mentally ill persons because problems of attention, motivation, question comprehension, and literacy are likely to interfere with direct self-report procedures (for example, see Dworkin, 1992). At the study site we had evidence that standard scales, such as the SCL-90-R (Derogatis, 1993), had much lower completion rates when self-administered than when used in the interviewer-administered format. Some of the scales have overlapping items, and we asked each of the overlapping questions once.

Structured interviews for substance use disorder. We also incorporated portions of the Life-Style Risk Assessment Interview (Graham,

1991), the Alcohol Research Foundation Intake Interview (Lettieri, Nelson, & Sayers, 1985), and the Addiction Severity Index (McLellan et al., 1980). The Life-Style Risk Assessment Interview was designed to be nonthreatening and to detect alcohol use disorder in medical settings where patients' presenting complaints are not related to substance use disorder. We incorporated the nine introductory questions from this scale to reduce subject defensiveness. The Alcohol Research Foundation Intake Interview deals with legal and treatment history, alcohol consumption patterns, quantity, social context, beverage preference, recent drug use, and adverse consequences of alcohol use. The Addiction Severity Index sections on drug and alcohol use, family and social relationships, and family history of substance use disorder were also included.

Cognitive function. The Mini-Mental State examination (Folstein, Folstein, & McHugh, 1975) is a brief screen for assessing cognitive functioning. It consists of 11 questions. The maximum score is 30, and a score of less than 23 is generally taken to indicate cognitive impairment.

Procedures

Researchers tracked all admissions to New Hampshire Hospital daily to determine study eligibility. Hospital charts were reviewed to determine probable diagnosis and prior connections with community mental health centers, and staff nurses provided initial estimates of current mental status, ability to provide informed consent, and approachability. Hospital psychologists and trained clinicians, independent from the research interviewers, administered the SCID, including the alcohol and substance use module. Once probable eligibility was determined, the project coordinator contacted potential subjects to explain the nature of the study, to obtain written informed consent, and to administer the Mini-Mental State examination. When appropriate, consent from legal guardians was also obtained.

Trained research interviewers administered the composite substance use disorder interview, which averaged less than 1 hour. Interrater reliability was checked throughout the study on every 10th patient. To simulate usual clinical procedures, the subjects were informed that information gleaned during the interview would be shared with their clinical team at the hospital and treated as part of the clinical record.

Figure I

Receiver Operating Characteristic Curves for the Dartmouth Assessment of Lifestyle Instrument Alcohol Screen and Other Alcohol Screens for an Index Group of Hospitalized Patients with Severe Mental Illness (N = 247)

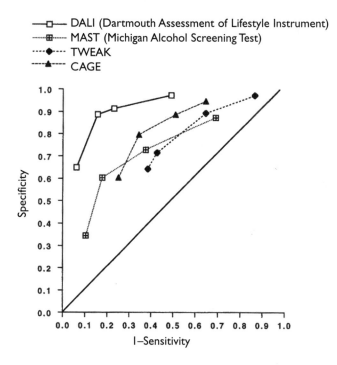

Statistical Analyses

When a reliable and valid criterion measure exists, discriminative procedures are preferable to traditional instrument-development techniques (Kraemer, 1992). Starting with the criterion diagnoses of alcohol use disorder and drug use disorder (cannabis or cocaine), we used standard logistic regression procedures to identify the optimal set of items from the existing screens to form the DALI. We then tested the DALI on an independent group of patients, using receiver operating characteristic curves to compare the DALI with other screens. Receiver operating characteristic procedures allow the comparison of two continuous screening measures with different blends of sensitivity and specificity to determine optimum cutoff points for detection. Receiver operating characteristic curves plot false alarms (1 minus sensitivity) against specificity. The area under the curve provides a comparison of scales (Hanley & McNeil, 1982).

Figure 2

Receiver Operating Characteristic Curves for the Dartmouth Assessment of Lifestyle Instrument Alcohol Screen and Other Alcohol Screens for a Validation Group of Hospitalized Patients with Severe Mental Illness (N = 73)

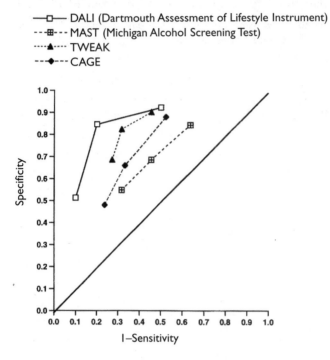

Results

Alcohol Use Disorder Screen

In the index study group of 247 patients, our procedures for establishing a criterion diagnosis identified 96 patients (38.9%) as meeting the *DSM-III-R* criteria for current (past 6 months) alcohol use disorder (abuse or dependence). Using stepwise logistic regression with the criterion alcohol diagnosis as the dependent variable, we identified the best items ($p<0.01$) from each of the 10 scales. The individual instruments contained between 4 and 50 questions each, and the stepwise logistic regression generally yielded between zero and four items per scale, for a total of 28 best items. These 28 items were included in a final stepwise logistic regression that yielded nine items and correctly classified 85.4% (170 of 199) of the patients as to their status on alcohol use disorder.

We next compared the DALI screen for alcohol use disorder with traditional instruments by using receiver operating characteristic curves. The standard interview and self-report measures of alcohol use disorder yielded overall classification accuracies varying between 61.1% and 74.1%, with different mixtures of sensitivity and specificity. Curves for the DALI and three of the common measures that performed best are shown in figure 1.

The DALI enjoys an inherent advantage, in comparisons with the existing scales from which it was drawn, in the index group from which it was derived. To eliminate this bias, we next assessed the DALI alcohol items in the validation group of 73 patients, which contained 22 patients (30.1%) with alcohol use disorder. The classification accuracy in the validation group was a comparable 83.1% (49 of 59). Figure 2 shows the performance of the alcohol DALI, in comparison with traditional instruments, in the validation group.

We carried out additional statistical comparisons of the various alcohol scales, using the approximation procedures described by Hanley and McNeil (Hanley & McNeil, 1982; Hanley & McNeil, 1983). Because the scores on the DALI and the other alcohol scales came from the same patients, we used the corrected formula for the combined standard error described by Hanley and McNeil (Hanley & McNeil, 1983). The corrected formula involves the calculation of r on the basis of the correlation between two separate sets of scores for the abusers and nonabusers and the areas under the two respective curves. The value of that r from the index group was 0.44. Using these procedures, we compared the DALI to all of the other alcohol scales. Pairwise z values appear in table 1.

A number of statistics besides sensitivity, specificity, and overall classification accuracy are commonly used to compare the accuracy of screens, and these include positive predictive value, negative predictive value, and likelihood ratio. The comparisons of the DALI to the other alcohol use disorder scales based on scores from the validation group are shown in table 2.

Table I

Pairwise Comparisons of Areas Under Receiver Operating Characteristic Curves for the Dartmouth Assessment of Lifestyle Instrument Alcohol Screen (DALI) and Other Alcohol Screens for an Index Group of Hospitalized Patients with Severe Mental Illness ($N = 247$)

Alcohol Screen	Pairwise z Value[a]					
	DALI	TWEAK	T-ACE	NET	CAGE	MAST
DALI Alcohol Screen		4.27	5.12	5.46	5.50	5.40
TWEAK	—		2.05	2.98	3.68	2.93
T-ACE	—	—		0.51	1.26	1.00
NET	—	—	—		0.96	0.78
CAGE	—	—	—	—		0.08
Michigan Alcohol Screening Test (MAST)	—	—	—	—	—	

a. From a nonparametric test comparing the areas under all possible pairs of receiver operating characteristic curves for the different screens. The test is equivalent to a series of Wilcoxon tests and has been recommended by Hanley and McNeil (1982). Because of the number of tests carried out, it is necessary to use a conservative criterion, such as $p < 0.01$. Therefore, z values greater than 2.58 are significant.

Cannabis or Cocaine Use Disorder Screen

The same procedures were then followed to develop a screen for cannabis and cocaine use disorders (abuse and dependence). In the index study group, 49 patients (19.8%) had current cannabis use disorder and 16 (6.5%) had current cocaine use disorder. Because of overlaps, 54 (21.9%) had cannabis or cocaine use disorder.

Using the same procedures to combine the best items from other scales, we developed the DALI drug questions. The DALI cannabis/cocaine screen consists of eight items, two of which are shared with the DALI alcohol screen. This scale yielded an overall classification accuracy for current cannabis or cocaine use disorder in the index study group of 89.5%. Figure 3 shows the receiver operating characteristic performance of the Drug Abuse Screening Test and Reasons for Drug Use Screening Test as compared to the DALI cannabis/cocaine questions in the index study group.

Among the validation group of 73 patients, 11 had cannabis use disorder, eight had cocaine use disorder, and owing to overlaps, 15 (20.5%) had drug use disorder overall. The classification accuracy of the DALI for cannabis or cocaine use disorder in the holdout group was 89.7% (61 of 68). Figure 4 displays the receiver operating characteristic curves for the DALI, the Reasons for Drug Use Screening Test, and the Drug Abuse Screening Test for the validation group.

Table 2

Performance of the Dartmouth Assessment of Lifestyle Instrument Alcohol Screen and Other Alcohol Screens in a Validation Group of Hospitalized Patients with Severe Mental Illness (n = 73)

Measure	Area Under the Curve	SE	Specificity	Sensitivity	Overall Classification Accuracy	Likelihood Ratio	Positive Predictive Value	Negative Predictive Value
DALI Screen	0.838	0.058	0.846	0.800	0.832	5.20	0.776	0.864
TWEAK	0.754	0.071	0.769	0.700	0.748	3.03	0.669	0.794
T-ACE	0.682	0.074	0.564	0.700	0.604	1.61	0.517	0.738
MAST	0.697	0.069	0.667	0.550	0.630	1.65	0.524	0.690
CAGE	0.715	0.073	0.667	0.700	0.680	2.10	0.583	0.769

Table 3

Performance of the Dartmouth Assessment of Lifestyle Instrument Cannabis/Cocaine Screen and Other Drug Abuse Screens in a Validation Group of Hospitalized Patients with Severe Mental Illness (n = 73).

Measure	Area Under the Curve	SE	Specificity	Sensitivity	Overall Classification Accuracy	Likelihood Ratio	Positive Predictive Value	Negative Predictive Value
DALI Screen	0.927	0.030	0.800	1.000	0.880	5.00	0.556	1.000
Reasons for Drug Use Screening Test	0.854	0.044	0.793	0.733	0.769	3.54	0.470	0.922
Drug Abuse Screening Test	0.700	0.077	0.684	0.667	0.679	2.11	0.345	0.891

Figure 3

Receiver Operating Characteristic Curves for the Dartmouth Assessment of Lifestyle Instrument Cannabis/Cocaine Screen and Other Drug Screens for an Index Group of Hospitalized Patients with Severe Mental Illness (N = 247)

—□— DALI (Dartmouth Assessment of Lifestyle Instrument)
---◆--- Drug Abuse Screening Test
·····○····· Reasons for Drug Use Screening Test

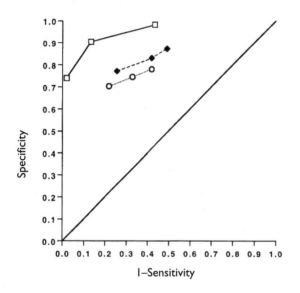

We then followed the same procedures in order to compare the performance of the DALI drug scale to the performance of the other two drug abuse measures. The pairwise z value of the area under the curve for the DALI drug screen was significantly greater than the area under the curve for either the Drug Abuse Screening Test or the Reasons for Drug Use Screening Test (p <0.001), and the latter two areas were not significantly different from each other.

As with the alcohol screens, to compare the accuracy of the drug screens we calculated several commonly used statistics, including positive predictive value, negative predictive value, and likelihood ratio. The comparison of the DALI to the other drug use disorder scales based on the validation group is shown in table 3.

Figure 4

Receiver Operating Characteristic Curves for the Dartmouth Assessment of Lifestyle Instrument Cannabis/Cocaine Screen and Other Drug Screens for a Validation Group of Hospitalized Patients with Severe Mental Illness (N = 73)

—□— DALI (Dartmouth Assessment of Lifestyle Instrument)
---◆--- Drug Abuse Screening Test
······O······ Reasons for Drug Use Screening Test

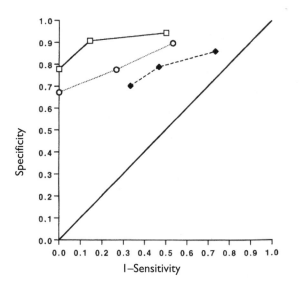

Description of DALI

The DALI is presented to patients as an 18-item, interviewer-administered scale. Three items, drawn from the Life-Style Risk Assessment Interview (Graham, 1991), are designed to reduce subject defensiveness and are not scored. Starting the screening interview in this manner was well received by the respondents. The remaining 15 items in the DALI are drawn from the Reasons for Drug Use Screening Test, TWEAK, CAGE, Drug Abuse Screening Test, Addiction Severity Index, and Life-Style Risk Assessment Interview. As in the original scales, many of the items do not explicitly refer to a specific time period (e.g., "How many drinks can you hold without passing out?") but are useful in predicting current use disorder. Although the items have differential weighting in the discriminant function equation, the reported classification accuracy is achieved by using equal weightings for all questions. The average time for administering the scale to a patient is approximately 6 minutes.

The DALI questionnaire, including scoring instructions and scale cutoff points, can be obtained directly from the authors, either by mail or directly from the New Hampshire-Dartmouth Psychiatric Research Center Web site (http://www.dartmouth.edu/dms/psychrc/). Interrater reliability, calculated for 40 interviews and five different interviewers, was as follows: alcohol questions, kappa=0.96; cannabis and cocaine questions, kappa=0.98; total scale, kappa=0.97. Test-retest reliability, calculated for 26 interviews, yielded a kappa coefficient of 0.90.

To evaluate how the DALI was affected by patient characteristics, we combined the two study groups (N=320) and examined gender, cognitive functioning (Mini-Mental State examination score $\geq$23), and diagnosis in relation to classification accuracy, using the Hanley and McNeil method (Hanley & McNeil, 1982). These analyses revealed no significant differences in classification accuracy according to any of these patient characteristics.

Discussion

The DALI functioned well as a brief screen for detecting substance use disorder among psychiatric patients entering a state hospital in New Hampshire. It is short and easy to administer; it classified patients with a degree of accuracy that is comparable to the accuracy of screening tests used for other populations; and it outperformed existing brief screens in one validation group. Additional work is needed to evaluate its performance in other settings and with other groups of psychiatric patients. A self-administered version, using either paper and pencil or computer procedures, may be more efficient with less acutely ill respondents.

This study had several advantages over existing approaches. The criterion measure of substance use disorder provides the best approximation of a diagnostic "gold standard" for this population. The existence of a reliable, valid criterion measure permitted us to use current discriminative procedures for developing the screen. The study used a relatively large number of patients, and the 90.9% participation rate was higher than rates reported for other studies of similar populations. Finally, the study maximized generalizability by using a real-world setting where assessment is difficult and by assessing the majority of regularly admitted patients. We also used confidentiality procedures that matched those generally used in acute-care settings.

Unlike traditional methods of test construction, the logistic regression procedures used in this study were not intended to identify face-valid items or items from specific domains of assessment, such as pattern of use or consequences of use. Although many face-valid items were included in the candidate items, most of the optimal items were slightly indirect: "Have you ever attended an AA meeting?" or "Have you used marijuana in the past six months?" The final set of items in the DALI did address several dimensions of substance use disorder: patterns of use, loss of control, the physiological syndrome of dependence, consequences of use, and subjective distress. Many of the final items focus on use versus nonuse and on attempts to control use, rather than on quantity of use or frequency of use. These findings are consistent with observations that patients with severe mental illness are vulnerable to adverse consequences with relatively small amounts of use (Lieberman, Kinon, & Loebel, 1990). The included items that reflect consequences emphasize relationships with family, and this focus is consistent with evidence showing that patients with severe mental illness have small social networks and often depend on families as their major supports (Cresswell, Kuipers, & Power, 1992).

The DALI was developed with a predominantly Caucasian, English-speaking, rural, New England population, in an inpatient setting, and in an environment where the rate of cocaine use is lower than rates in urban areas. Its generalizability to other populations and other settings obviously needs to be assessed. Establishing the validity of the DALI for different patient populations and in different settings is critical before the screening instrument enters general use. However, the results thus far provide encouragement that the DALI may be a more accurate screening instrument for substance use disorder in the psychiatric population than other currently available screens.

References

Ananth, J., Vandewater, S., Kamal, M., Brodsky, A., Gamal, R., Miller, M. (1989). Missed diagnosis of substance abuse in psychiatric patients. *Hospital and Community Psychiatry, 40*, 297–299.

Barbee, J. G., Clark, P. D., Craqanzano, M. S., Heintz, G.C., Kehoe, C. E. (1989). Alcohol and substance abuse among schizophrenic patients presenting to an emergency service. *Journal of Nervous and Mental Disease, 177*, 400–407.

Barry, K. L., Fleming, M. F., Greenley, J., Widlak, P., Kropp, S., McKee, P. (1995). Assessment of alcohol and other drug disorders in the seriously mentally ill. *Schizophrenia Bulletin, 21*, 313–321.

Bottoms, S. F., Martier, S. S., Sokol, R.J. (1989). Refinement in screening for risk drinking in reproductive aged women: The NET results (abstract). *Alcoholism, 13,* 339.

Carey, K. B., Cocco, K. M., Simons, J. S. (1996). Concurrent validity of clinicians' ratings of substance abuse among psychiatric outpatients. *Psychiatric Services, 47,* 842–847.

Comtois, K. A., Ries, R., Armstrong, H. E. (1994). Case manager ratings of the clinical status of dually diagnosed outpatients. *Hospital and Community Psychiatry, 45,* 568–573.

Coulehan, J.L., Zettler-Segal, M., Block, M., McClelland, M., Schulberg, H.C. (1987). Recognition of alcoholism and substance abuse in primary care. *Archives of Internal Medicine, 147,* 349–352.

Cournos, F., Empfield, M., Horwath, E., McKinnon, K., Meyer, I., Schrage, H., Currie, C., Agosin, B. (1991). HIV seroprevalence among patients admitted to two psychiatric hospitals. *American Journal of Psychiatry, 148,* 1225–1230.

Cresswell, C., Kuipers, L., Power, M. (1992). Social networks and support in long-term psychiatric patients. *Psychological Medicine, 22,* 1019–1026.

Derogatis, L.R. (1993). *The SCL-90-R.* Baltimore, MD: Clinical Psychometric Research.

Drake, R.E., McHugo, G. M., Clark, R. E., Teague, G. M., Ackerson, T. H., Xie, H., Miles, K. M. (in press). A clinical trial of assertive community treatment for patients with dual disorders. *American Journal of Orthopsychiatry.*

Drake, R. E., Osher, F. C., Noordsy, D. L., Hurlbut, S. C., Teague, G. B., Beaudette, M.S. (1990). Diagnosis of alcohol use disorders in schizophrenia. *Schizophrenia Bulletin, 16,* 57–67.

Drake, R. E., Osher, F. C., Wallach, M. A. (1989). Alcohol use and abuse in schizophrenia: A prospective community study. *Journal of Nervous and Mental Disease, 177,* 408–414.

Drake, R. E., Yovetich, N. A., Bebout, R. R., Harris, M., McHugo, G. M. (1997). Integrated treatment for dually diagnosed homeless adults. *Journal of Nervous and Mental Disease, 185,* 298–305.

Dworkin, R. J. (1992). Researching persons with mental illness: *Applied social research methods series. (Vol. 30).* Newbury Park, CA: Sage Publications.

Folstein, M. F., Folstein, S. E., McHugh, P. R. (1975). "Mini-mental state": A practical method for grading the cognitive state of patients for the clinician. *Journal of Psychiatric Research, 12,* 189–198.

Galletley, C. A., Field, C. D., Prior, M. (1993). Urine drug screening of patients admitted to a state psychiatric hospital. *Hospital and Community Psychiatry, 44,* 587–589.

Goldfinger, S. M., Schutt, R. K., Seidman, L. J., Turner, W. M., Penk, W. E., Tolomiczenko, G. S. (1996). Alternative measures of substance abuse among homeless mentally ill persons in the cross-section and over time. *Journal of Nervous and Mental Disease, 184,* 667–672.

Graham, A. W. (1991). Screening for alcoholism by life-style risk assessment in a community hospital. *Archives of Internal Medicine, 151,* 958–964.

Grant, B., Hasin, D. S., Harford, T. C. (1988). Screening for current drug use disorders in alcoholics: An application of receiver operating characteristic analysis. *Drug and Alcohol Dependence, 21,* 113–125.

Hanley, J. A., McNeil, B. J. (1982). The meaning and use of the area under a receiver operating characteristic (ROC) curve. *Radiology, 143,* 29–36.

Hanley, J. A., McNeil, B. J. (1983). A method for comparing the areas under receiving operating characteristic curves derived from some cases. *Radiology, 148,* 839–843.

Haywood, T. W., Kravitz, H. M., Grossman, L. S., Cavanaugh Jr., J. L., Davis, J. M., Lewis, D. A. (1995). Predicting the "revolving door" phenomenon among patients with schizophrenic, schizoaffective, and affective disorders. *American Journal of Psychiatry, 152,* 856–861.

Hedlund, J. L., Vieweg, B. W. (1984). The Michigan Alcoholism Screening Test (MAST): A comprehensive review. *Journal of Operational Psychiatry 15,* 55–65.

Irvin, E. A., Flannery, R. B., Penk, W. E., Hanson, M. A. (1995). The alcohol use scale: Concurrent validity data. *Journal of Social Behavior and Personality, 10,* 899–905.

Kraemer, H. (1992). *Evaluating medical tests: Objective and quantitative guidelines.* Newbury Park, CA: Sage Publications.

Lehman, A. F., Myers, C. P., Dixon, L. B., Johnson, J. L. (1996). Detection of substance use disorders among psychiatric inpatients. *Journal of Nervous and Mental Disease, 184,* 228–233.

Lettieri, D., Nelson, J. E., Sayers, M. A. (1985). *Treatment handbook series: Alcoholism treatment assessment research instruments.* Washington, DC: National Institute on Alcohol and Alcohol Abuse.

Lieberman, J., Kinon, B., Loebel, A. (1990). Dopaminergic mechanisms in idiopathic and drug-induced psychoses. *Schizophrenia Bulletin, 16,* 97–110.

Linszen, D., Dingemans, P., Lenoir, M. (1994). Cannabis abuse and the course of recent-onset schizophrenic disorders. *Archives of General Psychiatry, 51,* 273–279.

Mayfield, D., McLeod, G., Hall, P. (1974). The CAGE questionnaire: Validations of a new alcoholism screening instrument. *American Journal of Psychiatry, 131,* 1121–1123.

McLellan, A. T., Luborsky, L., Woody, G. E., O'Brien, C. P. (1980). An improved diagnostic evaluation instrument for substance abuse patients: The addiction severity index. *Journal of Nervous and Mental Disease, 168,* 26–33.

Mueser, K. T., Nishith, P., Tracy, J. I., DeGirolamo, J., Molinaro, M. (1995). Expectations and motives for substance use in schizophrenia. *Schizophrenia Bulletin, 21,* 367–378.

Mueser, K. T., Yarnold, P. R., Bellack, A. S. (1992). Diagnostic and demographic correlates of substance abuse in schizophrenia and major affective disorder. *Acta Psychiatrica Scandinavica, 85,* 48–55.

Mueser, K. T., Yarnold, P. R., Levinson, D. F., Singh, H., Bellack, A. S., Kee, K., Morrison, R. I., Yalalam, K. G. (1990). Prevalence of substance abuse in schizophrenia: demographic and clinical correlates. *Schizophrenia Bulletin, 16,* 31–56.

Regier, D. S., Farmer, M. E., Rae, D. S., Locke, B., Keith, S., Judd, L., Goodwin, F. (1990). Comorbidity of mental disorders with alcohol and other drug abuse. *Journal of the American Medical Association, 264,* 2511–2518.

Russell, M., Martier, S. S., Sokol, R.J., Mudar, P., Bottoms, S., Jacobson, S., Jacobson, J. (1994). Screening for pregnancy risk-drinking. *Alcoholism Clinical and Experimental Research, 18,* 1156–1161.

Searles, J. S., Alterman, A. I., Purtill, J. J. (1990). The detection of alcoholism in hospitalized schizophrenics: A comparison of the MAST and MAC. *Alcoholism Clinical and Experimental Research, 14,* 557–560.

Selzer, M. (1971). The Michigan alcoholism screening test: The quest for a new diagnostic instrument. *American Journal of Psychiatry, 127,* 1653–1658.

Shaner, A., Khalsa, M. E., Roberts, L., Wilkins, J., Anglin, D., Hsieh, S.C. (1993). Unrecognized cocaine use among schizophrenic patients. *American Journal of Psychiatry, 150,* 758–762.

Skinner, H. A. (1982). The drug abuse screening test. *Addictive Behavior, 7,* 363–371.

Sokol, R.J., Martier, S. S., Ager, J.W. (1989). The T-ACE questions: Practical prenatal detection of risk drinking. *American Journal of Obstetrics and Gynecology, 160,* 863–870.

Spitzer, R. L., Williams, J.B.W., Gibbon, M., First, M.B. (1988). *Instruction manual for the structured clinical interview for DSM-III-R (SCID).* New York, NY: State Psychiatric Institute, Biometrics Research.

Stone, A., Greenstein, R., Gamble, G., McLellan, A. T. (1993). Cocaine use in chronic schizophrenic outpatients receiving depot neuroleptic medications. *Hospital and Community Psychiatry, 44,* 176–177.

Teague, G. B., Drake, R. E., McHugo, G. M., Vowinkle, S. (1994). *Alcohol and substance abuse, housing, and vocational status in a statewide survey of severely mentally ill clients: Final report to the National Institute on Alcohol Abuse and Alcoholism.* Rockville, MD: NIAAA.

Test, M. A., Wallisch, L. S., Allness, D. J., Ripp, K. (1989). Substance use in young adults with schizophrenic disorders. *Schizophrenia Bulletin, 15,* 465–476.

Toner, B. B., Gillies, L. A., Prendergast, P., Cote, F. H., Browne, C. (1992). Substance use disorders in a sample of Canadian patients with chronic mental illness. *Hospital and Community Psychiatry, 43,* 251–254.

Wolford, G. L., Rosenberg, S. D., Oxman, T. E., Drake, R. E., Mueser, K. T., Hoffman, D., Vidaver, R. M. (1996). Evaluating existing methods for detecting substance use disorder in persons with severe mental illness. In *Book of Abstracts, 1996 Midwinter Meeting of the Society for Personality Assessment.* Falls Church, VA: Society for Personality Assessment.

Assessment of Alcohol and Other Drug Disorders in the Seriously Mentally Ill

Kristen L. Barry, Michael F. Fleming, James Greenley, Prudence Widlak, Svetlana Kropp & David McKee

This article originally appeared in *Schizophrenia Bulletin*, 1995, 21(2), 313–321, and is reprinted with permission.

Kristen L. Barry, Ph.D., is Associate Scientist, Michael F. Fleming, M.D., M.P.H., is Associate Professor, and Svetlana Kropp, M.S., is a Programmer Analyst, Department of Family Medicine, University of Wisconsin, Madison, WI; James Greenley, Ph.D., is Professor, Department of Psychiatry, Clinical Sciences Center, University of Wisconsin; Prudence Widlak, Ph.D., is Institutional Data Analyst, College of DuPage, Glen Ellyn, IL; and David McKee, Ph.D., is Associate Scientist, Mental Health Research Center, Department of Sociology, University of Wisconsin.

Brief assessment methods are needed to determine the presence of alcohol and drug problems in persons with severe mental illness. The purposes of this study were to determine the prevalence of alcohol and other drug problems in a rural population of 253 clients with severe mental illness and to determine the accuracy of case manager responses to specific alcohol and drug assessment questions about their clients. Clients were assessed for the presence of past and present alcohol and drug disorders by means of a face-to-face diagnostic interview. The specific questions the case managers were asked to complete were designed to assess the quantity and frequency of recent alcohol and drug use and the presence of three criteria for alcohol or drug dependence and to differentiate present versus past history of substance problems. On the basis of the Diagnostic Interview Schedule–Revised, 35% of the clients met current *DSM-III-R* alcohol or drug criteria for abuse, dependence, or both. There were differences between client and case manager reports on the clients' use of alcohol, marijuana, cocaine, narcotics, and unprescribed tranquilizers in the last year. The best predictor of a client's present alcohol or drug problem was whether the case manager thought that the client had substance use problems at some time in his or her life (sensitivity = 0.86, specificity = 0.75). This report provides additional evidence that case manager reports are a valid method of determining the prevalence of substance use problems in persons with severe mental illness.

The use of nonprescribed mood-altering substances is a major problem among adults with serious mental illnesses. Basing mental health treatment in the community allows easy access to alcohol and marijuana. A variety of substances interact in complex ways with the symptoms and problems associated with schizophrenia, bipolar disorders, and other forms of chronic mental illness. Alcohol dependence with withdrawal can produce psychotic symptoms, including delusions and hallucinations (Mott et al., 1965; Shuckit, 1989). Cannabis abuse (Knudsen & Vilmar, 1984; Treffert, 1978), and amphetamine abuse (Janowsky & Davis, 1976) have been shown to exacerbate symptoms in schizophrenia patients.

Despite increasing clinical concern about substance abuse in the chronically mentally ill, available information is based largely on clinical observations. Research data are limited. Existing studies assessing alcohol and drug problems in chronically mentally ill patients have generally not used standardized criteria or structured diagnostic interviews to test their screening questionnaires. The populations studied have generally been inpatient or outpatient samples in Department of Veterans Affairs programs, rather than community-based populations receiving treatment in community support programs (see Mueser et al., 1990 for a review of the literature). The failure to use standardized criteria assessed through a structured interview greatly increases information variance and the risk of misclassification (Alterman et al., 1984).

Determining substance abuse and dependence can be difficult in any population, but diagnostic clarity is especially challenging in a population whose everyday functioning is impaired by psychiatric illness. Strategies to improve the accuracy of diagnoses include comprehensive structured interviews with patients, the use of standardized criteria such as *DSM-III-R* criteria (American Psychiatric Association, 1987) for alcohol and drug abuse and dependence, and corroborative interviews with case managers. However, there is also a need in the mental health field to have valid screening questions that can be completed by case managers as opposed to lengthy diagnostic interviews with clients.

Drake et al. (1990) found that clinicians working with schizophrenia patients over time were able to accurately identify problem drinking. Clinicians' identification of substance abuse is important because the data can be used to assess the prevalence of alcohol and drug problems in this at-risk population, providing the basis for systematic studies of the consequences of use and correlates of health-related problems, and to assess cost and service differences between clients with and without alcohol-related problems. There has, however, been little validation of both specific (quantity and frequency, blackouts, inability to stop, other's concern about drinking) and more general (perception of a past problem, perception of a present problem) screening questions for this population that can quickly be used by case managers.

The specific aim of this study was to determine the usefulness of specific alcohol and drug assessment questions completed by case managers of chronically mentally ill consumers of community mental health services. These questions were designed to assess the quantity and frequency of recent alcohol and drug use and the presence of three criteria for alcohol or drug dependence and to differentiate present and past history of substance problems. In particular, this study assessed which questions posed to case managers were the best proxy for a present alcohol or drug problem in the clients as assessed by a structured diagnostic interview based on *DSM-III-R* criteria for alcohol abuse and dependence.

Methods

A cross-sectional study was conducted with a sample of 253 chronically mentally ill clients participating in two community-based mental health programs in Appleton and Wausau, Wisconsin. Both are midsized cities serving larger rural areas. Following Internal Review Board guidelines at the University of Wisconsin, staff from the mental health programs asked patients to participate. Each participant signed a consent form. Of the 358 clients originally asked to participate, 105 refused, for a 71% response rate.

The mean age of the sample was 44 (range = 20–77), the mean education level was 12 years (range = 8–17), and 51% ($n = 129$) were male. The racial composition of the rural Wisconsin counties studied was reflected in the sample, which was 97.0% white, 2.5% Native American, and 0.5% Hispanic. Fifty-two percent of the clients were diagnosed with schizophrenia; 25% with schizoaffective, 14% with depressive, 6% with bipolar, and 2% with borderline personality disorders; 1% had other diagnoses. Each client was paid $5 for participating.

The clients received a face-to-face diagnostic substance abuse interview with a member of the research team lasting approximately 45 to 55 minutes. Researchers received group and individual training in administering the interview schedule. The interview schedule included three sections: (1) alcohol abuse and dependence subscales of the Diagnostic Interview Schedule-Revised (DIS–R; Robins et al., 1989), based on *DSM-III-R* criteria; (2) illicit drug abuse and dependence subscales of the DIS–R; and (3) questions assessing substance use in the last year, including quantity and frequency, blackouts, inability to stop, other's concern (relative, friend, doctor, health care worker) about drinking, perception of a past problem, and perception of a present problem (over the last year). Robins et al. (1989) established interrater reliability in the administration of the DIS–R. The completed DIS–R is entered into a computer and the diagnosis is generated by a computer program. Interviewers were not responsible for making a diagnosis.

As part of a larger assessment of clients' health and services, case managers also completed the questions assessing each client's substance use in the last year. Case managers were chosen to provide information about the clients because of the intensity of their involvement with the clients. More than 90% of the clients had been served by the mental health organization for more than 1 year. Clients met with case managers an average of five times in the month before sampling (standard deviation = 4.9; median = 4). Case managers received inservice training about alcohol and other drug problems.

The drug use questions addressed the clients' use of cannabis; stimulants (e.g., amphetamines); cocaine, heroin, opioids (e.g., codeine, meperidine, propoxyphene, and aspirin/oxycodone); PCP; psychedelics (e.g., LSD); inhalants (e.g., glue, gasoline); and other drugs (nitrous oxide, amyl nitrite).

DSM-III-R criteria for alcohol or drug dependence include three or more of the following: (1) use of the substance in larger amounts over longer periods of time than intended; (2) unsuccessful efforts to cut down or control use; (3) large amounts of time spent in activities to get the substance or to recover from use; (4) frequent intoxication or withdrawal when expected to fulfill major obligations; (5) giving up of social, occupational, or recreational activities because of substance use; (6) continued use despite social, psychological, or physical problems caused by use; (7) marked tolerance—a need for increased amounts of the substance to achieve the desired effect or diminished effect with the same use; (8) withdrawal symptoms; and (9) substance taken to avoid withdrawal symptoms. These symptoms must have persisted for more than 1 month or the subject must have experienced recurrent episodes of these symptoms.

DSM-III-R criteria for alcohol or drug abuse include one or both of the following: (1) continued use despite social, psychological, or physical problems caused by use or (2) recurrent use in situations in which use is physically hazardous (e.g., driving while intoxicated). These symptoms must have persisted for more than 1 month or recurred over time.

Subjects who met three of the nine *DSM-III-R* criteria for alcohol or drug dependence and whose symptoms persisted over time were considered *DSM-III-R* positive for dependence. Those who met one of the two criteria for abuse and whose symptoms persisted over time were considered *DSM-III-R* positive for abuse. Past and present dependence and abuse can be ascertained from *DSM-III-R* alcohol and drug criteria.

Correlations, kappas, and tau-b measures of association were used to determine the relationship between case manager reports on the screening questions and client *DSM-III-R* criteria as assessed by the DIS-R. Because case manager data were available for only 200 of the 253 clients in the study, the analysis comparing case manager and client reports includes those 200 cases. Kappa (K) was used to assess the reliability of the questions because it is a measure of reliability that corrects for chance agreement. Since screening measures, such as the questions answered by the case managers, often have goals (such as high sensitivity) that differ from the goals of criterion measures such as the DIS-R, the two approaches frequently yield different marginal distributions on the same sample. One result is that the maximum possible kappa (K_m) will be less than 1.00. Thus, we include kappa divided by maximum kappa (K/K_m), which is a coefficient indicating the possible proportion of agreement in excess of chance (Cohen 1960). To illustrate the level of agreement as a representation of concurrent validity, Kendall's tau-b measures of association were also chosen.

The assessment questions about clients' alcohol and drug use were completed by both clients and their case managers (figure 1). The questions selected for testing with this population were adapted primarily from the Alcohol Use Disorders Identification Test (AUDIT) and the Health Screening Survey (HSS; Fleming & Barry, 1991). The AUDIT was developed as part of a large multicountry study with the World Health Organization for use as a multicultural screening test that would offer information on consumption patterns as well as selected criteria for alcohol dependence (Saunders et al., 1993). The HSS was developed on the basis of work by Wallace et al. (1988) for a large primary care clinical trial of brief physician advice with heavy drinkers.

Figure I

Alcohol and other drug screening questions completed by case managers

1. We would like to know what drugs the client uses (*excluding nicotine and caffeine*), and how frequently he/she uses them. For each drug, please write how many days per month, in the last year, the client used the drug and how much he/she used each time (drinks, joints, lines, etc.). If the client does not use a particular drug, please enter "0" for days per month. (*Give your best estimate.*)

Drug	How Many Days/Month?	How Much Per Day?
a Alcohol (drinks)	/month	/day
b Cocaine (lines)	/month	/day
c Marijuana (joints)	/month	/day
d Narcotics (pills)	/month	/day
e Tranquilizers (pills)	/month	/day
f Other	/month	/day
g	/month	/day
h	/month	/day
i	/month	/day

2. Do you think the client has ever had a drinking or other drug problem? Would you say definitely, probably, or not at all?
   o 1. *Definitely*
   o 2. *Probably*
   o 3. *Not at all* (Skip to 3.)

3. Do you think the client had a past problem only, or has he/she had alcohol or other drug problems within the last year?
   o 1. *Past only*
   o 2. *Within last year*

4. Has the client ever been unable to remember what happened the night before because of drinking alcohol or using other drugs?
   o 1. *Yes*
   o 2. *No* (Skip to 5.)

5. During the past year, has the client been unable to stop drinking alcohol or using other drugs once he/she has started? (GIVE YOUR BEST ESTIMATE.)
   o 1. *Yes*
   o 2. *No*

6. Has a relative, friend, doctor, or other health worker been concerned about the client's drinking and/or other drug use or suggested cutting down?
   o 1. *Yes*
   o 2. *No*

The assessment questions used in the present study included questions about (1) the quantity and frequency of use of alcohol, marijuana, cocaine, narcotics, tranquilizers, and stimulants; (2) past history of a substance use problem; (3) perception of a substance use problem in the past only or in the last year; (4) blackouts; (5) inability to stop in the last year, and (6) concerns of others about use (relative, friend, doctor, health care worker).

These questions were tested with this population for the following reasons. The first question assesses current use and binge use. There is a strong linear correlation between use and associated health problems. The greater the alcohol consumption, drug use, or both, the greater the number of consequences (Anderson et al., 1993). From a public health and prevention perspective, persons who are at-risk users of alcohol and drugs are a much larger health problem than persons who are alcohol or drug dependent. Even though the epidemiological data are clear, consumption questions are not included in other commonly used alcohol and drug screening tests (e.g., CAGE[1] [Mayfield et al., 1974], the Michigan Alcohol Screening Test [Selzer, 1971]) because of the assumption that self-report consumption data are invalid. There is considerable evidence, however, for the validity of self-report consumption data in substance abuse treatment populations (Babor et al., 1990; Maisto et al., 1990).

The second question inquires about past substance use problems ("Do you think the client has ever had a drinking or a drug problem?"). This question is purposely vague, as the potential list of problems is immense and depends on social, cultural, and health norms. The question specifically addressing past alcohol problems was tested in the HSS (Fleming & Barry, 1991) and found to have the highest sensitivity of the alcohol questions asked (questions included questions about consumption, CAGE, trauma, past problems, and present problems) in three samples—two treatment samples and one in a primary care setting (sensitivities = 0.95, 0.94, 0.57)—and in the Health Screening Questionnaire (Wallace et al., 1988). A question about past problems was also tested by Cyr & Wartman (1988) in a general medical population and found to be the best predictor of alcohol problems in that setting.

1. CAGE is an acronym for four questions: (1) Have you felt you should *cut* down or stop drinking?; (2) Have you been *annoyed* by someone telling you to cut down or stop drinking?; (3) Have you felt *guilty* or bad about how much you drink?; and (4) Have you been waking up in the morning wanting to have an alcoholic drink *(eyeopener)*?

The third question asks about problems in the last year. This question was included because the prevalence of past alcohol and drug problems is approximately twice that of current problems. Many persons with a history of problem use as young adults stop or decrease use with age. Others in this group may be recovering alcoholics. While the clinical importance of previous problems has not been clearly defined, current problems may be expected to have a stronger correlation with adverse health effects. The question appears to have been first used in a large-scale study by Wallace et al. (1988).

The presence of blackouts (assessed by the fourth question) is a sensitive marker for alcohol problems. Studies in college student and primary care samples found that as many as one-third of males had experienced at least one blackout in their lifetimes (Fleming & Barry, 1991; Fleming et al., 1991). A blackout is a period of amnesia associated with a heavy drinking episode; it is not the same as intoxication. While a single blackout is not diagnostic, it can indicate an abnormal physiological response to alcohol.

The fifth question, on inability to stop, was included because repeated episodes of loss of control can suggest alcohol or drug dependence.

The final question asks about the concerns of others about the person's alcohol or drug use. Family members and friends are often the first to recognize an alcohol or drug disorder. This is one of the *DSM-III-R* criteria and is used in many screening and diagnostic instruments.

Results

DSM-III-R Criteria: Alcohol and Other Drugs: Client Report

Of the total sample of 253 clients, 39.5% ($n = 100$) met *DSM-III-R* criteria for past alcohol abuse; 18.5% ($n = 47$) met *DSM-III-R* criteria for past alcohol dependence; and 15.0% ($n = 38$) met criteria for past drug abuse or dependence. Since the questions of interest in this study tapped current substance use, alcohol and drug diagnoses were combined.

Forty-one percent ($n = 104$) of the clients met criteria for past alcohol or drug problems. The percentage of clients who reported using drugs consistently for at least 2 weeks at some time in their lives was as follows: marijuana, 16% ($n = 40$); cocaine, 2% ($n = 6$); narcotics, 2% ($n = 6$); tranquilizers, 2% ($n = 6$); and stimulants, 3% ($n = 8$). Three of the clients who met criteria for drug abuse or dependence did not also meet alcohol abuse or dependence criteria.

Thirty-five percent ($n = 89$) of the clients met criteria for alcohol or drug abuse or dependence in the last year.

Screening Question Results: Comparison of Client and Case Manager Reports

Nineteen percent ($n = 47$) of the client sample reported abstinence from alcohol in the last year. Clients drank an average of four drinks per week (range = 0–135). Ten percent ($n = 25$) of the clients reported drinking 12 or more drinks per week; case managers thought that 9.7% ($n = 23$) drank at that level. Clients who met *DSM-III-R* criteria for alcohol abuse drank an average of eight drinks per week. Those who met *DSM-III-R* criteria for dependence drank 11 drinks per week. There were some differences between case manager and client reports of how many clients were currently using marijuana (clients, $n = 3$, case managers, $n = 12$) and cocaine (clients, $n = 1$; case managers, $n = 2$) in the last year. While case managers reported that one client was using narcotics and two were using unprescribed tranquilizers, clients reported no narcotic or unprescribed tranquilizer use in the previous year. Case managers accurately identified each of the clients who reported their own illicit drug use. Further statistics were not calculated for cocaine, narcotic, and unauthorized tranquilizer use because both clients and case managers reported little or no use. The reports of little or no use may be related to case managers' lack of awareness and clients' underreporting of illicit drug use; however, they may also reflect the low rates of illicit drug use in smaller, more rural communities by clients with little access to discretionary funds.

Thirty percent of the clients thought they had a past substance use problem and 5% reported a present problem. By comparison, case managers thought that 38% of the clients had past alcohol or drug problems and that 17% were continuing to experience present substance use problems.

Table 1 shows the agreement between case manager and client reports on the items in the screening questionnaire. Case manager and client responses to each of the individual screening questions were significantly correlated. Highest kappas in relationship to the maximum kappas possible were in perceptions of past ($K = 0.51$; $K_m = 0.65$; $K/K_m = 0.78$) or present ($K = 0.22$; $K_m = 0.31$; $K/K_m = 0.71$) substance use problems.

Table 1

Agreement between client and case manager responses to alcohol and drug screening questions

	K	K_m	K/K_m	Tau-b
Substance use				
Alcohol	0.31	0.63	0.49	0.33
Marijuana	0.50	0.87	0.57	0.50
Lifetime substance use problem	0.51	0.65	0.78	0.54
Current substance use problem	0.22	0.31	0.71	0.31
Blackouts	0.32	0.87	0.37	0.32
Loss of control	0.19	0.75	0.25	0.20
Others concerned	0.54	0.88	0.61	0.54

Note. Statistics were not calculated for cocaine, narcotic, and unauthorized tranquilizer use because both client and case manager reported little or no use. K = kappa; K_m = maximum kappa. All kappa and tau-b measures are significant at the $p < 0.001$ level except for the kappa for loss of control, which is significant at the $p < 0.005$ level.

Table 2 shows how well case manager and client reports corresponded to DIS–R diagnosis. Maximum kappas are also reported. The kappas and tau-b analyses for all of the case manager items were variable but showed reliability and validity. In addition, each of the client items was significantly related to whether or not the client met *DSM-III-R* alcohol or drug criteria. Both clients and case managers tended to assess client alcohol and drug problems accurately on the basis of *DSM-III-R* criteria for a substance use problem.

The sensitivities, specificities, and positive and negative predictive values of each of the case manager and client items are listed in table 3 by whether or not the client met current alcohol or drug *DSM-III-R* criteria. The best prediction of a client's meeting current *DSM-III-R* criteria was the case manager's perception that the client had had a substance use problem in his or her past (sensitivity = 0.86, specificity = 0.75; positive predictive value = 0.80, negative predictive value = 0.71). The best predictor of a substance use problem by the client was the perception that others were concerned about his or her use. Sensitivities and specificities were calculated for each question and for combinations of the questions. No combination of the six questions provided better sensitivity and specificity than the individual question about lifetime problems.

Discussion

Alcohol and drug abuse and dependence in consumers of community-based mental health care are significant problems with important clinical implications for treatment and long-term management. Although most of the previous studies assessing substance abuse in chronically mentally ill subjects were conducted in inpatient or urban Department of Veterans Affairs outpatient settings, the findings of this study confirm the high rates of past alcohol and drug abuse or dependence found in those studies (Barbee et al., 1989; Mueser et al., 1990). Forty percent of the clients in this midsized-city sample receiving community-based care met *DSM-III-R* criteria for past alcohol abuse, and 19% met dependence criteria. In addition, 15% met criteria for past drug abuse or dependence. Of more importance to this study was the finding that 35% of the clients met alcohol or drug abuse or dependence criteria in the last year.

This study assessed the use of six substance use screening questions completed by case managers for a best proxy of clients' present alcohol or drug problems. There were differences between client and case manager reports in how much clients were drinking and how many were using marijuana, cocaine, narcotics, and unprescribed tranquilizers in the last year.

Tests of association between case manager and client responses indicated the strongest relationship on global questions of past and present problems. Sensitivity and specificity tables comparing case manager reports and whether or not the clients currently met *DSM-III-R* criteria revealed that the best predictor of a client's present alcohol or drug problem was whether the case manager thought that the client had had a substance use problem at some time in his or her life ($K = 0.57$, $p < 0.001$; sensitivity $= 0.86$, specificity $= 0.75$).

Cyr and Wartman (1988) and Fleming and Barry (1991) found that a simple question asking about past problems was one of the better predictors of alcohol problems in general medical settings. This study extends that finding to a specific population in which small amounts of alcohol use may have more serious consequences than those seen in more general medical settings. Questions that require specific information about the client's behavior (e.g., blackouts, inability to stop, amount of substances used) provide a less accurate assessment of present problems.

Table 2

Measure of agreement with kappa and tau-b: Client and case manager responses to screening questions compared with DSM-III-R alcohol or drug criteria

	Case manager				Client			
	K	K_m	K/K_m	Tau-b	K	K_m	K/K_m	Tau-b
Substance use								
Alcohol	0.34	0.69	0.49	0.36	0.13	0.92	0.14	0.13
Marijuana	0.14	0.21	0.67	0.24	0.18	0.26	0.69	0.26
Lifetime substance use problem	0.57	0.78	0.73	0.59	0.57	0.89	0.64	0.57
Current substance use problem	0.36	0.65	0.55	0.39	0.15	0.17	0.88	0.27
Blackouts	0.44	0.65	0.67	0.47	0.50	0.73	0.68	0.52
Loss of control	0.23	0.55	0.42	0.25	0.40	0.72	0.56	0.41
Others concerned	0.44	0.79	0.56	0.45	0.58	0.94	0.62	0.59

Note. Statistics were not calculated for cocaine, narcotic, and unauthorized tranquilizer use because both client and case manager reported little or no use; DSM-III-R = Diagnostic and Statistical Manual of Mental Disorders (American Psychiatric Association, 1987); K = kappa; K_m = maximum kappa. All kappa and tau-b measures are significant at the $p < 0.001$ level.

Table 3

Sensitivity and specificity of client and case manager responses to screening questions compared with clients' current DSM-III-R alcohol or drug criteria

	Case Manager				Client			
	Sen	Spec	PPV	NPV	Sen	Spec	PPV	NPV
Substance use								
Alcohol	0.43	0.88	0.68	0.74	0.47	0.66	0.43	0.69
Marijuana	0.13	0.98	0.80	0.68	0.17	0.98	0.79	0.68
Lifetime substance use problem[1]	0.86	0.75	0.80	0.71	0.66	0.89	0.77	0.83
Current substance use problem	0.43	0.91	0.72	0.72	0.13	0.99	0.92	0.68
Blackouts	0.47	0.93	0.79	0.75	0.53	0.93	0.80	0.78
Loss of control	0.31	0.89	0.63	0.69	0.47	0.89	0.71	0.76
Others concerned	0.54	0.88	0.72	0.77	0.70	0.88	0.76	0.84

Note. Statistics were not calculated for cocaine, narcotic, and unauthorized tranquilizer use because both client and case manager reported little or no use. *DSM-III-R* = *Diagnostic and Statistical Manual of Mental Disorders* (American Psychiatric Association, 1987); Sen = sensitivity; Spec = specificity; PPV = positive predictive value; NPV = negative predictive value.

1. Best individual case manager question predicting a current client alcohol or drug problem.

Of interest was the finding that case managers identified more current marijuana use than did clients ($n = 12$ vs. 3) and that they identified present substance use problems at a higher rate (17% vs. 5%). This tendency of clients to minimize present use and problems supports the use of case manager reports, which may be more accurate and more useful predictors of actual ongoing client problems with substance use. Clients may be reluctant to disclose present use because they may fear losing services or receiving further intervention.

Since few studies to date have been conducted in community-based treatment programs and used standardized criteria for alcohol and drug abuse and dependence, caution must be used in extrapolating these results to other community-based consumers of mental health care. Further studies with larger populations in rural-based community mental health treatment settings are necessary. In addition, geographical area must be taken into account. The State of Wisconsin has a high alcohol abuse rate (National Institute on Alcohol Abuse and Alcoholism, 1987), and the high rate of reported alcohol-related problems in this study may reflect the geographical area in which the study was conducted as well as characteristics of consumers of community-based mental health care.

These results, however, suggest that alcohol- and drug-related problems may be as common in rural community-based programs serving chronically mentally ill clients as they are in urban inpatient programs. Since administering instruments based on *DSM-III-R* criteria to clients is costly and time-consuming in community-based mental health centers, the use of simple screening questions administered to case managers may prove important in determining who needs further assessment and treatment.

Further studies with standardized research methodologies are necessary to determine prevalence and to tease out issues of self-medication. These studies may provide a basis for the development of applicable alcohol and drug abuse programs designed for the special needs of clients living in smaller community settings.

References

Alterman, A. I., Ayers, F. R., & Williford, W. O. (1984). Diagnostic validation of conjoint schizophrenia and alcoholism. *Journal of Clinical Psychiatry, 45,* 300–303.

American Psychiatric Association. (1987). *DSM-III-R: Diagnostic and Statistical Manual of Mental Disorders. 3rd ed., revised.* Washington, DC: The Association.

Anderson, P., Cremona, A., Paton, A., Turner, C., & Wallace, P. (1993). Alcohol and risk. *Addiction, 88,* 1493–1508.

Babor, T., Brown, J., & DelBoca, F. (1990). The validity of self-reports in applied research on addictive behaviors: Fact or fiction. *Behavioral Assessment, 12,* 5–31.

Barbee, J. G., Clark, P. D., Crapanzano, M. S., Heintz, G. C., & Kehoe, C. E. (1989). Alcohol and substance abuse among schizophrenic patients presenting to an emergency psychiatric service. *Journal of Nervous and Mental Disease, 177,* 400–407.

Cohen, J. (1960). A coefficient of agreement for nominal cases. *Educational and Psychological Measurement, 20*(1), 37–47.

Cyr, M. G., & Wartman, S. A. (1988). The effectiveness of routine screening questions in the detection of alcoholism. *Journal of the American Medical Association, 259,* 51–54.

Drake, R., Osher, F., Noordsy, D., Hurlbut, S., Teague, G., & Beaudett, M. (1990). Diagnosis of alcohol use disorders in schizophrenia. *Schizophrenia Bulletin, 16*(1), 57–67.

Fleming, M., & Barry, K. (1991). A three-sample test of an alcohol screening questionnaire. *Alcohol and Alcoholism, 26*(1), 81–91.

Fleming, M., Barry, K., & MacDonald, R. (1991). The Alcohol Use Disorders Identification Test in a college sample. *International Journal of Addiction, 26*(11), 1173–1185.

Janowsky, D. S., & Davis, J. M. (1976). Methylphenidate, dextroamphetamine, and levamphetamine. *Archives of General Psychiatry, 33,* 304–308.

Knudsen, P., & Vilmar, T. (1984). Cannabis and neuroleptic agents in schizophrenia. *Acta Psychiatrica Scandinavica, 69,* 162–174.

Maisto, S., McKay, J., & Connors, J. (1990). Self-report issues in substance abuse: State of the art and future directions. *Behavioral Assessment, 12,* 117–134.

Mayfield, D., McLeod, G., & Hall, P. (1974). The CAGE questionnaire: Validation of a new alcoholism screening instrument. *American Journal of Psychiatry, 131,* 1121–1123.

Mott, R.H., Small, I. F., & Anderson, J. M. (1965). A comparative study of hallucinations. *Archives of General Psychiatry, 12,* 595–601.

Mueser, K. T., Yarnold, P. R., Levinson, D. F., Singh, H., Bellack, A. S., Kee, K., Morrison, R. L., & Yadalam, K. G. (1990). Prevalence of substance abuse in schizophrenia: Demographic and clinical correlates. *Schizophrenia Bulletin, 16*(1), 31–56.

National Institute on Alcohol Abuse and Alcoholism. (1987). *Special Report to Congress on Alcohol and Health.* Rockville, MD: The Institute.

Robins, L., Helzer, J., Cottler, L., & Goldring, E. (1989). *NIMH Diagnostic Interview Schedule: Version III, Revised.* St. Louis, MO: Washington University.

Saunders, J., Aasland, O., Babor, T., de la Fuenta, J., & Grant, M. (1993). Development of the Alcohol Use Disorders Identification Test (AUDIT): W.H.O. collaborative project on early detection of persons with harmful alcohol consumption—II. *Addiction, 88*(6), 791–804.

Selzer, M. (1971). The Michigan Alcoholism Screening Test: The quest for a new diagnostic instrument. *American Journal of Psychiatry, 127,* 1653–1658.

Shuckit, M. A. (1989). *Drug and alcohol abuse. 3rd ed.* New York, NY: Plenum Press.

Treffert, D. A. (1978). Marijuana use in schizophrenia: A clear hazard. *American Journal of Psychiatry, 135,* 1213–1215.

Wallace, P., Cutler, S., & Haines, A. (1988). Randomized controlled trial of general practitioner intervention in patients with excessive alcohol consumption. *British Medical Journal, 297,* 663–668.

Chapter Three: Treatment

Intervention Strategies for People with Dual Diagnosis

Kenneth Minkoff

This article originally appeared in *Innovations and Research,* 2(4), 11–17, 1993, and is reprinted with permission.

Kenneth Minkoff, M.D., is Chief of Psychiatric Services at Choate Health Systems, Inc., in Woburn, MA., and Medical Director of the Culfield Center, an integrated psychiatry and addiction hospital.

During the past 15 years, individuals with dual diagnosis of serious mental illness and substance disorder have become increasingly visible in service delivery systems. The Epidemiologic Catchment Area (ECA) survey found that 55% of people with schizophrenia in treatment—and 62% of people with affective illness—had lifetime diagnoses of substance disorder (Regier et al., 1990). These figures are even more striking when we consider that the true prevalence may be underreported because of the limitations in any survey of substance use in penetrating subject's denial, and when we consider that caffeine and nicotine were not included as substances of abuse. Numerous studies have reported similar results (Pepper et al., 1981; Schwartz & Goldfinger, 1981; Alterman, 1985; Safer, 1987; Caton, et al., 1989; Drake et al., 1989). Taken in total, these data suggest that the prevalence of "dual diagnosis" in people with serious mental illness is so high, that it must be considered an expectation, rather than an exception.

The high prevalence of substance disorders among individuals with serious mental illness is particularly problematic because of the deleterious effects of even relatively mild substance abuse on the course and outcome of major mental illness. Psychoactive substances, including alcohol, caffeine, and nicotine, can be particularly destabilizing to the brains of people with psychiatric disabilities, whose equilibrium is already fragile. Both caffeine and nicotine have been shown to interfere with absorption and to facilitate the excretion of psychotropic medication. Numerous studies have demonstrated that substance abusing mentally ill individuals have more severe psychiatric symptoms (Osher, et al., 1991), more self-destructive, violent, disruptive, and criminal behavior (McCarrick, et al., 1985; Drake et al., 1989; Safer, 1987), more housing instability and homelessness (Drake & Wallach, 1989; Minkoff & Drake, 1993), and more non-compliance with medication and treatment (Drake

& Wallach, 1989; Pristach & Smith, 1990). Consequently, they are more at risk for continuing relapse, with revolving door admissions, poor community tenure, and difficulty in engaging in stabilizing treatment support systems.

Despite the clearly harmful effects of substance abuse and dependence among the seriously mentally ill, efforts to develop and provide successful treatment interventions to "dual diagnosis" patients have been extremely frustrating. One major area of difficulty is at the systems level. The alcohol and drug abuse treatment systems and the mental health system are organized separately at the federal, state, and local levels, and often have apparently conflicting philosophies of treatment (Ridgely, et al., 1990). Consumers often experience themselves as "systems misfits" (Bachrach, 1987) as they receive "ping-pong therapy," bouncing back and forth between two systems of care, each of which excludes them because of comorbidity (Ridgely, et al., 1990). Families, already burdened by concern and care for a mentally ill relative, feel more than doubly overwhelmed when the problem of substance abuse is also present, not only because of fear about the clinical risk involved with such behavior, but also because of anger at the relative for engaging in apparently wilful destructive behavior and frustration at feeling powerless to "get him (or her) to stop." Mental health professionals feel similarly overwhelmed, because neither their training (usually in mental health or substance abuse, not both) nor the systems in which they work facilitate the provision of integrated, simultaneous mental health and substance abuse services to dually diagnosed individuals.

Even where integrated programs do exist, however, successful treatment outcomes are difficult to achieve. Many dually diagnosed individuals consider their substance abuse to be a choice, not a problem (despite the concerns of their families and caregivers). Some deny that they even use substances; others resent any mention of substance use. Caring suggestions by loved ones to stop using are often rebuffed angrily; efforts by caregivers to control substance behavior are subverted passively; angry remarks and guilt-inducing pleas are not only unsuccessful, they often seem to make the situation worse.

The purpose of this paper is to briefly present a unified conceptual framework to facilitate an integrated understanding of the assessment, diagnosis, and treatment of dual diagnosis, and then to utilize the principles of this conceptual framework to describe methodologies for initial intervention to engage these individuals in substance abuse treatment.

Unified Conceptual Framework: Disease and Recovery Model

Minkoff (1989) first described a unified conceptual framework in which substance disorders and mental illnesses are both viewed as primary disorders when they coexist, each requiring specific and intensive treatment. Moreover, both substance dependence and major mental illness are regarded as examples of primary, biologic, chronic mental illnesses which both fit into a disease and recovery model of treatment. Specifically, both diseases, despite differences in specific symptoms and treatments, share certain common characteristics. Some characteristics are related to the illness itself: for example, both are brain diseases characterized by lack of control of thought, behavior, and emotion which are hereditary, chronic, progressive, and treatable but incurable. Other characteristics, however, are related to the individual's—and family's—reaction to the illness: for example, both diseases are characterized by denial and minimization of both the disease and its chronicity, and are associated with enormous feelings of shame, guilt, failure, weakness, and stigma, all of which play a major role in preventing successful participation in treatment.

Recovery, in this model, defines a hopeful process of growth and change in the face of a serious, persistent, and often disabling disease. The recovery process defines the individual's recovery of self-worth and pride in the face of a stigmatizing disease, through increased recognition and acceptance of the reality of the disease and disability, and increased ability to focus energy on managing the disease creatively to prevent relapse, and on enhancing one's strengths and abilities to maximize rehabilitation. Recovery is a positive state of mind that can be attained by even the most severely disabled individuals with the poorest objective outcomes. Minkoff (1989, 1991) describes four distinct phases of recovery for each disease:

1. Acute Stabilization (Stabilization of acute psychosis; detoxification)

2. Engagement in Active Treatment (Initial engagement in a treatment process, as by taking medication to control mental illness, or by participating in treatment groups or 12-step programs to control substance use)

3. Relapse Prevention to Maintain Prolonged Stabilization (Ongoing participation in psychiatric or addiction treatment with a focus on learning techniques for prevention of relapse)

4. Rehabilitation and Recovery (Once stability of both illnesses is more secure, to begin to develop new skills for managing one's life to replace the deficits that result from either disease.)

Individuals do not proceed through these phases simultaneously. More commonly, patients will stabilize one illness first—usually the psychiatric disorder—while engagement in treatment for the other may not take place until much later. An important principle that derives from this model, therefore, is the following:

There is no one type of treatment program or intervention for dual diagnosis. The proper treatment interventions for each individual depends on the phase of recovery, as well as the level of acuity, severity, disability, and motivation for treatment associated with each primary disease (Minkoff, 1991).

Intervention Strategies for Engagement in Substance Treatment

Using this model, we can now focus particular attention on the problem described earlier; namely, that substance-abusing mentally ill individuals are frequently resistant to participating in treatment, and, in fact, are resistant to even acknowledging that their substance use is a problem. Most commonly, these individuals are involved in psychiatric treatment in the prolonged stabilization phase of recovery for their mental illness, but are not yet in the engagement phase regarding substance abuse.

To address this problem, therefore, we need to define specific intervention strategies to begin engagement of mentally ill substance abusers and addicts. Because substance abuse and dependence are distinct primary diagnoses, these strategies must be specifically directed at substance using behavior. However, because the patients are engaged in treatment for psychiatric illness only, and may see no reason to address substance use separately, these interventions must be integrated into the context of their ongoing mental health programs.

Osher and Kofoed (1989) have described the process of engagement as beginning with empathy, and moving through phases of persuasion or education, to participation in active treatment, and ultimately relapse prevention. The substance abuse literature offers more refinement in discussing intervention strategies, emphasizing that empathy must be combined with detachment from assuming responsibility for the other person's substance behavior or its consequences, and ultimately with confrontation of the individual with the consequences of continued substance use. The "intervention" process usually includes family members and other concerned individuals, not just professionals, and may involve techniques such as contingency contracting to define choices and consequences more clearly. Note that many of these strategies are commonly applied to foster the engagement of individuals in treatment for mental illness as well.

Sciacca (1991) has noted that intervention strategies must also take into account that people don't move from complete denial to complete acceptance of treatment in one step. Engagement is often a stepwise time-consuming process in which individuals slowly come to recognize that they have a problem and need help, as follows:

1. I have no problem, I don't want to change, I need no help.

2. I may have a problem, I don't want to change, I need no help.

3. I have a problem, I may want change, but not now, and I need no help.

4. I have a problem, I only want to cut down, not stop, and I'll do it myself.

5. I have a problem, I tried to stop but couldn't, and I probably need help, but I'm not ready.

6. I have a problem, I want to stop using, and I need help.

There are many additional steps and variations to this progression.

Four-Step Intervention Strategy for Engagement

The following discussion describes a four-step intervention strategy that describes the general tasks and challenges of the engagement process. This strategy is applicable to be used not only by treatment programs and by professionals, but also by peers and family members.

Step 1: Acknowledge your powerlessness.

This step is deceptively simple, but extremely important. No one has the power to "get anyone sober." No one has the power to make someone want to change his/her substance abusing behavior. Accepting your powerlessness means accepting that dual diagnosis patients choose to use substances—or not, choose to get help or not, choose to acknowledge a problem—or not. Accepting your powerlessness means you must accept choices you may disagree with, and see your role as helping the individual to make better choices for himself, not to get him to control his behavior so you will feel less worried or more successful.

Step 2: Establish empathic detachment.

An empathetic relationship is a prerequisite to a successful intervention; experiencing genuine caring and concern from others is a powerful motivator in enhancing willingness to explore options for change—even if the importance of that concern is not acknowledged directly.

Empathy with a dually diagnosed individual requires two elements: understanding the reasons for using substances, and respecting the choice to use substances for those reasons. Research on reasons for substance use by mentally ill people indicate that these reasons are often complex, and may include efforts to alleviate, or self-medicate, symptoms of mental illness (Shneier & Siris, 1987), to facilitate socialization (Bergman & Harris, 1985), and to develop an identity more acceptable than that of mental patient (Lamb, 1982; Drake, et al., 1991). Commonly, people with schizophrenia report reasons for use not unlike those of non-mentally ill substance abusers, involving relief of dysphoria, boredom, anxiety, and isolation, regardless of effect on psychosis (Dixon, et al., 1990; Noordsy et al., 1991).

Even though it may seem that it is clearly harmful for an individual to use substances for these reasons, it is essential to respect those reasons and to join the person empathically in understanding the enormous pain of his life in which these reasons make sense: the loneliness and despair of having a serious and prolonged mental illness. It is important not to feel that all those problems must be fixed, and it is important not to offer a lot of suggestions—just to let the person know that you may disagree with this choices, but you understand his pain, respect his choices, and respect his right to continue his behavior if it works for him. This type of statement will often precipitate, for the first time, some comments about why the substance use is not working as well as was hoped.

Step 3: Initiate an educational process.

The focus of education at this stage is not to lecture on the dangers of substance abuse but to help the individual learn more about substances in order to make better choices about substance use as part of dealing with mental illness in general.

Education can be provided in individual sessions, but has had most demonstrated effectiveness in peer group discussions. Koefoed (1986) and Sciacca (1991) have described a model for introducing substance abuse engagement and education groups into any mental health setting. The group leader is usually a mental health clinician who is not an expert in substance abuse, and is able to join the group in the learning process. Individuals may be included in these groups who are in complete denial of substance use, on the basis that they might acquire useful knowledge or offer help to others. The leader encourages open discussion of substance use in a non-judgmental manner through providing reading material, videos, and outside speakers. Discussions can be extended to include the use of caffeine, nicotine, and psychotropic medication. Group members are encouraged to evaluate the material critically, to form their own opinions about substance use, in order to make better choices. Generally, over a period of months, the group begins to evolve into a culture encouraging control of substance use, and, ultimately, abstinence.

Sciacca (1991) has also described the development of MICAA-non programs for families of dually diagnosed individuals, incorporating both education about substances and support to help families maintain a stance of empathic detachment.

Step 4: Develop opportunities for empathic confrontation.

Confrontation of the individual with negative consequences of substance use frequently is necessary as leverage to encourage him/her to accept substance abuse treatment. Confrontation, as used here, does not mean verbal attack. For confrontation of dually diagnosed individuals to be successful, it must occur within the context of a caring relationship, and involve genuine (not contrived) consequences of substance abuse. The essential element of a confrontation is that the individual is offered a "forced choice" between accepting help to change substance-abusing behavior or accepting the negative consequences of continued use. In a well-constructed confrontation, the consequences can be enforced fully and comfortably, and the confronter does not "lose" if the individual continues to use substances.

Confrontations can be performed by individual clinicians, by programs, by external agencies (e.g. courts), and by families or peers. For example, a psychiatrist might refuse to lower a patient's antipsychotic medication dosage unless s/he demonstrated abstinence for 3 months, or might refuse to prescribe an anti-depressant until s/he was substance free. Similarly, a case manager might withhold referral to a vocational rehabilitation program for a patient who had lost previous jobs due to substance abuse. Each of these situations must be thought through carefully to ensure that the confrontation makes sense for that particular individual, and is not simply a means of coercion.

Family members often feel that confrontation means threatening to kick their relative out onto the street; this is not the case. Families often provide many comforts (rides, cigarettes, new clothes, extra money) that can be made contingent on eliminating disruptive behavior related to substance use. Again, the confrontation must fit the behavior; setting limits on someone who becomes verbally abusive when drunk is very different than trying to enforce abstinence in someone whose drinking presents no obvious problem. Families may seek professional advice in order to construct these interventions properly.

Peer influence can often be a powerful confrontation. If peers (e.g. other clubhouse members) are genuinely concerned by someone's substance abusing behavior, they can caringly let him know that they can't be around him when he drinks, and urge him to get help. For many clients, their connection to a day or residential program is so important that caring confrontation in that setting can create a powerful impetus for change.

Confrontation in program settings can be somewhat more complex, however, because the contingencies enforced must not primarily reflect the needs of the client, but must reflex the needs of the program to maintain an environment that supports the safety of all clients and supports the achievement of program goals for everyone. Such contingencies must be applied uniformly to all clients, and not have certain clients singled out. The ideal mechanism for developing such confrontation is to develop a set of policies and procedures that defines problematic behavior, including problematic substance abusing behavior, and specifies a hierarchy of interventions to address violations. (See figure 1 for an example of such a policy.)

Conclusion

The four-step intervention process defines a general method of structuring an intervention for a particular group of dual diagnosis patients—those who are engaged in psychiatric treatment, but are resist-

Figure 1

Development of Substance Abuse Policies and Contracts for Dual Diagnosis Patients in Treatment Programs

Principle

Substance Abuse Policy must be designed to fit the needs of the program. It can be flexible, but must be applied consistently to all clients. Too much flexibility will undermine the power and effectiveness of the policy.

Step 1: Identify whether a policy for your program is to have all clients be totally abstinent, or just to be abstinent on the premises.

Step 2: Define a "violation," and develop a progressive hierarchy of interventions for clients that have repeated violations.

Step 3: Include a method for verification of substance abuse.

Step 4: Require the patient, not the staff, to be responsible for his own sobriety and the success of his substance abuse treatment.

Step 5: At the point of suspension or termination, always define the conditions for return to the program.

Sample Policy

Residents may use substances off premises in moderation, though abstinence is encouraged. However, any use or possession on premises, and/or any use which leads to being intoxicated on premises, and/or leads to any behavior which is dangerous to self or others in the program will be regarded as a violation. Confirmation of substance use by urine screen can be requested by staff at any time; refusal is the same as a positive result. Consequences are as follows:

First offense in a 6-month period: 24-hour suspension and offer of referral for substance treatment.

Second offense (if less than 6 months since first offense): 3-7 day suspension and offer of referral.

Third offense (if less than 6 months since second offense): 30-day suspension, plus mandatory successful completion of a substance abuse treatment program before return to the house.

Fourth offense: Minimum 60-day suspension, plus mandatory treatment, plus a minimum of 60 days of complete abstinence prior to return to the house, plus an abstinence contract in the house.

Fifth offense: Minimum of 90-day suspension, plus must have 3 months of abstinence before return to house.

Sixth offense: Termination, plus must have 6 months of documented abstinence before being eligible for reconsideration.

N.B. This contract depends on observable behavior and leaves it up to the patient to take responsibility for participation in treatment while in residence (e.g. going to AA). Note also that the specific lengths of punishment and numbers of steps are fairly arbitrary and can be adjusted according to the needs, comfort, and enforcement capability of each program.

ant to addressing substance abuse. Application of this process requires a great deal of explicit empathy and respect on the part of caregivers, as well as an array of resources to provide substance abuse education (at Step 3) and active substance abuse or addiction treatment (following confrontation at Step 4). This intervention strategy is derived from a unified conceptual framework based on the disease and recovery model, in which the following principles apply: (1) for mentally ill individuals, substance abuse is a distinct primary disorder which requires specific intervention; and, (2) intervention strategies must be specific to the phase of recovery, as well as the level of acuity, severity, disability, and motivation for treatment for each primary disease.

References

Alterman, A. I. (1985) (Edited). *Substance abuse in psychiatric patients in substance abuse and psychopathology.* New York: Plenum.

American Psychiatric Association. (1987). *Diagnostic and statistical manual of mental disorders, 3rd Edition, Revised.* Author:Washington, D.C.

Bachrach, L.L. (1987) The context of care for the chronic mental patient with substance abuse. *Psychiatric Quarterly, 58,* 3–14.

Bergman, H. C., & Harris, M. (1985). Substance use among young adult chronic patients. *Psychosocial Rehabilitation Journal, 9*(2), 49–54.

Carroll, K. M., Rounsaville, B. J., & Keller, D. S. (1991). Relapse prevention strategies for the treatment of cocaine abuse. *American Journal of Drug and Alcohol Abuse, 17,* 249–266.

Caton, C. L. M., Grainick, A., Bender, S., et al. (1989). Young chronic patients and substance abuse. *Hospital and Community Psychiatry, 40,* 1037–1040.

Dixon, L.; Haas, G.; Weiden, P., et al. (1990). Acute effects of drug abuse in schizophrenic patients: Clinical observations and patients' self-reports. *Schizophrenic Bulletin, 16,* 69–79.

Drake, R. E., Osher, F. C., & Wallach, M. A. (1989). Alcohol use and abuse in schizophrenia: A prospective community study. *Journal of Nervous and Mental Disease, 177,* 408–414.

Drake, R. E., & Wallach, M.A. (1989). Substance abuse among the chronically mentally ill. *Hospital and Community Psychiatry, 40,* 1041–1046.

Drake, R. E., McLaughlin, P., Pepper, B., et al. (1991). *Dual diagnosis of major mental illness and substance disorder: An overview in dual diagnosis of major mental illness and substance disorder.* San Francisco: Jossey-Bass.

Drake, R. E., Antosca, L. M., Noordsy, D. L., et al. (1991). New Hampsire's specialized services for the dually diagnosed. In K. Minkoff and R. E. Drake (Eds.), *An overview in dual diagnosis of major mental illness and substance disorder.* San Francisco: Jossey-Bass.

Evans, K., & Sullivan, J. M. (1990). *Dual diagnosis: Counseling the mentally ill substance abuser.* New York: Guildford Press.

Kline, J., Harris, M., Bebout, R. R., et al. (1991). Contrasting integrated & linkage models of treatment for homeless, dually diagnosed adults. In K. Minkoff and R. E. Drake (Eds.), *An overview in dual diagnosis of major mental illness and substance disorder.* San Francisco: Jossey-Bass.

Kofoed, L., Kania, J., Walsh, T., et al. (1986). Outpatient treatment of patients with substance abuse & coexisting psychiatric disorders. *American Journal of Psychiatry, 143,* 867–872.

Kofoed, L. (1991). Assessment of comorbid psychiatric illness and substance disorders. In K. Minkoff and R. E. Drake, *An overview in dual diagnosis of major mental illness and substance disorder.* San Francisco: Jossey-Bass.

Lamb, H. R. (1982). Young adult chronic patients: The new drifters. *Hospital and Community Psychiatry, 33,* 465–468.

Lehmann, A. F., Myers, C. P., Corty, E. (1989). Assessment & classification of patients with psychiatric & substance abuse syndromes. *Hospital and Community Psychiatry, 40,* 1019–1025.

McCarrick, A. K., Manderscheid, R. W., & Bertolucci, D. E. (1985). Correlates of acting-out behaviors among young adult chronic patients. *Hospital and Community Psychiatry, 44,* 259–261.

McLaughlin, P., & Pepper, B. (1991). Modifying the therapeutic community for the mentally ill substance abuser. In K. Minkoff and R. E. Drake (Eds.), *An overview in dual diagnosis of major mental illness and substance disorder.* San Francisco: Jossey-Bass.

Minkoff, K., Lamb, H. R., Goldfinger, S., et al. (1993). Ensuring services for persons with chronic mental illness under national health care reform. *Hospital and Community Psychiatry, 44,* 545–546.

Minkoff, K. (1989). An integrated treatment model for dual diagnosis of psychosis and addiction. *Hospital and Community Psychiatry, 40, 1031–1036.*

Minkoff, K. (1991). Program components of a comprehensive integrated care system for seriously mentally ill patients with substance disorders. In K. Minkoff and R. E. Drake (Eds), *An overview in dual diagnosis of major mental illness and substance disorder.* San Francisco: Jossey-Bass.

Noordsy, D. L., Drake, R. E., Teague, G. B., et al. Subjective experiences related to alcohol use among schizophrenics. *Journal of Nervous Mental Disease,* In Press.

Osher, F. C., Drake, R. E., Noordsy, D. L. et al. (1991). *Correlates of alcohol abuse among rural schizophrenic patients.* Unpublished Manuscript, New Hampshire-Dartmouth Psychiatric Research Center.

Osher, F. C., & Kofoed, L. (1989). Treatment of patients with psychiatric and psychoactive substance abuse disorders. *Hospital and Community Psychiatry, 40,* 1025–1030.

Pepper, B., Kirshner, M. C., & Ryglewicz, H. (1981). The young adult chronic patient: Overview of a population. *Hospital and Community Psychiatry, 32,* 463–469.

Pristach, C. A., & Smith, C. M. (1990). Medication compliance & substance abuse among schizophrenic patients. *Hospital and Community Psychiatry, 41,* 1345–1348.

Regier, D. A., Farmer, M. E., Rae, D. S., et al. (1990). Comorbidity of mental disorders with alcohol and other drug abuse. *Journal of American Medical Association, 264,* 2511–2518.

Ridgely, M. S., Goldman, H. H., Talbott, J. A. (1986). *Chronic mentally ill young adults with substance abuse problems: A review of the literature & creation of a research agenda.* Baltimore, Mental Health Policy Studies, University of Maryland School of Medicine.

Ridgely, M. S., Osher, F. C., & Talbott, J. A. (1986). *Chronic mentally ill young adults with substance abuse problems: Treatment and training issues.* Baltimore, University of Maryland School of Medicine.

Ridgely, M. S. (1991). Creating integrated programs for severely mentally ill persons with substance disorders. In K. Minkoff and R. E. Drake (Eds.), *An overview in dual diagnosis of major mental illness and substance disorder.* San Francisco: Jossey-Bass.

Safer, D. (1987). Substance abuse by young adult chronic patients. *Hospital and Community Psychiatry, 38,* 511–514.

Schneier, F. R., & Siris, S. G. (1987). A review of psychoactive substance use & abuse in schizophrenia: Patterns of drug choice. *Journal of Nervous and Mental Disease, 175,* 641–652.

Schwartz, S. R., & Goldfinger, S. M. (1981). The new chronic patient: Clinical characteristics of an emerging sub group. *Hospital and Community Psychiatry, 32,* 470–474.

Sciacca, K. (1991). An integrated treatment approach for severely mentally ill individuals with substance disorders. In K. Minkoff and R. E. Drake (Eds.), *An overview in dual diagnosis of major mental illness and substance disorder.* San Francisco: Jossey-Bass.

Seizer, M. L. (1971). The Michigan alcoholism screening test: The quest for a new diagnostic instrument. *American Journal of Psychiatry, 127,* 89–94.

Turner, Wm., & Tsuang, M. T. (1990). Impact of substance abuse on the course and outcome of schizophrenia. *Schizophrenic Bulletin, 16,* 87–95.

Psychosocial Approaches to Dual Diagnosis

Robert E. Drake & Kim T. Mueser

This article originally appeared in the *Schizophrenia Bulletin,* 2000, 26(1), 105–118 and is reprinted with permission.

Robert E. Drake, M.D., Ph.D., and Kim T. Mueser, Ph.D., are Professors of Psychiatry at the New Hampshire Dartmouth Psychiatric Research Center, Lebanon, NH.

This review was supported by U.S. Public Health Service grants MH–80039 and MH–56147 from the National Institute of Mental Health.

Recent research elucidates many aspects of the problem of co-occurring substance use disorder (SUD) in patients with severe mental illness, which is often termed dual diagnosis. This paper provides a brief overview of current research on the epidemiology, adverse consequences, and phenomenology of dual diagnosis, followed by a more extensive review of current approaches to services, assessment, and treatment. Accumulating evidence shows that comorbid SUD is quite common among individuals with severe mental illness and that these individuals suffer serious adverse consequences of SUD. The research further suggests that traditional, separate services for individuals with dual disorders are ineffective, and that integrated treatment programs, which combine mental health and substance abuse interventions, offer more promise. In addition to a comprehensive integration of services, successful programs include assessment, assertive case management, motivational interventions for patients who do not recognize the need for substance abuse treatment, behavioral interventions for those who are trying to attain or maintain abstinence, family interventions, housing, rehabilitation, and psychopharmacology. Further research is needed on the organization and financing of dual-diagnosis services and on specific components of the integrated treatment model, such as group treatments, family interventions, and housing approaches.

Over the past two decades there has been a growing awareness of the problem of co-occurring substance use disorder in persons with severe mental illnesses such as schizophrenia, schizoaffective disorder, and bipolar disorder. In this article, the terms dual diagnosis, dual disorders, and SUD comorbidity are used interchangeably to denote the problem of co-occurring SUD and severe mental illness. Following a brief overview of the epidemiology, phenomenology, and correlates of dual diagnosis, we review current approaches and research related to service organization, assessment, and treatment.

Epidemiology, Phenomenology, and Correlates of SUD

Numerous studies have shown that persons with severe mental illness are at increased risk for comorbid SUD (see Cuffel, 1996 and Mueser et al., 1995a for reviews). For example, in the most comprehensive study of comorbidity in severe mental illness conducted to date, the Epidemiologic Catchment Area study, the rate of lifetime SUD in the general population was 17%, compared with 48% for persons with schizophrenia and 56% for persons with bipolar disorder (Regier et al., 1990). In addition to the high rate of lifetime SUD in persons with severe mental illness, rates of recent alcohol and drug use disorders are also high. Most studies suggest that between 25 and 35% of persons with a severe mental illness have manifested SUD over the past 6 months (Mueser et al., 1995a). Thus, SUD is common among persons with severe mental illness, with about half of all patients experiencing substance-related problems sufficient to warrant a diagnosis at some time in their lives, and about one-quarter to one-third of patients having a recently active SUD.

Dual diagnosis tends to be more common in those severely mentally ill patients who are young, male, single, and less educated (Cuffel, 1996; Mueser et al., 1995a); in those with histories of conduct disorder (Mueser et al., 1999); and in those with family histories of SUD (Noordsy et al., 1994). Those who are homeless or in jail or who present to an emergency room or hospital setting are also more likely to have SUD than other patients (Galanter et al., 1988). To the extent that these characteristics pertain, patients are at especially high risk for SUD.

SUD in people with severe mental illness both resembles and differs from SUD in the general population. For both groups, alcohol is the most common substance of abuse, followed by cannabis and cocaine (e.g., Barry et al., 1995; Lehman et al., 1996; Mueser et al., 1992). Other similarities are that SUD tends to be a social behavior for both groups and is associated with problems of disinhibition and psychosocial instability (for reviews, see Dixon et al., 1990; Drake & Brunette, 1998). Further, despite considerable speculation that patients with psychiatric illness may be "self-medicating" symptoms of illness or side effects of medications through their use of substances (Khantzian, 1997), the evidence shows that psychiatric patients' self-reported reasons for use tend to be very similar to the reasons cited by others with SUD (reviewed in Mueser et al., 1998b). In other words, patients with severe mental illness typically report that they use alcohol and other substances to combat loneliness, social anxiety, boredom, and insomnia rather than specific symptoms of mental illness or side effects of medications. Finally, as with SUD in the general population, the available evidence indicates that SUD in persons with severe mental illness tends to be a chronic, relapsing disorder with persistence over many years for most dual-disorder patients (Drake et al., 1996).

How then does SUD manifest differently in people with severe mental illness? The central difference appears to be that people with severe mental illness have a heightened sensitivity to the effects of psychoactive substances (see Mueser et al., 1998b for a recent review of this issue). Several consistent observations are accounted for by the phenomenon of heightened sensitivity. First, numerous case reports and surveys indicate that the use of relatively small amounts of alcohol and other drugs by persons with severe mental illness adversely affects their psychiatric stability (exacerbations of illness) and psychosocial adjustment (problems of behavior, relationships, finances, and housing) (see Drake & Brunette, 1998 for a review). Second, people with severe mental illness are relatively unlikely to develop the physiological syndrome of dependence (Drake et al., 1990) or to develop medical sequelae of SUD (Wolford et al., 1999), both of which require sustained heavy use. Third, few persons with severe mental illness (probably less than 5%) are able to sustain moderate use of alcohol or other drugs without negative consequences, and a high proportion, approximately 50%, choose abstinence (Drake & Wallach, 1993). Both of these percentages are quite different from general population figures (Hilton, 1987). Finally, individuals with severe mental illness and SUD comorbidity are unlikely to be able to return to social or recreational use of alcohol or other drugs (Drake et al., in preparation). This last observation may be more similar in the general population, although long-term followup studies consistently show that a significant percentage of individuals with SUD are able to return to moderate use of substances without impairment (Vaillant, 1995).

People with severe mental illness are not only more sensitive to the effects of psychoactive substances, but are also more likely to encounter such substances (Drake et al., 1998a). As a result of deinstitutionalization and other risk factors such as poverty, poor education, poor social skills, lack of vocational skills and opportunities, and residence in drug-infested neighborhoods, they experience a high rate of regular exposure to psychoactive substances and of social pressures to use them.

Another way in which SUD is distinctive in individuals with severe mental illness is that they predictably suffer adverse consequences that are somewhat different from those encountered by others in the general population (see review by Drake & Brunette, 1998). More than 100 studies indicate that dual diagnosis is associated with higher rates of specific negative outcomes: severe financial problems resulting from poor money management; unstable housing and homelessness; medication noncompliance, relapse, and rehospitalization; violence, legal problems, and incarceration; depression and suicide; family burden; and high rates of sexually transmitted diseases. Many common problems related to SUD in the general population, such as marital and vocational difficulties, are less frequent in persons with severe mental illness. One important consequence of the clinical and social effects of SUD in this population is that dually diagnosed patients tend to use more psychiatric services than singly diagnosed patients, particularly costly services such as emergency room visits and inpatient hospitalizations (Bartels et al., 1993; Dickey & Azeni, 1996).

Because of the high prevalence and chronicity of SUD in persons with severe mental illness, the serious negative effects of dual diagnosis on the course of illness and on social problems, and the high cost of treatment, the development of more effective interventions for dual diagnosis has been a high priority since the mid-1980s. Current approaches to the care of persons with dual disorders involve substantive changes in traditional methods of service organization and clinical intervention.

Service Issues

Early reviews of dual-diagnosis services (e.g., Ridgely et al., 1987) identified two fundamental problems. First, most patients with dual diagnosis received no SUD treatment, largely because of difficulties in accessing services. Second, when they did receive SUD treatment, it was not tailored to the needs of persons with a comorbid mental illness. Poor access and inadequate treatment were attributed to the historical split between mental health and substance abuse treatment services.

Traditional Services

In the United States and many other countries, mental health and substance abuse treatment services have been separated for years. Different organizations provide mental health and substance abuse services; financing mechanisms are separate and often compete for scarce public health funds; education, training, and credentialing procedures differ between the two systems; and eligibility criteria for receipt of services differ as well. As a consequence of these factors, two general approaches to the treatment of patients with dual diagnosis predominated until recently. In the sequential treatment approach, patients were directed to obtain definitive treatment in one system before entering treatment in the other system. For example, a person with a mental illness might have been told that his or her SUD should be completely in remission before mental health treatment would be appropriate. In the parallel treatment approach, patients were directed to pursue independent treatments in each of the two systems. In other words, a patient in treatment in one system might be referred for an evaluation at a separate agency in the other treatment system. Both approaches placed the burden of integrating services entirely on patients rather than on providers, and ignored the need to modify mental health and SUD services for persons with comorbid disorders.

In practice, most patients with severe mental illness were quickly extruded from substance abuse treatment programs if they sought services. On the other hand, they experienced poor outcomes in the mental health system because their SUD was undetected or untreated. Even worse, patients with dual diagnosis were sometimes excluded from both systems because of having comorbid disorders. For example, the dually diagnosed individual could be determined ineligible for mental health hospitalization or housing because of SUD and simultaneously ineligible for SUD hospitalization or housing because of psychosis. Thus, sequential and parallel approaches defended providers' professional and financing boundaries but did not serve patients well.

By the end of the 1980s, several reviews had documented these problems with traditional dual-diagnosis treatment services and called for the formation of integrated programs that combined mental health and substance abuse services (e.g., Ridgely et al., 1990). Consequently, new models with a primary aim of integrating services have rapidly developed and evolved since the mid-1980s (e.g., Carey, 1996; Dailey et al., 1993; Lehman & Dixon, 1995; Mercer-McFadden et al., 1997; Miller, 1994; Minkoff, 1989; Osher & Kofoed, 1989; Solomon et al., 1993; Ziedonis & Fisher, 1994).

Integrated Treatment

The essence of integration is that the same clinicians or teams of clinicians, working in one setting, provide coordinated mental health and substance abuse interventions. Clinicians take responsibility for combining the interventions so that they are tailored for the presence of comorbidity. Integration is often accomplished through the use of multidisciplinary teams that include both mental health and substance abuse specialists who share responsibility for treatment and cross-training. Integration must be supported and sustained by a common administrative structure and confluent funding streams (Mercer et al., 1998). For the dually diagnosed individual, the services appear seamless, with a consistent approach, philosophy, and set of recommendations; the need to negotiate with separate systems, providers, or payers disappears.

Integration involves modifications of traditional approaches to both mental health and substance abuse treatment (Mueser et al., 1998a). For example, skills training focuses on the need to develop meaningful relationships and the need to deal with social situations involving substance use. Pharmacotherapy takes into account not only the need to control symptoms but also the potential of some medications for abuse. SUD interventions are modified in accordance with the vulnerability of patients with severe mental illness to confrontational interventions, their need for support, and their typical lack of motivation to pursue abstinence.

Numerous models for providing integrated treatment have evolved. Although the models vary, programs that have demonstrated positive outcomes have several common service features, beyond the basic commitment to integration of organization and financing mechanisms (Drake et al., 1998b). First, they are almost always developed within outpatient mental health programs, primarily because adding substance abuse treatment to the existing array of community support services already available for persons with severe mental illness is more feasible than reproducing all of these services within a substance abuse treatment context (Mercer-McFadden et al., 1997).

Second, awareness of SUD is insinuated into all aspects of the existing mental health program rather than isolated as a discrete substance abuse treatment intervention (Drake et al., 1993a). As described below, components such as case management, assessment, individual counseling, group interventions, family psychoeducation, medication management, money management, housing, and vocational rehabilitation incorporate special features that reflect awareness of dual diagnosis.

Third, successful programs address the difficulty that dually diagnosed patients have in linking with services and maintaining treatment adherence by providing continuous outreach and close monitoring techniques, which are described below (Mercer-McFadden et al., 1997). These approaches enable patients to access services and to maintain needed relationships with a consistent program over months and years. Without such efforts, noncompliance and dropouts are high (Hellerstein et al., 1995).

Fourth, integrated programs recognize that recovery tends to occur over months or years in the community (Drake et al., 1996). People with severe mental illness and SUD do not develop stable remission quickly, even in intensive treatment programs (Drake et al., 1998c). Rather, they seem to develop stable remission over longer periods, with a cumulative percentage of approximately 10 to 15% attaining stable remissions per year, in conjunction with a consistent dual-diagnosis program. Successful programs therefore take a long-term, outpatient perspective.

Fifth, most dual-diagnosis programs recognize that the majority of psychiatric patients have little readiness for abstinence-oriented SUD treatments (Carey, 1996; Mercer-McFadden et al., 1997; Test et al., 1989; Ziedonis & Trudeau, 1997). Rather than just treat the highly motivated patients, these programs incorporate motivational interventions designed to help patients who either do not recognize their SUD or do not desire substance abuse treatment become ready for more definitive interventions aimed at abstinence. Motivational interventions involve helping the individual to identify his or her own goals and then to recognize that using psychoactive substances interferes with attaining those goals (Miller & Rollnick, 1991).

Research evidence for the effectiveness of integrated treatments continues to mount. Ten recently completed studies support the effectiveness of integrated treatments (Drake et al., 1998c). The basic findings of these studies are that integrated programs are consistently able to engage dually diagnosed patients in services and to help them to reduce SUD behaviors and attain stable remission. Other outcomes related to hospital use, psychiatric symptoms, and quality of life are positive but less consistent.

Despite the encouraging findings regarding integrated treatment programs and the widespread acceptance that integrated treatment is superior to nonintegrated treatment for this population (e.g., Smith & Burns, 1994), implementation continues to be slow because of problems related to the organization and financing of programs. Organizational guidelines have been developed for dual-diagnosis programs (Mercer et al., 1998), but few large systems have successfully integrated services. Further services research is needed to clarify and resolve barriers.

Assessment

Several interlocking steps compose the standard approach to assessment of SUD: detection, classification, specialized (or functional) assessment, and treatment planning (Donovan, 1988). Each of these requires some modification for patients with schizophrenia.

Detection

Screening is critical because SUD tends to be covert and treatment depends on detection. SUD frequently goes undetected in psychiatric care settings (Ananth et al., 1989; Shaner et al., 1993; Stone et al., 1993), mainly because many mental health programs do not screen at all. When screening is attempted, other problems emerge. Acutely ill psychiatric patients are frequently unable to complete lengthy structured interviews (Barbee et al., 1989). Many psychiatric patients deny, minimize, or fail to perceive the consequences of SUD when responding to interviews (Test et al., 1989). Available screening instruments sometimes focus on amounts of use or on consequences that are inappropriate for this population (Wolford et al., 1999). Medical exams also have poor detection rates in psychiatric patients, possibly because these patients do not have the long histories of heavy drinking that produce medical sequelae (Wolford et al., 1999).

Research suggests three helpful approaches to the problem of detection. First, clinicians in mental health settings should ask all clients about their substance use and related problems. The basic step of establishing formal screening procedures increases detection (Appleby et al., 1997). Perhaps the most efficient method is with a new screening instrument, the Dartmouth Assessment of Lifestyle Instrument (DALI), which has been developed specifically for persons with severe mental illness. Initial studies show that the DALI performs much better than traditional SUD screening instruments for this population (Rosenberg et al., 1998).

Second, clinicians should maintain a high index of suspicion for SUD, even in the face of denial, particularly among young male patients with other characteristics that suggest SUD (Mueser et al., 1999). Denial of SUD in situations of symptomatic or psychosocial instability should lead to multimodal assessment, such as urine drug screens, interviews with collaterals, and longitudinal observations in the community. Laboratory tests may yield false negatives and are ineffective when there are delays between drug use and testing, but they often detect current use that is denied by patients (Shaner et al., 1993; Stone et al., 1993). Similarly, several studies indicate that collateral reports from trained case managers are an effective way of identifying SUD in psychiatric patients (Barry et al., 1995; Carey et al., 1996; Drake et al., 1990). Case managers have the opportunity to synthesize medical information from various assessment contacts, direct observations of the patient in the community, collateral reports from relatives, and self-reports over multiple occasions, leading to higher sensitivity to SUD.

Finally, all patients who have a past history of SUD or a current self-report of any regular use of alcohol or other substances should be followed carefully. Several pieces of evidence support this approach. SUD tends to be a chronic, relapsing disorder so that currently nonabusing patients with a history of SUD may be highly vulnerable (Drake et al., 1996). Psychiatric patients may be more likely to acknowledge past rather than current SUD (Barry et al., 1995). Moreover, they often acknowledge use but do not perceive or acknowledge the effects of their use (Test et al., 1989). Thus, their reports of recent use may indicate need for treatment better than their satisfaction of diagnostic criteria (Dixon et al., 1993). Also, patients with severe mental illness are unlikely to sustain substance use without developing related impairments (Drake & Wallach, 1993).

Classification

The classification of SUD is relatively straightforward. If a person repeatedly uses a psychoactive substance that results in medical, emotional, social, or vocational impairments or physical danger, a diagnosis of SUD should be made (American Psychiatric Association, 1994). Clinical opinion suggests that substance abuse, as opposed to substance dependence, is common in persons with severe mental illness and that the distinction may have important treatment implications (Minkoff, 1997). Furthermore, we also recommend using the classification of "use without impairment" as a marker for potential problems (Drake et al., 1990).

Few longitudinal data bear on these issues. As described above, the threshold for entertaining a SUD diagnosis in this population is low because considerable evidence indicates that small amounts of use may lead to atypical consequences, which are not perceived by the patient but should nevertheless qualify for a diagnosis. There is also some research evidence that schizophrenia patients who use alcohol without impairment are likely to develop SUD over time (Drake & Wallach, 1993), that patients with substance abuse rather than substance dependence have a better long-term course (Bartels et al., 1995), and that those with less severe alcohol dependence are more likely to respond to dual-diagnosis treatment (Drake et al., in preparation).

Although diagnosing SUD is relatively straightforward, comorbid psychiatric symptoms, syndromes, and diagnoses are often difficult to sort out because psychiatric symptoms of all kinds can occur as a result of SUD (Rounsaville, 1989). *DSM-IV* criteria specify making a diagnosis only after observing the patient for 1 month without substance use and without medications (American Psychiatric Association, 1994). Although standardized and simple, this recommendation has little empirical basis and is unrealistic for patients who have psychotic symptoms because they usually require immediate medications and are often not abstinent for sufficient time to observe them. Rather than the simple *DSM* rule, Weiss et al. (1992) recommend using more specific abstinence criteria based on the known effects of particular substances of abuse in relation to the disorders being classified. They also recognize that longitudinal evaluation, corroborating data from collaterals, and multiple data sources are often necessary to make accurate diagnoses.

Attempts to classify individuals with SUD and co-occurring psychotic symptoms have been fraught with difficulties and have found that many patients fall into an uncertain category (Lehman et al., 1996; Rosenthal et al., 1992; Shaner et al., 1998). Moreover, longitudinal data suggest that patients with persistent psychosis in the face of chronic

SUD more closely resemble schizophrenia patients than primary SUD patients in terms of course of illness and functioning (Turner & Tsuang, 1990). In practice, many clinicians treat these patients as though they have severe mental illness, withdraw medications when feasible, and reassess the diagnosis if and when they attain stable abstinence (Shaner et al., 1998).

Specialized Assessment

A specialized, or functional, assessment of substance use behavior is the cornerstone upon which dual-diagnosis treatment planning is based (Carey & Teitelbaum, 1996; Carey & Correia, 1998). Specialized assessment entails a detailed evaluation of the patient's SUD, including motives for use, expectancies related to specific substances, and motivation for change; of how the patient's SUD interacts with adjustment in different domains of functioning, including housing, relationships, illness management, and work; and of the patient's personal goals. All of these factors help the clinician to develop an individualized treatment plan, consistent with the patient's personal strengths and goals, that identifies specific targets and intervention approaches.

This type of behavioral analysis assumes that motivating factors sustain continued substance use and that addressing these factors will facilitate substance use reduction and abstinence. For example, dual diagnosis patients often report that substance use enhances social opportunities, helps them deal with boredom, anxiety, and dysphoria, and is an important source of recreation (Addington & Duchak, 1997; Baigent et al., 1995; Carey & Carey, 1995; Mueser et al., 1995b; Noordsy et al., 1991). Substance abuse treatment addresses specific, individual problems of this type.

While the details of specialized assessment are beyond the scope of this article, it should be clear that the assessment covers areas such as social relationships with family and friends, leisure and recreational activities, work and education, financial matters, legal involvement, and spirituality. One goal is to evaluate the patient's strengths and potential resources. For example, if the patient expresses a strong desire to work, treatment can focus on securing competitive work and developing strategies for reducing the impact of substance use on getting or maintaining employment.

Another goal is to assess the patient's awareness of negative consequences associated with substance use, insight into having a substance abuse problem, motivation for change, and preferences for treatment. Many patients need interventions specifically designed to help them develop motivation. Moreover, other interventions are keyed to the patient's stage of treatment participation (McHugo et al., 1995; Mueser et al., 1998a). The concept of stage of treatment is based on the four-stage model developed by Osher and Kofoed (1989): engagement (no regular contact with dual-diagnosis clinician), persuasion (contact with clinician but no reduction in substance abuse), active treatment (significant reduction in substance abuse), and relapse prevention (no problems with substance abuse in past 6 months). Treatment goals are determined partly by the patient's stage of treatment. In the *engagement* stage, patients have no working relationship with a clinician and are not motivated to change their substance use behavior, and therefore treatment goals primarily focus on establishing regular contact and helping patients get their basic needs met. At the *persuasion* stage, patients have regular contact with their clinicians, but are minimally invested in changing their substance use behavior. In this stage of treatment, patients are often motivated to learn more and talk about their substance use behavior, and to work on other goals that are personally relevant. In *active treatment* patients have begun to reduce their substance use and are motivated to achieve further reduction or abstinence. In *relapse prevention* patients have not recently had problems related to substance use, and there is motivation to keep the substance abuse in remission and to work on other areas.

Although there is a growing consensus regarding the importance of conducting a specialized assessment of substance use behavior in dual-diagnosis patients, little research has evaluated the benefits of such assessment. Since specialized assessment is part of the treatment process, evaluation will need to focus on intermediate goals, such as the development of specific, individualized treatment plans.

Treatment Planning

The final step in assessment, treatment planning, involves combining and integrating information obtained during the first three steps of assessment into a coherent set of actions to be taken by the clinicians. Treatment plans may involve interventions that either directly address SUD (e.g., developing motivation to reduce or cease substance use) or address other areas that impact on SUD (e.g., helping the patient find competitive work in order to decrease opportunities for using substances and improve self-esteem).

The treatment plan must of course address pressing needs, such as a grave risk to the patient or others; problems with housing, food, or clothing; untreated medical conditions; social network crises; and lack of psychiatric stabilization. More important, however, is the long-term plan to target behaviors for change based on the specialized assessment. Long-term goals might include, for example, changing the patient's social network, finding a job, and learning behavioral techniques to handle social anxiety. A wide variety of treatment strategies are available for achieving changes in target behaviors (Mueser et al., 1998a).

The research base for specific treatment plans includes studies showing that dual-diagnosis patients report specific expectancies and motives (Addington & Duchak, 1997; Baigent et al., 1995; Carey & Carey, 1995; Mueser et al., 1995b; Noordsy et al., 1991) and that they tend to recover from SUD in a stagewise fashion (McHugo et al., 1995; Drake et al., in preparation). We are aware of no studies of outcomes in relation to individualized treatment plans.

Treatment

As described above, the integration of mental health and substance abuse services involves organization and financing. Within the integrated treatment paradigm, however, a variety of specific components have been developed and are currently being refined. Individual components have different targets and are therefore often designed to be used in combination. For example, within a dual-diagnosis program, case management and close monitoring are used to link dually diagnosed individuals with treatment, substance abuse treatments to address SUD behaviors, family psychoeducation and housing supports to ensure that the environment supports stability and abstinence, rehabilitation to promote functioning in meaningful roles, and medications to target symptoms of mental illness and to inhibit SUD behaviors.

Before discussing individual components, we reiterate that dual-diagnosis programs are primarily focused on the outpatient setting. Inpatient care is reserved for stabilization, assessment, and linkage with the outpatient program (Drake & Noordsy, 1995; Greenfield et al., 1995). The research base for this focus is twofold. First, there is little evidence that hospital-based treatment is, by itself, effective in helping dual-diagnosis patients to achieve stable remission (Bachman et al., 1997; Ribisl et al., 1996). Patients who attain abstinence and participate in inpatient substance abuse treatment tend to relapse soon after discharge, suggesting that SUD is an environmentally sensitive condition and that patients need to learn to be abstinent in their long-term living setting. Second, the longitudinal evidence on recovery suggests that dual-diagnosis patients attain stable remission of SUD over months and years while living in the community (Drake et al., 1996; Drake et al., in preparation). Furthermore, since inpatient treatment is expensive, its overuse (for example, keeping patients in the hospital to prevent their access to substances) inevitably diminishes needed resources for outpatient care, even when costs are not capitated and individual programs are able to shift costs.

We have described the process of clinical care elsewhere (Mueser et al., 1998a). Here we will briefly describe the common components of integrated treatment and summarize the relevant research.

Case Management

The most common approach to integrating mental health and substance abuse treatments and to linking dual-diagnosis patients with outpatient services is through the use of multidisciplinary case management teams (Drake & Noordsy, 1994; Fariello & Scheidt, 1989). To integrate services, mental health and substance abuse specialists on the same team blend their respective skills into common procedures by sharing training experiences, responsibility for care, and the onus of developing a melded philosophy. To link dually diagnosed patients with services and maintain treatment relationships, teams rely heavily on outreach, practical assistance, and sharing decision making with the patient (Mercer-McFadden et al., 1997). After multidisciplinary teams are created, they require about 1 year of training to mature. Specific criteria for assessing the quality of dual-diagnosis treatment can be used to guide and monitor implementation (Teague et al., 1998).

The centrality of case management in dual-diagnosis programs is based on several pieces of evidence. When substance abuse treatment is integrated into mental health care without case management, the majority of patients drop out of the program (Hellerstein et al., 1995). In contrast, intensive case management has repeatedly demonstrated its capacity to engage and retain dual-diagnosis patients in outpatient services and to reduce their use of the hospital (Mercer-McFadden et al., 1997;

Morse et al., 1992). Further, when dual-diagnosis treatments are delivered in the context of intensive case management, patients also reduce their SUD behaviors and develop stable remissions (Detrick & Stiepock, 1992; Drake et al., 1993b, 1997, 1998b; Durell et al., 1993; Godley et al., 1994; Meisler et al., 1997). There is also emerging evidence that the quality of dual-diagnosis services predicts substance abuse treatment outcomes (Jerrell & Ridgely, 1999; McHugo et al., 1999).

Close Monitoring

In addition to outreach and direct substance abuse treatment, dual-diagnosis teams often provide a variety of interventions that can be described by the rubric "close monitoring" (Drake et al., 1993a). Close monitoring techniques include medication supervision, protective pay-eeships, guardianships for medications, urine drug screens, supported housing staff, and outpatient commitments. Many of these approaches rely on the patient's cooperation, while others assume some degree of coerciveness based on the patient's incapacity to manage his or her own affairs or on the need to protect the patient and others from dangerousness (Noordsy et al., 2002).

The evidence on specific approaches to close monitoring is meager because, although common, these interventions are rarely studied. The evidence on outpatient commitment is mixed (O'Keefe et al., 1997; Policy Research Associates, 1998). The most common close monitoring intervention, representative payeeship, has received little or no empirical study (Rosen & Rosenheck, 1999).

Substance Abuse Treatment

Once patients are engaged in outpatient services, all dual-diagnosis programs provide some form of substance abuse treatment. Because the patients are often unmotivated to pursue abstinence, most programs focus initially on education, harm reduction, and increasing motivation rather than on abstinence (Drake et al., 1993a; Carey, 1996; Mercer-McFadden et al., 1997; Ziedonis & Trudeau, 1997). As described above, motivational approaches are designed to help the patient to recognize that SUD is interfering with his or her own goals and thereby to nurture the patient's desire to reduce and then eliminate substance use. The other common approach to substance abuse treatment involves some form of cognitive-behavioral counseling. The two approaches are often combined or offered in stages so that skills for achieving and maintaining abstinence are taught after motivation is developed (e.g., Bellack & DiClemente, 1999).

Substance abuse interventions can be provided in individual, group, or family formats. Clinicians on multidisciplinary teams often use all of these approaches based on the patient's preference and a shared decision-making model (Mueser et al., 1998a). In practice, most dual-diagnosis programs assume that the peer-oriented group is a powerful vehicle and address substance-abusing behaviors in one or more types of professionally led groups. The groups vary in orientation from 12-step to educational-supportive to social skills training to stage based (Mueser & Noordsy, 1996).

An adjunctive approach to substance abuse treatment is linkage with self-help groups in the community such as Alcoholics Anonymous (Osher & Kofoed, 1989) or with self-help groups specifically for dual-diagnosis patients such as Double Trouble (Bricker, 1994). Clinical experience suggests that these linkages require some preparation and debriefing by mental health staff and that they are more effective once patients are actively pursuing abstinence (Noordsy et al., 1996).

The research on specific substance abuse treatments for dual-diagnosis patients is in its infancy. Early studies were limited by difficulties measuring SUD in this population, the lack of motivational interventions, and failure to tailor substance abuse treatments for people with severe mental illness (Mercer-McFadden et al., 1997). In addition, substance abuse treatment components are typically embedded in an overall dual-diagnosis program and are not assessed as independent interventions.

Nevertheless, the research base for substance abuse treatment of dual-diagnosis patients contains several relevant findings. First, case management by itself without a specific component of substance abuse treatment has little or no effect on SUD (Bond et al., 1991; Morse et al., 1992). Second, when substance abuse treatment is provided in the context of assertive case management, rates of stable remission improve steadily over at least 3 years (Drake et al., 1998b). Third, patients who attend dual-diagnosis groups tend to have good outcomes (Hellerstein & Meehan, 1987; Kofoed et al., 1986; Nigam et al., 1992). Fourth, there is no evidence that one type of group is more effective than another (Mueser & Noordsy, 1996). Although one study suggested that patients who participated in cognitive-behavioral skills training groups had better outcomes than those in case management and 12-step programs

(Jerrell & Ridgely, 1995), the results were probably best explained by quality of implementation (Jerrell & Ridgely, 1999).

Thus far there has been no research on individual or family interventions for dual-diagnosis patients. Minimal research on linking dual-diagnosis patients with self-help groups in the community suggests that only a minority (approximately 20%) sustain their involvement with the groups and that patients with mood disorders are more able to do so than those with schizophrenia (Noordsy et al., 1996). As far as we know there are no studies of Double Trouble groups.

Rehabilitation

Recovery from SUD involves building a new life rather than just avoiding substances (Vaillant, 1995). Stable abstinence usually requires major alterations in how one handles internal and external stress, social networks, habits, self-perceptions, and vocational activities. Because most dual-diagnosis patients have become entangled in the social scene of substance abuse over years, their recovery from SUD also takes years (Drake et al., 1998b). Many dual-diagnosis programs attempt to substitute day treatment, rehabilitation groups, or sheltered work for previous activities and relationships. The weakness of these approaches is that mental health activities are difficult to sustain over time and, more important, patients do not value them and often find them demeaning (Alverson et al., 1995; Estroff, 1981; Quimby et al., 2001). A more promising approach is community-based rehabilitation, such as supported education or supported employment, which helps patients to succeed in normal roles in the community. For example, standard approaches to supported employment can support the patient's movement toward abstinence (Becker & Drake, 1994).

There are currently no controlled studies of supported employment or any other approach to rehabilitation for dual-diagnosis patients. However, six independent studies of vocational or dual-diagnosis programs have shown that patients with dual disorders are as likely to succeed in working as those without SUD or those with remitted SUD (Sengupta et al., 1998). Moreover, many patients report that working is an important motivational step in their SUD recovery program (Alverson et al., 1995).

Housing

Since dual-diagnosis patients commonly have difficulties maintaining housing and since living in drug-infested housing settings often sustains their SUD, housing has been a specific focus of dual-diagnosis interventions, particularly for the homeless (Osher & Dixon, 1996). Patients, even those who are homeless, tend to prefer independent housing (Schutt & Goldfinger, 1996). Some housing specialists have argued on ideological grounds that independent housing is preferable, while others have argued that the special vulnerabilities of dual diagnosis can be addressed only in structured living situations that include close monitoring by professional staff. One well-known program has created a housing continuum that allows dual-diagnosis patients to enter housing while they are still actively abusing substances but also provides a range of staffed and supported housing arrangements for those who are in varying stages of recovery (Bebout, 1999).

The research on housing for dual-diagnosis patients is inchoate. Relevant findings include the following: First, dual-diagnosis patients are prone to be extruded from independent and congregate housing situations because of the behaviors attendant to their SUD (Center for Mental Health Services, 1994). Second, the great majority of dual-diagnosis patients are not able to participate in residential treatment or do not make the transition from residential treatment to independent housing (Bartels & Drake 1996; Blankertz & Cnaan, 1994; Burnam et al., 1995; Rahav et al., 1995). Third, in one study, for those who gained access to decent housing, making some progress in substance abuse treatment was a critical mediating step toward maintaining stable housing (Bebout et al., 1997). Fourth, the same study found that a housing continuum connected to integrated dual-diagnosis services resulted in better housing outcomes when compared with a nonintegrated system of housing, mental health, and substance abuse services (Drake et al., 1997).

Pharmacological Approaches

Although this review emphasizes psychosocial approaches, psychopharmacology is also a critical component of dual-diagnosis programs. Relevant topics include medication adherence, antipsychotic medications, mood stabilizers, antianxiety medications, abuse of prescribed medications, and antidipsomanic medications.

Medication nonadherence correlates with comorbid SUD (Miner et al., 1997; Swartz et al., 1998), perhaps in part because dually diagnosed individuals are often told that using alcohol or street drugs in addition to their prescribed medications poses a grave health risk. On the other hand, clinical experience suggests that medication adherence and symptom control are often prerequisites to successful SUD treatment. Most programs therefore adopt efforts to improve compliance by providing education, medication management skills training, medication supervision, use of depot forms of antipsychotic medications, and coercive means such as outpatient commitment and guardianship. There are, however, almost no data on whether these techniques actually improve medication adherence, symptom control, or outcomes among dual-diagnosis patients.

For patients with schizophrenia or psychotic symptoms, antipsychotic medications are the mainstay of pharmacological treatment. Typical antipsychotic medications, per se, probably do not decrease SUD behaviors and, according to several clinical opinions, may actually precipitate or worsen SUD (Siris, 1990; Voruganti et al., 1997). Few relevant data exist, although one study showed that patients starting a traditional antipsychotic drug increased nicotine use (McEvoy et al., 1995). On the other hand, there is emerging evidence that the atypical antipsychotic drug clozapine may reduce SUD in dual-diagnosis patients (Drake et al., in press; Zimmet et al., 2000). We are aware of no data on other atypical antipsychotic medications in relation to SUD.

Mood stabilizers are also a mainstay of treatment of severe mental illness and are frequently prescribed for dually disordered patients. Studies of adjunctive antidepressants for patients with comorbid schizophrenia and SUD have produced mixed results (Siris et al., 1993; Ziedonis et al., 1992). We are unaware of studies of mood stabilizers or newer antidepressants in dual-diagnosis patients.

Another critical issue in dual-diagnosis treatment concerns the effectiveness of antianxiety medications and their potential for abuse (Center for Substance Abuse Treatment, 1994). Clinical discussions of pharmacology for dual diagnosis inevitably produce strong but mixed opinions about whether long-acting benzodiazepines are helpful or harmful. There is also concern about the potential for abuse of antiparkinsonian medications. We are unaware of any data on these topics.

Finally, many psychiatrists prescribe antidipsomanic medications to help dual-diagnosis patients achieve stable remission. Kofoed et al. (1986) reported the usefulness of adjunctive disulfiram in an open clinical trial, but no controlled studies have examined disulfiram, naltrexone, or other medications that reduce psychoactive substance use or craving.

Conclusions

Comorbid SUD is a common complication of severe mental illness and is associated with serious adverse consequences. Over the past two decades the health care field has recognized the ineffectiveness of providing care in two separate service systems and has rapidly developed service models that integrate mental health and substance abuse treatments. Recent evidence regarding the general integrated treatment approach is consistent and positive, but much work remains to be done on the organization and financing of integrated programs. Furthermore, the basic components of integrated treatment—case management, close monitoring, substance abuse treatment, family psychoeducation, rehabilitation, housing, and medications—are still being developed and refined. Research is needed to address the effectiveness and proper combinations of these components.

References

Addington, J., & Duchak, V. (1997). Reasons for substance use in schizophrenia. *Acta Psychiatrica Scandinavica, 96,* 329–333.

Alverson, M., Becker, D. R., & Drake, R. E. (1995). An ethnographic study of coping strategies used by persons with severe mental illness participating in supported employment. *Psychosocial Rehabilitation Journal, 18,* 115–128.

American Psychiatric Association (1994). *DSM-IV: Diagnostic and Statistical Manual of Mental Disorders, 4th ed.* Washington, DC: The Association.

Ananth, J., Vanderwater, S., Kamal, M., Brodsky, A., Gamal, R. & Miller, M. (1989). Missed diagnosis of substance abuse in psychiatric patients. *Hospital and Community Psychiatry, 4,* 297–299.

Appleby, L., Dyson, V., Luchins, D. J., & Cohen, L. C. (1997). The impact of substance use screening on a public psychiatric inpatient population. *Psychiatric Services, 48,* 1311–1316.

Bachman, K. M., Moggi, F., Hirsbrunner, H. P., Donati, R., & Bridbeck, J. (1997). An integrated treatment program for dually diagnosed patients. *Psychiatric Services, 48,* 314–316.

Baigent, M., Holme, G., & Hafner, R. J. (1995). Self reports of the interaction between substance abuse and schizophrenia. *Australian and New Zealand Journal of Psychiatry, 29,* 69–74.

Barbee, J. G., Clark, P. D., Crapanzano, M. S., Heintz, G. C., & Kehoe, C. E. (1989). Alcohol and substance abuse among schizophrenic patients presenting to an emergency psychiatric service. *Journal of Nervous and Mental Disease, 177,* 400–407.

Barry, K. L., Fleming, M. F., Greenley, J., Widlak, P., Kropp, S., & McKee, D. (1995). Assessment of alcohol and other drug disorders in the seriously mentally ill. *Schizophrenia Bulletin, 21*(3), 313–321.

Bartels, S. J., & Drake, R. E. (1996). A pilot study of residential treatment for dual diagnosis. *Journal of Nervous and Mental Disease, 184,* 379–381.

Bartels, S. J., Drake, R. E., & Wallach, M. A. (1995). Long-term course of substance use disorders among patients with severe mental illness. *Psychiatric Services, 46,* 248–251.

Bartels, S. J., Teague, G. B., Drake, R. E., Clark, R. E., Bush, P., & Noordsy, D. L. (1993). Substance abuse in schizophrenia: Service utilization and costs. *Journal of Nervous and Mental Disease, 181,* 227–232.

Bebout, R. R. (1999). Housing solutions: The Community Connections Housing Program—Preventing homelessness by integrating housing and supports. *Alcoholism Treatment Quarterly, 17,* 93–112.

Bebout, R. R., Drake, R. E., Xie, H., McHugo, G. J., & Harris, M. (1997).Housing status among formerly homeless, dually diagnosed adults in Washington, DC. *Psychiatric Services, 48,* 936–941.

Becker, D. R., & Drake, R. E. (1994). Individual placement and support: A community mental health center approach to vocational rehabilitation. *Community Mental Health Journal, 30,* 193–206.

Bellack, A. S., & DiClemente, C. C. (1999). Treating substance abuse among patients with schizophrenia. *Psychiatric Services, 50,* 75–80.

Blankertz, L. E., & Cnaan, R. A. (1994). Assessing the impact of two residential programs for dually diagnosed homeless individuals. *Social Service Review, 68,* 536–560.

Bond, G. R., McDonel, E. C., Miller, L. D., & Pensec, M. (1991). Assertive community treatment and reference groups: An evaluation of their effectiveness for young adults with serious mental illness and substance abuse problems. *Psychosocial Rehabilitation Journal, 15*(2), 31–43.

Bricker, M. (1994). The evolution of mutual help groups for dual recovery. *Tie-Lines, 6*(2), 1–4.

Burnam, M. A., Morton, S. C., McGlynn, E. A., Petersen, L. P., Stecher, B. M., Hayes, C., & Vaccaro, J. V. (1995). An experimental evaluation of residential and nonresidential treatment for dually diagnosed homeless adults. *Journal of Addictive Diseases, 14,* 111–134.

Carey, K. B. (1996). Substance use reduction in the context of outpatient psychiatric treatment: A collaborative, motivational, harm reduction approach. *Community Mental Health Journal, 32,* 291–306.

Carey, K. B., & Carey, M. P. (1995). Reasons for drinking among psychiatric outpatients: Relationship to drinking patterns. *Psychology of Addictive Behaviors, 9,* 251–257.

Carey, K. B., Cocco, K. M., & Simons, J. S. (1996). Concurrent validity of clinicians' ratings of substance abuse among psychiatric outpatients. *Psychiatric Services, 47,* 842–847.

Carey, K. B., & Correia, C. J. (1998). Severe mental illness and addictions: Assessment considerations. *Addictive Behaviors, 23,* 735–748.

Carey, K. B., & Teitelbaum, L. M. (1996). Goals and methods of alcohol assessment. *Professional Psychology, 27,* 1–6.

Center for Mental Health Services (1994). *Making a difference: Interim status report of the McKinney Research Demonstration Program for Homeless Mentally Ill Adults.* Rockville, MD: Center for Mental Health Services, Substance Abuse and Mental Health Services Administration.

Center for Substance Abuse Treatment (1994). Assessment and treatment of patients with coexisting mental illness and alcohol and other drug abuse. *(Treatment Improvement Protocol [TIP] Series.)* Rockville, MD: U.S. Department of Health and Human Services, Substance Abuse and Mental Health Services Administration, Center for Substance Abuse Treatment.

Cuffel, B. J. (1996). Comorbid substance use disorder: Prevalence, patterns of use, and course. In Drake, R. E., & Mueser, K. T., eds. *Dual diagnosis of major mental illness and substance disorder: II. Research and clinical implications.* San Francisco, CA: Jossey-Bass. pp. 93–105.

Dailey, D. C., Moss, H. B., & Campbell, F. (1993). *Dual disorders: Counseling clients with chemical dependency and mental illness.* Center City, MN: Hazelden.

Detrick, A., & Stiepock, V. (1992). Treating persons with mental illness, substance abuse, and legal problems: The Rhode Island experience. In: Stein, L. I., ed. *Innovative community mental health programs.* San Francisco, CA: Jossey-Bass. pp. 65–77.

Dickey, B., & Azeni, H. (1996). Persons with dual diagnosis of substance abuse and major mental illness: Their excess costs of psychiatric care. *American Journal of Public Health, 86,* 973–977.

Dixon, L., Dibietz, E., Myers, P., Conley, R., Medoff, D., & Lehman, A. F. (1993). Comparison of *DSM-III-R* diagnoses and a brief interview for substance use among state hospital patients. *Hospital and Community Psychiatry, 44,* 748–752.

Dixon, L., Haas, G., Weiden, P., Sweeney, J., & Frances, A. (1990). Acute effects of drug abuse in schizophrenic patients: Clinical observations and patients' self-reports. *Schizophrenia Bulletin, 16*(1), 69–79.

Donovan, D. M. (1988). Assessment of addictive disorders: Implications of an emerging biopsychosocial model. In: Donovan, D.M., and Marlatt, G.M., eds. *Assessment of addictive behavior.* New York, NY Guilford Press. pp. 3–48.

Drake, R. E., Bartels, S. B., Teague, G. B., Noordsy, D. L., & Clark, R. E. (1993a). Treatment of substance use disorders in severely mentally ill patients. *Journal of Nervous and Mental Disease, 181,* 606–611.

Drake, R. E., & Brunette, M. F. (1998). Complications of severe mental illness related to alcohol and other drug use disorders. In: Galanter, M., Ed. *Recent developments in alcoholism. Vol. 14. Consequences of alcoholism.* New York: Plenum. pp. 285–299.

Drake, R. E., Brunette, M. F., & Mueser, K. T. (1998a). Substance use disorder and social functioning in schizophrenia. In: Mueser, K. T., & Tarrier, N., eds. *Handbook of social functioning in schizophrenia.* Boston, MA: Allyn and Bacon. pp. 280–289.

Drake, R. E., McHugo, G. M., Clark, R. E., Teague, G. B.; Ackerson, T.; Xie, H.; & Miles, K. M. (1998b). A clinical trial of assertive community treatment for patients with co-occurring severe mental illness and substance use disorder. *American Journal of Orthopsychiatry, 68,* 201–215.

Drake, R. E., McHugo, G. J., & Noordsy, D. L. (1993b). Treatment of alcoholism among schizophrenic outpatients: 4-year outcomes. *American Journal of Psychiatry, 150,* 328–329.

Drake, R. E., McHugo, G. J., Teague, G. B., Xie, H., Mueser, K. T., Wallach, M. A., & Vaillant, G. E. *A five-year study of treated substance use disorder among patients with severe mental illness.* In preparation.

Drake, R. E., Mercer-McFadden, C., Mueser, K. T., McHugo, G. J., & Bond, G. R. (1998c) Treatment of substance abuse in patients with severe mental illness: A review of recent research. *Schizophrenia Bulletin, 24*(4), 589–608.

Drake, R. E., Mueser, K. T., Clark, R. E., & Wallach, M. A. (1996). The course, treatment, and outcome of substance disorder in persons with severe mental illness. *American Journal of Orthopsychiatry, 66,* 42–51.

Drake, R. E., & Noordsy, D. L. (1994). Case management for people with coexisting severe mental disorder and substance use disorder. *Psychiatric Annals, 24,* 427–431.

Drake, R. E., & Noordsy, D. L. (1995). The role of inpatient care for patients with co-occurring severe mental disorder and substance use disorder. *Community Mental Health Journal, 31,* 279–282.

Drake, R. E., Osher, F. C., Noordsy, D., Hurlbut, S. C., Teague, G. B., & Beaudett, M. S. (1990). Diagnosis of alcohol use disorders in schizophrenia. *Schizophrenia Bulletin, 16*(1), 57–67.

Drake, R. E., & Wallach, M. A. (1993). Moderate drinking among people with severe mental illness. *Hospital and Community Psychiatry, 44,* 780–782.

Drake, R. E., Xie, H., McHugo, G. J., & Green, A. I. (2000). The effects of clozapine on alcohol and drug use disorders among schizophrenia patients. *Schizophrenia Bulletin, 26*(2) 441-449.

Drake, R. E., Yovetich, N. A., Bebout, R. R., Harris, M., & McHugo, G. J. (1997). Integrated treatment for dually diagnosed homeless adults. *Journal of Nervous and Mental Disease, 185,* 298–305.

Durell, J., Lechtenberg, B., Corse, S., & Frances, R. J. (1993). Intensive case management of persons with chronic mental illness who abuse substances. *Hospital and Community Psychiatry, 44,* 415–416, 428.

Estroff, S. (1981). *Making it crazy.* Berkeley, CA: University of California Press.

Fariello, D., & Scheidt, S. (1989). Clinical case management of the dually diagnosed patient. *Hospital and Community Psychiatry, 40,* 1065–1067.

Galanter, M., Castaneda, R., & Ferman, J. (1988). Substance abuse among general psychiatric patients. *American Journal of Drug and Alcohol Abuse, 14,* 211–235.

Godley, S. H., Hoewing-Roberson, R., & Godley, M. D. (1994). *Final MISA Report.* Bloomington, IL: Lighthouse Institute.

Greenfield, S. F., Weiss, R. D., & Tohen, M. (1995). Substance abuse and the chronically mentally ill: A description of dual diagnosis treatment services in a psychiatric hospital. *Community Mental Health Journal, 31,* 265–277.

Hellerstein, D., & Meehan, B. (1987). Outpatient group therapy for schizophrenic substance abusers. *American Journal of Psychiatry, 144,* 1337–1340.

Hellerstein, D. J., Rosenthal, R. N., & Miner, C. R. (1995). A prospective study of integrated outpatient treatment for substance abusing schizophrenic patients. *American Journal on Addictions, 4,* 33–42.

Hilton, M. D. (1987). Drinking patterns and drinking problems in 1984: Results from a general population survey. *Alcoholism, Clinical and Experimental Research, 11,* 167–175.

Jerrell, J. M., & Ridgely, M. S. (1995). Comparative effectiveness of three approaches to serving people with severe mental illness and substance abuse disorders. *Journal of Nervous and Mental Disease, 183,* 566–576.

Jerrell, J. M., & Ridgely, M. S. (1999). Impact of robustness of program implementation on outcomes of clients in dual diagnosis programs. *Psychiatric Services, 50,* 109–112.

Khantzian, E. J. (1997). The self-medication hypothesis of substance use disorders: A reconsideration and recent applications. *Harvard Review of Psychiatry, 4,* 231–244.

Kofoed, L., Kania, J., Walsh, T., & Atkinson, R. M. (1986). Outpatient treatment of patients with substance abuse and coexisting psychiatric disorders. *American Journal of Psychiatry, 143,* 867–872.

Lehman, A. F., & Dixon, L., Eds. (1995). *Double jeopardy: Chronic mental illness and substance abuse.* New York, NY: Harwood Academic Publishers.

Lehman, A. F., Myers, C. P., Dixon, L. B., & Johnson, J. L. (1996). Detection of substance use disorders among psychiatric inpatients. *Journal of Nervous and Mental Disease, 184,* 228–233.

McEvoy, J. P., Freudenreich, O., Levin, E. D., & Rose, J. E. (1995). Haloperidol increases smoking in patients with schizophrenia. *Psychopharmacology, 119,* 124–126.

McHugo, G. J., Drake, R. E., Burton, H. L., & Ackerson, T. H. (1995). A scale for assessing the stage of substance abuse treatment in persons with severe mental illness. *Journal of Nervous and Mental Disease, 183,* 762–767.

McHugo, G. J., Drake, R. E., Teague, G. B., Xie, H., & Sengupta, A. (1999). The relationship between model fidelity and client outcomes in the New Hampshire Dual Disorders Study. *Psychiatric Services, 50,* 818–824.

Meisler, N., Blankertz, L., Santos, A. B., & McKay, C. (1997). Impact of assertive community treatment on homeless persons with co-occurring severe psychiatric and substance use disorders. *Community Mental Health Journal, 33,* 113–122.

Mercer, C. C., Mueser, K. T., & Drake, R. E. (1998). Organizational guidelines for dual disorders programs. *Psychiatric Quarterly, 69,* 145–168.

Mercer-McFadden, C., Drake, R. E., Brown, N. B., & Fox, R. S. (1997). The Community Support Program demonstrations of services for young adults with severe mental illness and substance use disorders. *Psychiatric Rehabilitation Journal, 20*(3), 13–24.

Miller, N. S., Ed. (1994). *Treating coexisting psychiatric and addictive disorders.* Center City, MN: Hazelden.

Miller, W. R., & Rollnick, S. (1991). *Motivational interviewing: Preparing people to change addictive behavior.* New York, NY. Guilford Press.

Miner, C. R., Rosenthal, R. N., Hellerstein, D. J., & Muenz, L. R. (1997). Prediction of compliance with outpatient referral in patients with schizophrenia and psychoactive substance use disorders. *Archives of General Psychiatry, 54,* 706–712.

Minkoff, K. (1989). An integrated treatment model for dual diagnosis of psychosis and addiction. *Hospital and Community Psychiatry, 40,* 1031–1036.

Minkoff, K. (1997). Substance abuse versus substance dependence. *Psychiatric Services, 48,* 867.

Morse, G. A., Calsyn, R.J., Allen, G., Tempelhoff, B., & Smith, R. (1992). Experimental comparison of the effects of three treatment programs for homeless mentally ill people. *Hospital and Community Psychiatry, 43,* 1005–1010.

Mueser, K. T., Bennett, M., & Kushner, M. G. (1995a). Epidemiology of substance use disorders among persons with chronic mental illnesses. In: Lehman, A.F., and Dixon, L., eds. *Double jeopardy: Chronic mental illness and substance abuse.* New York, NY. Harwood Academic Publishers. pp. 9–25.

Mueser, K. T., Drake, R. E., & Noordsy, D. L. (1998a). Integrated mental health and substance abuse treatment for severe psychiatric disorders. *Journal of Practical Psychiatry and Behavioral Health, 4,* 129–139.

Mueser, K. T., Drake, R. E., & Wallach, M. A. (1998b). Dual diagnosis: A review of etiological theories. *Addictive Behaviors, 23,* 717–734.

Mueser, K. T., Nishith, P., Tracy, J. I., DeGirolamo, J., & Molinaro, M. (1995b). Expectations and motives for substance use in schizophrenia. *Schizophrenia Bulletin, 21*(3), 367–378.

Mueser, K. T., & Noordsy, D. L. (1996). Group treatment for dually diagnosed clients. In: Drake, R.E., & Mueser, K.T., eds. Dual diagnosis of major mental illness and substance abuse disorder: II. Recent research and clinical implications. *New Directions for Mental Health Services. Vol. 70.* San Francisco, CA: Jossey-Bass. pp. 33–51.

Mueser, K. T., Rosenberg, S. D., Drake, R. E., Miles, K., Wolford, G., Vidaver, R., & Carrieri, K. (1999). Conduct disorder, antisocial personality disorder and substance use disorders in schizophrenia and major affective disorders. *Journal of Studies on Alcohol, 60*(2), 278–284.

Mueser, K. T., Yarnold, P. R., & Bellack, A. S. (1992). Diagnostic and demographic correlates of substance abuse in schizophrenia and major affective disorder. *Acta Psychiatrica Scandinavica, 85,* 48–55.

Nigam, R., Schottenfeld, R., & Kosten, T. R. (1992). Treatment of dual diagnosis patients: A relapse prevention group approach. *Journal of Substance Abuse Treatment, 9,* 305–309.

Noordsy, D. L., Drake, R. E., Biesanz, J. C., & McHugo, G. J. (1994). Family history of alcoholism in schizophrenia. *Journal of Nervous and Mental Disease, 182,* 651–655.

Noordsy, D. L., Drake, R. E., Teague, G. B., Osher, F. C., Hurlbut, S. C., Beaudett, M. S., & Paskus, T. S. (1991). Subjective experiences related to alcohol use among schizophrenics. *Journal of Nervous and Mental Disease, 179,* 410–414.

Noordsy, D. L., Mercer, C. C., & Drake, R. E. (2002). Involuntary interventions in dual disorders programs. In: Cutler, D. L. and Backlar, P., eds. *Ethics in community mental health care: Commonplace concerns.* Williston, VT: Gordon and Breach.

Noordsy, D. L., Schwab, B., Fox, L., and Drake, R. E. (1996). The role of self-help programs in the rehabilitation of persons with mental illness and substance use disorders. *Community Mental Health Journal, 32,* 71–81.

O'Keefe, C., Potenza, D. P.; & Mueser, K. T. (1997). Treatment outcomes for severely mentally ill patients on conditional discharge to community-based treatment. *Journal of Nervous and Mental Disease, 185,* 409–411.

Osher, F. C., & Dixon, L. B. (1996). Housing for persons with co-occurring mental and addictive disorders. In: Drake, R. E., and Mueser, K. T., eds. *Dual diagnosis of major mental illness and substance abuse, Vol. 2. Recent research and clinical implications.* San Francisco, CA: Jossey-Bass. pp. 53–64.

Osher, F. C., & Kofoed, L. L. (1989). Treatment of patients with psychiatric and psychoactive substance abuse disorders. *Hospital and Community Psychiatry, 40,* 1025–1030.

Policy Research Associates (1998). *Research study of the New York City Involuntary Outpatient Commitment Pilot Program.* Delmar, NY: Policy Research Associates.

Quimby, E., Drake, R. E., & Becker, D. R. (2001). Ethnographic findings from the Washington, DC, Vocational Services Study. *Psychiatric Rehabilitation Journal, 24*(4) 368-374.

Rahav, M., Rivera, J. J., Nuttbrock, L., Ng-Mak, D., Sturz, E. L., Link, B. G., Struening, E. L., Pepper, B., & Gross, B. (1995). Characteristics and treatment of homeless, mentally ill, chemical-abusing men. *Journal of Psychoactive Drugs, 27,* 93–103.

Regier, D. A., Farmer, M. E., Rae, D. S., Locke, B. Z., Keith, S. J., Judd, L. L., Goodwin, F. K. (1990). Comorbidity of mental disorders with alcohol and other drug abuse. *Journal of the American Medical Association, 264,* 2511–2518.

Ribisl, K. M., Davidson, W. S., Luke, D. A., Mowbray, C. T., & Herman, S. H. (1996). *The role of social networks and psychopathology in predicting substance abuse treatment outcome in a dual diagnosis sample.* Unpublished manuscript.

Ridgely, M. S., Goldman, H. H., & Willenbring, M. (1990). Barriers to the care of persons with dual diagnoses. *Schizophrenia Bulletin, 16*(1), 123–132.

Ridgely, M. S., Osher, F. C., Goldman, H. H., & Talbott, J. A. (1987). *Executive summary: Chronic mentally ill young adults with substance abuse problems: A review of research, treatment, and training issues.* Baltimore, MD: Mental Health Services Research Center, University of Maryland School of Medicine.

Rosen, M. I., & Rosenheck, R. (1999). Substance use and assignment of representative payees. *Psychiatric Services, 50,* 95–98.

Rosenberg, S. D., Drake, R. E., Wolford, G. L., Mueser, K. T., Oxman, T. E., Vidaver, R. M., & Carrieri, K. (1998). The Dartmouth Assessment of Lifestyle Instrument (DALI): A substance use disorder screen for people with severe mental illness. *American Journal of Psychiatry, 155,* 232–238.

Rosenthal, R. N., Hellerstein, D. J., & Miner, C. R. (1992). Integrated services for treatment of schizophrenic substance abusers: Demographics, symptoms, and substance abuse patterns. *Psychiatric Quarterly, 63,* 3–26.

Rounsaville, B. J. (1989). Clinical assessment of drug abusers. In: Kleber, H.D., ed., *Treatment of drug abusers (nonalcohol): A task force report of the American Psychiatric Association.* Washington, DC: American Psychiatric Association Press. pp. 1183–1191.

Schutt, R. K., & Goldfinger, S. M. (1996). Housing preferences and perceptions of health and functioning among homeless mentally ill persons. *Psychiatric Services, 47,* 381–386.

Sengupta, A., Drake, R. E., & McHugo, G. J. (1998). The relationship between substance use disorder and vocational functioning among people with severe mental illness. *Psychiatric Rehabilitation Journal, 22,* 41–45.

Shaner, A., Khaka, E., Roberts, L., Wilkins, J., Anglin, D., & Hsieh, S. (1993). Unrecognized cocaine use among schizophrenic patients. American *Journal of Psychiatry, 150,* 777–783.

Shaner, A., Roberts, L. J., Eckman, T. A., Racenstein, J. M., Tucker, D. E., Tsuang, J. W., & Mintz, J. (1998). Sources of diagnostic uncertainty for chronically psychotic cocaine abusers. *Psychiatric Services, 49*, 684–690.

Siris, S. G. (1990). Pharmacological treatment of substance-abusing schizophrenic patients. *Schizophrenia Bulletin, 16*(1), 111–122.

Siris, S. G., Mason, S. E., Bermanzohn, P. C., Shuwall, M. A., & Aseniero, M. A. (1993). Adjunctive imipramine in substance-abusing dysphoric schizophrenic patients. *Psychopharmacology Bulletin, 29*, 127–134.

Smith, G. R., & Burns, B. J. (1994). Recommendations of the Little Rock Working Group on Mental Health and Substance Abuse Disorders in Health-Care Reform. *Journal of Mental Health Administration, 20*, 247–253.

Solomon, J., Zimberg, S., & Shollar, E., Eds. (1993). *Dual diagnosis: Evaluation, treatment, training, and program development.* New York, NY. Plenum.

Stone, A. M., Greenstein, R. A., Gamble, G., & McLellan, A. T. (1993). Cocaine use by schizophrenic outpatients who receive depot neuroleptic medication. *Hospital and Community Psychiatry, 44*, 176–177.

Swartz, M. S., Swanson, J. W., Hiday, V. A., Borum, R., Wagner, H. R., & Burns, B. J. (1998). Violence and severe mental illness: The effects of substance abuse and nonadherence to medication. *American Journal of Psychiatry, 155*, 226–231.

Teague, G. B., Bond, G. R., & Drake, R. E. (1998). Program fidelity in assertive community treatment. *American Journal of Orthopsychiatry, 68*, 216–232.

Test, M. A., Wallisch, L. S., Allness, D. J., & Ripp, K. (1989). Substance use in young adults with schizophrenic disorders. *Schizophrenia Bulletin, 15*(3), 465–476.

Turner, W. M., & Tsuang, M. T. (1990). Impact of substance abuse on the course and outcome of schizophrenia. *Schizophrenia Bulletin, 16*(1), 87–95.

Vaillant, G. E. (1995). *The natural history of alcoholism revisited.* Cambridge, MA: Harvard University Press.

Voruganti, L. N. P., Heslegrave, R. J., & Awad, A. G. (1997). Neuroleptic dysphoria may be the missing link between schizophrenia and substance abuse. *Journal of Nervous and Mental Disease, 185*, 463–465.

Weiss, R. D., Mirin, S. M., & Griffin, M. L. (1992). Methodological considerations in the diagnosis of coexisting psychiatric disorders in substance abusers. *British Journal of Addiction, 87*, 179–187.

Wolford, G., Rosenberg, S., Oxman, T., Drake, R., Mueser, K., Hoffman, D., & Vidaver, R. (1999). Evaluating existing methods for detecting substance use disorder in persons with severe mental illness. *Psychology of Addictive Behaviors, 13*, 313–326.

Ziedonis, D. M., & Fisher, W. (1994). Assessment and treatment of comorbid substance abuse in individuals with schizophrenia. *Psychiatric Annals, 24*, 477–483.

Ziedonis, D. M., Richardson, T., Lee, E., Petrakis, I., & Kosten, T. (1992). Adjunctive desipramine in the treatment of cocaine-abusing schizophrenics. *Psychopharmacology Bulletin, 28,* 309–314.

Ziedonis, D. M., & Trudeau, K. (1997). Motivation to quit using substances among individuals with schizophrenia: Implications for a motivation-based treatment model. *Schizophrenia Bulletin, 23*(2), 229–238.

Zimmet, S. V., Strous, R. D., Burgess, E. S., Kohnstamm, S., & Green, A. I. (2000). Effects of clozapine on substance use in patients with schizophrenia and schizoaffective disorders. *Journal of Clinical Psychopharmacology, 20*(1) 94-98.

Integrated Mental Health and Substance Abuse Treatment for Severe Psychiatric Disorders

Kim T. Mueser, Robert E. Drake & Douglas L. Noordsy

This article is reprinted with permission from the *Journal of Practice in Psychiatry and Behavioral Health*, May 1998, 4, 129–139.

Kim T. Mueser, Ph.D., is with the New Hampshire-Dartmouth Psychiatric Research Center, Concord, NH. Robert E. Drake, M.D., PhD, is with the New Hampshire-Dartmouth Psychiatric Research Center, Concord, NH. Douglas L. Noordsy, M.D., is with the New Hampshire-Dartmouth Psychiatric Research Center, Concord, NH.

Widespread recognition of the problem of dual disorders, defined here as coexisting substance use disorder (substance abuse or substance dependence) and severe mental illness, has led to the development of programs that integrate mental health and substance abuse treatments. In this article, the authors provide a brief summary of problems related to traditional treatment approaches for persons with dual disorders. They then define integrated dual-disorders treatment and describe common components of these programs: assertive outreach, comprehensiveness, long-term perspective, shared decision-making, stagewise treatment, and pharmacotherapy. The authors elaborate on the concept of stages of treatment (engagement, persuasion, active treatment, relapse prevention), including the specific goals of each stage, and provide examples of clinical interventions for achieving designated goals. Research on integrated treatment is then briefly summarized.

Over the past two decades, there has been a growing awareness of the problem of dual disorders, which refer to co-occurring substance use disorder (abuse or dependence) and severe mental illness (such as schizophrenia and bipolar disorder). As evidence has accumulated demonstrating that traditional, separate services for individuals with dual disorders are ineffective, new treatment approaches have been developed based on the theme of integrating previously disparate treatment services.

In this article, we provide an overview of integrated treatment as it has evolved over the past decade. We begin with a brief review of the prevalence of substance use disorders in persons with severe mental illness, followed by a discussion of common clinical correlates of substance use disorders in this population. We briefly discuss the natural history of dual disorders and review the problems associated with traditional approaches to treating dually diagnosed patients. After defining integrated treatment, we describe common elements of effective integrated treatment programs, with special emphasis on the concept of stages of dual diagnosis treatment. Last, we provide a brief summary of research on integrated dual diagnosis treatment and conclude with a discussion of future directions for clinical work and research in this area.

Prevalence of Substance Use Disorders in Severe Mental Illness

Numerous studies have shown that persons with severe mental illness are at increased risk for having comorbid substance use disorders (Cuffel, 1996). In the most comprehensive study of comorbidity in severe mental illnesses conducted to date, the Epidemiologic Catchment Area (ECA) study, the rate of lifetime substance use disorders in the general population was 17%, compared to 48% among persons with schizophrenia and 56% among persons with bipolar disorder (Regier et al., 1990). The ECA study found that, in general, all psychiatric disorders were associated with higher rates of substance use disorders compared to the general population, with individuals with severe mental illness having the highest rates.

In addition to the high rate of lifetime substance use disorders in persons with severe mental illness, rates of recent alcohol and drug use disorders are also high. Most studies suggest that between 25% and 35% of persons with severe mental illness have had a substance use disorder during the past 6 months (Mueser, Bennett, & Kushner, 1995). Thus, substance use disorders are common among persons with severe mental illness, with about half of all patients experiencing problems related to substance use at some time in their lives, and about one quarter to one third of patients having an active substance use disorder.

The prevalence and incidence rates of substance use disorder in the psychiatric population can vary as a function of sampling location and the demographic characteristics of the population. Persons with severe mental illness who are homeless, in jail, or who are assessed in an emergency room or acute care setting are more likely to have substance use disorders than other patients (Galanter, Castaneda, Ferman, 1988). In addition, substance use disorders tend to be more common in patients who are male, young, single, less educated, and have a family history of substance use disorder (Barry et al., 1996; Lambert, Griffith, Hendrickse,

1996; Menezes et al., 1996; Mueser, Bennett, & Kushner, 1995). To the extent that any sample of persons with severe mental illness is overrepresented among those with these demographic characteristics, patients may be more likely to have comorbid substance use disorders.

Clinical Correlates of Dual Diagnosis

Substance use disorders in persons with severe mental illness have been correlated with a wide range of negative outcomes. In fact, there is some evidence suggesting that substance abuse simply exacerbates all the negative outcomes that frequently occur in persons with severe mental illness. More specifically, substance use disorders have been found to be associated with higher rates of relapse and rehospitalization, medication noncompliance, violence, suicide, financial strain, family difficulties, HIV risk behaviors, and legal problems (Caton et al., 1994; Dixon, McNary, Lehman, 1995; Drake & Brunette, in press; Lindqvist & Allebeck, 1989; Linszen, Dingemans, & Lenior, 1994).

As a consequence of the clinical and social effects of substance use disorders in this population, dually diagnosed patients tend to utilize more psychiatric services then singly diagnosed patients, especially costly services such as emergency room visits and inpatient hospitalizations (Dickey & Azeni, 1996). Because of the high prevalence of substance use disorders in persons with severe mental illness, the wide ranging negative effects of substance abuse on the course of illness and the high cost of treatment, the development of more effective treatment programs for dual diagnosis has been a high priority since the mid-1980s.

Natural History of Dual Disorders

Although few studies have examined the long-term course of dual disorders, the available evidence suggests that, for most dual-disorder patients, substance use disorders are persistent with low rates of spontaneous remission (Drake et al., 1996). Bartels and colleagues (Bartels, Drake, Wallach, 1995) followed up a cohort of 148 patients in an intensive case management program 7 years later and found a stable rate of current substance use disorder. Using data from the ECA study described above (Regier et al., 1990), Cuffel et al. (Cuffel & Chase, 1994) found very similar rates of active substance use disorder in persons with schizophrenia assessed twice over a 1-year period. In the longest follow-up study to date, Kozaric-Kovacic et al. (1995) found remarkable persistence of alcoholism in a sample of 312 patients with schizophrenia followed up after approximately 20 years in Croatia.

Thus, the limited available evidence suggests the long-term persistence of substance use disorders in this population. Since most of the patients in these follow-up studies have received standard psychiatric care, their poor long-term outcome provides an indirect indictment of traditional treatment practices for dual disorders. Indeed, as discussed in the next section, numerous problems with traditional approaches to the treatment of dual diagnosis have been documented.

Problems with Traditional Treatment of Dual Diagnosis

In the United States and abroad, there has for many years been a division between mental health and substance use disorder treatment services. Consequently, two different treatment systems oversee and provide services for these two types of disorders. Education, training, and credentialing procedures differ between the two systems; eligibility criteria for patients to receive services also differ. Because of this separation of mental health and substance use disorder services, two general approaches to the treatment of dual diagnosis have predominated until recently: the sequential treatment approach and the parallel treatment approach. Each of these approaches is associated with a variety of problems.

The *sequential treatment* approach is a common clinical justification for exclusion from treatment rather than an explicit treatment model. In this approach, dually diagnosed patients are told they are not eligible for treatment in one part of a nonintegrated system until they resolve the other problem first. This approach defends programmatic boundaries while ignoring individual patients and larger systems needs. For example, an individual with schizophrenia and an alcohol use disorder might be informed by a substance abuse counselor that his alcohol problem cannot be effectively treated until the schizophrenia has been successfully treated or stabilized. Alternatively, an individual with bipolar disorder and a concurrent substance use disorder presenting for treatment to a mental health professional might be informed that it is unsafe to prescribe medications for her bipolar disorder until she stops using substances. Because substance use disorders rarely remit spontaneously and can worsen the course of psychiatric illness, and the severity of psychiatric illness can contribute to substance abuse (e.g., acute mania can increase substance abuse), attempts to treat one disorder before attending to the other are invariably doomed to failure.

In the *parallel treatment* approach, mental health and substance use disorders are treated simultaneously by different professionals, who usually work for different agencies. In theory, providers of separate services should attempt to coordinate their services by regular contacts and reaching consensus concerning the essential elements of the treatment plan. In practice, however, parallel treatment services have not involved such collaboration between professionals, and the burden of integration has either fallen on the patient, or, more likely, has not occurred at all. Although a variety of explanations may account for the poor integration of services in the parallel treatment approach, one possible factor is the different philosophies of treatment held by mental health and substance abuse treatment providers. For example, the use of affectively charged, confrontational approaches has been common among substance abuse treatment providers, while there is a general consensus that such emotionally charged approaches are counterproductive when working with individuals with severe mental illnesses such as schizophrenia and bipolar disorder.

In addition to the problems inherent in the sequential and parallel treatment approaches, dually diagnosed patients have often encountered funding barriers that interfere with access to treatment for one or the other of their disorders. Nonintegrated approaches generally rely on the dually diagnosed patient seeking treatment from both the mental health and substance abuse treatment systems. However, many individuals lack awareness of or motivation for treatment for one or both of their disorders. Consequently, some individuals with a dual diagnosis have failed to receive services for one of their disorders. Other individuals have failed to receive services for *either* disorder, "falling between the cracks" of available services as mental health and substance abuse service providers have deemed such individuals inappropriate for their type of service.

By the end of the 1980s, several comprehensive literature reviews had documented these and other problems with traditional dual diagnosis treatment services (e.g., Ridgely et al.) (Ridgely, Goldman, Willenbring, 1990). By that time, there was also overwhelming evidence documenting the poor prognosis for dually diagnosed patients and suggesting higher rates of costly service utilization (Dickey & Azeni, 1996).

As these facts became more widely recognized new programs began to be developed with the primary aim of integrating mental and substance abuse services in order to improve the long-term outcome for persons with a dual diagnosis.

Integrated Mental Health and Substance Abuse Treatment

An *integrated treatment program* can be defined as a program in which the same clinician (or team of clinicians) provides treatment for both the mental illness and the substance use disorder at the same time. This clinician assumes responsibility for integrating the mental health and substance abuse treatments so that the interventions are selected, modified, combined, and tailored for the specific patient. Because the educational and prescriptive message is integrated, there is no need for the patient to reconcile two messages—the approach appears seamless to the patient. It should be clear that integration does not mean that two agencies or programs merely agree to collaborate.

A variety of different integrated treatment programs have been developed in recent years to meet the needs of dually diagnosed patients. Many of these programs share a common philosophy, as well as core components of intervention. The essential components of integrated treatment programs for dually diagnosed patients are: assertive outreach, comprehensiveness, shared decision making, long-term commitment, stage-wise treatment; and pharmacotherapy. We describe each of these components in the following sections.

Assertive Outreach

Assertive outreach refers to the provision of services in patients' natural living environments, rather than in the clinic. Assertive outreach is an essential component of integrated treatment because many dually diagnosed patients tend to drop out of outpatient treatment due to the chaos in their lives, cognitive impairment, or low motivation. If these patients are to be engaged in treatment and progress is to be made towards reducing substance use and related outcomes, clinicians must reach out to patients by providing more community-oriented services and fewer clinic-based services. In addition to facilitating the engagement process, assertive outreach is helpful in monitoring the course of dual disorders since it can provide clinicians with more information about patients' functioning, as well as about social and other environmental factors that may influence the outcome of the disorders. Without assertive outreach, many dually diagnosed patients never receive the integrated services necessary to improve their disorders.

Comprehensiveness

Although a fundamental goal of integrated treatment is to decrease and eliminate substance abuse, achieving this goal typically involves more than changing behaviors directly related to substance use. To achieve long-term abstinence, individuals must not only stop using alcohol and other drugs but must also learn to lead an abstinent life. Maintaining abstinence for more than a few days is difficult precisely because it involves changing habits, activities, expectations, beliefs, friendships, and ways of dealing with internal distress—indeed, almost everything about one's life. Individuals who are dually diagnosed typically have a wide range of needs, such as improving the quality of their family and social relationships, work, capacity for independent living, leisure and recreational pursuits, and ability to manage anxiety and depression. Competent integrated treatment programs are necessarily *comprehensive* because they assume that the recovery process occurs longitudinally in the context of making many life changes and they address this broad range of needs.

In fact, every stage of treatment involves a comprehensive approach. Clients can make progress even before they acknowledge their substance abuse or develop motivation to reduce alcohol and drug use by improving their skills and supports. These improvements will increase their hopefulness about making positive changes and will facilitate their subsequent efforts to attain abstinence. As they attempt to live their lives without alcohol and drugs, they must be able to handle distress, to find meaningful activities, to have a constructive social network including rewarding friendships, and to live in a safe setting. Otherwise, they are very unlikely to maintain abstinence.

Shared Decision Making

A fundamental value of the integrated treatment approach is its goal of shared decision making among all critical stakeholders. A major premise of integrated treatment is that dually diagnosed patients, like others with severe mental illness, are capable of playing a critical role in the management of their disorders and in making progress towards achieving their goals. Such a philosophy is consistent with the recent emphasis on

Table 1

Stages of treatment

Stage	Definition	Goal
Engagement	Patient does not have regular contact with dual diagnosis clinician	To establish a working alliance with the patient
Persuasion	Patient has regular contact with clinician, but does not want to work on reducing substance abuse	To develop the patient's awareness that substance use is a problem and create motivation to change
Active Treatment	Patient is motivated to reduce substance use as indicated by reduction in substance use for at least 1 month but less than 6 months	To help the patient further reduce substance use and, if possible, attain abstinence
Relapse Prevention	Patient has not experienced problems related to substance use for at least 6 months (or is abstinent)	To maintain awareness that relapse could happen and to extend recovery to other areas (e.g., social relationships, work)

consumerism, illness self-management, community integration, quality of life rehabilitation, and recovery for persons with severe mental illness.

Shared decision making also recognizes the critical role that many families play in the lives of persons with severe mental illness. Since they are often involved as caregivers and serve to buffer patients from many of the negative effects of stress, families also need to be engaged and involved in making decisions.

For a number of medical illnesses, shared decision making has resulted in better educated patients, greater treatment compliance, higher satisfaction with care, and improved biomedical outcomes (Wennberg, 1991). Similar benefits are expected in mental health care. Making decisions collaboratively requires that patients and their families have as much information as possible about illnesses and treatments to facilitate better decisions. Providers assume the burden of getting information to patients and their families so that they can become more effective participants in the treatment process. Shared decision making maximizes the chances that treatment plans will be followed since different stakeholders are involved in selecting and implementing solutions to identified problems. Over the long run, patients and families become more able to advocate for themselves and to work collaboratively with professional providers. The goal, of course, is for the person with dual disorders to become responsible for recognizing and managing his or her own illnesses, using families for support and professionals for specific consultations and treatment. Patients and families are satisfied with care as they learn more and take responsibility for implementing care plans that they understand and have chosen. Shared decision making assumes that more knowledge, greater choice of treatment, increased responsibility for self-management, and higher satisfaction with care will produce better outcomes, including less severe symptoms, better social and vocational functioning, and a better quality of life.

Long-Term Commitment

If left untreated or treated by traditional service approaches, the longitudinal course of dual disorders is both chronic and severe. Available research on integrated treatment programs suggests that these programs can have a beneficial effect on decreasing substance use disorders and related negative outcomes in dually diagnosed patients.

However, research also suggests that integrated treatment programs do not produce dramatic changes in most patients over short periods of time; rather, patients gradually improve over time, with approximately 10-20% per year achieving stable remission of their substance use disorders (Drake et al., in press). These findings are consistent with other data on recovery, including longitudinal research on attaining stable remission from alcoholism (Vaillant, 1983) and on the long-term effects of rehabilitation for those with severe mental illness (Bellack & Mueser, 1993). Learning to lead an abstinent lifestyle, just like developing the skills and supports needed to manage one's illnesses and to attain satisfaction with activities and relationships, requires major life changes over months and years. It makes no sense to believe that recovery from two intertwined disorders might be faster than from either one alone.

Stage-Wise Treatment

A central feature of integrated treatment is the concept of stages of treatment. Clinicians and researchers have for a long time proposed that changes in maladaptive behavior occur in a series of different stages (Mahoney, 1991; Prochaska, 1984). Stages differ in terms of patients' motivational states, orientation towards change, goals, and the interventions that are most likely to be effective. Recognition of the stages of

Table 2

Examples of clinical interventions for the engagement stage

Outreach
Practical assistance (e.g., housing, benefits, transportation, medical care)
Crisis intervention
Support and assistance to social networks
Stabilization of psychiatric symptoms

treatment can provide clinicians with valuable information as to which interventions are most likely to be successful at a particular point in the course of recovery from a dual diagnosis.

Based on observations of the natural course of recovery of individuals with a dual diagnosis, Osher and Kofoed (Osher & Kofoed, 1989) described four common stages: (1) engagement, (2) persuasion, (3) active treatment, and (4) relapse prevention.

Osher and Kofoed observed that most patients who recovered progressed through each stage (although relapses and return to prior stages were common). Each of the different stages can be defined in terms of the patient's use of alcohol or drugs and the nature of their relationship with a dual diagnosis clinician. By determining a patient's stage of treatment, appropriate treatment goals can be identified. Clinicians have a variety of different treatment options they can use at each stage to help patients achieve a particular goal. The different stages of treatment have been operationalized in behavioral terms with a rating scale to facilitate reliable ratings between clinicians (McHugo et al., 1995).

In what follows, we define each stage of treatment, describe the goals of that stage, and provide examples of interventions that can be used to achieve those goals. Table 1 summarizes the definitions and goals of each stage. Tables 2–5 outline possible clinical interventions at each stage. After describing the four stages, we briefly highlight the clinical utility of the stages concept.

Engagement. Engagement is defined by the lack of a working alliance between the patient and the dual diagnosis clinician. Because the clinician cannot help the patient modify his or her substance use behavior without a therapeutic relationship, the goal of the engagement stage is to establish such an alliance, which is operationally defined as meeting voluntarily on a regular (at least weekly) basis. Patients who are not actively engaged in dual diagnosis treatment often attend clinics on an inconsistent, sporadic basis and never establish a trusting relationship with a single clinician. Therefore, outreach is often necessary in order to establish a therapeutic relationship with a patient.

The process of engagement typically begins with practical assistance in securing food, clothing, shelter, crisis intervention, or support. While rendering practical assistance, sensitivity and skill are required to understand and respond to the patient's language, behavior, and unspoken needs so that some trust and openness develop. During the engagement stage, the clinician typically does not address substance use directly, focusing instead on learning about the patient's world and developing a relationship that will later serve as a basis for modifying substance use behavior. Premature attempts to push patients into abstinence are often unsuccessful because they fail to recognize that the patient must develop the motivation, skills, and supports to lead an abstinent lifestyle. By the end of the engagement stage, the therapeutic alliance should allow discussion of the client's substance use and mental illness symptoms to facilitate the work of the persuasion stage.

Persuasion. After establishing regular contact and a working relationship with a dual diagnosis clinician, many patients still do not acknowledge that substance use has negative effects nor do they attempt to modify their substance use behavior. These behavioral steps of acknowledgment and modification constitute motivation; patients who are behaviorally unmotivated are in the persuasion stage. The goals of persuasion are to help the patient recognize that substance use is problematic, develop hopefulness that life can be improved by reducing substance use, and demonstrate motivation by attempting to change behavior. The tasks of persuasion are distinguished from directly helping the patient to acquire skills and supports for reducing substance use, which occurs during the next stage of treatment.

A variety of different strategies can be used to help patients understand that their substance use is a problem. Active psychiatric symptoms are stabilized at the same time as the patient receives substance abuse counseling to minimize interference from grandiosity, psychosis, or thought disorder. Patients and family members often benefit from education regarding psychiatric illness, substances of abuse, interactions between psychiatric illness and substances, and principles of treatment. Individual counseling is based on motivational interviewing (Miller & Rollnick, 1991) which enables patients to identify their own personal

Table 3

Examples of clinical interventions for the persuasion stage

Individual and family education

Motivational interviewing

Peer groups (e.g., "persuasion" groups)

Social skills training to address situations not related to substance use

Structured activity

Sampling constructive social and recreational activities

Psychological preparation for lifestyle changes necessary to achieve remission

Safe "damp" housing (i.e., tolerant of some substance abuse)

Select medications to treat psychiatric illness that may have a secondary effect on craving/addiction (e.g., selective serotonin reuptake inhibitors, tricyclic antidepressants, atypical antipsychotics, buspirone, buproprion)

---

goals and to discover how their use of substances interferes with attaining those goals. Group interventions help many patients to develop motivation to address substance-related problems (Ridgely, 1990). Persuasion groups are designed to provide an open forum in which patients can discuss their experiences with alcohol and drugs, both positive and negative, with peers. Family interventions and the sampling of healthy recreational and social activities are also frequently used as strategies during persuasion.

Coercive interventions such as involuntary hospitalizations, guardianship, or commitment to community treatment are sometimes necessary to stabilize the dangerously ill dually diagnosed patient. It is important to recognize that the prevention of harm and compulsory compliance that involuntary measures may provide do not constitute treatment and that such controls can only hold a patient static at best (O'Keefe, Potenza, Mueser, 1997). The most helpful aspects of involuntary measures may be increased access to the patient and psychiatric stabilization. For the patient to progress through the persuasion process, the clinician must still establish a therapeutic alliance and proceed with motivational development.

The term persuasion is sometimes misleading. The essence of persuasion is empowering the patient to have the insight, courage, and desire to change his or her substance disorder, not forcing the patient into abstinence by instituting behavioral controls. Motivation for abstinence must reside *in the patient,* not in the clinician or family. This distinction is often misunderstood and frequently leads to frustration on the part of dual diagnosis clinicians.

Understanding that motivation must exist in the patient helps providers recognize that many other important changes may occur during the persuasion stage. For example, it is possible to improve social skills, constructive activities, and social supports before there is any expressed motivation for abstinence; these changes will help to nurture motivation and will be needed by the patient in developing an abstinent lifestyle down the road. Note that the emphasis is on empowering the patient to make healthful changes rather than on coercive or involuntary interventions.

Active Treatment. A patient is defined as motivated to reduce substance use, and hence in the active treatment stage, when he or she has changed behaviors by significantly reducing substance use for more than 1 month and by actively seeking to sustain or enhance reductions.

The goal of this stage is to help the patient reduce substance use to the point of eliminating negative consequences or to attain abstinence for a prolonged period of time. Although research data indicate that abstinence is a much more successful remission strategy than occasional or moderate use (Drake et al., 1998), the decision to pursue abstinence must come from the patient.

A wide variety of different clinical strategies can be used to help patients further reduce their substance use or attain abstinence. These strategies involve the traditional rehabilitation dyad of increasing skills and improving supports, and they can be accomplished in a variety of settings. Individual counseling uses behavioral techniques for enhancing abstinence skills and networks that support abstinence (Monti et al., 1989). Active treatment groups and social skills training groups can help patients reduce substance use by developing skills for dealing with high-risk situations or compensatory skills for meeting needs in ways other than using substances (Mueser & Noordsy).

Self-help groups, such as Alcoholics Anonymous, can be useful for patients who endorse abstinence as a goal and wish to take advantage of the wide availability of such groups in most communities. Patients may affiliate most readily with self-help groups tailored to the dually diagnosed population (e.g., "Double-Trouble" or "Dual Recovery" groups). Family problem solving can be used to identify possible triggers of sub-

Table 4

Examples of clinical interventions for the active treatment stage

Family problem solving
Peer groups (e.g., "active treatment" groups)
Social skills training to address substance-related situations
Self-help groups (e.g., Alcoholics Anonymous)
Individual cognitive-behavioral counseling
Substituting activities (e.g., work, sports)
Pharmacologic treatments to support abstinence (e.g., disulfiram, naltrexone)
Safe housing
Outpatient or inpatient detoxification
Contingency management

---

stance use, to help patients get involved in alternative activities, to structure their time in order to decrease opportunities to use substances, and to provide behavioral rewards for achieving target goals. Contingency management strategies, such as monetarily reinforcing patients for not using substances (Shaner, et al., 1997), can be useful in helping patients reduce substance use and experience the benefits of sobriety.

Although the explicit goal during this stage is to reduce substance use, clinicians recognize that sustained behavioral change involves more than avoiding substances; it includes all the lifestyle changes described above under comprehensiveness. Therefore, interventions during active treatment may need to address the broader changes needed to achieve a different lifestyle that does not rely on drugs. Clinicians expand upon the persuasion process to develop patients' recognition of and motivation for addressing these changes. This process determines which areas are addressed during active treatment and which are saved for future work.

Relapses or slips back into active substance use are common in the active treatment stage. Relapses are not viewed as failures, but rather as part of the course of the chronic illness. Relapses are used as opportunities to learn more about what each individual will need to achieve sustained abstinence. The patient and clinician examine the relapse in microscopic detail, gleaning information about relapse triggers and the sequence of events leading to substance use. They use this information to refine their active treatment interventions and to identify new areas of lifestyle change that need attention.

If the patient has a relapse into sustained active substance use, the clinician should shift back into persuasion-stage work, only returning to active treatment interventions when the patient again demonstrates motivation for abstinence or reduced substance use. Many patients will choose to reduce substance use rather than to adopt abstinence during early active treatment. This strategy often fails to sustain remission, but the experience can be helpful in the long-term process of recovery because the patient learns experientially that moderate use of alcohol or drugs is not viable, thereby developing motivation to pursue abstinence.

Relapse Prevention. The patient is defined as having reached the relapse prevention stage when he or she has not experienced negative consequences related to substance use (or has been abstinent) for at least 6 months. The goals of this stage are to maintain an awareness that relapse of the substance use disorder could still happen, to prepare to respond to relapse, and to continue to expand the recovery to other areas of functioning, such as social relationships, work, and health. After abstinent patients achieve an extended period of sobriety, they often develop the confidence that they can resume controlled substance use. This strategy usually fails, since few patients with severe mental illness are capable of sustaining moderate use of alcohol or drugs without incurring negative consequences (Drake & Wallach, 1994). Helping patients in the relapse prevention stage maintain an awareness of their high vulnerability to relapse and developing monitoring strategies are critical goals of this stage of treatment. As is true at every stage, the patient's choices are paramount in how these goals are accomplished. Some patients will attend self-help groups, some will continue in dual diagnosis groups, some will review their status with their clinicians, and some will use other community-integrated support networks.

The overarching goal of this stage is to develop a meaningful recovery process. Clinicians facilitate a shift in focus from giving up substances to gaining a healthy life. When a remission of the substance use disorder has lasted for over 6 months, it becomes increasingly important to help patients achieve goals in other areas of functioning. The more patients are able to derive natural rewards from normative activities such as work, social relationships, and leisure pursuits, the less susceptible they will be to relapses of their substance use disorder. Therefore, strategies such as supported employment and social skills training may be used to help patients to achieve these goals.

At the same time, preparing for relapse is also an important skill during relapse prevention. The patient must know how to accept relapse

Table 5
Examples of clinical interventions for the relapse prevention stage

Supported or independent employment

Peer groups (e.g., "active treatment" groups)

Self-help groups

Social skills training to address other areas

Family problem solving

Lifestyle improvements (e.g., smoking cessation, healthy diet, regular exercise, stress management techniques)

Independent housing

and begin working on abstinence right away rather than experiencing failure, developing hopelessness, and giving in to a prolonged relapse. Education and knowledge about the long-term process of recovery may be helpful in preparing for relapse.

Clinical Utility of the Stages of Treatment. The most important feature of the concept of stages of treatment is that it helps clinicians identify appropriate goals and strategies at a particular point of treatment. Paying attention to the stage of treatment ensures that interventions will be optimally timed to fit a patient's current motivational state. For example, if a clinician attempts to help a patient discover that his or her substance use is destructive (a goal of the persuasion stage) before a therapeutic relationship with the patient has been established (engagement stage), he or she may unwittingly drive the patient away from treatment. Similarly, if the clinician tries to help the patient reduce his or her substance use (a goal of the active treatment stage) before the patient sees substance use as a problem (persuasion stage), the patient may become disenchanted and convinced that the clinician does not really "understand" him, and drop out of treatment. Therefore, the concept of stages helps clinicians increase the chances of selecting interventions with the greatest immediate relevance for patients at a particular point during their treatment.

Pharmacotherapy

Medications for both psychiatric illness and substance disorder should be integrated with psychosocial interventions in a complementary approach. Failure to prescribe needed medications or undermedication of severe psychiatric illness can promote psychiatric deterioration and/or relapse of substance use disorder. Because of the potential risks of medication abuse and of interactions between medications and drugs of abuse, however, caution is generally encouraged in prescribing psychoactive medications. In addition, due to the high rate of medication nonadherence in dually diagnosed patients, close monitoring of medication adherence in the community, for example by outreach nurses, is often recommended.

The Center for Substance Abuse Treatment has developed several guidelines for integrating pharmacotherapy with psychosocial approaches (Center for Substance Abuse Treatment, 1994):

1. Begin with nonpharmacologic approaches to manage emerging symptoms of a less severe nature, such as anxiety and mild depression and add medications if the symptoms do not respond. At the same time, recognize that acute and severe symptoms associated with mania, psychotic depression, and schizophrenia require immediate medications.

2. Encourage the use of medications with a low abuse potential. This conservative dictum should again be moderated by the dangers of acute and severe symptoms.

3. Be aware of specific interactions between drugs of abuse or withdrawal syndromes and medication effects. For example, alcohol intoxication and withdrawal can disturb electrolyte balance and affect lithium levels.

Specific pharmacotherapies for dual diagnosis are only now emerging. One experimental trial showed that schizophrenic patients with cocaine disorder did better with adjunctive desipramine (Ziedonis et al., 1992). Two nonexperimental reports suggest that clozapine may be superior to other antipsychotic drugs for dually diagnosed patients with schizophrenia by exerting a specific effect on substance use (Drake et al., submitted for publication; Zimmet et al., submitted for publication). Clinicians often recommend parenteral antipsychotic drugs (i.e., long-acting injections) for dually diagnosed patients who are seriously nonadherent, but we are unaware of any research on this practice. Anecdotally, clinicians have also reported success in using disulfiram or naltrexone with individual dual-diagnosis patients, but there are no controlled studies of these medications either (Koefed et al., 1986).

Research on Integrated Treatment

With the proliferation of integrated treatment programs for dually disordered patients over the past decade, the effectiveness of these programs has become the subject of substantial research. Early studies on integrated treatment usually involved before and after treatment assessments (i.e., no experimental control group) or quasi-experimental control groups. Although the research methods employed in these studies were limited, and many programs were relatively brief in duration, several trends were evident (Drake et al., in press). First, research suggested that integrated dual diagnosis programs were capable of engaging the vast majority of dually diagnosed patients in treatment and retaining them in treatment for 1 year or more. Second, engagement in integrated treatment programs was associated with greater improvement in substance use outcomes compared to patients who were not engaged or who dropped out. Third, brief, intensive programs and programs that failed to use motivation-based interventions tended to have poor outcomes.

More recent research on integrated treatment programs has employed appropriate control groups and has evaluated programs over longer periods of time (e.g., 1.5-3 years). Research from these studies has provided further encouragement concerning the effectiveness of integrated treatment programs (Drake et al., in press). Research on integrated treatment that is provided over a period of several years has shown that dually diagnosed patients demonstrate a consistent gradual progression towards substance use reduction and abstinence. Most research on traditional (parallel or sequential) treatment approaches for dual disorders indicate annual rates of sustained remission of less than 5%. In comparison, recent research on integrated treatment programs suggests significantly higher rates of remission, with 10%-20% of dually diagnosed patients achieving stable remission per year. These remission rates approximate those seen among people with substance use disorders without mental illness in substance abuse treatment, suggesting that integrating treatment for dual disorders may eliminate the adverse effect of mental illness on remission from substance abuse. There is also evidence that improvements in substance use outcomes are associated with gains in a variety of other areas, such as enhanced quantity and quality of community residence, decreased victimization, and increased life satisfaction (Drake et al., 1998). Finally, research on integrated treatment suggests that most dually diagnosed patients can be engaged in treatment for extended periods of time, well beyond the relatively brief intervals studied in earlier research (e.g., less than 1 year).

Summary and Recommendations

The treatment of dually diagnosed individuals has evolved tremendously over the past two decades, and advances continue to be made in this newly emergent field. There are several practical implications of this new growth in knowledge for clinicians who treat individuals with dual disorders.

First, clinicians must be aware of the high prevalence of substance use disorders in patients with severe mental illness. Substance use disorders can be hidden and may develop at any time during the life cycle. Therefore, assessment for substance use disorders must be ongoing. In order to detect dual disorders, clinicians need to be familiar with the common consequences of substance use in patients with severe mental illness, including relapse and rehospitalization, legal problems, family conflict, homelessness, money problems, suicidality, and violence. Due to the biological vulnerability that is presumably the basis of major mental illnesses, negative consequences may occur in these patients following even small amounts of substance use.

Second, clinicians need to strive to provide *integrated mental health and substance use disorder treatment* to individuals who are dually diagnosed. At the most basic level, integrated treatment means that the clinician or treatment team treats both disorders simultaneously, with an eye towards addressing the possible interactions between disorders. The clinician, not the patient, assumes the burden of integrating treatments. When skillfully done, such integration is seamless.

Third, clinicians who treat dually diagnosed patients need to be mindful that effective integrated treatment requires several core elements, including *assertive outreach* to patients in their natural environments, *comprehensiveness* (i.e., addressing areas such as work, housing, and social relationships), *shared decision making* (including patients, families, and significant others), *pharmacotherapy* to treat severe mental illness and (possibly) addiction, and *long-term commitment* (i.e., years rather than months). The success of an integrated treatment program rests on the incorporation of these basic components.

Fourth, integrated treatment programs that embrace the concept of stages of treatment *(engagement, persuasion, active treatment, and relapse prevention*) will optimize the timing of interventions by matching them to patients' current motivational states. The four stages of treatment are behaviorally defined with respect to patients' use of substances, and each stage has a unique goal that is the clinician's primary therapeutic aim. Multiple treatment options exist for clinicians to help patients accomplish the goal of each stage.

The lives of dually diagnosed patients are often miserable; these patients create havoc in their social relationships with relatives and others and are challenging and sometimes frustrating to treat. However, as the technology of integrated treatment has developed over the past decade, the outlook for dually diagnosed persons has brightened considerably. Many of these individuals enjoy positive outcomes and a favorable prognosis with the concerted efforts of dedicated clinicians. We are encouraged by both research and clinical experience that integrated treatment is a valuable approach for helping dually diagnosed patients progress towards a healthier lifestyle and achieve personally valued goals.

References

Barry, K. L., Fleming, M. F., Greenley, J. R., Kropp, S., & Widlak, P. (1996). Characteristics of persons with severe mental illness and substance abuse in rural areas. *Psychiatric Services, 47,* 88–90.

Bartels, S. J., Drake, R. E., & Wallach, M. A. (1995). Long-term course of substance use disorders among patients with severe mental illness. *Psychiatric Services, 46,* 248–51.

Bellack, A. S. & Mueser, K. T. (1993). Psychosocial treatment for schizophrenia. *Schizophrenia Bulletin, 19,* 317–36.

Caton, C. L. M., Shrout, P. E., Eagle, P. F., Opler, L. A., Felix, A., & Dominguez, B. (1994). Risk factors for homelessness among schizophrenic men: A case-control study. *American Journal of Public Health, 84,* 265–70.

Center for Substance Abuse Treatment (1994). Assessment and treatment of patients with coexisting mental illness and alcohol and other drug abuse. *Treatment improvement protocol (TIP) series 9.* Rockville, MD: U.S. Department of Public Health.

Cuffel, B. J. & Chase, P. (1994). Remission and relapse of substance use disorder in schizophrenia: Results from a one-year prospective study. *Journal of Nervous and Mental Disease, 182,* 342–8.

Cuffel, B. J. (1996). Comorbid substance use disorder—Prevalence, patterns, of use and course. In R. E. Drake & K. T. Mueser (Eds.), Dual diagnosis of major mental illness and substance abuse, Vol. 2: Recent research and clinical implications. *New directions for mental health services* (pp. 93–105). San Francisco: Jossey-Bass.

Dickey, B. & Azeni, H. (1996). Persons with dual diagnoses of substance abuse and major mental illness: Their excess costs of psychiatric care. *American Journal of Public Health, 86,* 973–7.

Dixon, L., McNary, S., & Lehman, A. (1995). Substance abuse and family relationships of persons with severe mental illness. *American Journal of Psychiatry, 152,* 456–8.

Drake, R. E., Musser, K. T., Clark, R. E., & Wallach, M. A. (1996). The course, treatment, and outcome of substance disorder in persons with severe mental illness. *American Journal of Orthopsychiatry, 66,* 42–51.

Drake, R. E. & Brunette, M. E. (in press). Complications of severe mental illness related to alcohol and drug use disorders. In M. Galanter (Ed.), *Recent developments in alcoholism, Vol. 14: The consequences of alcohol.* New York: Plenum.

Drake, R. E. & Wallach, M. A. (1994). Moderate drinking among people with severe mental illness. *Hospital and Community Psychiatry, 44,* 780–2.

Drake, R. E., McHugo, G. J., Xie, H., Teague, G. B., Mueser, K. T., & Vaillant, G. E. (1998). *The five-year course of treated substance use disorder in patients with severe mental illness.* Manuscript submitted for publication.

Drake, R. E., Mercer-McFadden, C., Mueser, K. T., McHugo, G. J., & Bond, G. R. (in press). A review of integrated mental health and substance abuse treatment for patients with dual disorders. *Schizophrenia Bulletin.*

Drake, R. E., Xie, H., McHugo, G. J., & Green, A. I. *The effects of clozapine on alcohol and drug use disorders among schizophrenic patients.* Manuscript submitted for publication.

Galanter, M., Castaneda, R., & Ferman, J. (1988). Substance abuse among general psychiatric patients. *American Journal of Drug and Alcohol Abuse, 14,* 211–35.

Koefed, L., Kania, J., Walsh, T., & Atkinson, R. M. (1986). Outpatient treatment of patients with substance abuse and coexisting psychiatric disorders. *American Journal of Psychiatry, 42,* 948–9.

Kozaric-Kovacic, D., Folnegovic-Smalc, V., Folnegovic, Z., & Marusic, A. (1995). Influence of alcoholism on the prognosis of schizophrenic patients. *Journal of Studies on Alcohol, 56,* 622–7.

Lambert, M. T., Griffith, J. M., & Hendrickse, W. (1996). Characteristics of patients with substance abuse diagnoses on a general psychiatry unit in a VA medical center. *Psychiatric Services, 47,* 1104–7.

Lindqvist, F. & Allebeck, P. (1989). Schizophrenia and assaultive behaviour: The role of alcohol and drug abuse. *Acta Psychiatrica Scandinavica, 82,* 191–5.

Linszen, D. H., Dingemans, P.M., & Lenior, M. E. (1994). Cannabis abuse and the course of recent-onset schizophrenic disorders. *Archives of General Psychiatry, 51,* 273–9.

Mahoney, M.J. (1991). *Human change processes: The scientific foundations of psychotherapy.* Delran, NJ: Basic Books.

McHugo, G.J., Drake, R.E., Burton, H.L., & Ackerson, T.H. (1995). A scale for accessing the stage of substance abuse treatment in persons with severe mental illness. *Journal of Nervous and Mental Disease, 183*, 762–7.

Menezes, P. R., Johnson, S., Thornicroft, G., et al. (1996). Drug and alcohol problems among individuals with severe mental illnesses in South London. *British Journal of Psychiatry, 168*, 612–9.

Miller, W. R. & Rollnick, S. (1991). *Motivational interviewing: Preparing people to change addictive behavior.* New York: Guilford Press.

Monti, P. M., Abrams, D. B., Kadden, R. M., & Cooney, N. L. (1989). *Treating alcohol dependence.* New York: Guilford Press.

Mueser, K. T. & Noordsy, D. L. (1996). Group treatment for dually diagnosed clients. In R. E. Drake & K. T. Mueser (Eds.) Dual diagnosis of major mental illness and substance abuse, Vol. 2: Recent research and clinical implications. *New directions for mental health services No. 70.* (pp. 33–51). San Francisco: Jossey-Bass.

Mueser, K. T., Bennett, M., & Kushner, M. G. (1995). Epidemiology of substance abuse among persons with chronic mental disorders. In A.F. Lehman, L. Dixon (Eds.), *Double jeopardy: Chronic mental illness and substance abuse* (pp. 9–25). New York: Harwood Academic Publishers.

O'keefe, C., Potenza, D. P., & Mueser, K. T. (1997). Treatment outcomes for severely mentally ill patients on conditional discharge to community-based treatment. *Journal of Nervous and Mental Disease, 185*, 409–11.

Osher, F. C. & Kofoed, L. L. (1989). Treatment of patients with psychiatric and psychoactive substance abuse disorders. *Hospital and Community Psychiatry, 40*, 1025–30.

Prochaska, J. O. (1984). *Systems of psychotherapy. A transtheoretical analysis.* Homewood, IL: Dorsey.

Regier, D. A., Farmer, M. E., Rae, D. S., et al. (1990). Comorbidity of mental disorders with alcohol and other drug abuse. *Journal of the American Medical Association, 264*, 2511–8.

Ridgely, M. S., Goldman, H. H., & Willenbring, M. (1990). Barriers to the care of persons with dual diagnoses: Organizational and financing issues. *Schizophrenia Bulletin, 16*, 123–32.

Shaner, A., Roberti, L. J., Eckman, T. A., et al. (1997). Monetary reinforcement of abstinence from cocaine among mentally ill patients with cocaine dependence. *Psychiatric Services, 48*, 807–10.

Vaillant, G. E. (1983). *The natural history of alcoholism revisited.* Cambridge, MA: Harvard University Press.

Wennberg, J. E. (1991). Outcomes research, patient preferences, and the primary care physician. *Journal of the American Board of Family Practice, 4*, 365–7.

Ziedonis, D. M., Richardson, T., Lee, E., Petrakis, I., & Kosten, T. (1992). Adjunctive desipramine in the treatment of cocaine abusing schizophrenics. *Psychopharmacology Bulletin, 28*, 309–14.

Zimmet, S. U., Strous, R. D., Kohnstamm, S., & Green, A. E. *Effects of clozapine on substance use in patients with schizophrenia and schizoaffective disorder: A retrospective study.* Manuscript submitted for publication.

Treating Substance Abuse Among Patients with Schizophrenia

Alan S. Bellack & Carlo C. DiClemente

This article originally appeared in *Psychiatric Services*, 1999, 50, 75–80 and is reprinted with permission.

Dr. Bellack is professor of psychiatry and director of psychology at the University of Maryland School of Medicine, Baltimore, Maryland.
Dr. DiClemente is professor and chair of the department of psychology at the University of Maryland, Baltimore County.

Preparation of this manuscript was supported by grant DA09406 from the National Institute on Drug Abuse to Dr. Bellack.

Although substance abuse has reached epidemic proportions among people with schizophrenia, relatively little is known about the critical elements of effective treatment of substance abuse in this population. The authors discuss common assumptions about treatment of substance abuse and review the features of the transtheoretical model of change, which is based on the view that behavior change is a longitudinal process consisting of several stages. In this model, substance abusers must first be persuaded to reduce substance use and then be engaged in treatment before they can be taught the skills necessary to become and remain abstinent. The authors suggest an adaptation of the model that attempts to minimize the impact of the cognitive and motivational deficits associated with schizophrenia. The 6-month treatment protocol contains four modules focusing on social skills and problem solving, education about the causes and dangers of substance use, motivational interviewing and goal setting for decreased substance use, and training in behavioral skills for relapse prevention. In the 90-minute, twice weekly sessions, behavioral rehearsal is emphasized, and complex social repertoires, such as refusing substances, are divided into smaller behavioral elements.

Drug and alcohol abuse by people with schizophrenia has become one of the most significant problems facing agencies and clinicians involved in their treatment. The lifetime prevalence rate of substance abuse among persons with schizophrenia is close to 50% (Mueser, Bennett, & Kushner, 1995; Regier, Farmer, Rae, et al., 1990), and estimates of recent or current substance abuse range from 20 to 65% (Drake, Osher, & Wallach, 1989; Mueser, Yarnold, & Bellack, 1992). Anecdotal evidence suggests that substance abuse in many inner-city areas may be even higher.

Excessive substance use by people with schizophrenia has most of the same adverse social, health, economic, and psychiatric consequences as it does for other individuals. Moreover, it has additional serious consequences for these multiply handicapped patients. Substances of abuse tend to increase dopaminergic activity (Koob, 1992), thereby increasing the risk of symptom exacerbation and relapse and compromising the efficacy of neuroleptic medications (Drake et al., 1989). Substance use is also thought to decrease compliance with treatment and often serves as a source of conflict in families, a pernicious circumstance for patients with schizophrenia, who are highly vulnerable to heightened stress (Hooley, 1985).

People with serious mental illness, the majority of whom have schizophrenia, are now one of the highest risk groups for HIV (Cournos & McKinnon, 1997). Ample data indicate that substance use substantially increases the likelihood of unsafe sex practices (Carey, Carey, & Kalichman, 1997), the primary source of infection in this population. Women who abuse substances also are at increased risk of physical and sexual abuse (Goodman, Rosenberg, Mueser, et al., 1997). Substance use also has deleterious cognitive effects, a particularly serious consequence for people with schizophrenia, as their information-processing system is already compromised by the illness (Bellack, 1992).

Substance Abuse Among Patients with Schizophrenia

It is widely assumed that patients with schizophrenia use substances to reduce psychotic symptoms and alleviate the sedating side effects of neuroleptics. However, the most common reasons given for use of alcohol and other drugs are to "get high" and to reduce negative affective states including social anxiety and tension, dysphoria and depression, and boredom (Dixon, Haas, Weiden, et al., 1991; Noordsy, Drake, Teague, et al., 1991).

Empirical data do not document a consistent relationship between substance use and specific forms of symptomatology (Dixon et al., 1991; Mueser, Bellack, Douglas, et al., 1991). Alcohol is the most commonly abused substance among people with schizophrenia, as well as in the general population. Preference for street drugs varies over time and as a function of the demographic characteristics of the sample. For example,

Mueser and associates (Mueser et al., 1992) reported that from 1983 to 1986 cannabis was the most commonly abused illicit drug among patients with schizophrenia, whereas from 1986 to 1990 cocaine became the most popular drug, a change in drug use pattern similar to that in the general population (Pope, Ionescu-Pioggia, Aizley, et al., 1990). For many patients, availability of substances appears to be more relevant than the specific effects on the central nervous system.

Treatment Issues

The problem of substance abuse in schizophrenia has generated a large literature, but to date few well-controlled trials of specific interventions to deal with this pernicious combination have been done. Several recent pilot and demonstration projects have yielded mixed results (Blankertz & Cnaan, 1994; Drake, McHugo, & Noordsy, 1993; Jerrell & Ridgely, 1995; Lehman, Herron, Schwartz, et al., 1993).

Despite the absence of definitive data on specific intervention techniques, researchers appear to have broad agreement about some general requirements for effective treatment. First and foremost is the contention that dually diagnosed patients need a special program that integrates and coordinates elements of both psychiatric and substance abuse treatment (Carey, 1996; Drake et al., 1989; Lehman & Dixon, 1995). A related caveat is that the confrontational, highly affective style of many traditional substance abuse treatments is contraindicated for people with schizophrenia.

A second assumption is that treatment is best conceptualized as an ongoing process that involves a number of relatively distinct stages in which motivation to reduce substance use waxes and wanes. For example, Osher and Kofoed (Osher & Kofoed, 1989) hypothesized that treatment entails four stages: engagement, persuasion, active treatment, and relapse prevention. McHugo and colleagues (McHugo, Drake, Burton, et al., 1995) further elaborated this model into eight stages through subdivision of the four stages into early and late phases.

These two models may have considerable clinical utility, but they are more descriptive than explanatory. They provide operational definitions for the treatment focus—for example, a patient who is not currently interested in reducing substance use must first be persuaded to reduce use, and an individual who has recently become abstinent needs help in preventing substance use relapse. However, the models fail to explain how or why an individual becomes motivated to change, and they fail to predict what types of persuasion, engagement, or active treatment will be effective at any particular point in time.

Transtheoretical Model

A more elaborate conceptualization of the stages of treatment is provided by the transtheoretical model of change (Prochaska & DiClemente, 1992; Prochaska, DiClemente, & Norcross, 1992). This model has posited several dimensions for understanding the process of intentional change of problem behaviors, which includes both interventions and self-initiated change in the natural environment.

The basic dimensions of the model are stages and processes of change. The stages of change represent the temporal, motivational aspect of the process of change. The processes are the strategies or coping mechanisms that move individuals through the stages. A third dimension, levels of change, represents the multidimensional nature of the problems for each individual that complicates the process of change for any single problem (DiClemente, 1993; Prochaska & DiClemente, 1984, 1992; Prochaska et al., 1992).

A series of studies by Prochaska, DiClemente, and others (DiClemente, 1991, 1993, 1994; Prochaska et al., 1992) has demonstrated that individuals can be classified as being at various points in the stages of change and seem to move systematically through five stages. The first stage is precontemplation, when individuals either are unconvinced that they have a problem or are unwilling to consider change. The second is contemplation, when individuals are considering change in the future, in 6 months to a year. The third stage is preparation, when individuals have a more proximal goal to change in the next month and make a commitment and initial plans to change the behavior. The fourth is an action stage, in which individuals take effective action to make the change. The fifth is a maintenance stage, where the task is to consolidate the change and integrate it into the individual's lifestyle.

The course of progression through this linear series of stages is often cyclical in the short term for most individuals, and relapse and recycling through these stages is the norm (Prochaska et al., 1992). Over time, many individuals move through this cyclical process repeatedly until they are able to successfully attain sustained change of the problem behavior. Thus both short-term and long-term perspectives are needed to understand movement through this process of change.

Several other variables are also important in the process of change. Decisional balance refers to an individual's subjective evaluation of the pros and cons of engaging in the problem behavior versus changing. Considerations of decisional balance have been important indicators that the individual is in an early stage of change or is moving through the early stages of change (DiClemente, 1991; Velicer, DiClemente, Prochaska, et al., 1985).

Self-efficacy deals with the individual's subjective sense of competence to perform specific behaviors, such as resisting temptations to use drugs. Self-efficacy has been shown to be salient as a predictor in the later stages of change (DiClemente, Fairhurst, & Piotrowski, 1995).

Several recent studies have supported the validity of components of the transtheoretical model with heterogeneous groups of psychiatric patients (Rothfleisch, 1997; Velaquez, 1997). Although patients with schizophrenia were included in these samples, the applicability of the model for schizophrenia was not specifically tested.

Schizophrenia is characterized by deficits in a variety of neurobiological, cognitive, and behavioral capacities that may limit the applicability of the model with this population. For example, the model deals with change in intentional behavior, but patients with schizophrenia have significant difficulty sustaining intentional behavior. The model posits that change entails ongoing judgments about the pros and cons of substance use and one's ability to make changes, but schizophrenia is marked by cognitive deficits that interfere with both introspection and complex problem solving. The model also assumes a set of coping skills—the processes of change—that may not be in the repertoire of many individuals with schizophrenia.

Obstacles To Change

An extensive body of research on substance abuse and addiction in the general population indicates that critical factors in abstinence and controlled use of addictive substances include high levels of motivation to quit, the ability to exert self-control in the face of temptation or urges, cognitive and behavioral coping skills, and social support or social pressure (Hall, Wasserman, & Havassy, 1991; Miller, 1989; Rounsaville &

Carroll, 1992; Sandberg & Marlatt, 1991). Unfortunately, the abuser with schizophrenia often has limitations in each of these areas.

First, several factors can be expected to diminish motivation among patients with schizophrenia. Most patients suffer from some degree of generalized avolition and anergia as a function of hypodopaminergia in the frontal cortex (Weinberger, 1987), medication side effects or other social, psychological, and biological factors that contribute to negative symptoms (Andreasen, Flaum, Swayze, et al., 1985; Carpenter, Heinrichs, & Alphs, 1985). Thus they may lack the internal drive to initiate the complex behavioral routines required for abstinence. Another negative symptom, anhedonia, may compromise the experience of positive affect, thereby limiting patients' ability to experience pleasure and positive reinforcement in the absence of sub-stance use and restricting patients' appraisal of the advantages of absti-nence (Blanchard, Mueser, & Bellack, 1998). There are extensive data documenting that people with schizophrenia can learn a variety of skills and acquire new information (Bellack & Mueser, 1993), but there is scant evidence that they use acquired skills in the community—that is, that they are motivated to apply what they have learned—or that they can sustain motivation in the absence of short-term reinforcement, such as that provided by awarding tokens (Paul & Lentz, 1977).

A second factor that might compromise the applicability of the transtheoretical model for people with schizophrenia is the profound and pervasive cognitive impairment that characterizes the disorder. Research in the last 10 years has documented that patients with schizo-phrenia have prominent deficits in attention, memory, and higher-level cognitive processes such as abstract reasoning. They also have deficits in maintenance of set, which is the ability to sustain focus on a strategy or goals, and in the ability to integrate situational context or previous expe-rience into ongoing processing—that is, to use previous experience to direct current behavior—as well as in other executive functions (Gray, Feldon, Rawlins, et al., 1991). They have been shown to have profound deficits in problem-solving ability on both neuropsychological tests (Goldberg & Gold, 1995) and more applied measures of social judgment (Bellack, Morrison, & Mueser, 1989).

Several lines of evidence suggest that cognitive impairment is large-ly independent of symptoms and that many of these higher-level deficits may result from a subtle neurodevelopmental anomaly that is reflected in frontal-temporal lobe dysfunction (Bellack et al., 1989; Goldberg & Gold, 1995; Saykin, Shtasel, Gur, et al., 1994). Moreover, cognitive performance deficits are not substantially ameliorated by treatment with typical antipsychotic medications (Spohn & Strauss, 1989). The new atypical antipsychotic medications may have a more beneficial effect on cognition (Green, Marshall, Wishing, et al., 1997), but overall the data on this issue are mixed.

The higher-level cognitive deficits would make it very difficult for patients with schizophrenia to engage in the complex processes thought to be central to intentional change in behavior and the transtheoretical model. They have difficulty engaging in self-reflection or evaluating previous experiences to formulate realistic appraisals of self-efficacy. Deficits in the ability to draw connections between past experience and current stimuli (Hemsley, 1995) may impede the ability to relate their substance use to negative consequences over time and to modify their decisional balance accordingly.

Deficits in problem-solving capacity and abstract reasoning may impede the ability to evaluate the pros and cons of substance use or formulate realistic goals. Motivation to change and inclination to resist urges and social pressure vary over time for anyone coping with substance abuse, but people with schizophrenia have the added burden of being unable to reliably recall their intentions and commitments to change. Frontal-temporal impairments are associated with a phenomenon referred to as "forgetting to remember," which may make it difficult for patients to recall commitments to change or to use coping skills in the face of temptations or cravings to use substances.

Another constraint on change is related to the marked social impairment that characterizes the illness. People with schizophrenia are often unable to fulfill basic social roles, they have difficulty initiating and maintaining conversations, and they frequently are unable to achieve goals or have their needs met in situations requiring social interaction (Morrison & Bellack, 1987). The precursors of adult social disability can often be discerned in childhood (Lewine, Watt, Prentky, et al., 1980) and may be associated with early attentional impairments (Cornblatt, Lenzenweger, Dworkin, et al., 1992). Pronounced social impairment would leave patients with schizophrenia and substance abuse vulnerable in a number of ways: they would have difficulty developing social relationships with individuals who do not use drugs, resisting social pressure to use drugs, and developing the social support system needed to reduce use.

A New Treatment Approach

Many patients do reduce their use of substances, with or without treatment, so sustained motivation and self-directed behavior change is clearly possible. However, existing treatment models do not adequately account for the specific learning and performance deficits that are characteristic of the illness. We have developed a new treatment approach that takes into account the unique deficits in motivation, cognitive ability, and social skills associated with schizophrenia.

The treatment protocol contains four modules that are implemented sequentially. First, social skills and problem-solving training enables patients to develop social contacts with others who do not abuse substances and to be able to refuse social pressure to use substances. The second module focuses on education about the reasons for substance use, including habits, triggers, and craving, and the particular dangers of substance use for people with schizophrenia. The third module consists of motivational interviewing, goal setting for decreased substance use, and development of contingency contracts for clean urine screening tests. The fourth module consists of training in behavioral skills for coping with urges and high-risk situations and training in relapse prevention skills.

The basic training techniques have been used effectively for more than 20 years to teach social skills to persons with schizophrenia (Bellack & Mueser, 1993) and include instruction, modeling, role play, feedback and positive reinforcement, and homework. Patients repeatedly rehearse both behavioral skills, such as refusing unreasonable requests, and didactic information, such as information about the role of dopamine. They receive social reinforcement for their efforts.

Training is done in a small-group format, with six to eight participants, to ensure sufficient individual attention and opportunities to rehearse skills within the session. The 90-minute sessions are held twice a week for approximately 6 months. This treatment duration allows time for participants to develop motivation to change and work toward their goals. As an accommodation to the disorganization and life problems that are typical of these patients, make-up sessions are offered as needed.

Several steps are taken in consideration of cognitive deficits. Sessions are highly structured, and there is a strong emphasis on behavioral rehearsal. The didactic material is broken down into small units. Complex social repertoires, such as making friends and refusing substances, are divided into component elements, such as maintaining eye contact and being able to say no. Patients are first taught to perform the elements, and then gradually learn to combine them.

The intervention emphasizes over-learning of a few specific and relatively narrow skills that can be used automatically, thereby minimizing the cognitive load for decision making during stressful interactions. Extensive use is made of learning aides, including handouts and flip charts, to reduce the requirements on memory and attention. Patients are prompted as many times as necessary, and there is also extensive repetition of material within and across sessions.

The module focused on motivational interviewing is based on work done by Miller and Rollnick (1991). We have found it difficult to engage patients in discussions of the general benefits of continuing to use substances versus quitting. Rather than attempting to make a broad shift in the decisional balance about substance use, we attempt to identify one or two specific negative consequences that have a strong impact on the patient and that can serve as a prompt for change. For example, a patient who is on conditional release from jail may be engaged in a discussion of how continued substance use may lead to a return to jail. These negative consequences then serve as a stimulus for patients to make and adhere to substance use goals.

Because many patients with schizophrenia may not be able or willing to accept complete abstinence as a goal (Lehman et al., 1993; Test, Wallisch, Allness, et al., 1989), identifying more modest goals that the patient is comfortable with is particularly important. Consistent with a harm-avoidance model (Carey, 1996), we attempt to shape behavior by gradually encouraging the patient to focus on increasing periods of abstinence or on using less drugs or alcohol.

The motivational interviewing sessions are supplemented by a financial contingency for clean urine screening tests. The reward for clean tests is $1 during initial sessions and increases to $2 over successive sessions. The urine testing helps ensure honest reporting of drug use and also adds a modest incentive for abstinence. Clients whose urine samples are positive for drugs receive training in coping skills to help prevent future slips.

We do not require patients to set any goals about substance use when they enter the program. Rather, we first attempt to engage them in the program. One factor that deters many patients from committing to reduced use is low self-efficacy based on a long history of failure in achieving any goals. Consequently, we first attempt to enhance a sense of efficacy by building the experience of success into the program. Patients first achieve success in learning skills that are directed at starting conversations and refusing unreasonable requests. Only then is the focus shifted to social situations involving substance use. Patients have the opportunity to practice before they make a commitment to saying no. Hence, when we do help them to set goals, they have already had some success in practicing some of the skills needed to achieve their goals.

The content of the sessions on coping skills and relapse prevention is adapted from substance abuse programs based on social learning theory that have proven to be effective with less impaired patients (Annis & Davis, 1989; Hester & Miller, 1989; Marlatt & Gordon, 1985). Patients with schizophrenia have considerable difficulty with abstract concepts and in generalizing principles of action across situations. Rather than teaching generic problem-solving skills and coping strategies that can be adapted to a variety of situations, we focus on specific skills that are effective for handling a few key high-risk situations—for example, what to do when your brother or a specific friend offers you cocaine, rather than what to do when anyone offers it to you. Similarly, management of negative affect and interpersonal distress is addressed concretely using scenarios provided by the patient to practice alternate responses and highlight behaviors that could evoke more satisfying interactions.

Our treatment approach has evolved in the context of a behavioral treatment development grant from the National Institute on Drug Abuse. Between May 1996 and January 1998, a total of 80 patients have been enrolled in the program. We have been highly successful in engaging and retaining participants: the attrition rate of 38.5% compares very favorably with rates for other substance abuse programs reported in the literature, and no subject who completed the first 3 weeks of the program dropped out after that.

We have also been able to teach therapists to conduct the treatment according to a detailed manual. Independent ratings of adherence to the manual have averaged 96.6±4.9%, and ratings of competence in presenting the material in the manual have averaged 5±.2 on a 5-point scale. The results for the first 12 subjects to complete the entire finalized protocol are quite promising. Based on the in-session urine testing, six of the 12 had negative tests an average of 90.8% of the time (range=72.7 to 100%) over a 4.5-month period. Subjects who had good outcomes attended 80.9% of all sessions. Subjects who had poor outcomes attended 73.2% of sessions before urine testing began and only 43.6% afterwards, suggesting it had a pronounced impact. The next phase of the treatment development process will be a controlled clinical trial.

Further research is needed to elucidate why people with schizophrenia abuse drugs and alcohol, how they reduce substance use on their own, and how cognitive deficits influence the process of change. We are currently evaluating which elements of intentional change are relevant for individuals with schizophrenia who abuse substances and how to adapt constructs of the transtheoretical model of change for this population, including how to modify specific decisional considerations that will promote reduction of substance use and which processes of change are used most frequently. The findings will offer insight into how people with schizophrenia change their behavior and the extent to which traditional and innovative approaches are appropriate.

References

Andreasen, N. C., Flaum, M., Swayze, V. W., et al. (1985). Positive and negative symptoms in schizophrenia: A critical reappraisal. *Archives of General Psychiatry, 47*, 615–621.

Annis, H. M., & Davis, C. S. (1989). Relapse prevention. In R. K. Hester & W. R. Miller (Eds.), *Handbook of alcoholism treatment approaches.* New York: Pergamon.

Bellack, A. S. (1992). Cognitive rehabilitation for schizophrenia: Is it possible? Is it necessary? *Schizophrenia Bulletin, 18*, 43–50.

Bellack, A. S., Morrison, R. L., & Mueser, K. T. (1989). Social problem solving in schizophrenia. *Schizophrenia Bulletin, 15*, 101–116.

Bellack, A. S., & Mueser, K. T. (1993). Psychosocial treatment for schizophrenia. *Schizophrenia Bulletin, 19*, 317–336.

Blanchard, J. J., Mueser, K. T., & Bellack, A. S. (1998). Anhedonia, positive and negative affect, and social functioning in schizophrenia. *Schizophrenia Bulletin, 24*, 413–424.

Blankertz, L. E., & Cnaan, R. A. (1994). Assessing the impact of two residential programs for dually diagnosed homeless individuals. *Social Service Review, 68*, 536–560.

Carey, K. B. (1996). Substance use reduction in the context of outpatient psychiatric treatment: A collaborative, motivational, harm reduction approach. *Community Mental Health Journal, 32,* 291–306.

Carey, M. P., Carey, K. B., & Kalichman, S. C. (1997). Risk for human immunodeficiency virus (HIV) infection among persons with severe mental illnesses. *Clinical Psychology Review, 17,* 271–291.

Carpenter, W. T. J., Heinrichs, D. W., & Alphs, L. D. (1985). Treatment of negative symptoms. *Schizophrenia Bulletin, 11,* 440–452.

Cornblatt, B. A., Lenzenweger, M. F., Dworkin, R. H., et al. (1992). Childhood attentional dysfunctions predict social deficits in unaffected adults at risk for schizophrenia. *British Journal of Psychiatry, 161*(18), 59–64.

Cournos, F., & McKinnon, K. (1997). HIV seroprevalence among people with severe mental illness in the US: A critical review. *Clinical Psychology Review, 17,* 259–269.

DiClemente, C. C. (1991). Motivational interviewing and the stages of change. In W. R. Miller & S. Rollnick (Eds.), *Motivational interviewing: Preparing people to change addictive behavior.* New York: Guilford.

DiClemente, C. C. (1993). Changing addictive behaviors: A process perspective. *Current Directions in Psychological Science, 2,* 101–106.

DiClemente, C. C. (1994). If behaviors change, can personality be far behind? In T. Heatherton & J. Weinberger (Eds.), *Can personality change?* Washington, DC: American Psychological Association.

DiClemente, C. C., Fairhurst, S. K., & Piotrowski, N. A. (1995). The role of self-efficacy in the addictive behaviors. In J. Maddux (Ed.), *Self-Efficacy, adaption and adjustment: Theory, research and application.* New York: Plenum.

Dixon, L. B., Haas, G., Weiden, P. J., et al. (1991). Drug abuse in schizophrenic patients: Clinical correlates and reasons for use. *American Journal of Psychiatry, 148,* 224–230.

Drake, R. E., McHugo, G. J., & Noordsy, D. L. (1993). Treatment of alcoholism among schizophrenia outpatients: 4-year outcomes. *American Journal of Psychiatry, 150,* 328–329.

Drake, R. E., Osher, F. C., & Wallach, M. A. (1989). Alcohol use and abuse in schizophrenia: A prospective community study. *Journal of Nervous and Mental Disease, 177,* 408–414.

Goldberg, T. E., & Gold, J. M. (1995). Neurocognitive deficits in schizophrenia. In S. R. Hirsch & D. R. Weinberger (Eds.), *Schizophrenia.* Cambridge, England: Blackwell Science.

Goodman, L. A., Rosenberg, S. D., Mueser, K. T., et al. (1997). Physical and sexual assult history in women with serious mental illness: Prevalence, impact, treatment, and future research directions. *Schizophrenia Bulletin, 23,* 685–696.

Gray, J. A., Feldon, J., Rawlins, J. N. P., et al. (1991). The neuropsychology of schizoprenia:. *Behavioral and Brain Sciences, 14,* 1–84.

Green, M. F., Marshall, B. D., Wishing, W. C., et al. (1997). Does risperidone improve verbal working memory in treatment-resistant schizophrenia. *American Journal of Psychiatry, 154,* 799–804.

Hall, S. M., Wasserman, D. A., & Havassy, B. E. (1991). Relapse prevention. In R. W. Pickens & C. G. Leukefeld & C. R. Schuster (Eds.), *Improving drug abuse treatment.* Rockville, MD: NIDA Research Monograph 106 National Institute on Drug Abuse.

Hemsley, D. R. (1995). Schizophrenia: A cognitive model and its implications for psychological intervention. *Behavior Modification, 20,* 139–169.

Hester, R. K., & Miller, W. R. (1989). Self-control training. In R. K. Hester & W. R. Miller (Eds.), *Handbook of alcoholism treatment approaches.* New York: Pergamon.

Hooley, J. (1985). Expressed emotion: A review of the critical literature. *Clinical Psychology Review, 5,* 119–140.

Jerrell, J. M., & Ridgely, M. S. (1995). Comparative effectiveness of three approaches to serving people with severe mental illness and substance abuse disorders. *Journal of Nervous and Mental Disease, 183,* 566–576.

Koob, G. F. (1992). Drugs of abuse: Anatomy, pharmacology, and function of rewards pathways. *TiPS, 13,* 177–184.

Lehman, A. F., & Dixon, L. B. (1995). *Double jeopardy: Chronic mental illness and substance use disorders.* Newark, NJ: Harwood Academic.

Lehman, A. F., Herron, J. D., Schwartz, R. P., et al. (1993). Rehabilitation for young adults with severe mental illness and substance use disorders. *Journal of Nervous and Mental Disease, 181,* 86–90.

Lewine, R. J., Watt, N. F., Prentky, R. A., & et al. (1980). Childhood social competence in functionally disordered psychiatric patients and in normals. *Journal of Abnormal Psychology, 89,* 132–138.

Marlatt, G. A., & Gordon, J. R. (1985). *Relapse prevention: Maintenance strategies in the treatment of addictive behaviors.* New York: Guilford.

McHugo, G. J., Drake, R. E., Burton, H. L., et al. (1995). A scale for assessing the stage of substance abuse treatment in persons with severe mental illness. *Journal of Nervous and Mental Disease, 183,* 762–767.

Miller, W. R. (1989). Increasing motivation to change. In R. K. Hester & W. R. Miller (Eds.), *Handbook of alcoholism treatment approaches.* New York: Pergamon.

Morrison, R. L., & Bellack, A. S. (1987). The social functioning of schizophrenic patients and research issues. *Schizophrenia Bulletin, 13,* 715–726.

Mueser, K. T., Bellack, A. S., Douglas, M. S., et al. (1991). Prediction of social skill acquisition in schizophrenic and major affective disorder patients from memory and symptomatology. *Psychiatry Research, 32,* 281–296.

Mueser, K. T., Bennett, M., & Kushner, M. G. (1995). Epidemiology of substance use disorders among persons with chronic mental illness. In A. F. Lehman & L. B. Dixon (Eds.), *Double jeopardy: Chronic mental illness and substance use disorders.* Newark, NJ: Harwood Academic.

Mueser, K. T., Yarnold, P. R., & Bellack, A. S. (1992). Diagnostic and demographic correlates of substance abuse in schizophrenia and major affective disorder. *Acta Psychiatrica Scandinavica, 85,* 48–55.

Noordsy, D. S., Drake, R. E., Teague, G. B., et al. (1991). Subjective experiences related to alcohol use among schizophrenics. *Journal of Nervous and Mental Disease, 179,* 410–414.

Osher, F. C., & Kofoed, L. L. (1989). Treatment of patients with psychiatric and psychoactive substance abuse disorder. *Hospital and Community Psychiatry, 40,* 1025–1030.

Paul, G. L., & Lentz, R. J. (1977). *Psychosocial treatment of chronic mental patients: Milieu versus social-learning programs.* Cambridge, MA: Harvard University Press.

Pope, H. G., Ionescu-Pioggia, M., Aizley, H. G., et al. (1990). Drug use and life style among college undergraduates in 1989: A comparison with 1969 and 1978. *American Journal of Psychiatry, 147,* 998–1001.

Prochaska, J. O., & DiClemente, C. C. (1984). *The transtheoretical approach: Crossing the traditional boundaries of therapy.* Malabar, FL: Krieger.

Prochaska, J. O., & DiClemente, C. C. (1992). Stages of change in the modification of problem behaviors. In M. Hersen & R. M. Eisler & P. M. Miller (Eds.), *Progress in behavior modification No. 28.* New York: Academic.

Prochaska, J. O., DiClemente, C. C., & Norcross, J. C. (1992). In search of how people change: Applications to addictive behaviors. *American Psychologist, 47*(9), 1102–1114.

Regier, D. A., Farmer, M. E., Rae, D. S., et al. (1990). Comorbidity of mental disorders with alcohol and other drug abuse. *JAMA, 264,* 2511–2518.

Rothfleisch, J. (1997). *Comparison of two measures of stages of change among drug abusers.* University of Houston, Department of Psychology Unpublished doctoral dissertation.

Rounsaville, B. J., & Carroll, K. M. (1992). Individual psychotherapy for drug abusers. In J. H. Lowinson & P. Ruiz & R. B. Millman et al. (Eds.), *Substance abuse: A comprehensive textbook.* Baltimore, MD: Williams & Wilkins.

Sandberg, G. G., & Marlatt, G. A. (1991). Relapse prevention. In D. A. Ciraulo & R. I. Shader (Eds.), *Clinical manual of chemical dependence.* Washington, DC: American Psychiatric Press.

Saykin, A. J., Shtasel, D. L., Gur, R. E., & et al. (1994). Neuropsychological deficits in neuroleptic naive patients with first-episode schizophrenia. *Archives of General Psychiatry, 51,* 124–131.

Spohn, H. E., & Strauss, M. E. (1989). Relation of neuropleptic and anticholinergic medication to cognitive functions in schizophrenia. *Journal of Abnormal Psychology, 4,* 367–380.

Test, M. A., Wallisch, L. S., Allness, D. J., et al. (1989). Substance use in young adults with schizophrenic disorders. *Schizophrenia Bulletin, 15,* 465–476.

Velaquez, M. (1997). *Psychiatric severity and behavior change in alcoholism: The relation of the transtheoretical model variables to psychiatric distress in dually diagnosed patients.* University of Texas, School of Public Health Unpublished doctoral dissertation.

Velicer, W. F., DiClemente, C. C., Prochaska, J. O., et al. (1985). Decisional balance measure for assessing and predicting smoking status. *Journal of Personality and Social Psychology, 48,* 1279–1289.

Weinberger, D. R. (1987). Implications of normal brain development for the pathogenesis of schizophrenia. *Archives of General Psychiatry, 44,* 660–669.

Group Treatment for Dually Diagnosed Clients

Kim T. Mueser and Douglas L. Noordsy

This article originally appeared in *New Directions for Mental Health Services,* Summer 1996, 70, 33–51 and is reprinted with permission.

Kim T Mueser, Ph.D., is associate professor of psychiatry and community and family medicine at Dartmouth Medical School and a senior researcher at the New Hampshire-Dartmouth Psychiatric Research Center. Douglas L. Noordsy, M.D., is assistant professor of psychiatry at Dartmouth Medical School and a research psychiatrist at the New Hampshire-Dartmouth Psychiatric Research Center.

Group treatment is a widely practiced intervention for persons with dual diagnoses. This chapter reviews the rationale for group treatment and discusses four different approaches to group intervention: 12-step, educational-supportive, social skills, and stagewise treatment.

It is now widely accepted that dually diagnosed individuals require interventions that simultaneously address both mental health and substance use disorders. In addition to recognizing the need to treat both dual disorders when present, integrated treatment models have embraced the concept of *stages of recovery* from substance use disorder. Accordingly, treatment must motivate clients to address their substance abuse prior to attempting to reduce substance use (Miller & Rollnick, 1991; Prochaska, Velicer, DiClemente, & Fava, 1988). Drake et al. (1993) have proposed four stages of treatment designed to provide maximally relevant interventions: engagement (client is not engaged in treatment), persuasion (client is engaged in treatment but is not convinced of the importance of reducing substance use), active treatment (client is attempting to reduce substance use), and relapse prevention (client has reduced or stopped substance use and is trying to prevent relapses). The stage concept provides a heuristic to clinicians by identifying the critical goals at each stage, and leads to the selection of stage-specific interventions (for example, at the persuasion stage the clinician works to establish awareness of the consequences of substance use).

A core component of integrated treatment programs is the inclusion of group-based intervention. There are three reasons for including group treatment. First, there is a strong tradition of nonprofessional self-help groups such as Alcoholics Anonymous (AA) in the primary addiction field. The group format is an ideal setting for capitalizing on the common need for support and identification shared by persons with an addiction. Second, substance abuse among psychiatric clients frequently occurs in a social context (Dixon et al., 1991; Test, Wallisch, Allness, & Ripp, 1989). Addressing substance use-related issues in a group setting makes it clear to clients that they are not alone and provides an opportunity for the sharing of experiences and coping strategies. Third, there are economical advantages to offering group therapy rather than individual therapy because less clinician time is required.

Models of Group Treatment

Different approaches to group treatment can be divided into four general models: 12-step, broad-based educational-supportive, social skills training, and stagewise. Although this categorization facilitates the discussion of different group methods, many interventions are hybrids of more than one model (for example, stagewise treatment may include elements of 12-step, social skills training, and educational-supportive models). Furthermore, for group intervention to be effective it must be provided in the context of a comprehensive treatment program, including elements such as ongoing assessment, case management, and pharmacotherapy (Drake et al., 1993).

Twelve-Step Models

Twelve-step models are based on the self-help group approach popularized by AA and adapted for other substances or disorders (narcotics addiction or gambling, for instance). A number of different approaches to dual diagnosis include aspects of 12-step programs, such as clinician-led groups that prepare clients for community AA-type meetings and consumer-led self-help meetings with a focus on individuals with dual diagnoses. The clinician-led models, described by Minkoff (1989) and Bartels and Thomas (1991), include 12-step principles and philosophy adapted from the AA model blended with education and support for mental illness management. Treatment is usually delivered by clinicians with some personal or professional experience with the 12-step model working in a mental health system. Their focus is on integrating substance abuse treatment with mental health care. These groups promote supplementary attendance at AA meetings but attempt to deliver comprehensive treatment through the group to those who never attend.

Professionally Assisted Pre-AA Group

We have previously described the difficulty persons with dual disorders have linking to self-help groups for substance abuse (Noordsy, Schwab, Fox, & Drake, 1996). We therefore designed a pre-AA model of group treatment for the New Hampshire study of dual diagnosis. This model is designed to facilitate the linkage of clients to self-help treatment in the community by developing an awareness of the consequences of substance use, motivation for treatment, and familiarity with the 12-step approach. Although initial work in this model parallels the persuasion model by necessity (see section on stagewise treatment), the language and milieu of the group differ. Twelve-step concepts such as denial, rationalization, working the steps, and surrender are central to the pre-AA group but not in persuasion groups. Members are also encouraged to attend self-help meetings and listen to others' stories to further their motivation to change.

The group discusses typical barriers clients experience to attending self-help groups, such as social discomfort, the emphasis on religion, and the negative stance some AA members have toward psychotropic medications, and strategies for overcoming those barriers. Members' attendance at self-help meetings and their reactions to them are regularly reviewed. Although pre-AA groups are clearly distinguished from 12-step meetings, some rituals, such as reading aloud from 12-step books and closing meetings by holding hands and reciting a prayer together, are practiced in group to increase members' comfort with them and to stimulate discussion. The active treatment phase of this model is attending AA or other self-help meetings with sobriety as a goal. Members in this phase are encouraged to continue attending the pre-AA group to serve as mentors to their peers.

Several authors have described 12-step self-help groups that specialize in serving a membership with dual disorders (Bricker, 1994; Hendrickson & Schmal, 1994). These include groups initiated by community AA volunteers (Kurtz et al., 1995; Woods, 1991) and groups initiated by professionals (Caldwell & White, 1991). The former follow a standard AA format but also include discussion of "recovery" from mental illness (Kurtz et al., 1995). The latter generally follow an AA format with some modifications, such as allowing professional involvement.

Broad-Based Educational-Supportive Models

This approach posits that change in substance abuse occurs because of education about the effects of substances and social support from others experiencing similar difficulties. An explicit educational curriculum is provided, interspersed with the sharing of personal experiences and open discussion of recent substance abuse. Other than a shared focus on education and engendering social support among group members, applications of this model vary widely in terms of their eligibility requirements, duration of treatment, and specific clinical methods employed (for example, psychoeducational techniques, skills training, and problem solving).

Some approaches limit participation in the group to persons who are motivated to reduce substance abuse (Hellerstein & Meehan, 1987; Hellerstein, Rosenthal, & Miner, 1995), whereas others do not (Alfs & McLellan, 1992; Sciacca, 1987; Straussman, 1985). The approach described by Hellerstein, Rosenthal, and Miner differs from others in that groups are offered on a time-unlimited basis. Common across the different educational-supportive group treatments is avoidance of direct confrontation, maintaining an affectively benign and supportive milieu, helping clients understand how substance abuse affects their psychiatric illness, and familiarizing clients with how AA-type groups in the community work. For example, in Sciacca's (1987) group, speakers from AA and Narcotics Anonymous (NA) are invited to describe their groups to members.

In general, the educational-supportive model is the least theoretically distinct model of integrated group treatment for dually diagnosed individuals. The approach is compatible with stagewise treatments without explicitly endorsing the stage model of recovery. For example, the approaches of Alfs and McClellan (1992), Sciacca (1987), and Straussman (1985) resemble persuasion groups, whereas Hellerstein and Meehan's (1987) groups resemble active treatment groups (described below). Members are encouraged to try AA and other self-help groups, but the main purpose of educational-supportive groups is not to prepare clients for self-help groups in the community. Finally, although some skills training techniques may be used in some of these groups, they do not embrace a social-learning conceptualization of treating dual disorders.

Social Skills Training

Social skills training (SST) refers to a social learning approach to improving interpersonal competence through modeling, role-playing, positive and corrective feedback, and homework assignments (Liberman, DeRisi, & Mueser, 1989). SST procedures have traditionally been used to teach interpersonal skills, but can also be used to teach self-care skills such as grooming and hygiene. Although SST methods are employed by other group models, the SST model differs in two respects. First, the SST model conceptualizes the needs of dually diagnosed persons in terms of skill deficits that interfere with the ability to develop a lifestyle free from substance abuse. Thus, deficits in areas such as the ability to resist offers to use substances, recreational skills, or skill in managing interpersonal conflicts are thought to contribute to substance abuse. Second, because the focus of SST is on teaching new skills or relearning old ones, an emphasis is placed on *explicit* modeling of skills and repeated behavioral rehearsals, guided by the principle that over-practice of skills is necessary to achieving mastery (Ericsson & Charness, 1994). In contrast, other group models are more likely to facilitate skill development by *implicit* use of modeling (for example, skills are used by leaders, but are not specifically demonstrated for participants) and talking about skills, with only occasional use of role plays and behaviorally based feedback.

In order to teach an array of specific skills to clients, SST models employ detailed, preplanned curricula and follow a specific agenda. Despite the structure of the groups, the SST approach places high value on fostering supportive relationships between group members, improving understanding about the effects of substances, and addressing the emergent needs of clients (Jerrell & Ridgely, 1995). As with other models, specific SST programs vary in their content, format, and structure. Nikkel (1994) has described a long-term SST program based on training modules developed by Liberman et al. (1987), with skills taught in areas such as relationships, resisting offers to use substances, self-care, money management, sleep hygiene, leisure, and vocational and educational functioning. The group format and other formats (for example, family psychoeducation and individual therapy) are used to teach skills. Carey, Carey, and Meisler (1990) describe a skills training approach in which problem-solving skills are systematically taught to outpatients to enable them to more effectively manage stress and interpersonal situations. We have recently developed a time-limited inpatient SST group with a focus on teaching interpersonal skills, strategies for managing negative emotions, and alternative recreational activities (Mueser et al., 1995).

As with the educational-supportive group model, a key distinction between the social skills model and stagewise treatment is that the skills approach does not formally incorporate the distinction between persuasion and active treatment into the group. Similarly, skills training and other behavioral strategies are typically included in stagewise treatment (as indicated in the following section), as well as a range of other clinical methods. Consistent with the other group models, the SST model incorporates education into the curriculum and endorses the potential benefits of self-help groups such as AA (for example, Nikkel, 1994).

Stagewise Treatment

Stagewise treatment refers to group interventions designed to meet the unique needs of clients at different stages of recovery from substance abuse. Over the past several years, we have developed and implemented stagewise group treatments at different community mental health centers throughout New Hampshire (Noordsy & Fox, 1991). Although four different stages of recovery have been proposed, for the purposes of group treatment, clients in the second stage (persuasion) participate in one type of group (a *persuasion group*), and clients in the last two stages (active treatment and relapse prevention) participate in a second type of group (an *active treatment group*). Clients in the engagement phase may attend some persuasion groups, but regular attendance does not typically occur until they complete this stage.

The unique feature of this approach is recognition that many individuals with dual diagnoses lack motivation for treatment, and that motivation must be developed for treatment to succeed. This approach draws on the techniques of the other three group intervention models, using them as they are relevant for individuals within groups and subdividing their use across two motivational stages. Leaders must be skilled in the techniques of the other approaches to be able to use them when needed.

Persuasion Groups. By definition, clients in the engagement and persuasion stages of recovery do not recognize that they have a substance abuse problem, and do not endorse the goal of reducing substance use. Therefore the primary goal of persuasion groups is to develop clients' awareness of how substances complicate their lives. A combination of clinical strategies is employed to assist participants in examining the consequences of their substance use, including education and motivational interviewing techniques (Miller & Rollnick, 1991), such as empathic listening and helping clients perceive the discrepancy between their personal goals and substance use. Persuasion groups can be conducted either with inpatients (Kofoed & Keys, 1988) or outpatients (Noordsy & Fox, 1991). We provide below a brief description of how these groups are conducted on an outpatient basis at several community mental health centers in New Hampshire.

The optimal format for groups is to have two leaders, one with expertise in treating mental illness and the other with expertise in addictive disorders. Groups are held weekly, often shortly after the weekend so that periods of heavy substance use are likely to be fresh in clients' minds. Some groups run for 45–60 minutes, whereas others have two 20–30 minute sessions separated by a short break. Brief sessions reduce the intensity and enable clients with limited attention spans to participate. Groups are open to all clients and weekly attendance is encouraged but not required. Because initial attendance is usually a problem, the groups serve refreshments, include activities (for example, community trips and videos), and are extremely supportive. Clients need not acknowledge a problem with substances in order to attend and those who have been using substances are allowed to attend group if they behave appropriately.

Persuasion groups are not confrontational. They assume instead that recognition of a substance abuse problem occurs over time in the context of peer group support and education. The stated goal of the group is to help members learn more about the role that alcohol and drugs play in their lives. Group leaders provide didactic material on substances and mental illness, but they spend most of their effort facilitating peer interactions and feedback about substance use. Leaders actively limit the level of affect, monitor psychotic behaviors, and maintain the group's focus on substance abuse. Members who turn up at group inebriated are allowed to participate (if they are not disruptive), and members are permitted to leave early if they choose. Those who are reluctant to participate are invited to contribute at least once or twice during each meeting. The overriding theme is to encourage participation in the group and to gently, repeatedly expose members to opportunities to explore the reinforcing and destructive effects of their substance use.

Persuasion group sessions often begin with a review of each member's use of substances over the previous week. This discussion is nonjudgmental so that members feel safe in reporting their use honestly. As a member discusses a recent period of intoxication, others help to identify antecedents, including internal emotional states, and consequences of use. All members are encouraged to contribute to this process, perhaps offering advice or relating a similar experience. Leaders field questions and provide brief information on addiction, the effects of various substances on physical and mental health, and the interactions between drugs and medications. Relevant films, short readings, or group outings are occasionally used to stimulate interest and discussion if needed, although lengthy didactic presentations are avoided. Group members often ask leaders about their own use of substances. Leaders are typically open about their use; those who are recovering from addiction may share their own experiences, and those who are not honestly relate their past experimentation, subsequent consequences if any, and current choices, facilitating discussion of distinctions between use and abuse.

Active Treatment Groups. These groups are focused, behavioral, and aimed at reducing substance use and promoting abstinence. Members working toward a common goal of abstinence actively give each other feedback and support. Unlike persuasion groups, there is an assumption of sobriety during participation in active treatment groups. Although not required, members are encouraged to try out self-help meetings as a form of active treatment work or one route to sobriety. Members often accompany each other to meetings. The group work includes review of members' experiences using self-help and focuses on developing the skills to successfully negotiate a self-help program (at times similar to pre-AA groups).

Behavioral principles of addiction treatment (Monti, Abrams, Kadden, & Cooney, 1989) guide active treatment groups. This approach is less stimulating than some others and addresses the development of skills that dually diagnosed clients often lack. Members learn social skills through role plays and group interaction and use one another for support and assistance in attending self-help meetings. They are trained in assertiveness, giving and receiving criticism, drink or drug refusal skills, making new friends, and managing thoughts about alcohol or other drug use. Clients learn to develop constructive substitutes for substance use, to manage craving, difficult emotions, or symptoms. Another common focus of these groups is on learning coping strategies. For example, clients experiencing cravings for substances may be taught the use of imagery by transforming positive images for a desired substance into negative images, such as hangovers, psychotic relapses, or fights.

Clients also learn to recognize situations that increase their risk of substance use and to use relapse prevention techniques for managing these situations (Marlatt & Gordon, 1985). For example, relaxation training and principles of sleep hygiene are used to regain control over anxiety and insomnia that may lead to the use of substances. Many members need help with concrete situations such as learning how to set limits on substance-abusing friends. The cognitive and behavioral chain of events leading up to episodes of craving or substance use are identified and strategies for preventing future episodes are developed. Members are encouraged to write down their internal or interpersonal struggles during the week so that they can work on them in the group. Leaders help them discover and label strategies for managing emotional experiences that they had been obliterating with substance use and to appreciate the gradual improvements in their mental health and stability that come with sobriety. Members often gain a greater sense of responsibility for managing both of their illnesses during this process. When relapses do occur, group members offer support and help in developing plans to minimize the severity of the relapse in order to arrest the backslide to substance abuse and dependence.

Combined Persuasion and Active Treatment Groups. In some settings where persuasion and active treatment groups have been running for several years, it may be advantageous to combine the two formats into a single group, despite the fact that all clients participate in the same group, intervention is tailored to the specific stage of recovery for each client. We provide several clinical vignettes illustrating stagewise treatment in a combined group.

Clinical Vignettes
The following vignettes illustrate typical interactions at different stages of group development in the stagewise model.

Beginning the Group
The leaders start group by asking each member to describe their use of substances or craving for them over the past week. This exercise

is used to provide continuity from group to group and to develop material for the session.

Leader: Good morning. Let's go ahead and get started. How was your week, George?

George: I'm still drinking and smoking and I just can't stop. I'm awake half the night because I can't breathe, and I cough and hack my guts out every morning. I've got to stop. It's killing me.

Leader: You've been struggling with this for a while. Would you like to develop a plan for quitting in group today? There's a lot of experience in this room that you could put to work for you.

George: Couldn't hurt.

Leader: Good, we'll get back to that. How was your week, Jim?

Jim: This has been a pretty intense week for me. I didn't sleep much over the weekend and I got pretty manic.

Leader: Were you using?

Jim: I haven't had a drink in 3 months. Drinking didn't have anything to do with how I was feeling this weekend. I was going through some intense personal exploration and my medications got all screwed up.

Leader: You have often mentioned smoking pot to the group.

Jim: Well, sure I was smoking, but that had nothing to do with it. I smoke less when I'm manic because I don't need it as much.

Leader: Would it be fair to look at that some more later?

Jim: Fair enough.

Leader: How was your week, Brian?

Brian: Pretty lousy. I couldn't sleep good and I had pains in my neck and back and shoulders. I hurt all over.

Leader: Were you using?

Brian: No, it's been a year since I've had a drink or a drug. I didn't want to wreck that, but I sure was thinking that a beer would help kill the pain.

Developing a Plan to Quit

George is a 52-year-old divorced male with diagnoses of schizophrenia and alcohol dependence. His psychotic illness had onset in his mid-thirties and was characterized by frequent medication discontinuation and episodes of behaviorally disruptive psychosis. He has used alcohol heavily since his teens except for 5 years during his marriage when his wife disallowed it. During one severe episode of drinking and psychosis he stole a car in response to his delusions. He was convicted of auto theft and his probation required medication compliance and abstinence. Since the probation ended 3 years ago he has remained medication compliant and has not had another severe psychotic episode, but he returned to daily drinking. He attended the stagewise group regularly during his probation, but now drops out for a month or two at a time. He is in group for the first time in 5 weeks today. He has repeatedly identified an abstinence goal and made attempts at quitting drinking, placing him in the early active treatment stage.

Leader: George, you mentioned a lot of problems related to smoking and drinking. Would you like some help figuring out how to change?

George: Well, I'm moving to a new place so I was thinking of quitting then. Is that what you mean?

Leader: That's excellent. Starting in a new place would help to avoid craving being triggered by the reminders of using around your old home. Would you like to pick a quit date?

George: I'm going to be way out in the boonies. I just won't bring it with me and I won't go out to see anyone anymore. Everyone I know drinks and smokes, even my girlfriend. I've had enough of her. I wish someone would just lock me up in detox for a few weeks, but they don't do that anymore. I can't do it around my friends.

Bill: I wouldn't be alone. That'll drive you to drink.

Mary: Won't you get bored? I'd be pacing the floor thinking about using the whole time.

George: No, I like to be alone. When I quit before, 9 years ago, I just went out in the woods for a few weeks and quit everything, even medication.

Leader: How did that work out?

George: Well I ended up in the hospital, but I didn't drink for 2 years.

Jim: You don't want to end up back in there. Besides, you'll need to go to the store sometime and there's always beer there begging you to take it home. I think you should go to AA.

Leader: Maybe we can develop a plan using the things that worked for you before and some of these other suggestions to help you get to your goal. One thing that might help is establishing a date and time now for starting your new healthy lifestyle. You are less likely to just keep using out of habit and miss the opportunity of using your move to help you if you make a clear plan for yourself.

George: Well, I'm moving this weekend.

Leader: Would you like to be using during the move?

George: Yeah, I'll probably be drinking some that day. I'll be all in by Saturday night.

Leader: Would you like to stop using then?

George: Yeah, that's it. I'll stop using Saturday night at, say six o'clock.

Leader: What other things have helped people to get sober?

Jim: I needed to have people to talk to get through it. Sober people. That's why I went to AA.

George: The guy I'm renting from is real nice and he doesn't drink or smoke. I can hang around with him. I guess I could try AA again. I went years ago on probation but it just made me want to drink more to hear all those stories.

Leader: It might be worth trying AA again. You might hear those stories differently now that you want to quit. Could you use any family members for support?

George: They're all drunks too for the most part except for my sister. She quit about 3 years ago. She goes to AA actually.

Jim: You could talk to her for support and ask her to take you to a few meetings, too.

Leader: Would the folks in this group be willing to help George out if he needed support?

Jim: Sure, call me anytime George. We could have coffee and talk.

Mary: I'd be happy to help out, but I don't have a phone. I still live in the same place.

Brian: Yeah, I'll help.

Leader: I'll make sure your case manager knows about this plan so she can work with you on it, too. You know, Mary mentioned craving before. Maybe we can generate a list of things to do to get through a craving.

George: When I get craving a drink I can just taste it. It's hard to think of anything else. That's what gets me.

Mary: You could keep a list with you that tells you what to do.

Leader: You know, Mary's right. It's hard to think when you are in the middle of a craving, but if you have a list handy you can just read it. Why don't each of us come up with a personal list of things to do to get through a craving. I'll pass around index cards and let's each write down ten things we could do to get through a craving and then we'll go around the room and share ideas....

Persuasion Work

Jim is a 35-year-old man with advanced degrees in philosophy who has been diagnosed with a bipolar affective disorder. He used alcohol and other drugs extensively throughout his postsecondary schooling and subsequent employment. He suffered a head injury in a car accident at age twenty-five and subsequently developed chronic bipolar symptoms with psychotic features exacerbated by severe alcoholism and marijuana abuse. Jim has attended stagewise treatment groups intermittently in the last 2 years. Initially he did persuasion stage work in group, recognized severe physical consequences of his alcohol use, and developed a goal of abstinence from alcohol. He developed active treatment plans in individual and group settings and used AA meetings as well. During this time his group participation became erratic, attending for several sessions after each relapse back to alcohol use and psychosis. After several state hospital admissions he reestablished an abstinence goal and has been attending group regularly for 9 months. He had a brief, severe relapse to drinking 3 months ago and has been abstinent from alcohol since. He continues marijuana use. He is therefore doing relapse prevention work around alcohol, but still requires persuasion stage work focusing on his marijuana use.

Leader: Jim, you mentioned that you had a rough weekend with some medication problems and mania, and you were smoking some too.

Jim: Nothing different from usual. Actually when I'm manic I smoke less; I don't need it as much. It's just that I cut back on the lithium for a little while and things got a little out of hand. I got pretty psychotic, but I just took some [chlorpromazine] and got back in control. I'm all set now.

Leader: How much were you smoking?

Jim: Oh, you know, whenever I got the chance. Marijuana has been a really positive drug for me. I don't look at it as a drug for me any more than I would psychiatric medications. It's a tool that helps me have insights and understand life.

Leader: Were you smoking any more than usual last week?

Jim: Well, I did get a good supply last week so you could say that I was smoking a fair amount until it ran out.

Leader: When did it run out?

Jim: Friday night.

Leader: When did you get psychotic?

Jim: I don't know. I guess it started Friday during the day.

Leader: Do you like being psychotic?

Jim: It's interesting to a point but I don't like getting real paranoid. I usually quit smoking before it gets too bad.

Leader: But you didn't this time. How come?

Jim: It was really good stuff and I had a lot of it. I guess I just didn't want to stop badly enough.

Leader: What do you think, Brian?

Brian: I don't know. Sounds like he couldn't stop.

Leader: George?

George: I know where he's coming from. It's hard to say no when it's right there under your nose.

Leader: And you usually don't feel the consequences until it's too late. Jim, no one can decide what's right for you except yourself but it sounds like your pot use wasn't all that pleasurable this week.

Jim: Yeah, I was pretty hurting by the end.

Leader: What did it cost you to buy?

Jim: Forty bucks.

Leader: Was it worth it?

Jim: If you'd have asked me Thursday I would have said yes. I don't know now.

Common and Unique Factors in Group Models

Different models of integrated group treatment share many common characteristics. All the approaches educate clients about the effects of substance use and avoid the confrontation typical of many programs for primary substance abuse. Each of the models strives to create a supportive social milieu within the group and encourages socialization between members outside of the group. All the models also recognize the role that psychiatric disorders play in increasing clients' risk to substance abuse (for example, symptoms, stigma, and lack of leisure activities) and attempt to address illness-related factors that may contribute to this vulnerability through education, skills training, and supportive techniques. Finally, all the models endorse the potential benefits of self-help organizations such as AA in aiding clients in their recovery from substance use disorders.

The models of group treatment can be distinguished primarily in their philosophy of recovery. By its very nature, only stagewise treatment explicitly identifies goals and targets interventions based on the client's stage of recovery and focuses on self-assessment of motivational development as a prerequisite to sobriety-oriented work. Twelve-step groups have a strong orientation toward recovery based on the traditional AA model and toward trying to engage clients in self-help groups available in the community. The skills training approach places a premium on the acquisition of new skills and downplays the possible role of insight in aiding recovery. Although none of these foci are unique to one model, their emphasis differs across the models. Thus the 12-step, educational-supportive, stagewise, and social skills models are each based on somewhat different but compatible philosophies. Overall, the integrated approaches to group treatment have more in common than they are unique.

Research on Group Treatment

Over the past decade a number of studies have examined the effectiveness of group treatment in the context of integrated programs for dually diagnosed persons. The results of these studies are summarized in table 1. As can be seen from inspection of this table, research has been limited by the paucity of controlled studies, especially those involving random assignment to treatment groups. None of the three studies in which clients were randomly assigned to group treatment and no group treatment categories found an added effect for the group intervention (Carey, Carey, & Meisler, 1990; Hellerstein, Rosenthal, & Miner, 1995; Lehman, Herron, Schwartz, & Myers, 1993). These studies were limited, however, by the relatively brief intervention period (ranging from 6 weeks to 1 year), small sample sizes (ranging from 29 to 54), and nonattendance in the group condition (for example, Lehman, Herron, Schwartz, & Myers, 1993). Bond, McDonel, Miller, and Pensec's (1991) quasi-experimental study was unique in that clients who received group treatment over 18 months improved more in substance abuse outcomes than clients who received either ACT or standard treatment. It is possible that nonrandom assignment of clients to treatment condition con-

Table I

Summary of Research on Group Treatment for Dually Diagnosed Clients

Investigator	Number of Clients	Treatment Groups	Duration of Treatment	Research Design	Outcomes
Kofoed et al. (1986)	32	Educational-supportive	Up to 2 years (weekly sessions)	Pre-post	35% of clients remained in treatment for more than 3 months. Clients who remained in treatment spent less time in hospital.
Hellerstein and Meehan (1987)	10	Educational-supportive	1 year (weekly sessions)	Pre-post	50% of clients remained in treatment 1 year. Clients who remained in treatment spent less time in hospital.
Kofoed and Keys (1988)	109	Stagewise (persuasion)	Inpatient-brief (2 sessions/wk.)	Non-experimental comparison of two	Clients in treatment group referred for outpatient substance abuse treatment more than clients who did not receive treatment group. No differences in rehospitalization over 6 months.
	109	No inpatient group treatment			
Carey et al. (1990)	17	Social skills training (problem solving)	6 weeks (2 sessions/wk.)	Random assignment to group/no group treatment	At 1-month follow-up, no difference in problem-solving skills between groups.
	12	No group treatment			

Table 1 *(continued)*

Investigator	Number of Clients	Treatment Groups	Duration of Treatment	Research Design	Outcomes
Bond et al. (1991)	23	Educational-supportive	18 months (variable group session frequency)	Quasi-experimental	Group treatment and ACT clients remained in treatment longer.
	31	Assertive community treatment (ACT) (no group treatment)			Group treatment clients had fewer hospitalizations; ACT clients spent less time in hospital.
	43	Control (no group treatment)			Group treatment clients used less alcohol and drugs. All clients improved in quality of life.
Noordsy and Fox (1991)	18	Stagewise (weekly sessions)	3 years	Pre-post	Approximately 60% of all clients attained stable abstinence and 80% of group attendance.
Alfs and McClellan	145	Educational-supportive	6–8 weeks (daily meetings in day hospital; weekly evening aftercare)	Pre-post	66% clients completed program 33% of clients in active treatment relapsed.
Lehman et al. (1993)	29	Educational-supportive and 12-step and intensive case management	1 year (daily sessions)	Random assignment to group/no group treatment.	Clients in group treatment attended 20% of the groups. No differences or changes in symptoms, substance abuse, or life satisfaction.

Investigator	Number of Clients	Treatment Groups	Duration of Treatment	Research Design	Outcomes
(continued)					
Lehman et al. (1993)	25	Control (no group treatment)			
Hellerstein et al.(1995)	24	Educational-supportive	8 months (2 sessions/week)	Random assignment to group/no group treatment	36% of clients remain in treatment. Clients improved in substance abuse and symptoms, but no differences between group treatment and controls.
	23	Control (standard, non-integrated, no group treatment)			
Jerrell and Ridgely (1995)	39	12-step	18 months	Quasi-experimental	Clients improved on most measures of substance abuse, symptoms, social functioning, and service utilization. Clients in SST tended to do best, followed by CM, followed by 12-step.
	45	Case management (CM) and sporadic educational groups			
	48	Social skills training (SST)			
Drake et al. (1996)	158	Integrated treatment and cognitive-behavioral groups	18 months	Quasi-experimental	Clients in integrated treatment improved more in alcohol abuse, spent less time in hospitals, and had more stable housing. Clients in both treatments improved in symptoms and quality of life.
	59	Standard treatment with 12-step groups			

tributed to the differential outcome in substance abuse. Jerrell and Ridgely's (1995) study suggests that different approaches to integrated treatment produce similar results, with some advantage for the skills training model. By and large, however, the outcomes for the different integrated treatments in this study were similar. In a recently completed study, Drake et al. (1996) reported that integrated substance abuse and mental health treatment, with a heavy reliance on cognitive-behavioral groups, resulted in better alcohol abuse and housing outcomes for homeless dually diagnosed persons than standard services that employed 12-step groups. Similar to Jerrell and Ridgely's (1995) study, however, the two treatment conditions studied by Drake et al. differed in a variety of respects other than the group models used, so it is difficult to ascribe differences in outcomes to the group models employed.

Although the experimental evidence supporting the added benefits of group treatment is meager, more naturalistic pre-post study designs suggest that group treatment, when provided with other elements of integrated treatment, is associated with improved outcomes compared to standard care. There is also a trend for integrated treatments that include groups to more successfully engage and retain clients in treatment, which is associated with better outcomes (Drake, McHugo, & Noordsy, 1993, Hellerstein & Meehan, 1987; Hellerstein, Rosenthal, & Miner, 1995; Kofoed & Keys, 1988; Kofoed, Kania, Walsh, & Atkinson, 1986). These findings are consistent with the positive results of the NIMH Community Support Program Demonstration Studies of Services for Young Adults with Severe Mental Illness and Substance Abuse (Mercer-McFadden & Drake, 1993), which examined the effects of integrated treatment, including group intervention, across thirteen different sites.

It appears that one obstacle to demonstrating the effects of group treatment is that integrated approaches are so powerful that it is difficult to show the added advantage of a single component of the model. At the same time, a systematic dismantling of the different components of integrated treatment models is a formidable task, both because of the sheer number of components (for example, case management, family intervention, group models, use of monitoring techniques, control over contingencies such as funds, housing, and hospitalization) and because of the variety of articulated integrated treatment models. An additional research problem is that only 50 to 75% of dually diagnosed clients will attend groups even minimally, and 30 to 50% regularly. Therefore the group must have very strong effects to exceed the "noise" of nonattenders.

Recommendations for Future Research on Group Treatment

Significant progress has been made over the past decade in the treatment of dually diagnosed persons. Coincident with the recognition that these individuals need comprehensive interventions that simultaneously address both disorders, an understanding has developed that short-term treatments produce short-term benefits, and that long-term strategies are required for meaningful results to accrue. Group intervention has consistently been included as a vital component of integrated treatment programs, yet there are scant data to support this important role. In fact, only two controlled studies suggest added benefits of group treatment, and both included quasi-experimental, not fully randomized designs (Bond et al., 1991; Jerrell & Ridgley, 1995).

Several avenues of research may shed light on the effects of group treatment. First, there is a pressing need for more controlled research that compares the effects of integrated treatment with versus without group therapy. In order for such research to be meaningful, the treatments must be provided long-term (preferably at least 18 months), the group model must be sufficiently specified, and a moderate proportion of the clients must attend the groups. Studies in which few clients regularly attend groups tell us little about the efficacy of group intervention (for example, Lehman, Herron, Schwartz, & Myers, 1993). It may be fruitful to identify characteristics of clients most likely to attend treatment groups so that research on the efficacy of group treatment can focus primarily on these clients, and clinicians can explore strategies for increasing attendance at groups.

Second, there is a need to examine whether specific client attributes are predictive of clinical response to group treatment in general or to specific models of group intervention. For example, it might be argued that social skills deficits will predict a better response to social skills training, an external locus of control will be related to improvements in a 12-step approach, whereas antisocial personality characteristics predict a poor response to all group interventions. Although such correlational research is necessarily speculative, it can form the basis for hypothesis generation that can be subsequently evaluated in experimental designs.

Finally, research into group treatment may provide valuable insights into the relationship between specific dimensions of client participation in the group (for example, level of participation and specific content of verbal contributions) and their current and future clinical functioning. At present, there is little available information to aid clinicians in understanding when and for whom the group intervention is working. Research on client group behavior and patterns of substance abuse may assist clinicians in identifying clients who are ready to begin tapering their substance use, who are at increased risk for relapse, or who may be on the verge of dropping out. Such information would enable clinicians to take proactive steps to enhance outcomes.

Substantial advances have been made in treating this difficult population. The positive effects of many different interventions that have included a group treatment component bode well for the efficacy of this modality. Despite this, the benefits of group treatment remain to be empirically demonstrated. The recent specification of a number of coherent group treatment models poises the field to address this important question.

References

Alfs, D. S. & McClellan, T. A. (1992). A day hospital program for dual diagnosis patients in a VA Medical Center. *Hospital and Community Psychiatry, 43,* 241–244.

Bartels, S. J. & Thomas, W. N. (1991). Lessons from a pilot residential treatment program for people with dual disorders of severe mental illness and substance use disorder. *Psychosocial Rehabilitation Journal, 15,* 19–30.

Bond, G., McDonel, E. C., Miller, L. D., & Pensec, M. (1991). Assertive community treatment and reference groups: An evaluation of their effectiveness for young adults with serious mental illness and substance use problems. *Psychosocial Rehabilitation Journal, 15,* 31–43.

Bricker, M. (1994). The evolution of mutual help groups for dual recovery. *TIE-Lines, 11,* 1–4.

Caldwell, S. & White, K. K. (1991). Co-Creating a Self-Help Recovery Movement. *Psychosocial Rehabilitation Journal, 15,* 91–95.

Carey, M. P., Carey, K. B., & Meisler, A. W. (1990). Training mentally ill chemical abusers in social problem solving. *Behavior Therapy, 21,* 511–518.

Dixon, L., Haas, G., Weiden, P., Sweeney, J., & Frances, A. (1991). Drug abuse in schizophrenic patients: Clinical correlates and reasons for use. *American Journal of Psychiatry, 148,* 224–230.

Drake, R. E., Bartels, S. B., Teague, G. B., Noordsy, D. L., & Clark, R. E. (1993). Treatment of substance abuse in severely mentally ill patients. *Journal of Nervous and Mental Disease, 181,* 606–611.

Drake, R. E., McHugo, G. J., & Noordsy, D. L. (1993). Treatment of alcoholism among schizophrenic outpatients: Four-year outcomes. *American Journal of Psychiatry, 150,* 328–329.

Drake, R. E., Yovetich, N. A., Bebout, R. R., Harris, M., & McHugo, G. J. (1996). *Integrated treatment for dually diagnosed homeless adults.* Unpublished manuscript.

Ericsson, K. A. & Charness, N. (1994). Expert performance: Its structure and acquisition. *American Psychologist, 49,* 725–747.

Hellerstein, D. J. & Meehan, B. (1987). Outpatient group therapy for schizophrenic substance abusers. *American Journal of Psychiatry, 144,* 1337–1339.

Hellerstein, D. J., Rosenthal, R. N., & Miner, C. R. (1995). A prospective study of integrated outpatient treatment for substance-abusing schizophrenic patients. *American Journal on Addictions, 4,* 33–42.

Hendrickson, E. & Schmal, M. (1994). Dual disorder. *Tie-Lines, 11,* 10–11.

Jerrell, J. M. & Ridgely, M. S. (1995). Comparative effectiveness of three approaches to serving people with severe mental illness and substance abuse disorders. *Journal of Nervous and Mental Disease, 183,* 566–576.

Kofoed, L. L., Kania, J., Walsh, T., & Atkinson, R. M. (1986). Outpatient treatment of patients with substance abuse and coexisting psychiatric disorders. *American Journal of Psychiatry, 143,* 867–872.

Kofoed, L. L. & Keys, A. (1988). Using group therapy to persuade dual-diagnosis patients to seek substance abuse treatment. *Hospital and Community Psychiatry, 39,* 1209–1211.

Kurtz, L. F., Garvin, C. D., Hill, E. M., Pollio, D., McPherson, S., & Powell, T. J. (1995). Involvement in alcoholics anonymous by persons with dual disorders. *Alcoholism Treatment Quarterly, 12,* 1–18.

Lehman, A. F., Herron, J. D., Schwartz, R. P., & Myers, C. P. (1993). Rehabilitation for adults with severe mental illness and substance use disorders: A clinical trial. *Journal of Nervous and Mental Disease, 181,* 86–90.

Liberman, R. P., DeRisi, W. J., & Mueser, K. T. (1989). *Social skills training for psychiatric patients.* Needham Heights, Mass.: Allyn & Bacon.

Liberman, R. et al. (1987). *Psychiatric rehabilitation of the chronic mental patient.* Washington, D.C.: American Psychiatric Press.

Marlatt, G. A. & Gordon, J. R. (1985). *Relapse prevention maintenance strategies in the treatment of addictive behaviors.* New York: Guilford Press.

Mercer-McFadden, C. & Drake, R. E. (1993). *A review of NIMH demonstration programs for young adults with co-occurring severe mental illness and substance use disorder.* Center for Community Mental Health Services, SAMSHA. Rockville, Md.: U.S. Department of Health and Human Services.

Miller, W. R. & Rollnick, S. (1991). *Motivational interviewing: Preparing people to change addictive behavior.* New York: Guilford Press.

Minkoff, K. (1989). An integrated treatment model for dual diagnosis of psychosis and addiction. *Hospital and Community Psychiatry, 40,* 1031–1036.

Monti, P. M., Abrams, D. B., Kadden, R. M., & Cooney, N. L. (1989). *Treating alcohol dependence.* New York: Guilford Press.

Mueser, K. T., Fox, M., Kenison, L. B., & Geltz, B. L. (1995). *The Better Living Skills Group treatment manual.* Available from New Hampshire-Dartmouth Psychiatric Research, Main Building, 105 Pleasant St., Concord, NH, 03301.

Nikkel, R. E. (1994). Areas of skills training for persons with mental illness and substance use disorders: Building skills for successful living. *Community Mental Health Journal, 30,* 61–72.

Noordsy, D. L. & Fox, L. (1991). Group intervention techniques for people with dual disorders. *Psychosocial Rehabilitation Journal, 1991,* 15, 67–78.

Noordsy, D. L., Schwab, B., Fox, L., & Drake, R. E. (1996). The role of self-help programs in the rehabilitation of persons with severe mental illness. *Community Mental Health Journal, 32,* 71–78.

Prochaska, J. O., Velicer, W. F., DiClemente, C. C., & Fava, J. (1988). Measuring processes of change: application to the cessation of smoking. *Journal of Consulting and Clinical Psychology, 56,* 520–528.

Sciacca, K. (1987). New initiatives on the treatment of the chronic patient with alcohol/substance use problems. *TIE-Lines, 4,* 5–6.

Straussman, J. (1985). Dealing with double disabilities: Alcohol use in the club. *Psychosocial Rehabilitation Journal, 8,* 8–14.

Test, M. A., Wallisch, L., Allness, D. J., & Ripp, K. (1989). Substance use in young adults with schizophrenic disorders. *Schizophrenia Bulletin, 15,* 465–476.

Woods, J. D. (1991). Incorporating services for chemical dependency problems into clubhouse model programs: A description of two programs. *Psychosocial Rehabilitation Journal, 15,* 107–112.

A Relapse Prevention Group for Patients with Bipolar and Substance Use Disorders

Roger D. Weiss, Lisa M. Najavits & Shelly F. Greenfield

This article originally appeared in the *Journal of Substance Abuse Treatment*, 1998, 16(1), 47–54 and is reprinted with permission.

Roger D. Weiss, M.D., Lisa M. Najavits, Ph.D., & Shelly F. Greenfield, M.D., M.P.H., Alcohol and Drug Abuse Program, McLean Hospital, Belmont, MA; and Department of Psychiatry, Harvard Medical School, Boston, MA.

Although bipolar disorder is the Axis I disorder associated with the highest risk of having a coexisting substance use disorder, no specific treatment approaches for this dually diagnosed patient population have thus far been developed. This paper describes a 20-session relapse prevention group therapy that the authors have developed for the treatment of patients with coexisting bipolar disorder and substance use disorder. The treatment uses an integrated approach by discussing topics that are relevant to both disorders and by highlighting common aspects of recovery from and relapse to each disorder.

Studies of community samples (Kessler et al., 1997; Regier et al., 1990) and treatment populations (Brady, Casto, Lydiard, Malcolm, & Arana, 1991; Keller et al., 1986; Mirin, Weiss, Griffin, & Michael, 1991; Ross, Glaser, & Germanson, 1988; Rounsaville et al., 1991) have consistently shown a high rate of co-occurrence of bipolar disorder and substance use disorders. Indeed, the National Institute of Mental Health Epidemiologic Catchment Area study (Regier et al., 1990) revealed that bipolar disorder was the Axis I disorder associated with the highest risk of having a coexisting substance use disorder; the likelihood of an individual with bipolar disorder having a substance use disorder (SUD) was six times greater than that of the general population (i.e., odds ratio = 6.6). People with bipolar-I disorder (i.e., those who have been hospitalized for mania) had an even higher risk of having an SUD, with an odds ratio of 7.9.

Studies of clinical populations have also revealed high rates of comorbidity between bipolar disorder and substance use disorders. Surveys of patients being treated for bipolar disorder have revealed prevalence rates of substance use disorders ranging from 21 to 31% (Brady et al., 1991; Hasin, Endicott, & Lewis, 1985; Keller et al., 1986; Miller, Busch, & Tanenbaum, 1989; Reich, Davies, & Himmelhoch, 1974). In addition, patients seeking treatment for substance abuse or dependence have an elevated rate of bipolar disorder (Hesselbrock, Meyer, & Keener, 1985; Mirin et al., 1991; Ross et al., 1988; Rounsaville et al., 1991). While epidemiologic studies (Kessler et al., 1994; Weissman et al., 1988) have shown that 1.2 to 1.6% of the United States population have a lifetime diagnosis of bipolar disorder, studies of treatment-seeking substance abusers have typically shown prevalence rates of bipolar disorder ranging from 2 to 9% (Hesselbrock et al., 1985; Mirin et al., 1991; Ross et al., 1988; Rounsaville et al., 1991).

There is some evidence that the coexistence of bipolar disorder and SUD worsens prognosis. Keller et al. (1986), for example, found that patients who had bipolar disorder with associated alcoholism had an increased likelihood of rapid cycling and a slower time to recovery from affective episodes. Morrison (1974) and Feinman and Dunner (1996) have both reported a substantially increased rate of suicide attempts among alcoholic patients with bipolar disorder, when compared with nonalcoholic bipolar patients. Reich et al. (1974) and Brady et al. (1991) found that patients with coexisting bipolar and substance use disorders were twice as likely as patients with bipolar disorder alone to require hospitalization. Keck, McElroy, Strakowski, Bourne, and West (1997) and Maarbjerg, Aagaard, and Vestergaard (1988) have reported that having a substance use disorder increased the likelihood of medication noncompliance in patients with bipolar disorder. Finally, in a 4-year prospective follow-up study of 75 patients who recovered from an index manic episode, Tohen, Waternaux, and Tsuang (1990) found that a history of alcoholism was a predictor of poor outcome for the bipolar disorder.

Despite the high prevalence rate of substance use disorders among patients with bipolar disorder and the poor prognosis associated with this dually diagnosed population, there have been very few studies of treatment for patients with coexisting substance use and bipolar disorders. Indeed, we know of only three small open pharmacotherapy trials (Brady, Sonne, Anton, & Ballenger, 1995; Gawin & Kleber, 1984; Nunes, McGrath, Wager, & Quitkin, 1990), with a total sample size of 24 patients; we are aware of no trials of psychotherapeutic treatment for this population.

Until recently, psychotherapeutic approaches to patients with bipolar disorder received scant research attention. Jamison, Gerner, and Goodwin (1979) found that patients with bipolar disorder were far more likely to value psychotherapy than were physicians who treated bipolar patients, despite the fact that most of the physicians surveyed were practicing psychotherapists. Psychotherapy for patients with substance use disorder, which was similarly long held in disfavor (Vaillant, 1981), has also recently been the subject of renewed interest (Najavits & Weiss, 1994). Although promising new approaches for patients with bipolar disorder (Frank et al., 1994; Miklowitz & Goldstein, 1990; Miklowitz, 1996) and substance use disorder (Najavits & Weiss, 1994; Onken, Blaine, & Boren, 1993; Project MATCH Research Group, 1997) have been developed, these have not specifically focused on patients with these coexisting disorders. Since this patient population is quite prevalent and typically has a particularly poor prognosis, we decided to focus on developing a treatment approach for this group.

We chose group therapy as a promising intervention for this patient population because group therapy is a staple of substance abuse treatment, and because several reports (Cerbone, Mayo, Cuthbertson, & O'Connell, 1992; Davenport, Ebert, Adland, & Goodwin, 1977; Graves, 1993; Kripke & Robinson, 1985; Volkmar, Bacon, Shakir, & Pfefferbaum, 1981; Wulsin, Bachop, & Hoffman, 1988) have shown encouraging results for patients with bipolar disorder who receive group therapy in conjunction with pharmacotherapy. Previous studies of group therapy for patients with bipolar disorder have had certain characteristics in common. These have included (a) an emphasis on educating patients about bipolar disorder, (b) a forum for patients to share their experiences with the illness and offer mutual support, (c) discussion about medications, ambivalence about taking them, and the importance of complying with the prescribed regimen despite this ambivalence, (d) difficulties with interpersonal relationships, and (e) the importance of accepting one's illness despite the wish to deny it. However, none of these studies specifically addressed the issue of drug use; only one (Kripke & Robinson, 1985) mentioned alcohol use; and one (Graves, 1993) excluded patients with substance use disorders. Moreover, manuals were neither developed nor employed in any of these studies.

Why should we develop a specific treatment for this population, rather than relying on either a more generalized dual diagnosis treatment approach, an approach that is geared toward depression, or a treatment strategy that is aimed at chronically psychotic patients with substance use disorders? We have previously argued (Weiss, Mirin, & Frances, 1992) that the term *dual diagnosis* is an oversimplification, and, in actuality, represents a heterogeneous group of patients with various combinations of types and severity of both substance use disorders and other psychiatric illnesses. Moreover, bipolar disorder has certain unique characteristics that would theoretically make patients with this disorder and substance use disorder especially suitable for a specific treatment intervention. First, there is some evidence that patients with bipolar disorder are at higher risk to use drugs or alcohol when hypomanic or manic, as opposed to when depressed (Weiss, Mirin, Griffin, & Michael, 1988; Zisook & Schuckit, 1987). Second, patients with bipolar disorder differ from those with unipolar depression in that substance use and noncompliance with medication regimens in the former group are often related to their *positive* attitudes toward their hypomanic symptoms. Jamison et al. (1979), for example, found that bipolar patients were more likely to comply with medication due to a fear of depression rather than a fear of mania. Indeed, in studies of patients hospitalized for cocaine dependence, we have previously reported that the majority of the patients with bipolar spectrum disorder whom we interviewed claimed to use cocaine primarily when hypomanic, in part to enhance their endogenous symptomatology (Weiss et al., 1988; Weiss, Mirin, Michael, & Sollogub, 1986). We decided to offer a separate group for bipolar patients rather than a heterogeneous group including patients with schizophrenia, because, unlike the latter group, when patients are in remission from a bipolar episode, they may experience few symptoms. Indeed, this absence of symptoms can be a major reason for medication noncompliance (Jamison et al., 1979).

The use of treatment manuals is widespread in the field of psychotherapy research. Treatment manuals are believed to assist the therapist by providing a theoretically based rationale for a set of therapeutic techniques, a detailed description of techniques, and a logical organization of treatment content. They also provide a documented treatment that can be replicated in future studies, thus enhancing the rigor of treatment outcome research (Rounsaville, O'Malley, Foley, & Weissman, 1988). Although manuals for relapse prevention treatment of substance use disorders exist (Daley, 1986; Wanigaretne, Wallace, Pullin, Keaney, & Farmer, 1990), we are aware of no manuals that have been developed specifically for patients with coexisting substance use and bipolar disorders.

Our goal was to develop an *integrated* treatment of the two disorders. The treatment of dually disordered patients frequently occurs in either sequential (e.g., the patient receives substance abuse treatment, after which he/she is treated for bipolar disorder) or parallel (the patient simultaneously receives treatment for each disorder at two different clinics) fashion (Weiss & Najavits, 1998). A number of clinicians and researchers have recommended integrated treatment of dually diagnosed patients, that is, treatment of both disorders at the same time in the same setting by the same clinicians who are familiar with both disorders (Mueser, Bellack, & Blanchard, 1992). Although this approach has been advocated for a number of years, there have been relatively few empirical studies of integrated treatment for dually diagnosed patients (Drake, McHugo, & Noordsy, 1993; Hellerstein, Rosenthal, & Miner, 1995; Kofoed, Kania, Walsh, & Atkinson, 1986; Lehman, Herron, & Schwartz, 1993; Najavits, Weiss, & Liese, 1996).

Finally, we decided to develop a manual based on a relapse prevention approach for several reasons. First, this cognitive-behavioral treatment modality, which seeks to prevent relapse through the use of self-control strategies, skill training, identification of high-risk situations, impulse control, advantage-disadvantage analysis, and lifestyle changes, has been used with some success in the treatment of patients with a variety of substance use disorders (Carroll et al., 1994; Project MATCH Research Group, 1997). Second, the flexibility of relapse prevention therapy and its adaptability for a variety of populations (Carroll, Rounsaville, & Keller, 1991) is an advantage; relapse prevention techniques have been directly modified for use with certain other Axis I disorders (Gossop, 1989). Third, relapse prevention treatment addresses some of the major issues that patients with both substance use disorder and bipolar disorder frequently face, including ambivalence about complying with treatment; coping with high-risk situations; self-monitoring of drug craving, moods, and thought patterns; and modifying lifestyle to improve self-care and develop better interpersonal relationships. Finally, Cochran (1984) has provided empirical evidence of the potential utility of a cognitive-behavioral intervention for patients with bipolar disorder. She found that a six-session course of modified cognitive-behavioral therapy significantly enhanced lithium compliance in 14 bipolar patients, when compared with an equal number of patients who did not receive this treatment. Basco and Rush (1996) have recently published a cognitive-behavioral manual for the treatment of patients with bipolar disorder, although it is not specifically tailored for patients with coexisting substance use disorder.

Development of the Treatment

The overall goal of our project has been the development and pilot testing of an integrated manualized relapse prevention group therapy for patients with coexisting bipolar disorder and substance use disorder. The group has been designed to focus on and integrate themes that are relevant to each disorder. The treatment, which is described below, has been developed as part of a Stage I (i.e., developmental and pilot testing) study, conducted under the auspices of the National Institute on Drug Abuse Behavioral Therapies Development Program. Future papers will discuss the outcome of this treatment.

Characteristics of the Patient Population

The group treatment is designed for men and women between the ages of 18 and 65 who have current *Diagnostic and Statistical Manual of Mental Disorders, 4th edition (DSM-IV);* (American Psychiatric Association, 1994) diagnoses of both bipolar disorder and psychoactive substance use disorder. In order to enroll in the group, patients need to be in remission from their most recent episode of bipolar disorder because the group is not appropriate for patients with acute symptoms of the disorder. Rather, it requires a level of attention and concentration generally not present in patients with acute symptoms of bipolar disorder. In order to enter the group, patients must be seeing a psychiatrist who is prescribing their medication, and must give us permission to contact their psychiatrist if necessary (e.g., if a patient arrives at a group acutely manic or suicidal). Patients have been recruited while hospitalized at McLean Hospital, and they then begin the group after they have been discharged.

Characteristics of the Therapists

Thus far, therapists who have conducted the group have met the following criteria: a master's or doctoral degree in an area that includes training in psychopathology (e.g., MSW, PhD, MD); at least 1 year of experience in a general psychiatric setting; at least 1 year of substance use disorder treatment experience; and at least 1 year of group therapy experience. Therapists are supervised weekly, based on videotaped group sessions; supervision has emphasized keeping patients engaged in treatment, maintaining a compassionate, nonconfrontational attitude toward patients, following the relapse prevention model, and presenting an integrated approach to the treatment of the two disorders.

The major goals of the group program are as follows:

1. Educate patients about the nature and treatment of their two illnesses.

2. Help patients gain further acceptance of their illnesses.

3. Help patients offer and receive mutual social support in their effort to recover from their illnesses.

4. Help patients desire and attain a goal of abstinence from substances of abuse.

5. Help patients comply with the medication regimen and other treatment recommended for their bipolar disorder.

Structure of Group Sessions

The group therapy consists of 20 hour-long weekly sessions, each devoted to a specific topic. Several topics of particular importance are repeated (see below), but most are covered in one session. Each session consists of several core components, similar to a group therapy model our group has developed for women with posttraumatic stress disorder and substance use disorder (Najavits et al., 1996). The group begins with a "check-in," in which group members report how they are progressing with the major goals of the treatment. In this part of the session, all members say whether or not they used any drugs or alcohol in the preceding week; how their overall mood was during the week; whether they took their medications as prescribed; whether they experienced any high-risk situations; whether they used any positive coping skills that they have learned in the group; and whether they anticipate any high-risk situations in the upcoming week. Patients have approximately 2 minutes apiece for their check-in reports.

After the check-in, the group leader reviews the highlights of the previous week's session, and then introduces the current group topic. The remainder of the group consists of a didactic session and a discussion of the day's topic. At each group, patients receive a session handout that summarizes the major points of the group in approximately two pages. Resource lists are also available at each session; these include information about self-help groups for substance abuse, bipolar disorder, and dual diagnosis issues.

Content of Sessions

Whenever feasible, group sessions are designed to discuss topics that are relevant to both disorders. Each session is designed to function independently so that the treatment can be carried out in an "open" format, that is, patients can enter at any time; the group sessions thus cycle, rather than building on each other. We chose an open format because one of the difficulties inherent in recruiting patients for group treatment is the fact that a therapy group needs a critical mass of patients in order to begin. If the period of time from initial recruitment until the actual start of the group is too lengthy, then recruited patients may lose interest in the group. However, since our waiting period has been kept to 1 to 4 weeks, we have been able to recruit patients and retain them until the beginning of the group. A list of topics and a brief description of each session follows.

Specific Session Topics

"It's Two Against One, But You Can Win." The relationship between substance use disorder and bipolar disorder is reviewed; the session emphasizes the capacity of certain drugs to trigger manic or depressive episodes; the potential adverse effect of substance use on medication adherence; the effect of manic or depressed thinking on judgment, including decision-making about substance use (Beck, Wright, Newman, & Liese, 1993); and the similarity between addictive, depressive, and manic thinking (e.g., irrationality, failure to consider the consequences of one's actions).

"Identifying and Fighting Triggers" (2 Sessions). Patients are taught about the nature of "triggers," that is, high-risk situations. They are taught about both internal (depression, anger) and external (seeing one's drug dealer) triggers. Patients are asked to identify major triggers for their substance use, depression, and mania. Mechanisms for coping with triggers are reviewed, including using the "3As" (e.g., *avoiding* triggers when possible, avoiding facing triggers while *alone,* and distracting oneself with *activities*).

"Managing Bipolar Disorder Without Abusing Substances" (2 Sessions). The concept of depressive thinking and manic thinking are reviewed. Characteristics of depressive and manic thinking (e.g., irra-

tionality, difficulty with priorities, pathological pessimism/optimism) are discussed. Patients are taught ways to cope with mood changes, with an emphasis on both behavioral methods (e.g., identifying and fighting the urge to "give up") and the importance of reporting early mood changes to one's psychiatrist.

"Dealing With Friends and Family Members" (2 Sessions). The purpose of this module is to help patients understand the common difficulties that people with bipolar disorder and substance use disorder frequently experience in their relationships with family members and friends. Patients are helped to put their own experiences in perspective by hearing what other group members have gone through, and they are helped to identify ways in which they can improve their family relationships. This topic typically elicits more affect—especially sadness— than any other session, as patients often report that their families have "given up" on them. The therapist tries to help patients to accept what they can and cannot expect from their friends and family members.

"Denial, Ambivalence, Admitting, and Acceptance." The concepts of denial, ambivalence, admitting, and acceptance are all reviewed. Patients are taught that having ambivalent feelings about sobriety and bipolar disorder treatment is very common. However, they are told that while acknowledging feelings of ambivalence can be helpful, acting on these feelings by using substances or stopping bipolar disorder treatment can be quite dangerous. Patients are taught to identify their ambivalent feelings and their early manifestations of denial.

"Reading Your Signals: Recognizing Early Signs of Trouble." Typical early warning signs of relapse to mania, depression, and substance abuse are discussed. Patients are taught to monitor their moods and their desire for substance use as a way of identifying these early warning signs. The concept of the "abstinence violation effect" is reviewed in this session, and the difference between a "lapse" (slip) and a relapse is discussed (Marlatt & Gordon, 1985).

"Refusing Alcohol and Drugs." Alcohol- and drug-refusal skills are discussed in this session. Patients are told that they need to know what they will say if someone offers them a drink or a drug. This group emphasizes the idea that alcohol and drug refusal skills are the last line of defense against using. Rather, avoiding high-risk situations and using other people for support can help reduce the likelihood of being offered drugs or alcohol.

"Using Self-Help Groups." Self-help groups for addiction and for bipolar disorder are both discussed. Patients' experiences in these groups are reviewed, with an emphasis on both positive and negative experiences that patients have encountered. Much of the group is devoted to a discussion of how they can overcome some of the common problems that dually diagnosed patients face when attending addiction self-help groups. For example, patients may be told by other self-help group attendees that their psychiatric symptoms are merely a result of their substance use, and that they should therefore stop taking their prescribed medication. This session focuses on how to distinguish between good and bad advice emanating from self-help groups, and emphasizes the importance of seeking the opinions of professionals when dealing with psychiatric issues.

"Taking Medication" (2 Sessions). This session focuses on taking medication for both bipolar disorder (e.g., mood stabilizers) and for substance use disorder (e.g., naltrexone, disulfiram). The group focuses on the difficulties that patients have had with medications, and tries to generate solutions to these problems. Common problems that are discussed include ambivalence about whether one needs to take medication at all; the stigma of being on psychotropic medications; physical and psychological side effects; and conflicts with one's prescribing psychiatrist.

"Recovery Versus Relapse Thinking." This session focuses on the differences between the type of thinking process that is characteristic of recovery versus relapse. The concept of "may as well" thinking is reviewed ("I may as well get high, I may as well stay in bed all day," etc.); this is contrasted with a recurring theme of the group, that "it matters what you do," that is, it matters whether one takes medication or not, and whether one decides to drink alcohol or not.

"Taking Care of Yourself." This group reviews two aspects of self-care: sleep hygiene and human immunodeficiency virus (HIV) risk behaviors. Sleep difficulties can increase the risk of relapse to bipolar disorder (Goodwin & Jamison, 1990) and are common in substance use disorder; concrete skills for establishing a healthy sleep pattern are thus reviewed. The increased likelihood of HIV-related risk behaviors associated with both bipolar disorder and substance use disorder is also discussed. We have found that by incorporating the discussion of HIV risk into a general discussion of self-care, patients are willing to discuss this very sensitive topic more openly.

"Balancing Recovery with the Rest of Your Life." This group reviews two common problems patients face as they try to balance their early recovery with other important aspects of their life. Commonly, people are busy with other life obligations, leaving little time for their treatment. Conversely, others spend so much time on treatment that they lose touch with the rest of their lives. The latter situation may lead patients to resent treatment, and some may suddenly stop treatment as a result. This session reviews the different stages of treatment and recovery, and discusses ways to recognize an imbalance between recovery and the rest of one's life. Potential strategies to overcome this lack of balance are reviewed.

"Getting Support From Other People for Recovery." The importance of developing healthy relationships and avoiding problematic relationships (e.g., relationships with active substance users) is discussed. Patients are taught that people who develop healthy relationships are more likely to have a successful recovery than are those who stay involved in their old, troubled relationships. Ways to develop supportive relationships are discussed, including the use of self-help groups, therapy groups, and the use of supportive friends and family members.

"Weighing the Pros and Cons of Recovery." In this session, patients are encouraged to discuss both the positive and negative aspects of their substance use disorder and bipolar disorder. The similarities between addictive thinking and bipolar disorder thinking are emphasized. Patients are taught ways of fighting this type of thinking through a concept known as "hanging up your disease." Addictive thoughts (e.g., "It's okay to get high") are likened to a telephone salesperson trying to sell someone something that he or she does not want; patients are taught to "hang up" rather than engage in this internal discussion.

"Taking the Group With You." This session discusses how patients can continue their recovery successfully after completing the group. Patients are given several guidelines to help them continue successfully after terminating from the group. These include building up other supports, either through individual or group therapy or self-help groups; continuing to review session handouts even after the group has ended; and identifying the recovery thoughts and recovery plans that specifically work well for them.

"Stabilizing Your Recovery: Thinking Through Your Decisions." The difficulties involved in early recovery from bipolar disorder and

substance use disorder are discussed. These include resolving problems left over from their recent acute episode (e.g., debts from a manic spending spree); trying to break long-standing addictive habits; and difficulties related to long-standing poor decision-making. The idea of "thinking through solutions" is emphasized in order to help people to identify problems and develop better solutions. Patients are taught to think through the consequences of their behavior, and to discuss their decisions with other people who are supportive of their recovery.

Major Themes

Although a number of different topics are discussed in the group, several major themes have emerged. The first is the "central recovery rule," which is discussed in every group: "Don't drink, don't use drugs, and take your medication as prescribed, *no matter what.*" The central recovery rule is held up as an example of "recovery thinking," which is contrasted with "relapse thinking," whereby patients give themselves permission to abuse substances in certain situations (for example, if they feel depressed, if they feel a need to "reward" themselves, or if they have been mistreated by a family member).

As stated above, the concept of "may as well" thinking is also discussed regularly as an example of relapse thinking, and is contrasted with the idea that "it matters what you do." This pattern of thinking is discussed with respect to both bipolar disorder and substance abuse. For example, some patients who continue to experience mood symptoms despite taking their medication as prescribed say, "Why bother taking these medications at all? If I'm going to get depressed or manic anyway, I may as well stop them altogether." Of course, this type of decision-making only exacerbates these patients' problems. Discussing "may as well" thinking is an example of our adaptation of the abstinence violation effect (which was described by Marlatt and Gordon [1985] for the treatment of substance abuse) for bipolar disorder. This is one way in which the themes of recovery and relapse that are common to both disorders are discussed in an integrated fashion.

Future Directions

The treatment that we have developed is the first known psychotherapeutic approach designed specifically for patients with bipolar disorder and substance use disorder. We are currently carrying out a research study to evaluate the effectiveness of this treatment when compared with a group of patients who meet the same diagnostic criteria, but who do not receive the group therapy. If these preliminary results are encouraging, we hope to conduct a controlled trial in the future to further test the efficacy of this treatment. It is our hope that this group therapy will prove to be an effective modality that clinicians in the field can use in the treatment of this patient population.

References

American Psychiatric Association. (1994). *Diagnostic and statistical manual of mental disorders (4th ed.).* Washington, DC: Author.

Basco, M.R., & Rush, A.J. (1996). *Cognitive-behavioral therapy for bipolar disorder.* New York: The Guilford Press.

Beck, A.T., Wright, F.D., Newman, C.F., & Liese, B.S. (1993). *Cognitive therapy of substance abuse.* New York: The Guilford Press.

Brady, K., Casto, S., Lydiard, R.B., Malcolm, R., & Arana, G. (1991). Substance abuse in an inpatient psychiatric sample. *American Journal of Drug and Alcohol Abuse, 17,* 389–397.

Brady, K.T., Sonne, S.C., Anton, R., & Ballenger, J.C. (1995). Val proate in the treatment of acute bipolar affective episodes complicated by substance abuse: A pilot study. *Journal of Clinical Psychiatry, 56,* 118–121.

Carroll, K.M., Rounsaville, B.J., Gordon, L.T., Nich, C., Jatlow, P., Bisighini, R.M., & Gawin, F.H. (1994). Psychotherapy and pharmacotherapy for ambulatory cocaine abusers. *Archives of General Psychiatry, 51,* 177–187.

Carroll, K., Rounsaville, B., & Keller, D. (1991). Relapse prevention strategies for the treatment of cocaine abuse. *American Journal of Drug and Alcohol Abuse, 17,* 249–265.

Cerbone, M.J.A., Mayo, J.A., Cuthbertson, B.A., & O'Connell, R.A. (1992). Group therapy as an adjunct to medication in the management of bipolar affective disorder. *Group, 16*(3), 174–187.

Cochran, S.D. (1984). Preventing medical noncompliance in the outpatient treatment of bipolar affective disorders. *Journal of Consulting and Clinical Psychology, 52,* 873–878.

Daley, D. (1986). *Relapse prevention workbook: For recovering alcoholics and drug dependent persons.* Holmes Beach, FL: Learning Publications.

Davenport, Y.B., Ebert, M.H., Adland, M.L., & Goodwin, F.K. (1977). Couples group therapy as an adjunct to lithium maintenance of the manic patient. *American Journal of Orthopsychiatry, 47,* 495–502.

Drake, R.E., McHugo, G.J., & Noordsy, D.L. (1993). Treatment of alcoholism among schizophrenic outpatients: 4-year outcomes. *American Journal of Psychiatry, 150,* 328–329.

Feinman, J.A., & Dunner, D.L. (1996). The effect of alcohol and substance abuse on the course of bipolar affective disorder. *Journal of Affective Disorders, 37,* 43–49.

Frank, E., Kupfer, D.J., Ehlers, C.L., Monk, T.H., Cornes, C., Carter, S., & Frankel, D. (1994). Interpersonal and social rhythm therapy for bipolar disorder: Integrating interpersonal and behavioral approaches. *Behavior Therapist, 17,* 143–149.

Gawin, F.H., & Kleber, H.D. (1984). Cocaine abuse treatment: Open pilot trial with desipramine and lithium carbonate. *Archives of General Psychiatry,* 41, 903–909.

Goodwin, F.K., & Jamison, K.R. (1990). *Manic-depressive illness.* New York: Oxford University Press.

Gossop, M. (Ed.) (1989). *Relapse and addictive behavior.* London and New York: Tavistock/Routledge.

Graves, J.S. (1993). Living with mania: A study of outpatient group psychotherapy for bipolar patients. *American Journal of Psychotherapy, 47,* 113–126.

Hasin, D., Endicott, J., & Lewis, C. (1985). Alcohol and drug abuse in patients with affective syndromes. *Comprehensive Psychiatry, 26,* 283–295.

Hellerstein, D., Rosenthal, R., & Miner, C. (1995). A prospective study of integrated outpatient treatment for substance-abusing schizophrenic patients. *American Journal on Addictions, 4,* 33–42.

Hesselbrock, M., Meyer, R., & Keener, J. (1985). Psychopathology in hospitalized alcoholics. *Archives of General Psychiatry, 42,* 1050–1055.

Jamison, K.R., Gerner, R.H., & Goodwin, F.K. (1979). Patient and physician attitudes toward lithium: Relationship to compliance. *Archives of General Psychiatry, 36,* 866–869.

Keck, P., McElroy, S., Strakowski, S., Bourne, M., & West, S. (1997). Compliance with maintenance treatment in bipolar disorder. *Psychopharmacology Bulletin, 33,* 87–91.

Keller, M.B., Lavori, P.W., Coryell, W., Andreasen, N.C., Endicott, J., Clayton, P.J., Klerman, G.L., & Hirschfeld, R.M. (1986). Differential outcome of pure manic, mixed/cycling, and pure depressive episodes in patients with bipolar illness. *Journal of the American Medical Association, 255,* 3138–3142.

Kessler, R.C., Crum, R.C., Warner, L.A., Nelson, C.B., Schulenberg, J., & Anthony, J.C. (1997). Lifetime co-occurrence of *DSM-III-R* alcohol abuse and dependence with other psychiatric disorders in the National Comorbidity Survey. *Archives of General Psychiatry, 54,* 313–321.

Kessler, R.C., McGonagle, K.A., Zhao, S., Nelson, C.B., Hughes, M., Eshleman, S., Wittchen, H.-U., & Kendler, K.S. (1994). Lifetime and 12-month prevalence of *DSM–III–R* psychiatric disorders in the United States: Results from the national comorbidity survey. *Archives of General Psychiatry, 51,* 8–19.

Kofoed, L., Kania, J., Walsh, T., & Atkinson, R.M. (1986). Outpatient treatment for patients with substance abuse and coexisting psychiatric disorders. *American Journal of Psychiatry, 143,* 867–872.

Kripke, D.F., & Robinson, D. (1985). Ten years with a lithium group. *McLean Hospital Journal, 10,* 1–11.

Lehman, A., Herron, J., & Schwartz, R. (1993). Rehabilitation for young adults with severe mental illness and substance use disorders: A clinical trial. *Journal of Nervous and Mental Disease, 181,* 86–90.

Maarbjerg, K., Aagaard, J., & Vestergaard, P. (1988). Adherence to lithium prophylaxis: I. Clinical predictors and patient's reasons for nonadherence. *Pharmacopsychiatry, 21,* 121–125.

Marlatt, G.A., & Gordon, J.R. (1985). *Relapse prevention: Maintenance strategies in the treatment of addictive behaviors.* New York: The Guilford Press.

Miklowitz, D.J. (1996). Psychotherapy in combination with drug treatment for bipolar disorder. *Journal of Clinical Psychopharmacology, (Suppl. 1), 16,* 56S–66S.

Miklowitz, D., & Goldstein, M. (1990). Behavioral family treatment for patients with bipolar affective disorder, *Behavior Modification, 14,* 457–489.

Miller, F.T., Busch, F., & Tanenbaum, J.H. (1989). Drug abuse in schizophrenia and bipolar disorder. *American Journal of Drug and Alcohol Abuse, 15,* 291–295.

Mirin, S.M., Weiss, R.D., Griffin, M.L., & Michael, J.L. (1991). Psychopathology in drug abusers and their families. *Comprehensive Psychiatry, 32,* 36–51.

Morrison, J.R. (1974). Bipolar affective disorder and alcoholism. *American Journal of Psychiatry, 131,* 1130–1133.

Mueser, K.T., Bellack, A.S., & Blanchard, J.J. (1992). Comorbidity of schizophrenia and substance abuse: Implications for treatment. *Journal of Consulting and Clinical Psychology, 60,* 845–856.

Najavits, L., & Weiss, R. (1994). The role of psychotherapy in the treatment of substance use disorders. *Harvard Review of Psychiatry, 2,* 84–96.

Najavits, L.M., Weiss, R.D., & Liese, B.S. (1996). Group cognitivebehavioral therapy for women with PTSD and substance use disorder. *Journal of Substance Abuse Treatment, 13,* 13–22.

Nunes, E.V., McGrath, P.J., Wager, S., & Quitkin, J.M. (1990). Lithium treatment for cocaine abusers with bipolar spectrum disorders. *American Journal of Psychiatry, 147,* 655–657.

Onken, L.S., Blaine, J.D., & Boren, J.J. (1993). *Behavioral treatments for drug abuse and dependence.* Rockville, MD: U.S. Department of Health and Human Services.

Project MATCH Research Group. (1997). Matching alcoholism treatments to client heterogeneity: Project MATCH posttreatment drinking outcomes. *Journal of Studies on Alcohol, 58,* 7–29.

Regier, D.A., Farmer, M.E., Rae, D.S., Locke, B.Z., Keith, S.J., Judd, L.L., & Goodwin, F.K. (1990). Co-morbidity of mental disorders with alcohol and other drug abuse: Results from the Epiderniologic Catchment Area (ECA) study. *Journal of the American Medical Association, 264,* 2511–2518.

Reich, L.H., Davies, R.K., & Himmelhoch, J.M. (1974). Excessive alcohol use in manic-depressive illness. *American Journal of Psychiatry, 131,* 83–86.

Ross, H.E., Glaser, F.B., & Germanson, T. (1988). The prevalence of psychiatric disorders in patients with alcohol and other drug problems. *Archives of General Psychiatry, 45,* 1023–1031.

Rounsaville, B.J., Anton, S.F., Carroll, K., Budde, D., Prusoff, B.A., & Gawin, F. (1991). Psychiatric diagnoses of treatment-seeking cocaine abusers. *Archives of General Psychiatry, 48,* 43–51.

Rounsaville, B.J., O'Malley, S., Foley, S., & Weissman, M.M. (1988). Role of manual-guided training in the conduct and efficacy of interpersonal therapy for depression. *Journal of Consulting and Clinical Psychology, 56,* 681–688.

Tohen, M., Waternaux, C.M., & Tsuang, M.T. (1990). Outcome in mania: A 4-year prospective follow-up of 75 patients utilizing survival analysis. *Archives of General Psychiatry, 47,* 1106–1111.

Vaillant, G. (1981). Dangers of psychotherapy in the treatment of alcoholism. In M. Bean & N. Zinberg (Eds.), *Dynamic approaches to the understanding and treatment of alcoholism* (pp. 36–54). New York: The Free Press.

Volkmar, F.R., Bacon, S., Shakir, S.A., & Pfefferbaum, A. (1981). Group therapy in the management of manic-depressive illness. *American Journal of Psychotherapy, 35,* 226–234.

Wanigaretne, S., Wallace, W., Pullin, J., Keaney, F., & Farmer, R. (1990). *Relapse prevention for addictive behaviours.* Oxford: Blackwell Scientific Publications.

Weiss, R., & Najavits, L. (1998). Overview of treatment modalities for dual diagnosis patients: Pharmacotherapy, psychotherapy, twelve-step programs. In H. Kranzler & B. Rounsaville (Eds.), *Dual diagnosis: Substance abuse and comorbid medical and psychiatric disorders* (pp. 87–105). New York: Marcel Dekker, Inc.

Weiss, R.D., Mirin, S.M., & Frances, R.J. (1992). The myth of the typical dual diagnosis patient. *Hospital and Community Psychiatry, 43,* 107–108.

Weiss, R.D., Mirin, S.M., Griffin, M.L., & Michael, J.L. (1988). Psychopathology in cocaine abusers: Changing trends. *Journal of Nervous and Mental Disease, 176,* 719–725.

Weiss, R.D., Mirin, S.M., Michael, J.L., & Sollogub, A. (1996). Psychopathology in chronic cocaine abusers. *American Journal of Drug and Alcohol Abuse, 12,* 17–29.

Weissman, M.M., Leaf, P.J., Tischler, G.L., Blazer, D.G., Kamo, M., Bruce, M.L., & Florio, L.P. (1988). Affective disorders in five United States communities. *Psychological Medicine, 18,* 141–153.

Wulsin, L., Bachop, M., & Hoffman, D. (1988). Group therapy in manic-depressive illness. *American Journal of Psychotherapy, 42,* 263–271.

Zisook, S., & Schuckit, M.A. (1987). Male primary alcoholics with and without family histories of affective disorder. *Journal of Studies on Alcohol, 48,* 337–344.

Trauma and Posttraumatic Stress Disorder in Severe Mental Illness

Kim T. Mueser, Lisa B. Goodman, Susan L. Trumbetta,
Stanley D. Rosenberg, Fred C. Osher, Robert Vidaver, Patricia Auciello,
& David W. Foy

This article originally appeared in the *Journal of Consulting and Clinical Psychology*, 1998, 66(3), 493–499 and is reprinted with permission.

Kim T. Mueser, Susan L. Trumbetta, Stanley D. Rosenberg, & Robert Vidaver, Department of Psychiatry, Dartmouth Medical School, New Hampshire–Dartmouth Psychiatric Research Center, and New Hampshire Hospital, Concord, NH; Lisa B. Goodman, Department of Psychology, University of Maryland, College Park; Fred C. Osher, Department of Psychiatry, University of Maryland School of Medicine; Patricia Auciello, Mental Health Center of Greater Manchester, NH; David W. Foy, Department of Psychology, Pepperdine University and West Los Angeles Veterans Affairs Medical Center, Malibu, CA.

This research assessed the lifetime prevalence of traumatic events and current posttraumatic stress disorder (PTSD) in 275 patients with severe mental illness (e.g., schizophrenia and bipolar disorder) receiving public mental health services in Concord and Manchester, New Hampshire, and Baltimore, Maryland. Lifetime exposure to traumatic events was high, with 98% of the sample reporting exposure to at least 1 traumatic event. The rate of PTSD in our sample was 43%, but only 3 of 119 patients with PTSD (2%) had this diagnosis in their charts. PTSD was predicted most strongly by the number of different types of trauma, followed by childhood sexual abuse. The findings suggest that PTSD is a common comorbid disorder in severe mental illness that is frequently overlooked in mental health settings.

Abundant evidence documents the high rate of trauma, especially interpersonal violence, in the lives of persons with severe mental illnesses. Surveys indicate that between 34% and 53% of patients with severe mental illness report childhood sexual or physical abuse (Greenfield, Strakowski, Tohen, Batson, & Kolbrener, 1994; Ross, Anderson, & Clark, 1994), and estimates of their lifetime exposure to such types of interpersonal violence vary between 48% and 81% (Hutchings & Dutton, 1993; Jacobson & Richardson, 1998). These rates of trauma clearly exceed rates reported for the general population (Breslau, Davis, Andreski, & Peterson, 1991; Kessler, Sonnega, Bromet, Hughes, & Nelson, 1995).

Trauma has been related to a variety of negative outcomes in persons with severe mental illness. Patients with trauma histories tend to have more severe symptoms, are more likely to have substance use disorders, and tend to use higher cost psychiatric services, such as hospitalizations (e.g., Briere, Woo, McRae, Foltz, & Sitzman, 1997; Carmen, Rieker, & Mills, 1984). These findings suggest that further research is needed to understand the effects of trauma on patients with severe mental illness and the treatment needs of these individuals.

Although the high rate of trauma in severely mentally ill patients has often been reported, less research has examined posttraumatic stress disorder (PTSD) in this population. The apparent neglect of PTSD in severely mentally ill patients is surprising considering how widely PTSD is studied in the general population. However, two studies suggest that PTSD rates are also high in the severely mentally ill population. Craine, Henson, Colliver, and MacLean (1988) reported that 34% of women admitted to state hospitals had PTSD secondary to childhood sexual abuse (66% of the exposed sample). Cascardi, Mueser, DeGirolomo, and Murrin (1996) found that 29% of recently admitted psychiatric patients had PTSD related to domestic violence over the past year (48% of the exposed sample). These PTSD rates also appeared higher than the 8% to 9% rates reported in the general population (Breslau et al., 1991; Kessler et al., 1995). Of equal importance, none of the patients in the Craine et al. (1988) or Cascardi et al. (1996) studies had a PTSD diagnosis in their charts.

Although the studies by Craine et al. (1988) and Cascardi et al. (1996) suggest high rates of PTSD in patients with severe mental illness, neither assessed lifetime exposure to trauma, resulting in a possible underestimation of PTSD. Evaluating the prevalence of PTSD in patients with severe mental illness, as well as its underdetection in chart records, could have important clinical implications. Unrecognized (and hence untreated) PTSD may lead to a worse course of severe mental illness and point to a need to develop interventions that target PTSD in this population. To address these questions, we evaluated trauma history and PTSD in a large cohort of patients with severe mental illness receiving psychiatric services. Analyses focused on evaluating the presence of PTSD as a function of demographic and diagnostic differences.

In addition, we examined relationships between different types of trauma and PTSD diagnosis to determine whether similar associations were found as have been reported for the general population. Such findings would lend further support to the validity of PTSD diagnoses in the severely mentally ill population, and would suggest that theoretical models and treatments for PTSD developed in the general population may be useful for the severely mentally ill population.

Method

The study was designed to assess lifetime trauma history and PTSD in a large sample of patients with severe mental illness receiving public sector psychiatric services. As no research to our knowledge has examined PTSD in the severely mentally ill population on the basis of lifetime trauma exposure, we sought to assess as broad a sample of patients as possible, including patients in rural and urban settings, inpatients receiving acute care services, and outpatients, while imposing minimal diagnostic criteria for inclusion in the study. This sampling framework was intended to maximize the generalizability of findings to other samples of severely mentally ill patients receiving public sector services.

The study included 275 patients assessed in Concord and Manchester, New Hampshire (50 inpatients, 67 outpatients), or Baltimore, Maryland (42 inpatients, 116 outpatients). Inpatients were consecutive admissions, and outpatients were convenience samples. Inclusion criteria were patients (a) between 18 and 60 years old; (b) with a primary *Diagnostic and Statistical Manual of Mental Disorders (4th ed.; DSM-IV*; American Psychiatric Association [APA], 1994) diagnosis other than substance abuse or dependence; (c) who met state definitions of severe mental illness (a psychiatric illness resulting in significant impairment in ability to care for oneself, work, or meet other role obligations—all patients were receiving Social Security Disability Insurance or Supplementary Security Income); (d) who were fluent in English; and (e) who were willing to provide written informed consent to participate in the research assessments. About 10% of patients declined to participate in the assessments. Demographic and diagnostic characteristics of the patients are summarized in table 1. Psychiatric diagnoses were based on chart records, except for the patients assessed at the New Hampshire Hospital (NHH; $n = 52$, 19%), where diagnoses other than PTSD were determined by the Structured Clinical Interview for the *DSM-IV*

Table 1

Sample Demographics

Demographic	New Hampshire		Maryland		Total	
	n	%	n	%	N	%
Gender	(n = 117)		(n = 158)		(N = 275)	
Male	34	29	88	56	122	44
Female	83	71	70	44	153	56
Race	(n = 106)		(n = 145)		(N = 251)	
White	103	97	46	32	149	59
Hispanic	2	2	0	0	2	1
Black	1	1	98	67	99	39
Native American	0	0	1	1	1	1
Education	(n = 106)		(n = 130)		(N = 236)	
< High school graduate	28	26	67	52	95	40
High school graduate	41	39	38	29	79	34
Some college	26	24	17	13	43	18
College graduate	7	7	8	6	15	6
> College graduate	4	4	0	0	4	2
Marital status	(n = 107)		(n = 139)		(N = 246)	
Single	47	44	87	63	134	55
Married	22	21	6	4	28	11
Separated	6	5	17	12	23	9
Divorced	28	26	22	16	50	20
Widowed	4	4	7	5	11	5
Patient status	(n = 117)		(n = 158)		(N = 275)	
Inpatient	50	43	42	27	92	34
Outpatient	67	57	116	73	183	66
Diagnosis	(n = 117)		(n = 158)		(N = 275)	
Schizophrenia	15	13	49	31	64	23
Schizoaffective disorder	11	9	19	12	30	11
Bipolar disorder	21	18	29	18	50	18
Depression[a]	32	28	33	21	65	24
Borderline personality disorder	19	16	3	2	22	8
All other personality disorders	7	6	3	2	10	4
Other	12	10	22	14	34	12
Mean age (and SD)[b]	39.64	(12.56)	40.25	(10.84)	40.00	(11.57)

a. Includes major depression (58%), depressive disorder not otherwise specified (26%), dysthymia (8%), adjustment disorder with depressed mood (6%), and mood disorder due to medical condition (2%).

b. ns were 114, 158, and 272 for patients in New Hampshire, patients in Maryland, and total sample, respectively.

(SCID; First, Spitzer, Gibbon, & Williams, 1996). A common assessment protocol was administered by trained interviewers at each site. All instruments were conducted by interview, including self-report instruments. Interviews were completed between January and September 1996. The procedures for patient recruitment and assessment at each site are described below.

New Hampshire

Outpatients were assessed at the Greater Manchester Mental Health Center (GMMHC) and inpatients were assessed at the NHH. The GMMHC is the lead agency funded by the state for serving patients with severe mental illness in the Manchester area. Patients participating in the community support program at the GMMHC were recruited by their clinicians to participate in the study assessments. These clinicians also conducted the study assessments, after receiving training from Kim T. Mueser and Stanley D. Rosenberg on the administration of the instruments. The NHH is the only state hospital in New Hampshire and the primary site for acute care of psychiatric inpatients with severe mental illness. Patients were admitted to the NHH from any 1 of 10 local community mental health centers in New Hampshire. The average length of stay for acute admissions was approximately 10 days. Assessments at the NHH were conducted by clinicians following completion of other intake information. These clinicians received the same training in the administration of the research instruments as the clinicians at the GMMHC. Patients at the GMMHC and the NHH were not paid for participating in the assessments.

Baltimore

Outpatients in Baltimore were assessed at the Walter P. Carter Community Mental Health Center, which serves residents of south and west Baltimore. The sample was drawn from patients receiving traditional clinic services and those assigned to an assertive community treatment team. Inpatients were assessed on the units of the Institute for Psychiatry and Human Behavior. Both programs are components of the University of Maryland Department of Psychiatry. Assessments were conducted by two research interviewers, both clinicians who had experience working with severely mentally ill patients. They received training from Lisa B. Goodman on the administration of the study instruments. Outpatients were recruited to participate in the assessments either by their clinicians or by direct contact with the interviewers. All participants were paid $10 for their participation.

Measures

Lifetime exposure to traumatic events was assessed with the Trauma History Questionnaire (THQ; Green, 1996) and selected items from the Community Violence Scale (CVS; Foy et al., in press). Events meeting the *DSM–IV* Criterion A definition of traumatic event for PTSD (i.e., exposure to events involving actual or threatened death, serious injury, or threat to self or others, in which the person experienced intense fear, horror, or helplessness; APA, 1994) were coded as present. This definition of a traumatic event is comparable with the definition from the *DSM* (3rd ed., rev.; *DSM–III–R;* APA, 1987) used by the Breslau et al. (1991) and Kessler et al. (1995) studies, although *DSM–IV* specifies an immediate negative reaction to the event, whereas the *DSM–III–R* does not. In line with the observation that many patients with severe mental illness deny experiencing physical or sexual abuse, but admit exposure to events such as sexual or physical assaults (e.g., Cascardi et al., 1996; Goodman, Rosenberg, Mueser, & Drake, 1997), questions regarding trauma history on these measures are behaviorally specific and avoid use of words such as abuse.

Exposure to traumatic events based on the THQ was recorded separately for childhood (occurring before age 16) and for adulthood. Lifetime exposure to other *DSM–IV* qualifying traumatic events not elicited in the THQ was assessed during administration of the CVS. Age of exposure to these events was not obtained. For statistical analyses, traumas were grouped into the following categories: sexual assault (unwanted sexual contact or, for children, sexual contact with someone who is more than 4 years older), physical attack (without a weapon), attack with a weapon, witnessing a killing or serious injury to another, accident, disaster, and having a close friend or relative either murdered or killed by a drunk driver. Exposure to events that involved more than one type of trauma was coded for the single type of trauma most likely to result in PTSD, on the basis of research on the general population (Kessler et al., 1995): sexual traumas first, followed by physical assault, followed by witnessing.

PTSD was assessed with the PTSD Checklist (PCL–S, Weathers, Litz, Herman, Huska, & Keane, 1993). The PCL–S requires participants to indicate on a 4-point scale the degree of distress they have experienced for the different symptoms of PTSD included in the *DSM–IV.* The PCL–S was completed for the single traumatic event that patients judged most severe. In practice, because of the many types of *DSM–IV* qualifying traumatic events reported, patients reported difficulty describing their reactions to a single event, although they were requested to attempt this nevertheless. For the purposes of establishing a PTSD diagnosis, symptoms that were rated as moderately severe or greater were classified as present. The PCL–S has good reliability with structured interviews for PTSD; a recent study of victims of motor vehicle accidents or sexual assault indicated that the correlation between the PCL–S and the Clinician-Administered PTSD Scale (CAPS; Blake et al., 1995) was .929 (Blanchard, Jones-Alexander, Buckley, & Forneris, 1996). In this study, the PCL–S had good internal reliability, with a coefficient alpha of .87 for reexperiencing, .81 for physiological arousal, and .80 for avoidance. Although the PCL–S was administered in an interview format, it is not a structured interview like the CAPS or the SCID. Therefore, the PTSD diagnoses derived in the present study may be regarded as probable or presumptive diagnoses, to the extent that diagnoses of PTSD based on structured interviews are considered more valid.

Results

We first examined site differences in the demographic and diagnostic variables, followed by rates of trauma and PTSD. Next, we evaluated gender differences in exposure to different types of trauma, and the relationships between type of trauma, number of traumas, and PTSD. Last, we explored whether rates of PTSD differed as function of psychiatric diagnosis. To facilitate comparison of findings with the general population, our analytic strategy follows that of Kessler et al.'s (1995) analysis of the National Comorbidity Survey.

Site Differences

A number of site differences between the New Hampshire and Maryland samples emerged. Patients assessed in New Hampshire compared with those in Maryland were more likely to be female (70% vs. 44%), ever married (56% vs. 36%), non-Hispanic White (97% vs. 32%), high school graduates (74% vs. 48%), to have a diagnosis of borderline personality disorder (16% vs. 2%), and were less likely to have diagnoses of schizophrenia (13% vs. 31%), $ps < .05$. There were no site differences in age.

The sites also differed in the exposure to different types of trauma. Chi-square analyses indicated that patients in New Hampshire were more likely than patients in Maryland to report physical (25% vs. 13%) and sexual assault in childhood (53% vs. 39%) and were less likely to report a relative or close friend murdered or killed by a drunk driver in childhood (3% vs. 11%) or adulthood (18% vs. 29%) or to report being attacked with a weapon as an adult (32% vs. 49%), $ps < .05$. There were no significant site differences in exposure to other types of trauma. These site differences appear to reflect the general tendency toward more community violence in Baltimore and the greater percentage of women assessed in New Hampshire, although women in New Hampshire were more likely to report childhood sexual assault than women in Maryland, χ^2 (1, $N = 152$) = 4.32, $p = .04$. Rates of PTSD also differed by site, with 51% of the New Hampshire sample having PTSD, compared with 38% of the Maryland sample. The different rates of PTSD between the two sites appears to be due to exposure to different types of trauma which contribute to PTSD, as indicated below.

Trauma Exposure

The rates of lifetime exposure to traumatic events in this sample are presented separately for men and women in table 2. The overall rate of trauma exposure in this sample was high, with the majority of patients reporting exposure to more than one type of traumatic event. Almost all of the patients in the sample (98%) reported exposure to at least one traumatic event over their lives, with patients experiencing an average of 3.5 different types of traumatic events (counting events that occurred in childhood and adulthood separately).

There were no gender differences in the number of different types of trauma to which patients were exposed. However, there were significant differences in the specific types of trauma experienced. Women were more likely to have experienced sexual abuse as a child (35% in men, 52% in women), odds ratio (OR) = 1.99, $p < .006$, and sexual abuse as an adult (26% in men, 64% in women), OR = 5.07, $p < .001$, whereas men were more likely to have been attacked with a weapon (49% in men, 36% in women), OR = 1.55, $p < .05$, and to have witnessed a killing or serious injury to another (43% in men, 24% in women), OR = 2.34,

Table 2

Prevalence of Trauma Exposure

Trauma	Men (n = 122)			Women (n = 153)			Total (N = 275)		
	%	SE (%)	n	%	SE (%)	n	%	SE (%)	N
Childhood									
Sexual assault	35.5	4.4	43	52.0	4.1	79	44.7	3.0	122
Physical attack without weapon	20.8	3.7	25	16.3	3.0	25	18.3	2.4	50
Attack with weapon	17.2	3.4	21	16.7	3.1	25	16.9	2.3	46
Witness killing or serious injury of another	17.7	3.5	21	13.9	2.8	21	15.6	2.1	42
Close friend or relative murdered or killed by a drunk driver	9.4	2.7	11	6.1	2.0	9	7.3	1.6	20
Car or work accident	13.3	3.1	16	15.1	2.9	23	14.3	2.1	39
Natural or human-made disaster	8.3	2.5	10	9.2	2.4	14	8.7	1.7	24
Adulthood									
Sexual assault	25.9	4.1	30	63.6	4.0	91	46.7	3.0	121
Physical attack without weapon	39.7	4.6	46	36.3	4.0	53	37.8	3.0	99
Attack with weapon	49.2	4.6	58	36.6	4.0	53	42.2	3.0	111
Witness killing or serious injury of another	42.6	4.6	49	23.8	3.6	34	32.2	2.9	83
Close friend or relative murdered or killed by a drunk driver	25.6	4.1	30	23.1	3.5	34	24.2	2.6	64
Car or work accident	45.3	4.6	53	41.2	4.1	61	43.0	3.1	114
Natural or human-made disaster	16.7	3.4	20	12.2	2.7	18	14.2	2.1	38

$p < .002$, as an adult. Gender, differences in the other types of traumatic events were not significant.

Prevalence of PTSD

The rate of current PTSD was 43% (with an SE of 3.0%). Despite the high prevalence of PTSD, chart diagnoses ascertained PTSD in only 3 of 119 patients, suggesting a marked underdetection of PTSD in this sample of severely mentally ill patients. To evaluate the association between demographic characteristics and PTSD, we performed a logistic regression analysis, predicting PTSD diagnosis from age, gender, marital status, and their interactions. None of the effects were significant, indicating no relationship between diagnosis of PTSD and gender (men, 44%, women, 43%), marital status (never married, 39%; married, 43%; previously married, 49%), and age; neither was PTSD related to inpatient–outpatient status, as determined by a chi-square test.

To evaluate whether other psychiatric diagnoses were related to a PTSD diagnosis, we computed a chi-square test (omitting the other diagnosis category). This test was significant, χ^2 (7, $N = 275$) = 15.24, p = .033, indicating diagnostic differences in PTSD. The rate of PTSD was highest in patients with depression (58%) and borderline personality disorder (54%), followed by other diagnosis (47%), bipolar disorder (40%) and all other personality disorders (40%), and lowest in schizoaffective disorder (37%) and schizophrenia (28%).

Differences Across Traumas in Probability of PTSD

Patients reported exposure to multiple types of trauma. To determine whether certain types of trauma were more consistently related to PTSD than others, as has been reported in the general population, we evaluated the relationships between exposure to different types of traumatic events in childhood, adulthood, and over the life span and current PTSD diagnosis. It can be seen from Table 3 that exposure to certain types of trauma was more consistently related to PTSD than other types. In childhood, sexual assault was most strongly related to PTSD for both men and women. For women, attack without a weapon and witnessing a killing or injury in childhood were also related to PTSD. For men, no specific trauma types in adulthood were related to PTSD, whereas for women PTSD was related to sexual assault and witnessing a killing or serious injury. Over a lifetime, having a close friend or relative murdered or killed by a drunk driver was the only trauma related to PTSD for

Table 3

Odds Ratio for Posttraumatic Stress Disorder Given Exposure to Specific Traumatic Events in Childhood, Adulthood, and Over Lifetime

Trauma	Men (n = 122)			Women (n = 153)		
	Childhood	Adulthood	Lifetime	Childhood	Adulthood	Lifetime
Sexual assault	2.89*	0.84	1.59	4.73*	2.77*	4.29*
Physical attack without weapon	1.03	1.85	1.63	3.43*	1.89	2.64*
Attack with weapon	1.55	1.31	1.46	1.52	1.91	1.82
Witness killing or serious injury of another	1.47	1.48	1.47	3.10*	2.19*	2.78*
Close friend or relative murdered or killed by a drunk driver	2.56	1.49	2.25*	1.05	1.40	1.24
Car or work accident	1.31	1.73	1.90	0.67	1.58	1.25
Natural or man-made disaster	2.04	0.66	0.93	0.72	1.36	1.03

men, whereas for women PTSD was related to sexual assault, physical assault without a weapon, and witnessing a killing or serious injury.

To explore the total number of types of trauma to which a patient was exposed or the specific types or trauma that were most predictive of PTSD, we conducted three forward stepwise logistic regression analyses, one for the whole group and one for each gender separately. For each regression, the dependent variable was PTSD diagnosis, and the independent variables were number of types of trauma (counting traumas in childhood and adulthood separately), and each type of trauma (coded as either present or absent). For the overall sample, both the number of types of trauma experienced (Wald $[W] = 10.95, p = .0009$), and sexual assault as a child ($W = 8.15, p = .0043$) were significant predictors of PTSD, $\chi^2 (1, N = 225) = 8.19, p = .0042$, resulting in correct classification of 69% of the cases. The same results were found for women: Number of types of trauma ($W = 6.50, p = .0108$) and sexual abuse in childhood ($W = 4.50, p = .0338$) were significant, with the model correctly classifying 73% of the sample, $\chi^2 (1, N = 123) = 8.74, p = .0031$. For men, only the number of types of trauma predicted PTSD, $\chi^2 (1, N = 102) = 7.04, p = .008$, a correct classification of 58%, although sexual abuse in childhood narrowly missed the $p < .05$ level for entry into the regression model ($p = .07$).

Discussion

On the basis of lifetime trauma history, the rate of PTSD in this mixed sample of inpatients and outpatients with severe mental illness was 43% higher than the rates of 29% and 34%, respectively, for PTSD reported for severely mentally ill inpatients by Cascardi et al. (1996) and Craine et al. (1988), whose studies were based on selected trauma histories. However, considering that the lifetime prevalence of PTSD in the general population has been estimated to be 8 to 9% (Breslau et al., 1991; Kessler et al., 1995), this study and the studies of Craine et al. and Cascardi et al. suggest that patients with severe mental illness are at increased risk for having PTSD. The higher rate of PTSD in the severely mentally ill patients we studied is consistent with their increased reported exposure to traumatic events over the lifetime. We found 98% of the patients in our sample reported exposure to at least one traumatic event over their lives, compared with rates of 39–56% of lifetime exposure to trauma in the general population (Breslau et al., 1991; Kessler et al.,

1995), using a similar definition of traumatic event. Thus, PTSD appears to be a common comorbid disorder for patients with severe mental illness.

Despite the high rate of PTSD in these patients, chart diagnoses ascertained only 3 of 119 patients (2%) with PTSD. The gross underdetection of PTSD in the present sample is consistent with other studies: Craine et al. (1988) and Cascardi et al. (1996) both reported that PTSD diagnoses were not documented in any of the charts of their patients with severe mental illness, even though current rates of PTSD in their samples were 34% and 29%, respectively. Although many studies have documented the high rate of interpersonal trauma in the lives of patients with severe mental illness (e.g., Briere et al., 1997; Carmen et al., 1984; Greenfield et al., 1994), relatively few studies of severe mental illness have explored one of the most widely examined consequences of trauma in the general population, PTSD.

Failure to diagnose PTSD as a comorbid disorder in severely mentally ill patients could have important implications for assessment and management of their illnesses. For example, PTSD could increase patients' vulnerability to substance use disorders (Stewart, 1996), leading to a worse course of severe mental illness (Drake, Mueser, Clark, & Wallach, 1996). Similarly, PTSD-related avoidance because of interpersonal trauma could contribute to social isolation and loss of social support, increasing vulnerability to relapse in persons with severe mental illness (Cresswell, Kuipers, & Power, 1992). Research is needed to evaluate whether PTSD in severely mentally ill patients is related to a more severe course of illness. If PTSD and a worse outcome of severe mental illness are related, then attention will need to be directed toward developing and evaluating interventions for PTSD in this population.

Although rates of exposure to traumatic events and PTSD in this sample of patients with severe mental illness were higher than reports in the general population, patterns in the types of trauma experienced between the severely mentally ill and general populations were consistent. Similar to the finding in the National Comorbidity Survey (Kessler et al., 1995), women with severe mental illness were more likely to experience sexual assault, both in childhood and adulthood, whereas men were more likely to have been attacked with a weapon and to have witnessed the killing or serious injury of another. Also in line with Kessler et al. (1995), severely mentally ill patients in our study who had been exposed to traumatic events tended to have been multiply traumatized, with exposure to an average of 3.5 different types of trauma.

Furthermore, trauma exposure in our sample of patients with severe mental illness was related to PTSD in a similar fashion to the general population. The only type of traumatic event that was related to PTSD for both men and women was sexual assault in childhood. There is abundant evidence indicating that childhood sexual abuse is strongly predictive of PTSD in adults (e.g., Greenwald, Leitenberg, Cado, & Tarran, 1990; O'Neill & Gupta, 1991, Rodriguez, Ryan, Van De Kemp, & Foy, 1997). The logistic regression analyses indicated that the number of types of trauma experienced was the most important predictor of PTSD, both in the overall sample and within each gender as well, with childhood sexual abuse also significant for women, and marginally significant for men. This finding is consistent with studies in the general population indicating that the number of traumas experienced is predictive of PTSD (Astin, Ogland-Hand, Coleman, & Foy, 1995; King, King, Foy, & Gudanowski, 1996; Resnick & Kilpatrick, 1994). Considering the strong associations between both childhood sexual abuse and number of types of trauma and PTSD, it appears that sexual abuse in childhood may increase vulnerability to subsequent trauma over the lifetime, resulting in the retraumatization phenomenon (Polusny & Follette, 1995).

The similarity in the pattern in trauma exposure and the relationship between trauma and PTSD between this sample of severely mentally ill patients and studies of trauma and PTSD in the general population lends support for the validity of the assessments in the present study. In addition, the high rate of comorbid PTSD in patients with another psychiatric diagnosis is also consistent with Kessler et al. (1995), who reported that, in the general population, 83% of persons with PTSD had another psychiatric disorder. Thus, the comorbidity between PTSD and other psychiatric disorders appears to be high.

What accounts for this high rate of PTSD in patients with other psychiatric disorders? Because our study and others examining the prevalence of PTSD in the general population (e.g., Kessler et al., 1995) are limited by their reliance on retrospective reports of traumatic experiences, it is impossible to sort out the causal relationships between PTSD and other psychiatric disorders. For example, it is possible that trauma and PTSD, especially at an early age, increase vulnerability to the development of other comorbid psychiatric disorders. Alternatively, persons with psychiatric symptoms such as depression might be more likely to remember past traumatic experiences and their effects, leading to PTSD symptoms that are at least partly secondary to other psychiatric symptoms. Of course, each of these explanations may be correct for different people. Understanding the interactions between trauma, PTSD, and other psychiatric disorders is an extremely complex task requiring prospective research over the life span, presumably beginning in childhood when some of the most important traumas occur. Prospective research of a less ambitious nature on the interrelationships among trauma, PTSD symptoms, and severe mental illness would provide valuable information as to whether a PTSD diagnosis has an effect on the course of the other psychiatric illnesses and whether changes in psychiatric status affect trauma recall and the severity of PTSD symptoms.

Diagnosis was significantly related to the rate of PTSD in this sample, with PTSD being lowest in patients with schizophrenia and schizoaffective disorder and highest in patients with depression and borderline personality disorder. The relatively low rates of PTSD in schizophrenia and schizoaffective disorder could be due to a variety of factors, such as problems related to memory (e.g., Goldman-Rakic, 1994), which could limit intrusive memories or avoidance of traumatic events or social withdrawal leading to a lower vulnerability to interpersonal (re)victimization. Further research on random samples of patients with severe mental illness is needed to explore the relationships between psychiatric diagnosis and PTSD.

Several limitations of our study need to be acknowledged. The instrument we used to diagnose PTSD (the PCL–S) was developed as a self-report scale. Although we administered it in the form of an interview, it is a less rigorous approach to the diagnosis of PTSD than the use of structured clinical interviews. Although we attempted to elicit from patients their PTSD symptoms resulting from a single traumatic event, many reported that their experience with multiple traumas made this process difficult. A preferable alternative may be to have patients report their psychological responses to several qualifying traumatic events, rather than to a single event. Our study was also limited by the lack of structured clinical interviews for psychiatric diagnosis for most patients and the use of clinicians as interviewers in New Hampshire. Finally, we studied a convenience sample, rather than a randomly selected sample, limiting conclusions that can be drawn about the prevalence of trauma and PTSD in the more general population of patients with psychiatric disorders.

Our study found that patients with severe mental illness receiving mental health services in the public sector had high rates of lifetime trauma exposure and high rates of current PTSD. Despite the apparent prevalence of PTSD in our sample, it was rarely diagnosed, with only 3 of 119 patients receiving a chart diagnosis of PTSD. There is a need to conduct more research aimed at understanding the scope of the problem of PTSD in this population and to determine whether the course of severe mental illness is influenced by comorbid PTSD. If PTSD is found to be related to a worse course of psychiatric illness, then treatment programs will need to be developed to address this unmet need.

References

American Psychiatric Association. (1987). *Diagnostic and statistical manual of mental disorders (3rd ed., rev.).* Washington, DC: Author.

American Psychiatric Association. (1994). *Diagnostic and statistical manual of mental disorders (4th ed.).* Washington, DC: Author.

Astin, M. C., Ogland-Hand, S. M., Coleman, E. M., & Foy, D. W. (1995). Posttraumatic stress disorder and childhood abuse in battered women: Comparisons with maritally distressed women. *Journal of Consulting and Clinical Psychology, 63,* 308–312.

Blake, D. D., Weathers, F. W., Nagy. L. M., Kaloupek, D. G., Charney, D. S., & Keane, T. M. (1995). *Clinician-Administered PTSD Scale for DSM–IV.* Boston and West Haven, CT: National Center for Posttraumatic Stress Disorder.

Blanchard, E. B., Jones-Alexander, J., Buckley, T. C., & Forneris, C. A. (1996). Psychometric properties of the PTSD Checklist. *Behaviour Research and Therapy, 34,* 669–673.

Breslau, N., Davis, G. C., Andreski, P., & Peterson, E. (1991). Traumatic events and posttraumatic stress disorder in an urban population of young adults. *Archives of General Psychiatry, 48,* 216–222.

Briere, J., Woo, R., McRae, B., Foltz, J., & Sitzman, R. (1997). Lifetime victimization history, demographics, and clinical status in female psychiatric emergency room patients. *Journal of Nervous and Mental Disease, 185,* 95–101.

Carmen, E., Ricker, P. R., & Mills, T. (1984). Victims of violence and psychiatric illness. *American Journal of Psychiatry, 141,* 378–383.

Cascardi, M., Mueser, K. T., DeGirolomo, J., & Murrin, M. (1996). Physical aggression against psychiatric inpatients by family members and partners: A descriptive study. *Psychiatric Services, 47,* 531–533.

Craine, L. S., Henson, C. E., Colliver, J. A., & MacLean, D. G. (1988). Prevalence of a history of sexual abuse among female psychiatric patients in a state hospital system. *Hospital and Community Psychiatry, 39,* 300–304.

Cresswell, C. M., Kuipers, L., & Power, M. J. (1992). Social networks and support in long-term psychiatric patients. *Psychological Medicine, 22,* 1019–1026.

Drake, R. E., Mueser, K. T., Clark, R. E., & Wallach, M. A. (1996). The course, treatment, and outcome of substance disorder in persons with severe mental illness. *American Journal of Orthopsychiatry, 66,* 42–51.

First, M. B., Spitzer, R. L., Gibbon, M., & Williams, J. B. W. (1996). *Structured Clinical Interview for Axes I and II DSM–IV Disorders—Patient Edition, (SCID–I/P).* New York: Biometrics Research Department, New York State Psychiatric Institute.

Foy, D. W., Guevara, M. V., Camilleri, A. J., Leskin, G., Layne, C. M., Gaba, R. J., Raia, J., & Wood, J. L. (in press). Community violence. In D. J. Miller (Ed.), *Handbook of posttraumatic stress disorders.*

Goldman-Rakie, P. S. (1994). Working memory dysfunction in schizophrenia. *Journal of Neuropsychiatry and Clinical Neurosciences, 6,* 348–357.

Goodman, L., Rosenberg, S. D., Mueser, K. T., & Drake, R. E. (1997). Physical and sexual assault history in women with serious mental illness: Prevalence, impact, treatment, and future directions. *Schizophrenia Bulletin, 23,* 685–696.

Green, B. L. (1996). Trauma History Questionnaire. In B. H. Stamm (Ed.), *Measurement of stress, self-report trauma, and adaptation* (pp. 366–368). Lutherville, MD: Sidran Press.

Greenfield, S. F., Strakowski, S. M., Tohen, M., Batson, S. C., & Kolbrener, M. L. (1994). Childhood abuse in first-episode psychosis. *British Journal of Psychiatry, 164,* 831–834.

Greenwald, E., Leitenberg, H., Cado, S., & Tarran, M. J. (1990). Childhood sexual abuse: Long-term effects on psychological and sexual functioning in a nonclinical and nonstudent sample of adult women. *Child Abuse and Neglect, 14,* 504–513.

Hutchings, P. S., & Dutton, M. A. (1993). Sexual assault history in a community mental health center clinical population. *Community Mental Health Journal, 29,* 59–63.

Jacobson, A., & Richardson, B. (1987). Assault experiences of 100 psychiatric inpatients: Evidence of the need for routine inquiry. *American Journal of Psychiatry, 144,* 508–513.

Kessler, R. C., Sonnega, A., Bromet, E., Hughes, M., & Nelson, C. B. (1995). Posttraumatic stress disorder in the National Comorbidity Survey. *Archives of General Psychiatry, 52,* 1048–1060.

King, D. W., King, L. A., Foy, D. W., & Gudanowski, D. M. (1996). Prewar factors in combat-related posttraumatic stress disorder: Structural equation modeling with a national sample of female and male Vietnam veterans. *Journal of Consulting and Clinical Psychology, 64,* 520–531.

O'Neill, K., & Gupta, K. (1991). Post-traumatic stress disorder in women who were victims of childhood sexual abuse. *Irish Journal of Psychological Medicine, 8,* 124–127.

Polusny, M. A., & Follette, V. M. (1995). Long-term correlates of child sexual abuse: Theory and review of the empirical literature. *Applied and Preventive Psychology, 4,* 143–166.

Resnick, H. S., & Kilpatrick, D. G. (1994). Crime-related PTSD: Emphasis on adult general population samples. *PTSD Research Quarterly, 5,* 1–3.

Rodriguez, N., Ryan, S. W., Van De Kemp, H., & Foy, D. W. (1997). Posttraumatic stress disorder in adult female survivors of childhood sexual abuse: A comparison study. *Journal of Consulting and Clinical Psychology, 65,* 53–59.

Ross, C. A., Anderson, G., & Clark, P. (1994). Childhood abuse and the positive symptoms of schizophrenia. *Hospital and Community Psychiatry, 45,* 489–491.

Stewart, S. H. (1996). Alcohol abuse in individuals exposed to trauma: A critical review. *Psychological Bulletin, 120,* 83–112.

Weathers, F. W., Litz, B. T., Herman, D. S., Huska, J. A., & Keane, T. M. (1993, October). *The PTSD Checklist: Reliability, validity, and diagnostic utility.* Paper presented at the annual meeting of the International Society for Traumatic Stress Studies, San Antonio, TX.

Effectiveness of Treatment for Substance Abuse and Dependence for Dual Diagnosis Patients: A Model of Treatment Factors Associated with One-Year Outcomes

Franz Moggi, Paige Crosby Ouimette, John W. Finney & Rudolf Moos

This article originally appeared in the *Journal of Studies on Alcohol,* 1999, 60, 856–866 and is reprinted with permission.

Franz Moggi, Ph.D., Paige Crosby Ouimette, Ph.D., John W. Finney, Ph.D,. & Rudolf H. Moos, Ph.D., Program Evaluation and Resource Center and HSR&D Center for Health Care Evaluation, Veterans Affairs Palo Alto Health Care System & Stanford University Medical Center, Palo Alto, CA.

The project was supported by the Department of Veterans Affairs Mental Health Strategic Health Group and the Health Services Research and Development Service, and by the Swiss National Science Foundation grant 823B-050302 to Franz Moggi for a fellowship at the Department of Psychiatry and Behavioral Sciences, Stanford Univerity.

Objective: This study examines a model of treatment for substance abuse and dependence for patients with substance use disorders and concomitant psychiatric disorders. The model focuses on five interrelated sets of variables (social background, intake functioning, dual diagnosis treatment orientation, patients' change on proximal outcomes, and aftercare participation) that are hypothesized to affect dual diagnosis patients' 1-year posttreatment outcomes. Method: A total of 981 male dual diagnosis patients completed assessment at intake, discharge and 1-year follow-up. The relative importance of each set of variables as predictors of outcome was estimated by constructing block variables and conducting path analyses. Results: Dual diagnosis patients had a higher abstinence rate at follow-up (39%) than at intake (2%); they also improved on freedom from psychiatric symptoms (from 60% to 68%) and employment (from 20% to 29%). At follow-up, patients in programs with a stronger dual diagnosis treatment orientation showed a higher rate of freedom from psychiatric symptoms (71%) than did patients in weaker dual diagnosis treatment oriented programs (65%); they also were more likely to be employed (34% vs 25%). More change on proximal outcomes and more aftercare participation were also associated with better 1-year outcomes. Patients with less severe psychiatric disorders improved more and responded better to dual diagnosis oriented treatments than did patients with more severe psychiatric disorders. Conclusion: Treatment programs for substance use disorders that adhere to principles of dual diagnosis treatment obtain better outcomes for dual diagnosis patients, especially for patients with less severe psychiatric disorders.

About one third of individuals with alcohol use disorders and one half of individuals with drug use disorders have a comorbid psychiatric diagnosis (Regier et al., 1990). These "dually diagnosed" individuals seek treatment services more often (Kiesler et al., 1990; Moos et al., 1994a,b; Regier et al., 1993) and have worse outcomes after treatment than individuals with only substance use disorders (Moos et al., 1994a,b; Ouimette et al., 1997a; Peterson et al., 1994; Rounsaville et al., 1987; Swindle et al., 1995).

Recently, general guidelines have been proposed for the treatment of dual diagnosis patients (Drake et al., 1993; Evans & Sullivan, 1990; Lehman et al., 1989; Minkoff, 1991; Mueser et al., 1992; Osher & Kofoed, 1989; Ries, 1993). Evaluations of inpatient programs based on these guidelines suggest that integrated treatment for substance abuse and dependence and psychiatric disorders is effective (Cuffel & Chase, 1994; Fisher & Bentley, 1996; Franco et al., 1995; Hoffman et al., 1993; Jerrell, 1996; Moggi et al., in press; Ries & Ellingson, 1990). However, in the current era of cost containment, most treatment programs for substance use disorders will not have the resources to create dual diagnosis specialty programs. Patients with substance use and psychiatric disorders will most likely receive treatment in primary programs for substance abuse and dependence. Thus, research on aspects of treatment for substance abuse and dependence that are particularly beneficial for dual diagnosis patients is important.

The present study focuses on the 1-year outcomes of patients with a substance use disorder who had a comorbid psychiatric disorder and participated in a naturalistic multisite study of Department of Veterans Affairs treatment programs for substance use disorders. Our overall goal is to examine a model of substance abuse and dependence treatment outcomes for dual diagnosis patients that will highlight treatment factors related to enhanced posttreatment functioning.

A Model of Treatment Factors Associated with Outcome in Dual Diagnosis Patients

Clinicians who work with dual diagnosis patients emphasize several interrelated key factors in treatment. Contrary to traditional substance abuse or dependence treatment philosophy, dual diagnosis treatment experts recommend more liberal use of psychotropic medications in order to address psychiatric symptoms (Ridgely, 1991; Sheehan, 1993; Siris, 1990). In addition, they recommend encouraging patients' active participation in program activities (Franco et al., 1995; Lehman et al., 1993; Minkoff, 1991; Osher & Kofoed, 1989), maintaining a well organized program structure and providing clear rules (Drake et al., 1993; Mowbray et al., 1995; Osher & Kofoed, 1989). Supportive approaches, rather than confrontation (Mueser et al., 1992; Osher & Kofoed, 1989), and a practical orientation in terms of working on future goals are seen as advantageous for dual diagnosis patients (Zweben, 1992). Intensive programs that offer treatment and counseling to address a variety of issues like substance use, psychiatric symptoms, housing issues, employment issues, and legal, family and medical problems are also recommended for these patients (Drake et al., 1993; Mowbray et al., 1995; Ryglewicz, 1991).

Clinicians focusing on treatment of dual diagnosis patients emphasize change on cognitive and behavioral factors assumed to underlie substance use (Evans & Sullivan, 1990; Nigam et al., 1992; Zweben, 1992). As for patients with primarily substance use disorders, changing cognitive factors, such as expectancies for substance use, have also been noted as important for dual diagnosis patients (Mueser et al., 1995). Behavioral factors that are emphasized include patients' skills in relapse prevention and involvement in 12-step programs (Evans & Sullivan, 1990; Fisher & Bentley, 1996; Jerrell & Ridgely, 1995). Programs with dual diagnosis treatment orientation, as outlined above, are considered to be more conducive to changing these cognitive and behavioral factors (Minkoff, 1991; Osher & Kofoed, 1989).

Participation in services after discharge and continuing case management are also considered necessary components for successful treatment of dual diagnosis patients (Mason & Siris, 1992; Minkoff, 1991; Osher & Kofoed, 1989; Roberts et al., 1992; Wolpe et al., 1993). Dual diagnosis patients who attend more aftercare show a greater reduction in substance use and psychiatric symptoms (Jerrell & Ridgely, 1995), have lower readmission rates (Moos et al., 1996; Swindle et al., 1995) and increased functioning at work (Jerrell & Ridgely, 1995).

Using the clinical and research literature on the treatment of dual diagnosis patients as a framework, we propose a working model of treatment outcome for dual diagnosis patients. An understanding of treatment outcome is hypothesized to require an assessment of a set of interrelated factors, including patient pretreatment characteristics, dual diagnosis treatment orientation, changes on relevant proximal outcomes,

Figure I
Conceptual model of factors associated with outcome in dual diagnosis patients

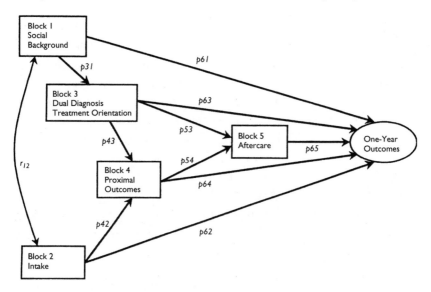

and aftercare participation. The model shown in figure 1 depicts the relationships among the following variables that are hypothesized to predict treatment outcome for dual diagnosis patients:

- Social background (Block 1), including age, marital status, education and ethnicity.

- Intake functioning on outcome criterion (Block 2).

- Dual diagnosis treatment orientation (Block 3), including dual diagnosis treatment climate reflected by a program's relative adherence to a more supportive, well-organized environment that encourages patients' involvement and practical goals, and espouses clear rules; an active treatment orientation as measured by the intensity of services provided; and a medication focus assessed by the access to prescribed psychotropic medications.

- Proximal outcomes (Block 4), or during-treatment change on positive reinforcement expectancies for substance use, positive expectancies for quitting substance use, self-efficacy for preventing relapse, and 12-step group involvement.

- Aftercare (Block 5), including the amount of participation in 12-step meetings and outpatient mental health treatment.

Social background (Block 1) and intake functioning (Block 2) represent characteristics of the patient at treatment entry. These variables are presumed to be intercorrelated (represented by r_{12}) (Jerrell & Ridgely, 1995; Moos et al., 1990b) and associated with a patient's outcome after treatment (paths p_{61} and p_{62}). Higher social background, including older age, and higher psychosocial functioning at intake are related to better outcomes among dual diagnosis patients (Cuffel & Chase, 1994; McLellan et al., 1983; Rounsaville et al., 1987). Social background generally is assumed to influence the type of program a patient enters (Block 3), as specified by path p_{31} (Connors et al., 1996; Moos et al., 1990b). Patients higher in social background attend treatment programs with characteristics that are similar to dual diagnosis treatment climate (e.g., more support, practical orientation and organization) (Timko & Moos, 1998).

Proximal outcomes (Block 4) are affected by patients' intake functioning and dual diagnosis treatment orientation (paths p_{42} and p_{43}). Higher psychosocial functioning at intake (McLellan et al., 1983) and dual diagnosis treatment orientation are expected to promote more "positive" changes in proximal outcomes (Mueser et al., 1992; Osher & Kofoed, 1989).

Aftercare participation (Block 5) is influenced by dual diagnosis treatment orientation, and proximal outcomes, as specified by paths p_{53} and p_{54}. Supportive, well-organized and task-oriented intensive programs, encouraging patients' involvement in treatment, as well as changes in cognitive and behavioral factors underlying substance use, are thought to promote participation in aftercare (Carey, 1996; Osher & Kofoed, 1989). Medication use is also expected to enhance compliance with aftercare (Sheehan, 1993).

All of the treatment-related variables, such as dual diagnosis treatment orientation ($p63$), better proximal outcomes ($p64$) and more aftercare ($p65$), are expected to be associated with better outcomes (e.g., Drake et al., 1993; Evans & Sullivan, 1990; Osher & Kofoed, 1989).

This model allows us to extend prior work by examining a network of interrelated variables and enabling us to partition explained variance of outcomes into unique and shared variance of specific variables and combinations of variables. We also extend prior work by examining the severity of the psychiatric disorder (psychotic vs nonpsychotic) and its effect on dual diagnosis patients' response to treatment. McLellan and colleagues (1983) found that level of psychiatric severity predicted response to treatment for substance abuse and dependence. Patients high in psychiatric severity did not improve at a 6-month follow-up, whereas patients low in psychiatric severity did improve. Here, we examine whether treatment effects vary for patients with more severe (i.e., schizophrenic, paranoid and affective psychosis) versus patients with less severe (i.e., anxiety, depressive and personality disorders) psychiatric disorder diagnoses.

Method

Participants

Male patients (N = 981) with a substance use disorder and diagnosed with a comorbid psychiatric disorder participated in a multisite evaluation of Department of Veterans Affairs inpatient programs for substance use disorders. Fifteen treatment programs in the VA Health Care System were selected from a pool of 174 programs. Patients were recruited after they completed medical detoxification and were admitted to the programs. Women were excluded due to their small numbers (for more detail see Ouimette et al., 1997b).

Dually diagnosed participants were on average ($\pm SD$) 43 ± 8.47 years of age and had a high school education (mean = 12.82 ± 1.80 years); the majority was unemployed (80.2%; n = 787). For those patients with some income (n = 561), their average annual income was approximately $10,051 ± 9,146. About 58% were white, 35% black and the remaining 7% were Hispanic/Latino, Native American, Asian or other. Only 17% of the participants were married; 42% were divorced, 21% were never married, 17% were separated and 3% were widowed. At intake, about 19% of the patients were on probation or parole; 33% had been arrested in the past 12 months.

Patients' discharge diagnoses were abstracted from the VA Patient Treatment File (PTF), a national VA patient database. These diagnoses are based on the ninth revision of the International Classification of Diseases (ICD-9-CM; DHHS, 1991). Overall, 413 patients (42.1%) had an alcohol use disorder, 106 patients (10.8%) had a drug use disorder and 462 patients (47.1%) had both an alcohol and a drug use disorder diagnosis. Nine hundred seventy-one patients had a substance dependence diagnosis (99%) and 10 patients had a substance abuse diagnosis (1%).

This overall group of patients was further subdivided into two broad categories. One hundred forty-two patients (14.5%) were diagnosed with a comorbid psychotic disorder, including schizophrenia, paranoid psychosis and affective psychosis. Eight hundred thirty-nine patients (85.5%) had a nonpsychotic psychiatric disorder, including depressive disorders, anxiety disorders and personality disorders.

Treatment Programs

The programs had a 21- to 28-day desired length of stay. Programs were based on cognitive-behavioral/12-step or mixed cognitive-behavioral/12-step treatment principles. Traditional 12-step programs included treatment activities such as participating in 12-step groups, working on steps and reading the "Big Book." Cognitive-behavioral programs included relapse prevention and/or coping skills groups.

Measures

Selected scales and items were taken from the Intake Information Form (IIF), the Discharge Information Form (DIF) and the Follow-up Information Form (FIF; Ouimette et al., 1997b). Unless otherwise noted, all questions were asked in reference to the prior 3 months. Three of the four outcomes were dichotomized to provide more clinically meaningful indices.

Outcome measures. Abstinence from substance use was assessed using questions from the Health and Daily Living Form (HDL; Moos et al., 1990a) and the Treatment Outcome Prospective Study (TOPS; Hubbard et al., 1989) inventories. On the HDL items, participants indicated the amount of beer, wine and distilled spirits that they had consumed, and on the TOPS items they reported the frequency of use of various illicit drugs on a five-point scale (i.e., 0 = never to 4 = every day). Patients received a score of 1 if they reported no substance use; otherwise, they were coded 0.

Psychiatric symptoms were measured by items of the Paranoid Ideation (e.g., "Feeling others are to blame for most of your troubles"; Cronbach's α = .81) and Psychoticism scale (e.g., "The idea that you should be punished for your sins"; α = .77) from the Brief Psychiatric Symptom Inventory (Derogatis & Melisaratos, 1983). We focused primarily on psychotic symptoms, because we were interested in patients' more severe symptoms of psychiatric disorders. Patients received a score of 0 if they endorsed 4 or more of the 10 items at the level of "quite a bit" or "extremely"; otherwise, they were coded 1 for being free of significant psychiatric symptoms.

Employment: Patients were asked if they were employed at intake and at follow-up. Patients were scored 1 if they were employed full or part time and 0 if they were not employed.

Community tenure: The number of months the patient remained in the community after discharge was obtained from the VA Patient Treatment File (PTF). Scores range from 1 to 13, with 13 indicating remaining in the community (i.e., having no hospital readmission for a mental health diagnosis, including substance use disorders) during the entire follow-up period.

Predictor variables. Social background was represented by four variables: age; marital status (0 = not married; 1 = married); years of education; and ethnicity (0 = not white; 1 = white).

Dual diagnosis treatment orientation: To create a *program-level* measure of dual diagnosis treatment orientation, we used three indices: dual diagnosis treatment climate, active treatment orientation, and medication focus. We used responses from all patients with a substance use disorder who participated in the overall evaluation of the multisite study and completed a Discharge Information Form, regardless of whether or not they had a comorbid psychiatric disorder (N = 3,328; Ouimette et al., 1997b). The mean of each measure/variable described below was determined for all patients. Programs (N = 15) were then classified by whether their patients' mean score fell above or below the overall mean.

(a)   The involvement (α= .75), support (α = .70), practical orientation (α = .57), order and organization (α= .68), and program clarity (α = .68) subscales of the Community Oriented Program Environment Scale (Moos, 1996) measured a program's dual diagnosis treatment climate. If the program mean was above the overall patient mean score for three or more scales, the program was classified as dual diagnosis treatment oriented (eight programs, coded 1); otherwise, it was classified as not dual diagnosis treatment oriented (seven programs, coded 0).

(b) Active treatment orientation was measured by the total number of treatment and counseling sessions in which patients participated, including sessions devoted to substance use problems, vocational issues, housing situation, legal problems, family problems and so on. Six programs fell above the overall patient mean (coded 1); nine programs fell below that mean (coded 0).

(c) The proportion of patients receiving psychotropic medication in the overall sample assessed *medication-focus* for mental health problems. Seven programs had a higher proportion of patients on psychotropic medication than did the overall sample (coded 1), whereas eight programs had fewer such patients (coded 0).

Proximal outcomes were measured by changes between intake and discharge of patients' positive reinforcement expectancies, positive expectancies for quitting substance use, self-efficacy to resist substance use in high-risk situations, and "taking" the 12 steps.

(a) Patients' positive reinforcement expectancies for consuming alcohol and drugs were measured with 12 items adapted from the Alcohol Expectancy Questionnaire (AEQ; Brown et al., 1980; $\alpha = .82$). Two items from each of six AEQ factors were selected and modified to include both alcohol and drug expectancies. The scoring of the items was reversed, so that higher scores indicate less positive reinforcement expectancies for the consequences of substance use.

(b) Positive expectancies for quitting substance use were measured with 12 items taken from the Outcomes Expectancies Scale (Solomon & Annis, 1989, 1990; $\alpha = .74$) and modified for patients who used alcohol and/or drugs. Two subscales of six items each measured the costs and the benefits of quitting. Higher scores on the overall score indicate expectation of greater benefits from and fewer costs of quitting.

(c) Self-efficacy to resist substance use in high-risk situations was measured by 14 items adapted from the Situational Confidence Questionnaire (SCQ; Annis & Davis, 1988; Miller et al., 1989; $\alpha = .95$). Two items were selected from each of seven SCQ subscales and reworded to assess answers in regard to both alcohol and drug use.

(d) Patients were asked to indicate how many of the 12 steps they had taken in the last 12 months before intake and since they had started treatment.

Aftercare was represented by two variables: outpatient mental health visits and 12-step meetings. Using data from the VA outpatient clinic file, the number of outpatient visits for mental health and substance use problems in the year after treatment was obtained. On the FIF, 12-step group attendance was assessed by the following question: "In the past 3 months, how many AA/NA/CA meetings did you attend?" Responses were recorded on a five-point scale: 0 = none; 1 = 1–9; 2 = 10–19; 3 = 20–29; and 4 = 30 or more. In analyses predicting community tenure, only the number of outpatient mental health visits up to readmission was used. Twelve-step group attendance was omitted, because this item refers only to 3 months before follow-up.

Data Analytic Plan

Patient improvement. McNemar's tests for categorical data (Tabachnick & Fidell, 1989) paired *t* tests were used to determine significant changes on the four outcome variables from intake to follow-up. Percent improved (e.g., the proportion of patients who were not abstinent at intake and who were abstinent at follow-up) and deteriorated (e.g., the proportion of patients who were abstinent at intake and who were not abstinent at follow-up) are presented as indices of treatment effects. Group comparisons (e.g., nonpsychotic vs psychotic group) on treatment effects were examined via logistic regression for dichotomous outcomes, and via analysis of covariance for community tenure using social background and the corresponding intake value as covariates.

Path analysis. To test the hypothesized associations among dual diagnosis treatment orientation, proximal outcomes, aftercare and 1-year outcomes, path analytic techniques were used (see Alwin & Hauser, 1975; Connors et al., 1996; Cronkite & Moos, 1978). The distribution of each variable was checked for normality. In the path analysis for community tenure, three scores required transformations: aftercare (i.e., inverse transformation) and community tenure at intake and at follow-up (i.e., logarithm transformation) (Tabachnick & Fidell, 1989). All variables were converted to z scores to create a common measurement scale. Then, the block variables were created by regression analyses in which each set of independent variables predicted the dependent variable. The standardized beta weights from these regression models were used to create the block variables. Each participant's standard score for a variable in a set was multiplied by the corresponding standardized beta weights. This procedure was repeated for each variable in a set and then the products were summed. The net result is the individual's composite score or block score for that variable set (Coleman, 1975).

All of the direct, indirect and total effects corresponding to the model in Figure 1 were estimated for the four outcome criteria. For simplicity, we used linear regressions to examine the models. To note, the patterns of results remained the same when logistic regression was used for the dichotomous outcomes.

Results

Patient Improvement

Table 1 presents proportions and means for the four outcomes. Compared to intake, a higher proportion of patients was abstinent, did not have psychiatric symptoms and was employed at follow-up. In contrast, patients remained on average 1 month less in the community subsequent to discharge than prior to intake. Results were similar among patients with nonpsychotic disorders. The patients with psychotic disorders improved only on abstinence.

The nonpsychotic group improved more on psychiatric symptoms (χ^2 improvement $= 4.02$, 1 df, p $< .05$, $n = 981$) and on employment (χ^2 improvement $= 7.79$, 1 df, p $< .01$, $n = 977$) than did the psychotic group. No significant differences were found for abstinence (χ^2 improvement $= 0.60$, 1 df, $p > .05$, $n = 979$) and community tenure ($F = 0.34$, 1/980 df, $p > .05$).

Dual Diagnosis Treatment Orientation and Outcomes

Patients in stronger dual diagnosis treatment oriented programs (i.e., mean $= > 1.5$) improved more on psychiatric symptoms (χ^2 improvement $= 5.76$, 1 df, $p < .05$, $n = 975$), on employment (χ^2 improvement $= 13.27$, 1 df, $p < .01$, $n = 973$) and on community tenure ($F = 68.81$, 1/974 df, $p < .01$) than did patients in weaker dual diagnosis treatment oriented programs (i.e., mean $= < 1.5$). No significant difference was found for abstinence. At follow-up, patients in stronger dual diagnosis treatment oriented programs showed a higher rate of freedom from psychiatric symptoms (71.4% vs 64.5%, respectively), had more employ-

Table I

Dual diagnosis patient improvement after inpatient treatment for substance abuse and dependence

Variable	Whole sample (N = 981)					Patients with psychotic disorders (n = 142)					Patients with nonpsychotic disorders (n = 839)				
	Intake	Follow-up	t/χ^2	% Imp.	% Det.	Intake	Follow-up	t/χ^2	% Imp.	% Det.	Intake	Follow-up	t/χ^2	% Imp.	% Det.
% Abstinent	1.7	38.5	341.77†	37.6	<1	2.1	40.1	50.16†	38.7	<1	1.7	38.2	289.71†	37.4	<1
% No significant psychiatric symptoms	60.2	67.9	17.61†	19.7	12.0	54.2	59.2	0.61	23.2	18.3	61.3	69.4	17.81†	19.1	11.0
% Employed	19.7	29.3	32.76†	18.3	8.7	14.8	20.4	2.53	9.9	4.2	20.5	30.8	29.61†	19.7	9.4
Community tenure (1–13)[a]															
Mean	9.01	8.07	-4.51†	27.1	35.1	7.55	7.45	-.18	35.2	35.2	9.26	8.17	-4.80†	25.8	35.0
(SD)	(5.21)	(5.07)				(5.21)	(5.07)				(5.06)	(5.20)			

Note: Imp. = improvement; Det. = deterioration.

a «Mean number of months the patient remained in the community in the year prior to intake, or during the follow-up, with 13 indicating remaining in the community without hospital admission.

† p<.01.

Table 2

Interrelationship among the block variables: Direct, indirect and total effects on dual diagnosis treatment orientation, proximal outcomes and aftercare

Dependent variable	Independent variable	Type of intake and outcome criterion			
		Abstinence	No psychiatric symptoms	Employment	Community tenure
Dual diagnosis treatment orientation (TO)	Social background: Direct & total (p_{31})	.016	-.045	-.010	.069*
Proximal outcomes (PO)	Social background: Via TO & total (p_{31}, p_{43})	.001	-.001	-.001	.001
	Intake: Direct & total (p_{42})	-.065*	.029	.064*	.087†
	Dual diagnosis treatment orientation Direct & total (p_{43})	.035	.014	.045	.018
Aftercare (AC)	Social background Via TO (p_{31}, p_{53})	.004	-.004	-.001	.005
	Via TO, PO (p_{31}, p_{43}, p_{54})	-.000	-.000	-.000	.000
	Total	.004	-.004	-.001	.005
	Intake: Via PO & total (p_{42}, p_{54})	.002	.003	.006	.001
	Dual diagnosis treatment orientation Direct (p_{53})	.228†	.087†	.077*	.065*
	Via PO (p_{43}, p_{54})	-.001	.001	.004	.000
	Total	.227	.088	.083	.065
	Proximal outcomes: Direct & total (p_{54})	-.036	.086†	.093†	.012
Correlations between intake and social background		.06	.13†	.13†	-.01

Note: Significance tests are calculated for direct effects only. * p <.05. † p <.01.

ment (33.8% vs 25.1%) and their average community tenure was longer (mean [$\pm SD$] = 8.67 ± 5.00 vs 6.13 ± 5.48).

Relationship of Patient Characteristics to Treatment Variables

Table 2 presents the estimated direct, indirect and total effects of preceding variables on dual diagnosis treatment orientation, proximal outcomes and aftercare. Correlations between social background and intake values are also shown.

Determinants of dual diagnosis treatment orientation. The composite background variable generally was not an important determinant of the type of program a patient enters; three of the four estimates of p_{31} were small and nonsignificant. The general absence of significant findings may be the result of the VA patient population and service delivery system. VA treatment programs for substance use disorders generally serve low-income veterans who attend the program that is located nearest to their residence (i.e., veterans usually do not have a choice of multiple programs). However, in the path analysis for community tenure, patients with more advantageous social backgrounds were more likely to be in a dual diagnosis treatment oriented program.

Determinants of change in proximal outcomes. Three of the four estimates of direct effects of the intake functioning variable on proximal outcomes (p_{42}) were significant (table 2). Two of these findings (employment and community tenure) suggest that patients who are higher functioning at intake show somewhat greater changes in proximal outcomes. The significant negative path coefficient suggests that patients who were abstinent at intake show less change on proximal outcomes. Participation in a more dual diagnosis treatment oriented program (p_{43}) was not associated with greater change on proximal outcomes.

Determinants of aftercare participation. All estimates of dual diagnosis treatment orientation on aftercare participation were significant (p_{53}), suggesting that dual diagnosis treatment orientation is associated with more aftercare participation (table 2). Greater change on proximal outcomes was associated with more aftercare participation (p_{54}) in the models for psychiatric symptoms and employment.

Relationship of Patients' Characteristics and Treatment to Outcomes

Table 3 presents the direct, indirect and total effects of the five predictor variables hypothesized to affect outcome.

A Model of Treatment Factors Associated with One-Year Outcomes

Table 3

Direct, indirect and total effect of patients' social background, intake, dual diagnosis treatment orientation, proximal outcomes and aftercare on outcomes

Independent variable	Type of intake and outcome criterion			
	Abstinence	No psychiatric symptoms	Employment	Community tenure
Direct effects				
Social background (p_{61})	.111†	.024	.201†	.071*
Intake (p_{62})	.051	.310†	.263†	.160†
Dual diagnosis treatment orientation (p_{63})	.025	.075*	.108†	.265†
Proximal outcomes (p_{64})	.037	.091†	.021	.078*
Aftercare (p_{65})	.289†	.048	.029	.295†
Indirect effects				
Social background: Via TO (p_{31}, p_{63})	.000	-.003	-.001	.018
Via TO, PO (p_{31}, p_{43}, p_{64})	.000	-.000	-.000	.000
Via TO, AC, (p_{31}, p_{53}, p_{65})	.001	-.000	-.000	.001
Via TO, PO, AC ($p_{31}, p_{43}, p_{54}, p_{65}$)	-.000	-.000	-.000	.000
Intake: Via PO (p_{42}, p_{64})	-.002	.003	.001	.007
Via PO, AC (p_{42}, p_{54}, p_{65})	.001	.000	.000	.000
Dual diagnosis treatment orientation: Via PO (p_{43}, p_{64})	.001	.001	.001	.001
Via AC (p_{53}, p_{65})	.066	.004	.002	.019
Via PO, AC (p_{43}, p_{54}, p_{65})	-.000	.000	.000	.000
Proximal outcomes: Via AC (p_{54}, p_{65})	-.010	.004	.003	.004
Total				
Social background (q_{61})	.112	.021	.200	.090
Intake (q_{62})	.050	.313	.264	.167
Dual diagnosis treatment orientation (q_{63})	.092	.080	.111	.285
Proximal outcomes (q_{64})	.027	.095	.024	.082
Aftercare (q_{65})	.289	.048	.029	.295
Total variance explained	.10†	.12†	.11†	.20†

Notes: Significance tests are calculated for direct effects only. TO = Dual diagnosis treatment orientation; PO = Proximal outcomes; AC = Aftercare.
*p <.05. †p <.01.

Direct effects. Three of the four estimates of social background on outcomes (p_{61}) were significant. A more advantageous social background was associated with a higher likelihood of abstinence and employment, and with slightly longer community tenure. Excluding abstinence, each of the direct effects of other aspects of intake functioning on their respective outcomes were positive and significant.

Three of four estimates of dual diagnosis treatment orientation effects on outcomes (p_{63}) were significant. A stronger dual diagnosis treatment orientation was associated with a higher likelihood of being free of significant psychiatric symptoms, being employed and having longer community tenure (table 3). More change on proximal outcome during treatment was significantly associated with a lower likelihood of psychiatric symptoms and longer community tenure. More aftercare participation was strongly associated with abstinence and longer community tenure (p_{65}).

In comparing the relative strength of the direct effects of each block on outcomes, no consistent pattern emerges across the four models. Intake functioning was the strongest predictor of psychiatric symptoms and employment, although dual diagnosis treatment orientation was also important. Treatment variables were most strongly associated with two of the criteria: aftercare predicted abstinence and community tenure, and dual diagnosis treatment orientation predicted community tenure.

Indirect and total effects. Table 3 presents estimates of the indirect effects for each model of outcome. None of the indirect effects was notable. Thus, we did not find mediation of the direct effects. Consequently, the total effect of each predictor variable on outcome was generally the same as the direct effect. Total variance explained for the four models ranged from 10% to 20%.

Patients with and without Psychotic Disorders

The four path models were examined separately for patients with and without psychotic disorders. The pattern of findings for patients with nonpsychotic disorders was similar to the overall dual diagnosis patient sample. In contrast, for patients with psychotic disorders, the magnitude of most path coefficients was smaller than for the patients with nonpsychotic disorders. For patients with psychotic disorders, only three treatment effects on outcomes were significant. More aftercare participation was associated with abstinence and longer community tenure, and greater dual diagnosis treatment orientation predicted longer community tenure. Employment and longer community tenure at intake were also associated with better outcomes. Proximal outcomes were not related to 1-year outcomes. Thus, the model appears to better explain outcomes for patients with nonpsychotic disorders than those with psychotic disorders.

Dual Diagnosis Treatment Orientation and Treatment Motivation

One potential confound is that dual diagnosis treatment orientation may reflect patients' motivation for treatment. Hence, we examined motivation by the Stages of Change Readiness and Treatment Eagerness Scale (Miller, unpublished manuscript) subscales "determination" and "action." Among the dual diagnosis patients, there was little or no correlation between motivation and dual diagnosis treatment orientation. In addition, motivation was not associated with the 1-year outcomes. Thus, we conclude that patients' motivation does not account for the findings.

Discussion

This study focused on a dual diagnosis model of treatment for substance abuse and dependence outcomes in a sample of male veterans seeking VA inpatient substance abuse and dependence treatments. Findings showed that dual diagnosis treatment orientation, proximal outcomes and aftercare were associated with 1-year outcomes for dual diagnosis patients.

Patient Improvement

Dual diagnosis patients improved from intake to 1-year following treatment for substance abuse and dependence. One year after treatment, dual diagnosis patients were more likely to be abstinent, employed and free of significant psychiatric symptoms than they were prior to treatment. At follow-up, almost 39% of the dual diagnosis patients were abstinent, 68% reported no significant psychiatric symptoms and 29% were employed. The abstinence rate is quite high for these types of patients, who are typically described as being likely to have poor substance use outcomes (Bartels et al., 1995; Rounsaville et al., 1987). Hence, dual diagnosis patients can benefit from substance abuse and dependence treatments that are primarily designed for patients with only substance use disorders (Ouimette et al., 1997b).

Compared to abstinence, psychiatric symptoms were less likely to improve (20%) and more likely to deteriorate (12%). This result suggests that dual diagnosis patients need treatments that also directly address psychiatric symptoms (Osher & Kofoed, 1989). In addition, dual diagnosis patients may need more intensive and longer treatment to show improvement on psychiatric symptoms than do patients with only psychiatric disorders (Drake et al., 1993; Mueser et al., 1992). The least improvement was found for employment status. As with psychiatric symptoms, more improvement may be evident over longer follow-ups (Evans & Sullivan, 1990; Mueser et al., 1992). However, dually diagnosed patients often are not functioning well enough to maintain employment and are less likely to be employed than are patients with only substance use disorders (Ouimette et al., 1997a).

Similar to previous work (McLellan et al., 1983), patients with more severe psychiatric disorders showed less overall improvement than did patients with less severe psychiatric disorders. Importantly, patients with psychotic disorders improved on abstinence, but not on psychiatric symptoms or employment. The severity of psychotic disorders, relative to nonpsychotic disorders, may have weakened substance abuse and dependence treatment effects on these outcome criteria. Psychotic patients may be a specific patient group that should be targeted for integrative treatments that provide intensive interventions for both disorders (Lehman et al., 1994).

A Model of Treatment Outcome for Dual Diagnosis Patients

The most important finding in the overall path model is that dual diagnosis treatment orientation had significant direct effects on three of four outcomes. Well-organized programs with practical orientation that were supportive and encouraged active participation (Minkoff, 1991; Osher & Kofoed, 1989), addressed a variety of problems (Drake et al., 1993) and allowed more liberal use of psychotropic medication (Sheehan, 1993) were associated with freedom from significant psychiatric symptoms, being employed and having longer community tenure. These findings are also consistent with previous work that has shown the general benefits of well-structured, supportive and intensive programs for patients with severe psychiatric disorders and poor functioning (Moos, 1997; Ouimette et al., 1998a; Timko et al., in press).

More change on proximal outcomes was associated with two 1-year outcomes, suggesting that a short-term inpatient program improvement on substance-related cognitive and behavioral variables has an effect on posttreatment functioning. Had we used a broader range of proximal outcomes, we might have found stronger associations between proximal outcomes and 1-year functioning. For example, improvement in skills to cope with psychiatric symptoms or improvement in social skills have been proposed as crucial for improvement in dual diagnosis patients' functioning (Lehman et al., 1989; Mueser et al., 1992).

Dual diagnosis treatment clinicians and researchers emphasize the importance of aftercare for dual diagnosis patients (Mason & Siris, 1992; Minkoff, 1991; Moos et al., 1996). Consistent with previous work (Ouimette et al., 1998b), our findings showed that more participation in aftercare resulted in a greater likelihood of abstinence at the 1-year follow-up. In addition, more aftercare was associated with longer community tenure. Osher and Kofoed (1989) proposed that relapse prevention should be part of aftercare. We cannot determine from our data whether this type of treatment was offered. Lehman et al. (1989) emphasized the need for a broad array of services to maintain treatment effects. Our measure captured mental health service use. Other types of services should be measured and examined in regard to outcomes.

Psychiatric symptoms were the least responsive to treatment. The relatively small effect of dual diagnosis treatment orientation and aftercare on psychiatric symptoms is surprising given the emphasis on these variables in the dual diagnosis literature. However, the treatment measured here was offered in the context of a treatment program for substance use disorders. These findings suggest that treatment programs for substance use disorders need to add counseling that is specific to these symptoms (Woody et al., 1990) or offer integrated dual diagnosis services (Lehman et al., 1994; Ries, 1993).

Dual diagnosis treatment orientation did not affect proximal outcomes, implying that, when delivered in the context of treatment programs for substance use disorders, it does not enhance changes in cognitive and behavioral factors underlying substance use. Treatment programs for substance use disorders directed at changing proximal outcomes may already be sufficiently effective. Integrated treatments for dual diagnosis patients are normally designed for a longer stay than 20 to 28 days (Swindle et al., 1995). Dual diagnosis treatment orientation may be more effective if treatments are of longer duration. Moos et al. (1996) found that patients with substance use disorders and concomitant psychiatric disorders benefit more from longer residential care.

Dual diagnosis treatment orientation was associated with aftercare. Patients in a program oriented more to dual diagnosis treatment participated more in aftercare, including both mental health outpatient visits and 12-step meetings (Evans & Sullivan, 1990; Roberts et al., 1992). Thus, dual diagnosis oriented programs appear to encourage active aftercare participation (Drake et al., 1993; Minkoff, 1991; Osher & Kofoed, 1989). Accordingly, dual diagnosis patients' compliance with aftercare may be improved if they are involved in well-structured and intensive programs that provide support by staff and mutual help among patients, working on future goals, and appropriate medication.

We also examined model differences among subgroups of dual diagnosis patients, differentiating patients with more severe (i.e., psychotic disorders) from those with less severe (i.e., nonpsychotic disorders) disorders. The findings for dual diagnosis patients suffering from depression, anxiety or personality disorders were similar to the findings for the overall sample of dual diagnosis patients. Thus, these patients benefit from treatment programs for substance use disorders with characteristics of integrated dual diagnosis treatment (Woody et al., 1985). In contrast, among dual diagnosis patients with psychotic disorders, only two treatment-related factors influenced outcomes: aftercare was linked to abstinence and community tenure, and dual diagnosis treatment orientation was related to longer community tenure. Mueser and colleagues (1992) argued that psychotic disorders include cognitive deficits that hinder the effectiveness of substance abuse or dependency treatments. For patients with psychotic disorders, integrative models including treatment for psychotic symptoms may be necessary (Lehman et al., 1994; Ries, 1993).

Indirect effects generally played little or no role in the models, suggesting that the block variables did not share substantial amounts of variance. The four path models explained 10% to 20% of the variance in the outcomes, indicating that other unmeasured variables are contributing to treatment outcomes. Such variables as social resources, life stressors and coping responses will be examined in future analyses of the data.

Several other cautions are noted. We focused on male patients participating in treatment for substance abuse and dependence in the Veteran Affairs health care system. These patients generally have few social resources (e.g., lower income, less education and less social support). Future studies are needed to examine the generalizability of these findings to women and nonveteran populations that have more social resources.

Patients' diagnoses were derived from regular clinical interviews rather than structured interviews or self-report instruments, and psychiatric severity was defined according to these diagnoses; their reliability and validity are unknown. However, the diagnoses may be considered more ecologically valid, because, in standard practice, assessments usually are based on clinical interviews. Also, attempts were made to verify patients' self-reports in the overall sample. The conditions under which data were collected and biological test data (i.e., alcohol and drug tests) support the validity of the self-report data (Ouimette et al., 1997b). However, our results await replication in future research using more structured assessments and ongoing biological test data.

In the absence of a validated dual diagnosis treatment orientation scale, we created a composite score consisting of three variables that have been widely proposed in the literature. Hence, the construct validity of our dual diagnosis treatment orientation index is unknown and needs to be examined in further studies. Importantly, dual diagnosis treatment orientation did not seem to reflect patients' treatment motivation. The dual diagnosis treatment orientation construct may include other dimensions. For example, tolerance to patients' problem behavior (e.g., noncompliance) has been proposed as a criterion of dual diagnosis treatment orientation (Osher & Kofoed, 1989) and has been associated with lower readmission rates (Swindle et al., 1995).

In conclusion, dual diagnosis patients improved after treatment for substance abuse and dependence on several outcomes, including psychiatric status. Programs that hold and encourage treatment practices consistent with dual diagnosis treatment models are associated with better outcomes for patients with dual diagnoses. Patients with less severe psychiatric disorders improved more than those with more severe psychiatric disorders. Future research needs to focus on these less responsive patients and identify program factors that improve their outcomes.

References

Alwin, D.F. & Hauser, R.M. (1975). The decomposition of effects in path analysis. *American Sociological Review 40*, 37–47.

Annis, H.M. & Davis, C.S. (1988). Assessment of expectancies. In Donovan, D.M. & Marlatt, G.A. (Eds.) *Assessment of addictive behaviors,* New York: Guilford Press, pp. 84–111.

Bartels, S.J., Drake, R.E. & Wallach, M.A. (1995). Long-term course of substance use disorders among patients with severe mental illness. *Psychiatric Services, 46,* 248–251.

Brown, S.A., Goldman, M.S., Inn, A. & Anderson, L.R. (1980). Expectations of reinforcement from alcohol: Their domain and relation to drinking patterns. *Journal of Consulting and Clinical Psychology, 48,* 419–426.

Carey, K.B. (1996). Treatment of co-occurring substance abuse and major mental illness. In: Drake, R.E. & Mueser, K.T. (Eds.) Dual diagnosis of major mental illness and substance abuse, Vol. 2: Recent research and clinical implications. *New Directions for Mental Health Services, 70,* San Francisco, CA: Jossey-Bass, Inc. pp. 19–31.

Coleman, J.S. (1975). Methods and results in the IEA studies of effects of school on learning. *Review of Education Research, 45,* 355–386.

Connors, G.J., Maisto, S.A. & Zywiak, W.H. (1996). Understanding relapse in the broader context of post-treatment functioning. *Addiction, 91* (Suppl.), S173–S189.

Cronkite, R.C. & Moos, R.H. (1978). Evaluating alcoholism treatment programs: An integrated approach. *Journal of Consulting and Clinical Psychology, 46,* 1105–1119.

Cronkite, R.C. & Moos, R.H. (1980). Determinants of the posttreatment functioning of alcoholic patients: A conceptual framework. *Journal of Consulting and Clinical Psychology, 48,* 305–316.

Cuffel, B.J. & Chase, P. (1994). Remission and relapse of substance use disorders in schizophrenia: Results from a one-year prospective study. *Journal of Nervous and Mental Disease, 182,* 342–348.

Department of Health and Human Services. (1991). *International classification of diseases, 9th Revision, Clinical modification (ICD-9CM) (4th ed.),* DHHS Publication No. (PHS) 91-1260, Washington: Government Printing Office.

Derogatis, L.R. & Melisaratos, N. (1983). The Brief Symptom Inventory: An introductory report. *Psychol. Med., 13,* 595–605.

Drake, R.E., Bartels, S.J., Teague, G.B., Noordsy, D.L. & Clark, R.E. (1993). Treatment of substance abuse in severely mentally ill patients. *Journal of Nervous and Mental Disease, 181,* 606–611.

Evans, K. & Sullivan, J.M. (1990). *Dual Diagnosis: Counseling the mentally ill substance abuser,* New York: Guilford Press.

Fisher, M.S. & Bentley, K.J. (1996). Two group therapy models for clients with a dual diagnosis of substance abuse and personality disorder. *Psychiatric Services, 47,* 1244–1250.

Franco, H., Galanter, M., Castaneda, R. & Patterson, J. (1995). Combining behavioral and self-help approaches in the inpatient management of dually diagnosed patients. *Journal of Substance Abuse Treatment, 12,* 227–232.

Hoffman, G.W., DiRito, D.C. & McGill, E.C. (1993). Three-month follow-up of 28 dual diagnosis inpatients. *American Journal of Drug and Alcohol Abuse, 19,* 79–88.

Hubbard, R.L., Marsden, M.E., Cavanaugh, J.V. & Ginzburg, H.M. (1989). *Drug and abuse treatment: A national study of effectiveness,* Chapel Hill, NC: Univ. of North Carolina Press.

Jerrell, J.M. (1996). Cost-effective treatment for persons with dual disorders. In Drake, R.E. & Mueser, K.T. (Eds.) Dual diagnosis of major mental illness and substance abuse, Vol. 2: Recent research and clinical implications, *New Directions for Mental Health Services, 70,* San Francisco, CA: Jossey-Bass, Inc., pp. 79–91.

Jerrell, J.M. & Ridgely, M.S. (1995). Comparative effectiveness of three approaches to serving people with severe mental illness and substance abuse disorders. *Journal of Nervous and Mental Disease, 183,* 566–576.

Kiesler, C.A., Simpkins, C. & Morton, T. (1990). Predicting length of hospital stay for psychiatric inpatients. *Hospital and Community Psychiatry, 41,* 149–154.

Lehman, A.F., Herron, J.D., Schwartz, R.P. & Myers, C.P. (1993). Rehabilitation for adults with severe mental illness and substance use disorders: A clinical trial. *Journal of Nervous and Mental Disease, 181,* 86–90.

Lehman, A.F., Myers, C.P. & Corty, E. (1989). Assessment and classification of patients with psychiatric and substance abuse syndromes. *Hospital and Community Psychiatry, 40,* 1019–1025.

Lehman, A.F., Myers, C.P., Dixon, L.B. & Johnson, J.L. (1994). Defining subgroups of dual diagnosis patients for service planning. *Hospital and Community Psychiatry, 45,* 556–561.

McLellan, A.T., Luborsky, L., Woody, G.E., O'Brien, C.P. & Druley, K.A. (1983). Predicting response to alcohol and drug abuse treatments: Role of psychiatric severity. *Archives of General Psychiatry, 40,* 620–625.

Mason, S.E. & Siris, S.G. (1992). Dual diagnosis: The case for case management. *American Journal of Addiction, 1,* 77–82.

Miller, P.J., Ross, S.M., Emmerson, R.Y. & Todt, E.H. (1989). Self-efficacy in alcoholics: Clinical validation of the Situational Confidence Scale. *Addictive Behaviors 14,* 217–224.

Miller, W.R. (1991). *The stages of change readiness and treatment eagerness scale,* Albuquerque: University of New Mexico, unpublished manuscript.

Minkoff, K. (1991). Program components of a comprehensive integrated care system for serious mentally ill patients with substance disorders. *New Directions for Mental Health Services, 50,* 13–27.

Moggi, F., Hirsbrunner, H.P., Brodbeck, J. & Bachmann, K.M. One-year outcome of an integrative inpatient treatment for dual diagnosis patients. *Addictive Behaviors,* in press.

Moos, R.H. (1996). *Community-Oriented Programs Environment Scale manual, (3rd ed.).* Palo Alto, CA: Mind Garden.

Moos, R.H. (1997). *Evaluating treatment environments: The quality of psychiatric and substance abuse programs, (2nd ed.).* New Brunswick, NJ: Transaction Publishers.

Moos, R.H., Brennan, P.L. & Mertens, J.R. (1994a). Diagnostic subgroups and predictors of one-year readmission among late-middle-aged and older substance abuse patients. *Journal of Studies on Alcohol, 55,* 173–183.

Moos, R.H., Cronkite, R.H. & Finney, J.W. (1990a). *Health and Daily Living Form manual, (2nd ed.).* Palo Alto, CA: Mind Garden.

Moos, R.H., Finney, J.W. & Cronkite, R.C. (1990b). *Alcoholism treatment: Context, process, and outcome,* New York: Oxford Univ. Press, Inc.

Moos, R.H., King, M.J. & Patterson, M.A. (1996). Outcomes of residential treatment of substance abuse in hospital- and community-based programs. *Psychiatric Services, 47,* 68–74.

Moos, R.H., Mertens, J.R. & Brennan, P.L. (1994b). Rates and predictors of four-year readmission among late-middle-aged and older substance abuse patients. *Journal of Studies on Alcohol, 55,* 561–570.

Mowbray, C.T., Solomon, M., Ribisl, K.M., Ebejer, M.A., Deiz, N., Brown, W., Bandla, H., Luke, D.A., Davidson, W.S. & Herman, S. (1995). Treatment for mental illness and substance abuse in a public psychiatric hospital: Successful strategies and challenging problems. *Journal of Substance Abuse Treatment, 12,* 129–139.

Mueser, K.T., Bellack, A.S. & Blanchard, J.J. (1992). Comorbidity of schizophrenia and substance abuse: Implications for treatment. *Journal of Consulting and Clinical Psychology, 60,* 845–856.

Mueser, K.T., Nishith, P., Tracy, J.I., DeGirolamo, J. & Molinaro, M. (1995). Expectations and motives for substance use in schizophrenia. *Schizophrenia Bulletin, 21,* 367–378.

Nigam, R., Schottenfeld, R. & Kosten, T.R. (1992). Treatment of dual diagnosis patients: A relapse prevention group approach. *Journal of Substance Abuse Treatment, 9,* 305–309.

Osher, F.C. & Kofoed, L.L. (1989). Treatment of patients with psychiatric and psychoactive substance abuse disorders. *Hospital and Community Psychiatry, 40,* 1025–1030.

Ouimette, P.C., Ahrens, C., Moos, R.H. & Finney, J.W. (1997a). Posttraumatic stress disorder in substance abuse patients: Relationship to 1-year post-treatment outcomes. *Psychology of Addictive Behavior. 11,* 34–47.

Ouimette, P.C., Ahrens, C., Moos, R.H. & Finney, J.W. (1998a). During treatment changes in substance abuse patients with posttraumatic stress disorder: The influence of specific interventions and program environments. *Journal of Substance Abuse Treatment, 15,* 555–564.

Ouimette, P.C., Finney, J.W. & Moos, R.H. (1997b). Twelve-step and cognitive-behavioral treatment for substance abuse: A comparison of treatment effectiveness. *Journal of Consulting and Clinical Psychology, 65,* 230–240.

Ouimette, P.C., Moos, R.H. & Finney, J.W. (1998b). Influence of outpatient treatment and 12-step group involvement on one-year substance abuse treatment outcomes. *Journal of Studies on Alcohol, 59,* 513–522.

Peterson, K.A., Swindle, R.W., Phibbs, C.S., Recine, B. & Moos, R.H. (1994). Determinants of readmission following inpatient substance abuse treatment: A national study of VA programs. *Med. Care, 32,* 535–550.

Regier, D.A., Farmer, M.E., Rae, D.S., Locke, B.Z., Keith, S.J., Judd, L.L. & Goodwin, F.K. (1990). Comorbidity of mental disorders with alcohol and other drug abuse: Results from the Epidemiological Catchment Area (ECA) study. *JAMA, 264,* 2511–2518.

Regier, D.A., Narrow, W.E., Rae, D.S., Manderscheid, R.W., Locke, B.Z. & Goodwin, F.K. (1993). The de facto US mental and addictive disorders service system: Epidemiologic Catchment Area prospective 1-year prevalence rates of disorders and services. *Archives of General Psychiatry, 50,* 85–94.

Ridgely, M.S. (1991). Creating integrated programs for severely mentally ill persons with substance disorders. *New Directions for Mental Health Services, 50,* 29–41.

Ries, R. (1993). Clinical treatment matching models for dually diagnosed patients. *Psychiat. Clin. No. Amer., 16,* 167–175.

Ries, R.K. & Ellingson, T. (1990). A pilot assessment at one month of 17 dual diagnosis patients. *Hospital and Community Psychiatry, 41,* 1230–1233.

Roberts, L.J., Shaner, A., Eckman, T.A., Tucker, D.E. & Vaccaro, J.V. (1992). Effectively treating stimulant-abusing schizophrenics. Mission impossible? *New Directions for Mental Health Services, 53,* 55–65.

Rounsaville, B.J., Dolinsky, Z.S., Babor, T.F. & Meyer, R.E. (1987). Psychopathology as a predictor of treatment outcome in alcoholics. *Archives of General Psychiatry, 44,* 505–513.

Ryglewicz, H. (1991). Psychoeducation for clients and families: A way in, out, and through in working with people with dual diagnosis. *Psychosocial Rehabilitation Journal, 15,* 79–89.

Sheehan, M.F. (1993). Dual diagnosis. *Psychiatric Quarterly, 64,* 107–134.

Siris, S.G. (1990). Pharmacological treatment of substance-abusing schizophrenic patients. *Schizophrenia Bulletin, 16,* 111–122.

Solomon, K.E. & Annis, H.M. (1989). Development of a scale to measure outcome expectancy in alcoholics. *Cog. Ther. Res. 13,* 409–421.

Solomon, K.E. & Annis, H.M. (1990). Outcome and efficacy expectancy in the prediction of post-treatment drinking behaviour. *British Journal of Addiction, 85,* 659–665.

Swindle, R.W., Phibbs, C.S., Paradise, M.J., Recine, B.P. & Moos, R.H. (1995). Inpatient treatment for substance abuse patients with psychiatric disorders: A national study of determinants of readmission. *Journal of Substance Abuse, 7,* 79–97.

Tabachnick, B.G. & Fidell, L.S. (1989). *Using multivariate statistics (2nd ed.).* New York: Harper & Row.

Timko, C. & Moos, R.H. (1998). Determinants of the treatment climate in psychiatric and substance abuse programs: Implications for improving patient outcomes. *Journal of Nervous and Mental Disease, 186,* 96–103.

Timko, C., Moos, R.H. & Finney, J.W. Models of matching patients and treatments. In: Craik, K., Price, R. & Walsh, W.B. (Eds.) *New Directions in Person-Environment Psychology, (2nd ed.).* Mahwah, NJ: Lawrence Erlbaum Assocs., Inc., in press.

Wolpe, P.R., Gorton, G., Serota, R. & Sanford, B. (1993). Predicting compliance of dual diagnosis inpatients with aftercare treatment. *Hospital and Community Psychiatry, 44,* 45–49.

Woody, G.E., McLellan, A.T., Luborsky, L. & O'Brien C.P. (1985). Sociopathy and psychotherapy outcome. *Archives of General Psychiatry, 42,* 1081–1086.

Woody, G.E., McLellan, A.T. & O'Brien, C.P. (1990). Research on psychopathology and addiction: Treatment implications. *Drug Alcohol Depend., 25,* 121–123.

Zweben, J.E. (1992). Issues in the treatment of the dual-diagnosis patient. In Wallace, B.C. (Ed.) *The chemically dependent: Phases of treatment and recovery,* Bristol, PA: Brunner/Mazel Publishing, pp. 298–309.

Use of Exclusion Criteria in Selecting Research Subjects and Its Effect on the Generalizability of Alcohol Treatment Outcome Studies

Keith Humphreys & Constance Weisner

This article originally appeared in the *American Journal of Psychiatry*, 2000, 157(4), 588–594 and is reprinted with permission.

Keith Humphreys, Ph.D., and Constance Weisner, Dr.P.H., Center for Health Care Evaluation, VA Palo Alto Health Care System, Department of Psychiatry and Behavioral Sciences, Stanford University School of Medicine, Stanford, California.

The research was supported by National Institute on Alcohol Abuse and Alcoholism grant AA-09750 and by the VA Mental Health Strategic Health Group.

Objective: Researchers have not systematically examined how exclusion criteria used in selection of research subjects affect the generalizability of treatment outcome research. This study evaluated the use of exclusion criteria in alcohol treatment outcome research and its effects on the comparability of research subjects with real-world individuals seeking alcohol treatment. Method: Eight of the most common exclusion criteria described in the alcohol treatment research literature were operationalized and applied to large, representative clinical patient samples from the public and private sectors to determine whether the hypothetical research samples differed substantially from real-world samples. Five hundred ninety-three consecutive individuals seeking alcohol treatment at one of eight treatment programs participated. A trained research technician gathered information from participants on demographic variables and on alcohol, drug, and psychiatric problems as measured by the Addiction Severity Index. Results: Large proportions of potential research subjects were excluded under most of the criteria tested. The overall pattern of results showed that African Americans, low-income individuals, and individuals who had more severe alcohol, drug, and psychiatric problems were disproportionately excluded under most criteria. Conclusions: Exclusion criteria can result in alcohol treatment outcome research samples that are more heavily composed of white, economically stable, and higher-functioning individuals than are real-world samples of substance abuse patients seen in clinical practice, potentially compromising the generalizability of results. For both scientific and ethical reasons, in addition to studies that use exclusion criteria, outcome research that uses no or minimal exclusion criteria should be conducted so that alcohol treatment outcome research can be better generalized to vulnerable populations.

Most clinical research studies in psychiatry and other areas of medicine exclude some potential subjects on the basis of predefined criteria. Use of exclusion criteria can optimize internal validity, make a study more feasible (e.g., by excluding patients who are nonadherent to treatment) (Pablos-Mendez, Barr, & Shea, 1998), reduce cost (e.g., by excluding patients who would be difficult to follow up), and serve ethical functions (e.g., by excluding patients who might be harmed by study participation). At the same time, exclusion criteria can have negative implications for the generalizability (or "external validity") of results to real-world practice settings. Because by definition patients meeting a study's exclusion criteria differ from those not excluded, the results of the study cannot be assumed to apply to excluded patients. Further, clinicians may be less likely to administer an intervention if the patients they typically treat differ from the subset of patients who met predefined criteria in research that supported the intervention's efficacy. Such concerns were a key reason for development of the National Institutes of Health guidelines encouraging inclusion of women and members of ethnic minority groups as subjects in clinical research (Department of Health and Human Services, 1994); the guidelines are intended to ensure that both the burden and the benefits of treatment research are fairly distributed throughout society.

The implications of exclusion criteria for the external validity and clinical utility of findings in various areas of research have not been systematically examined. The study reported here assessed whether exclusion criteria affect the generalizability of research findings in one important area of psychiatric research—treatment for alcohol problems. On October 1, 1997, approximately 625,000 individuals were receiving specialty alcohol treatment services in the United States (Substance Abuse and Mental Health Services Administration, 1999). The large number of treated individuals underscores the importance of clinical alcohol research's being relevant to real-world practice.

Meta-analyses of alcohol treatment research by Finney and Monahan (Finney & Monahan, 1996; Monahan & Finney, 1996) have indicated that 74.9% of outcome studies (254 of 339 studies conducted between 1980–1992) reported using exclusion criteria. This proportion is a conservative estimate because researchers do not always report the use of exclusion criteria; they may believe that exclusion procedures "go without saying" and do not need to be described, or they may be unaware that exclusion criteria have been implemented (e.g., when treatment staff surreptitiously discourage more severely disabled patients from participating in a clinical trial) (Devine, Brody, & Wright, 1997). The nine most common exclusion criteria used in the alcohol treatment studies reviewed by Finney and Monahan were psychiatric/emotional problems, noncompliance/lack of motivation, serious medical problems, neurological impairment (e.g., organic brain syndrome), drug abuse problems, lack of success in prior alcohol treatment, residence far from the treatment facility, social instability (e.g., unmarried, unemployed), and residential instability.

To examine the effect of exclusion criteria on the generalizability of findings from alcohol treatment research, the present study operationalized eight of these commonly used exclusion criteria and then applied them to real-world samples of patients seeking treatment at representative alcohol programs in the public and the private sector. By comparing patients who were excluded or not excluded under each rule, we estimated how exclusion criteria changed the samples in question, in other words, the extent to which the criteria produced research samples that differed from real-world clinical samples.

Method

Patients

Participants were individuals ($N = 593$) seeking treatment at one of eight alcohol treatment programs that were representative of public and private-for-profit programs in a northern California county (Weisner & Schmidt, 1995). In terms of the demographic characteristics of the population and the treatment services available, this county is representative of many counties in the United States. To be considered eligible for participation, patients had to be at least 18 years old and able to complete a structured, in-person interview (i.e., non-English-speaking patients and patients suffering from cognitive impairment or delirium were excluded). During the period of fieldwork, 690 of 739 consecutive admissions (93.4%) met inclusion criteria for the study. Of the 338 study-eligible individuals admitted to the public programs, 298 (88.2%) were asked to participate and consented. Of the 352 study-eligible individuals admitted to the private programs, 295 (83.8%) were asked to participate and consented. A chi-square analysis indicated that this difference in participation rate between public and private systems was not significant ($\chi^2 = 2.71$, $df = 1$, $p > 0.05$). Of the 97 eligible patients who did not agree to participate in the study, 57 (58.8%) were non-Hispanic Caucasian and 62 (63.9%) were male. These proportions are similar to those of the study sample, as described below.

Men ($N = 391$) composed slightly under two-thirds of the sample (65.9%). At intake, 211 (35.6%) participants were separated or divorced, and 167 (28.2%) were married or living in a marriage-like relationship. About two-thirds of the sample ($N = 380$, 64.1%) were unemployed. The most common racial/ethnic backgrounds were non-Hispanic Caucasian (51.9%, $N = 308$) and African American (34.2%, $N = 203$). The mean age of the participants was 39.0 years ($SD = 10.5$).

Programs

Alcohol treatment programs were selected on the basis of size (more than one admission per week) and primary funding source. The six publicly funded programs included two detoxification units, two residential facilities, and two outpatient clinics. At the time of the study, public county substance abuse services in California were mainly funded by federal block grants and matching funds from the state and its counties. Almost all patients in the public programs either had no insurance or had publicly funded insurance such as Medicaid. The two private programs were large, for-profit, hospital-based units that offered both inpatient and outpatient services and were primarily funded by fee-for-service insurance. These programs drew clients from all parts of the county and were representative of private programs in the county.

Procedure

Trained research staff independent from the treatment programs recruited participants on-site. Research staff described the study to eligible patients and made it clear that the decision of whether to participate in the study would have no impact on treatment services they would receive. After the study was fully explained, written, informed consent was obtained from the 593 patients who decided to participate. For each completed interview, $20 was paid either to the participant or to the residents' fund at the treatment program.

The widely used Addiction Severity Index (McLellan et al., 1980) served as the core assessment instrument. The Addiction Severity Index produces continuous composite scores (range = 0–1) for alcohol, drug, and psychiatric problems. It has excellent concurrent reliability and has been shown to have discriminant and concurrent validity across a variety of substance-abusing populations (McLellan et al., 1985). The Addiction Severity Index was supplemented with questions from the Diagnostic Interview Schedule for Psychoactive Substance Dependence (Robins et al., 1989) that assessed the presence or absence of nine drug dependence symptoms (e.g., tolerance, withdrawal symptoms, disruption of important daily activities) in the past 30 days. Finally, participants were asked to report the dates and types of any prior alcohol and psychiatric treatment episodes.

Operationalization and Analysis of Exclusion Criteria

Using the data gathered, eight of the nine commonly used exclusion criteria were operationalized: psychiatric/emotional problems, noncompliance/lack of motivation, medical problems, drug dependence, lack of success in prior alcohol treatment, residence distant from the treatment facility, social instability, and residential instability (table 1). The effect of an exclusion criterion for neurological impairment on the characteristics of samples could not be evaluated here because neurological impairment was an exclusion criterion in the present study. Operationalizations were chosen to be the same or similar to widely employed operationalizations in the literature, within the constraints of the data of the present study.

For each dependent variable, the eight exclusion rules were applied individually within the group of public sector subjects, and then within the group of private sector subjects. Thus all tests and comparisons were made separately within service systems rather than across them. For each exclusion rule, the proportion of patients excluded was calculated, and then the characteristics of the excluded and the included patients were compared. For categorical dependent variables (race, sex, and income), statistical significance was assessed using a chi-square test. For continuous variables (drug, alcohol, and psychiatric problems), statistical significance was assessed with independent samples t tests. For chi-square analyses, a threshold of $p < 0.01$ was used to judge significance, whereas for the more statistically powerful t test analysis, a threshold of $p < 0.005$ was employed. In practical terms, statistically significant

Table 1
Operationalization of Exclusion Criteria Widely Used in Clinical Research on Alcohol Treatment

Criterion	Operationalization
Psychiatric/emotional problems	Any of the following: inpatient psychiatric treatment in the past year; current treatment with psychotropic medication, hallucinations not directly attributable to substance use in the past 30 days, serious thoughts of suicide not directly attributable to substance use in the past 30 days
Noncompliance/lack of motivation	Patient rating of treatment for current substance abuse problem less than "considerably important" on a 5-point Addiction Severity Index item
Medical problems	Addiction Severity Index medical composite problem score two or more standard deviations higher than the norm for the general population (McLellan, Weisner, & Hunkler; in press)
Drug dependence	Three or more NIMH Diagnostic Interview Schedule (Robins et al., 1989) drug dependence symptoms in past 30 days
Unsuccessful prior alcohol treatment	Treatment for substance abuse prior to current treatment episode
Residence distant from treatment facility	Residence outside of the county in which the treatment program was located
Social instability	Both unmarried and unemployed
Residential instability	Not living in a house or apartment at intake

results in this study indicate that when a particular exclusion criterion is applied in a real-world treatment system, patients who are excluded from the resulting hypothetical research sample are significantly different on the variable of interest (e.g., race, sex) than patients who would be included in the research sample.

Results

The proportion of patients excluded under each criterion was as follows: noncompliance/lack of motivation (10.7% [N = 32] of public sector patients; 7.5% [N = 22] of private sector patients), residential instability (44.0% [N = 131], public sector; 16.9% [N = 50], private sector), medical problems (22.5%, [N = 67], public; 39.3% [N = 116], private), residence distant from treatment (19.8% [N = 59], public; 50.8% [N = 150], private), psychiatric/emotional problems (34.6% [N = 103], public; 50.5% [N = 149], private), drug dependence (55.4% [N = 165], public; 55.3% [N = 163], private), social instability (72.5% [N = 216], public; 40.7% [N = 120], private), and unsuccessful prior alcohol treatment (74.8% [N = 223], public; 57.6% [N = 170], private). Overall, large proportions of patients in both systems were excluded under most rules. Thus, in a treatment outcome study conducted using these exclusion criteria, many or most of these treated patients would not be eligible to participate.

Race

Of the 298 patients treated in public programs, 117 (39.3%) were white, 137 (46.0%) were African American, and 44 (14.8%) had other racial/ethnic backgrounds. For six of the exclusion criteria, excluded and included patients did not differ on race. However, under the drug dependence criterion, a significantly higher proportion of African Americans were in the excluded group (χ^2 = 38.16, df = 2, p<0.0001). Specifically, in the excluded group (N = 165), 25.5% of the patients (N = 42) were white and 61.8% (N = 102) were black, whereas in the included group (N = 133), 56.4% of the patients (N = 75) were white and 26.3% (N = 35) were black. In addition, under the exclusion criterion of distance from treatment, the tendency for blacks to be disproportionately excluded approached significance (χ^2 = 6.45, df = 2, p = 0.04): 59.3% (N = 35) of the 59 excluded patients were black versus 42.7% (N = 102) of the 239 included patients.

Of the 295 patients treated in the private sector programs, 191 (64.7%) were white, 66 (22.4%) were black, and 38 (12.9%) had other racial/ethnic backgrounds. In the private sector group, exclusion criteria also disproportionately affected black patients. There were significant differences in the racial characteristics of excluded and included patients for the psychiatric/emotional problem criterion (44 of 149 excluded patients [29.5%] were black versus 22 of 145 included patients [15.2%]; $\chi^2 = 10.25$, $df = 2$, $p < 0.01$), the drug dependence criterion (50 of 163 excluded patients [30.7%] were black versus 16 of 131 included patients [12.2%]; $\chi^2 = 15.50$, $df = 2$, $p < 0.001$), the social instability criterion (42 of 120 excluded patients [35.0%] were black versus of 24 of 174 included patients [13.8%]; $\chi^2 = 18.48$, $df = 2$, $p < 0.0001$), and the residential instability criterion (18 of 50 excluded patients [36.0%] were black versus 48 of 245 included patients [19.6%]; $\chi^2 = 8.54$, $df = 2$, $p < 0.01$).

Overall, in both service systems, but particularly in the private sector, the application of exclusion criteria tended to reduce the proportion of African Americans (and, obviously, increase the proportion of Caucasians) in hypothetical research samples. In other words, exclusion criteria often created treatment research samples that had different racial characteristics than do real-world treatment samples.

Sex

All but one exclusion criteria had no significant effect on the sex ratio of samples in either service system. The sole exception was the residential instability criterion, under which the proportion of males in public programs who were excluded (105 of 131 patients, 80.2%) was significantly higher than those who were included (101 of 167 patients, 60.5%) ($\chi^2 = 13.31$, $df = 1$, $p < 0.0001$).

Income

In the public sector, 289 of the 298 patients (97.0%) provided data on annual income. Of these, 184 (63.7%) had an annual income of less than $10,000, 69 (23.9%) had an income between $10,000 and $35,000, and 36 (12.5%) had an income of $35,000 or more. Of the 213 patients excluded under the social instability criteria, 157 (73.7%) had less than $10,000 income, 40 (18.8%) had an income between $10,000 and $35,000, and 16 (7.5%) had an income greater than $35,000. In contrast, the 76 patients included under this criteria had significantly higher incomes: 27 (35.5%) had less than $10,000, 29 (38.2%) had between

Table 2

Mean composite drug, alcohol, and psychiatric problem scores of patients in public sector and private sector alcohol treatment programs who were excluded from or included in hypothetical research samples by using common exclusion criteria[a]

Exclusion Criterion and Patient Group	Public Sector							Private Sector						
	N	Drug Mean	SD	Alcohol Mean	SD	Psychiatric Mean	SD	N	Drug Mean	SD	Alcohol Mean	SD	Psychiatric Mean	SD
Total sample	298	0.13	0.13	0.34	0.32	0.37	0.24	295	0.15	0.14	0.43	0.34	0.43	0.24
Psychiatric/emotional problems														
Excluded patients	103	0.16	0.13	0.41*	0.32	0.56*	0.19	149	0.18*	0.15	0.44	0.33	0.56*	0.20
Included patients	195	0.12	0.12	0.30	0.31	0.27	0.20	145	0.12	0.13	0.42	0.35	0.28	0.19
Noncompliance/lack of motivation														
Excluded patients	32	0.11	0.10	0.37	0.23	0.34	0.20	22	0.15	0.11	0.43	0.31	0.49	0.23
Included patients	266	0.14	0.13	0.33	0.33	0.38	0.24	273	0.15	0.14	0.43	0.34	0.42	0.24
Medical problems														
Excluded patients	67	0.16	0.14	0.48*	0.30	0.46*	0.25	116	0.15	0.15	0.48	0.35	0.49*	0.22
Included patients	231	0.12	0.12	0.29	0.31	0.34	0.23	179	0.14	0.13	0.39	0.33	0.38	0.24
Drug dependence														
Excluded patients	165	0.21*	0.11	0.34	0.31	0.43*	0.23	163	0.24*	0.11	0.29*	0.33	0.47*	0.24
Included patients	133	0.03	0.05	0.33	0.33	0.30	0.24	131	0.00	0.01	0.59	0.28	0.38	0.24
Unsuccessful prior alcohol treatment														
Excluded patients	223	0.14	0.13	0.36	0.33	0.38	0.24	170	0.16	0.14	0.46	0.34	0.46*	0.23
Included patients	75	0.12	0.11	0.28	0.27	0.35	0.24	125	0.13	0.14	0.38	0.34	0.37	0.25

(continued)

Table 2 (continued)

Exclusion Criterion and Patient Group	Public Sector							Private Sector						
	N	Drug Mean	SD	Alcohol Mean	SD	Psychiatric Mean	SD	N	Drug Mean	SD	Alcohol Mean	SD	Psychiatric Mean	SD
Residence distant from treatment facility														
Excluded patients	59	0.14	0.12	0.47	0.30	0.38	0.22	150	0.15	0.15	0.43	0.33	0.44	0.23
Included patients	239	0.13	0.13	0.30	0.31	0.37	0.25	145	0.14	0.13	0.43	0.35	0.41	0.25
Social instability														
Excluded patients	216	0.13	0.13	0.34	0.32	0.37	0.24	120	0.16*	0.14	0.42	0.34	0.45*	0.24
Included patients	82	0.13	0.13	0.21	0.25	0.50	0.28	174	0.01	0.11	0.48	0.35	0.34	0.23
Residential instability														
Excluded patients	131	0.13	0.13	0.34	0.31	0.37	0.22	50	0.17	0.14	0.39	0.32	0.47	0.22
Included patients	167	0.13	0.12	0.34	0.32	0.38	0.26	245	0.14	0.14	0.44	0.35	0.42	0.24

a. Drug, alcohol, and psychiatric problems assessed by using the Addiction Severity Index (McLellan et al., 1980). Comparisons of excluded and included patients under each criterion were conducted within each system (public and private) by using t tests (df = 296 for public program comparisons and df = 293 for private program comparisons). Total N = 294 for some analyses in the private sector because of one subject with some missing data.

* $p \leq 0.005$.

$10,000–$35,000, and 20 (26.3%) had greater than $35,000 ($\chi^2 = 37.54$, *df* = 2, *p* < 0.0001). Similarly, under the residential instability criterion, the 126 excluded patients had significantly lower incomes ($\chi^2 = 8.91$, *df* = 2, *p* < 0.01) than the 163 included patients (e.g., 73.0% of excluded patients [*N* = 92] had less than $10,000 income versus 56.4% of included patients [*N* = 92]). Under the criterion of noncompliance/lack of motivation, the tendency for excluded patients (*N* = 32, 11.1%) to have lower incomes than included patients (*N* = 257, 88.9%), approached but did not attain significance ($\chi^2 = 6.72$, *df* = 2, *p* = 0.03).

In the private sector, 289 of the 295 patients provided income data. Of these, 83 (28.7%) had less than $10,000 annual income, 84 (29.1%) had between $10,000–$35,000 income, and 122 (42.2%) had an income of over $35,000. In general, the eight exclusion criteria disproportionately excluded low-income patients. The pattern of those results approaching or attaining significance can most easily be summarized by reporting the proportion of excluded and included patients under each criterion that lived in extreme poverty (i.e., had less than $10,000 annual income): psychiatric/emotional problems (66 of 149 excluded patients [44.3%] lived in poverty versus 17 of 140 included patients [12.1%]; $\chi^2 = 37.25$, *df* = 2, *p*<0.0001), medical problems (37 of 115 excluded patients [32.2%] versus 47 of 175 included patients [26.9%]; $\chi^2 = 6.59$, *df* = 2, *p* = 0.04), drug dependence (57 of 160 excluded patients [35.6%] versus 26 of 128 included patients [20.3%]; $\chi^2 = 10.00$, *df* = 2, *p* < 0.01), unsuccessful prior alcohol treatment (65 of 167 excluded patients [38.9%] versus 18 of 122 included patients [14.8%]; $\chi^2 = 25.94$, *df* = 2, *p* < 0.0001), social instability (64 of 117 excluded patients [54.7%] versus 19 of 171 included patients [11.1%]; not a significant difference), and residential instability (26 of 50 excluded patients [52.0%] versus 57 of 239 included patients [23.8%]; not a significant difference).

To summarize, in both service systems and particularly in private programs, exclusion criteria significantly reduced the proportion of low-income patients who would have been eligible to participate in a hypothetical research study.

Drug, Alcohol, and Psychiatric Problems

Differences in the frequency of drug, alcohol, and psychiatric problems (as assessed by the Addiction Severity Index) among excluded and included patients under each exclusion criterion are presented in table 2. In public programs, patients excluded (*N* = 103) under the psychiatric/emotional problems criterion had significantly higher scores for alcohol and psychiatric problems than included patients ($N = 195$). Patients excluded under the medical problems criterion ($N = 67$) had significantly higher scores for alcohol and psychiatric problems than included patients ($N = 231$). Finally, patients excluded under the drug dependence criterion ($N = 165$) had significantly higher scores for drug and psychiatric problems than patients included under this criterion ($N = 133$).

Parallel effects were evident within the private sector. Excluded patients had higher scores for drug problems than included patients under the psychiatric/emotional problems, drug dependence, and social instability criteria. Similarly, excluded patients had higher scores for psychiatric problems than included patients under the psychiatric/emotional problems, medical problems, drug dependence, unsuccessful prior alcohol treatment, and social instability criteria. The only exception to the overall trend for exclusion criteria to differently affect more severely disabled patients was for the drug dependence criterion. When this criterion was applied in private programs, included patients had more severe alcohol-related problems than excluded patients.

Overall, the effects identified are of considerable magnitude, with the problem severity of excluded patients exceeding that of included patients by three or more standard deviations in some cases. The findings underscore the difficulty of excluding patient problems in only a single domain. For example, although it is not surprising that an exclusion criterion for psychiatric/emotional problems would reduce the frequency of psychiatric problems in a sample, the extent to which the same criterion can significantly alter the frequency of drug and alcohol problems of the samples is striking.

Sensitivity Analyses

A variety of alternative operationalizations were chosen for the exclusion rules to determine if the pattern of findings was significantly affected. These operationalizations ranged from substantially more restrictive (e.g., requiring that three of the four psychiatric problem indicators be present for the psychiatric/emotional problems criterion, requiring multiple prior treatments for the unsuccessful prior alcohol treatment criterion) to substantially more liberal (e.g., excluding all patients who had used drugs in the past 30 days, even if they did not have a diagnosis of drug dependence) than those applied here. These results (not shown here but available from the first author) indicated that, as would be expected, more liberal operationalizations resulted in larger proportions of patients being excluded than did more conservative operationalizations. However, across operationalizations, the pattern of disproportionate exclusion of African American, low-income, and more severely disabled patients continued to hold.

Discussion

The study reported here was stimulated by our observation that clinicians and administrators in alcohol treatment programs frequently speculate openly about whether the patients in their programs are similar to the research subjects who provided the data that is supposed to guide clinical intervention. This study operationalized common exclusion criteria and applied them to a real-world sample of patients seeking alcohol treatment. The results suggest that, in terms of sex ratios, samples of real-world patients are similar to samples of research subjects. However, the results indicate that exclusion criteria can produce research samples in which African American, low-income, and severely disabled patients are underrepresented. The differences between excluded and included patients were more pronounced in private programs because of the relative heterogeneity of the caseloads in these programs, which included both well-off patients with private insurance as well as poor, disabled patients with fee-for-service alcohol treatment coverage through Medicare. However, the differences were still of significant concern in public programs. The study results have yet to be replicated in other service systems and in other parts of the country, but given the size of the study samples, the representativeness of the county and the programs, and impressive size of the effects generated by the exclusion criteria, it would be unwise to ignore these results in the interim, particularly because race, socioeconomic status, and problem severity have been shown to influence alcohol treatment outcome (Gibbs & Flanagan, 1977).

One might argue that our operationalization of the exclusion criteria was too liberal and tended to overstate effects. However, this result seems unlikely, given that most of the criteria were quite strict (e.g., having medical problems of a severity more than two standard deviations higher than the mean for the general population), and sensitivity analyses indicated that alternative operationalizations produced similar results. Further, the exclusion criteria were applied singly. Applying criteria singly has a smaller effect on research samples than applying multiple exclusion criteria, which is done in most studies of alcohol interventions. To take a recent, well-known example, Project MATCH (Matching Alcoholism Treatments to Client Heterogeneity, 1997), the largest randomized trial of alcohol treatment ever conducted, excluded potential participants who were unwilling to complete an extensive assessment battery, had used intravenous drugs in the past 6 months, were dependent on any drug other than marijuana, were currently a danger to themselves or others, had probation or parole requirements that would interfere with protocol participation, were residentially unstable, could not identify a collateral contact who would assist in locating them at follow-up, were acutely psychotic, had severe organic impairment, or had planned or current involvement in treatment other than that provided in the study (as well as, of course, patients who were unwilling to be randomly assigned to treatment). As a result, more than 60% of the patients presenting for alcohol treatment were excluded from that study, which is unsurprising given the data presented here.

The higher likelihood that African Americans, low-income individuals, and more severely troubled patients will be excluded from clinical alcohol research can have significant scientific, clinical, and ethical consequences. From a scientific viewpoint, exclusion criteria can enhance internal validity and thereby facilitate evaluation of treatment "efficacy" (i.e., how well a treatment works under ideal conditions) (Wells, 1999). At the same time, exclusion criteria weaken our ability to assess treatment "effectiveness" (i.e., how well a treatment works in the real world of day-to-day clinical practice) (Wells, 1999). For example, African Americans constitute about one-fourth of substance abuse patients in the United States (Substance Abuse and Mental Health Services Administration, 1999), so to the extent that substance abuse treatment research does not include them, it becomes less useful as a method for assessing treatment effectiveness (and for that matter, informing health care policy decisions that affect African Americans). Further, whether a study is primarily aimed at assessing treatment efficacy or treatment effectiveness, the results presented here suggest that some exclusion criteria can make a study more difficult to complete. Because some criteria exclude many potential research participants, fieldwork time may need to be extended until enough nonexcluded patients are admitted to the recruitment site.

Clinically, the differences produced by exclusion criteria between research and real-world samples of patients with alcohol problems may help explain the commonly described "research-practice gap." Many treatment providers work in alcohol programs where the majority of patients are low-income persons with minority racial/ethnic background who have comorbid psychiatric and drug problems; in short, the very type of patient who is particularly likely to be excluded from alcohol treatment research. Practitioners may be understandably wary about applying findings from samples that have been "creamed" through exclusion criteria to omit such disadvantaged and troubled patients.

As for ethical consequences, the medical research community has already reached consensus that African Americans and more severely troubled individuals have a legitimate expectation that publicly funded medical science will be relevant to them (Department of Health and Human Services, 1994). We do not believe that the tendency of exclusion criteria to reduce the number of poor and African American individuals in treatment samples has been an outcome intended by researchers. We are sure that researchers are committed to having their work be useful in the treatment of vulnerable populations; thus we have pointed out how exclusion criteria can inadvertently subvert this goal.

Obviously, exclusion criteria are sometimes necessary. However, we concur with Wells (1999) that the scientific process of evaluating interventions is not complete until studies with minimal or no exclusion criteria are conducted, such as is more often the case in the burgeoning field of health services research. Funding agencies can help treatment researchers conduct such studies by recognizing that loosening or eliminating exclusion criteria may in some cases raise the cost of conducting outcome research (Wells, 1999) (e.g., more funds may be needed to locate more severely troubled participants at follow-up). Because it seems unlikely that alcohol treatment research is the only area of research in which exclusion criteria may compromise generalizability, we urge other psychiatric and medical researchers to undertake systematic analysis of these issues in their own fields of intervention research.

References

Department of Health and Human Services (1994). National Institutes of Health Guidelines on the inclusion of women and minorities in clinical research. *Federal Register 59,* 11146.

Devine, J. A., Brody, C. J., & Wright, J. D. (1997). Evaluating an alcohol and drug treatment program for the homeless: an econometric approach. *Evaluation and Program Planning, 20,* 205–215.

Finney, J. W. & Monahan, S. C. (1996). The cost-effectiveness of treatment for alcoholism: A second approximation. *Journal of Studies on Alcohol, 57,* 229–243.

Gibbs, L. & Flanagan, J. (1977). Prognostic indicators of alcoholism treatment outcome. *International Journal of Addiction, 12,* 1097–1141.

Matching Alcoholism Treatments to Client Heterogeneity. (1997). Project MATCH posttreatment drinking outcomes. *Journal of Studies on Alcohol, 58,* 7–29.

McLellan, A. T., Luborsky, L., Cacciola, J., Griffith, J., Evans, F., Barr, H. L., & O'Brien, C. P. (1985). New data from the Addiction Severity Index: Reliability and validity in three centers. *Journal of Nervous and Mental Disease, 173,* 412–423.

McLellan, A. T., Luborsky, L., Woody, G. E., & O'Brien, C. P. (1980). An improved diagnostic evaluation instrument for substance abuse patients: The Addiction Severity Index. *Journal of Nervous and Mental Disease 168,* 26–33.

McLellan, A. T., Weisner, C., & Hunkler, E. (in press). Data from general membership and treated samples of HMO members: One case of norming the Addiction Severity Index. *Journal of Substance Abuse Treatment.*

Monahan, S. C. & Finney, J. W. (1996). Explaining abstinence rates following treatment for alcohol abuse: A quantitative synthesis of patient, research design and treatment effects. *Addiction, 91,* 787–805.

Pablos-Mendez, A., Barr, R. G., & Shea, S. (1998). Run-in periods in randomized trials: Implications for the application of results in clinical practice. *JAMA, 279,* 222–225.

Robins, L. N., Helzer, J. E., Cottler, L., & Golding, E. (1989). *National Institute of Mental Health Diagnostic Interview Schedule, version III, revised.* St. Louis: Washington University, Department of Psychiatry.

Substance Abuse and Mental Health Services Administration (1999). *Uniform Facilities Dataset (UFDS).* Washington, DC: Office of Applied Studies, Substance Abuse and Mental Health Services Administration.

Weisner, C. & Schmidt, L. (1995). The Community Epidemiology Laboratory: Studying alcohol problems in community and agency-based populations. *Addiction, 90,* 329–341.

Wells, K. B. (1999). Treatment research at the crossroads: The scientific interface of clinical trials and effectiveness research. *American Journal of Psychiatry, 156,* 5–10.

First Person Account: Insight from a Schizophrenia Patient with Depression

Chris L. Fleshner

This article originally appeared in the *Schizophrenia Bulletin,* 1995, 21(1), 703–707.

Chris L. Fleshner has an AAS degree in computer programming from Western Iowa Technical Community College, Sioux City, Iowa. He was a systems programmer analyst at a major insurance company and was also involved in contract programming. He has completed classes in Auto Cad, and he is currently using that program to do computerized drawings of inventions for a patent law firm. Mr. Fleshner has two brothers, two sisters, and parents who have been very supportive and understanding of his illness since his first treatment in October 1987.

Nearly every person I've talked with who has a mental illness can come up with a date that it began. What they really meant was, the date when it got so bad they could no longer function. Around July of 1987 I was doing a lot of self-examination. I became obsessed with the Bible, particularly the book of Revelation. Up to that point I had not really studied much of the Bible. But it seemed as though my life was coming to an end, so what better book to read than Revelation? At that time I was working on an entirely new reality, one with mysticism in it, one with emotional gratification beyond any reasonable comprehension. In fact, I experienced it, but I also experienced terror and hell. This was all due to my illness.

It was during this time of reading the Bible and fasting that I had my first emotional trauma coupled with a hallucination. At the time I thought it was evil. I thought people could transfer themselves, their thoughts and minds, from one body to the next, but it was more complex than that. In fact when this transfer occurred you would actually "see" the person from whom the transfer had been taken. For example, you imagine person A transferring his or her mind to person B. Although in "reality" person B is the physical entity before you, person A is the one you actually "see." I could actually see both (hence the hallucination). Deception thus existed because of this mind switch. In reality I was looking at a co-worker and nothing more.

I think it was later in the week when I began to have more serious delusions. I was responsible for loading copies of programs for the online system programmers. This authority was given to one person to consolidate the process and avoid costly errors. It was usually quite stressful on Fridays because the online transfer would happen Thursday night. This meant the freshly changed program might develop problems the following morning, thus requiring a "dynamic load" to change the erroneous copy to a working copy. So one Friday, I imagined that the end of the world was coming and those programmers who wanted their names in "the book of life" (Rev. 20:12) would have to go through me to save their lives, or was it the end of their lives? I didn't know. It was so real. I felt as though I was a demon and a savior, holding the key to all these people's lives, and that the computer was actually determining their fate via every key I punched. I imagined the file cabinets (full of microfiche) were in fact transcripts of every thought and every state-ment anybody had ever made—the necessary "goods" by which to judge each individual's salvation. Instead of a merciful judgment, it was a financial enterprise in which corruption pervaded every corner. The "higher-ups" would have the power to manipulate records that would incriminate or discredit them.

I dealt with the concept of killing the people (via the dynamic load process) by denying it was actually happening and being totally unaware of the killing. I was imagining myself a pawn in a giant game of decep-tion against humanity. I lived all this as if it were reality. It was terrify-ing. However, now I know this was all due to my then undiagnosed mental disorder.

Back then my delusions caused tearfulness at times and conse-quently my boss suggested I see a psychiatrist. I did go and see one, but I was too sick by then to be able to realize all this was in my imagina-tion. I was certain the therapist did not have my best interest in mind and in fact considered him a part of the corrupt system of knowledge/ judgment that I referred to earlier. Trusting your therapist is essential in getting on the road to mental health.

These thoughts and others caused my breakdown and finally my decision to quit the company I was working for. Unfortunately, I lost my disability benefits when I made that poor decision. I decided to go back to school to get a bachelor's degree. I struggled further with my mental illness at Wichita State University and could not complete the first semester. Finally my parents came from Oklahoma and picked me up. I went to a clinic and had my second experience with the mental health profession. The clinic first gave me talk therapy from a psychologist. Next I'd be ushered into a room where the doctor prescribed medication; my first was Mellaril. Later, a "friend" of mine, curious about my problems, called and I told him I was taking the Mellaril. He, being a pot smoker, just laughed and thought I was doing it for kicks. I have since discontinued my friendship with him. Disassociation with friends that use drugs is highly advisable.

The problems I have are not easily understood. They have pretty much rendered me unemployable for any length of time. In some cases, I think my illness aided me in dealing with abstract programming applications. But I would gladly give up the abstract thoughts and creativity for emotional receptiveness, stability, and energy.

My brother said the other day, "You are very creative." He went on to say I should write a book about my illness so people could try to understand. In fact, it is true that this illness enriches my imagination, but it can be very frightening and at times debilitating. It seems my mental illness will not just go away. It is a chronic situation in which the complications are mental and not physical. With the body, when an organ fails, sometimes complications develop in another part of the body. With the mind, it is a thought or thoughts pervading the conscious and/or subconscious that build up, yielding false beliefs.

I would like to describe the few delusions I've had in the past to help others understand how frightening and real these thoughts can be. They are a thumbs up from President Clinton on TV, a nip on the thumb from a dog, a smile from my mother while my nephew had difficulty swallowing a piece of potato. I now recognize all these past delusions as false, caused mainly by my condition stabilizing with the medications I take.

The sign from Clinton stems from my uncertainty about whether to vote for the Governor. I was wavering between Clinton and Perot. On the morning of the vote, as I drove to the polls, I decided to vote for Clinton. (Most of the time I felt that I would vote for him anyway.) When I went to the polls, voting was not by machine but rather by ballot. After receiving instructions on how to fill out the ballot I thought I heard the registrar say to initial it in the lower right-hand corner. I wondered why I would have to initial a ballot. It is supposed to be a secret ballot. Immediately I suspected that my vote and my vote alone would determine the destiny of the presidency for election year 1992. (In fact there were initials on the form itself, which needed to appear through the ballot holder so the ballot would go into the ballot box face down.) Later thoughts of my "sentencing" those individuals at work to death (the computer incident) crept in. I thought Clinton was the power boss who controlled everything including this "evil empire." So later, while watching TV, I saw what I perceived to be a rather sheepish, maybe slightly devilish glance from Clinton and a thumbs up (presumably at me) for having cast my vote the way I did. You see I had an additional delusion that while watching TV the subject being televised can peer right into your living room (which, by the way, is not far down the road technologically). In my deluded mind, the thumbs up was for me personally for voting as I did. I thus made myself responsible for voting in somebody who at the time I felt participated in the knowledge/ judgment system of corruption I described earlier. The Clinton delusion stemmed from the "voice" that said to initial the ballot.

The nip on the thumb was my mother's thumb, not my own, but it caused me mental pain just as well. I was having a rather open discussion about God with my sister and Mom, and my mind had been wandering. I had just told my sister how God operates in my life. I had been attending a support group, which has helped quite a bit. At times it seems as though God works through the people there. Anyway, I was beginning to tell her this when my sister's dog nipped my mom. Immediately, I thought it was a sign from God that my going to the support group was wrong. It was further reinforced by the blood that was coming out of her finger, analogous to Christ's crucifixion. This was a delusion. I was distraught, and it didn't end there. My sister said innocently, "God doesn't give signs that often." I thought to myself, "True. I haven't seen a sign in a long time, and there it was—the dog bite—so I'd better pay heed." Then I said, "Maybe it was a sign from the devil." My sister said, "He wouldn't bother." What she meant was that the devil would not bother with" such a trivial sign as a little nip on the thumb, but what I perceived was that the devil wouldn't bother with me because I was too sinful to worry about. This only furthered the self-destructive paranoid delusion.

The last delusion I mentioned stemmed from when I was in Wichita. There was a job service called "Man Power," a name that can take on additional connotations if taken into an ill mind. The incident with my nephew occurred during a rather stress-filled day. My sister and her husband's mom and dad were here for a visit and dinner. I occasionally suffer from paranoia regarding food; for example, it is evil to eat food and barbaric to eat meat. My Mom had fixed a large meal and everybody had helped themselves to some of the meat. My cute little nephew Sam sat in his highchair next to my mom, and my sister watched as mom fed him a few potatoes. He was having difficulty swallowing the potatoes, and my sister was concerned. She wasn't yelling or anything, just a little nervous about him being able to swallow what he had in his little mouth. Just then I looked up at my mom and she smiled at me. I thought it was an evil smile and that she purposely fed him too much so he would choke and die. She had been changing his diapers all day long, caring for him the way grandmothers do, and I thought she was doing harm to him. I was certain of it then, but now I am certain it was a delusion brought about by my mental illness. My paranoia sometimes tells me that children are born to provide a vessel for a future inhabitant who is aging. This was reinforced by the delusion I had about the "Man Power" company. In my mind I thought that a child is not his own person, but rather a "pawn" in this corrupt company. The corruption in my mind extended all the way up to the President of the United States. My nephew Sam was going to be a vessel for me. It was terrifying! As I write this I wonder whether this thought will extend to God being corrupt too! Writing this enables me to detect this line of thinking and understand it as fiction, a wild imagination coupled with mental illness.

Nevertheless, the story about my nephew is very disturbing. I believed it and even acted on it. I got up out of my chair, walked out, and hitched a ride to the Psychiatric Crisis Center. I even accused my mother of child abuse. It was a few hours before I realized that the whole thing was in my mind. I called my brother in Seattle and he talked me through it. I came home to a worried family and my snoozing nephew.

It probably isn't comforting hearing these things but it is possible to find relief. The key is to be able to detect these false beliefs and reinforce them as fiction at a later time. Unfortunately, these thoughts snowball. I can't control the snowball effect (cause) but I can control the snowball affect (influence).

If I could control the cause, I would be able to help a lot of people suffering from schizophrenia. I'll leave that up to researchers who are studying schizophrenia and related disorders.

What I can do is give information about the current mental state of a person diagnosed with schizophrenia. I can also give some tips on how to help yourself if you suffer from schizophrenia.

While not an extremely common aspect of mental disorders, it is a problem nonetheless. Judgment and decision-making are greatly affected by your emotions. If you lack emotion people might consider you cruel or insensitive. Cruel is definitely not the case. In the most literal sense, insensitive basically hits the nail on the head—insensitive in the sense that the emotional sense is defective. This is not by choice, however. The minds of individuals with schizophrenia simply do not respond to feelings on the level that a normal mind does. I cannot imagine quite what it would be like to have good emotions the majority of the time. I do know what it is like to have a low mood or a high mood. However, emotions have a great influence on the normal person's life and ultimately what they do from day to day. As a psychiatrist aptly put it, "It is difficult to feel."

Here is a dilemma. I do not know if it is possible to build up emotional sensitivity with my mental illness. I know that the medications can have a rather large impact on how one feels. So it is important, perhaps, to continue with research on better drugs for mental disorders. Flat emotions are an apparent trade-off for reduced psychotic symptoms. It has been my experience that flat emotions make one feel emotions to a lesser degree than a normal person.

In the meantime, is there anything you can do to help yourself? One main method is to reach out to others for support. Sometimes this is very difficult for people to do. Maybe they don't feel comfortable socially with the situation. Sometimes, it is not possible to meet with people and discuss problems for fear of being shunned.

The solution to the above-mentioned problems is trained mental health professionals. They can help if you will let them.

"Bad" or troubling thoughts contribute to a person's state of mind. The majority of the time the thoughts evoke shame, guilt, and anxiety. It is curious that we have these thoughts at all. My mother once told me, "Thoughts are free." It is true. They don't cost you a thing, so they shouldn't affect you in a negative way when they are troubling or bad. I've learned that the source of these thoughts is unimportant. Everybody has them from time to time. What you can do is treat them as a learning experience and learn to identify an aspect of your personality that perhaps the thoughts can be made analogous to. Then draw a positive picture from those thoughts. You may ask, how can you draw a positive picture from a negative thought? Well, you have to learn to accept that you are not perfect and those imperfections make up part of you anyhow. In many cases, those negative thoughts don't manifest themselves in your personality to any real degree, so why give them any more credence than a mere passing thought. These thoughts are a mechanism by which you can learn to grow by accepting your shortcomings.

I can't emphasize enough how destructive negative thoughts can be. It is no more comforting either, for somebody simply to say "Don't think that way," because after all, "thoughts are free." Without thoughts, what would we be? With all "good" thoughts, would our life not be rather mundane? I'm not advocating seeking out bad thoughts to enrich one's life. On the contrary, what I see is that these discomforting thoughts are instead a bit of anger surfacing, anger about not being willing to accept one's own faults or constructive criticism. Sometimes criticism is not constructive, and the same is true of some thoughts. Hence, some "bad" thoughts are present. The trick is to let these negative thoughts enrich your life, rather than destroy or control your life. It is possible to grow from negative thoughts.

The best part of all about life is that there are good thoughts to reflect on and to experience. On that note, I would like to say some positive things. The mentally ill, despite having to deal with stigma issues, have it better than they ever have. There are psychiatrists and trained counselors to help us. There are medications that lessen suffering. There are social programs to help the mentally ill. The public is slowly being educated. We need to keep all this going strong! I am very lucky because my parents and family are very supportive of me. Also, I have a support group and the people there to help me get well. The computer groups that I lead help my self-esteem. I set socialization goals in my first review and achieved them by the second. I am determined to continue to grow as a person and educate myself as much as I can about my condition. I am giving myself credit for my happiness, but a large part of this happiness is due to the people and case workers at the support group. Also, the psychiatrists I've had over the years have played a major role in improving my mental health.

Chapter Four: **Cognitive-Behavioral Approaches**

Cognitive Restructuring and the 12-Step Program of Alcoholics Anonymous

Fran Steigerwald & David Stone

This article originally appeared in the *Journal of Substance Abuse Treatment,* 1999, 16(4), 321–327 and is reprinted with permission.

Fran Steigerwald, M.Ed. and David Stone, Ph.D., Department of Counseling and Higher Education, Ohio University, Athens, OH.

Alcohol addiction affects many clients that enter the offices of traditional mental health professionals. Their recovery is impacted by what goes on inside the office, in treatment, as well as by involvement outside the office, in 12-step programs as Alcoholics Anonymous (AA). This article examines alcoholism as a thought disorder and cognitive restructuring as an effective model of treatment. Cognitive restructuring occurs in therapy and in AA. It can, therefore, be the bridge that encourages understanding and cooperation between the two factors influencing recovery.

Introduction

Alcohol addiction affects many of the clients that are seen in the day-to-day practice of mental health. It is estimated that 10 million men, women, and children suffer from alcoholism in the United States, and another 14 to 18 million adults are problem drinkers (National Council on Alcoholism, 1989). A federal survey by the National Center for Health Statistics (1991) found that 4 in 10 Americans have been exposed to alcoholism in their families. Miller and McCrady (1993) estimated that 1 in 10 Americans have attended an Alcoholics Anonymous (AA) meeting and 1 in 8 have attended a 12-step program.

Treatment and recovery for alcohol addiction involves multifaceted approaches, usually including both addiction treatment and participation in AA. Treatment of addictions, which involves a cognitive focus through restructuring ineffective thinking, has been used in the offices of many mental health practices (Brown, 1985; Haaga & Allison, 1994; Henman & Henman, 1990; Pecsok & Fremouw, 1988; Sylvain & Ladoucheur, 1992). Recovery of addictions also moves outside the office practice to include AA involvement. Brown, Peterson, and Cunningham (1988) surveyed inpatient alcohol treatment programs and found that 95% incorporated AA and Narcotics Anonymous (NA) into their programs of recovery. According to Johnson, Phelps, and McCuen (1990) programs such as AA serve as a resource to 15 to 20% of clients/patients in health-professional offices and 30% of general hospital patients. These stated percentages are based on clients who meet the criteria for addiction to alcohol and drugs. Further, Valliant (1983) found attendance at AA meetings to be a significant variable factor (28%) impacting positive clinical results, even over other important variables, such as employment and marital status.

Since effective alcohol addiction treatment is clearly multifaceted, counselors and other professionals in the field of mental health need to have a thorough understanding of what AA and other 12-step programs do for individuals caught in the throes of alcohol or drug addiction. Counselors' awareness and understanding of the local recovery support community as a valuable tool, impacts the recovery of the addicted as well as those in relationship with the addicted (Johnson & Chappel, 1994).

Participation in AA is far-reaching; but, Henman and Henman (1990) stated that there is often a "subtle and often overt mistrust" between traditional counselors and 12-step-program people. This mistrust often discourages counseling, inhibits recovery, and reflects the lack of counselor training in alcoholism addiction, as well as the lack of understanding of the principles of 12-step anonymous programs. Competent and supportive counselors need to understand the therapeutic interventions that occur both inside the counseling office and in the 12-step support groups, in order to maximize client recovery.

This article will explore the benefits derived from participation in AA as a therapeutic strategy of cognitive restructuring. This cognitive intervention will be defined and examined in terms of its effectiveness with various populations in general, and, specifically, with alcoholics. Therapeutic gains will be discussed considering areas of participation in the 12-step program such as, meetings, sponsorship, and working the 12 steps.

Cognitive Restructuring

This section examines the history and development of cognitive restructuring, including definition, goal, and procedures, and concludes with populations and issues that have been impacted successfully by cognitive restructuring.

Traditional therapy utilizes cognitive approaches. Cognitive counseling regards thinking errors as the basis for emotional upsets and inappropriate behaviors, and focuses on internal dialogue as a foundation for a person's reaction to a life event. Beck (1976) is often credited with first using cognitive therapy for treatment of depression in the early 1960s. Since then, cognitive treatment has been used with a wide variety of client problems and populations.

Ellis, Beck, Meichenbaum, and Burns all address cognitive restructuring. Ellis (1962) explained "rational and irrational thinking." When thought, assumptions, and expectations are inaccurate, false, or irrational, clinical intervention into the thought process, rather than the responses to it, is appropriate. An individual learns some psychological distance in cognitive restructuring, in order to examine thoughts, see them as misconceptions in light of rational evidence, and change the perception. Cognitive restructuring helps a client control emotions and, ultimately, behaviors, by convincing the client that certain ideas are irrational and by teaching more rational, less defeating ideas. Beck (1976) described "automatic thoughts." These are thoughts that spring up without deliberate reasoning, usually unaware to the client or uncritically accepted as true, and cause negative emotions. He identified four patterns: dichotomous thinking (things are either good or bad), overgeneralization (arriving at conclusions based on little data), magnification (catastrophizing), and arbitrary inference (arriving at conclusions without evidence). Meichenbaurn (1977) discussed "self-instructions." His cognitive-behavioral modification is self-instructional therapy. The client is taught to focus on self-talk and to modify the instructions. Cognitive restructuring plays a central role in this theory by helping the client to reorganize aspects of thinking and to become in control, or his or her own "Executive Processor," and direct the restructured thoughts. Burns (1980) outlined "distorted thinking." His cognitive approach begins with understanding that a person feels the way one thinks. Once the connection is made between thought and feeling, the next step is to examine the illogical thoughts that contribute to the bad feelings. Burns put these distorted thoughts into 10 categories: all-or-nothing thinking, overgeneralization, mental filter, discounting the positives, jumping to conclusions (mind-reading and fortune-telling), magnification or minimization, emotional reasoning, should statements, labeling, and blame. In summary, cognitive therapists believe that a person needs to be taught to attend to shifts in affect, and that if a person is helped to effectively and positively think about life events, then negativity and behavior, which causes disruption, will lessen, allowing the client to have the goal of moving forward with a happier and more fulfilling life (Patterson & Welfel, 1994).

This goal is reiterated by Kaarsemaker, Jedding, and Lange (1986), with further clarification of how this is therapeutically achieved. They defined the goal of cognitive restructuring as a verbal intervention that challenges the client to find a new way of seeing his or her situation and to begin to effect positive change. They examined the verbal and behavioral interventions used by therapists in the cognitive restructuring process. They devised seven exclusive categories in this process: making comparisons, stressing consequences, giving assignments, providing information, reformulation, gathering information, and challenging the language of the client. Lange and Van Woudenberg (1994) further examined these categories in therapeutic settings, concluding that therapists used a particular intervention according to the therapy model they most practiced. Goldfried's (1988) research stated that there was no empirical support for any one therapeutic restructuring procedure over another. However, he translated several general principles that underline the therapeutic procedure for cognitive restructuring into a four-step process: (a) helping the client to see that thoughts affect emotional responses, (b) helping the client to see unrealistic beliefs and to offer alternatives to those beliefs, (c) exploring deeper awareness into beliefs and developing a hierarchical structure, and (d) helping the client to reevaluate beliefs and provide guidelines and practice for change and mastery.

This cognitive restructuring goal and these procedures have been successful with many populations with diverse issues such as, anxiety, depression, suicidal ideation, obsessions, relationship issues, and addictions. These issues all correlate with issues endemic to the alcoholic population. Goldfried (1988) discussed the theoretical application of using cognitive restructuring for symptom reduction in anxiety-based disorders. He considered it an appropriate intervention for a variety of forms of anxiety, especially "forms of social-evaluative anxiety" where there is "excessive concern" over other peoples' negative reactions (p. 66). Beck's (1976) cognitive restructuring approach in working with people who suffer from depression was that faulty thoughts were causal to the basic symptom of depression. Patsiokas and Clum (1985) studied the effects of cognitive restructuring on suicide attempters, often with accompanying depression, and noted significant improvements with this intervention. Suicide ideations are filled with distorted cognitions and faulty perceptions. Simos and Dimitriou (1994) used cognitive restructuring with obsessional rumination. Difficulty in realizing thoughts as irrational was also complicated by a culturally implied superstition. Cognitive restructuring involved realistic perceptions of responsibility, while attending to cultural beliefs. Huber and Milstein (1985) found the use of cognitive restructuring particularly beneficial in the couple's therapy and relationship difficulties. It helped to modify the underlying unrealistic beliefs couples held about their partners and their relationships and to restructure realistic goals and understandings.

Many addictive behaviors are also often treated successfully with cognitive restructuring. The Sylvain and Ladoucheur (1992) study showed some impact from the use of cognitive restructuring on the faulty thoughts and perceptions of gamblers in decreasing faulty verbalizations, increasing adequate verbalizations, thus decreasing frequency of gambling in controlled gambling situations. Haaga and Allison (1994) studied smokers' relapses in reference to cognitive coping tactics. They found that cognitive restructuring was used more consistently by abstainers then lapsers, and was associated with maintaining abstinence. Pecsok and Fremouw (1988) evaluated the effect of cognitive restructuring in binge eating among restrained eaters and found the intervention beneficial in reducing the magnitude of the binges. Effective treatments for bulimia nervosa have included cognitive restructuring as a major component, based on the fact that dysfunctional thinking and irrational perceptions lie at the root of binge-eating and purging behaviors (Fairburn, 1981; Wilson, 1984).

Cognitive Restructuring and the 12 Steps of AA

Alcoholic treatment utilizes cognitive restructuring. Henman and Henman (1990) discussed their model of counseling alcoholics, which encourages 12-step program participation with a therapy based on cognitive behavioral modification and neuro-linguistic programming (NLP) called, Cognitive-Perceptual Reconstruction (CPR). This model helps the alcoholic work interactively with the counselor to "explore and reframe" (cognitive restructuring) the old faulty alcoholic "assumptions, beliefs, attitudes, perceptual filters, internal dialogue, and unconscious patterns of processing information" (p. 107). The client is taught awareness of internal thought and dialogue and the process that is needed to challenge and change dysfunctional thinking.

Brown (1985) stated that with the progression of alcohol addiction, certain changes in cognitions occur, which form what has been commonly referred to as "alcoholic thinking." These are ways of thinking and rationalizations that are also accompanied by characteristics of "grandiosity, omnipotence, and low frustration tolerance" (p.97). Denial of these cognitive changes grows with the addiction and creates emotional immaturity, self-centeredness, and irresponsibility. Henman and Henman (1990) have also stated that alcohol addiction is a thought disorder and that these characteristic qualities contain the alcoholic's primary defenses.

These defenses are discussed by Bean-Bayog (1993) as three basic cognitive distortions that are held by active alcoholics: (a) they deny that they cannot control drinking; (b) they believe they drink abnormally because of pain and that drinking relieves pain, they do not see that drinking becomes the source of pain; and (c) they are ignorant and hopeless about solving this problem. Typical reactions to suggestions of recovery through AA are met most often by the alcoholic with furtive interest as well as fascination, and overtly with fear, shame, repression, revulsion, and rage. Abstinence from alcohol and changes in thinking along with actions that stabilize the commitment to change are necessary ingredients for recovery.

These necessary ingredients to recovery are best introduced at AA meetings, which provide an atmosphere in which cognitive restructuring can take place. Khantzian and Mack (1994) refer to AA meetings as a reprogramming process. The 12-step group encourages and supports alcoholics to explore and own selfish, self-seeking, and self-centered thinking, which brought them to AA in the first place. Members hear other members tell stories of their drunken thoughts, feelings, and behaviors. These narratives are familiar to all alcoholics in AA meetings and provide the drinkers with mounting external evidence that something was and is not right about their drinking and their cognitions, which underlie their substance abuse. Attendance at meetings provides alcoholics with "emotional arousal, hope, and dependence on others for relief" (George, 1990, p. 167). In the presence of fellow alcoholics for whom self-regulation has been an ongoing struggle, alcoholics learn that dependence on others is key to gaining strength for continued abstinence.

Attendance at AA meetings also allows members to learn the messages of cognitive restructuring. In AA, there are numerous and often-used slogans that have been gleaned from the AA literature. The slogans reflect some of the issues, like control, power, and distorted thinking, which alcoholics have struggled with while drinking. Repeatedly hearing these catch phrases assists recovering alcoholics to fight old ways of thinking. Robertson (1988) suggested that alcoholics cannot think straight and that these slogans provide extra protection. These sayings include, but are not limited to: "Let go and let God"; "Live and let live"; "Easy does it"; "Keep it simple"; and "One day at a time." Drinking alcoholics are in a battle for control over their drinking behavior, denying that they cannot control the behavior, only to lose control when they do drink. This distorted thinking about self-control can be dismantled with the slogans, which teach about relinquishing control.

Sponsorship is an additional area that operates as a cognitive strategy for change. Sponsors play a pivotal role in members working a solid program of recovery. AA sponsors serve as mentors and teachers for newcomers and assist in the development of new cognitions. Sponsorship is of paramount importance. Chapel (1993) found that 85% of AA members have sponsors. Sponsorship also serves a dual purpose. Sheerer (1988) found that the most important predictor of stable sobriety was being a sponsor.

The 12 steps of AA formulate the basis for cognitive restructuring and abstinence. DiClemente (1993) examined the 12-step program and indicated that it addressed significant problems for alcoholics with faulty beliefs and maladaptive cognitions, which need to be identified and changed in recovery. AA phrases like "stinking thinking" are commonly used in program to identify thought patterns that lead to relapse and interfere with sobriety.

According to AA's *Twelve Steps and Twelve Traditions* (Alcoholics Anonymous, 1981), the 12 steps, "are a group of principles, spiritual in their nature, which is practiced as a way of life, can expel the obsession to drink and enable the sufferer to become happily and usefully whole" (p. 15). *Alcoholics Anonymous* commonly referred to as *The Big Book* (Alcoholics Anonymous World Services, Inc., 1986), discussed the necessity for thoroughness and honesty in following the 12 steps, in order to change lives. The necessity to restructure thinking is addressed: "Some of us have tried to hold onto our old ideas and the result was nil until we let go absolutely" (p. 58). The letting go of old ideas and the turning of lives over to a higher power, a newly structured thought for most alcoholics, is fundamental to the 12-step recovery process. "This concept was the keystone of the new and triumphant arch through which we passed to freedom" (p. 62).

Fowler (1993) created an understanding of cognitive and affective recovery using a 12-step commitment, based on and expanding the work of Brown's (1985) phases of recovery, a progression from the drinking phase, through transition, early recovery, and ongoing recovery. The initial drinking phase cognitions are compartmentalized, with denial, defensiveness, manipulation, and selective screening operant. Object attachment is to alcohol. The therapeutic strategy is to try to break through the denial and faulty belief system. The transition phase is characterized by the admission of loss of control and alcoholism and is pivotal with the beginning of learning a new language (restructured cognitions) of recovery and relinquishing the old faulty thinking. The therapeutic strategies are concrete guidance, imitation, and reimaging, moving the object attachment from alcohol to AA meetings, slogans, and Steps 1 to 3. The early recovery phase starts with the beginning of an integration of new attitudes (restructured cognitions) resulting in new behaviors, moving from the isolated self-reliance based in old faulty thinking and ways of acting that perpetuated the addiction, to the ability to ask for help, rely upon a group, become teachable, and begin to reimage the self. The therapeutic strategies are 12-step self-exploration and therapy, grasping the paradox of freedom through dependence. Object attachment moves to include sponsorship, AA principles, and a higher power. The ongoing recovery phase begins with the realization that the 12 steps are a continuing life process. Identification of character defects and distorted life patterns using family of origin work and the 12 steps as tools for restructuring and reconstructing the past. Therapeutic strategies are based on critical reflection on beliefs and practices using the object attachment of sponsors, groups, friends, therapy, books, higher power, and meetings, to formulate a new recovering alcoholic identity that has an executive system that helps to activate and monitor integrated cognitions and continual ongoing practices. Henman and Henman (1990) create, in their CPR treatment, what they call a "new program adult" utilizing the new recovering cognitions to monitor the old irresponsible alcoholic "2-year-old" personality.

George (1990) stated that in order to get and maintain sobriety, first, one does not go through these 12 steps in a simple linear process. A new member of AA may, in fact, take them initially one after the other, but soon learns that recovery is a continual cycling through the various steps, with ongoing work, study, and discussion within the AA program. Second, step work involves effort and a commitment to the AA program. "Effort simply means to be willing to think new thoughts, to try new behaviors, to make an effort to do those things which are necessary to 'working the program'" (p. 169).

The program is a unified process. The 12 steps cannot be taken individually. The first three steps together provide the basis for a cognitive restructuring that allows for the distorted alcoholic cognitions, emotions, and behaviors to change. Step 1 challenges the cognitive distortions of grandiosity, defiance, and isolation by admitting powerlessness together with other alcoholics, "we admitted we were powerless..." Step 2 restructures this powerlessness into reliance and hope through belief in a higher power. Step 3 is the action step that cuts out self-will and begins dependence upon this higher power.

Step 1. We admitted we were powerless over alcohol—that our lives had become unmanageable.

Tiebout (1953), Bateson (1971), and Brown (1993) examined the beliefs about power and control with maintenance of abstinence and life-long change. Distorted faulty beliefs concerning the power of self and control form the basis of addiction. Brown (1993) stated that the recovery process paradoxically is based in relinquishing that self-power to find true power and freedom. "Recovery involves relinquishing the core belief of power over self and accepting the reality of loss of control over one's drinking or use of substance. Drinking alcoholics often believe they are empowered by alcohol when in fact they are victimized by it. Recovering alcoholics acknowledge that they have no power over alcohol and are, in turn, empowered by the truth and their acceptance of it" (p. 138).

Twelve Steps and Twelve Traditions (Alcoholics Anonymous, 1981) elaborated:

Who cares to admit complete defeat? Practically no one, of course. Every natural instinct cries out against this idea of personal powerlessness... Upon entering A.A. we soon take quite another view of this absolute humiliation. We perceive that only through utter defeat are we able to take our first steps toward liberation and strength. Our admission of personal powerlessness finally turn out to be firm bedrock upon which happy and purposeful lives may be built.... Our sponsors declared that we were victims of a mental obsession so subtly powerful that no amount of human willpower could break it....We stand ready to do anything that will lift the merciless obsession from us. (pp. 21–24)

Brown (1993) stated that powerlessness alone does not lead to sobriety. However, powerlessness acknowledged within a "complementary schema" does. Recovering alcoholics do not recover in isolation.

Step 2. Came to believe that a Power greater than ourselves could restore us to sanity.

Brown (1993) reflected how the reliance on a higher power offers alcoholics a continual challenge to that "alcoholic thinking" of omnipotence, grandiosity, and defiance. Bateson (1971) stated:

Implicit in the combination of these two steps is an extraordinary, and I believe correct idea: the experience of defeat not only serves to convince the alcoholic a change is necessary; it is the first spiritual experience. The myth of self-power is thereby broken by the demonstration of greater power. (p. 3)

He further elaborated that alcoholics are steeped in pride and in "symmetrical, competitive" relationships with themselves and others. This is based on distorted dichotomous thinking of winning and losing, which is permeated with control and power. Steps 1 and 2, admitting powerlessness and then reliance on a higher power, allow alcoholics to shift to complementary thinking and relationships, becoming of "service rather than dominance" (p. 16) and laying the foundations for the remaining steps.

Step 3. Made a decision to turn our will and lives over to the care of God as we understand Him.

The step is often referred to as the action step within the first three steps. It is directly linked to cognitive restructuring. Here, the concept of self-will is challenged and removed and dependency on a higher power is cultivated. Brown (1993) stated that the "first three steps are a direct assault on pathological egocentricity or narcissism, a condition that includes an inflated unrealistic belief in self-power" (p. 146), which needs to be changed for recovery to ensue.

Twelve Steps and Twelve Traditions (Alcoholics Anonymous, 1981) claims that the effectiveness of a recovery program depends upon how thoroughly this step is taken. The program alludes to a dissolving of egotism. The alcoholic challenges self-sufficiency and instead claims dependency. The difficulty and misunderstanding of this step with traditional psychology is discussed in AA literature. Dependency of any type is often viewed by mental health professionals as pathological. AA calls for a reexamination of the concept that all forms of dependency are wrong and suggests the need for an understanding of dependency in program as a process of bringing one's will in conformity with that of a higher power's will. "In times of emotional disturbance and indecision, we can pause, ask for quiet, and in the stillness simply say: 'God, grant me the serenity to accept the things I cannot change, courage to change the things I can, and wisdom to know the difference'"(pp. 40–41). The flexibility this step allows in using one's own understanding of a higher power, be it person, idea, or concept, helps make this step easier for many people who do have the traditional Judeo-Christian concepts of God, and thereby works to exclude no one from the recovery options offered (George, 1990).

Step 4. Made a searching and moral inventory of ourselves.

Step 5. Admitted to God, to ourselves, and to another human being the exact nature of our wrongs.

Step 6. Were entirely ready to have God remove all these defects of character.

Step 7. Humbly asked Him to remove our shortcomings.

Step 8. Made a list of all persons we had harmed, and became willing to make amends to them all.

Step 9. Made direct amends to such people whenever possible, except when to do so would injure them or others.

Steps 4 though 9 are often referred to as the "housecleaning" steps. These steps involve beginning with a personal moral inventory done with thoroughness and rigorous honesty, working with others to address interpersonal problems and increase awareness of personal defects. Most practicing alcoholics do not think to use introspection to focus on their defects. Introspection is integral both for recovery and as insurance against relapse by listing defects and persons that have been harmed with the destructive alcoholic behaviors and attitudes and making amends to them, while continuing to look for and resolve interpersonal problems (DiClemente, 1993). Guilt from past actions or omissions are decreased by confession, atonement, and making amends, so there is less need for defenses, projections, and distorted cognitions (Bean-Bayog, 1993).

> *Step 10. Continued to take personal inventory and when we were wrong promptly admitted it.*

> *Step 11. Sought through prayer and meditation to improve our conscious contact with God, as we understand Him, praying only for knowledge of His will for us and the power to carry that out.*

> *Step 12. Having had a spiritual awakening as the result of these Steps, we tried to carry this message to others, and to practice these principles in all our affairs.*

Steps 10, 11, and 12 are often referred to as the "maintenance" steps (Alcoholics Anonymous, 1981). Using a present time focus, these steps call for a restructured self, based on restructured cognitions, as the alcoholic moves through the stages of recovery. These steps require a continuing vigilance, spiritual development, a contact and reliance on a higher power, and attitudinal and characteristic trait changes that can help recovering alcoholics awaken to and maintain ego reduction, honesty, humility, gratitude, and responsibility, while being connected to something greater than themselves (Brown, 1993). In the 12th step, a recovering person moves toward altruism and uses his or her personal recovery to help others (Bean-Bayog, 1993).

Conclusion

Alcoholism needs to be thought of as a thinking disorder, with participation in AA and professional treatment working together to provide effective establishment and maintenance of abstinence. It is necessary that this unified action between AA and therapy be encouraged to facilitate client recovery. Attendance at AA meetings, obtaining, using, and eventually becoming a sponsor, and working the 12 steps provide a mechanism through which alcoholics learn new cognitions of recovery that can then be supported in counseling.

Mental health professionals who work with addicted persons need to possess knowledge of AA's 12 steps to ensure sound, ethically competent treatment. Information on how to access clients' local AA recovery support systems, and how to maximize their impact on the recovery process is necessary for those working with persons seeking assistance with recovery from chemical dependency.

Additional empirical research needs to be undertaken that calls for verification of AA's 12-step program as cognitive restructuring and discusses correlation of recovery with sound collaborative working arrangements of counseling professionals and AA, specifically addressing and working to further understand those areas that claim to have been historically problematic, such as spirituality, powerlessness, dependency, and alcoholic identification.

References

Alcoholics Anonymous. (1981). *Twelve steps and twelve traditions.* New York: Alcoholics Anonymous World Services, Inc.

Alcoholics Anonymous World Services, Inc. (1986). *Alcoholics Anonymous (3rd ed.)* New York: Author.

Bateson, G. (1971). The cybernetics of self. A theory of alcoholism. *Psychiatry 34,* 1–18.

Bean-Bayog, M. (1993). AA processes and change: How does it work? In B. S. McCrady & W. R. Miller (Eds.), *Research on Alcoholics Anonymous* (pp. 113–135). New Brunswick, NY: Rutgers Center of Alcohol Studies.

Beck, A. T. (1976). *Cognitive therapy and emotional disorders.* New York: International Universities Press.

Brown, H. P., Peterson, J. H., & Cunningham, O. (1988). Rationale and theoretical basis of a behavioral/cognitive approach to spirituality. *Alcoholism Treatment Quarterly, 5,* 47–59.

Brown, S. (1985) *Treating the alcoholic, a development model of recovery.* New York: John Wiley & Sons.

Brown, S. (1993). Therapeutic processes in Alcoholics Anonymous. In B.S. McCrady & W.R. Miller (Eds.), *Research on Alcoholics Anonymous* (pp. 113–135). New Brunswick, NJ: Rutgers Center of Alcohol Studies.

Burns, D. D. (1980). *Feeling good: The new mood therapy.* New York: William Morrow and Company.

Chappel, J. N. (1993). Working a program of recovery in Alcoholics Anonymous. *Journal of Substance Abuse Treatment, 11,* 99–104.

DiClemente, C. C. (1993). Alcoholics Anonymous and the structure of change. In B. S. McCrady & W. R. Miller (Eds.), *Research on Alcoholics Anonymous* (pp. 113–135). New Brunswick, NJ: Rutgers Center of Alcohol Studies.

Ellis, A. (1962). *Reason and emotion in psychotherapy.* New York: Lyle Stuart.

Fairburn, C. G. (1981). A cognitive-behavioral approach to the treatment of bulimia. *Psychological Medicine, 11,* 707–711.

Fowler, J. W. (1993). Alcoholics anonymous and faith development. In B. S. McCrady & W. R. Miller (Eds.), *Research on Alcoholics Anonymous* (pp. 113–135), New Brunswick, NJ: Rutgers Center of Alcohol Studies.

George, R. L. (1990). *Counseling the chemically dependent: Theory and practice.* Boston: Allyn and Bacon.

Goldfried, M. R. (1988). Application of rational restructuring to anxiety disorders. The *Counseling Psychologist, 16,* 50–68.

Haaga, D. A., & Allison, M. L. (1994). Thought suppression and smoking relapse: A secondary analysis of Haaga (1989). *British Journal of Clinical Psychology, 33,* 327–331.

Henman, J. O., & Henman, S. (1990). Cognitive-perceptual reconstruction in the treatment of alcoholism. In C. M. Sterman (Ed.), *Neurolinguistic programming in alcoholism treatment* (pp. 105–124). New York: Haworth Press.

Huber, C. H., & Milstein, B. (1985). Cognitive restructuring and a collaborative set in couples' work. *American Journal of Family Therapy 3*(2), 17–27.

Johnson, N. P., & Chappel. J. N. (1994). Using AA and other 12-Step programs more effectively. *Journal of Substance Abuse Treatment, 11,* 137–142.

Johnson, N. P., Phelps, G. L., & McCuen, S. K. (1990). Never try to carry a drunk by yourself. Effective use of self-help groups. *Journal of the South Carolina Medical Association, 86,* 27–31.

Kaarsemaker, M., Jedding, B., & Lange, A. (1986). Cognitief herstructureen, een inhoudsanalyse van 24 therapeizittingen [Cognitive restructuring, a content analysis of 24 therapy sessions]. *Directieve Therapie 6,* 294–308.

Khantzian, E. J., & Mack, J. E. (1994). Alcoholics Anonymous and contemporary psychodynamic theory. In M. Galanter (Ed.), *Recent developments in alcoholism, 7,* 67–89. New York: Plenum Press.

Lange, A., & Van Woudenberg, M. (1994). Cognitive restructuring in behavior therapy and in psychoanalytical therapy: A content analysis of therapy sessions. *Behavioural and Cognitive Psychotherapy, 22,* 65–73.

Meichenbaum, D. (1977). *Cognitive-behavior modification: An integrative approach.* New York: Plenum Press.

Miller, W. R., & McCrady, B. S. (1993). The importance of research on Alcoholics Anonymous. In B.S. McCrady & W.R. Miller (Eds.), *Research on Alcoholics Anonymous* (pp. 3–11). New Brunswick, NJ: Rutgers Center of Alcohol Studies.

National Center for Health Statistics. (1991). Alcohol impacts four of ten adults. Lincoln. [*NE] Star,* p. 3.

National Council on Alcoholism. (1989). *Facts about alcohol.* New York: Author.

Patsiokas, A. T., & Clum, G. A. (1985). Effects of psychotherapeutic strategies in the treatment of suicide attempters. *Psychotherapy, 22,* 281–290.

Patterson, L. E., & Welfel, E. R. (1994). *The counseling process.* Pacific Grove, CA: Brooks/Cole Publishing.

Pecsok, E. H., & Fremouw, W. J. (1988). Controlling laboratory binging among restrained eaters through self-monitoring and cognitive restructuring procedures. *Addictive Behaviors, 13,* 37–44.

Robertson, N. (1988). *Getting better: Inside Alcoholics Anonymous,* New York: Morrow.

Sheeren, M. (1988). The relationship between relapse and involvement in Alcoholics Anonymous. *Journal of Studies in Alcoholism, 49,* 104–106.

Simos, G., & Dimitriou, E. (1994). Cognitive-behavioral treatment of culturally bound obsessional ruminations: A case report. *Behavioral and Cognitive Psychotherapy, 22,* 325–330.

Sylvain, C., & Ladoucheur, R. (1992). Correction cognitive et habitudes de jeu chez les joueurs de poker video. *Canadian Journal of Behavioral Science, 24,* 479–489.

Tiebout, H. M. (1953). Surrender vs. compliance in therapy with special reference to alcoholism. *Quarterly Journal of Studies on Alcohol, 14,* 58–68.

Valliant, G. E. (1983). *The natural history of alcoholism.* Cambridge, MA: Harvard University Press.

Wilson, G. T. (1984). Toward the understanding and treatment of binge eating. In R. C. Hawkins, W. J. Fremouw, & P. F. Clement (Eds.), *The binge-purge syndrome: Diagnosis, treatment, and research* (pp. 264–289). New York: Springer.

Evaluating Substance Abuse Treatment Process Models: 1. Changes on Proximal Outcome Variables During 12-Step and Cognitive-Behavioral Treatment

John W. Finney, Charlotte A. Noyes, Adam I. Coutts, & Rudolf H. Moos

This article originally appeared in the *Journal of Studies and Alcohol, 59*, 371–380, 1998, and is published with permission.

John W. Finney, Ph.D., Charlotte A. Noyes, M.P.H., Adam I. Coutts, B.A., & Rudolf H. Moos, Ph.D., Program Evaluation Resource Center, HSR&D Center for Health Care Evaluation, Veterans Affairs Palo Alto Health Care System and Stanford University Medical Center, Palo Alto, CA.

Objective: This article provides data on the early linkages in the treatment process chains that are thought to underlie two prevalent approaches to substance abuse treatment—traditional 12-step treatment and cognitive-behavioral treatment. The focus is on the during-treatment changes on "proximal outcomes" that, according to the treatment theory underlying each modality, patients are supposed to undergo or achieve in order to experience a positive "ultimate outcome." Method: In all, 3,228 men receiving treatment in 15 Department of Veterans Affairs substance abuse treatment programs were assessed at treatment entry and at or near discharge from inpatient programs that had desired lengths of stay of 21–28 days. Results: Between intake and discharge, patients in 12-step programs improved more than did C-B patients on proximal outcome variables assumed to be specific to 12-step treatment (e.g., attending 12-step meetings, taking steps), whereas patients in cognitive-behavioral programs made no greater change (and in a few cases, less change) than did 12-step patients on proximal outcome variables assumed to underlie cognitive-behavioral treatment (e.g., self-efficacy, coping skills). Conclusions: These findings suggest that the proximal outcomes thought to be specific to cognitive behavioral treatment are actually general proximal outcomes of both 12-step and cognitive-behavioral treatment.

Substance abuse treatment is assumed to set in motion a therapeutic process chain that, although varying in the nature of the linkages for different modalities, connects a patient's entering treatment to a positive outcome (e.g., abstinence or reduced substance use) at a later point. As reflected in the current emphasis on patient-treatment matching (Mattson et al., 1994), the process underlying a given treatment modality is not assumed to be effective for every patient. However, treatment programs are presumed by their proponents to be effective, *if a patient complies with the treatment.* With respect to 12-step treatment, for example, the "Big Book" (Alcoholics Anonymous, 1976) states: "Rarely have we seen a person fail who has thoroughly followed our path" (p. 58).

Although studies of substance abuse treatment effectiveness have become commonplace, relatively few have investigated the processes underlying the effects of different treatment modalities (Morley et al., 1996). In this article, we provide data on the early linkages in the treatment process chains that are thought to underlie two prevalent approaches to substance abuse treatment—traditional 12-step treatment and cognitive-behavioral (C-B) treatment. More specifically, we focus on during-treatment changes on "proximal outcomes" (Rosen & Proctor, 1981). Proximal outcomes, sometimes referred to as "sub outcomes," are the specific changes in attitudes, beliefs and behaviors, that, according to a treatment theory, patients are supposed to undergo or achieve. Improvement on proximal outcome variables is assumed to lead to better "ultimate outcomes," such as reduced substance use.

Theory-Specified During-Treatment Changes in Traditional 12-Step Treatment

Traditional 12-step treatment combines the 12-step approach of Alcoholics Anonymous (AA), Narcotics Anonymous (NA) and Cocaine Anonymous (CA) with the disease model of addiction. It assumes that, as a result of a biological and/or psychological vulnerability, patients have lost control over use of the abused substance. Treatment attempts to bring about the patient's acceptance of the disease model of addiction, of an "alcoholic" or "addict" identity, and of abstinence as a treatment goal, as well as involvement in 12-step activities (e.g., attending meetings, getting a sponsor, working the steps).

Although several studies have assessed traditional 12-step proximal outcomes and attempted to link such proximal outcomes with ultimate outcomes (Brown & Peterson, 1991; Carroll, 1993; Christo & Franey, 1995; Gilbert, 1991; McKay et al., 1994; Montgomery et al., 1995), we found only two that examined during-treatment changes on 12-step proximal outcomes. In one study, patients who completed a 12-step based, Minnesota Model inpatient treatment program were less likely to see themselves as responsible for their addiction and less likely to consider their addiction as being due to internal (e.g., "I must be weak") or external (e.g., "domestic problems") factors than they were at treatment intake (Morojele & Stephenson, 1992). Rejection of such attributions is consistent with the disease model of addiction and, indeed, agreement with the statement "My addiction is a disease" increased significantly during treatment.

In the second study, Morgenstern and his colleagues (1996) assessed seven proximal outcomes among patients from two programs that employed a "traditional chemical dependency treatment" (TCDT) approach. Scores on proximal outcome measures conceptualized as specific to TCDT (acknowledgment of powerlessness over substance use, belief in a higher power, commitment to affiliate with Alcoholics Anonymous or Narcotics Anonymous, acknowledgment of having a disease of alcoholism or addiction, and belief that slips inevitably lead to a full-blown relapse) increased moderately, but significantly, during treatment. However, scores on proximal outcomes that are thought to be in common with those found in other forms of treatment (commitment to abstinence and intention to avoid high-risk situations) did not change significantly during treatment.

Although these two studies detected some expected changes on proximal outcome variables during the course of 12-step treatment, no study that we are aware of has examined whether changes on such variables occur to a greater extent in 12-step versus some other form of treatment. It is crucial to examine the therapeutic processes in more than one type of treatment if processes specific to a particular treatment approach are to be differentiated from more general processes (Hollon et al., 1987). In this study, we examine whether patients exposed to traditional 12-step treatment change more than patients in C-B programs on disease model beliefs, acceptance of alcoholic or addict identity, acceptance of abstinence as a treatment goal, attendance at 12-step meetings, having a sponsor, having friends in 12-step groups, reading 12-step materials and taking the 12 steps.

Theory-Specified During-Treatment Changes in C-B Treatment

Cognitive-behavioral treatment assumes that substance abuse is a learned behavior, whose onset and perpetuation is influenced by distorted beliefs about the effects of the abused substance and by reliance on substance use as a (maladaptive) coping behavior. Primary cognitive

proximal outcomes of C-B treatment are an enhanced sense of self-efficacy to remain abstinent in high-risk situations, decreased positive anticipated consequences of drinking or using drugs (positive substance use
expectancies), and increased expectancies regarding the benefits of quitting or reducing drinking behavior or drug use and reduced expectancies
regarding the costs of such outcomes (positive outcome expectancies).
In addition, most C-B programs attempt to impart cognitive and behavioral coping skills that clients can use to avoid drinking, drinking exces-
sively or using drugs in situations that previously had been associated
with heavy drinking or drug use. Many C-B programs also teach
patients general methods for coping with stressful situations.

With respect to during-treatment changes on cognitive proximal
outcomes, Rychtarik et al. (1992) found that patients' sense of self-efficacy increased during the course of inpatient treatment that employed a
cognitive-behavioral approach. McKay et al. (1993) reported a trend for
patient self-efficacy to decline less among patients receiving behaviorally
oriented aftercare following Behavioral Marital Therapy than among
patients receiving no aftercare. Aftercare participants initially low in self-
efficacy were more likely to exhibit increased self-efficacy by a 6-month
follow-up than were nonparticipants.

In terms of changes in coping skills, Monti and colleagues (1990)
observed that patients treated in communications skills training
improved more on the rated effectiveness of their coping responses than
did persons treated in a mood management condition. No differences
were found on other observer-rated dimensions of coping, however.

General Mediators of Treatment Effects

Proximal outcomes conceptualized as specific to a particular form
of treatment may, in fact, be general mediators of the effects of multiple
treatment modalities (Hollon et al., 1987). Variables that have been conceptualized as proximal outcomes of C-B treatment also may be proximal outcomes of other types of treatment, including traditional 12-step
treatment (McCrady, 1994). For example, patients in 12-step treatment
may develop an enhanced sense of being able to abstain in relapse-
inducing situations. Indeed, self-efficacy was conceived of by Bandura
(1977) as a general mediator of intervention effects. Likewise, patients in
12-step treatment may change their substance use and outcome
expectancies and may acquire cognitive and/or behavioral skills to cope
with relapse-inducing situations. In this regard, Morojele and

Stephenson (1992) reported that patients were more likely to believe that abstinence would result in positive outcomes at the end of their Minnesota Model treatment than at the start of treatment. Wells et al. (1994) found no difference in coping-skills acquisition among patients who used cocaine and were exposed to either relapse prevention or 12-step treatment. Finally, Snow et al. (1994) observed that persons currently involved in AA indicated that they used stimulus control and behavior management coping processes to a greater extent than did persons who had never been in AA or had been involved only in the past. Overall, we hypothesize that the proximal outcomes focused on in C-B treatment are more general proximal outcomes of substance abuse treatment, including 12-step treatment.

Method

Research Participants

Patients were recruited for a multisite evaluation of Department of Veterans Affairs (VA) substance abuse treatment services. In all, 3,228 men from 15 substance abuse treatment programs located at 13 VA medical centers provided information at intake to treatment and at treatment discharge or shortly thereafter. Eligibility criteria were that patients be in the standard treatment program (e.g., not a former patient participating in the program again for a short time as a "booster" episode to avoid relapse) and be a male (only 1–2% of VA substance abuse patients are women).

The patients were an average of 43 years old; 48% were black, 46% were white; 17% were married and 17% were separated. Across all patients, an average of about $10,600 was earned in an average of 19 weeks of work in the year prior to entering treatment; however, 76% of the patients were unemployed at treatment entry. Based on International Classification of Diseases-9th Revision (ICD-9-CM) (Health Care Financing Administration, 1991) information in the VA Patient Treatment File (a national VA patient database), 51% of the patients had both alcohol and drug abuse/dependence diagnoses, 36% had only alcohol abuse/dependence diagnoses and 13% had only drug abuse/ dependence diagnoses. Patients who drank alcohol (93%) reported consuming an average of 11 ounces of ethanol per day. In the 3 months prior to treatment, 48% of the patients snorted, injected or smoked cocaine or crack; 39% smoked marijuana; and 13% used heroin, street methadone or other opiates. In the 2 years prior to treatment intake, 32% of the patients had received inpatient substance abuse treatment (not including detoxification only) and 21% had received outpatient substance abuse treatment.

Procedure

Patients were invited to participate in the evaluation after they had completed detoxification and were admitted to a Program (usually within 72 hours of admission). Consecutive admissions were recruited at some programs; at larger Programs, every second or third admission was asked to participate. Of 4,193 patients approached to participate in the evaluation (90% of those eligible), 494 (12%) declined to do so, leaving an initial intake sample of 3,699 patients.

Patients completed an Intake Information Form (IIF, in some cases with assistance from a local member of the evaluation team, shortly after intake to treatment. At a point within 72 hours of their expected discharge after a typical 21- or 28-day stay in treatment, patients were scheduled to complete a Discharge Information Form (DIF). Most patients who completed the discharge form did so at this point. For patients who left treatment unexpectedly, an attempt was made to obtain the discharge information from them in the community. In all, 3,228 (87%) of the 3,699 recruited patients completed a DIF prior to discharge or within 30 days after leaving treatment.

We compared the patients who provided discharge information with those who did not on age, education, ethnicity, income, employment status, amount of alcohol consumed per day, alcohol dependence symptoms, use of cocaine, heroin injection, consequences of substance use, prior inpatient detoxification or treatment, prior outpatient treatment and symptoms of depression. No significant differences were found using a $p < .001$ significance threshold to adjust for the number of tests.

Measures

Proximal outcome variables. The key variables of interest are proximal outcomes that have been implicated in the treatment process models associated with 12-step and C-B treatment. These variables were assessed at intake to treatment and at discharge. Several of the measures are briefer, modified versions of established scales. Items were selected to provide coverage of some or all of the subscales in the original measures. Available psychometric data (e.g., factor loadings) were taken into account in determining which items should be included. Where needed, items were modified to refer to both alcohol consumption and drug use.

Traditional 12-step proximal outcomes. Some of the proximal outcomes for 12-step treatment refer to cognitive variables. *Disease model beliefs* were tapped using four modified items (e.g., "Every alcoholic or addict is one drink or one hit away from a relapse") from the 21-item Disease Model Beliefs subscale of the Understanding of Alcoholism Scale (Humphreys et al., 1996; Moyers, 199 1; Moyers and Miller, 1993). Responses on a 0–4 scale ranged from "strongly disagree" to "strongly agree"; total scores potentially could vary from 0 to 16. An internal consistency reliability estimate (Cronbach's alpha) was .70 for this scale in the entire intake sample. Acceptance of an *Alcoholic identity* or *Addict identity* was assessed with a single item: "Do you consider yourself to be an alcoholic [addict]?" (yes/no). Commitment to an *Abstinence goal* was determined by whether or not the respondent indicated that he wanted "to achieve total abstinence and never use alcohol or drugs again." Those indicating commitment to this goal were coded 1; the remaining respondents were coded 0.

The remaining 12-step proximal outcomes refer to 12-step behaviors or activities. Attendance at *12-step meetings* was tapped by the following item: "How many AA/NA/CA meetings have you attended since you started treatment?" (at intake, the timeframe was the past 3 months). A 0–4 frequency response format, which allowed for more meeting attendance in the 3 months prior to intake than during treatment, was converted to number of meetings by taking (near) midpoints of the specified frequency ranges. For example, the " 1–4 meetings" category on the DIF (originally coded 1) was converted to 3 meetings. The questionnaire also asked: "Do you currently have an AA/NA/CA *Sponsor?*" (yes/no). To assess *12-step friends,* patients were asked: "How many of your close friends are active in AA, NA, or CA?" The response categories, which ranged from "none" to "four or more," were coded 0–4. *Reading 12-step materials* was assessed by asking: "How often do you read the "Big Book," *24 Hours A Day,* or other 12-step (AA/NA/CA) materials?" Respondents could indicate "never" (scored "0") to "several times a week" (scored 4). Finally, each of the 12 steps was presented and the patient was asked: "Have you taken this step?" (yes/no). The *Number of steps* taken is the sum of the "yes" responses.

Cognitive-behavioral general proximal outcomes. Many of the C-B/general proximal outcomes were cognitive variables, although behavioral variables in the form of some coping skills also were assessed.

Fourteen of the 39 items from the Situational Confidence Questionnaire (Annis and Graham, 1988) were used to assess *Self-efficacy*. Responses could range from "not confident at all" (0% confidence scored 0) to "very confident" (100% confidence scored 5), so total scores could range from 0 to 70. Cronbach's alpha was .96 for the intake sample. Twelve modified items from the 90-item Alcohol Expectancy Questionnaire (Brown et al., 1980; alpha = .82) were used to tap *Positive substance use expectancies* regarding pleasurable consequences of continued use of alcohol or drugs. Responses were "yes" (scored 1) or "no" (scored 0); total scores had a potential range of 0–12. *Positive outcome expectancies* regarding desirable consequences of quitting substance use were assessed using 12 of the 34 items from the Outcome Expectancy Scale developed by Solomon and Annis (1989, 1990). Cronbach's alpha for the 12-item scale was .72. Patients could respond on a five-point scale, from "strongly disagree" (scored 0) to "strongly agree" (scored 4); scores potentially could range from 0 to 48.

Coping responses specific to substance use were assessed by a 15-item modified form of the 40-item *Processes of Change* scale (Prochaska et al., 1988) originally developed to assess change processes in smoking cessation. The original measure had 10 subscales; five were assessed in the present study. Three of the four original items on each subscale were selected to assess *Self-liberation* ("I tell myself I can choose to drink/use or not"; alpha = .70), Stimulus control ("I remove things from my home that remind me of drinking or using"; alpha = .65), *Counter conditioning* ("Instead of drinking or using, I engage in some physical activity"; alpha = .76), *Self-reevaluation* ("I remind myself that my dependency on drugs or alcohol makes me feel disappointed with myself"; alpha = .67) and *Reinforcement management* ("I reward myself when I don't drink or use"; alpha = .77). Each item was rated on a frequency scale, from "never" (coded 0) to "often" (coded 4), and item responses were summed to construct the overall scale and the five subscales. For the total scale, alpha was .88.

Four of the eight subscales from the Coping Responses Inventory (Moos, 1993) were selected to assess the general methods with which a patient coped with a stressful or challenging life situation in the year prior to intake. At discharge, the patient was asked how he expected to cope with the most important problem or stressful situation anticipated in the next 12 months. Six items each were used to assess responses in terms of *Positive reappraisal* (e.g., "Remind yourself how much worse things could be"; alpha = .76), *Problem-solving* ("Make a plan of action and follow it"; alpha = .79), *Cognitive avoidance* ("Try to forget the whole thing"; alpha = .74) and *Emotional discharge* coping ("Yell or shout to let off steam"; alpha = .63). Responses to items ranged from "no" (scored 0) to "fairly often" (scored 3), so scores on each scale could range from 0 to 18.

Precontemplation stage of change. Precontemplation was assessed by four modified items from the eight-item precontemplation subscale of the Stages of Change Readiness and Treatment Eagerness Scale (Version 5; Miller and Tonigan, 1996). Items were scored 0–4, total scores had a potential range of 0–16, and Cronbach's alpha was .57.

Results

Designation and Verification of Program Type

The first step in determining differences across treatment types in changes on proximal outcomes was to identify the type of treatment offered at the 15 treatment programs. Although programs were selected initially because they were thought to employ either a 12-step, C-B, or eclectic (combined 12-step and C-B) approach (for more details on the program selection process, see Ouimette et al., 1997), we used a two-step empirical process to classify programs in terms of their therapeutic orientation. First, we examined program directors' responses to questions concerning the number of treatment hours devoted to 12-step activities and C-B activities. In addition, program directors had responded to the Drug and Alcohol Program Treatment Inventory (DAPTI) (Peterson et al., 1994; Swindle et al., 1995) that inquires about therapeutic goals and activities that are characteristic of 12-step and C-B treatment. Based on those responses, we classified five programs as 12-step, five as C-B and five as eclectic (combining both 12-step and C-B treatment elements).

Second, we verified our classification of programs into three types by examining the responses of staff ($N = 327$) at the 15 programs to the DAPTI (Swindle et al., 1995) and an adapted and shorter version of the Disease Model Beliefs subscale developed by Moyers and Miller (1993) (see also Humphreys et al., 1996; Moyers, 1991). Those data supported the validity of our program type designations (for more details, see Ouimette et al., 1997). In all, 970 patients were treated in 12-step programs, 1,067 patients in eclectic programs, and 1, 191 patients in C-B programs.

Pre- to Posttreatment Changes in Proximal Outcomes

Table 1 gives the intake and discharge scores for patients in each of the three types of programs. In general, the data in table 1 indicate that patients in the three program types already exhibited some differences on proximal outcomes—particularly the 12-step proximal outcomes—at the time of the intake assessment. Those differences may reflect the rapid inculcation of patients with respect to the treatment orientation between their admission to the program and the intake assessment (a period, typically, of 72 hours or less). Alternatively, the variation among program types in intake proximal outcome scores could indicate that somewhat different patients were attracted or assigned to the three types of programs. In either case, the data indicate the need to control for intake scores on proximal outcomes before comparing proximal outcomes at discharge.

Prior to comparing changes in proximal outcomes across the three types of programs, we examined changes on proximal outcomes for patients within each of the program types. The superscript daggers in table 1 indicate the significance of such during-treatment patient changes as determined by paired t tests.

12 -step patients. Using a $p < .001$ level of significance as an adjusted significance threshold given multiple tests, we found that patients in the 12-step programs improved on all but one of the proximal outcomes conceptualized as specific to 12-step treatment. Specifically, on the cognitive outcomes, they increased their disease model beliefs and were more likely to identify themselves as alcoholics or addicts at discharge (85% and 66%, respectively) than at intake (78% and 59%, respectively). With respect to 12-step behaviors, they attended more 12-step meetings during treatment than they had in the 3 months prior to treatment, and 47% of the patients had a sponsor when they completed the DIF versus 11% at treatment entry. Patients also made more close friends in 12-step groups, increased their reading of 12-step materials and took an additional 1.8 steps.

Patients in 12-step programs likewise exhibited significant changes over time on almost all of the proximal outcomes commonly implicated in C-B treatment. They significantly increased their sense of self-efficacy, decreased their positive expectancies for substance use and acquired more substance-specific and general coping skills, as indicated by increased scores on all the Processes of Change subscales, and by increases in positive reappraisal and problem-solving and decreases in cognitive avoidance and emotional discharge coping.

Eclectic program patients. The patients in the eclectic programs increased significantly on all the proximal outcomes specific to 12-step treatment, except for adherence to an abstinence goal. They, too, had a significantly enhanced sense of self-efficacy at the end of treatment and had significantly improved on all measures of substance use-specific and general coping skills.

C-B patients. C-B patients made expected changes on all of the proximal outcomes associated with C-B treatment. They increased their sense of self-efficacy, decreased their positive expectancies for substance use, enhanced their positive expectancies for quitting substance use, and acquired more substance use-specific and general coping skills. The C-B patients also made significant changes on the proximal outcome measures assessing 12-step behaviors, but not the 12-step cognitive outcomes. Specifically, C-B patients increased their 12-step involvement in terms of attendance at 12-step meetings, having a sponsor and more 12-step friends, reading 12-step materials and taking the steps. However, in contrast to the patients in the other two program types, they indicated significantly lower endorsement of disease model beliefs, significantly less commitment to abstinence as a treatment goal, and no change in terms of accepting an alcoholic or addict identity at discharge in comparison with their scores at intake.

Relationship to length of stay. We examined whether the amount of change on some proximal outcomes was related to patients' length of stay (LOS) in treatment. The average (±SD) LOS was 24.0 ± 4.9 days in 12-step programs, 23.4 ± 7.3 days in eclectic programs and 24.5 ± 5.9 days in C-B programs.

To examine LOS-proximal outcome relationships, we computed partial correlations, controlling for the intake score on the proximal outcome variable and using a $p < .001$ significance threshold to adjust for multiple significance tests. Significant partial correlations indicated that 12-step patients (n = 964-967 for the analyses reported here) with longer stays adhered more to abstinence as a treatment goal (r = .11), attended more 12-step meetings ($r = .38$), were more likely to have a 12-step sponsor ($r = .19$) and close 12-step friends ($r = .16$), and read more 12-step materials ($r = .37$). Likewise, 12-step patients who remained longer in treatment had a stronger sense of self-efficacy ($r = .11$) and scored higher on the Processes of Change scale ($r = .14$) and its stimulus control ($r = .19$), counter conditioning ($r = .15$), and reinforcement management ($r = .11$) subscales.

For the eclectic program patients ($n = 1,059–1,062$ for the analyses reported here), longer stays were significantly associated with attending more 12-step meetings ($r = .23$), reading more 12-step materials ($r = .19$), having a stronger sense of self-efficacy ($r = .12$), and using more counter-conditioning ($r = .10$) as a process of change.

C-B patients ($n = 1,185$-$1,186$ for the analyses reported here) who had longer stays scored significantly higher on the Processes of Change scale ($r = .15$), and its stimulus control ($r = .11$), self-reevaluation ($r = 10$) and reinforcement management ($r = .20$) subscales. Surprisingly, C-B patients who stayed longer tended to have higher positive substance use expectancies ($r = .10$) than patients with shorter stays. There was no relationship between LOS and the Other C-B/general proximal outcomes (self-efficacy, outcome expectancies and general coping responses). However, patients who remained in C-B treatment longer showed significant increases on some of the 12-step proximal outcomes—specifically, disease model beliefs ($r = .17$), attendance at 12-step meetings ($r = .56$), and number of steps taken ($r = .21$). Overall, the analyses indicate some relationships between treatment duration and amount of change on proximal outcomes. However, most of the significant relationships were modest in magnitude.

Between-Program Differences in Changes on Proximal Outcomes

The major focus of this research was to determine if patients in the three types of programs showed different levels of change on proximal outcome variables during the course of treatment. With patient self-selection or other nonrandom treatment allocation processes, differences on patient pretreatment characteristics are possible across program types. Such pre-existing patient differences should be controlled to increase confidence that differences in the amount of change on proximal outcomes by patients in the three program types reflect the effects of treatment. We examined an array of patient intake variables for such

Table I

Intake and discharge mean scores on proximal outcome variables for patients in 12-step, eclectic and cognitive-behavioral programs

Proximal outcome variable (scale)	12-Step (n = 970)		Eclectic (n = 1,067)		Cognitive-behavioral (n = 1,191)	
	Intake	Discharge	Intake	Discharge	Intake	Discharge
	(1/956–969 df)		(1/1051–1064 df)		(1/1175–1189 df)	
Traditional 12-step						
Cognitive variables						
Disease model beliefs (0–16)	14.33	14.76[‡]	13.95	14.53[‡]	12.78	11.40[‡]
Alcoholic identity (% yes; 0–1)	78	85[‡]	76	80[‡]	72	70
Addict identity (% yes; 0–1)	59	66[‡]	53	56[‡]	43	42
Abstinence goal (% yes; 0–1)	77	78	70	68	62	52[‡]
Behavioral variables						
12-step meetings[a]	4.73	12.07[‡]	6.29	12.55[‡]	5.32	7.42[‡]
Have sponsor (% yes; 0–1)	11	47[‡]	14	19[‡]	8	12[‡]
12-step friends (0–4)	0.95	1.58[‡]	1.13	1.42[‡]	0.84	1.22[‡]
Read 12-step materials (0–4)	1.08	3.06[‡]	1.13	2.76[‡]	0.74	1.17[‡]
Number of steps taken (0–12)	4.37	6.16[‡]	5.02	6.79[‡]	4.21	5.52[‡]

(continued)

Table 1 *(continued)*

Proximal outcome variable (scale)	12-Step (n = 970)		Eclectic (n = 1,067)		Cognitive-behavioral (n = 1,191)	
	Intake (1/956–969 df)	Discharge	Intake (1/1051–1064 df)	Discharge	Intake (1/1175–1189 df)	Discharge
Cognitive-behavioral/general						
Self-efficacy (0–70)	47.18	55.96‡	43.29	53.04‡	42.82	52.63‡
Pos. substance use expectancies (0–12)	7.08	6.26‡	6.96	6.72	6.98	6.27‡
Positive outcome expectancies (0–48)	31.99	32.37	30.81	31.13	30.56	31.48‡
Processes of change (0–60)	30.09	46.51‡	29.89	46.13‡	29.13	44.53‡
Self-liberation (0–15)	7.17	8.55‡	7.03	9.02‡	7.28	9.32‡
Stimulus control (0–15)	5.09	10.16‡	5.31	9.93‡	4.85	8.90‡
Counterconditioning (0–15)	5.95	10.66‡	5.84	10.27‡	5.85	10.05‡
Self-reevaluation (0–15)	7.31	9.05‡	7.26	9.30‡	7.04	8.67‡
Reinforcement management (0–15)	4.57	8.10‡	4.43	7.58‡	4.12	7.58‡
General coping responses						
Positive reappraisal (0–18)	10.69	13.80‡	10.22	13.51‡	9.50	12.99‡
Problem-solving (0–18)	10.66	15.70‡	10.41	15.43‡	10.15	14.91‡
Cognitive avoidance (0–18)	10.15	6.91‡	9.69	6.94‡	9.44	6.76‡
Emotional discharge (0–18)	7.28	5.23‡	7.00	5.01‡	6.78	4.95‡

a Scoring range at discharge was 0–15; scoring range at intake was 0–35.

‡ $p < .001$ differences between intake and discharge scores as determined by within-group, paired t test. Ns vary slightly due to missing data.

differences and used some of them as covariates in the analyses of covariance (ANCOVAS) reported below.

We selected covariates with a three-stage process. First, patient pretreatment variables that were most strongly related to program type were identified. Second, intercorrelations among those variables were examined. Third, among more highly correlated variables, one was selected. After employing this approach, seven baseline covariates were identified: black ethnicity, education level, level of precontemplation stage of change, inpatient detoxification or treatment for substance use in the prior 2 years, outpatient treatment in the prior 2 years, amount of ethanol consumed per day and heroin injection (yes/no). Means for these seven variables by program type are given in table 2.

We conducted two multivariate analyses of covariance (MANCO-VAS) to test the overall relationship between program type and the set of 12-step-related proximal outcomes and the set of C-B-related proximal outcomes. These analyses controlled for the covariates listed above and the intake values of all of the proximal outcomes within the specific set. The results of the two MANCOVAS indicated significant relationships between program type and the sets of both 12-step-related (Pillai's Approximate $F = 67.98$, 144/28,611 df, $p < .001$) and C-B-related (Pillai's Approximate $F = 19.93$, 228/37,884 df, $p < .001$) outcome variables.

To probe the relationship of program type to the individual proximal outcome variables, univariate ANCOVAS were carried out. These controlled for the seven covariates and the intake score on the proximal outcome variable of interest. The results of these analyses can be interpreted as assessing differential "change" across program types, in that the adjusted discharge mean scores assume patients in the three program types had the same scores on the baseline covariates and the same intake score on the proximal outcome variable.

The ANCOVAS indicated significant between-program variation on (changes in) all of the proximal outcomes assumed to be specific to 12-step treatment. The covariate-adjusted means in table 3 indicate that disease model beliefs increased less (they actually decreased slightly) among patients in the C-B programs than among those in the 12-step or eclectic programs. The increase in the proportion of patients accepting alcoholic and addict identities was greater among the 12-step patients than among patients in the other two program types. In addition,

Table 2

Mean scores by program type on patient pretreatment variables used as covariates

Patient pretreatment variable	12-step (n = 970)	Eclectic (n = 1,067)	Cognitive-behavioral (n = 1,191)	F (2/3234–3325 df)
Black (% yes)	58[a]	56[a]	34[b]	80.08‡
Education (years)	12.90[a]	12.49[b]	12.78[a]	15.39‡
Precontemplation stage	1.46[a]	1.71	1.84[b]	8.09‡
Prior inpatient detox. or treatment (% yes)	30[a]	49[b]	40[c]	38.57‡
Prior outpatient treatment (% yes)	16[a]	24[b]	22[b]	10.27‡
Amount of ethanol per day (ozs)	11.47[a]	14.47[b]	11.71[a]	21.44‡
Heroin injection (% yes)	3[a]	7[b]	5	6.07†

Note: Ns varied slightly across analyses due to missing data. Means or percentages that have different superscripts differ significantly ($p < .001$).

† $p < .01$.
‡ $p < .001$.

Table 3

Covariate-adjusted discharge mean scores assessing "change" on proximal outcome variables for patients in 12-step, eclectic and cognitive-behavioral programs

Proximal outcome variable	12-step (n = 970)	Eclectic (n = 1,067)	Cognitive-behavioral (n = 1,191)	F (2/3173–3211 df)
Traditional 12-step				
Cognitive variables				
Disease model beliefs	14.39[a]	14.30[a]	12.00[b]	193.10[‡]
Alcoholic identity (% yes)	84[a]	79[b]	72[c]	41.34[‡]
Addict identity (% yes)	60[a]	54[b]	50[c]	34.98[‡]
Abstinence goal (% yes)	74[a]	68[a]	58[b]	40.50[‡]
Behavioral variables				
12-step meetings	11.96[a]	12.45[a]	7.63[b]	432.65[‡]
Have sponsor (% yes)	47[a]	18[b]	13[b]	245.33[‡]
12-step friends	1.58[a]	1.31[b]	1.32[b]	12.51[‡]
Read 12-step materials	2.97[a]	2.69[b]	1.32[c]	453.51[‡]
Number of steps taken	6.08	6.55[a]	5.84[a]	11.12[‡]

(continued)

Table 3 *(continued)*

Proximal outcome variable	12-step (n = 970)	Eclectic (n = 1,067)	Cognitive-behavioral (n = 1,191)	F (2/3234–3325 df)
Cognitive-behavioral/general				
Self-efficacy	54.64	53.87	53.12	3.13
Pos. substance use expectancies	6.30	6.71	6.25	6.12
Positive outcome expectancies	31.78	31.42	32.80	1.34
Processes of change	46.16	45.98	45.03	5.09
Self-liberation	8.52[a]	9.07[b]	9.30[b]	19.65[‡]
Stimulus control	10.07[a]	9.85[a]	9.08[b]	49.73[‡]
Counterconditioning	10.57[a]	10.27[b]	10.14[b]	12.79[‡]
Self-reevaluation	9.01	9.26[a]	8.75[b]	13.53[‡]
Reinforcement management	7.97[a]	7.52[b]	7.77	5.94
General coping responses				
Positive reappraisal	13.62	13.48	13.19	4.58
Problem-solving	15.59[a]	15.48	14.98[b]	13.80[‡]
Cognitive avoidance	6.93	6.82	6.87	0.17
Emotional discharge	5.27	4.94	4.97	3.37

Note: Ns varied slightly across analyses due to missing data. Means that have different superscripts differ significantly ($p < .001$).

‡ $p < .001$.

patients in the eclectic programs were more likely to indicate an alcoholic/addict identity at discharge than were the C-B patients. Adherence to an abstinence goal and attendance at 12-step meetings during the course of treatment were significantly lower for C-B patients than for those in 12-step and eclectic programs. The 12-step patients acquired a 12-step sponsor in more cases, increased the number of their 12-step friends and read more 12-step materials during treatment in comparison to patients in the other two program types. Eclectic program patients also read more 12-step materials during treatment than did C-B patients. Finally, patients in the eclectic programs took more steps during treatment than did the C-B patients.

There were fewer significant differences across program types with respect to changes on the proximal outcome variables conceptualized as either specific to C-B treatment or more general in nature. Patients in all three program types experienced similar changes in their sense of self-efficacy, positive substance use expectancies, positive outcome expectancies, total processes of change scores and the general coping skills of positive reappraisal, cognitive avoidance and emotional discharge.

With respect to specific change processes, however, there were some differences across program types. Patients in the C-B and eclectic programs increased their use of self-liberation processes more than did patients in the 12-step programs, a finding consistent with the personal responsibility orientation of C-B treatment and the powerlessness orientation of 12-step treatment. Stimulus control coping was greater among 12-step patients and eclectic program patients at discharge than among C-B patients. Counterconditioning, as a method for coping with relapse-inducing situations, improved more among 12-step patients than among eclectic or C-B patients. The use of self-reevaluation increased more among the eclectic program patients than among the C-B patients; reinforcement management skills improved more among 12-step than eclectic patients. Finally, 12-step patients made greater gains in problem-solving, as a general coping skill, than did C-B patients.

Discussion
We have examined the gains that patients are supposed to make during treatment on proximal outcomes implicated in the treatment process models for traditional 12-step and C-B treatment.

Within-Program Type Change

Our findings with respect to some aspects of 12-step treatment process are similar to those reported by Morgenstern et al. (1996). Overall, many patients entering these substance abuse treatment programs were already immersed in some of the aspects of the traditional 12-step treatment model, especially cognitive 12-step process variables. For example, the mean for all patients on our abbreviated measure of disease model beliefs was 13.6 at intake to treatment; the highest possible score was 16. At intake, 75% of all patients described themselves as alcoholics. The average patient indicated at intake that he had already taken 4.5 of the 12 steps. On the other hand, only 11% of patients indicated that they had a 12-step sponsor, and scores for the measures of 12-step friends and reading 12-step materials were relatively low.

Overall, patients in the 12-step and eclectic programs show significant increases on both the cognitive and behavioral (activity) 12-step proximal outcomes. In contrast, patients in the C-B programs exhibited modest decreases or no change on the cognitive 12-step outcomes (disease model beliefs, adherence to an abstinence goal and acceptance of an alcoholic or addict identity), even though they showed increases in attending 12-step meetings, having a sponsor, having close friends involved in 12-step groups, reading more 12-step materials and taking the steps. The changes reflect some 12-step participation among patients in C-B programs, but suggest that their participation did not result in an internalization of 12-step beliefs.

On the C-B/general proximal outcome variables, patients in all three types of programs significantly enhanced their sense of efficacy in dealing with high-risk situations and were better equipped at treatment discharge to cope with relapse inducing and stressful situations, as indicated by their changes on the Processes of Change and the Coping Responses Inventory subscales. However, only C-B and 12-step patients showed a significant decrease in expectancies for positive consequences for substance use, and only C-B patients exhibited a significant increase in their expectancies for positive consequences from reducing or quitting drinking and drug use.

Overall, these findings indicate that patients made significant changes on proximal outcomes during substance abuse treatment. As noted earlier, the magnitude of some of the changes was modestly associated with how long patients remained in treatment. These same patients exhibited improvement (e.g., reduced substance use) at a follow-up approximately 1 year after treatment (see Ouimette et al., 1997). Future analyses will determine if maintenance of the gains on proximal outcomes during the course of treatment, shown here, is linked to improvement on 1-year ultimate outcome variables.

Differential Change Across Program Types

With one exception, patients in the traditional 12-step programs evidenced greater improvement than did C-B patients on both the cognitive and behavioral proximal outcome variables assumed to be specific to 12-step treatment. In contrast, patients in the C-B programs made no greater change (and, on three variables, less change) than did 12-step patients on the proximal outcome variables that have been referred to in C-B treatment process models. This pattern suggests that the proximal outcomes sometimes examined with respect to C-B treatment may be general proximal outcomes of psychosocial substance abuse treatment, or at least of 12-step and C-B treatment. In this vein, Kazdin (1986) noted that "comparative studies [of psychotherapies] often reveal that ... the reactions of clients, and the outcome results are not as diametrically opposed as the theories underlying the alternative techniques would suggest" (p. 96).

One potential extrapolation of the results presented here is that, because patients in the 12-step programs made more of the desired changes on proximal outcomes than did patients in the C-B programs, they may experience better outcomes at follow-up (e.g., reduced substance use). Such an extrapolation would be based on an assumption that the sets of proximal outcome thought to be specific to the two different forms of treatment were equivalent in terms of the domains covered and responsiveness to treatment. However, as noted earlier, the 12-step proximal outcomes were quite specific to 12-step treatment and many focused on 12-step behaviors or activities (attending 12-step meetings, reading 12-step materials). In contrast, the proximal outcomes highlighted in descriptions of C-B treatment were more general in nature, referring to broader cognitions (e.g., expectancies) and behaviors (behavioral coping skills) and not to specific treatment activities. Had we assessed C-B treatment activities (e.g., "performed a functional analysis," "did homework assignments") as proximal outcomes, it is likely that C-B patients would have shown significantly more change on such measures than would 12-step or eclectic program patients.

Accordingly, our results do not necessarily point to more favorable outcomes for 12-step patients at longer-term follow-ups. Given that patients in 12-step and eclectic programs made at least as much improvement on most C-B/general proximal outcomes as C-B patients did, however, one could reasonably expect that 12-step patients would fare at least as well as patients in the other two types of programs on outcome variables assessed at follow-up. Examination of 1-year follow-up outcomes for patients in the three types of treatment programs (Ouimette et al., 1997) indicates little difference on an array of outcome variables, although 12-step patients were more likely to be abstinent from alcohol and drugs than patients in the other two types of programs.

Limitations

Although it employed a large, representative multisite patient sample and stringent statistical significance thresholds to examine important proximal outcome variables thought to underlie two prevalent forms of substance abuse treatment, the present study has limitations. First, not all relevant 12-step (e.g., spirituality) and C-B (e.g., functional analyses) proximal outcome variables were assessed. Second, as noted earlier, the domains covered by the proximal outcomes for 12-step and cognitive-behavioral treatment were not equivalent. Some of the 12-step proximal outcomes assessed relatively specific behaviors or activities (e.g., attending 12-step meetings, reading 12-step materials). In contrast, the C-B proximal outcomes were more general in nature, assessing cognitive variables, such as sense of self-efficacy and coping skills. Future comparative studies of during-treatment changes should ensure that, to the extent possible while maintaining treatment representativeness, proximal outcomes for different treatment approaches tap similar domains of variables (e.g., activities, beliefs and skills).

Third, because patients were not randomly assigned to program types, one has to be concerned whether the differential changes in proximal outcomes across program types actually reflect the effect of differences in patient pretreatment characteristics for the three program types. Although we attempted to control for patient pretreatment differences by adjusting our results for seven covariates, as well as the intake score of the proximal outcome variable, it is possible that those variables did not tap all relevant differences across patients in the three program types. Finally, it is unknown to what extent our findings would generalize to patient populations other than male veterans.

Conclusion

Overall, the analyses presented here represent the first step in our examination of substance abuse treatment models and treatment processes. The significant changes exhibited by patients in all three types of treatment suggest that the interventions offered were successful in bringing about desired proximal outcomes. Future process analyses will examine the relationships of 12-step and C-B/general proximal outcomes to ultimate outcomes (e.g., substance use at follow-up). The findings will provide important additional evidence about the stability of during-treatment changes and the adequacy of the theories that underlie these two prevalent forms of substance abuse treatment.

References

Alcoholics Anonymous. (1976). *Alcoholics anonymous: The story of how many thousands of men and women have recovered from alcoholism, 3rd Edition,* New York: Alcoholics Anonymous World Services, Inc.

Annis, H. M. & Graham, J. M. (1988). *Situational confidence questionnaire (SCQ–39) User's Guide.* Toronto: Addiction Research Foundation.

Bandura, A. (1977). Self-efficacy: Toward a unifying theory of behavioral change. *Psychological Review, 84,* 191–215.

Brown, H. P., Jr. & Peterson, J. H., Jr. (1991). Assessing spirituality in addiction treatment and follow-up: Development of the Brown-Peterson Recovery Process Inventory (B-PRPI). *Alcoholism Treatment Quarterly, 8*(2): 21–50.

Brown, S. A., Goldman, M. S., Inn, A., & Anderson, L. R. (1980). Expectations of reinforcement from alcohol: Their domains and relation to drinking patterns. *Journal of Counseling and Clinical Psychology, 48,* 419–426.

Carroll, S. (1993). Spirituality and purpose in life in alcoholism recovery. *Journal of Studies on Alcohol, 54,* 297–301.

Christo, G. & Franey, C. (1995). Drug users' spiritual beliefs, locus of control and the disease concept in relation to Narcotics Anonymous attendance and six-month outcomes. *Drug and Alcohol Dependendency, 38,* 51–56.

Gilbert, F. S. (1991). Development of a "Steps Questionnaire." *Journal of Studies on Alcohol, 52,* 353–360.

Health Care Financing Administration. (1991). *The international classification of diseases, 9th revision, clinical modification (ICD-9-CM), 4th Edition,* DHHS Publication No. (PHS) 91–1260, Washington: Government Printing Office.

Hollon, S. D., DeRubeis, R. J., & Evans, M. D. (1987). Causal mediation of change in treatment for depression: Discriminating between nonspecificity and noncausality. *Psychological Bulletin, 102,* 139–149.

Humphreys, K., Greenbaum, M. A., Noke, J. M., & Finney, J. W. (1996). Reliability, validity, and normative data for a short version of the Understanding of Alcoholism Scale. *Psychology of Addictive Behaviors, 10*, 38–44.

Kazdin, A. E. (1986). Comparative outcome studies of psychotherapy: Methodological issues and strategies. *Journal of Counseling and Clinical Psychology, 54*, 95–105.

McCrady, B. S. (1994). Alcoholics Anonymous and behavior therapy: Can habits be treated as diseases? Can diseases be treated as habits? *Journal of Counseling and Clinical Psychology, 62*, 1159–1166.

McKay, J. R., Alterman, A. I., McLellan, A. T., & Snider, E .C. (1994). Treatment goals, continuity of care, and outcome in a day hospital substance abuse rehabilitation program. *American Journal of Psychiatry, 151*, 254–259.

McKay, J. R., Maisto, S. A., & O'Farrell, T. J. (1993). End-of-treatment Self efficacy, aftercare, and drinking outcomes of alcoholic men. *Alcoholism, Clinical and Experimental Research, 17*, 1078–1083.

Mattson, M.E., Allen, J. P., Longabaugh, R., Nickless, C. J., Connors, G. J., & Kadden, R. M. (1994). A chronological review of empirical studies of matching alcoholic clients to treatment. *Journal of Studies on Alcohol, Supplement No. 12*,16–29.

Miller, W. R. & Tonigan, J. S. (1996). Assessing drinkers' motivations for change: The Stages of Change Readiness and Treatment Eagerness Scale (SOCRATES). *Psychology of Addictive Behaviors, 10*, 81–89.

Montgomery, H. A., Miller, W. R., & Tonigan, J. S. (1995). Does Alcoholics Anonymous involvement predict treatment outcome? *Journal of Studies on Alcohol, 12*, 241–246.

Monti, P.M., Abrams, D. B., Binkoff, J. A., Zwick, W. R., Liepman, M. R., Nirenberg, T. D., & Rohsenow, D. J. (1990). Communication skills training, communication skills training with family and cognitive behavioral mood management training for alcoholics. *Journal of Studies on Alcohol, 51*, 263–270.

Moos, R. H. (1993). *Coping responses inventory professional manual.* Fla: Psychological Assessment Resources.

Morgenstern, J., Frey, R. M., McCrady, B. S., Labouvie, E., & Neighbors, C. J. (1996). Examining mediators of change in traditional chemical dependency treatment. *Journal of Studies on Alcohol, 57*, 53–64.

Morley, J. A., Finney, J. W., Monahan, S. C., & Floyd, A. S. (1996). Alcoholism treatment outcome studies, 1980–1992: Methodological characteristics and quality. *Addictive Behaviors, 21*, 429-443.

Morojele, N. K. & Stephenson, G. M. (1992). The Minnesota Model in the treatment of addictions: A social psychological assessment of changes in beliefs and attributions. *Journal of Community and Applied Social Psychology, 2*, 25-41.

Moyers, T. B. (1991). *Therapists' conceptualizations of alcoholism: Implications for treatment decisions.* Ph.D. dissertation, University of New Mexico.

Moyers, T. B. & Miller, W. R. (1993). Therapists' conceptualizations of alcoholism: Measurement and implications for treatment decisions. *Psychology of Addictive Behaviors, 21, 7,* 238–245.

Ouimette, P. C., Finney, J. W., & Moos, R. H. (1997). Twelve-step and cognitive behavioral treatment for substance abuse: A comparison of treatment effectiveness. *Journal of Counseling and Clinical Psychology, 65,* 230–240.

Peterson, K. A., Swindle, R. W., Paradise, M. A., & Moos, R. H. (1994). *Substance abuse treatment programming in the VA: Program structure and treatment processes.* Palo Alto, CA: Program Evaluation and Resource Center.

Prochaska, J. O., Velicer, W. F., DiClemente, C. C., & Fava, J. (1988). Measuring processes of change: Applications to the cessation of smoking. *Journal of Counseling and Clinical Psychology, 56,* 520–528.

Rosen, A. & Proctor, E. K. (1981). Distinctions between treatment outcomes and their implications for treatment evaluation. *Journal of Counseling and Clinical Psychology, 49,* 418–425.

Rychtarik, R. G., Prue, D. M., Rapp, S. R., & King, A. C. (1992). Self-efficacy, aftercare and relapse in a treatment program for alcoholics. *Journal of Studies on Alcohol, 53,* 435–440.

Snow, M. G., Prochaska, J. O., & Rossi, J. S. (1994). Processes of change in Alcoholics Anonymous: Maintenance factors in long-term sobriety. *Journal of Studies on Alcohol, 55,* 362–371.

Solomon, K. E. & Annis, H. M. (1989). Development of a scale to measure outcome expectancy in alcoholics. *Cognitive Therapy Research, 13,* 409–421.

Solomon, K. E. & Annis, H. M. (1990). Outcome and efficacy expectancy in the prediction of post-treatment drinking behaviour. *British Journal of Addiction, 85,* 659–665.

Swindle, R. W., Peterson, K. A., Paradise, M. J., & Moos, R. H. (1995). Measuring substance abuse program treatment orientations: The Drug and Alcohol Program Treatment Inventory. *Journal of Substance Abuse, 7,* 61–78.

Wells, E. A., Peterson, P. L., Gainey, R. R., Hawkins, J. D., & Catalan, R. F. (1994). Outpatient treatment for cocaine abuse: A controlled comparison of relapse prevention and Twelve Step approaches. *American Journal of Drug and Alcohol Abuse, 20,* 1–17.

Substance Dependence Posttraumatic Stress Disorder Therapy: An Integrated Cognitive-Behavioral Approach

Elisa Triffleman, Kathleen Carroll & Scott Kellogg

This article originally appeared in the *Journal of Substance Abuse Treatment*, 1999, 17(1–2), 3–14, and is reprinted with permission.

Elisa Triffleman, Kathleen Carroll & Scott Kellogg, Department of Psychiatry, Yale University School of Medicine, New Haven, CT

Support for this project came from National Institute of Drug (NIDA) grants 5K12 DA06963 and NIDA 1P50 DA09241.

While substance abuse and posttraumatic stress disorder (PTSD) are known to frequently co-occur, there have been few published clinical trials evaluating integrated approaches for this form of dual diagnosis. This article describes Substance Dependence PTSD Therapy (SDPT), the first manualized individual treatment to undergo a controlled clinical trial. SDPT is a 5-month, twice-weekly, two-phase individual cognitive-behavioral treatment utilizing (a) relapse prevention and coping skills training for substance abuse; and (b) psychoeducation, stress inoculation training, and in vivo exposure for PTSD. SDPT is also unique in having been designed for use in mixed-gendered civilians with varied sources of trauma. Design considerations and the format, structure, and content of therapy sessions are discussed. Open trial pilot data indicates efficacy in reducing PTSD severity.

The comorbidity of posttraumatic stress disorder (PTSD) (American Psychiatric Association, 1994) and substance dependence is common in the general population, among the traumatized, and in addicted persons. In epidemiological samples, PTSD is itself a ubiquitous syndrome, affecting up to 12.3% of the general community (Kessler, Sonnega, Bromet, Hughes, & Nelson, 1995; Resnick, Kilpatrick, Dansky, Saunders, & Best, 1993). Rates of up to 43% of co-occurrence of substance abuse and PTSD have been reported (Kessler et al., 1995; Breslau, Davis, Andreski, & Peterson, 1991). Rates of PTSD occurring in persons primarily identified with or in treatment for substance abuse vary from 20–59% (Triffleman, 1998). Despite this frequency, no "gold standard" treatment for this comorbidity yet exists.

However, consensus exists that the comorbidity of PTSD and substance abuse negatively affects the outcome of each of the component diagnoses. In a study that examined precipitants to relapse among male veterans (Abueg, Chun, & Lurie, 1990), 25% indicated that relapse occurred in the context of activated PTSD symptoms. That male inpatient veterans reported that cocaine worsened and opiates improved symptoms of PTSD in Bremner, Southwick, Darnell, and Charney (1996). Response to standard addictions treatment may also be affected by this comorbidity, resulting in shorter times to relapse, more treatment recidivism with lower treatment retention in each episode, and overall greater use of treatment services (Brown, Recupero, & Stout, 1995; Ouimette, Ahrens, Moos, & Finney, 1997). In comparison to those with substance abuse only, persons with PTSD-substance abuse also were less likely to be employed and expected fewer benefits from discontinuing substance use (Ouimette et al., 1997).

Thus, a need exists to examine treatment approaches for this dual diagnosis. A limited number of clinical approaches have been reported. Abueg and Fairbank (1992) developed a 1- to 2-year, phased-treatment approach for male Vietnam veterans based on Prochaska and DiClemente's (1983) stages of change model. Following detoxification and initial stabilization, a brief period of psychoeducation is followed by direct therapeutic exposure for PTSD, cue exposure, self-control training for addiction, and relapse prevention for both substance abuse and PTSD. Seidel, Gusman, and Abueg (1994) described a Veteran's Administration (VA) PTSD/Alcohol Dependence inpatient program with an average length of stay of 3 to 4 months, using a multimodal strategy. Patients are first introduced to cognitive-behavioral techniques designed to overcome dysfunctional cognitions associated with chronic PTSD and the denial associated with chronic alcohol abuse. Patients then move into trauma-focused exposure therapy and coping skills training, followed by reintegration into the community. Reportedly, 60% of patients remained abstinent at 3-month follow-up, although a controlled trial of this treatment has not yet been reported.

A 12-step–influenced treatment approach has also been described (Evans & Sullivan, 1995) based mainly in the treatment of childhood trauma, with individualized decision-making about when and how deeply to address the trauma. Satel, Becker, and Dan (1993) examined the dilemmas faced by outpatient substance-abusing veterans with PTSD in affiliating with Alcoholics Anonymous, such as difficulties dealing with a Higher Power or interpersonal estrangement. These may be serious obstacles to participation in 12-step programs, requiring specific therapeutic interventions.

The research literature regarding PTSD-substance abuse has also been limited. In the only medication trial to systematically monitor both PTSD and alcohol-dependence symptoms, Brady, Sonne, and Roberts (1995) reported, in an $N = 9$ series of civilian subjects, that the severity of both PTSD and alcohol-dependence symptoms declined significantly in response to 12 weeks of sertraline. In a psychosocial treatment study (Najavits, Weiss, Shaw, & Muenz, 1998), significant decreases in PTSD and substance-dependence symptoms were reported among treatment completers in an uncontrolled pilot trial of a fully integrated group therapy for civilian women with addictions and PTSD or Disorders of Extreme Stress Not Otherwise Specified (Herman, 1993; Najavits, Weiss, & Liese, 1996). Seventeen subjects received 36 therapist contact-hours over the course of 12 weeks. Interventions were largely cognitive and coping-skills–based, with emphases on self-safety and self-care, identifying and managing dysfunctional cognitions, and dealing with boundaries, among others. Behavioral interventions, such as flooding or in vivo exposure were not undertaken.

In this report, we describe a manualized outpatient cognitive-behavioral treatment (CBT) approach, developed during National Institute of Drug Abuse funded open (Triffleman, Kellogg, & Syracuse-Siewert, 1997) and controlled clinical trials (Triffleman, Kellogg, & Syracuse-Siewert, 1997) of civilian patients with PTSD and opiate and/or cocaine dependence. Substance-Dependence PTSD Therapy (SDPT; Triffleman & Kellogg, 1997; manual available from EGT) is an outpatient, two-phase, 20-week individual therapy and is an adaptation and integration of cognitive-behavioral and coping skills treatment for substance abuse (CBCST; Carroll, Donovan, Hester, & Kadden, 1993; Kadden et al., 1992; Marlatt & Gordon, 1985; Monti, Abram, Kadden, & Cooney, 1989), stress inoculation training (SIT; Foa, Rothbaum, Riggs, & Murdock, 1991; Meichenbaum & Cameron, 1983; Veronen & Kilpatrick, 1983) and in vivo exposure (Marks, Lovell, Noshirvani, Livanou, & Thrasher, 1998; Richards, Lovell, & Marks, 1994; Richards & Rose, 1991). While these treatment techniques are not new, both the integration of these existing elements and the use of these PTSD-treatment techniques in a substance-abusing population is unique. This report describes the goals and structure of SDPT; salient design considerations, including the timing of trauma work in treatment; the target population; and session format and content.

SDPT Treatment Goals, Overview, and Rationale

The goals of SDPT are: (a) initiation of abstinence from substance use through CBCST (Carroll et al., 1993; Kadden et al., 1992), (b) maintenance of substance abstinence during the course of PTSD treatment, and (c) reduction of PTSD symptom severity. These goals are accomplished through the use of a two-phase model of treatment. During the 12 weeks of Phase I, or the "Trauma-Informed, Addictions-Focused Treatment" phase, twin emphases are placed on (a) the establishment of abstinence; and (b) psychoeducation on and attention to PTSD symptoms, and the interactions between PTSD and the expression of substance abuse within the individual. This phase also allows time for a trusting therapeutic alliance to develop. Abstinence-oriented trauma-informed coping skills training includes examinations of craving-associated and dysphoria-associated cognitions; generation of alternative cognitions; and increasing management of emotional and physical states. Many of these skills are also useful adjunctive interventions in treating the secondary effects of PTSD.

Phase II, or the final 8 weeks, is the "Trauma-Focused, Addictions-Informed" phase. During this phase, the primary emphasis is placed on the treatment of PTSD through (a) an adaptation of SIT (Foa et al., 1991; Meichenbaum & Cameron, 1983), which provides cognitive strategies and coping skills for dealing with present-day situations symbolic of the trauma; and (b) in vivo (or live) exposure, focused on desensitizing patients to avoided trauma-related stimuli. This is paired with continuing active monitoring of the patient's substance use and abstinence status as the trauma work proceeds, along with pacing the exposure commensurate with the needs of addicted patients, for whom strong affects can be experienced as deeply destabilizing. To address this, in vivo exposure (Marks et al., 1998) is implemented in the form of a desensitization hierarchy, from least avoided/least upsetting situations through most avidly avoided/most upsetting situations.

The decision to transition a patient between Phase I and Phase II is made on clinical criteria. During the research trial, a continuous 2-week period of abstinence during Phase I was the initial threshold for transitioning a patient. It became clear, however, that it was difficult for some patients to remit from marijuana and low-frequency alcohol use within 12 weeks. It also became clear that there were patients who had markedly decreased their substance use even while not achieving complete abstinence, but who were able to tolerate Phase II work. On a practical basis, then, the decision to transition a given patient is that significant clinical progress has been made in decreasing substance abuse, and the patient appears ready to tolerate the negative affects arising during the course of Phase II treatment without major relapse.

SDPT is designed as a "stand-alone" therapy, in conjunction with substance-abuse-related medication administration (such as opiate agonists and antagonists). During the 20-week length of treatment, 55-minute sessions are scheduled twice weekly, to provide crisis containment, allow for "ventilation time" regarding lesser crises, and to increase the opportunities for a good therapeutic alliance to develop. In-session tasks (accompanied by handouts) and extra-session therapy "homework" are also assigned to increase the subject's ability to apply therapy-related concepts to their current lives. Urine toxicology screens may be taken either once or twice weekly as necessary.

Therapy was provided during the treatment trial by doctoral-level personnel experienced in substance abuse and PTSD treatment (including EGT and SK). However, this therapy could also be feasibly performed by masters'-level therapists with at least 5 years' previous experience in the treatment of trauma or substance abuse under doctoral-level supervision. Regardless of experience and educational attainment, weekly supervision is a necessity due to the patients' complexities and to prevent vicarious traumatization (Pearlman & Saakvitne, 1995; Triffleman, 1998).

Considerations in Developing SDPT

Timing: When the Substance Abuse Is Addressed, When the PTSD Is Addressed

There were many considerations in designing a treatment method for PTSD-substance abuse. A fundamental concern was when in treatment to address the PTSD. Those who advocate an immediate approach to the trauma note that (a) by not addressing symptoms early, relapse and dropout is a risk, as trauma-associated symptoms occur and the patient continues to struggle with them (Brown et al., 1995; Ouimette et al., 1997); (b) by addressing trauma symptoms early, suffering may be alleviated sooner; and (c) a potentially motivating factor in the patient's substance use may be removed, thereby facilitating abstinence.

Those who advocate a later approach to the trauma (often after 6 months of abstinence) note that (a) for the patient who has sought treatment primarily for addictions, addressing other issues may be threatening or inappropriate (Clark, 1986); (b) substance abusers frequently have a low tolerance for all types of negative affects without relapsing or dropping out of treatment, especially in early abstinence (Beck, Wright, Newman, & Liese, 1993); (c) discussing trauma necessitates the ability to withstand often powerful and conflicting affects and cognitions specific not only to re-experiencing the trauma, but also to the act of telling even the most empathic listener (McFarlane, 1994; Silove, Chang, & Manicavasagar, 1995); (d) therapeutic interventions directed at underlying conflicts in any disorder, including PTSD, often prove less successful in persons continuing to use substances (Perconte & Griger, 1991); (e) a proportion of PTSD severity may subside with abstinence, just as in depressive symptoms associated with substance use (Dansky, personal communication); and (f) by delaying the discussion of trauma, a trusting therapeutic alliance may evolve, thereby allowing the patient to take the risks necessary to undertake trauma work without dropping out of treatment (Shalev, Bonne, & Spencer, 1996; van der Kolk, 1994).

SDPT, in its two-phase design, adopts a middle-ground stance similar to that of Abueg and Fairbank (1992). As noted above, the first phase does not ignore the presence of PTSD, but rather incorporates understanding and education about PTSD symptoms as part of the overall approach to the induction of abstinence. The second phase similarly allows for continued work on substance-related abstinence, while primarily targeting PTSD symptoms.

Considerations Regarding PTSD-Related Treatment Techniques

In part, the debate regarding early versus late onset of trauma treatment in PTSD-substance abuse is conditioned by the fears staff and patients may have regarding PTSD treatment techniques. Coping-skills based treatments for PTSD, such as SIT are seen as less stressful, inasmuch as SIT focuses on practical, daily-living skills with a lesser focus on memories of the traumatic event per se. In contrast, in-session imaginal exposure (Boudewyns & Hyer, 1990; Cooper & Clum, 1989; Foa, Rothbaum, Riggs, & Murdock, 1991; Keane, Fairbank, Caddell, & Zimering, 1989) requires the patient to discuss his/her experiences repetitively, to allow full processing of the memory (Foa, Steketee, & Rothbaum, 1989) and to generate alternative, healthier meanings from the experience (Foa, Molilar, & Cashman, 1995). While imaginal exposure permits the patient to maintain control regarding the content and pacing of sharing with the therapist and the observing self, it may appear to be overwhelmingly stressful to staff or patients, and thus, would not necessarily be acceptable to either. Indeed, in one uncontrolled case series (Pitman et al., 1991), of six patients who had psychiatric complications after imaginal flooding, four had current or past histories of substance abuse. Three of the four relapsed to substances during the course of flooding. The study's authors concluded that the presence of a history of substance abuse requires preparation and monitoring beyond that usually required by PTSD patients.

However, in studies contrasting several CBTs in rape victims (Foa et al., 1991; Foa, Rothbaum, & Molnar, 1995), after 9 weeks of treatment, imaginal exposure showed equal efficacy to SIT and emergent additional therapeutic effects at 3-month follow-up. In these studies, subjects with active substance use were excluded, and monitoring of substance use through the trial was not undertaken (Foa, personal communication). More recently, Marks et al. (1998) found that subjects receiving combined in vivo and in-session imaginal exposure did as well as subjects receiving cognitive restructuring across global measures of PTSD severity, with continued improvement over 6 months follow-up. In a case series (Richards & Rose, 1991), and a subsequent small trial (Richards et al., 1994), combined in vivo and imaginal exposures were found to specifically decrease phobic avoidance and intrusive symptoms, sustained over 12-month follow-up. Phobic avoidance, however, decreased specifically in response to live and not imaginal exposure. Subjects were excluded whose substance abuse began prior to the trauma, and level of current substance abuse at baseline or throughout the trial were not reported. The finding that PTSD symptoms are well-treated with live exposure is consistent with studies in other anxiety disorders (De Araujo & Marks, 1996; de Beurs, Van Balkom, Lange, Koele, & van Dyck, 1995; Hellstrom & Lars-Goran, 1995).

Overall, exposure-based PTSD treatments appear to be effective on a sustained basis in decreasing PTSD severity, although, to date, these approaches have not been evaluated in the context of substance abuse. Thus, in designing a treatment method for PTSD-substance abuse, a dilemma emerged regarding the effectiveness of exposure-based PTSD treatment versus approaches that might be more consistent with initiating and maintaining substance-related abstinence as well as be more broadly acceptable to patients and treatment providers. In SDPT, SIT provides both a useful transition from CBCST for substance abuse to PTSD treatment, with its emphasis on cognitions and skills, and useful preparatory techniques prior to undertaking in vivo exposure.

The rationale for in vivo exposure, implemented as a desensitization hierarchy, from a theoretical standpoint originates in theories of information processing in PTSD (Foa, 1997; Foa, Steketee, & Rothbaum, 1989, Horowitz, 1974): that PTSD represents a *forme fruste* of normal memory processing, intrusions representing attempts by the brain to process the traumatic memory and avoidance precluding this processing. In this framework, in order to treat PTSD, the full traumatic memory must be activated to permit completion of processing and storage as normal memory (Foa & Kozak, 1986). In live exposure, approaching those real-life cues that are associated with or are symbolic of the traumatic events is hypothesized to activate those memories as well as presenting here-and-now countervailing information to the memory. Exposure by definition involves initially generating increased arousal, which, with further contact with an identified, otherwise safe stimulus, generally subsides (Ross, 1996).

On a practical level, in vivo exposure is also useful in this patient population in that it (a) allows the patient to maintain control over the pace of treatment and degree of arousal experienced, and (b) enables the patient to reintegrate valued life activities into their routines, which (c) may alter the patient's trauma-related self-perceptions of shame and ineffectuality. Additionally, the types of traumas experienced by substance-abusing patients are diverse (Ellason, Ross, Sainton, & Mayran, 1996; Grice, Brady, Dustan, Malcolm, & Kilpatrick, 1995; Triffleman, Marmar, Delucchi, & Ronfeldt, 1995). Live exposure is readily adaptable for a broad range of traumatic events.

Design Considerations Regarding the Treatment of Substance Abuse

In developing SDPT, the substance abuse treatment techniques selected had to have both proven efficacy and congruence with the PTSD interventions selected. CBCST for substance abuse has been shown to be effective in trials across several patient populations (Crits-Christoph & Siqueland, 1996; Project MATCH Research Group, 1997; Woody et al., 1983) and to have emergent, durable treatment effects

(Carroll, Nich, & Rounsaville, 1995). As Najavits et al. (1996) cogently noted, CBCST is also useful in this patient population by (a) offering realistic, easily manageable skills alternatives, b) challenging the underlying beliefs that would make such skills seemingly unattainable and creating facilitative alternative cognitions, and (c) increasing identification of and tolerance to negative affective and physical states, thereby decreasing trauma-related dissociation and alexithymia (Haviland, Shaw, MacMurray, & Cummings, 1988; Hyer, Woods, & Boudewyns, 1991). CBCST techniques (and content areas) are used in SDPT, including in-session role playing, identification of dysfunctional and alternative cognitions, and covert role modeling.

Contrasts with Other Approaches and the Role of Self-Help Groups

Given the above considerations, SDPT differs from standard CBCST for substance abuse in several ways: (a) the explicit focus from day one that the patient has issues referable both to the processes of substance abuse and to traumatic experiences; (b) explicit discussion between patient and therapist regarding whether and what types of overlaps exist for the individual patient between PTSD and substance abuse-related problems, including how PTSD changes during the course of abstinence; (c) the use of phase-specific interventions; (d) the inclusion of PTSD-specific therapeutic techniques; and (e) in the frequency (twice weekly) and duration of this individual therapy. SDPT differs from existing CBT-based PTSD treatments by (a) maintaining explicit focus on substance abuse, abstinence, and maintenance; (b) monitoring substance use through urine toxicological screening and self-report; (c) pacing the PTSD interventions, with appropriate slowing as needed in the event of relapse or destabilizing cravings; and (d) increasing duration over which exposure occurs to accommodate substance-related therapeutic goals.

SDPT also stands in contrast to 12-step–based approaches (Evans & Sullivan, 1995). SDPT does not utilize 12-step treatment techniques or philosophy. In the context of the clinical trials (Triffleman et al., 1998), explicit references to the 12 steps, 12-step meetings, or slogans were proscribed as: (a) 12-step–based therapies are active therapies in their own right (Project MATCH Research Group, 1997); (b) consistency of therapeutic approach has been demonstrated to directly effect substance abuse treatment outcomes (Ouimette, Finney, & Moos, 1997); and (c) 12-Step Facilitation Therapy (Nowinski, Baker, & Carroll, 1992; Baker & Triffleman, 1998) was the contrasting condition for this study. However, participation in 12-step and other peer addictions-related support groups often provide useful social supports and support for abstinence. Given this, the SDPT therapist may: (a) *briefly* suggest or recommend that the patient seek out and attend 12-step meetings (or other substance-use support groups) for intersession support; or (b) use any experiences in peer support groups as a vehicle for further SDPT-style discussions of social interactions during appropriate SDPT topic sessions.

Referrals to self-help groups for ongoing traumas are made on a need-now basis. For example, if a patient is in a battering relationship, the therapist should provide the patient with information regarding domestic violence services and shelters. This is consistent with SDPT goals for facilitating the patient's freedom from ongoing trauma, and substance abstinence. Another contrasting therapeutic approach which has currency in the PTSD treatment field is that of psychodynamic psychotherapy (Brom, Kleber, & Defares, 1989). It is important to distinguish between treatment techniques used during the therapy hour and the SDPT therapist's internal framework for understanding the patient. Patients with PTSD-substance abuse are frequently complex and fragile individuals, capable of generating strong transference-countertransference states, and often have multilayered defense systems (Wilson & Lindy, 1994). It is important that SDPT therapists have experience and knowledge of such issues, and be able to identify transference, resistance, projections, and projective identification as they occur. However, explicit interpretation of transference phenomena to the patient is not part of SDPT. In addition, SDPT therapists are active, directive, and frequently didactic, in contrast to stances sometimes found in psychodynamic psychotherapy.

Target Population

SDPT has been designed to accommodate both genders and persons of diverse ethnic and socioeconomic backgrounds, given that such diversity is found in treatment programs. Indications for this approach include (a) either a current or lifetime history of substance dependence, and (b) lifetime full PTSD and at least current subsyndromal PTSD (Carlier & Gersons, 1995). SDPT accommodates a variety of traumas. Many substance-abusing patients have experienced both childhood and adulthood trauma, and find the emphasis on pragmatic approaches under their personal control to be helpful. However, persons seeking treatment primarily for a history of prolonged and repeated childhood sexual or combined sexual-physical abuse may not find this brief, highly symptom-focused treatment satisfying. Frequently, such individuals have profound difficulties with relationships and maintaining self-safety. In these instances, SDPT may serve as an introduction to therapy and to the process of examining trauma. Referrals may then be made for continuing therapy thereafter.

In addition to PTSD-substance abuse, patients may have other psychiatric problems as well (McFarlane & Papay, 1992; Southwick, Yehuda, & Giller, 1993). However, persons with current severe major depression, hypomania, or mania should not begin SDPT until stabilized on medications for at least 8 weeks. Chronic psychotic disorders, such as schizophrenia, are a contraindication to SDPT. Persons with *minor* psychotic symptoms, consistent with personality disorders (such as hearing one's name called sporadically) may be treatable after medication stabilization, but the therapist should monitor such symptoms closely as the PTSD interventions are undertaken. Dissociative identity disorder is also a contraindication, as it is likely to impair the patient's ability to undertake and tolerate the exposure component.

SDPT may be used in patients with many types of primary substance use disorders. In opiate-dependent patients, stabilization on opiate agonist or antagonist medication prior to starting therapy is optimal, while other patients may require detoxification prior to therapy initiation. Medication-free opiate-dependent patients may be treated with SDPT if they have maintained abstinence from opiates for at least 2 months prior to treatment entry. However, current nontherapeutic benzodiazepine dependence is a contraindication, as our experience is that these patients' ability to register information is often significantly impaired and they may require multiple episodes of detoxification during outpatient therapy.

Persons in the extremes of homelessness—residing on a day-in, day-out basis at temporary shelters, or "on the street"—may not do well, as the exigencies of daily living become paramount, and keeping an appointment at a fixed time may not be feasible. Such individuals need assertive outreach and placement in a more stable environment prior to undertaking SDPT (Milby et al., 1996; Stahler, 1995). Residence in a nonusing friend or family member's home, however, often provides adequate stability. Similarly, therapists should also be cautious about attempting to treat patients with clear secondary gain from continuing PTSD or addictions. Patients applying for or receiving disability or other compensation for these disorders should be monitored regarding the meaning of impairment to them and the economic and emotional risks of improvement.

Typical Session Format

SDPT sessions are highly structured. During one session per week, the session should open by interviewing the patient regarding the previous 7 days' substance use, and having the patient fill out a measure of PTSD symptomatology such as the Impact of Events Scale-Revised (Weiss & Marmar, 1997) or the Posttraumatic Diagnostic Scale (Foa, Cashman, Jaycox, & Perry, 1997). A urine toxicology screen should be obtained at least once a week. The therapist then uses these sources of information in therapy to ascertain and discuss with the patient her/his current level of substance use, and the degree to which PTSD symptoms are currently impairing the patient, and to provide appropriate support and determine the trajectory of symptom course.

Before, during, and after the questionnaires, patients often present general issues regarding current life problems. This portion should last no longer than 15 to 20 minutes, as this is the point at which the therapy can easily become derailed. The therapist will have to make judgment calls about the duration of these discussions, which, while often reflective of very real problems, may at times also represent various defensive processes by the patient, as in "I don't want to discuss my relapse," or "I don't want to do that scary PTSD stuff; you're so mean." The therapist should also bear in mind that "crises" can represent chronic patterns resolvable through therapeutic attention to PTSD symptoms or substance abuse. Where this is the case, the therapist should identify the chronic pattern to the patient, so that both parties may refocus on and, if necessary, redetermine appropriate treatment goals. However, on occasion, it is necessary to break with formal structure as true crises emerge, and as the patient requires containment and/or "ventilation" time.

The next step after the initial questionnaires and check-in is for the therapist to inquire about out-of-session assignments. The work is reviewed and problems or progress are evaluated. A decision to continue with that topic focus or move onto another one is then made on the basis of patient's progress and understanding, and current clinical applicability.

The session's topic focus is then introduced. This may be either a continuation from the previous session or the introduction of a new theme or skill. The patient's understanding and application of the topic is discussed, as the therapist actively elicits patient participation and experiences. Key words and phrases from the topic focus are written on an oversized paper pad (Najavits et al., 1996), so that (a) both therapist and patient may view them as the session progresses, and (b) so that this may be given to the patient at session's end, as a further reminder of topic discussed and conclusions reached. The patient should also be invited to write responses on the pad, such as the positive consequences of abstinence, possible alternative cognitions, etc. Doing so increases the chances that the patient will remain engaged, and emphasizes that agency and responsibility for change is shared—that SDPT is something done *with* the patient and not *to* her/him. Manual-based informational handouts are reviewed throughout the session as appropriate, and in-session exercises, including role-plays, imagining situations, and problem-solving takes place. Toward the end of session, "homework" assignments are explained, and anticipated problems with completion are examined.

Overview of Therapy Content

The content of session modules changes with the phase of treatment. During Phase I, topics include: (a) Introduction to SDPT, (b) Coping with Craving, (c) Relaxation Training, (d) Anger Awareness and Management, (e) Depression and Managing Negative Thoughts, (f) Handling Emergencies, (g) HIV Awareness, (h) Assertiveness Training, and (i) Social Supports. Of these, Handling Emergencies, Assertiveness Training, Increasing Social Support Networks, and Depression and Managing Negative Moods are implemented as described elsewhere (Carroll et al., 1993; Kadden et al., 1992). The remainder were especially adapted for SDPT and are described in detail below. These modules create and reinforce a solid foundation for substance abstinence and for handling the stresses encountered during Phase II of treatment. Each module lasts 1 to 4 sessions, as clinically indicated. In general, Introduction to SDPT followed by Coping with Craving are the first modules, as Coping with Craving contains cornerstone techniques for all other SDPT substance-related interventions. Other modules are then done in an order consistent with the patient's clinical needs.

Phase I modules should be done even with those patients who have a solid foundation of abstinence for several reasons: (a) by design, Phase I topics overlap common trauma-related deficits, such as those in anger management (Chemtob, Novaco, Hamada, Gross, & Smith, 1997) or assertiveness; (b) reinforcing knowledge and skills creates an opportunity for both patient and therapist to proactively identify and address areas in which difficulties can be anticipated, especially as the trauma-specific interventions are undertaken; and (c) module topics can serve as a springboard for examinations of previously unidentified problems in the patient's functioning.

In Phase II, the initial approach to dealing with trauma-related avoidance, Anti-Avoidance (I) lasts between 2 to 4 sessions. Anti-Avoidance (II), during which patients implement the exposure hierarchy, lasts between 6 to 12 sessions. Therapists should continue to monitor substance-abuse patterns and PTSD-related status, and adjust the pacing of the exposure hierarchy as needed.

Phase I Modules: Substance-Focused, Trauma-Informed Therapy

An Introduction to SDPT

During this module, SDPT as a therapy is described. Substance dependence and the symptoms of PTSD are defined. The nature of CBCST is described, including the antecedents-beliefs-consequences model (Beck, Rush, Shaw, & Emery, 1979), what SIT is and that live exposure will be used during the PTSD section. The patient's and therapist's goals and expectations for treatment are then reviewed, including the primary goal of abstinence from substance use.

Coping with Craving and Drug-Use Triggers

Craving for substances and contact with associated triggers often lead to slips and relapses. In this session, subjective experiences of craving and withdrawal are explored in the physical, emotional and affective realms (Carroll et al., 1993; Marlatt & Gordon, 1985). Triggers (both internal states and external cues) and typical drug-using situations are reviewed. Included is an explicit, detailed review of the ways (if any) external cues and internal states symbolic of her/his trauma have served as triggers for substance use. Such trauma-substance triggers can include nightmares or other intrusive symptoms, or an anticipated contact with a trauma-associated setting, for example. The positive and negative consequences of substance use and the anticipated positive and negative consequences of abstinence are explored, including the patient's observations regarding changes in PTSD symptoms during periods of use and abstinence. Emphasized here is that while patients may have experienced transient or lasting PTSD exacerbations during abstinence, abstinence is a necessary step toward more permanently reducing the severity of PTSD recurrences.

Tools used here include assignments to monitor craving over the following weeks. Subjects are also taught to engage in healthy avoidance of drug-using triggers; and to use distractions and alternative cognitions when experiencing craving. "Urge-surfing" (Carroll et al., 1993), a technique of localizing craving and maintaining awareness of it, coupled with alternative cognitions, and consciously allowing the craving to pass, is practiced in session and as part of therapy homework.

Relaxation Training

Relaxation training (Bernstein & Borkovec, 1973; Davis, Eshelman, & McKay, 1995) is taught as a means to deal with craving and urges to use, and as a general stress management tool in these patients for whom a resting state is sometimes delimited by continuing PTSD-related hypervigilance and intrusions. Under the rubric of stress management, relaxation skills are also framed as a partial means of dealing with trauma-related stimuli (Marks et al., 1998; Watson, Tuorila, Vickers, Gearhart, & Mendex, 1997). The patient's prior knowledge and attempts at attaining a relaxed state are reviewed, as are the human circulatory system and oxygen utilization patterns. Deep breathing is then taught, followed by progressive muscle relaxation. Patients are asked to identify and visualize in detail a "safe space" from their past, a place or situation associated with calm sensations. Therapists often play an active role in (a) guiding patients away from designating as safe spaces situations where substances were used or that are trauma-associated, and (b) helping the most traumatized patients to simply imagine a perhaps never-experienced calm situation.

HIV Risk Behaviors

During this module, drug-related and sex-related HIV risk behaviors (Avants, DePhilippis, Nickou, & Weiss, 1995; Sternberg, 1997) are discussed. The patient's knowledge regarding prevention of HIV transmission, previous HIV education, testing and HIV-related health maintenance is first reviewed. Where necessary, basic education is given, including that sexual abuse histories and PTSD along with substance abuse may be risk factors for engaging in HIV-transmissible behaviors (Bartholow et al., 1994; Stiffman, Dore, Earls, & Cunningham, 1992; Zierler et al., 1991). A typical high-risk scenario is then elicited from the patient, along with associated cognitions, dissociative symptoms occurring during sex (especially among the sexually traumatized) or high-risk drug use, and difficulties along the axes of power, coercion, and responsibility in relation to engaging in self-safe behaviors and refusing high-risk activities. Links between intimacy, passion, and commitment are also explored with regard to sexual high-risk behaviors (Sternberg, 1997). Abstinence from drugs as a means of decreasing drug-related HIV risks is also emphasized. Referrals for further evaluation and testing are offered.

Anger Awareness and Management

Persons with PTSD-substance abuse often have dysfunctional styles around anger, especially given that irritability is a symptom of PTSD. On the one hand, some persons actively attempt to suppress anger expression (sometimes using substances in that attempt), while others explode with rage and irritability (Chemtob et al., 1997). Increasing awareness of the beginning stages of anger is presented as the first step to anger management. A brief anger history is taken with regard to extent of aggressive actions to person and property, other outlets for anger, substance use in relation to anger, and the physical sensations and cognitions associated with a typical instance of anger. Whether episodes of anger occur in situations symbolic of the patient's trauma or during intrusive memories is also explored. Patients are taught to identify the intensity of their anger on a "thermometer" scale of 0 to 100 (Reilly, 1993), to keep a log of situations in which anger occurred and how it was managed.

Anger management builds on this awareness (Carroll et al., 1993; Reilly, Clark, Shopshire, Lewis, & Sorensen, 1994). For subjects who suppress anger, interventions overlap that of assertiveness training. For anger suppressers and the enraged, emphasis is placed on addressing anger at as early a stage as possible. In a manner similar to SIT for trauma (see below), patients are encouraged to anticipate situations in which they become angered and consider options for handling matters prior to entry into the situation. Alternative cognitions, good communication skills, social supports, expression through creative arts, and leaving the situation where necessary, are all discussed for use when angry. An anger management log is kept to monitor change.

Phase II Modules: Trauma-Focused, Addictions-Informed Therapy

Anti-Avoidance (I) — Stress Inoculation

The symptoms of PTSD are reviewed again with the patient. Patients are taught that avoidance, as a concept, has both salutory and dysfunctional aspects in the person with PTSD-substance abuse. On the one hand, avoiding triggers to substance use is a necessary skill. Avoiding situations that objectively may result in retraumatization (such as high-crime districts) is also salutory. But anxiously avoiding situations that have low objective risk other than escalating PTSD symptoms may not be adaptive and is the target of Phase II. Theories of information processing in PTSD (Foa & Kozak, 1986; Foa et al., 1989; Horowitz, 1974) are reviewed: that avoidance of trauma-associated cues occurs as a method of coping with intrusions and hyperarousal, but intrusions recur as a result of incomplete memory processing. How the patient avoids PTSD-related external and internal cues is reviewed and discussed, including an explicit rediscussion of current substance use and coping with craving in relation to these "trauma triggers."

A list is then made of places, persons, and situations avoided due to PTSD. These are then numerically ranked by the patient according to the level of difficulty the patient anticipates in re-approaching the item. The therapist should also assess how much these avoidances are in fact interfering with the patient's life. For example, driving 45 minutes out of the way to avoid an otherwise safe street may be more salient on a daily basis than avoiding seeing friends who live 700 miles away. On the other hand, the latter situation may be a more meaningful problem to the patient. Therefore, the therapist must make ongoing judgments together with the patient throughout Phase II about which avoided items are preferentially addressed.

In preparation for dealing with the hierarchy, SIT strategies are taught (Foa et al., 1991; Meichenbaum & Cameron, 1983). Four stages of dealing with an avoided situation are reviewed: approaching it, confronting it, what to do if overwhelmed, and dealing with the aftermath. Positive cognitions specific to each stage are developed along with behavioral strategies, such as using relaxation skills, and rewarding oneself in healthy manner after dealing with the stressor. Patients then write up index cards with these strategies along with alternative cognitions, for use at the time of stressor approach.

Anti-Avoidance (II)—Continued Stress Inoculation and Hierarchical in Vivo Exposure

As a continuation of the above, the least upsetting, most easily accomplished avoidance task is then selected from the exposure hierarchy together by patient and therapist. The patient is asked to consider what negative cognitions, fears, and problems can be anticipated in relation to the task. In-session visualization and role-play in relation to each SIT stage is undertaken as a rehearsal for approaching the avoidance. (Unlike imaginal exposure, repetitive in-session reviews are not performed.) Patients may be asked to identify supportive others who can be available to accompany the subject to the site if necessary for additional support. (Patients are also given the option to call therapists after or during task completion.) Unlike treatment of nonaddicted patients, SDPT patients are encouraged to remain in the situation only as long as they can tolerate the arousal. Functionally, this may mean only 30 seconds or up to several minutes. Patients are counseled to leave the site if overwhelming intrusions or flashbacks occur. Such situations are then re-approached in a more gradual fashion or are reranked for increased difficulty (and hence, re-approach is delayed). The patient is also advised to identify and engage in a healthy self-reward after the task, such as eating a favorite food or calling a friend (or the therapist), so that a guaranteed positive consequence is experienced.

In-session discussions about hierarchy items include reviewing: (a) what the patient did during each of the four SIT stages; (b) specific cognitions, affects, and memories experienced at each stage; (c) the meaning of the experience to the patient; and (d) other associated memories. Frequently, in discussing and experiencing the hierarchy items, other previously unexamined thoughts about the trauma surface, which may then impart to both the patient and therapist a richer understanding of the meaning of the trauma, and the meaning of going on with life. A common problem is that patients may be fearful that they will become amnestic for the experience if their hyperarousal and intrusions diminish. Therapists should provide appropriate reassurances that this will not occur.

Increasingly difficult hierarchy items are then undertaken. If, during this process, patient or therapist discover that the identified trauma itself or the hierarchy items are either not compelling or are too overwhelming to the patient, another trauma or other hierarchy item that is better suited for this work should be identified. The opposite problem — that of the patient deciding to immediately take on their most anxiety-provoking item at the onset of the hierarchy — is not uncommon. SDPT therapists should caution patients against doing so, due to the risk of generating more arousal than the patient may be able to handle from either a PTSD standpoint or that of maintaining substance abstinence. If the patient chooses to attempt the most difficult item despite this, then the therapist should give support to the patient and discuss the attempt. If the targeted hierarchy is completed, and sufficient time in therapy remains, a second trauma and related hierarchy is identified and another exposure undertaken.

Therapists will also need to be careful regarding patient attempts to derail the anti-avoidance work by (a) multiple crises, or (b) through passive resistance, such as agreeing to do assignments and then not doing so. Such actions should be gently discussed in light of any underlying concerns and cognitions. Passive resistance may also reflect a need to identify and approach less-arousing hierarchy items. Throughout the anti-avoidance phase, the therapist should review with the patient any thoughts, cravings, slips, or relapses to substance use. Slips occurring specifically in relation to hierarchy assignments generally indicate a need to at least temporarily slow movement along the hierarchy, and to re-examine the patient's use of SIT and stress management skills. Toxicology screens should continue to be obtained on a weekly basis throughout this phase.

Termination

In SDPT, termination is a process occurring over several sessions, starting from the beginning of therapy. SDPT is designed as a 5-month treatment. Thus, from the beginning, termination is made explicit, with a clear statement of the time-limited treatment duration. Patients are again gently reminded of the limited treatment duration at the transition between phases.

The termination process is begun in earnest at the beginning of the fifth month, by first setting the stop date and then reviewing the therapist's and patient's perceptions of past gains and continuing difficulties. Preliminary recommendations and referrals for further treatment are also reviewed. This is then broadened to a discussion regarding the patient's past experiences with loss and endings. Past responses to endings are likely to have included substance relapses, but also may have included being incarcerated or otherwise unable to participate in such rituals as funerals. Recrudescence of PTSD symptoms or feelings of loss of control and abandonment are also not unusual during periods of objective loss. SDPT termination is framed as an opportunity to have a planful, nonchaotic loss without concurrent substance use, and with the opportunity to grow through the process. Initial patient responses to termination discussions may vary from nonplused dismissal or denial of affect, as in, "We're ending? Oh good, I need the time," to feelings of abandonment and re-experiencing of trauma. By simultaneously acknowledging the pain and hurt, and maintaining an emphasis on the patient's gains in therapy and future planning, healthy acceptance may occur.

Such discussions will then likely color the continuing sessions, but therapists should formally review both the patient's current state with regard to termination, and referrals and recommendations at 2 weeks to end, with a final goodbye on the last day of treatment. Patients may attempt to avoid termination by either (a) no-showing or canceling the last few sessions, or (b) discussing other urgent matters instead. Clearly, where a true emergency is present, the therapist should attend to it, but as with much else in SDPT, the therapist will need to differentiate between crises needing attention and those that distract from necessary therapy work.

Summary and Conclusion

SDPT is a unique integration of existing treatment techniques for patients with comorbid substance abuse and PTSD. Among these elements is the inclusion of live exposure for PTSD, which in our experience has good patient acceptability. Results of an open trial (Triffleman et al., 1997) have indicated the preliminary efficacy of this treatment method in reducing PTSD severity. Implicit in this and other treatment methods for PTSD-substance abuse is the patient-level acceptability of addressing trauma relatively early in treatment. Building on a solid therapeutic alliance is key to this acceptability, as trust in the therapist and the therapeutic process (along with continuing symptom monitoring) plays a critical role in the treatment of substance abuse (Belding, Iguchi, Morral, & McLellan, 1997; Bell, Montoya, & Atkinson, 1997) and PTSD (McFarlane, 1994).

More studies and more theoretical approaches in the treatment of PTSD-substance are needed. Little is known about which patients with PTSD-substance abuse benefit from concurrent treatment of both disorders, nor is it established which existing standard substance abuse treatments—or elements of existing treatment approaches—are most congruent with PTSD treatment, and vice versa. A review of the literature suggests, however, that many persons with civilian PTSD are readily treatable (Lazrove, Triffleman, Kite, McGlashan, & Rounsaville, 1998; Shalev, 1997; Triffleman, 1998) under the proper conditions. Continuing identification of optimal treatment conditions for the more "typical" outpatient, as well as the development of approaches for the hardest-to-treat—such as the traumatized, chronically psychotic substance-abusing patient—remain as continuing challenges.

References

Abueg, F. R., Chun, K., & Lurie, D. (1990). *Precipitants to alcohol relapse among PTSD-alcoholics.* Presentation at the American Psychological Association Annual Meeting, Boston, MA.

Abueg, F. R., & Fairbank, J. A. (1992). Behavioral treatment of the PTSD-substance abuser: A multidimensional stage model. In P. Saigh (Ed.), *Posttraumatic Stress Disorder: A behavioral approach to assessment and treatment* (pp. 111–147). NY: Pergamon Press.

American Psychiatric Association. (1994). *Diagnostic and statistical manual of mental disorders (4th ed.).* Washington, DC: American Psychiatric Association.

Avants, K., DePhilippis, D., Nickou, C., & Weiss, A. (1995). *Risk reduction group therapy (RRT) for HIV-positive intravenous drug users.* Unpublished masters' thesis.

Baker, S., & Triffleman, E. (1998). *Twelve-step facilitation therapy in the treatment of substance abusers with PTSD.* Manuscript submitted for publication.

Bartholow, B. N., Doll, L. S., Joy, D., Douglas, J. M., Bolan, G., Harrison, J. S., Moss, P. M., & Kirnan, D. (1994). Emotional, behavioral and HIV risks associated with sexual abuse among adult homosexual and bisexual men. *Child Abuse Neglect, 18,* 747–761.

Beck, A. T., Rush, A. J., Shaw, B. E., & Emery, G. (1979). *Cognitive therapy of depression.* New York: Guilford Press.

Beck, A. T., Wright, F. D., Newman, C. F., & Liese, B. S. (1993). *Cognitive therapy of substance abuse.* New York: Guilford Press.

Belding, M. A., Iguchi, M. Y., Mortal, A. R., & McLellan, A. T. (1997). Assessing the helping alliance and its impact in the treatment of opiate dependence. *Drug and Alcohol Dependence, 48,* 51–59.

Bell, D. C., Montoya, I. D., & Atkinson, J. S. (1997). Therapeutic connection and client progress in drug abuse treatment. *Journal of Clinical Psychology, 53,* 215–224.

Bernstein, D. A., & Borkovec, T. D. (1973). *Progressive relaxation training: A manual for the helping professions.* Champaign, IL: Research Press.

Boudewyns, P. A., & Hyer, L. (1990). Physiological response to combat memories and preliminary treatment outcome in Vietnam veteran PTSD patients treated with direct therapeutic exposure. *Behavior Therapy, 21,* 63–87.

Brady, K. T., Sonne, S. C., & Roberts, J. M. (1995). Sertraline treatment of comorbid posttraumatic stress disorder and alcohol dependence. *Journal of Clinical Psychiatry, 56,* 502–505.

Bremner, J. D., Southwick, S. M., Darnell, A., & Charney, D. S. (1996). Chronic PTSD in Vietnam combat veterans: Course of illness and substance abuse. *American Journal of Psychiatry, 153,* 369–375.

Breslau, N., Davis, G. C., Andreski, P., & Peterson, E. (1991). Traumatic events and posttraumatic stress disorder in an urban population of young adults. *Archives of General Psychiatry, 48,* 216–222.

Brom, D., Kleber, R. J., & Defares, P. B. (1989). Brief psychotherapy for posttraumatic stress disorders. *Journal of Consulting and Clinical Psychology, 57,* 607–612.

Brown, P. J., Recupero, P. R., & Stout, R. (1995). PTSD-substance abuse comorbidity and treatment utilization. Addictive Behavior, 20, 251–254.

Carlier, I. V. E., & Gersons, B. P. E. (1995). Partial posttraumatic stress disorder (PTSD): The issue of psychological scars and the occurrence of PTSD symptoms. *Journal of Nervous and Mental Disease, 183,* 107–109.

Carroll, K., Donovan, D., Hester, R., & Kadden, R. (1993). *Cognitive-behavioral coping skills program.* Unpublished manuscript.

Carroll K., Nich, C., & Rounsaville, B. J. (1995). Differential symptom reduction in depressed cocaine abusers treated with psychotherapy and pharmacotherapy. *Journal of Nervous and Mental Disease, 183,* 251–259.

Chemtob, C. M., Novaco, R. W., Hamada, R. S., Gross, D. M., & Smith, G. (1997). Anger regulation deficits in combat-related posttraumatic stress disorder. *Journal of Traumatic Stress, 10,* 17–36.

Clark, M. (1986). Alcoholism first. *Women and Therapy, 5,* 71–76.

Cooper, N. A., & Clum, G. A. (1989). Imaginal flooding as a supplementary treatment for PTSD in combat veterans: A controlled study. *Behavior Therapy, 20,* 381–391.

Crits-Christoph, P., & Siqueland, L. (1996). Psychosocial treatment for drug abuse: selected review and recommendations for national health care. *Archives of General Psychiatry, 53,* 749–756.

Davis, M., Eshelman, E. R., & McKay, M. (1995). *The relaxation and stress reduction workbook (4th ed.).* Oakland, CA: New Harbinger Publications, Inc.

De Araujo, L. A., & Marks, I. M. (1996). Early compliance and other factors predicting outcome of exposure for obsessive-compulsive disorder. *British Journal of Psychiatry, 169,* 747–752.

de Beurs, E., van Balkom, J. L. M., Lange, A., Koele, P., & van Dyck, R. (1995). Treatment of Panic disorder with agoraphobia: Comparison of fluvoxamine, placebo and psychological panic management combined with exposure and of exposure in vivo alone. *American Journal of Psychiatry, 152,* 683–691.

Ellason, J. W., Ross, C. A., Sainton, K., & Mayran, L. W. (1996). Axis I and II comorbidity and childhood trauma history in chemical dependency. *Bulletin of the Menninger Clinic, 60,* 39–51.

Evans, D., & Sullivan, J. M. (1995). *Treating addicted survivors of trauma.* New York, NY: Guilford Press.

Foa, E. B. (1997). Psychological processes related to recovery from a trauma and an effective treatment for PTSD. In R. Yehuda & A. C. McFarlane (Eds.), *Annals of the New York Academy of Sciences, 821,* 410–424.

Foa, E. B., Cashman, L., Jaycox, L., & Perry, K. (1997). The validation of a self-report measure of posttraumatic stress disorder: The Posttraumatic Diagnostic Scale. *Psychological Assessment, 9,* 445–451.

Foa, E. B., & Kozak, M. J. (1986). Emotional processing of fear: exposure to corrective information. *Psychological Bulletin, 99,* 20–35.

Foa, E. B., Molnar, C., & Cashman, L. (1995). Change in rape narratives during exposure therapy for posttraumatic stress disorder. *Journal of Traumatic Stress, 8,* 675–690.

Foa, E. B., Rothbaum, B., & Molnar, C. (1995). Cognitive-behavioral therapy of post-traumatic stress disorder. In M.J. Friedman, D.S. Chamey, & A.Y. Deutch (Eds.), *Neurobiological and clinical consequences of stress* (pp. 483–494). Philadelphia, PA: Lippincott-Raven.

Foa, E. B., Rothbaum, B. O., Riggs, D. S., & Murdock, T. B. (1991). Treatment of posttraumatic stress disorder in rape victim: A comparison between cognitive-behavioral procedures and counseling. *Journal of Consulting and Clinical Psychology, 59,* 715–723.

Foa, E. B., Steketee, G., & Rothbaum, B. O. (1989). Behavioral/cognitive conceptualizations of post-traumatic stress disorder. *Behavior Therapy, 20,* 155–176.

Grice, D. E., Brady, K. T., Dustan, L. R., Malcolm, R., & Kilpatrick, D. G. (1995). Sexual and physical assault history and posttraumatic stress disorder in substance-dependent individuals. *American Journal of Addictions, 4,* 297–305.

Haviland, M. G., Shaw, D. G., MacMurray, J. P., & Cummings, M. A. (1988). Validation of the Toronto Alexithymia Scale with substance abusers. *Psychotherapy and Psychosomatics, 50,* 81–87.

Hellstrom, K., & Lars-Goran, O. (1995). One-session therapist directed exposure vs. two forms of manual directed self-exposure in the treatment of spider phobia. *Behavior Research and Therapy, 33,* 959–965.

Herman, J. L. (1993). Sequelae of prolonged and repeated trauma: Evidence for a complex posttrauamtic syndrome (DESNOS). In J. R. T. Davidson & E. D. Foa (Eds.), *Post-traumatic stress disorder: DSM-IV and beyond* (pp. 213–228). Washington, DC: American Psychiatric Press, Inc.

Horowitz, M. (1974). Stress response syndromes: Character style and dynamic psychotherapy. *Archives of General Psychiatry, 31,* 768–781.

Hyer, L., Woods, M. G., & Boudewyns, P. (1991). PTSD and Alexithymia: Importance of emotional clarification in treatment. *Psychotherapy, 28,* 129–139.

Kadden, R., Carroll, K., Donovan, D., Cooney, N., Monti, P., Abram, D., Litt, M., & Hester, R. (1992). Cognitive-Behavioral Coping Skills Therapy manual: A Clinical research guide for therapists creating individuals with alcohol abuse and dependence. *NIAAA Project MATCH Monograph Series (vol. 3.).* Washington, DC: DHHS Pub No (ADM) 92-1895.

Keane, T. M., Fairbank, J. A.. Caddell, J. M., & Zimering, R. T. (1989). Implosive (flooding) therapy reduces symptoms of PTSD in Vietnam combat veterans. *Behavior Therapy, 20,* 245–260.

Kessler, R. C., Sonnega, A., Bromet, E., Hughes, M., & Nelson, C. (1995). Posttraumatic Stress disorder in the National Comorbidity Survey. *Archives of General Psychiatry, 52,* 1048–1060.

Lazrove, S., Triffleman, E., Kite, L., McGlashan. T., & Rounsaville, B. (1998). An open trial of EMDR as treatment for chronic PTSD. *American Journal of Orthopsychiatry, 68,* 601–608.

Marks, I. M., Lovell, K., Noshirvani, H., Livanou, M., & Thrasher, S. (1998). Treatment of posttraumatic stress disorder by exposure and/or cognitive restructuring. *Archives of General Psychiatry, 55,* 317–325.

Marlatt, G. A., & Gordon, J. R. (1985). *Relapse prevention.* New York, NY: Guilford Press.

McFarlane, A.C. (1994). Individual Psychotherapy for post-traumatic stress disorder. *Psychiatric Clinics of North America, 17,* 393–408.

McFarlane, A.C., & Papay, P. (1992). Multiple diagnosis in posttraumatic stress disorder in the victims of a natural disaster. *Journal of Nervous and Mental Disease, 180,* 498–504.

Meichenbaum, D., & Cameron, R. (1983). Stress inoculation training: Toward a general paradigm for training coping skills. In D. Meichenbaum & M.E. Jaremko (Eds.), *Stress reduction and prevention* (pp. 115–157). New York: Plenum Press.

Milby, J. B., Schumacher, J. E., Raczynski, J. M., Caldwell, E., Engle, M., Michael, M., & Carr, J. (1996). Sufficient conditions for effective treatment of substance abusing homeless persons. *Drug and Alcohol Dependence, 43,* 39–47.

Monti, P. M., Abram, D. B., Kadden, R., & Cooney, N. (1989). *Treating alcohol dependence: A coping skills training guide.* New York, NY: Guilford Press.

Najavits, L. M., Weiss, R. D., & Liese, B. S. (1996). Group cognitive-behavioral therapy for women with PTSD and substance use disorder. *Journal of Substance Abuse Treatment, 13,* 13–22.

Najavits, L. M., Weiss, R. D., Shaw, S. R., & Muenz, L. R. (1998). "Seeking safety": Outcome of a new cognitive-behavioral psychotherapy for women with posttraumatic stress disorder and substance dependence. *Journal of Traumatic Stress, 11,* 437–456.

Nowinski, J., Baker, S., & Carroll, K. M. (1992). Twelve step facilitation therapy manual: A Clinical research guide for therapists treating individuals with alcohol abuse and dependence. *NIAAA Project MATCH Monograph (vol. 1).* Washington, DC: Government Printing Office. DHHS Publication No. (ADM) 92-1893.

Ouimette, P.C., Ahrens, C., Moos, R. H., & Finney, J. W. (1997). Posttraumatic stress disorder in substance abuse patients: relationship to one-year post-treatment outcomes. *Psychology of Addictive Behavior, 11,* 34–47.

Ouimette, P. C., Finney, J. W., & Moos, R. H. (1997). Twelve-step and cognitive-behavioral treatment for substance abuse: A comparison of treatment effectiveness. *Journal of Consulting and Clinical Psychology, 65,* 230–240.

Pearlman, L. A., & Saakvitne, K. W. (1995). *Trauma and the therapist.* New York, NY: W.W. Norton and Co.

Perconte, S. T., & Griger, M. L. (1991). Comparison of successful, unsuccessful, and relapsed Vietnam veterans treated for posttraumatic stress disorder. *Journal of Nervous and Mental Disease, 179,* 558–562.

Pitman, R. K., Altman, B., Greenwald, E., Longpre. R., Macklin, M. L., Poire, R. E., & Steketee, G. S. (1991). Psychiatric complications during flooding therapy for posttraumatic stress disorder. *Journal of Clinical Psychiatry, 52,* 17–20.

Prochaska, J. O., & DiClemente, C. C. (1983). Stages and Processes of self-change of smoking: Toward an Integrative model of change. *Journal of Consulting Psychology, 51,* 390–395.

Project MATCH Research Group. (1997). Matching alcoholism treatments to client heterogeneity, Project MATCH posttreatment drinking outcomes. *Journal of Studies on Alcohol, 58,* 7–29.

Reilly, P. (1993). *Anger management for substance abuse.* Unpublished manuscript.

Reilly, P. M., Clark, H. W., Shopshire, M. S., Lewis, E. W., & Sorensen, D. J. (1994). Anger management and temper control: Critical components of posttraumatic stress disorder and substance abuse treatment. *Journal of Psychoactive Drugs, 26,* 401–407.

Resnick, H. S., Kilpatrick, D. G., Dansky, B. S., Saunders, B. E., & Best, C. L. (1993). Prevalence of civilian trauma and posttraumatic stress disorder in a representative national sample of women. *Journal of Consulting Clinical Psychology, 6,* 984–991.

Richards, D. A., Lovell, K., & Marks, I. M. (1994). Post-traumatic stress disorder: Evaluation of a Behavioral treatment program. *Journal of Traumatic Stress, 7,* 669–680.

Richards, D. A., & Rose, J. S. (1991). Exposure therapy for posttraumatic stress disorder: Four Case studies. *British Journal of Psychiatry, 158,* 836–840.

Ross, J. L. (1996). In vivo desensitization: Anxiety coping techniques. In C.G. Lindemann (Ed.), *Handbook of the treatment of the anxiety disorders (2nd. ed.,* pp. 293–302). Northvale, NJ: Jason Aronson, Inc.

Satel, S. L., Becker, B. R., & Dan, E. (1993). Reducing obstacles to affiliation with alcoholics anonymous among veterans with PTSD and alcoholism. *Hospital and Community Psychiatry, 44,* 1061–1065.

Seidel, R. W., Gusman, F. D., & Abueg, F. R. (1994). Theoretical and practical foundations of an inpatient post-traumatic stress disorder and alcoholism treatment program. *Psychotherapy, 31,* 67–78.

Shalev, A. (1997). Discussion: Treatment of prolonged posttraumatic stress disorder. *Journal of Traumatic Stress, 10,* 415–422.

Shalev, A. Y., Bonne, O., & Spencer, E. (1996). Treatment of posttraumatic stress disorder. *Psychosomatic Medicine, 58,* 165–182.

Silove, D., Chang, R., & Manicavasagar, V. (1995). Impact of recounting stories on the emotional state of Cambodian refugees. *Psychiatric Services, 46,* 1287–1288.

Southwick, S., Yehuda, R., & Giller, E. L. (1993). Personality disorders in treatment-seeking combat veterans with posttraumatic stress disorder. *American Journal of Psychiatry, 150,* 1020–1023.

Stahler, G.J. (1995). Social interventions for homeless substance abusers: Evaluating treatment outcomes. *Journal of Addictive Diseases, 14,* xv–xxvi.

Sternberg, R.J. (1997). Construct validation of a triangular love scale. European *Journal of Social Psychology, 27,* 313–335.

Stiffman, A.R., Dore, P., Earls, F., & Cunningham, R. (1992). The influence of mental health problems on aids-related risk behaviors in young adults. *Journal of Nervous and Mental Disease, 180,* 314–320.

Triffleman, E. (1998). *Vicarious traumatization among addictions treatment staff: A clinical consultation.* Manuscript submitted for publication.

Triffleman, E. (1998). An overview of trauma, PTSD and substance abuse. In H. Kranzler & B. Rounsaville (Eds.), *Dual diagnosis and treatment, (2nd ed.),* (pp. 263–316). New York, NY: Marcel Dekker.

Triffleman, E., & Kellogg, S. (1997). *Substance dependence post-traumatic stress disorder therapy (SDPT): A therapist's manual.* Unpublished manuscript.

Triffleman, E., Kellogg, S., & Syracuse-Siewert, G. (1997). *Pilot study findings: A controlled trial of psychosocial treatments in substance dependent patients with PTSD.* Presented at the 13th Annual Meeting of the International Society for Traumatic Stress Studies, Montreal, Quebec, Canada.

Triffleman, E., Kellogg, S., & Syracuse-Siewert, G. (1997). *A pilot study of psychosocial treatment for substance dependence and civilian post-traumatic stress disorder.* Unpublished manuscript.

Triffleman, E. G., Marmar, C. R., Delucchi, K. L., & Ronfeldt, H. (1995). Childhood trauma and posttraumatic stress disorder in substance abuse inpatients. *Journal of Nervous and Mental Disease, 183,* 172–176.

van der Kolk, B. (1994). Forward. In J. P. Wilson & J. D. Lindy (Eds.), *Countertransference in the treatment of PTSD (p*p. vii–xii.). New York, NY: Guilford Press.

Veronen, L. J., & Kilpatrick, D. G. (1983). Stress Management for rape victims. In D. Meichenbaum & M. E. Jaremko (Eds.), *Stress reduction and prevention* (pp. 341–374). New York, NY: Plenum Press.

Watson, C. G., Tuorila, J. R., Vickers, K. S., Gearhart, L. P., & Mendex, C. M. (1997). The efficacies of three relaxation regimens in the treatment of PTSD in Vietnam War veterans. *Journal of Clinical Psychology, 53,* 917–923.

Weiss, D. S., & Marmar, C. R. (1997). The Impact of Event Scale Revised. In J. P. Wilson & T. M. Keane (Eds.), *Assessing psychological trauma and PTSD* (pp. 399–411). New York, NY: Guilford Press.

Wilson. J. P., & Lindy, J. D. (Eds.) (1994). *Countertransference in the treatment of PTSD.* New York, NY: Guilford Press.

Woody, G. E., Luborsky, L., McLellan, A. T., O'Brien, C. P., Beck, A. T., Blaine, J., Herman, I., & Hole, A. (1983). Psychotherapy for opiate addicts: Does it help? *Archives of General Psychiatry, 40,* 639–645.

Zierler, S., Feingold, L., Laufer, D., Velentgas, P., Kantrowitz-Gordon, I., & Mayer, K. (1991). Adult survivors of childhood sexual abuse and subsequent risk of HIV infection. *American Journal of Public Health, 81,* 572–575.

Chapter Five: Clinical Issues

An Integrated Model for the Management of Co-Occurring Psychiatric and Substance Disorders in Managed-Care Systems

Kenneth Minkoff

This article originally appeared in *Disease Management Health Outcomes*, 2000, (5), 251–257, and is reprinted with permission by Adis Publications, Inc., New Zealand.

Kenneth Minkoff, M.D., is Chief of Psychiatric Services at Choate Health Systems, Inc., in Woburn, MA, and Medical Director of the Culfield Center, an integrated psychiatry and addiction hospital.

This article describes research-based principles of successful treatment interventions in individuals with co-occurring disorders. These principles are placed in the context of an integrated model of service delivery that utilises a common language or treatment philosophy that makes sense from the perspective of both mental health treatment and substance disorder treatment fields. The article begins with an overview of the clinical and programmatic dilemmas faced by clinicians in treating these "dually diagnosed" individuals and then enumerates 7 principles of treatment. These are: (i) dual diagnosis is an expectation, not an exception, within any of the 4 subtypes of comorbidity (using a subtyping model based on high/low severity of each disorder); (ii) the most significant predictor of treatment success is the provision of an empathic, hopeful, continuous treatment relationship in which integrated treatment and care coordination are provided over time; (iii) within the context of this relationship, caretaking and case management are balanced with empathic detachment, empowerment and confrontation at each point in time; (iv) within this ongoing treatment context, both mental illness and substance disorder are considered primary, and integrated dual primary treatment is provided; (v) both mental illness and addiction are examples of not just random primary disorders, but chronic biological mental illnesses which can be understood using a disease and recovery model; (vi) the model defines parallel phases of recovery, which themselves define phase-specific treatment interventions; as a result, there is no single correct intervention in this model. For each individual, the correct treatment must be matched to subtype, diagnosis, phase of treatment and extent of patient motivation and disability; and (vii) within a managed-care system, these interventions must be further individualised by a discrete level of care assessment for each disorder. These principles provide a template both for developing practice guidelines to determine individualised clinical treatment matching, as well as providing a template for large-scale system initiatives for the creation of comprehensive continuous integrated systems of care, and for assigning roles for each type of programme within those systems. These large systems initiatives are currently underway in several US states, and provide a laboratory for further research on this model.

During the past 2 decades, the problem of providing successful treatment to individuals with co-occurring psychiatric and substance disorders (ICOPSD) has emerged with considerable energy in both the mental health system and the substance disorder treatment system. Increasing volumes of data have supported the impression of clinical experience in both systems that ICOPSD have poorer outcomes across multiple domains, as well as being difficult to serve in traditional treatment venues. Specifically, ICOPSD are more likely to relapse and be rehospitalised, to be treatment resistant and noncompliant, medically involved (e.g. HIV infected), criminally involved, and homeless, as well as impulsive, suicidal and violent (Abram & Teplin, 1991; Bartels, Drake, & McHugo, 1992; Cournos, Empfield, Horwath, et al., 1991; Cuffel, Shumway, Chouljian, et al., 1994; Drake, Osher, & Wallach, 1991; RachBeisel, Scott, & Dixon, 1999). In addition, studies in managed-care systems have identified ICOPSD as being overrepresented in populations of high utilisers of scarce systems resources, in both public and private sector systems (Quinlivan & McWhirter, 1996; Hartman & Nelson, 1997).

Successful treatment and disease management of either substance disorders or psychiatric disorders separately is highly challenging. Both disorders are chronic, relapsing, stigmatising and potentially disabling. In addition, both disorders involve alteration of the individual's mental status, so that disease management strategies are targeted at someone who is cognitively impaired, possibly with poor reality testing, and who may not adequately recognise the seriousness of his or her condition.

When the two illnesses co-occur, the problems of disease management are compounded dramatically. This occurs not only because of the potential for the two types of disorders to interact and create mutual symptomatic exacerbation, but also because of the fact that ICOPSD are essentially "system misfits," who dare to have more than one disorder in systems of care that are designed to deal with a distinct primary mental health *or* substance disorder only (Bachrach, 1986-7). Furthermore, managed-care initiatives in behavioural health systems during the past decade have added a layer of funding complexity to the already difficult clinical, programmatic, and philosophical issues that result from inter-system conflict.

Fortunately, accumulating research—as well as clinical experi-ence—over the past 2 decades, addressing comorbidity in both popula-tions with serious mental illness and complex addicted populations (with less serious but still problematic co-occurring mental disorders), has begun to identify a variety of principles that guide successful interven-tion. These research and clinical findings have been sufficiently elaborat-ed to permit the development of expert consensus on an integrated model and standards of care for co-occurring disorder management in managed-care systems. This model, in turn, provides a template on which to base further clinical and systems research. The principles and standards, as well as the model, were disseminated in an expert consensus panel report generated by the Substance Abuse and Mental Health Services Administration, as part of its "managed-care initiative" (Minkoff, 1998).

This article reviews those principles and illustrates their applica-tion, both to the model and to strategies for system change.

Principles of Successful Treatment Intervention

First Principle
Comorbidity is an expectation, not an exception.
The first principle derives from epidemiological research on comorbidity conducted both in the 1980s (Regier, Farmer, & Rae, 1990) and the 1990s (Kessler, Nelson, McGonagle, et al., 1996). Both surveys illustrated that in a majority of individuals with serious mental illness, particularly those with unstable conditions, comorbid substance use disorders were present. Conversely, in individuals with substance disor-ders, 39 to 56% (according to one survey [Regier, Farmer, & Rae, 1990]) had any psychiatric diagnosis.

The implication of this first principle is that the most cost-effective systems intervention is to create a process for integrated system plan-ning to redesign the system so that all existing resources are used in accordance with this principle. This requires that all programmes are planned and designed to be competent in dealing with the people with comorbidity that they are already treating, and that all system clinicians are expected, over time, to attain minimum required levels of dual competency.

It is also important to note that this principle applies regardless of the subtype of dual disorder under consideration. The most common subtyping models are four quadrant models (Ries & Miller, 1993; National Association of State Mental Health Program Directors, National Association of State Alcohol and Drug Abuse Directors, 1998) involving high and low severity of psychiatric and substance disorders. In one model (Ries & Miller, 1993), the four subtypes are defined as follows: (i) severe and persistent mental disorder (SPMI) plus substance dependence; (ii) SPMI plus substance abuse; (iii) substance dependence plus non-SPMI psychiatric symptomatology; and (iv) substance abuse plus non-SPMI symptomatology. In each instance, the prevalence of comorbidity is significant.

Second Principle

Successful treatment requires most importantly the creation of welcoming, empathic, hopeful, continuous treatment relationships, in which integrated treatment and coordination of care are sustained through multiple treatment episodes.

This second principle is based on the findings of clinical research with hard-to-engage populations (Drake, Bartels, Teague, et al., 1993; Quinlivan & McWhirter, 1996). It emphasises that the first task of system and programme design is to foster opportunities for integrated continuity of clinical care, rather than to emphasise any particular "programme" model. Disease management for chronic disabling conditions is a continuing process, in which the risk of decompensation due to inadequate treatment adherence persists over time. This is especially true for comorbid conditions in which the capacity for treatment adherence is impaired by the symptoms of either disease, and in which system discontinuity promotes the possibility of individuals receiving inconsistent messages regarding their treatment needs. Integrated continuous care coordination shifts the burden of making sense of disparate input from the client to the clinician, and creates the possibility of continuous learning through repeated collaborative trial and error.

Third Principle

Within the context of the continuous integrated treatment relationship, case management and caretaking must be balanced with empathic detachment and confrontation in accordance with the individual's level of functioning, disability and capacity for treatment adherence.

This third principle addresses the apparent philosophical incompatibility between the nature of treatment relationships in mental health treatment and addiction treatment. In the former, the emphasis is on case management, care and continuous responsibility for the client; in the latter, the emphasis is on empathic detachment, confrontation and consequences, and the client's responsibility to bear consequences of his or her own decisions. However, research on the value of case management in successful interventions with complex addiction populations as well as with seriously mentally ill substance abusers (RachBeisel, Scott, & Dixon, 1999), plus the growing emphasis of the mental health consumer movement on the need for consumer empowerment, has led to recognition that these relationship styles are not incompatible at all. Instead, they are absolutely complementary.

The value of this clinical principle (although not yet fully research tested) is that philosophical battles about the "right" relational style can be reframed as clinical strategic discussions about the most appropriate place to draw the line between what to do for the client and what responsibility the client must bear on his or her own (Minkoff, 1989). The clinical challenge is that there is no "rule book" to tell clinicians where to draw the line; the balance must be derived in the context of an individual relationship, often through a process of trial and error over time. Individuals with more serious disabilities require considerably more structure; the particular challenge is to provide that structure in the context of behavioural contingencies which promote learning and responsibility. Recent research has introduced methods of utilising payeeships and other behavioural rewards to create this structure (Ries & Comtois, 1997).

Fourth Principle

When mental illness and substance disorder coexist, both disorders should be considered primary, and integrated dual primary treatment is required.

This fourth principle addresses the dilemma of determining which disorder should be considered primary. Each system's regulations and clinical philosophy support the concept that its disease should be primary, and considerable conflict may emerge between systems in trying to determine which is the client's "real" disease. Clients, in turn, often are caught in the middle of this split, experiencing what has been termed "ping-pong therapy" as they are bounced back and forth between mental health and addiction settings (Ridgely, Goldman, & Willenbring, 1990). Treatment is often "sequential" (each disorder considered primary in turn), or "parallel" (each disorder treated separately in isolation). The essence of integrated treatment, however, derives from principle 4.

Thus, in the context of the continuing integrated treatment relationship, integrated coordination of primary treatment interventions for both disorders is provided. In fact, even though mental illness and substance disorders are interactive, the significance of the interactions is small compared with the importance of ensuring adequate attention to each primary disorder and making sure treatment is adequate, given possible interference from the other disorder. Specifically, this means that it is important to maintain medication for serious mental illness (and in fact to use the best possible medication) even in the presence of continuing substance use (Minkoff, 1998). Similarly, it is also important to remember that individuals with psychiatric impairment require more addiction treatment to acquire recovery skills than comparably addicted individuals without impairment. This "additional" treatment often must be more simplified, not more complex, and provided in smaller increments with more support over a longer period of time in order to achieve comparable outcomes (Roberts, Shaner, & Eckman, 1999).

Fifth Principle

Both psychiatric illnesses and substance dependence are examples of chronic, biological mental illnesses which can be understood using a disease and recovery model. Each disorder is characterised by parallel phases of recovery, acute stabilisation, engagement and motivational enhancement, active treatment and prolonged stabilisation, rehabilitation and recovery (Minkoff, 1989).

This fifth principle expands on its predecessor to create a common language and integrated treatment philosophy that makes sense from the perspective of both the mental health system and the addiction system. In this model, both disorders are characterised by positive symptoms which can be stabilised through ongoing participation in a treatment regime (e.g. medication, Alcoholics Anonymous), and deficit symptoms which must be addressed through ongoing rehabilitation. Both disorders involve denial, despair, shame, guilt and stigma which inhibit treatment participation, yet both offer the hope of recovery despite incurability, potential persistent disability and risk of relapse. Recovery applies not to the disorder, but to the person who has the disorder, and involves recovering a sense of pride, self-worth, dignity and meaning in the face of an ongoing, stigmatising and possibly disabling disease (Deegan, 1988).

Sixth Principle

There is no single correct dual diagnosis intervention. Appropriate practice guidelines require that interventions must be individualised, according to the subtype of dual disorder, specific diagnosis of each disorder, phase of recovery/stage of change, and level of functional capacity or disability (Minkoff, 1998).

Advances in clinical research in both systems during the last decade have recognised not only the presence of stages of change (Prochaska, DiClemente, & Norcross, 1992) or phases of treatment (Osher & Kofoed, 1989) consistent with this model, but have demonstrated that successful interventions tend to be phase or stage-specific. Particular focus has been on the developing technology of motivational enhancement therapy (Miller & Rollnick, 1991), in which individuals are engaged at their own level of readiness to change, and assisted, through a combination of both collaboration and empathic confrontation, to make better choices over time. Consequently, it has gradually become more apparent that interventions must be appropriately matched along a variety of dimensions.

Consequently, interventions which are apparently incompatible, such as "harm reduction" and "abstinence orientation," can be seen as being valuable aspects of the same therapeutic armamentarium, provided that each is appropriately matched according to patient diagnosis and stage of change. In addition, this same model can be applied to designing a comprehensive system of care, in which there is a full range of available programmes to meet the needs of clients as they move through various phases of recovery with different levels of impairment and disability (Minkoff, 1991).

Seventh Principle

Within a managed-care system, any of the individualised phase-specific interventions can be applied at any level of care. Consequently, a separate multidimensional level of care assessment is required.

The integrated model can be applied to disease management interventions in managed-care systems. In both addiction and mental health treatment systems, level of care assessment decisions for each type of disorder separately have been guided less by well documented research than by clinically derived assessment instruments that utilise multiple dimensions of assessment to attempt to predict service intensity requirements. These assessment instruments have had, to date, only limited application to individuals with co-occurring disorders, but are beginning to be elaborated to better accommodate the needs of this population. Within the addiction system, for example, the most widely utilised level of care assessment instrument has been the American Society of Addiction Medicine (ASAM) Patient Placement Criteria (PPC 2) (American Society of Addiction Medicine [ASAM], 1995), which have recently been revised (ASAM PPC 2R) (American Society of Addiction Medicine [ASAM], in press, revised) to more appropriately incorporate individuals with co-occurring psychiatric impairment. Within the mental health system, the American Association of Community Psychiatrists has recently disseminated a more psychiatric-based multidimensional assessment tool (LOCUS 2.0) (American Association of Community Psychiatrists, 1998) which also includes a dimension evaluating substance-related, as well as medical, comorbidity.

Conclusions

This article has presented an integrated model for treatment of individuals with co-occurring disorders, derived from research-based model treatment initiatives, that permits the use of a common language or treatment philosophy for all subtypes of dually diagnosed individuals throughout both the mental health system and the addiction treatment system. This "integrated philosophy" emphasises that both substance disorders and psychiatric disorders are "primary" when they coexist, and that they both can be treated using a disease and recovery model, which defines parallel phases of treatment for each disorder, implying that clinical experience with the recovery process for one disorder can be informative regarding the recovery process for the other disorder.

In addition, this model provides a template for the development of individualised disease management strategies for individuals with co-occurring disorders that can be applied at multiple levels of care within a managed-care system. This template can be utilised to develop practice guidelines that assist clinicians in appropriately individualised clinical treatment matching (e.g., when to use harm reduction; when to use an abstinence orientation). This template can also be used at the systems level to design a comprehensive, continuous integrated system of care, in which each component of the system plays a role in the provision of appropriately matched treatment. The model implies that the prevalence and variability of dual disorders result in a need for "dual diagnosis competency" throughout the service system, and suggests that the most efficient approach is not only to develop specialised programmes but also to initiate large scale systems change in which *all* programmes in the system, at all levels of care, are expected to achieve this competency.

One of the major challenges that must be addressed in the application of this model is the development of well described, and, hopefully, formally evaluated strategies for real world implementation of the model at the systems level. Currently, some of the most exciting innovations in dual diagnosis treatment are the applications of this model to systems change initiatives at the state or regional level in a number of US states, including Arizona, Louisiana, Pennsylvania, Florida, Michigan, Illinois, New York and Massachusetts (Barreira, Espey, Fishbein, et al., 2000).

Although these initiatives are still in progress, early results seem to indicate that to overcome barriers to systems change, change efforts must address multiple levels of the system simultaneously. This can include:

- systems level changes (e.g. large scale consensus building [Barreira, Espey, Fishbein, et al., 2000], regulatory change to eliminate licensing and reimbursement barriers)

- programme level changes (e.g. creating structures for interprogramme care coordination, developing programme standards for both dual diagnosis-capable [DDC] and dual diagnosis enhanced [DDE] programmes [American Society of Addiction Medicine (ASAM), in press, revised] replicating established model programmes [Regier, Farmer, Rae, et al., 1990]).

- clinical practice changes (e.g., establishing practice guidelines for assessment or psychopharmacology (Minkoff, 1998), developing integrated screening tools)

- clinician changes (e.g. adopting system-wide mandatory competencies (Arbour Health System, 1998), developing advanced dual-diagnosis certification programmes, and creating systemic training initiatives emphasising continued "on the job" training (Blaser, 2000).

As these strategies are more widely tested, programme evaluation efforts at the systems level will hopefully be able to demonstrate which approaches to implementation are the most effective, as well as demonstrating the cost effectiveness of this model as a whole in promoting more successful disease management outcomes system-wide.

References

Abram, K. M., & Teplin, L. A. (1991). Co-occurring disorders among mentally ill jail detainees: implications for public policy. *American Psychologist, 46,* 1036–1045.

American Association of Community Psychiatrists. (1998). *Level of Care Utilization System (LOCUS) 2.0.* Dallas (TX): Author.

American Society of Addiction Medicine (ASAM). (In press). *ASAM patient placement criteria. 2nd rev. ed. (ASAM PPC 2R).* Washington, DC: Author.

American Society of Addiction Medicine (ASAM). (1995). *ASAM patient placement criteria. 2nd ed. (ASAM PPC 2).* Washington, DC: Author.

Arbour Health System. (1998). *Policy manual: Basic required dual diagnosis. Competencies for adult clinicians.* Boston (MA): Arbour Health System.

Bachrach, L. L. (1986-7). The context of care for the chronic mental patient with substance abuse. *Psychiatric Quarterly, 58,* 3–16.

Barreira, R., Espey, B., Fishbein, R., et al. (2000). Linking substance abuse and serious mental illness service delivery systems: initiating a statewide collaborative. *Journal of Behavioral Health Services Research, 27*(1), 107–113.

Bartels, S. J., Drake, R. E., & McHugo, G. J. (1992). Alcohol abuse, depression, and suicidal behavior in schizophrenia. *American Journal of Psychiatry, 149,* 394–395.

Blaser, B. (2000). MISA basic training curriculum completed. *The Illinois MISA Newsletter.* Springfield (IL): Illinois Department of Mental Health, 6.

Cournos, F., Empfield, M., Horwath, E., et al. (1991). HIV seroprevalence among patients admitted to two psychiatric hospitals. *American Journal of Psychiatry, 148,* 1225–1230.

Cuffel, B. J., Shumway, M., Chouljian, T. L., et al. (1994). A longitudinal study of substance use and community violence in schizophrenia. *Journal of Nervous and Mental Disease, 182,* 704–708.

Deegan, P. E. (1988). Recovery: the lived experience of rehabilitation. *Psychiatric Rehabilitation Journal, 11*(4), 11–19.

Drake, R. E., Bartels, S. B., Teague, G. B., et al. (1993). Treatment of substance use disorders in severely mentally ill patients. *Journal of Nervous and Mental Disease, 181,* 606–611.

Drake, R. E., Osher, F. C., & Wallach, M. A. (1991) Homelessness and dual diagnosis. *American Psychologist, 46,* 1149–1158.

Hartman, E., & Nelson, D. (1997). A case study of statewide capitation: The Massachusetts experience. In K. Minkoff & D. Pollack (Eds.). *Managed mental health care in the public sector: A survival manual.* Amsterdam: Harwood Academic Publishers.

Kessler, R. C., Nelson, C. B., McGonagle, K. A., et al. (1996). The epidemiology of co-occurring addictive and mental disorders: implications for prevention and service utilization. *American Journal of Orthopsychiatry, 66,* 17–31.

Miller, W. R., & Rollnick, S. (1991). *Motivational interviewing: preparing people to change addictive behavior.* New York: Guilford.

Minkoff, K. (1998, January). Center for Mental Health Services. Managed Care Initiative Panel on Co-Occurring Disorders. *Co-occurring psychiatric and substance disorders in managed care systems: standards of care, practice guidelines, workforce competencies, and training curricula.* Rockville (MD): Center for Mental Health Services.

Minkoff, K. (1991). Program components of a comprehensive integrated care system for serious mentally ill patients with substance disorders. In: K. Minkoff & R. E. Drake (Eds.). Dual diagnosis of serious mental illness and substance disorder. *New Directions for Mental Health Services No. 50.* San Francisco (CA): Jossey-Bass, 13–27.

Minkoff, K. (1989). An integrated treatment model for dual diagnosis of psychosis and addiction. *Hospital and Community Psychiatry; 40*(10), 1031–1036.

National Association of State Mental Health Program Directors, National Association of State Alcohol and Drug Abuse Directors. (1998, June). *National dialogue on co-occurring mental health and substance abuse disorders.* Washington DC, 16–17.

Osher, F. C., & Kofoed, L. (1999). Treatment of patients with psychiatric and substance use disorders. *Hospital and Community Psychiatry, 40,* 1025–1030.

Prochaska, J. O., DiClemente, C. C., & Norcross, J. C. (1992). In search of how people change: applications to addictive behaviors. *American Psychologist, 47,* 1102–1114.

Quinlivan, R., & McWhirter, D. P. (1996). Designing a comprehensive care program for high-cost clients in a managed care environment. *Psychiatric Services, 47*(8), 813–815.

RachBeisel, J., Scott, J., & Dixon, L. (1999). Co-occurring severe mental illness and substance use disorders: a review of recent research. *Psychiatric Services, 50*(11), 1427–1434.

Regier, D. A., Farmer, M. E., Rae, D. S., et al. (1990). Comorbidity of mental disorders with alcohol and other drug abuse. *Journal of the American Medical Association, 264,* 2511–2518.

Ridgely, M. S., Goldman, H. H., & Willenbring, M. (1990). Barriers to the care of persons with dual diagnosis: organizational and financing issues. *Schizophrenia Bulletin, 16*(1), 123–132.

Ries, R. K., & Comtois, K. A. (1997). Managing disability benefits as part of treatment for persons with severe mental illness and comorbid drug/alcohol disorders: a comparative study of payee and non-payee participants. *American Journal of Addictions, 6*(4), 330–338.

Ries, R. K., & Miller, N. S. (1993). Dual diagnosis: concept, diagnosis, and treatment. In: D. L. Dunner (Ed.). *Current psychiatric therapy.* Philadelphia (PA): W. B. Saunders, 131–138.

Roberts, L. J., Shaner, A, & Eckman, T. A. (1999). *Overcoming addictions: skills training for people with schizophrenia.* New York: W. W. Norton.

Principles Underlying a Model Policy on Relationships Between Staff and Service Recipients in a Mental Health System

William A. Fisher & Eric Goldsmith

This article originally appeared in *Psychiatric Services,* 1999, 50(11), 1447–1452, and is reprinted with permission.

Dr. Fisher is clinical director of Creedmoor Psychiatric Center and associate clinical professor of psychiatry at Columbia University College of Physicians and Surgeons in New York City. Dr. Goldsmith, formerly clinical director of Kirby Forensic Psychiatric Center in Wards Island, New York, currently is a partner at New York Forensic Psychiatric Associates, LLP, in New York City.

Objective: The authors participated in a work group to produce a model policy addressing the boundaries of relationships between staff and recipients of service in a public mental health system that provides and regulates services in a variety of treatment settings. Methods: The chief medical officer of the New York State Office of Mental Health assembled a work group of administrators, clinicians, state officials, and a representative of service recipients. The group reviewed the professional literature and existing ethics guidelines and policies addressing relationships between staff members and service recipients and made recommendations for a new policy. Results and conclusions: The work group formulated five guiding principles: prevention of the exploitation of recipients of services by staff; the right of recipients to be treated as competent autonomous human beings; recognition that certain developmental stages, treatment settings, and pre-existing relationships increase a service recipient's vulnerability to exploitation and call for more stringent regulation of staff actions; acceptance of a spectrum of permissible relationships for staff and recipients outside of the relationship dictated by the staff member's job description; and recognition of the difference between a relationship focused on treatment or service provision and other professional relationships between providers and current or former recipients. The principles were used to develop a model policy on relationships between staff and recipients that addresses both the organizational complexity and the recipient-centered rehabilitation model of a large state-operated mental health system.

The provision of mental health services is an organizationally complex undertaking involving myriad relationships between persons who receive services and persons who work for service providers or for other agencies that are regulated by those providers. As psychiatry continues to move away from psychoanalytic neutrality and custodial care into a broader range of service paradigms, many of which emphasize the empowerment of service recipients, the outlines of these relationships become increasingly blurred. Organizations, individual providers, and service recipients are often left in confusion, as the following vignettes illustrate.

A recipient of services is employed part time as a peer counselor at the clinic at which she receives services. The clinic holds a monthly staff dinner. Should she be invited?

A therapy aide at a rural psychiatric hospital moonlights as one of the few fishing guides in the area. A recently discharged patient wishes to hire him for a fishing trip. Should he refuse?

A psychiatric case manager has the job of coordinating concrete services, such as entitlements, housing, and medical care, for his clients. He and one of his clients find that they share common interests and a common outlook on life. In fact, both would rather just be friends and have someone else coordinate the client's concrete services. How should they proceed?

Clarifying the boundaries of such relationships is an especially challenging task for public mental health authorities, which encompass a complex array of services. Many public mental health authorities operate or regulate hospitals that provide acute, intermediate, and long-term care and also operate or regulate a variety of outpatient programs, including those offering comprehensive psychiatric emergency services, partial hospitalization, continuing day treatment, intensive psychiatric rehabilitation, intensive and supportive case management, clinical services, assertive community treatment, peer advocacy, and psychosocial clubs. In addition, public mental health authorities usually provide or regulate a range of housing alternatives for service recipients, including family or foster care, supervised and supportive community residences, and crisis residences.

Within this array of services, the types of relationships range from those involved in staff members' provision of involuntary treatment to service recipients in an emergency room to those involved in service recipients' participation in psychosocial, advocacy, and housing programs that are operated by other service recipients. Across this variety of relationships, state mental health authorities retain the obligation to ensure that service recipients are not exploited by staff. This obligation cannot be fulfilled without impinging on the rights of service recipients to make autonomous choices unless public mental health authorities have a clear understanding of the parameters of staff-recipient relationships that are applicable in any service setting.

This paper describes the efforts of a work group convened by the New York State Office of Mental Health to clarify appropriate relationships between staff members and service recipients. It discusses the principles identified by the work group that were incorporated into a proposed model policy addressing staff-recipient relationships.

Methods

To clarify the conceptualization of staff-recipient relationships, in 1994 the chief medical officer of the New York State Office of Mental Health appointed a work group to explore this issue and develop a model policy for staff's interaction with service recipients that would incorporate its findings. The work group met during 1994 and 1995 and submitted its final recommendations to the chief medical officer in 1996. The work group consisted of two psychiatric administrators, a psychiatric nurse, a psychiatrist, a therapy aide, a social work administrator, a recipient of services representing the Office of Mental Health's bureau of recipient affairs, and representatives of the Office of Mental Health's legal, investigative, operations, and quality assurance divisions.

The work group reviewed the literature about relationships between staff and service recipients, professional guidelines in this area, and existing policies on staff-recipient relations in effect in facilities operated by the Office of Mental Health. As a result of these activities and extensive discussions among work group members, the work group formulated basic guiding principles that were incorporated into a model policy.

The existing policies of state-operated psychiatric centers in New York outlined a range of levels of restrictiveness—from prohibitions on all personal or social relationships between current or former service recipients and staff to explicit prohibitions on a limited set of activities between staff and current recipients such as sexual activity, accepting gifts, or staff members' inviting recipients into their homes. This lack of uniformity was one of the issues the work group was convened to address. To create a framework for a uniform model policy, the work group elucidated basic principles that would be operationalized in the policy. Elucidating the basic principles was particularly important because of the potential for some principles to conflict with others. Failure to explicitly recognize the potential conflicts would result in a lack of clarity in any policy that would be developed.

Results

Literature Review

The literature on relationships between providers and recipients of mental health services is quite narrowly focused on the boundaries of the psychotherapist-patient relationship and focuses particularly on sexual relationships between therapists and patients. Even many of the general discussions of patient-therapist boundaries are framed around a "slippery-slope" hypothesis that categorizes all boundary violations as potential steps on the road to a sexual relationship between the therapist and the patient (Gutheil & Gabbard, 1993; Simon, 1992; Strasburger, Jorgenson, & Sutherland, 1992).

Some authors have discussed specific aspects of sexual relationships between therapists and patients—for example, relationships after termination of therapy (Appelbaum & Jorgenson, 1991; Lazarus, 1992)—and others have discussed the incidence of sexual contact in various settings such as residency training (Gartrell et al., 1988), inpatient units (Munsat & Riordan, 1990), or general psychiatric practice (Gartrell et al., 1986; Herman et al., 1987). Epstein and associates (Epstein, Simon, & Kay, 1992) used a self-assessment questionnaire—the Exploitation Index—as a survey instrument and educational tool to examine actual and potential boundary violations in the psychotherapeutic relationship.

Several authors have broadened the conceptualization of the relationship beyond that of therapist and patient. The concept of the "dual relationship"—the existence of any additional relationship between the patient and therapist—has been applied chiefly to psychotherapy and has been generally seen as harmful (Congress & Stern, 1994; Kagle & Giebelhausen, 1994). An example of a dual relationship is a therapist's employing a patient to paint his or her house. The work group used the concept of dual relationships as a basis for delineating a wider universe of provider-recipient relationships beyond the therapist-patient relationship. In this wider universe, dual relationships may not be as harmful as they are usually characterized.

Review of Professional Guidelines

Several mental health professions have addressed dual relationships. The focus of the guidelines varies from quite narrow to somewhat broader. Both the American Medical Association and the American Psychiatric Association define sexual activity with current patients as unethical. In its guidelines the American Psychiatric Association goes further, defining sexual activity with former patients as "almost always" unethical (American Psychiatric Association, 1992).

The American Psychological Association begins its guidelines with the premise that psychologists should avoid potentially harmful dual relationships but recognizes that such relationships are not always avoidable (Committee on Ethical Guidelines for Forensic Psychologists, 1991). For example, in small communities, a psychologist may have difficulty avoiding social contact with clients. The association's guidelines direct psychologists to remain alert to the potential of such relationships for reducing their effectiveness or harming the other party and to refrain from engaging in relationships that do so. Again sexual intimacy is singled out as harmful to the patient. In addition, the guidelines recommend a 2-year post-therapy ban on sexual activity with former patients, after which the psychologist must bear the burden of proof in demonstrating that such a relationship would not be exploitive (Committee on Ethical Guidelines for Forensic Psychologists, 1991).

The National Association of Social Workers instructs social workers to refrain from potentially exploitive or harmful dual relationships and explicitly prohibits sexual activities with clients (National Association of Social Workers, 1992). The American Nursing Association refers to respect for the dignity, worth, and self-determination of clients (American Nurses Association, 1985).

Legal Issues

Case law on the exploitation of recipients of services, like the mental health literature in this area, largely centers on sexual relationships. The mental health practitioner who indulges in sex with recipients of service can become embroiled in civil, ethical, professional, and even criminal disciplinary proceedings. The consequences of sex between practitioner and recipient are usually devastating for both parties. Practitioners stand to lose their reputation, professional license, and source of income following civil and criminal litigation. Professional organizations may undertake proceedings pursuant to ethical violations leading to expulsion and publication of a notice of the sexual misconduct.

Recipients of mental health services who have been sexually exploited by their therapists are exposed to a profound violation of trust. They have often experienced progressive boundary violations preceding the sexual act, and the act itself often produces a significant degree of psychological harm. Their treatment is interrupted, they are likely to regress in their psychiatric condition, and they may flee all mental health treatments. They may be unable to summon the trust necessary to develop a therapeutic alliance with another practitioner in the future.

Sexual exploitation may also result in a civil lawsuit against the employer of the provider. The courts have invoked the legal doctrine of "respondent superior" in holding hospitals or government institutions vicariously liable for the actions of individual providers as long as that person acted within the scope of his or her employment. Hospitals may argue that a therapist who sexually exploits a recipient did not do so within the scope of employment and that the hospital should not be held vicariously liable. Courts may in fact rule that as a matter of law, the sexual misconduct of an employee falls outside the scope of employment.

However, the law has been known to take a broad view of the meaning of scope of employment. In a recent case the court held that "the fact that an employee is not engaged in the ultimate object of his employment at the time of his wrongful act does not preclude attribution of liability to an employer" (*Alma v. Oakland Unified School District,* 1981). In some cases employers have been held vicariously liable for the sexual misconduct of their employees. In a 1990 case, a trial court upheld the doctrine of respondent superior, holding a pastoral counseling center liable for the actions of one of its counselors who sexually abused the petitioner (*Jane Doe v. Samaritan Counseling Center,* 1990). The court found that although the therapist "was not authorized to become sexually involved with his clients, that contact occurred in conjunction with his legitimate counseling activities."

A search of the case law yielded no cases involving the exploitation of a service recipient by nonprofessional staff. However, under the doctrine of respondent superior, a hospital could well be held vicariously liable for the behavior of nonprofessional members if that behavior fell within the scope of their employment.

Guiding Principles

The work group identified five principles that provided the framework for a model policy addressing relationships between staff of mental health agencies and recipients of services. The principles are listed below, and the model policy is shown in the box on the next page. (The model policy is a product of the staff-recipient relations work group and is not a policy of the New York State Office of Mental Health.)

- An agency is responsible for preventing the exploitation of recipients of its services by its staff.

- Recipients of services have the right to be treated as competent autonomous human beings in all their relationships with staff.

- Certain developmental stages, treatment settings, and pre-existing relationships increase a person's vulnerability to exploitation and call for more stringent regulation of staff actions.

- There is a spectrum of permissible relationships for staff and recipients that fall outside of those defined by the staff member's job description.

- There is a spectrum of vulnerability within the gamut of professional relationships between staff and recipients of services, with current treatment relationships at the most vulnerable end of that spectrum.

Discussion

The first principle identified by the work group was that agencies are responsible for preventing staff members from exploiting recipients. The work group's review of policies on staff-recipient relationships suggested that this principle is a traditional basis for such policies and that it is often the only underlying principle.

The work group operationalized exploitation as "the use by an employee of the Office of Mental Health of a recipient's person or property or of the treatment or service provision relationship in a manner that results in or is intended to result in personal profit or gain (beyond the employee's authorized compensation) or personal advantage for the

Figure I

Model policy addressing relationships between staff members and recipients of mental health services in a state-operated mental health system[1]

Definitions used in the policy statement

Close personal relationship: Spending substantial amounts of time together outside of the provision of services that constitute a recipient's treatment plan but excluding sexual contact.

Commercial advantage: The purchase or provision of goods or services at other than fair market value.

Commercial relationship: The purchase or provision of goods or services (other than mental health services) at fair market value.

Domestic partnership: A relationship that resembles marriage in all respects except that of legal sanction.

Exploitation: The use by an employee of a recipient's person or property or of the treatment or service provision relationship in a manner that results in or is intended to result in personal profit or gain (beyond the employee's authorized compensation) or personal advantage for the employee.

Sexual contact: Any touching of the sexual or other intimate parts of a person for the purpose of gratifying the desire of either party. Any verbal or written statements intended to promote or produce such physical contact.

Treatment or service provision relationship: The provision of mental health services or residential counseling or supervision services or participation in the specific planning of such services for an individual recipient. This relationship involves but is not necessarily limited to members of the recipient's treatment team.

Policy statement

Any relationship that involves the exploitation of a service recipient by an employee is explicitly prohibited.

Exploitation includes but is not limited to:
- Any sexual contact between any employee and any recipient of services who is under the age of 18.

- Any sexual contact between any employee and any individual receiving inpatient services with the exception of employees and recipients who have a pre-existing spousal or domestic partner relationship. In this case, the facility's policy on consensual sexual contact should apply.

- Any sexual contact between an employee in a treatment or service provision relationship (inpatient, outpatient, or residential) and the recipient of those services.

- Any close personal relationship between any employee and any recipient of inpatient services with the exception of pre-existing spousal, domestic partner, or close personal relationships.

- Any close personal relationship between an employee in a treatment or service provision relationship (inpatient, outpatient, or residential) and the recipient of those services.

- The establishment of a treatment or service provision relationship (inpatient, outpatient, or residential) in the context of a pre-existing sexual contact.

- The solicitation or acceptance by any employee of any commercial advantage from a recipient of services including the solicitation of any gifts or acceptance of gifts of more than token value.

- Any commercial relationship between any employee and any recipient of inpatient services with the exception of a pre-existing commercial relationship

In cases of the initiation of sexual contact between an employee and an individual with whom the employee had previously been in a service provision relationship, the burden of proof always resides with the employee to demonstrate that such sexual contact is not exploitive.

For employees in a non-inpatient treatment or service provision relationship with a recipient of services 18 years or older, should the potential for a non-exploitive close personal relationship arise, the employee and the recipient of services should mutually determine which of the two relationships shall be continued. If the treatment or service provision relationship is to be terminated, the burden of proof remains with the employee to demonstrate that the termination is done in a manner that does not injure the recipient or compromise his or her access to services, that the choice was made in a non-coercive and non-exploitive manner, and that the employee maintains the recipient's rights of confidentiality.

This policy applies equally to volunteers.

This policy applies equally to employees or volunteers who are also recipients of services.

Employees in any treatment or service provision setting with recipients under the age of 18 years are explicitly prohibited from having any sexual contact or close personal relationship with any such recipient. This prohibition applies both to the time services are provided and to any future involvement between the employee and such former recipient of service.

---

1. This model policy is a product of the staff-recipient relations work group and is not a policy of the New York State Office of Mental Health.

employee." This definition provided a broad foundation from which specific prohibitions could be elucidated. The work group struggled with the murkiness of the concept of "intent" but decided that it would be unfair to exonerate an employee simply because an attempt at exploitation had not succeeded.

The second and equally important principle was the right of recipients of services to be treated as competent autonomous human beings in both their treatment and their nontreatment relationships with staff. The work group felt that the traditional prohibitions on staff from having any relationship beyond that of treatment provider with current and former recipients of services served to perpetuate the view of recipients as infantile, totally vulnerable, and incompetent to make sound decisions about who they socialize with, do business with, or even fall in love with. The work group also believed that this view was perpetuated by extending traditional prohibitions to clerical and maintenance staff, staff members at other service sites operated by the same facility, and other staff members who were not directly involved in the treatment relationship.

The work group also decided that the relationships of service recipients who work as agency staff would be governed by the same policy that applies to the relationships of other staff members. The group noted that if service recipients are to have autonomy, they must also be responsible for their actions. To ask recipients who function as staff members to adhere to a different policy would undermine and infantilize them in their role as staff members.

The third principle was based on the idea that a spectrum of vulnerability to exploitation exists among service recipients. Recipients at certain developmental stages, recipients who receive services in certain treatment settings, or recipients who have certain pre-existing relationships may have increased vulnerability to exploitation and must be protected by more stringent regulation of staff actions. This principle led to a policy of absolute prohibition of staff members' having sexual contact or a close personal relationship with recipients who are under age 18 or former recipients who were under age 18 while receiving services. In addition, sexual contact between staff and recipients who are receiving inpatient services was prohibited. Further, staff members were prohibited from establishing treatment relationships with recipients with whom they had prior sexual contact.

The recognition of the power differential inherent in the inpatient treatment setting led to further prohibitions on staff members' establishing commercial or close personal relationships with recipients of inpatient services. The prohibition on close personal and commercial relationships between staff and inpatients was not extended to cases in which these relationships predated the inpatient services, as long as the staff member and recipient were not in a relationship involving treatment or provision of mental health services. A similar exception to the prohibition on sexual relationships was established in the case of a preexisting marriage or domestic partnership.

The difference between the policies on commercial relationships, close personal relationships, and sexual relationships implies the fourth underlying principle—that a spectrum of permissible relationships exists for staff and recipients outside of the relationship dictated by the staff member's job description. The work group concluded that the potential for abuse or harm varies with the type of relationship and so therefore must the stringency of the prohibitions or safeguards connected with each type. The work group defined a commercial relationship as "the purchase or provision of goods or services (other than mental health services) at fair market value." Commercial advantage was defined as a commercial relationship in which the principle of fair market value was not observed.

A close personal relationship was defined as "spending substantial amounts of time together outside of the provision of the services that constitute a recipient's treatment plan but excluding sexual contact." Sexual contact was defined as "any touching of the sexual or other intimate parts of a person for the purpose of gratifying the desire of either party" as well as "any verbal or written statement intended to promote or produce such physical contact."

The fifth principle recognized the existence of a spectrum of professional relationships between staff and recipients, with an associated spectrum of potential for harm. The elucidation of this principle involved differentiation between relationships focused on treatment or service provision and other forms of professional relationships between providers and current or former recipients. From the point of view of both psychodynamic theory and common sense, the potential for a sexual relationship between a recipient and staff member to be coercive and destructive varies depending on the nature of the professional relationship. It would be more harmful if the staff member is the recipient's therapist or an aide counseling the recipient on activities of daily living than if the staff member is a therapist in a different program or a clerical worker in the facility's business office.

The model policy prohibits sexual relationships and close personal relationships between staff members who are providing services or treatment and the recipients of those services. The work group included the concept of service provision with treatment to encompass the wide range of therapeutic, direct care, and support relationships in which both transferential and practical power imbalances increase the potential for harm. The work group defined a treatment or service provision relationship as "the provision of mental health services or residential counseling or supervision services or participation in the specific planning of such services for an individual recipient." The group noted that the service provision relationship "involves but is not necessarily limited to members of the recipient's treatment team."

The issue of sexual contact between staff and recipients with whom they have had a prior treatment or service provision relationship has been the subject of considerable controversy in the psychiatric literature (Appelbaum & Jorgenson, 1991; Lazarus, 1992). Cogent arguments can be made for lifetime prohibitions, time-limited prohibitions, or case-by-case analysis. Ultimately, the work group chose the last option with the additional caveat that the burden of proof rests with the employee to demonstrate to program administration that the sexual contact does not exploit the previous relationship. This approach was felt to be most consistent with placing value on both autonomy and protection.

Another related issue with which the work group grappled was how to proceed if the potential for a non-exploitive close personal relationship arose in the context of an existing outpatient treatment relationship. Here again the work group took its guidance from the principles of preventing exploitation while maximizing recipient autonomy. The first principle dictated that the two relationships could not coexist, the second that the decision about which relationship would be pursued must be made mutually by the staff member and service recipient.

In such situations, the staff member would bear the burden of proof to show that the relationship did not compromise the recipient's future access to services, that the recipient's choice to enter the relationship was not coerced, and that the recipient's confidentiality was maintained.

Although the idea of burden of proof is difficult to operationalize, including the term in a policy statement at least conveys the message that the choice to enter a close personal relationship should not be made lightly.

Conclusions

By identifying a set of underlying principles that apply to relationships between staff and recipients of services, the work group was able to draft a model policy that addresses both the organizational complexity and recipient-centered rehabilitation model of a large and diverse state-operated mental health system.

References

Alma W v Oakland Unified School District. (1981). 123 Cal App 3d 133, 139.

American Nurses Association. (1985). *Code for nurses.* Washington, DC: Author.

American Psychiatric Association. (1992). *Opinions of the ethics committee on the principles of medical ethics with annotations especially applicable to psychiatry.* Washington, DC: Author.

American Psychiatric Association. (1992). *The principles of medical ethics with annotations especially applicable to psychiatry.* Washington, DC: Author.

Appelbaum, P. S. & Jorgenson, L. (1991). Psychotherapist-patient sexual contact after termination of treatment: an analysis and a proposal. *American Journal of Psychiatry, 148,* 1466–1473.

Committee on Ethical Guidelines for Forensic Psychologists. (1991). Specialty guidelines for forensic psychologists. *Law and Human Behavior, 15,* 655–666.

Congress, E. P. & Stern, L. (1994). *Dilemmas of dual relationships.* Washington, DC: National Association of Social Workers.

Epstein, R. S., Simon, R. I., & Kay, G. G. (1992). Assessing boundary violations in psychotherapy: survey results with the Exploitation Index. *Bulletin of the Menninger Clinic, 56,* 150–166.

Gartrell, N., Herman, J., Olarte, S., et al. (1986). Psychiatrist-patient sexual contact: results of a national survey: I. prevalence. *American Journal of Psychiatry, 143,* 1126–1131.

Gartrell, N., Herman, J., Olarte, S., et al. (1988). Psychiatric residents' sexual contact with educators and patients: results of a national survey. *American Journal of Psychiatry, 145,* 690–694.

Gutheil, T. G. & Gabbard, G. O. (1993). The concept of boundaries in clinical practice: theoretical and risk-management dimensions. *American Journal of Psychiatry, 150,* 188–196.

Herman, J. L., Gartrell, N., Olarte, S., et al. (1987). Psychiatrist-patient sexual contact: results of a national survey: II. Psychiatrists' attitudes. *American Journal of Psychiatry, 144,* 164–169.

Jane Doe v Samaritan Counseling Center. (1990). 791 P2d 344.

Kagle, J. D. & Giebelhausen, P. N. (1994). Dual relationships and professional boundaries. *Social Work, 39,* 213–219.

Lazarus, J. A. (1992). Sex with former patients almost always unethical. *American Journal of Psychiatry, 149,* 855–857.

Munsat, E. M. & Riordan, J. J. (1990). Under wraps: prevalence of staff-patient sexual interactions on inpatient units. *Journal of Psychosocial Nursing, 28,* 23–26.

National Association of Social Workers. (1992). *Code of ethics.* Washington, DC: Author.

Simon, R. I. (1992). Treatment boundary violations: clinical, ethical, and legal considerations. *Bulletin of the American Academy of Psychiatry and the Law, 20,* 269–286.

Strasburger, L. H., Jorgenson, L., & Sutherland, P. (1992). The prevention of psychotherapist sexual misconduct: avoiding the slippery slope. *American Journal of Psychotherapy, 46,* 544–555.

Predicting the Therapeutic Alliance in Alcoholism Treatment

Gerard J. Connors, Carlo C. DiClemente, Kurt H. Dermen,
Ronald Kadden, Kathleen M. Carroll & Michael R. Frone

This article originally appeared in the *Journal of Studies on Alcohol,* 2000, 61, 139–149, and is reprinted with permission.

Gerard J. Connors, Ph.D., Kurt H. Dermen, Ph.D., & Michael R. Frone, Ph.D., Research Institute on Addictions, Buffalo, NY; Carlo C. DiClemente, Ph.D., Department of Psychology, University of Maryland–Baltimore County, Baltimore, MD; Ronald Kadden, Ph.D., Department of Psychiatry, University of Connecticut School of Medicine, Farmington, CT; Kathleen M. Carroll, Ph.D., Substance Abuse Center, Yale University School of Medicine, New Haven, CT.

This research was supported by a series of grants from the National Institute on Alcohol Abuse and Alcoholism.

Objective: Prediction of the therapeutic alliance in alcoholism treatment (as rated by the client and by the therapist) was examined in light of a range of potentially relevant factors, including client demographics, drinking history, current drinking, current psychosocial functioning and therapist demographics. Method: The data were gathered in Project MATCH. The present analyses were based on data from 707 outpatients and 480 aftercare clients assigned to one of the three Project MATCH treatments. Potential predictor variables were evaluated by first examining bivariate linear relationships between the variables and ratings of the alliance, and then entering blocks of these predictors into multiple linear regression equations with alliance ratings as the dependent variables. All analysis incorporated adjustments for the nonindependence of ratings pertaining to clients seen by the same therapist. Results: In simple regressions evaluating bivariate relationships, outpatients' ratings of the alliance were positively predicted by client age, motivational readiness to change, socialization, level of perceived social support and therapist age, and were negatively predicted by client educational level, level of depression, and meaning seeking. Therapist ratings in the outpatient sample were positively predicted by the client being female and by level of overall alcohol involvement, severity of alcohol dependence, negative consequences of alcohol use, and readiness to change. Among aftercare clients, ratings of the alliance were positively predicted by readiness to change, socialization and social support, and were negatively predicted by level of depression. Therapist ratings of the alliance in the aftercare sample were positively predicted by the client being female and therapist educational level, and were negatively predicted by pretreatment drinks per drinking day. Of the variables having significant bivariate relationships with alliance scores, only a few were identified as significant predictors in multiple regression equations. Among outpatients, client age and motivational readiness to change remained positive predictors and client education a negative predictor of client ratings of the alliance, while client gender remained a significant predictor of therapist ratings. Among aftercare clients, readiness to change and level of depression remained significant predictors of client ratings, while none of the variables remained a significant predictor of therapist ratings. Conclusions: While the data indicate that several client variables predict the nature of both the client's and therapist's perception of the therapeutic alliance, the significant relationships are of modest magnitude, and few variables remain predictive after controlling for causally prior variables. The strongest relationship identified in both the outpatient and aftercare samples is that between clients' motivational readiness to change and their ratings of the alliance.

It has long been recognized that establishment of a working relationship between the client and therapist is an important component of the behavior change process. This relationship has consistently predicted client response to psychotherapeutic interventions in a variety of clinical domains (Henry et al., 1994; Horvath & Greenberg, 1994). Most definitions of the therapeutic alliance have in common an emphasis on a collaborative relationship that consists of an emotional bond and shared attitudes regarding the tasks and goals of the treatment endeavor (e.g., Bordin, 1979; Greenson, 1967).

The therapeutic alliance has received specific research attention in the context of opioid dependence. For example, Luborsky et al. (1985) found that client ratings of the therapeutic alliance among male methadone maintenance clients were positively associated with better drug use outcomes, and Tunis et al. (1995) reported a positive relationship between client ratings of the helping alliance and better drug use outcomes in the latter stages of a 180-day opioid detoxification program. However, such a relationship was not found in a study by Belding et al. (1997) among methadone maintenance clients. They concluded that the helping alliance may be more a predictor of treatment progress than of drug outcomes. Nevertheless, whether a helping alliance enhances treatment progress or substance use outcomes, both represent clinically important events.

The role of the therapeutic alliance in predicting alcoholism treatment outcomes has also been examined in one recent study. Connors et al. (1997) evaluated the relationship between the therapeutic alliance and both treatment participation and drinking behavior during and after treatment among alcoholic outpatients and aftercare clients who participated in Project MATCH (Matching Alcoholism Treatments to Client Heterogeneity; Project MATCH Research Group, 1997a). Among outpatients, client ratings and therapist ratings of the therapeutic alliance were significant predictors of treatment participation (operationalized as weeks of treatment attended) and drinking behavior during treatment and throughout the 12 months following treatment. Higher ratings of the therapeutic alliance were associated with longer stays in treatment, higher percent days abstinent, and fewer drinks per drinking day during treatment and follow-up. However, among aftercare clients (who prior to their aftercare treatment had completed inpatient or day hospital treatment), client ratings of the alliance did not predict treatment participation or drinking outcomes, and therapist ratings predicted only abstinent days during treatment and follow-up. Thus, the therapeutic alliance was a consistent predictor of treatment participation and outcome among outpatient, but not aftercare, clients.

While the therapeutic alliance has been examined extensively in regard to treatment outcomes, less attention has been given to factors associated with the establishment of the therapeutic alliance itself. The limited information available suggests that both client and therapist variables may contribute to the nature of the alliance (Horvath, 1994), although most of the empirical research has attended more to client than therapist variables. Client variables were grouped by Horvath (1994) into three categories: interpersonal variables (e.g., family and social relationships), intrapersonal variables (e.g., motivation) and diagnostic variables (e.g., illness category and severity). The results of his review suggest that both interpersonal and intrapersonal variables predict the therapeutic alliance. Interestingly, illness symptomatology was not related to the reported establishment of the therapeutic alliance. Much less research has been conducted on therapist variables that might influence the therapeutic alliance. Although it has been assumed that a positive therapeutic alliance necessitates a therapist with good relational capabilities and the ability to be empathic and affirming (e.g., Orlinsky et al., 1994), there is little empirical work in this area.

Given the apparent importance of the therapeutic alliance to treatment participation and outcome, it would be useful to explore further what factors both client and therapist contribute to this alliance. While general models of the therapeutic alliance have been advanced (e.g., Henry & Strupp, 1994; Horvath, 1995), there has been little specification of potentially relevant variables. For this reason, we chose to examine a broad set of potential predictors of the alliance, many of which are unique to alcoholic clients. The data were gathered in Project MATCH, a national multisite clinical trial designed to evaluate hypotheses relating to patient-treatment matching.

Method

Overview of Project MATCH

Two independent but parallel matching studies were conducted, one with clients recruited from outpatient settings ($N = 952$), the other with clients receiving aftercare treatment following inpatient or day hospital care ($N = 774$). Following baseline assessments, clients were randomly assigned to one of three 12-week treatments: Twelve-Step Facilitation (TSF), Cognitive-Behavioral Coping Skills Treatment (CBT) or Motivational Enhancement Therapy (MET). There were several within-treatment process assessments, and the subjects were followed at 3-month intervals for the year following the treatment period. The trial has been described in greater detail by the Project MATCH Research Group (1993), and tests of the primary and secondary *a priori* matching hypotheses have been reported (Project MATCH Research Group, 1997a,b).

Participants

For the present analyses, subjects ($N = 1, 187$) were 707 outpatient (71% male) and 480 aftercare (79% male) clients with complete data for all independent variables and at least one of the two dependent variables. All met the *DSM-III-R* (APA, 1987) criteria for a current diagnosis of alcohol abuse or dependence (for aftercare clients, based on drinking during the period prior to admission to their inpatient or day hospital admission), as assessed using the alcohol section of the Structured Clinical Interview for *DSM-III-R* (SCID; Spitzer & Williams, 1985). The vast majority (>95%) met the criteria for alcohol dependence as

Table I

Descriptive information on clients in the outpatient and aftercare samples

Demographic	Outpatient			Aftercare		
	Men	Women	Total	Men	Women	Total
N	504 (71%)	203 (29%)	707	381 (79%)	99 (21%)	480
Age (mean [±SD] years)	39.3 ± 10.7	39.6 ± 11.1	39.4 ± 10.8	42.2 ± 10.7	42.6 ± 11.7	42.3 ± 10.9
Ethnicity (%)						
White	84	80	82	81	83	81
Black	4	8	5	13	13	13
Hispanic	11	7	10	3	3	3
Other	1	4	2	2	1	2
Education (mean [±SD] years)	13.5 ± 2.2	13.7 ± 2.0	13.6 ± 2.1	13.1 ± 2.1	13.2 ± 2.1	13.2 ± 2.1
Relationship status (%)[a]						
Married	42	31	38	40	26	37
Single	58	69	62	60	74	63
Employment (%)[b]						
Employed	58	40	53	50	43	49
Not employed	42	60	47	50	57	51
Prior alcohol treatment (%)						
Yes	44	37	42	62	56	61
No	56	63	58	38	44	39
Alcohol dependence symptoms[c]						
Mean (±SD)	5.7 ± 2.0	5.7 ± 1.8	5.7 ± 1.9	6.9 ± 1.9	6.5 ± 2.0	6.8 ± 1.9

a. Married = married and living with spouse at least 1 year; single = all others.
b. Employed = employed full time in same job continuously for past 6 months; not employed = all others.
c. Measured by the Structured Clinical Inventory for the DSM-III-R for the 90-day baseline period (range = 1–9).

opposed to alcohol abuse. Descriptive information for clients in each arm of the trial is provided in table 1.

The present sample represents 74% of the original cohort of Project MATCH outpatients and 62% of the aftercare clients. The main reasons for deletion of cases from the original population of 1,726 were missing Working Alliance Inventory (WAI) ratings (approximately 15%, mostly reflecting treatment dropouts) and missing therapist demographic information (approximately 10%). Comparisons of subjects in the present sample to those excluded for any reason (analyses by outpatient or aftercare arm) revealed three differences in the outpatient arm and none in the aftercare arm. Chi-square tests showed that outpatient clients included were less likely to be Hispanic and more likely to be white, were more likely to be married and had higher educational attainment, relative to those excluded.

Procedure

Considerable effort was taken to maintain comparability of procedures across the two (outpatient and aftercare) arms of the investigation. Outpatient clients were recruited from the community and from applicants to outpatient treatment centers; aftercare clients were recruited from inpatient or intensive day hospital treatment programs. The subjects were recruited through nine clinical research units (CRUs) across the country using a number of clinical sites.

Inclusion criteria for the outpatient sample were: a current *DSM-III-R* (APA, 1987) diagnosis of alcohol abuse or dependence; alcohol as the principal drug of abuse; active drinking during the 3 months prior to entrance to the study; minimum age of 18; and minimum sixth grade reading level. Inclusion criteria for the aftercare arm were identical except that symptoms of alcohol abuse or dependence and requisite drinking behavior were assessed for the 3-month period prior to the inpatient or day hospital admission, clients completed a program of at least 7 days of inpatient or intensive day hospital treatment (not simply detoxification), and clients were referred for aftercare treatment by the inpatient or day hospital staff. Exclusion criteria were: a *DSM-III-R* diagnosis of current dependence on sedative/hypnotic drugs, stimulants, cocaine, or opiates; any intravenous drug use in the past 6 months; currently a danger to self or others; probation/parole requirements that might interfere with protocol participation; acute psychosis or severe organic impairment; and current or planned involvement in alternative treatments for alcohol problems other than that provided by Project MATCH (defined as greater than 6 hours of nonstudy treatment, except for self-help groups, during the 3 months of study treatment).

Following an initial screen to evaluate inclusion/exclusion criteria, clients provided informed consent and participated in three intake sessions comprised of personal interviews, computer-assisted assessment, and completion of self-administered questionnaires (described elsewhere by Connors et al., 1994). Where possible, an interview was conducted with an individual familiar with the subject's drinking (a collateral). Assignment to treatment was performed using a computerized urn balancing program designed to minimize participant differences on variables such as critical demographic characteristics across the three study treatments at each site (Stout et al., 1994).

Each treatment lasted 12 weeks. Therapy sessions were videotaped to assure quality delivery of treatment and to provide the data needed for a detailed investigation of treatment process (Carroll et al., 1994; DiClemente et al., 1994b). In this regard, assessments in a variety of process domains were incorporated into the protocol (DiClemente et al., 1994b). Directly relevant to the purposes of the present report, the process assessment component included ratings of the therapeutic alliance.

Treatments

Three treatments were chosen for study in Project MATCH because of their potential relevance to matching, the evidence for their clinical efficacy, their distinctiveness from each other, feasibility of implementation, and their application within existing treatment systems (Donovan et al., 1994). The Twelve-Step Facilitation (TSF) treatment was based on the concept of alcoholism as a spiritual and medical disease, with stated objectives of fostering acceptance of the disease of alcoholism, developing a commitment to participate in AA and beginning to work the 12 steps. The Cognitive-Behavioral Coping Skills Treatment (CBT) was grounded in social learning theory and viewed drinking behavior as functionally related to major problems in an individual's life, with emphasis placed on overcoming skills deficits and increasing the ability to cope with situations that commonly precipitate relapse. The Motivational Enhancement Treatment (MET) was based on principles of motivational psychology and focused on producing internally motivated change. This treatment was not designed to guide the client step by step through recovery but, instead, employed motivational strategies to mobilize the individual's own resources. The TSF and CBT treatments involved 12 weekly treatment sessions; MET consisted of four sessions, occurring during the first, second, sixth, and twelfth weeks. The therapy protocol for each modality is described in detailed treatment manuals (Kadden et al., 1992; Miller et al., 1992; Nowinski et al., 1992).

All Project MATCH therapy sessions were videotaped and supervisors monitored 25% of the sessions (over 2,500) to ensure therapist adherence to the protocol (Project MATCH Research Group, 1993). Subsequent independent and blind tape ratings have supported the discriminability and integrity of the treatments (Carroll et al., 1998).

Therapists

Each therapist delivered only one type of treatment; therapists were selected based on their commitment to, and experience with, one of the three Project MATCH treatments. A training protocol for each therapy and standards for therapist certification and monitoring were developed. There were 80 therapists certified to administer one of the three treatments in the trial. For the present analyses, sufficient data were available for 42 therapists who treated clients in the outpatient arm and 35 therapists in the aftercare arm (24 in TSF, 29 in CBT and 24 in MET). Outpatient therapists had a mean ($\pm SD$) age of 39.2 ± 7.7 years and 64% were women; the aftercare therapists averaged 37.7 ± 7.1 years of age and 60% were women. Outpatient therapists treated a mean ($\pm SD$) of 16.8 ± 8.7 clients, whereas aftercare therapists treated an average of 14.0 ± 7.4 clients.

Measures

Client and therapist background characteristics. A variety of basic background information (e.g., demographics, education, current marital and employment status) was gathered from clients as part of the initial screening and a formal diagnostic evaluation interview session. Therapists completed a demographics questionnaire that yielded comparable information.

Treatment alliance and participation. The Working Alliance Inventory (WAI; Horvath & Greenberg, 1986) was used to assess the therapeutic alliance. The WAI is a 36-item measure consisting of subscales that address the goals of therapy (Goal), the tasks of therapy (Task) and the bond between the client and therapist (Bond). Ratings on

Table 2

Blocks and associated variables for the hierarchical multiple regression analyses

Block	Variables Comprising Block
Client demographics	Gender; age; ethnicity (black, Hispanic, white); education
Client drinking history	Number of years since onset of problem drinking; previous alcoholism treatment (number of previous outpatient and inpatient treatment episodes); Alcohol Use Inventory alcohol involvement score
Client current drinking	Baseline percentage of days abstinent (for 90-day pretreatment period prior to the client's last drink), baseline drinks per drinking day (for same pretreatment period); SCID alcohol dependence symptom count (range = 1–9) for the 90-day pretreatment period; drinking consequences (for 90-day pretreatment period, assessed using the DrInC)
Client current functioning	Motivational readiness to change (assessed using the URICA); Alcohol Abstinence Self-Efficacy score; Addiction Severity Index psychiatric severity scale score; Beck Depression Inventory score; Socialization Scale score from California Personality Inventory; Meaning-seeking score; Social Support Questionnaire score
Therapist demographics	Gender; age; education

Note: Ethnicity was effect coded. The baseline period for the clients in the aftercare study was the period prior to entry to their inpatient or day hospital treatment episode.

the extent to which the respondent agrees with the statement are made on a 7-point Likert-type scale (ranging from 1 = never to 7 = always), and a global score is calculated as the sum of the 36 items (after accounting for reverse-scored items). The WAI was selected for use for several reasons. First, the orientation of the WAI system is eclectic and thus suitable to the three treatments being evaluated. Second, the psychometric properties of the WAI are well established, with estimates of internal consistency, interrater reliability and validity at .85 and above on all subscales (Horvath & Greenberg, 1986; Safran & Wallner, 1991; Tracey & Kokotovic, 1989). Co-efficient alphas in the present data set also indicated satisfactory internal consistency (alphas > .70 for WAI client and therapist ratings in each arm of the study). Third, there are parallel forms of the WAI for ratings by both client and therapist. In this project, clients and therapists completed the WAI after the second treatment session. Ratings of the therapeutic alliance at the early stages of treatment have been more predictive of outcome than ratings taken later in the treatment process (Hartley & Strupp, 1983; Luborsky et al., 1983, 1985).

In isolated cases, the client and/or therapist did not complete the WAI at the second session. In such cases, several decision rules were used. First, if the WAI was mistakenly completed at the first session, the data were excluded ($n = 4$). Cases in which the WAI was completed at Session 4 or later (Session 3 in the case of the MET treatment) were also deleted ($n = 21$). WAI data collected at Session 3 for the weekly TSF and CBT treatments were included and treated as Session 2 reports ($n = 43$). Thus, all ratings of the alliance followed at least two treatment sessions but occurred no later than the third treatment session in TSF and CBT and the second treatment session in MET.

In the present study, the results are based on analyses using WAI total scores. This determination was made after evaluation of the intercorrelations among the WAI subscales. The intercorrelations among the subscales ranged from .68 to .92 (across client and therapist scores and the two samples). The correlations between the subscales and the total score ranged from .86 to .97. Further justification for the use of the WAI total scores is provided by the structural analysis of the WAI reported by Tracey and Kokotovic (1989), who found support for the use of the WAI to assess one general alliance dimension.

Client drinking history, alcohol consumption and related consequences. Several questionnaire and interview measures were used to gather information on clients' drinking and related consequences, including the alcohol section of the SCID (Spitzer & Williams, 1985), the Alcohol Use Inventory (AUI; Wanberg et al., 1977) and the Drinker Inventory of Consequences (DrInC; Miller et al., 1995). Estimates of alcohol consumption for the 90-day pretreatment period (for outpatient clients, the 90 days ending on the last drinking day prior to the interview; for aftercare clients, the 90 days ending on the last drinking day prior to entering inpatient or day hospital treatment) were obtained using the Form 90 (Miller, 1996). This interview procedure, which combined calendar memory cues from the time-line follow-back methodology (Sobell & Sobell, 1992) and drinking pattern estimation procedures (Miller & Marlatt, 1984), provides estimates of alcohol consumption for each day of the preceding period. Evidence from several sources suggests that the self-reports of drinking have acceptable levels of reliability and validity (Project MATCH Research Group, 1997a; Tonigan et al., 1997).

Table 3

Means and standard deviations for predictor variables and Working Alliance Inventory (WAI) client and therapist total scores

Variable	Outpatient sample Mean (±SD)	Aftercare sample Mean (±SD)
Client age	39.41 ± 10.85	42.28 ± 10.92
Client education	13.56 ± 2.11	13.15 ± 2.11
Years of problem drinking	13.80 ± 9.42	14.98 ± 10.21
Previous alcoholism treatments	1.00 ± 2.14	1.63 ± 2.49
Alcohol Use Inventory–Alcohol Involvement score	26.33 ± 10.77	33.17 ± 12.47
Pretreatment % days abstinent (transformed)	0.57 ± 0.39	0.46 ± 0.41
Pretreatment % days abstinent (raw)	0.34 ± 0.30	0.27 ± 0.30
Pretreatment drinks per drinking day (transformed)	3.46 ± 0.91	4.27 ± 1.25
Pretreatment drinks per drinking day (raw)	12.82 ± 7.01	19.75 ± 11.74
Alcohol dependence symptoms (SCID)	5.72 ± 1.93	6.80 ± 1.91
Drinking consequences (DrInC)	45.81 ± 21.71	58.93 ± 22.80
URICA Readiness	83.77 ± 13.50	89.61 ± 11.08
Abstinence self-efficacy	−0.26 ± 28.02	−9.76 ± 32.88
ASI psychiatric severity	0.19 ± 0.19	0.23 ± 0.21
Beck Depression Inventory	9.85 ± 7.93	10.34 ± 8.56
CPI Socialization Scale	24.02 ± 5.77	23.45 ± 6.04
Meaning-seeking	−17.55 ± 29.26	−11.52 ± 30.99
Social support	4.14 ± 1.80	4.06 ± 1.87
WAI client total score–client analyses[a]	211.77 ± 23.60	214.87 ± 23.20
WAI therapist total score–client analyses[b]	192.79 ± 24.36	192.89 ± 26.58
Therapist age[c]	39.21 ± 7.69	37.74 ± 7.12
Therapist education[c]	18.76 ± 2.93	18.43 ± 2.68
WAI client total score–therapist analyses[c]	212.86 ± 8.38	215.11 ± 12.17
WAI therapist total score–therapist analyses[c]	190.34 ± 16.36	193.93 ± 19.73

Note: Descriptions of variables provided in the text. Except as otherwise noted, outpatient sample: $n = 707$; aftercare sample: $n = 480$.

a. Outpatient sample: $n = 682$; aftercare sample: $n = 465$.

b. Outpatient sample: $n = 675$; aftercare sample: $n = 472$.

c. For these statistics, the unit of analysis is therapist. Thus, the means and standard deviations are unweighted with respect to number of clients seen by each therapist and the WAI data points used represent each therapist's average score across all clients seen by that therapist. Outpatient therapist: $n = 42$; aftercare therapist: $n = 35$.

Table 4

Simple and multiple regressions predicting client and therapist Working Alliance Inventory (WAI) scores for the outpatient sample

Predictors	Working Alliance–Client Scores				Working Alliance–Therapist Scores			
	Simple regressions	Multiple regression			Simple regressions	Multiple regression		
	Beta	ΔR^2	Beta	B	Beta	ΔR^2	Beta	B
Client characteristics[a]	(n = 682)				(n = 675)			
Block 1-demographics		.03**				.05**		
Gender	0.04		0.04	2.185	0.16**		0.16**	8.745
Age	0.09*		0.111**	0.241	0.00		-0.01	-0.025
Ethnicity								
White and other	-0.03		-0.01	-0.456	0.06		0.07	2.850
Black	-0.01		-0.03	-1.685	-0.01		-0.03	-1.923
Hispanic	0.05		0.06	2.142	-0.04		-0.02	-0.927
Education	-0.11**		-0.12**	-1.354	0.01		0.00	-0.011
Block 2-drinking history		.00				.01		
Years of problem drinking	0.06		0.02	0.057	0.02		0.05	0.117
Previous alcoholism treatment	0.02		0.00	-0.008	-0.02		-0.03	-0.539
Alcohol Use Inventory total score	-0.02		-0.03	-0.074	0.08**		0.07*	0.149
Block 3-current drinking		.02*				.01		
Pretreatment abstinent days	0.00		0.05	3.027	0.00		0.03	1.625
Pretreatment drinks per drinking day	0.03		0.00	-0.019	-0.01		-0.02	-0.480
Alcohol dependence symptoms (SCID)	0.07		0.11*	1.307	0.07*		0.05	0.576
Drinking consequences (DrInC)	0.05		0.12*	0.132	0.07*		0.06	0.072

(continued)

Table 4 (continued)

Predictors	Working Alliance–Client Scores				Working Alliance–Therapist Scores			
	Simple regressions	Multiple regression			Simple regressions	Multiple regression		
	Beta	ΔR^2	Beta	B	Beta	ΔR^2	Beta	B
Client characteristics[a]	(n = 682)				(n = 675)			
Block 4-current functioning		.08***				.03*		
URICA readiness	0.25***		0.24***	0.415	0.11***		0.06	0.100
Abstinence self-efficacy	-0.02		-0.09*	-0.073	-0.02		0.02	0.015
ASI psychiatric severity	-0.07		-0.03	-3.809	-0.02		-0.04	-5.388
Beck Depression Inventory	-0.10**		-0.05	-0.147	0.00		-0.01	-0.043
CPI socialization scale	0.10*		0.07	0.274	0.04		0.07	0.306
Meaning-seeking	-0.13***		-0.09	-0.077	0.01		0.02	0.018
Social support	0.12**		0.06	0.820	0.06		0.07*	0.980
Therapist characteristics[b]	(n = 42)				(n = 42)			
Demographics		.16				.03		
Gender	0.27		0.23	3.977	0.09		0.10	3.315
Age	0.33*		0.31*	0.333	0.01		0.01	0.018
Education	-0.03		0.02	0.052	0.15		0.15	0.861

Notes: Gender: 1 = male, 2 = female.

a. Analyses using client characteristics as predictors reflect pooled within-therapist relationships between the predictors and dependent variables. Multiple regression coefficients for client characteristics represent results from each block prior to entry of subsequent blocks.

b. Analyses using therapist characteristics as predictors were conducted using therapist as the unit of analysis; the dependent variables in these analyses are the WAI scores for each therapist, averaged across all clients seen by that therapist.

* $p < .05$; ** $p < .01$; *** $p < .001$.

Client psychosocial functioning. Several questionnaire measures were used to assess a variety of client characteristics. Cognitive factors related to drinking were provided by the University of Rhode Island Change Assessment scale (URICA; Carbonari et al., 1994; DiClemente & Hughes, 1990), which assesses readiness to change. Specifically, a motivational readiness to change score was calculated by summing the contemplation, action and maintenance subscale scores and subtracting the precontemplation subscale score (Carbonari et al., 1994). Temptation to drink and confidence in ability to abstain were assessed by subscales of the Alcohol Abstinence Self-Efficacy measure (AASE; DiClemente, 1986; DiClemente et al., 1994a). Strength of self-efficacy was operationalized in these analyses as the difference score between confidence to abstain and temptation to drink. Dimensions of psychological distress were measured by the Beck Depression Inventory (BDI; Beck et al., 1961) and the psychiatric severity section of the Addiction Severity Index (ASI; McLellan et al., 1980). Socialization was assessed using the Socialization Scale of the California Psychological Inventory (CPI; Gough, 1975), and meaning-seeking was measured by combining data from two measures: the Seeking of Noetic Goals scale (SONG; Crumbaugh, 1977) and the Purpose in Life scale (PIL; Crumbaugh & Maholik, 1976). Finally, perceived social support was assessed using the Social Support Questionnaire (Procidano & Heller, 1983), which measures support received from family and friends.

Analysis plan

For each sample (outpatient and aftercare), two dependent variables were predicted: the client WAI total score and therapist WAI total score. Evaluation of the relationship between potential predictor variables and ratings of the therapeutic alliance was conducted via ordinary least squares regression analyses. Because several clients were seen by each therapist, the data (especially therapists' ratings of the alliance) violate the assumption of independence of observations. This was dealt with in two ways. Analyses involving client characteristics as predictors (represented in the top section of tables 4 and 5) were conducted after removing between-therapist variance in each dependent variable. With respect to estimating regression coefficients and their standard errors, the fixed-effect regression procedure used was computationally equivalent to entering a set of dummy codes representing therapist ID prior to entering the client characteristic variables. This procedure provides the pooled within-therapist relationships between the client characteristic predictors and the dependent variables. It also provides standard errors that are adjusted for potential nonindependence in the data. Analyses involving therapist demographics as predictors were conducted separately. For these analyses (represented in the bottom section of tables 4 and 5), each therapist's average score for each dependent variable was computed from the scores for all clients seen by that therapist. These average scores were then regressed on the therapist demographic predictors. This between-therapist regression procedure adjusts for sample-size inflation and non-independence in the dependent variable score that would have occurred if client was used as the unit of analysis when evaluating the relationship of therapist characteristics to the dependent variables.

For each dependent variable, two sets of regression coefficients are presented. First, bivariate relationships between predictors and alliance ratings were evaluated by examining the beta weight (and its significance) of each predictor entered alone into a regression equation containing that predictor as the sole independent variable. Second, multiple regression analyses were conducted in which several predictor variables were entered together. Analyses in which client characteristics served as predictors were conducted using a hierarchical approach, organizing the predictor variables into four blocks. These blocks reflected, in order, client demographics, drinking history, current drinking and current functioning. The purpose of this hierarchical approach was partly to control for the inflation of alpha that arises from testing multiple bivariate relationships, and partly to assess the impact of each block of variables after covarying out the potentially confounded influence of causally prior variables (with causal priority determined primarily by temporal order). Although this approach leads to relatively conservative tests of the predictive power of variables entered later in the equation, it provides a useful counterpoint to the more liberal bivariate tests described earlier. Multiple regression analyses in which therapist demographics served as predictors contained just a single block of variables, which were entered simultaneously. Variables associated with each of the four blocks of client characteristics and the single block of therapist demographics are identified in table 2. Client ethnicity was represented as a group of effect-coded variables.

The means and standard deviations for the predictor variables (except client and therapist gender and client ethnicity) and the WAI

Table 5

Simple and multiple regressions predicting client and therapist Working Alliance Inventory (WAI) scores for the aftercare sample

Predictors	Working Alliance–Client Scores				Working Alliance–Therapist Scores			
	Simple regressions	Multiple regression			Simple regressions	Multiple regression		
	Beta	ΔR^2	Beta	B	Beta	ΔR^2	Beta	B
Client characteristics[a]	($n = 465$)				($n = 472$)			
Block 1-demographics		.01				.02		
Gender	0.02		0.02	1.169	0.07*		0.07*	4.360
Age	0.08		0.09	0.189	0.00		-0.01	-0.017
Ethnicity								
White and other	-0.06		-0.06	-3.059	-0.04		-0.04	-2.425
Black	-0.04		-0.04	-2.174	-0.01		-0.01	-0.530
Hispanic	0.10		0.11	5.232	0.05		0.05	2.955
Education	0.00		-0.01	-0.106	0.05		0.05	0.609
Block 2-drinking history		.01				.02		
Years of problem drinking	0.03		0.01	0.025	-0.03		-0.01	-0.034
Previous alcoholism treatment	-0.08		-0.10	-0.909	-0.05		-0.07	-0.747
Alcohol Use Inventory total score	-0.04		0.01	0.022	0.05		0.09*	0.188
Block 3-current drinking		.01				.02		
Pretreatment abstinent days	-0.02		0.02	0.852	-0.01		-0.01	-0.714
Pretreatment drinks per drinking day	-0.01		0.01	0.182	-0.07*		-0.11**	-2.267
Alcohol dependence symptoms (SCID)	0.03		0.09	1.119	0.03		0.04	0.622
Drinking consequences (DrInC)	-0.05		-0.05	-0.046	0.00		-0.05	-0.059

(continued)

Table 5 (continued)

Predictors	Working Alliance–Client Scores				Working Alliance-Therapist Scores			
	Simple regressions	Multiple regression			Simple regressions	Multiple regression		
	Beta	ΔR^2	Beta	B	Beta	ΔR^2	Beta	B
Client characteristics[a]	(n = 465)				(n = 472)			
Block 4-current functioning		.11***				.02		
URICA readiness	0.23***		0.25***	0.530	0.01		-0.01	-0.016
Abstinence self-efficacy	-0.09		-0.04	-0.026	-0.01		-0.02	-0.017
ASI psychiatric severity	-0.03		0.04	4.508	0.02		0.03	3.764
Beck Depression Inventory	-0.18***		-0.17**	-0.453	-0.06		-0.08*	-0.257
CPI socialization scale	0.14**		0.12	0.448	0.06		0.08	0.353
Meaning-seeking	-0.09		0.01	0.007	-0.02		0.01	0.012
Social support	0.14**		0.05	0.612	0.03		0.01	0.095
Therapist characteristics[b]	(n = 35)				(n = 35)			
Demographics		.07				.16		
Gender	-0.19		-0.20	-4.909	-0.17		-0.15	-5.917
Age	-0.01		0.01	0.024	-0.10		-0.05	-0.136
Education	-0.18		-0.19	-0.844	0.37*		0.36*	2.627

Notes: Gender: 1 = male, 2 = female.

a. Analyses using client characteristics as predictors reflect pooled within-therapist relationships between the predictors and dependent variables. Multiple regression coefficients for client characteristics represent results from each block prior to entry of subsequent blocks.

b. Analyses using therapist characteristics as predictors were conducted using therapist as the unit of analysis; the dependent variables in these analyses are the WAI scores for each therapist, averaged across all clients seen by that therapist.

*$p < .05$; **$p < .01$; ***$p < .001$.

client and therapist total scores are provided in table 3. It should be noted that variables such as percentage of days abstinent and drinks per drinking day often depart from normality due to floor/ceiling effects. Therefore, the percentage of days abstinent variable was subjected to an arcsin transformation and the drinks per drinking day variable to a square root transformation, in each case to improve the distribution.

Results

Outpatient Sample

The bivariate relationships between the four blocks of outpatient client characteristics and WAI scores are provided in the top panel of table 4, under the columns labeled "simple regressions." Although several relationships were statistically significant, they were, at most, of modest magnitude. The strongest relationship (beta = .25, $p < .001$) was between motivational readiness to change (URICA) and client WAI ratings. Outpatients' ratings of the alliance were also positively predicted by client age, socialization and level of perceived social support, and they were negatively predicted by client educational level, level of depression and meaning seeking. Therapist ratings in the outpatient sample were positively predicted by the client being female and by level of overall alcohol involvement, severity of alcohol dependence, negative consequences of alcohol use and readiness to change (URICA).

The bivariate relationships between outpatient therapist demographics and the WAI scores are provided in the bottom panel of table 4. Of these, only the relationship between therapist age and client WAI ratings was significant (beta = .33, $p < .05$).

The results of the multiple regression analyses for the outpatient clients are detailed in the remaining columns of table 4. Of the variables having significant bivariate relationships with alliance scores among outpatients, only a few were identified as significant predictors in these equations. Client age and motivational readiness to change remained positive predictors and client education a negative predictor of client ratings of the alliance, and client gender remained a significant predictor of therapist ratings. The adjusted total proportion of variance in WAI scores accounted for by all of the client-related predictors was .10 for client scores and .06 for therapist scores. Therapist demographic variables entered as a group did not account for a significant portion of variance in either client or therapist WAI scores.

Aftercare Sample

The bivariate relationships between aftercare client characteristics and WAI scores are provided in the top panel of table 5, under the columns labeled "simple regressions." As with the outpatient clients, the relationships were, at most, of modest magnitude, and the strongest relationship (beta = .23, $p < .001$) was between motivational readiness to change (URICA) and client WAI ratings. Aftercare clients' ratings of the alliance were also positively predicted by socialization and level of perceived social support, and were negatively predicted by level of depression. Therapist ratings in the aftercare sample were predicted positively by the client being female and negatively by pretreatment drinks per drinking day.

The bivariate relationships between aftercare therapist demographics and WAI scores are provided in the bottom panel of table 5. Only the relationship between therapist education and therapist WAI ratings was significant (beta = .37, $p < .05$).

The results of the multiple regression analyses for the aftercare clients are detailed in the remaining columns of table 5. Of the variables having significant bivariate relationships with alliance scores among aftercare clients, only two were identified as significant predictors in multiple regression equations. Motivational readiness to change remained a positive predictor and depression a negative predictor of client ratings of the alliance; none of the variables remained a significant predictor of therapist ratings. The adjusted total proportion of variance in WAI scores accounted for by client-related predictors was .10 for client scores and .04 for therapist scores. Therapist demographic variables entered as a group did not account for a significant portion of variance in either client or therapist WAI scores.

Discussion

The present study identified a variety of factors that may contribute to the therapeutic alliance. The simple regressions evaluating bivariate relationships showed that outpatients' ratings of the alliance were positively predicted by client age, motivational readiness to change, socialization, level of perceived social support, and therapist age, and negatively predicted by client educational level, level of depression, and meaning seeking. Therapist ratings in the outpatient sample were positively predicted by the client being female and by level of overall alcohol involvement, severity of alcohol dependence, negative consequences of alcohol use, and readiness to change. Among aftercare clients, ratings of the alliance were positively predicted by readiness to change, socialization, and social support, and negatively predicted by level of depression. Therapist ratings of the alliance in the aftercare sample were positively predicted by the client being female and therapist educational level, and negatively predicted by pretreatment drinks per drinking day. Of these variables, only a few were significant predictors in multiple regression equations. Among outpatients, client age and readiness to change remained positive predictors and client education a negative predictor of client ratings of the alliance, while client gender remained a significant predictor of therapist ratings. Among aftercare clients, readiness to change and level of depression remained significant predictors of client ratings, while none of the variables remained a significant predictor of therapist ratings. Taken together, the data indicate that several client and therapist variables predict the client's perception of the therapeutic alliance and that motivational readiness to change their drinking behavior is the most robust predictor among both outpatient and aftercare clients in relation to the other variables in these analyses.

The findings regarding motivation to change stand out. The role of motivation in ratings of the therapeutic alliance has not been systematically evaluated in prior studies. As such, it is plausible that motivation has mediated at least some of the previous findings relating therapeutic alliance to participation and outcome. Motivated clients are more likely to be invested in the process of change and see the therapy enterprise in a more positive light. They also appear to be more engaged in change and thus see themselves as more in synchrony with the therapist in terms of goals, tasks, and the bond of the working alliance. Further studies should incorporate assessment of client motivation when examining the processes and mechanisms of alcoholism treatment. Relatedly, it may be useful to explore strategies for engendering and/or maximizing client readiness to change.

It was notable that there was relatively little overlap between the variables that predicted clients' alliance ratings and those that predicted therapists' alliance ratings in both the simple and multiple regressions. The only exception was that ratings of the alliance provided by outpatient clients and by outpatient therapists were positively predicted by motivational readiness to change in the simple regressions. This general lack of overlap suggests that different factors influence clients' and therapists' perceptions of the working relationship in alcoholism treatment.

Among both outpatient and aftercare clients, ratings of the alliance appeared to be influenced at a bivariate level by intrapersonal (depression, level of socialization) and interpersonal (social support) indicators of functioning, but not by indices of past and current drinking or drinking-related problems. This finding seems consistent with previous research, which has suggested that severity of illness is not associated with rating of the therapeutic alliance (Horvath, 1994). In contrast, ratings of the alliance provided by the outpatient therapists were positively predicted by several indices of problem severity (i.e., overall alcohol involvement, severity of alcohol dependence and negative consequences of alcohol use). Alliance ratings by aftercare therapists, however, were *negatively* related to pretreatment drinks per drinking day.

In the present report, results of both simple regression analyses between the predictor variables and alliance scores and multiple regression analyses examining the unique predictive power of the variables were described. The fact that many of the bivariate relationships identified were no longer significant in the context of multiple regression analyses suggests that some of the relationships may not be independent of each other or may stem from prior shared causal factors, and that some may be unique to the current samples. Further research will be needed to replicate these findings and to explicate the interrelationships among these factors and measures of the working alliance. On the other hand, those bivariate relationships that were found to represent unique contributions to prediction (especially motivation to change, as noted earlier) are probably robust and provide clearer information regarding factors that contribute to a positive working alliance.

There are limits on the generalizability of these results that need to be acknowledged. First, these data were gathered as part of a clinical research protocol involving alcoholic clients who agreed to participate in such a trial and received treatment in the form of structured, manual-guided, time-limited interventions. The extent to which these results would be replicated in other clinical contexts and using other treatments (e.g., treatments less structured, treatments using different durations, treatments representing different intervention modalities) is not known. Second, the samples included only individuals who stayed in treatment at least through the second session and, as a result, do not include those clients who dropped out of treatment before the second session. Further, the aftercare sample did not include clients who failed to complete a more intensive treatment for alcoholism immediately before their involvement in the protocol. As such, these results cannot be immediately generalized to all clients who seek alcoholism treatment. Finally, using a range of client- and therapist-related variables, we were able in our multiple regression analyses to account for only between 4% and 10% of variance (adjusted R^2) in WAI scores. These findings suggest that other factors not reflected in the set of independent variables used here may also have an impact on the alliance.

In conclusion, while the data indicate that several client variables predict the nature of both the client's and therapist's perception of the therapeutic alliance, the significant relationships are of modest magnitude, and few variables remain predictive after controlling for causally prior variables. The strongest relationship identified in both the outpatient and aftercare samples is that between clients' motivational readiness to change and their ratings of the alliance. It may be useful in subsequent research on the therapeutic alliance to determine what, if any, key variables were not evaluated in the present analyses (e.g., dimensions of interpersonal functioning).

References

American Psychiatric Association. (1987). *Diagnostic and Statistical Manual of Mental Disorders (DSM-III-R),* Washington, DC.

Beck, A.T., Ward, C.H., Mendelson, M., Mock, J., & Erbaugh, J. (1961). An inventory for measuring depression. *Archives of General Psychiatry, 4,* 561–571.

Belding, M.A., Iguchi, M.Y., Morral, A.R., & McLellan, A.T. (1997). Assessing the helping alliance and its impact in the treatment of opiate dependence. *Drug and Alcohol Dependence, 48,* 51–59.

Bordin, E.S. (1979). The generalizability of the psychoanalytic concept of the working alliance. *Psychotherapy Theory, Research, and Practice, 16,* 252–260.

Carbonari, J.P., DiClemente, C.C., & Zweben, A. (1994). A readiness to change scale: Its development, validation and usefulness. In: DiClemente, C.C. (Chair) *Assessing Critical Dimensions for Alcoholism Treatment.* Symposium presented at the annual meeting of the Association for Advancement of Behavior Therapy, San Diego, CA.

Carroll, K.M., Connors, G.J., Cooney, N.L., DiClemente, C.C., Donovan, D.M., Kadden, R.R., Longabaugh, R.L., Rounsaville, B.J., Wirtz, P.W., & Zweben, A. (1998). Internal validity of Project MATCH treatments: Discriminability and integrity. *Journal of Counseling and Clinical Psychology, 66,* 290–303.

Carroll, K.M., Kadden, R.M., Donovan, D.M., Zweben, A., & Rounsaville, B.J. (1994). Implementing treatment and protecting the validity of the independent variable in treatment matching studies. *Journal of Studies on Alcohol, Supplement No. 12,* pp. 149–155.

Connors, G.J., Allen, J.P., Cooney, N.L., DiClemente, C.C., Tonigan, J.S., & Anton, R.F. (1994). Assessment issues and strategies in alcoholism treatment matching research. *Journal of Studies on Alcohol, Supplement No. 12,* pp. 92–100.

Connors, G.J., Carroll, K.M., DiClemente, C.C., Longabaugh, R., & Donovan, D.M. (1997). The therapeutic alliance and its relationship to alcoholism treatment participation and outcome. *Journal of Counseling and Clinical Psychology, 65,* 588–598.

Crumbaugh, J.C. (1977). The seeking of Noetic Goals Test (SONG): A complementary scale to the Purpose in Life Test (PIL). *Journal of Clinical Psychology, 33,* 900–907.

Crumbaugh, J.C. & Maholik, L.T. (1976). Purpose in Life Scale. Murfreesboro, TN: Psychometric Affiliates.

DiClemente, C.C. (1986). Self-efficacy and the addictive behaviors. *Journal of Social and Clinical Psychology, 4,* 302–315.

DiClemente, C.C., Carbonari, J.P., Montgomery, R.P.G., & Hughes, S.O. (1994a). The Alcohol Abstinence Self-Efficacy Scale. *Journal of Studies on Alcohol, 55,* 141–148.

DiClemente, C.C., Carroll, K.M., Connors, G.J., & Kadden, R.M. (1994b). Process assessment in treatment matching research. *Journal of Studies on Alcohol, Supplement No. 12,* pp. 156–162.

DiClemente, C.C. & Hughes, S.O. (1990). Stages of change profiles in outpatient alcoholism treatment. *Journal of Substance Abuse, 2,* 217–235.

Donovan, D.M., Kadden, R.M., DiClemente, C.C., Carroll, K.M., Longabaugh, R., Zweben, A., & Rychtarik, R. (1994). Issues in the selection and development of therapies in alcoholism treatment matching research. *Journal of Studies on Alcohol, Supplement No. 12,* pp. 138–148.

Gough, H.G. (1975). *Manual for the California Psychological Inventory.* Palo Alto, CA: Consulting Psychologists Press.

Greenson, R.R. (1967). *The technique and practice of psychoanalysis.* New York: International Universities Press.

Hartley, D.E. & Strupp, H.H. (1983). The therapeutic alliance: Its relationship to outcome in brief psychotherapy. In J.M. Masling (Ed.), *Empirical studies of psychoanalytical theories.* Mahwah, NJ: Lawrence Erlbaum, pp. 1–37.

Henry, W.P. & Strupp, H.H. (1994). The therapeutic alliance as interpersonal process. In A.O. Horvath & L.S. Greenberg (Eds.),*The working alliance: Theory, research, and practice.* New York: John Wiley & Sons, pp. 51–84.

Henry, W.P. Strupp, H.H., Schacht, T.E., & Gatson, L. (1994). Psychodynamic approaches. In A.E. Bergin & S.L. Garfield (Eds.) *Handbook of psychotherapy and behavior change, 4th edition.* New York: John Wiley & Sons, pp. 467–508.

Horvath, A.O. Research on the alliance. (1994). In A.O. Horvath & L.S. Greenberg (Eds.), *The working alliance: Theory, research, and practice.* New York: John Wiley & Sons, pp. 259–286.

Horvath, A.O. (1995). The therapeutic relationship: From transference to alliance. *In Session: Psychotherapy Practice 1,* 7–17.

Horvath, A.O. & Greenberg, L.S. (1986). The development of the Working Alliance Inventory. In L.S. Greenberg & W.M. Pinsof (Eds.), *The psychotherapeutic process: A research handbook.* New York: Guilford Press, pp. 529–556.

Horvath, A.O. & Greenberg, L.S. (Eds.) (1994). *The working alliance: Theory, research, and practice.* New York: John Wiley & Sons.

Kadden, R., Carroll, K., Donovan, D., Cooney, N., Monti, P., Abrams, D., Litt, M., & Hester, R. (1992). Cognitive-behavioral coping skills therapy manual: A clinical research guide for therapists treating individuals with alcohol abuse and dependence. *NIAAA Project MATCH Monograph Series, Vol. 3,* DHHS Publication No. (ADM) 92-1895, Washington: Government Printing Office.

LuBorsky, L., Crits-Christoph, P., Alexander, L., Margolis, M., & Cohen, M. (1983). Two helping alliance methods for predicting outcomes of psychotherapy: A counting signs vs. a global rating method. *Journal of Nervous and Mental Disease, 171,* 480–491.

LuBorsky, L., McLellan, A.T., Woody, G.E., O'Brien, C.P., & Auerbach, A. (1985). Therapist success and its determinants. *Archives of General Psychiatry, 42,* 602–611.

McLellan, A.T., LuBorsky, L., Woody, G.E., & O'Brien, C.P. (1980). An improved diagnostic evaluation instrument for substance abuse patients: The Addiction Severity Index. *Journal of Nervous and Mental Disease,* 168, 26–33.

Miller, W.R. (1996). Form 90: A Structured Assessment Interview for Drinking and Related Behaviors: Test manual. *NIAAA Project MATCH Monograph Series, Vol. 5,* NIH Publication No. 96–4004, Rockville, MD: Department of Health and Human Services.

Miller, W.R. & Marlatt, G.A. (1984). *The Comprehensive Drinker Profile.* Odessa, FL: Psychological Assessment Resources.

Miller, W.R., Tonigan, J.S., & Longabaugh, R. (1995). The Drinker Inventory of Consequences (DrInQ: An instrument for assessing adverse consequences of alcohol abuse (Test Manual). *NIAAA Project MATCH Monograph Series, Vol. 4,* NIH Publication No. 95–3911, Rockville, MD: Department of Health and Human Services,

Miller, W.R., Zweben, A., DiClemente, C.C., & Rychtarik, R.G. (1992). Motivational Enhancement Therapy manual: A clinical research guide for therapists treating individuals with alcohol abuse and dependence. *NIAAA Project MATCH Monograph Series, Vol. 2,* DHHS Publication No. (ADM) 92-1894, Washington: Government Printing Office.

Nowinski, J., Baker, S., & Carroll, K. (1992). Twelve-Step Facilitation Therapy manual: A clinical research guide for therapists treating individuals with alcohol abuse and dependence. *NIAAA Project MATCH Monograph Series, Vol. 1,* DHHS Publication No. (ADM) 92–1893, Washington: Government Printing Office.

Orlinsky, D.E., Grawe, K., & Parks, B.X. (1994). Process and outcome in psychotherapy: Noch einmal, In A.E. Bergin & S.L. Garfield (Eds.), *Handbook of psychotherapy and behavior change, 4th Edition.* New York: John Wiley & Sons, pp. 270–376.

Procidano, M.E. & Heller, K. (1983). Measures of perceived social support from friends and from family: Three validation studies. *American Journal of Community Psychology, 11,* 1–24.

Project MATCH Research Group. (1993). Project MATCH: Rationale and methods for a multisite clinical trial matching patients to alcoholism treatment. *Alcoholism, Clinical and Experimental Research, 17,* 1130–1145.

Project MATCH Research Group. (1997a). Matching alcoholism treatments to client heterogeneity: Project MATCH posttreatment drinking outcomes. *Journal of Studies on Alcohol, 58,* 7–29.

Project MATCH Research Group. (1997b). Project MATCH secondary a priori hypotheses. *Addiction 92,* 1671–1698.

Safran, J.D. & Wallner, L.K. (1991). The relative predictive validity of two therapeutic alliance measures in cognitive therapy. *Psychological Assessment, 3,* 188–195.

Sobell, L.C. & Sobell, M.B. (1992). Timeline follow-back: A technique for assessing self-reported alcohol consumption. In R.Z. Litten & J.P. Allen, (Eds.), *Measuring alcohol consumption: Psychosocial and biochemical methods.* Totowa, NJ: Humana Press, pp. 41–72.

Spitzer, R.L. & Williams, J.B.W. (1985). *Structured Clinical Interview for DSM-III-R, Patient Version,* New York: Biometric Research Department, New York State Psychiatric Institute.

Stout, R.L., Wirtz, P.W., Carbonari, J.P., & Del Boca, F.K. (1994). Ensuring balanced distribution of prognostic factors in treatment outcome research. *Journal of Studies on Alcohol, Supplement No. 12,* pp. 70–75.

Tonigan, J.S., Miller, W.R., & Brown, J.M. (1997). The reliability of Form 90: An instrument for assessing alcohol treatment outcome. *Journal of Studies on Alcohol, 58,* 358–364.

Tracey, T.J. & Kokotovic, A.M. (1989). Factor structure of the Working Alliance Inventory. *Psychological Assessment, 1,* 207–210.

Tunis, S.L., Delucchi, K.L., Schwartz, K., Banys, P., & Sees, K.L. (1995). The relationship of counselor and peer alliance to drug use and HIV risk behaviors in a six-month methadone detoxification program. *Addictive Behaviors, 20,* 395–405.

Wanberg, K.W., Horn, J.L., & Foster, F.M. (1977). A differential assessment model for alcoholism: The scales of the Alcohol Use Inventory. *Journal of Studies on Alcohol, 38,* 512–543.

Recovery Challenges Among Dually Diagnosed Individuals

Alexandre B. Laudet, Stephen Magura, Howard S. Vogel &
Edward Knight

This article originally appeared in *Journal of Substance Abuse Treatment*, 2000, 18, 321–329, and is reprinted with permission.

Alexandre B. Laudet, Ph.D., & Stephen Magura, Ph.D., National Development and Research Institutes, Inc., New York, NY. Howard S. Vogel, C.S.W., & Edward Knight, Ph.D., Mental Health Empowerment Project, Inc., Albany, NY.

The work reported here was supported by National Institute on Drug Abuse grant R01 DA 11240–01.

Although there is a high prevalence of co-occurring mental and substance abuse disorders, and empirical evidence shows the need to integrate multiple treatment services for dually diagnosed persons, service integration is relatively recent and often poorly implemented. Moreover, service providers and clients often hold divergent views of what constitute appropriate and feasible treatment goals. This paper presents interview data from an urban sample of dually diagnosed members of self-help groups ($N = 310$) concerning the challenges confronting them in their recovery, and discusses the interrelations of these issues. The findings indicate that most clients struggle with emotional and socioeconomic issues, which bear significantly on their ability to handle adequately other aspects of recovery.

Introduction

Individuals diagnosed with a mental disorder and chemical dependence present a unique challenge to service providers who usually are trained in one area only. Both clinical observation and formal research have shown the complexity of the relationships between substance abuse and psychiatric disabilities (Drake et al., 1993; Lehman et al., 1989, 1994; Meyer, 1988; Nunes & Deliyannides, 1993). Although the reasons for onset of substance use or psychiatric symptoms may vary, investigations have found that substance abuse and mental disorders may reinforce each other or describe relatively autonomous courses (Hein et al., 1993; Lehman et al., 1994). Thus, remediating either the substance use or mental disorder often will not automatically resolve the other. In fact, treatment of one condition (addiction or mental disorder) is often hampered by the symptoms of the other if the latter remains unaddressed or untreated; for instance, high levels of psychiatric severity are associated with little or no improvement in formal substance abuse treatment (e.g., Marks, 1990).

Recent research indicates that two thirds of dually diagnosed persons appear to have dual primary diagnoses, that these disorders can interact, and that the goal of recovery in these cases is synonymous with dual recovery (Hein et al., 1993). Mental health providers are becoming more aware of the need to address dual recovery issues holistically (for review, see Rosenthal et al., 1992) and the consensus seems to be towards integrating services into dual-diagnosis treatment programs (e.g., Center for Substance Abuse Treatment, 1994; Post Ahrens, 1998; Senay, 1998). However, because of the diversity of conditions and also, because each client experiences his/her dual-diagnosis differently, it is difficult to standardize treatment protocols to meet all clients' particular needs. Further, clients face different struggles and have different needs at various stages of the recovery process. Moreover, clients and service providers may have different views of what constitutes appropriate or important treatment goals (Sainfort et al., 1996). This article presents and discusses findings about the challenges with which dually diagnosed individuals report struggling in their recovery.

Prevalence of Dual-Diagnoses

Numerous studies of both community and patient samples have shown substantial rates of comorbid psychiatric (mental) and substance abuse disorders. The Epidemiologic Catchment Area (ECA) study findings for lifetime prevalences are: (a) among those with a mental disorder, 29% had a comorbid addictive disorder (odds ratio [OR] = 2.7), (b) among those with an alcohol disorder, 37% had a mental disorder (OR = 2.3), (c) among those with a drug disorder, 53% had a mental disorder (OR = 4.5). Cocaine users displayed the highest rates of comorbidity (Regier et al., 1990). The subsequent National Comorbidity study found that, of respondents with lifetime illicit drug abuse or dependence, 59% also had a lifetime mental disorder, and that those with lifetime comorbidity were more likely than those with only one disorder to experience major impairments in economic (e.g., unemployment, financial problems) and social roles (e.g., social isolation, interpersonal conflicts). The great majority of people with recent disorders have not received recent treatment (Kessler, 1995).

In a study of low income, inner city residents, 60% of patients in mental health clinics had lifetime dual diagnoses and 67% of patients in outpatient substance abuse treatment were dually diagnosed; about two thirds of the patients in both settings had dual primary diagnoses, in that their psychiatric and addictive disorders had independent or overlapping courses (Hein et al., 1993). Many studies of treatment-seekers in substance abuse and mental health programs have documented high rates of dual-diagnosis (Dixon et al., 1991; Gawin & Kleber, 1985; Greenfield et al., 1996; Hesselbrock et al., 1985; Kleinman et al., 1990; Magura et al., 1998; Marlowe et al., 1995; Mirin et al., 1988; Rounsaville et al., 1982, 1986, 1991; Weiss et al., 1986).

Consequences of Dual-Diagnosis

There is evidence that comorbid disorders are more severe and chronic than single, "pure" psychiatric disorders (Hagnell & Grasbeck, 1990; Hirschfeld et al., 1990; Kessler, 1995; Murphy, 1990). In the general population, persons with lifetime comorbidity are more likely than those with only one disorder to experience major impairments in economic (e.g., unemployment, financial problems, low education) and social roles (e.g., marital problems, social isolation, interpersonal conflicts; Kessler, 1995). The great majority of those with recent comorbid disorders have not had recent treatment, although they are more likely than others to obtain treatment (Kessler, 1995; Regier et al., 1990) However, comorbidity is a predictor of negative treatment outcomes. Among substance abuse patients, the severity of psychiatric symptoms is associated with poorer outcomes (McLellan et al., 1983; Rounsaville et al., 1986; Walker et al., 1983). Among opiate addicts the presence of any personality disorder is associated with more unemployment, family/social problems, legal problems and HIV risk, and with lower social judgment/sensitivity (Rutherford et al., 1994); antisocial personality disorder increases HIV risk among injecting drug users (Brooner et al., 1990). Among mental health patients, particularly persons with schizophrenia, a comorbid addictive disorder has been associated with various negative consequences: noncompliance with mental health treatment and medication, higher rehospitalization and emergency room visits, the need for higher dosages of neuroleptics, housing problems and homelessness, criminality and violence, suicide attempts, increased fluctuation and severity of psychiatric symptoms, legal problems, HIV infection and family stress (Bartels et al., 1993; Bergman & Harris, 1985; Drake & Brunette, 1998; Mueser et al., 1992; Osher & Kofoed, 1989; Osher et al., 1994; Westermeyer & Walzer, 1985). Different substances can have different symptomatic effects; for instance, alcohol has been implicated in organic brain symptoms, such as memory loss and hallucinations; marijuana can result in paranoia and more medication side effects; cocaine abuse can cause paranoia during use and suicidality during withdrawal, and decrease the effectiveness of neuroleptics; nicotine also reduces neuroleptic plasma levels (for a review, see Ziedonis & Fisher, 1994).

Method

Setting

Study participants were recruited from individuals attending Double Trouble in Recovery (DTR) meetings throughout New York City. DTR is a mutual-aid program adapted from the 12-step Alcoholics Anonymous (AA) model, specifically embracing those who have a dual-diagnosis of substance abuse/dependency and psychiatric disability. The DTR fellowship was started in New York State in 1989 and currently has over 100 DTR group meetings in the United States (some 40 in New York City, 20 more in New York State, as well as in Colorado, Georgia, Nebraska, New Mexico, and Pennsylvania). New DTR groups are being started continually, some initiated by consumers, others by professionals who feel that mutual help fellowships are a useful addition to formal treatment, especially for the hard-to-engage population of the dually diagnosed. DTR, Inc., a small nonprofit organization, supports this growth by training consumers to start and run groups and by providing ongoing support to existing groups. DTR developed as a grass-roots initiative and functions today with minimal involvement from the professional community. Groups meet in community-based organizations, psychosocial clubs, day treatment programs for mental health, substance abuse and dual-diagnosis, as well as in hospital inpatient units. All DTR groups are led by recovering individuals, even when groups meet in institutional settings (for a more detailed discussion of DTR, see Vogel et al., 1998).

Procedures

Prospective study participants were recruited at 25 DTR groups held in community-based organizations and day treatment programs through the five boroughs of New York City. All DTR members who had been attending for 1 month or more were eligible to participate in the study. Groups were visited approximately three times each during baseline data collection. An estimated 15% of group members declined to participate; the main reason cited for not wanting to be interviewed was a concern about confidentiality, especially in groups that are held in a treatment facility. A total of 310 baseline interviews were completed.

Client participation was voluntary based on informed consent. All data collected were confidential. The study was approved by National Development and Research Institute's Institutional Review Board and by the review processes of the various participating agencies where DTR groups are held. A federal Certificate of Confidentiality was obtained to protect data from intrusion. Administration of the baseline instrument takes approximately 2.5 hours; participants were given a $35 cash incentive.

Measures

The baseline interview is a semi-structured instrument covering sociodemographics and background, mental health status and history (including treatment and medication status and history), perception of stigma attached to having a dual-diagnosis, recovery challenges, history and experience of participating in DTR, and history and current status of substance use (including history and current treatment status).

For the Recovery Challenges section, subjects were presented with a list of 29 items and instructed thus: "Following are issues and situations that people may struggle with during their recovery from dual-diagnosis. Please rate each according to your own experience dealing with these issues in recovery." The answer categories were on a 4-point Likert-type scale: 1 = not at all difficult to deal with/to do, 2 = a little difficult, 3 = moderately difficult, and 4 = very difficult. As part of its effort to educate about dual-diagnosis, DTR regularly organizes dialogues where consumers and service providers are gathered around small round tables and given the opportunity to exchange ideas and concerns outside of the therapeutic environment. This process is guided through a series of questions attendees are asked to answer. One such question is: "What has been your most difficult struggle in your recovery from dual-diagnosis?" Proceedings from eight such meetings held in New York State in 1996 and 1997 representing about 150 participants were combined and categorized so as to eliminate redundancy. The resulting list of 29 items was incorporated into the baseline questionnaire.

Results

Sociodemographics and Background

The DTR participants were predominantly male (72%) and African American (58%), Hispanic (16%), non-Hispanic White (25%). Members' ages ranged from 20 to 63 years of age (*Mdn* = 39 years). Over one half (59%) finished high school or obtained a GED; almost all (95%) reported disability benefits (Supplemental Security Income [SSI] or Social Security Disability Income [SSDI]) as their primary source of income. Median income from all sources is $636 per month.

Over one half (52%) lived in a community residence or apartment program; 21% lived in their own apartment or house; 11% with friends/relatives, 10% in an Single Room Occupancy Residence (SRO), and 6% in a homeless shelter. The majority of subjects (62%) were single, 30% were separated, divorced, or widowed; 8% were married or in a common law marriage. Nearly one half (45%) reported physical abuse during childhood; 36%, sexual abuse. Most (91%) have no current involvement with the judicial system; 7% are on probation or parole. Six percent have tested positive for HIV.

Drug and Alcohol Use

DTR members' experiences with drugs and alcohol is extensive, starting with their first use at age 14 (median). The most often cited reason for starting to use was peer pressure ("to fit in," "to be accepted"), mentioned by 63% of the sample. Overall, crack/cocaine has been the primary substance for 42% of subjects; 34% cited alcohol as primary; 11%, heroin; 10%, marijuana; 2%, pills; and 1%, other drugs (including hallucinogens).

Nearly one half (47%) of the subjects reported having used drugs, alcohol, or both in the 12 months preceding the interview; 9% used drugs, alcohol, or both in the past month.

Mental Health

DTR members have a long history of mental health symptoms, reporting their first episode in adolescence (*Mdn* = 18 years). They did not seek or receive help for their symptoms until several years later (*Mdn* = 22 years). Almost all (96%) have been diagnosed with a mental health disorder; median age when first diagnosed is 30 years. The most prevalent diagnoses were schizophrenia (43%), bipolar disorder (25%), unipolar (major) depression (26%), schizoaffective (7%), and posttraumatic stress disorder (5%).

Over two thirds (70%) reported experiencing symptoms in the past year. In the past month, 10% reported being "very troubled" by emotional or mental health problems, 28% "moderately," 38% "somewhat troubled," and 24% "not at all troubled."

Association Between Substance Abuse and Mental Health

Over one third (38%) started experiencing mental health symptoms before they ever used drugs or alcohol while 50% showed the reverse pattern; 12% started experiencing symptoms and using drugs or alcohol at the same age. To assess the relationship between substance abuse and mental symptoms in this sample, subjects were asked their experiences of the interaction between the two. These responses suggest a strong connection: Two thirds (69%) reported that their mental health symptoms get worse when they are using drugs and alcohol, and 44% felt like using drugs or alcohol "very much" when they experience symptoms. In response to the question: "Overall, what has caused you the most problems?," one half (49%) reported that substance abuse and mental health had been "both equally" troublesome to them in their lives; 29% said that substance abuse had caused them more problems overall, while 17% said mental health; 6% didn't know or were not sure. When sharing at a DTR meeting, three quarters (76%) identify themselves as "dually diagnosed," compared to 6% as "alcoholic," 10% as "addict and alcoholic," and 8% in another way.

Formal Treatment

Subjects have extensive experience in treatment, both for substance abuse and mental health. On average, subjects first sought or received treatment for drugs or alcohol abuse at age 28 (median). Two thirds (71%) have received inpatient treatment for their addiction at least once, 24% more than five times; almost all (96%) have been enrolled in outpatient treatment for drug or alcohol abuse. Currently, three quarters (77%) are enrolled in an outpatient program for substance abuse or dual-diagnosis; median length of current enrollment is 8 months.

The majority of subjects (89%) have had one or more inpatient hospitalizations for mental health; nearly half (46%) have had over five. Almost all (97%) have been enrolled in outpatient treatment for mental health. Nine out of ten (91%) are currently enrolled in an outpatient mental health or dual-diagnosis treatment program; length of current outpatient enrollment is 9 months (median).

Self-help Participation

Many subjects heard about DTR while in the treatment system: from a counselor or therapist (41 %), while in treatment for alcohol or drug abuse (16%) or for mental health (8%). Other members came to DTR on the recommendation of a friend (19%), from the community (5%), from other 12-step fellowships (4%), or from other sources (7%). DTR attendance among study participants ranged from 1 month to 5 years or more; two thirds (68%) have been attending for 1 year or more. The majority of members attend regularly: 37% more than once a week, 60% once a week.

Three quarters (75%) also attend traditional 12-step meetings: 73% currently go to AA and 64% to Narcotics Anonymous (NA). Those who do not attend AA or NA report that it is because they feel uncomfortable, judged, or not accepted because of mental health issues or medications (17%), or because DTR meets their needs and no other group is necessary (15%). One half of DTR members who attend AA or NA do so to stay clean and sober and to focus on alcohol and drug use issues; 52% only of DTR members who attend AA or NA report discussing mental health issues at these meetings.

Challenges in Recovery

The analysis was performed in two stages: data reduction and individual items. First, a principal components factor analysis was selected as the data reduction procedure and performed on the 29 items. One dominant factor emerged, accounting for 48.2% of the variance; two other minor factors were extracted, each accounting for less than 5% of the variance. In the absence of two or more interpretable factors, the results are presented for individual items.

Table 1 presents difficulty ratings and mean difficulty ratings for all 29 items, ranked in descending order of rated difficulty. The "very difficult" rating ranged from 46% for both "Dealing with feelings (anger, pain, shame, guilt, etc.)" and "Working, finding work or keeping a job" to 15% for "Following a program such as the 12-steps" and 13% for "Accepting a Higher Power." The ranking of mean difficulty rating closely mirrors that of the individual rating percentages, with the mean rating ranging from 3.0 for "Dealing with feelings (anger, pain, shame, guilt, etc.)" to 1.9 for "Accepting a Higher Power."

Table I

Recovery challenges (N = 310): "Very difficult" rating in descending order

	Difficulty rating (%)				Mean[a]
	Very	Moderately	A little	Not at all	
Dealing with feelings (anger, pain, shame, guilt, etc.)	46	23	21	11	3.0
Working, finding work, or keeping a job	46	15	17	21	2.8
Fear of picking up	44	18	17	22	2.8
Having money problems	41	19	19	22	2.8
Dealing with inner conflicts	39	22	23	16	2.8
Not being understood	37	22	25	17	2.8
Things are not happening fast enough	37	27	23	12	2.9
Being bored	36	26	21	17	2.8
Feeling helpless	32	26	20	22	2.7
Not getting frustrated with the system	33	24	22	22	2.7
Overcoming fear of change, taking risks	33	20	20	27	2.6
Dealing with stability, with a clear head	32	25	24	19	2.7
Fear of never getting better	31	21	19	29	2.5
Overcoming confusion	30	20	24	26	2.5
Overcoming isolation	30	20	25	25	2.5
Identifying and dealing with triggers	29	20	25	27	2.5
Coping with mental disorder (managing/accepting symptoms)	25	20	27	28	2.4

(continued)

Table 1 (continued)

	Difficulty rating (%)				
	Very	Moderately	A little	Not at all	Mean[a]
Overcoming stigma of dual-diagnosis	25	24	22	30	2.4
Dealing with the system, with providers	24	31	17	28	2.5
Feeling good about yourself	24	24	20	32	2.4
Having or getting structure in your life	24	22	24	30	2.4
Accepting yourself and your dual-diagnosis	24	21	21	35	2.3
Admitting powerlessness	23	20	23	34	2.3
Dealing with medications (dosage, side effects, etc.)	23	17	19	40	2.2
Asking/accepting help and support	22	22	18	37	2.3
Being open-minded, listening	20	14	22	44	2.1
Not being accepted at other 12-step groups	19	18	22	41	2.1
Following a program such as the 12 steps	15	26	19	39	2.2
Accepting a "Higher Power"	13	16	17	54	1.9

a. 1 = not at all difficult to 4 = very difficult.

Discussion

Subjects in this sample, many of them members of an ethnic minority and at the bottom end of the socioeconomic ladder, have a long history of both substance abuse and mental health symptoms, and equally extensive experience with formal treatment in both areas. They are actively working on their recovery, as evidenced not only by the high percentage of current enrollment in formal treatment but also by sustained attendance at DTR and other 12-step fellowships.

The three areas rated as very difficult to deal with by most subjects are: dealing with feelings and inner conflicts, socioeconomic issues (work and money problems) and the maintenance of sobriety. The difficulty of dealing with feelings is understandable for individuals whose addiction is aggravated by mental disorders in which inappropriate affect regulation plays a large role (e.g., unipolar depression). Dealing with feelings such as anger, sadness, and loneliness that may have been previously masked by active addiction, and also feelings associated with entering recovery, such as shame, regret, and guilt, is a crucial area to work on in recovery. Dealing with feelings is particularly important and difficult for individuals with a history of childhood trauma, as is true for nearly half the sample. The importance of emotion management is heightened by the fact that how individuals deal with their feelings about the past (e.g., anger, shame, guilt, regret, sadness), the present (e.g., confusion, pain, isolation) and the future (e.g., fear, hopelessness) bears on their sobriety, another area many subjects rate as very difficult. In qualitative interviews, most subjects asked about slips and relapses to drug use cite an emotional cause: loneliness and isolation, and anger in particular.

Another area rated as very difficult to deal with by nearly one half of subjects is socioeconomic (working, finding and keeping a job, having money problems). This finding is consistent with empirical data indicating that, among psychiatric clients, getting a job is the most important self-reported goal (Boykin, 1998; Sainfort et al., 1996). The importance of socioeconomic issues is not surprising, given that the majority of subjects are receiving disability benefits averaging less than $700 a month from which room, board, and services are deducted by the community residence where many subjects live. Clients new in recovery from substance abuse are often placed on money management protocols whereby the caseworker handles the client's money, providing a weekly or daily allowance as low as $1 per day. (This is done so that clients are not tempted to use their resources to purchase drugs and alcohol at a time when they are not deemed able to handle money in a responsible way.) The finding that socioeconomic problems cause great difficulty in this sample is consistent with data indicating that vocational and employment issues are the most often cited goal for the next year in this sample (mentioned by 46% of subjects). Education, including earning a GED and going to college, is a close second, cited as a goal in the next year by one third of respondents (30%). Preliminary findings from qualitative interviews conducted for this study indicate that many subjects are gradually preparing to return to work with part-time positions in their residence or program (receptionist, maintenance), odd jobs (painting apartments), vocational and educational programs and school (ranging from GED programs to college-level courses).

Obstacles to returning to work are numerous. Some subjects have never worked or have not worked in many years and lack the job skills necessary to find a job. Symptoms and medication side effects may cause cognitive impairments that compound the difficulty of finding or retaining employment. Some subjects cite difficulties coping with people and poor impulse control as major obstacles to entering or reentering the workplace. Subjects may also need training in skills other than job-related ones, such as personal habits, time management, and social and workplace relations.

The stigma of dual-diagnosis may also represent an obstacle to finding employment. Subjects were asked to indicate their degree of agreement with a series of statements about what "most people believe." Three quarters (73%) of subjects disagreed that "most people would believe that a person with a dual-diagnosis is trustworthy" and over one half (55%) disagreed that "most people will hire a person with a dual-diagnosis if he or she is qualified for the job." There is little doubt that such beliefs, likely based on personal experiences, contribute to dually diagnosed individuals' feeling shut out of the workplace and, by extension, out of the larger society. Being employed, being a productive member of society, is highly valued and often defines one's social worth beyond the workplace itself.

Recovering individuals' stated desire and self-assessed readiness to work does not always coincide with service providers' assessments. In an outcome evaluation study of a comprehensive treatment program for drug-abusing mothers in treatment (Laudet et al., 1998; Magura et al., 1999), clients reported being frustrated with the programs' qualifying requirements for educational and vocational training: programs often require a minimum of 1 year of sobriety before a client can be considered eligible for training. Clients want to progress and voice the desire to return to work as a goal relatively early in their recoveries. This may not necessarily indicate that they are truly ready to work or even that they believe themselves ready. Rather, such clients may be expressing a commitment to strive for the outcome society seems to value most—to become productive members of society. Ironically, another obstacle to returning to work may be the entitlements system itself. In a discussion of vocational rehabilitation for clients with serious and persistent mental disorders, Harding (1996) quotes a client: "Entitlements had so many disincentives to go back to work that I did not" (p. 2). Receiving entitlements has been shown to affect one's sense of self as well as the outcome of treatment and of rehabilitation (Estroff, 1997). We should note that while entitlements in the form of disability benefits (SSI, SSDI) may act as a disincentive to return to work, recent reforms in the welfare system (Workfare) are meant as an incentive for individuals to return to work.

Individuals who feel stigmatized may not perceive themselves as potentially able and competent in the workplace. Self-efficacy theory predicts that individuals will not adopt new behaviors if they believe they are likely to fail (Bandura, 1995). Because work achievement is an important basis of positive self-esteem in our society, recovering individuals tend to devalue themselves as members of conventional, wage-earning society, although they may pride themselves on their ability to hustle and survive in a hostile environment. This, in turn, may lead to demoralization, whereby the individual gives up trying (for discussion, see Harding et al., 1987), thus threatening the possibility of successful recovery, which requires commitment and difficult emotional work.

Employment and financial status go beyond the socioeconomic domain, affecting how society perceives people and how people perceive themselves; unemployment and economic problems can make people feel incompetent. Such low self-efficacy or learned helplessness are associated with low self-esteem because social norms demand individuals to be personally effective, and inability to conform is distressing (Abramson et al., 1978; Bandura, 1995). Addiction and mental disorders do vary in course and severity, but societal views of both mental disorders and drug addiction as incurable, and the low expectations of clients held by some professionals, contribute to low self-efficacy in persons who are dually diagnosed (Leete, 1989). The far-reaching psychological implications of unemployment and poverty help explain the findings that dealing with issues in the socioeconomic domain is rated as most difficult by many of these dually diagnosed individuals.

A third area rated as very difficult by nearly one half of subjects is the maintenance of sobriety ("fear of picking up"). Most subjects in this sample began using drugs and alcohol in adolescence and have used almost continuously ever since. Many have used drugs and alcohol to help deal with painful feelings (low self-esteem, past traumas, perceived social inadequacy—see earlier discussion about dealing with feelings) and have known no other life until they entered the treatment system. Now faced with a new situation (abstinence, a new lifestyle) for which they do not yet have adequate coping strategies, individuals in recovery are having to face these challenges without resorting to drugs and alcohol. Recovery is very demanding on the individual, who must deal daily with old thought patterns, triggers, demands, and requirements of the new lifestyle (including treatment programs and community residences, and 12-step fellowships). These challenges cumulate with socioeconomic and emotional issues, and sometimes physical health issues as well (many emerge from years of addiction with serious, chronic health problems). Once the individual has made the commitment to enter recovery—following counselors' and peers' advice, staying away from drugs and alcohol and "doing the right thing"—it can be demoralizing to see how slow progress is at first. Many newcomers to recovery have difficulty coming to terms with the fact that years of addiction will not be erased or "fixed" in a few months of abstinence but, rather, it will take years of arduous self-work and determination to get a new "clean" life. Such popular 12-step program sayings as "one day at a time" and "easy does it" are much more than slogans; they are constant and comforting reminders that the recovery process cannot be rushed.

It is worth noting that while dealing with sobriety is rated as very difficult by nearly one half of subjects, only one quarter of subjects rated coping with mental disorder as very difficult. Perhaps the most plausible explanation for this finding is that the majority of participants are on psychiatric medication prescribed to control symptoms; since participants have a long history of symptoms and medication, they probably have developed strategies to cope with these issues. On the other hand, achieving and maintaining abstinence from drugs, alcohol, or both causes physical and psychological symptoms—cravings, urges, drug dreams—which are more novel, so that participants may not have developed effective coping strategies.

We now turn to the areas rated very difficult to deal with by the fewest subjects: asking for help and support, being open-minded, and working a program of recovery such as the 12-step program (including accepting a Higher Power). "Asking for and accepting help and support" and "being open-minded and listening," which are both rated very difficult by one fifth of subjects, are crucial to learning coping strategies. Asking for help and listening to others also enhances social skills and helps curb feelings of isolation and alienation. That few subjects report difficulty asking for help is encouraging because it indicates that they are empowered enough to advocate for themselves when necessary, rather than feeling helpless. While this may seem inconsistent with the earlier discussion of participants' possible low self-efficacy, the latter was introduced in the context of employment, a new and foreboding challenge for many. "Asking for and accepting help and support" and "being open-minded and listening" represent an underlying openness to the outside world, which is not predicated on perceived self-competence, but rather on an attitude toward others. This openness indicates that subjects are aware of needing help and motivated to seek it. Having an open mind and listening are both signs of cognitive and emotional tolerance, whereby new or different points of view are considered rather than rejected. One of the most crucial tasks in recovery is to let go of old thought patterns and habits and to adopt new ones modeled by counselors and more experienced peers.

The area rated as very difficult to deal with by the fewest subjects centers around the 12-step recovery program, "Accepting a Higher Power" and "Following a program such as the 12-steps." Accepting a Higher Power, Step Two of the 12-steps, indicates acceptance that "a power greater than self" can and will help if sought. In other words, it indicates that the person is psychologically ready to start working on recovery. In addition to working the 12-step steps, the program also encourages members to attend meetings and form a network of peers in which the more experienced act as role models for newcomers. It may be that participants' willingness to reach out for help helps them embrace the program. That few subjects reported difficulty "Not being accepted at other 12-step groups" can be explained by their membership in DTR, a 12-step group specifically designed to meet their dual-recovery needs and where they find acceptance and respect from peers. As noted earlier, DTR members who attend other 12-step fellowships (AA/NA) do so to work on their substance abuse issues only, and those who do not attend cite feeling uncomfortable and not accepted because of their mental health and medication issues as a reason for not attending.

The finding that reaching out to others and accepting the 12-step program are the least difficult areas to deal with is of particular interest in the context of this study, which focuses on effectiveness of self-help for persons with a dual-diagnosis. It is also important because there is evidence that participation in self-help facilitates the recovery process (for comprehensive review, see Kyrouz & Humphreys, 1997). For instance, participation in self-help has been found to increase the sense of security and self-esteem of mental health clients, decrease their existential anxiety, broaden their sense of spirituality, and increase their ability to accept problems without blaming themselves or others (Kennedy, 1990); to improve alcohol use, dependence symptoms, adverse consequences, days intoxicated and depression, both at 1- and 3-year follow-up among alcoholics (Humphreys & Moos, 1996); and to foster positive perception of self, personal well-being, autonomous decision-making, improved social functioning, pursuit of educational goals and employment opportunities, and sobriety and decreased recidivism (Carpinello & Knight, 1991). Markowitz et al. (1996) found that among mental health clients, while the effects of formal services on quality of life and on self-concept were small and negative, self-help had a modest significantly positive effect on self-concept and on interpersonal satisfaction. Outcome data from this ongoing longitudinal study of the effectiveness of self-help for the dually diagnosed may elucidate the role of self-help participation as a resource to face difficult recovery challenges.

Conclusions

We have presented data about the areas dually-diagnosed individuals report as difficult to deal with in the process of recovery. The data were obtained from a sample of New York City members of a self-help group, mostly minority group subjects living on disability benefits with long histories of addiction, mental health disorder and treatment. Individuals' service and treatment needs vary according to many factors, including history of disorder and treatment, age, gender, ethnicity and cultural background, socioeconomic status, and levels of support available. According to Senay (1998, p. 191), "although it has not yet been proven by scientific study, clinical experience suggests that the more strongly the level of response to the domains of need in a patient, the better the outcome." While the primary focus of treatment programs necessary is on medical supervision and symptom control, there is clearly a need for both medical and ancillary services (including educational and vocational services) if the goal is to be long-term rehabilitation (for discussion, see Room, 1998). This article is thus a first step toward documenting clients' viewpoints, needs, and struggles. As discussed by Diamond (1998), "the next step beyond acknowledging the differences in viewpoints [between clients and providers] is to take the patients' concerns seriously." It is important to ascertain what challenges dually diagnosed clients struggle with at various points in their recovery process, and to address these issues in an integrated way in order to promote joint recovery from substance abuse and mental disorders.

References

Abramson, L. Y., Seligman, M. E. P., & Teasdale, J. D. (1978). Learned hopelessness in humans: critique and reformulation. *Journal of Abnormal Psychology, 87,* 49–74.

Bandura, A. (1995). *Self-efficiency: The exercise of control.* New York: Freeman.

Bartels, S. J., Teague, G. B., Drake, R. E., Clark, R. E., Bush, P. W., & Noordsy, D. L. (1993). Substance abuse in schizophrenia: Service utilization and costs. *Journal of Nervous and Mental Disease, 181,* 227–232.

Bergman, H. C., & Harris, M. (1985). Substance abuse among young adult chronic patients. *Psychosocial Rehabilitation Journal, 9,* 49–54.

Boykin, Q. (1998). Parting words. NYC Office of Consumer Affairs. *From the Edge* 2(1), 16.

Brooner, R. K., Bigelow, G. E., Strain, E., & Schmidt, C. W. (1990). Intravenous drug abusers with antisocial personality disorder: increased HIV risk behavior. *Drug and Alcohol Dependence, 26,* 39–44.

Carpinello, S. E., & Knight, E. L. (1991). *A qualitative study of the perceptions of the meaning of self-help by self-help group leaders, members, and significant others.* Albany: New York State Office of Mental Health, Bureau of Evaluation and Services Research.

Center for Substance Abuse Treatment. (1994). *Assessment and treatment of patients with co-existing mental illness and alcohol or other drug abuse.* Washington. DC: U.S. Department of Health and Human Services.

Diamond, R. J. (1998). *Quality of life: What do clients tell us?* Symposium abstract presented at the American Psychiatric Association 50th's Institute on Psychiatric Services, Los Angeles, CA, October 2–6.

Dixon, L., Haas, G., Weiden, P. J., Sweeney, J., & Frances, A. J. (1991). Drug abuse in schizophrenic patients: clinical correlates and reasons for use. *American Journal of Psychiatry, 148,* 224–230.

Drake, R. E., & Brunette, M. F. (1998). Complications of severe mental illness related to alcohol and drug use disorders. In M. Galanter (Ed.). *Recent developments in alcoholism, Vol. 14: The consequences of alcohol* (pp. 285–299). New York: Plenum Press.

Drake, R. E., Bartels, S. J., Teague. G. B., Noordsy, D. L., & Clark, R. E. (1993). Treatment of substance abuse in severely mentally ill patients. *Journal of Nervous and Mental Disease, 181,* 606–611.

Estroff, S. (1997). No other way to go: application for disability income among persons with severe mental illness. In R. Bonnie & J. Monahan (Eds.). *Mental disorder, work disability and the law* (pp. 87–104). Chicago: University of Chicago Press.

Gawin, F. H., & Kleber, H. D. (1985). Cocaine abuse in treatment population: patterns and diagnostic distractions. In E. H. Adams & N. J. Kozel (Eds.), Cocaine use in America: epidemiologic and clinical perspectives (pp. 182–192). *NIDA Research Monograph Series. 61.* Washington, DC: National Institute on Drug Abuse.

Greenfield, S. F., Weiss, R. D., & Tohen, M. (1996). Substance abuse and the chronically mentally ill: a description of dual diagnosis treatment services in a psychiatric hospital. *Community Mental Health Journal, 31,* 265–277.

Hagnell, O., & Grasbeck. A. (1990). Comorbidity of anxiety and depression in the Lunby 25-year prospective study: the pattern of subsequent episodes. In J. D. Maser & C. R. Cloninger (Eds.), *Comorbidity of mood and anxiety disorders* (pp. 139–152). Washington. DC: American Psychiatric Press.

Harding, C. M. (1996). *Some things we've learned about vocational rehabilitation of the seriously and persistently mentally ill.* Presented at the Boston University Colloquium, Brookline, MA, April 17.

Harding, C. M., Brooks, G. W., Ashikaga. T., Strauss, J. S., & Landerl, P. D. (1987). Aging and social functioning in once-chronic schizophrenic patients 22–62 years after first admission: the Vermont story. In N. Miller & G. D. Cohen (Eds.). *Schizophrenia and aging* (pp. 160–166). New York: Guilford Press.

Hein, D., Zimberg, S., Weissman, S., First, M., & Ackerman, S. (1993). *Dual diagnosis subtypes in urban substance abuse and mental health clinics.* Presented in part at the American Psychiatric Association 148th Annual Meeting, San Francisco, June.

Hesselbrock, M. N., Meyer, R. E., & Keener, J. J. (1985). Psychopathology in hospitalized alcoholics. *Archives of General Psychiatry, 42,* 1050–1055.

Hirschfeld, R. M. A., Hasin, D., Keller, M. B., Endicott, J., & Wunder, J. (1990). Depression and alcoholism: comorbidity in a longitudinal study. In J. D. Maser & C. R. Cloninger (Eds.), *Comorbidity of mood and anxiety disorders* (pp. 293–304). Washington. DC: American Psychiatric Press.

Humphreys, K., & Moos, R. (1996). Reduced substance abuse-related health care costs among voluntary participants of Alcoholics Anonymous. *Psychiatric Services, 47,* 709–713.

Kennedy, M. (1990). *Psychiatric hospitalizations of GROWers.* Paper presented at the Second Biennial Conference on Community Research and Action, East Lansing, MI.

Kessler, R. C. (1995). The national comorbidity survey: preliminary results and future directions. *International Journal of Methods in Psychiatric Research, 5,* 139–151.

Kleinman, P. H., Miller, A. B., & Millman. R. B. (1990). Psychopathology among cocaine abusers entering treatment. *Journal of Nervous and Mental Disease, 178,* 442–447.

Kyrouz, E., & Humphreys, K. (1997). A review of research on the effectiveness of self-help mutual aid groups. *The Mental Health Network.* Available at: http://www.cmhc.com/articles/.

Laudet, A., Magura, S., & Whitney, S. (1998). *Effectiveness of intensive services for substance-using women with cocaine-exposed infants.* Paper presented at the 24th International Congress of Applied Psychology, San Francisco, August.

Leete, E. (1989). How I perceive and manage my illness. *Schizophrenia Bulletin, 15,* 197–200.

Lehman, A. F., Myers, O. P., & Corty, E. (1989). Assessment and classification of patients with psychiatric and substance abuse syndromes. *Hospital and Community Psychiatry, 40,* 1019–1025.

Lehman, A. F., Myers, C. P., Dixon, L. B., & Johnson, J. L. (1994). Defining subgroups of dual diagnosis patients for service planning. *Hospital and Community Psychiatry, 45,* 556–561.

Magura, S., Kami, S. Y., Rosenblum, A., Handlesman, L., & Foote, J. 1998). Gender differences in psychiatric comorbidity among cocaine-using opiate addicts. *Journal of Addictive Diseases, 17*(3), 49–61.

Magura, S., Laudet. A., Kang, S. Y., & Whitney, S. (1999). Effectiveness of intensive services for crack-dependent women with newborns and young children. *Journal of Psychoactive Drugs, 31,* 321–338.

Markowitz, F., DeMasi, M., Carpinello, S., Knight, E., Videka-Sherman, L., & Sofka, C. (1996). *The role of self-help in the recovery process.* Paper presented at the 6th Annual National Conference on State Mental Health Agency Services Research and Program Evaluation. Arlington, VA.

Marks, I. M. (1990). *Mental health care delivery: innovations, impediments and implementation.* Cambridge: Cambridge University Press.

Marlowe, D. B., Husband, S. D., Lamb, R. J., Kirby, K. C., Iguchi, M. Y., & Platt, J. J. (1995). Psychiatric comorbidity in cocaine dependence. *American Journal on Addictions, 4,* 70–81.

McLellan, A. T., Luborsky, L., Woody, G. E., O'Brien, C. P., & Druley, K. (1983). Predicting response to alcohol and drug abuse treatments: Role of psychiatric severity. *Archives of General Psychiatry, 40,* 620–625.

Meyer. R. E. (1988). Conditioning phenomena and the problem of relapse in opioid addicts and alcoholics. *NIDA Research Monograph, 84,* 161–179.

Mirin, S. M., Weiss, R. D., & Michael, J. (1988). Psychopathology in substance abusers: diagnosis and treatment. *American Journal of Drug and Alcohol Abuse, 14,* 139–157.

Mueser, K. T., Belluck. A. S., & Blanchard, J. J. (1992). Comorbidity of schizophrenia and substance abuse: implications for treatment. *Journal of Consulting and Clinical Psychology, 60,* 845–856.

Murphy, J. M. (1990). Diagnostic comorbidity and symptom co-occurrence: The Stirling County Study. In J. D. Maser & C. R. Cloninger (Eds.). *Comorbidity of mood and anxiety disorders* (pp. 153–176). Washington. DC: American Psychiatric Press.

Nunes, E. V., & Deliyannides, D. A. (1993). Research issues in dual diagnosis. In J. Solomon, S. Zimber, & E. Sholler (Eds.). *Dual diagnosis* (pp. 287–309). New York: Plenum Press.

Osher, F. C., Drake, R. E., & Noordsy, D. L. (1994). Correlates and outcomes of alcohol use disorder among rural outpatients with schizophrenia. *Journal of Clinical Psychiatry, 55,* 109–113.

Osher, F. C., & Kofoed, L. L. (1989). Treatment of patients with psychiatric and psychoactive substance use disorders. *Hospital and Community Psychiatry, 40,* 1025–1030.

Post Ahrens, M. (1999). A model for dual disorder treatment in acute psychiatry in a VA population. *Journal of Substance Abuse Treatment, 15,* 107–112.

Regier, D. A., Farmer, M. E., Rae, D. S., Locke, B. Z., Keith, S. J., Judd. L. L., & Goodwin, F. K. (1990). Comorbidity of mental disorders with alcohol and other drug abuse. *Journal of the American Medical Association, 264,* 2511–2518.

Room, J. A. (1998). Work and identity in substance abuse recovery. *Journal of Substance Abuse Treatment, 15,* 65–74.

Rosenthal, R., Hellerstein, D., & Miner, C. (1992). A model of integrated services for outpatient treatment of patients with comorbid schizophrenia and addictive disorders. *American Journal of the Addictions, 1,* 339–348.

Rounsaville, B. J., Anton, S. F., & Carroll, K. (1991). Psychiatric diagnoses of treatment-seeking cocaine abusers. *Archives of General Psychiatry, 48,* 43–51.

Rounsaville, B. J., Kosten, T. R., Weissman, M. M., & Kleber, H. D. (1986). Prognostic significance of psychopathology in treated opiate addicts. *Archives of General Psychiatry, 43,* 739–745.

Rounsaville, B. J., Weissman, M. M., Kleber, H. D., & Wilber, C. (1982). Heterogeneity of psychiatric diagnosis in treated opiate addicts. *Archives of General Psychiatry, 39,* 161–166.

Rutherford, M. J., Cacciola, J. S., & Alterman, A. I. (1994). Relationships of personality disorders with problem severity in methadone patients. *Drug and Alcohol Dependence, 35,* 69–76.

Sainfort, F., Becker, M., & Diamond, R. (1996). Judgements of quality of life of individuals with severe mental disorders: patients' self-report vs. providers' perspectives. *American Journal of Psychiatry, 4,* 497–502.

Senay, E. C. (1998). *Substance abuse disorders in clinical practice.* New York: Norton.

Vogel, H., Knight. E., Laudet, A., & Magura, S. (1998). Double trouble in recovery: self-help for the dually-diagnosed. *Psychiatric Rehabilitation Journal 21,* 356–364.

Walker, R. D., Donovan, D. M., Kiivahan, D. R., & O'Leary, M. R. (1983). Length of stay, neuropsychological performance, and aftercare: influences on alcohol treatment outcome. *Journal of Consulting and Clinical Psychology, 51,* 900–911.

Weiss, R. D., Mirin, S. M., & Griffin, M. L. (1986). Psychopathology in chronic cocaine abusers. *American Journal of Drug and Alcohol Abuse, 12,* 17–29.

Westermeyer, J., & Walzer, V. (1985). Sociopathology and drug abuse in a young psychiatric population. *Diseases of the Nervous System, 36,* 673–677.

Ziedonis, D. M., & Fisher, W. (1994). Assessment and treatment of comorbid substance abuse in individuals with schizophrenia. *Psychiatric Annals 24*(9), 477–483.

Pharmacotherapy of Schizophrenia Patients with Comorbid Substance Abuse

Jeffery N. Wilkins

This article originally appeared in *Schizophrenia Bulletin,* 1997, 23(2): 215–228, and is reprinted with permission

Jeffery N. Wilkins, M.D., is Chief, Clinical Psychopharmacology Laboratory, West Los Angeles Veterans Affairs Medical Center (VAMC) Medication Development Unit, and Medical Director, Comprehensive Homeless Programs, West Los Angeles VAMC, and Professor of Psychiatry and Biobehavioral Sciences, University of California School of Medicine, Los Angeles, CA.

This study was supported by National Institutes of Health grant R01 DA-06551 and the Veterans Affairs Medication Development Unit Program from the National Institute on Drug Abuse.

Substance abuse worsens the course of schizophrenia and significantly impairs the relationship between the patient and the health care team. Recent advances in laboratory studies of substance abuse and the pharmacology of schizophrenia open up new possibilities for pharmacotherapy of substance abuse in schizophrenia patients. D_1 dopaminergic receptor agonists may directly block the drive for stimulant use. D_2 dopaminergic receptor antagonists may indirectly block the drive for stimulant and nicotine use, while opioid antagonists appear to reduce the drive to use alcohol. New generations of neuroleptics with serotonin ($5\text{-}HT_2$) receptor antagonism and/or $5\text{-}HT_{1A}$ agonist activity may reduce substance abuse in schizophrenia patients who self-medicate negative symptoms or neuroleptic side effects. Pharmacotherapy efficacy may be enhanced by adding contingency management, social skills training, and other manualized programs. Tables are provided of potentially useful medications. Preliminary results are presented of cocaine-abusing schizophrenia patients treated with desipramine and traditional neuroleptics.

This review article focuses on the pharmacotherapy of substance abuse problems in patients manifesting schizophrenia. Substance abuse, common in schizophrenia patients (Brady et al., 1991; Shaner et al., 1993; Wilkins et al., 1991), worsens the course of schizophrenia and significantly impairs the relationship between the patient and the health care team. For example, substance-induced exacerbations of psychosis result in frequent hospitalizations for some patients. Shaner et al. (1995) have described a model that outlines the contributions of substance abuse to the "revolving door" phenomenon in individuals with schizophrenia (Haywood et al., 1995). In this model, hospital admission rates for cocaine-abusing patients with schizophrenia are linked temporally with the dispensation of disability checks. When disability funds are given directly to such patients, rather than to a representative payee, the money is used to purchase cocaine. The use of cocaine exacerbates psychosis, and the patient is subsequently admitted to the hospital—psychotic and out of funds.

Substance abuse also seems to result in an earlier onset of schizophrenia (Alterman & Erdlen, 1983; Breakey et al., 1974; Weller & Weller, 1986), and amphetamine use has been linked to the development and maintenance of psychosis (Baberg et al., 1996; Flaum & Schultz, 1996). Substances of abuse may also create neuroleptic refractoriness by altering mesolimbic dopaminergic systems (Bowers et al., 1990). In addition to exacerbating psychosis, alcohol and cannabinoids seem to aggravate and hasten the appearance of tardive dyskinesia (TD) (Dixon et al., 1992; Olivera et al., 1990). Even recreational use of marijuana or alcohol may increase the severity of TD in neuroleptic-treated patients with schizophrenia (Zaretsky et al., 1993).

Recommendations regarding the pharmacotherapy of schizophrenia patients with comorbid substance abuse are derived from four sources: pharmacotherapy studies of cocaine abuse in schizophrenia patients, pharmacotherapy studies of substance abuse in patients with non-Axis I comorbid illness, advances in the pharmacotherapy of schizophrenia, and advances in the neurosciences. For example, although still in an early phase of development, the pharmacotherapy of cocaine abuse and dependence in schizophrenia patients has shown progress. Study results at two centers suggest that treatment of schizophrenia in cocaine-abusing patients may be enhanced by administering supplementary desipramine (DMI). Additional studies are progressing on the use in schizophrenia patients of supplementary selegiline, a monoamine oxidase (MAO) type B inhibitor, flupenthixol, a dopamine (DA) D_2 autoreceptor and postsynaptic blocker, mazindol (Berger et al., 1989), a partial DA agonist, and the DA agonist bromocriptine. With support from the National Institute on Drug Abuse Medication Development Division, levo-alpha-acetylmethadol (LAAM), a long-acting opioid maintenance medication, and naltrexone, an opioid antagonist, have recently been approved by the Food and Drug Administration (FDA) for relapse prevention treatment of opioids and alcohol. Lists are provided of medications that may serve as useful pharmacotherapy adjuncts in the treatment of substance-abusing individuals with schizophrenia. Some of these medications have already been approved for administration to schizophrenia patients as antipsychotic or extrapyramidal symptom (EPS) reducing agents or have been administered to them as part of clinical studies. Others are medications approved for treatment of mental health or medical illness but are under evaluation for treatment of substance abuse. Progress attained in the pharmacotherapy of schizophrenia may also contribute to the pharmacotherapy of substance abuse in schizophrenia patients. Novel neuroleptics, including clozapine and risperidone, may reduce the drive to self-medicate the negative symptoms of schizophrenia or neuroleptic-induced side effects with substances of abuse. Adjunctive medications that target neuroleptic-induced side effects may have the same effect. In addition, new classes of agents are being discovered through basic research with the N-methyl-D-aspartate receptor complex, the gamma-aminobutyric acid system, and the DA, opiate, and other neurotransmitter transporter and receptor systems.

Pharmacotherapy Trials of Cocaine Abuse and Dependence in Schizophrenia Patients

In the main, pharmacotherapy of cocaine abuse or dependence has targeted dopaminergic receptor systems within the brain's reinforcement centers (reviewed by Kosten 1992). Recent animal research supports this approach. Self et al. (1996) have demonstrated that D_1-like agonists prevented cocaine-seeking behavior in rats that had already received priming doses of cocaine, while D_2-like agonists increased cocaine-seeking behavior.

Discussed below are the results of an open trial and a placebo controlled, double-blind trial of DMI, a tricyclic antidepressant that blocks dopamine reuptake, administered to persons who manifested cocaine abuse and schizophrenia or schizoaffective disorder.

DMI

Cocaine-dependent individuals without schizophrenia have been shown to reliably reduce ratings of craving and improve ratings of depression when administered DMI (Gawin & Ellinwood, 1988). Although further study has failed to demonstrate DMI-produced abstinence from cocaine (Arndt et al., 1992), recent studies suggest that it may be effective in special populations, such as methadone-maintained cocaine users (Kosten et al., 1992). In a 12-week open design study, Ziedonis et al. (1992) compared 12 cocaine-abusing schizophrenia patients treated with 100 to 150 mg of DMI and antipsychotic agents with 15 such patients treated with antipsychotic agents alone. The patients all received social skills training (Liberman et al., 1989) and were given lower dosages of DMI than usual because its metabolism is altered when used in combination with neuroleptics (Ziedonis et al., 1992). Patients receiving DMI were more likely to complete the study (83% vs. 60%), had fewer cocaine-positive urinalyses during the last 6 weeks of the study (20% vs. 50%, 10% vs. 56% during the last month), and had higher 6-week (58% vs. 33%) and 4-week abstinence rates (75% vs. 53%). Treatment retention was greater in the DMI group than in the no-DMI group (83% vs. 60%), and overall psychiatric symptoms and signs were reduced. Ziedonis et al. (1996) have extended this work by comparing DMI efficacy with the MAO type B inhibitor selegiline. Selegiline indirectly elevates DA levels and may decrease cocaine cravings and negative symptoms of schizophrenia. This 12-week open-label study compared cocaine-abusing schizophrenia patients treated with selegiline (5 to 10 mg, $n = 13$), DMI (100 to 150 mg, $n = 12$), or no medication (NOMED; $n = 15$). Subjects receiving DMI had significantly better outcomes than those in the selegiline and NOMED groups. For example, 83 percent of the DMI group completed the study compared with 53 percent of NOMED and 46 percent of selegiline subjects.

DMI has also been administered in a randomized, double-blind design over 12 weeks to 80 patients with cocaine abuse or dependence and schizophrenia or schizoaffective disorder as determined by the Structured Clinical Interview for *DSM-III-R* ratings (SCID, Spitzer et al., 1988; Wilkins et al., 1996). The patients were recruited following hospitalization for acute psychosis, received DMI for the first 3 weeks as inpatients, and were then followed for 15 months as outpatients. Before receiving the study medication, the participants were stabilized on neuroleptics. The dose of DMI was titrated upward with yoked adjustments aimed at achieving steady-state plasma levels between 175 and 250 ng/ml. DMI blood levels were performed during the 12 weeks of medication and 3 additional weeks to monitor washout of the medication.

The study was conducted as an affiliate investigation of the Clinical Research Center for Schizophrenia and Psychiatric

Rehabilitation. The study staff were trained through the Schizophrenia Clinical Research Center with regular determinations of kappa inter-rater reliability. All new study assessment staff received the same training before conducting assessments. After assessments to confirm schizophrenia and cocaine dependence by the SCID, assessments were conducted of current psychopathology (Brief Psychiatric Rating Scale [BPRS, Overall & Gorham, 1962], Beck Depression Inventory [BDI, Beck et al., 1961], Hamilton Anxiety Scale [Hamilton, 1959], Scales for Assessment of Negative and Positive Symptoms [SANS & SAPS; Andreasen, 1984a, 1984b]), medical condition (history and physical exam, blood and urine tests, electrocardiogram, and characteristics of recent drug use and psychosocial functioning [Addiction Severity Index, McLellan et al. 1980]). Assessments also focused on whether medication effects persisted once the medication was stopped and whether baseline subject characteristics predicted outcome (Wilkins et al., 1993).

Eighty-seven study participants were entered into the study, 80 received study medication. Seventy-three study participants (91% of all subjects) received study medication for at least 2 weeks, and 50 subjects (63%) completed study medication. Analysis of urine levels of the cocaine metabolite benzoylecgonine (BE) revealed an apparent treatment effect during study weeks 10 to 26 ($p = 0.035$, general estimated equation). Between weeks 10 and 26, a median of 47 patients (60% of subjects) were evaluated 11 times (weeks 10 to 19 and week 26). Semiquantitative urine levels of BE were higher in the placebo group in 10 of the 11 visits between weeks 10 and 26: They were more than three times as high at weeks 10 and 11, more than four times as high at week 17, and more than nine times as high at weeks 19 and 26. Consistent with this finding, Student t-tests revealed significant or near significant medication group differences at study weeks 11 ($p = 0.07$), 17 ($p = 0.05$), 19 ($p = 0.06$), and 26 ($p = 0.03$). (See figures 1 and 2.) Although not statistically significant when compared with the placebo group, the DMI group had twice the number of negative urinalyses at weeks 16 and 17 and 1.5 times as many at weeks 18 and 19. There was no difference in retention between the two medication groups. In addition, there was an interaction between a current visit's log BE and the total BDI score at the same visit ($p = 0.0001$) and at the prior visit ($p = 0.0113$), and between a current visit's log BE and the BPRS negative symptom subscale for each of the two prior visits ($p = 0.0219$ and $p = 0.0180$, respectively) (Wilkins et al., 1993).

Figure 1
Mean quantitative urine levels of the cocaine metabolite benzoylecgonine (all visits)

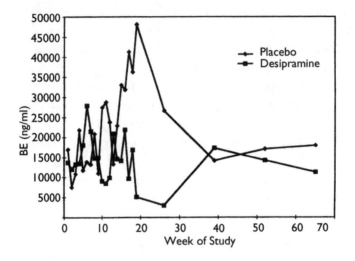

Figure 2
Percent of study participants with negative urinalyses

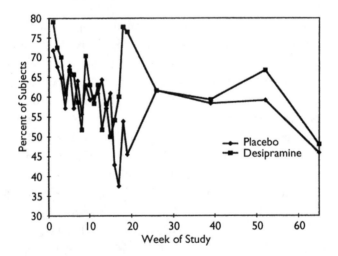

These preliminary results suggest that cocaine-abusing schizophrenia patients receiving DMI for 12 weeks used less cocaine in a 15-month period than schizophrenia patients who received placebo medication. This decrease in frequency and amount of cocaine use occurred between weeks 10 and 26. The timing of this apparent effect is of interest, since it extended for almost 2 months after the medication was discontinued. Investigation is under way to identify individual characteristics of those patients, including their steady state and washout DMI blood levels, who best responded to DMI. Particular focus will be on those study participants who manifested any negative urinalyses during weeks 10 to 26 (Wilkins et al., 1993).

In a preliminary study drawn from the above population, Pearson correlation coefficients from 29 of the patients with urines positive for cocaine and for cocaine and marijuana were characterized as manifesting either "positive" or "negative" correlation between urine values and the BPRS, BDI, and SANS scores. Almost all subjects in the cocaine only, but not the cocaine and marijuana group, had positive correlation with the BDI total depression score (12 positive, 1 negative vs. 6 positive, 8 negative, Fisher's statistic = 7.334, p = 0.013). A similar but inverse relationship was found with the BPRS negative symptom subscale (2 positive, 11 negative vs. 7 positive, 7 negative, Fisher's statistic = 3.483, p = 0. 103). Conversely, the cocaine only and cocaine and marijuana groups had similar positive correlation with the BPRS hostility/suspiciousness subscale (11 positive and 4 negative, 10 positive and 4 negative, Student t = 2.81, p = 0.009). The provisional conclusion from these results was that cocaine produces depression in schizophrenia patients but may reduce negative symptoms; cocaine and cocaine plus marijuana induce hostility and suspiciousness, but concomitant marijuana use prevents cocaine-induced depression. Therefore, patients who develop depression secondary to cocaine use may alleviate some of this depression with marijuana use. In addition, stimulation of the marijuana receptor may ameliorate depression, even in patients with depleted brain catecholamines.

Imipramine (IMI) and Flupenthixol

In parallel with the above studies, Siris et al. (1993) extended prior work with IMI treatment of postpsychotic depression (Siris et al., 1988a, 1988b) by administering IMI in an open design to schizophrenia subjects with substance abuse problems. Four of 11 patients receiving IMI were reported to have improved significantly, and none worsened in signs or symptoms of schizophrenia while receiving IMI. Flupenthixol, a depot or orally administered thioxanthene derivative combining DA type 2 (D_2) pre- and post-synaptic receptor blockade has been evaluated in an open-label trial by Levin et al. (submitted for publication) for the treatment of cocaine-abusing schizophrenia patients. Preliminary results in the 4-week inpatient, 6-week outpatient study of eight individuals administered 40 mg of flupenthixol every 2 weeks demonstrate increases in cocaine-negative urinalyses and clinic visits, and decreases in negative symptoms and BDI scores.

Pharmacological Advances in the Pharmacotherapy of Substance Abuse in Patients Without Schizophrenia

Various forms of substance abuse pharmacotherapy recommended for patients without schizophrenia (American Psychiatric Association, 1995) may be applicable to schizophrenia patients. For example, naltrexone, a long-acting opioid antagonist, was recently approved by the FDA for adjunctive pharmacotherapy in the treatment of relapse prevention in alcoholics. Opioid agonists and antagonists have been used experimentally in individuals with schizophrenia since the discovery of beta-endorphin and the enkephalins almost 20 years ago (reviewed by Marchesi et al., 1992; Welsh & Thompson, 1994). Similarly, the use of benzodiazepines for sedative-hypnotic withdrawal does not seem to be contraindicated in schizophrenia patients since these agents are recommended for treatment of their EPS (reviewed by Wolkowitz & Pickar, 1991).

Tables 1 and 2 list substances that are being evaluated or are under consideration for treatment of substance abuse (reviewed by Ling & Shoptaw, in press). Table 1 lists medications that are approved for the treatment of schizophrenia or that have already been involved in clinical studies with schizophrenia patients. Table 2 lists medications that are approved for the treatment of mental health or medical conditions other than substance abuse, but that are under evaluation or being considered for substance abuse treatment. Clinicians treating schizophrenia patients should use these medications for treatment of substance abuse only after reviewing FDA guidelines for administering substances for non-approved indications. Of clear concern is the risk of medication interactions (e.g., adjunctive medications taken to reduce substance use that alter neuroleptic levels or biological activity) or pharmacological interactions with abused substances. In addition, contingency management, demonstrated to be a powerful tool in diminishing cocaine use by schizophrenia patients (Shaner et al., in press) and nonschizophrenia patients (Higgins et al., 1994), along with social skills training (Liberman & Corrigan, 1993) should be considered important adjuncts to pharmacotherapy.

Table I

Medications already used in treatment and clinical research of schizophrenia that may also assist in treatment of substance abuse (SA)

Medication	Traditional Use	SA Mechanism of Action	SA Desired Pharmacological Effect
Amantadine	Alleviate EPS	DA agonist	Stimulant relapse prevention
Benzodiazepines	Alleviate EPS	GABA antagonist	Alcohol, opioid detoxification
Bromocriptine	Reduce hyperprolactinemia	D_2 agonist	Stimulant relapse prevention
Carbamazepine	Treat bipolar illness	Anticonvulsant	Stimulant, alcohol relapse prevention
Dextroamphetamine	Reduce negative symptoms	Sympathomimetic amine	Stimulant relapse prevention
Desipramine	Prevent cocaine relapse	DA, NE reuptake inhibitor	Stimulant relapse prevention
Disulfiram	Prevent alcohol relapse	Aldehydre dehydrogenase inhibitor	Alcohol relapse prevention
Flupenthixol	Antipsychotic, antidepressant	Autoreceptor/postsynaptic, DA antagonist	Cocaine relapse prevention
Mazindol	Anorectic	DA antagonist	Stimulant relapse prevention
Risperidone	Antipsychotic	D_2 and 5-HT_2 antagonist	Stimulant relapse prevention
Selegiline	Anti-Parkinson's disease	MAOI-B	Stimulant relapse prevention
Tiapride	Antipsychotic	D_2 antagonist	Alcohol relapse prevention

Note. EPS = extrapyramidal symptoms; DA = dopamine, GABA = gamma-aminobutyric acid, NE = norepinephrine; D_2 = dopamine type 2:5-HT_2 = serotonin-2; MAOI-B = monamine oxidase type B inhibitor.

Self-Medication as a Target for Pharmacotherapy

Traditional pharmacological treatment of substance abuse problems can be divided into seven configurations: (1) agonists to substitute for the substance during detoxification or maintenance (e.g., opioid or nicotine replacement); (2) antagonists (e.g., naloxone, naltrexone); (3) aversive agents (e.g., disulfiram); (4) anticraving agents; (5) antidrug-seeking agents (other than anticraving); (6) agents for comorbid psychiatric problems (either drug-induced or drug-independent); and (7) agents for comorbid medical problems (either drug-induced or drug-independent). Two additional areas may be appropriate for the pharmacotherapy of individuals with schizophrenia who have substance abuse problems: agents targeting negative symptoms and neuroleptic side effects that target the central nervous system receptor mechanisms underlying both schizophrenia and substance abuse.

The coexistence of substance abuse and diminished substance abuse has led many investigators to propose that a major motivation for substance abuse in schizophrenia patients is self-medication of negative symptoms (Schneier & Siris, 1987), neuroleptic-induced EPS (Knudsen & Vilmar, 1984; Miller & Tanenbaum, 1989; Treffert, 1978) or depression (Freed 1975; Siris et al., 1993). Because substance-abusing patients manifest less psychopathology than non-substance-abusing patients (Dixon et al., 1991; Mueser et al., 1990), it has been proposed that drug abuse is a behavior that requires higher function and that drug abuse may complicate a less severe case of schizophrenia. For example, in a study of 83 psychotic inpatients, approximately half of whom were substance abusers, the 41 patients who did abuse substances had less overall psychopathology (per the Global Assessment Scale [Endicott et al., 1976], BPRS, and negative symptom measures) at discharge from inpatient status, yet over the outpatient stabilization phase did no better than the non-substance-abusing patients (Dixon et al., 1991). A recent review of prevalence studies of stimulant abuse in schizophrenia patients (LeDuc & Mittleman, 1995) proposed that the primary reason for the increased presence of stimulant use by schizophrenia patients, as compared with other diagnostic groups, is self-medication to overcome neuroleptic-associated symptoms.

Stimulant Abuse

Stimulant use, which often arises as a form of self-medication to reduce negative symptoms, has also been shown to increase depression

(Serper et al., 1995; Sevy et al., 1990; Wilkins et al., 1993). Consistent with these findings, van Kammen and Boronow (1988) observed attenuation of negative symptoms in schizophrenia patients receiving intravenous dextro-amphetamine. In the study by Serper and colleagues, 15 cocaine-abusing and 22 cocaine-abstaining patients were evaluated within hours of their last cocaine use and between days 21 and 30 of inpatient admission. The schizophrenia patients using cocaine were found to have fewer negative symptoms on the Abnormal Involuntary Movement Scale (AIMS) (Guy, 1976) and increased anxiety/depression as measured by the BPRS. The significant difference in negative signs and mood symptoms at admission was attributed to the neurobiological impact of cocaine. In an earlier study (Brady et al., 1990), 17 male cocaine-abusing schizophrenia patients reported using cocaine to elevate their mood. After 1 year these patients were hospitalized more frequently, were more likely to have a diagnosis of the paranoid subtype, and were more likely to be depressed at the time of interview than the group that did not use cocaine. There was also a trend toward higher AIMS scores in the cocaine-abusing group (4.3 compared with 2.8 for nonabusers), suggesting that chronic cocaine use may produce a supersensitivity of DA receptors, which could then potentiate the neuroleptic-induced supersensitivity that some investigators think is responsible for TD.

Cannabinoids

The effects of marijuana on positive and negative symptoms of schizophrenia were studied by Peralta and Cuesta (1995). Marijuana-abusing individuals with schizophrenia ($n = 23$) scored significantly lower on the alogia subscale of the SANS than nonabusers, ($n = 72$) did, suggesting that schizophrenia patients may use marijuana to self-medicate negative symptoms. In an earlier study (Knudsen & Vilmar, 1984), 7 of 10 cannabis-using schizophrenia patients described initial experiences as feeling "inspired," "relaxed," "energized," or "active" and subsequent experiences of feeling "bad" or "aggressive." This finding is consistent with a survey in which 69 of 76 schizophrenia patients who used cannabis reported adverse psychic effects due to cannabis use (Negrete et al., 1986). In addition, marijuana use may accelerate the onset of schizophrenia or exacerbate a current episode (Andreasson et al., 1987). For example, in this study (Andreasson et al., 1987) the risk factors in marijuana users for development of schizophrenia were greater than those of nonusers by a factor of 4.

Table 2

Medications already used to treat mental health and medical illness that may also assist in treatment of schizophrenia patients with substance abuse (SA) problems

Medication	SA Mechanism of Action	Non-SA Traditional Clinical Use
Cocaine treatment		
Amoxapine	DA agonist, NE and 5-HT reuptake inhibitor	Antidepressant
Baclofen	GABAb antagonist	Antispasm
Bupropion	DA transporter inhibitor	Antidepressant
Butylcholinesterase	Increases metabolism of cocaine	Metabolic induction
Carbidopa/levodopa	DA precursor	Anti-Parkinson's disease
Ergoloid mesylates	D_1, D_2 partial agonist	Cognitive enhancer
Fenfluramine	Increases 5-HT turnover	Anorectic
Fluoxetine	SSRI	Antidepressant
GBR-12909	DA transporter inhibitor	Antidepressant, anti-Parkinson's disease
Lamotrigine	Sodium channel blocker	Anticonvulsant
Lisuride	DA partial agonist, 5-HT antagonist	Anti-Parkinson's disease
Methylphenidate	CNS stimulant	ADHD
Naltrexone	Mu opioid antagonist	Opioid, alcohol relapse prevention
Nefazodone	NE antagonist, $5\text{-}HT_2$ antagonist	Antidepressant
Pemoline	CNS stimulant	ADHD
Pergolide	D_1, D_2 agonist	ADHD
Alcoholism treatment		
Calcium acetylhomotaruinate	Analog of GABA	
Citalopram	SSRI	
Clonidine	Alpha-2-adrenergic agonist	Antihypertensive
Fluoxetine	SSRI	Antidepressant
(continued)		

Table 2 *(continued)*

Medication	SA Mechanism of Action	Non-SA Traditional Clinical Use
Alcoholism treatment *(continued)*		
Lofexidine	Alpha-2-adrenergic agonist	Antihypertensive
Naltrexone	Mu opioid antagonist	Opioid relapse prevention
Ondansetron	5-HT$_3$ antagonist	Antiemetic
Phenobarbital	CNS depressant	Anticonvulsant
Phenytoin	Sodium channel blocker	Anticonvulsant
Opiates/opioid treatment maintenance		
Buprenorphine	Mu opioid agonist	Under review by FDA
Buprenorphine/naloxone	Mu opioid agonist/antagonist	Under review by FDA
LAAM	Mu opioid agonist	1995 FDA approval
Methadone	Mu opioid agonist	Most common form of detoxification and maintenance
Others		
Captopril	ACE inhibitor	Antihypertensive
Dextromethorphan	NMDA receptor antagonist	Antitussive
Lofexidine	Alpha-2-adrenergic agonist	Antihypertensive
Memantine	NMDA receptor antagonist	None
Naltrexone	Mu opioid antagonist	
Nimodipine	Calcium channel antagonist	Antistroke

Note. DA = dopamine; NE = norepinephrine; 5-HT = serotonin; GABA = gamma aminobutyric acid; D$_2$ - dopamine type I; D$_2$ = dopamine type 2; SSRI selective serotonin reuptake inhibitor; CNS = central nervous system; ADHD = attention deficit hyperactivity disorder; FDA = Food and Drug Administration; ACE = angiotensin converting enzyme; NMDA = N-methyl-D-aspartic acid; LAAM = levo-alpha-acetylmethadol.

In a study of 93 relatively young patients consecutively admitted to the hospital with recent-onset schizophrenia—of whom 24 (26%) tested positive for cannabis—patients were assessed at baseline and at a 1-year followup visit (Linszen et al., 1994). The authors reported significantly more and earlier psychotic relapses in the cannabis-abusing group. This association became stronger when mild and heavy abuse were distinguished. In all but one patient, cannabis abuse preceded the onset of the first psychotic symptoms for the 1-year period of study. The authors concluded that cannabis abuse, particularly heavy abuse, can be considered a stressor eliciting relapse in patients with schizophrenia and related disorders and possibly may be a premorbid precipitant; they also reported that the results were not confounded by exposure to alcohol or any other psychoactive drugs, nor by differences in antipsychotic medication compliance and dosage.

Although two medications—L-tryptophan and SAAVE, a proprietary supplement made up of amino acid precursors of DA and serotonin (5-HT)—have been recommended for treatment of withdrawal symptoms from cannabinoids (Zweben & O'Connell, 1992), there is no controlled research to support their efficacy.

Nicotine

Over 90% of schizophrenia patients receiving inpatient treatment in an urban medical center were found to smoke cigarettes (Gritz et al., 1985). Schizophrenia patients who smoke have been reported to normalize schizophrenia-associated auditory dysfunction (Adler et al., 1993) as well as manifest significantly less neuroleptic-induced Parkinsonism, and a trend for diminished TD as measured by the AIMS (Goff et al., 1992). These findings reflect the central nervous system actions of nicotine coupled with nicotine's ability to induce hepatic microsomal metabolism of neuroleptics (reviewed by Ziedonis & George, 1997). Consistent with the metabolic findings, individuals with schizophrenia who smoke have been reported to receive significantly higher doses of neuroleptics (Leon et al., 1995).

In a study of 265 outpatients with schizophrenia ($n = 182$) or schizoaffective disorder ($n = 83$) (Ziedonis et al., 1994), smokers had an earlier onset of schizophrenia (age 24) than nonsmokers (age 28), had more positive symptoms of schizophrenia (heavy smokers: 9.1; light smokers: 5.5; nonsmokers: 4.3), and were prescribed higher levels of neuroleptic medication (590 mg of chlorpromazine for smokers vs. 375

mg for nonsmokers). As might be anticipated from the findings with individuals with schizophrenia who use cocaine or amphetamines, the heavy smokers also had less negative symptoms (5.9 compared with 7.0 for light smokers and 7.2 for nonsmokers).

Regarding treatment, schizophrenia patients wearing a nicotine-containing skin patch have been found to smoke significantly less than when wearing a placebo patch (Hartman et al., 1991). (The use of the nicotine patch has been summarized by the American Psychiatric Association, 1996.) Patients successfully treated with the patch will likely require a lowering of neuroleptic dose as they smoke less. Interestingly, traditional neuroleptics have been found to diminish cigarette smoking in non-schizophrenia patients (Caskey et al., in press).

Caffeine

Schizophrenia patients may ingest coffee as a form of self-medication but with attendant risks. For example, Hyde (1990) has demonstrated that there are subgroups of schizophrenia patients who require increasing doses of neuroleptic to "cover" coffee effects.

The pharmacological treatment of choice for individuals wishings to stop or attenuate caffeine use is a rapidly tapering regimen of caffeine; as yet there is no viable pharmacological substitute to offset caffeine withdrawal and diminish caffeine craving (Greden & Walters, 1992). The rationale for this approach is empirical, with support from the demonstration that coffee drinkers, after a week of drinking decaffeinated coffee, had no preference for caffeinated over decaffeinated coffee (Griffiths et al., 1986). Based on this approach, an individual who drinks six cups of coffee per day could be placed on the following 6-day tapering regimen: first day—five cups caffeinated coffee/one cup decaffeinated, second day—four cups caffeinated coffee/two cups decaffeinated, and so forth to the sixth day—no cups caffeinated coffee/six cups decaffeinated. The recommendation is detoxification to complete abstinence, since abstinence seems to be more effective in preventing relapse than reduction (Greden & Walters, 1992). Caffeine pills may be substituted, especially for those with severe caffeine dependence of 1 gram per day or more than eight cups of coffee per day. Treatment should also include education about the adverse consequences of chronic caffeine use and the various products and medications that contain caffeine. By having water and perhaps some sugarless mints readily available, the client may be better prepared to manage and alleviate craving.

Alcohol

Studies of the DA metabolite homovanillic acid (HVA) in individuals with schizophrenia should control for the use of alcohol because low HVA levels have been found in male alcoholics who have been abstinent for 3 weeks (Fulton et al., 1995). These findings also suggest that agents altering dopaminergic systems may prove useful in the treatment of schizophrenia patients who abuse alcohol.

While disufiram has been used extensively with patients manifesting schizophrenia, naltrexone may also be useful for this population. Recently approved by FDA for alcohol relapse prevention, naltrexone may help schizophrenia patients who have attained abstinence from alcohol. The FDA approval was based largely on studies from Volpicelli and colleagues (1992) at the Philadelphia Veterans Affairs Medical Center substance abuse programs and O'Malley and colleagues (1992) at the Yale substance abuse programs. Volpicelli et al. (1992) demonstrated in a double-blind study of 70 alcohol-dependent–only subjects that those who received naltrexone had significantly fewer cravings and a significantly lower rate of relapse than those who received the placebo. In addition, naltrexone treatment had no effect on psychopathological condition as assessed by the BPRS and the Hopkins Symptom Checklist–90 (Derogatis et al., 1973; SCL-90). Furthermore, naltrexone, as compared to placebo, significantly decreased the relapse rate for drinking once an individual had "slipped" (consumed any alcohol). In another study assessing the effects of naltrexone and coping skills or supportive therapy versus only coping skills or only supportive therapy, relapse rates for those receiving the medication plus therapy were again significantly lower than those receiving therapy only (O'Malley et al., 1992). The authors concluded that naltrexone was significantly superior to placebo, regardless of therapy received, on several treatment variables, including number of drinks consumed, abstinence and relapse rates, and problem severity as measured by the Addiction Severity Index on alcohol, drug, and employment problems.

Although there were early reports that the use of disulfiram is correlated with psychosis (Liddon & Satran, 1967), within narrow limits, it has been demonstrated to be effective and safe in schizophrenia patients (Kofoed et. al., 1986). The narrow limits are imposed due to disulfiram's apparent ability to increase central nervous system levels of DA, possibly through its blockage of DA beta hydroxylase, the enzyme that catalyzes the conversion of DA to norepinephrine. Kingsbury and Salzman (1990) noted that patients at least 40 years old and able to remain in psychiatric treatment despite a long history of alcohol abuse seem to be good candidates for treatment with disulfiram. Patients should not be acutely psychotic; should not have signs of organic mental impairment, depression, or impulsive behavior; and should be legally competent and able to give informed consent. They should also have demonstrated compliance with other medications and should be in a stable treatment program. The typical recommended daily dose is 250 to 500 mg, but lower doses seem to have fewer side effects. Disulfiram may interact with other drugs taken by individuals with schizophrenia because it increases the metabolism of neuroleptics. The authors note the absolute contraindication of pregnancy and relative contraindications of myocardial disease, liver disease, chronic renal failure, pulmonary insufficiency, and asthma.

Kofoed et al. (1986) reported the successful use of disulfiram with schizophrenia patients (reviewed by Galanter et al., 1988). Thirty-two patients with coexisting substance abuse and other psychiatric disorders were treated in an outpatient pilot program that used techniques drawn from both psychiatric and substances abuse treatment. Eleven patients remained in treatment for 3 or more months, and 7 completed a year or more of treatment. (Specific pharmacotherapies were not the main focus of this article, but a few important results involving disulfiram can be found in table 2.) No complications were reported in routine disulfiram administration to the dually diagnosed population. Overall disulfiram compliance rates and individual patterns of compliance were reported to be almost identical to those reported in alcoholics without other psychiatric illness.

Contributions to the Pharmacotherapy of Substance Abuse Arising from Advances in the Medication Treatment of Schizophrenia

Neuroleptics or other pharmacological agents that improve negative symptoms, target impaired affect (Hogarty et al., 1995), or reduce traditional neuroleptic side effects may reduce the drive for self-medication. For example, a reliable association has been made between use of traditional neuroleptics and stimulant abuse in schizophrenia patients (LeDuc & Mittleman, 1995).

Recent neuroscientific evidence strongly suggests that the DA receptor (D_1) is the primary receptor for reinforcement of cocaine and other substances of abuse. Thus, the ideal medication for pharmacotherapy of a stimulant-abusing schizophrenia patient would lessen negative symptoms while simultaneously targeting both the D_1 (reducing the drive to use cocaine) and D_2 receptors, the latter being largely responsible for the positive symptoms of schizophrenia. Clozapine seems to be the prototype for this ideal agent. It has D_1 blocking activity, with minimal D_2 blocking supplemented by blockade of serotonin-2 ($5\text{-}HT_2$) receptors. Clozapine has been shown to improve negative symptoms (Nordstrom et al., 1995) and thus may reduce the drive to self-medicate with substances of abuse. Although clozapine's ability to treat substance abuse requires further study, Buckley et al. (1994a, 1994b) have demonstrated that substance abusers and nonabusers showed similar improvements on measures of psychopathology and psychosocial functioning after 6 months of clozapine therapy. Two other neuroleptics that share mixed $5\text{-}HT_2/D_2$ antagonism are risperidone and remoxipride. Risperidone has been shown to inhibit phencyclidine (PCP)-induced stereotyped behaviors in rats in comparison with haloperidol and ritanserin, but with DA metabolite levels demonstrating less D_2 activity than haloperidol. Flupenthixol, a medication that may reduce cocaine craving (Gawin et al., 1989), balances D_1 with D_2 activity (Soyka & Sand, 1995).

The 5-HT system inhibits doparninergic function at the level of the origin of the DA system in the midbrain, as well as in the terminal doparninergic fields in the forebrain (Kapur & Remington, 1996). Serotonergic antagonists release the DA system from this inhibition. This disinhibition may alleviate neuroleptic-induced EPS, and a similar disinhibition in the prefrontal cortex may ameliorate negative symptoms. Serotonergic modulation of dopaminergic function is a viable mechanism to be explored for enhancing therapeutics in schizophrenia patients. There is evidence for a clear role for $5\text{-}HT_3$ receptors in the modulation of activity of mesolimbic and mesocortical DA neurons. Antagonists to the $5\text{-}HT_3$ receptor may have potential as novel antipsychotic agents and in treating psychoactive substance abuse (Hagan et al., 1993). They may prove to be among the first agents available to treat schizophrenia that are not D_2 antagonists and hence lack their side effects.

Although prior studies have failed to demonstrate the efficacy of neuroleptics in treating cocaine abuse in humans (Gawin, 1986), a recent study by Berger et al. (1996) illustrates the potential importance of blocking DA receptors for attenuating the physiological and neuroendocrine effects of cocaine-related cues. Reexposure to environmental cues (e.g., pharmaceutical aromas or money) associated with cocaine use can trigger craving and drug-seeking behavior. This craving may persist long after the period of initial drug abstinence (Gawin & Kleber, 1986), thereby increasing the risk of relapse (Childress et al., 1992). In a study evaluating the role of DA release by such cues, 20 male cocaine-dependent, veteran inpatients were randomized in a single-dose, crossover, placebo-controlled design to haloperidol (4 mg by mouth) and placebo (Berger et al., 1996). Plasma HVA, the principal DA metabolite, adrenocorticotrophic hormone (ACTH), and cortisol were assayed before and after cue (videotape) exposure. Craving and anxiety were also measured before and after cue exposure with visual analog scales. Cocaine cues significantly increased levels of anxiety, ACTH, cortisol, and HVA. Increases in anxiety and craving were significantly antagonized by pretreatment with haloperidol. Although the side effect profile of haloperidol makes it unlikely to be of value in patients who do *not* have schizophrenia and, for that matter, creates problems in schizophrenia patients, the cocaine cue-reactivity model may illustrate a mechanism relevant to the pharmacotherapy of stimulants and other drugs of abuse. Shorter-acting, better-tolerated DA antagonists or drugs that inhibit DA release may merit attention.

Adding anticholinergic medication, especially in the acute phase of psychosis (Tandon & DeQuardo, 1995, referring to Goff et al., 1995), seems to lessen negative symptoms significantly (Garcia, 1991). The addition of D-cycloserine to conventional neuroleptics seems to improve negative symptoms in schizophrenia patients for whom these symptoms are dominant (Goff et al., 1995). At a dose of 50 mg/day, D-cycloserine reportedly produced reductions in negative symptoms, and improved reaction times. In this preliminary study, the authors concluded that D-cycloserine may improve negative symptoms and cognitive deficits over a narrow dose range when added to conventional antipsychotic agents. As discussed in the following sections, reduction of negative symptoms may lessen the drive for self-medication with substances of abuse by schizophrenia patients.

Summary

Five themes have been discussed in this review: (1) The phenomenology of schizophrenia influences the patient's choice of substance, timing and amount used, and motivation for substance abuse treatment. (2) Schizophrenia patients use stimulants (cocaine, amphetamine, caffeine), cannabinoids, nicotine, and alcohol, partly to self-medicate the negative symptoms of schizophrenia or adverse experiences of neuroleptic treatment. (3) Self-medication with substances of abuse is only transiently effective, with subsequent development of untoward results, including depression, anxiety, and worsening of positive symptoms. (4) To be optimally successful, pharmacotherapy of schizophrenia patients with substance abuse problems must be combined with manual-based psychosocial strategies including contingency management of disability funds and social skills training. For example, contingency management of disability monies through the use of payees could be performed in concert with pharmacotherapy aimed at reducing substance abuse. (5) Pharmacotherapy with D_1 DA receptor agonists and partial D_2 DA receptor blockade may reduce the drive to use stimulants and nicotine, and the use of neuroleptics with $5\text{-}HT_2$ receptor antagonism or $5\text{-}HT_{1A}$ agonist activity may reduce substance abuse in schizophrenia patients who self-medicate.

References

Adler, L.E., Hoffer, L.D., Wiser, A., & Freedman, R. (1993). Normalization of auditory physiology by cigarette smoking in schizophrenic patients. *American Journal of Psychiatry, 150,* 1856–1861.

Alterman, A.I., & Erdlen, D.L. (1983). Illicit substance use in hospitalized psychiatric patients: Clinical observations. *Journal of Psychiatric Treatment and Evaluation, 5,* 377–380.

American Psychiatric Association. (1995). Practice guidelines for the treatment of patients with substance use disorders: Alcohol, cocaine, opioids. *American Journal of Psychiatry, 152(Suppl. 11),* 4–59.

American Psychiatric Association. (1996). Practice guidelines for the treatment of patients with nicotine dependence. *American Journal of Psychiatry, 153(Suppl. 10),* 1–31.

Andreasen, N.C. (1984a). *The Scale for the Assessment of Negative Symptoms (SANS).* Iowa City, IA: The University of Iowa.

Andreasen, N.C. (1984b). *The Scale for the Assessment of Positive Symptoms (SAPS).* Iowa City, IA: The University of Iowa.

Andreasson, S., Allebeck, P., Engstrom, A., & Rydberg, U. (1987). Cannabis and schizophrenia: A longitudinal study of Swedish conscripts. *Lancet, II,* 1483–1486.

Arndt, I.O., Dorozynsky, L., Woody, G.E., McLellan, A.T., & O'Brien, C.P. (1992). Desipramine treatment of cocaine dependence in methadone-maintained patients. *Archives of General Psychiatry, 49,* 893–898.

Baberg, H.T., Nelesen, R.A., & Dimsdale, J.E. (1996). Amphetamine use: Return of an old scourge in a consultation psychiatry setting. *American Journal of Psychiatry, 153*(6), 789–793.

Beck, A.T., Ward, C.H., Mendelson, M., Mock, J., & Erbaugh, J.K. (1961). An inventory for measuring depression. *Archives of General Psychiatry, 4,* 561–571.

Berger, S.P., Gawin, F., & Kosten, T.R. Treatment of cocaine abuse with mazindol. *Lancet, I,* 283.

Berger, S.P., Hall, S., Mickalian, J.D., Reid, M.S., Crawford, C.A., Delucchi, K., Carr, K., & Hall, S. (1996). Haloperidol antagonism of cue-elicited cocaine craving. *Lancet, 347,* 504–508.

Bowers, M.B., Mazure, C.M., Nelson, J.C., & Jadow, P.I. (1990). Psychotogenic drug use and neuroleptic response. *Schizophrenia Bulletin, 16*(1), 81–85.

Brady, K., Anton, R.A., Ballenger, J.C., Lydiard, R.B., Adinoff, B., & Selander, J. (1990). Cocaine abuse among schizophrenic patients. *American Journal of Psychiatry, 147*(9), 1164–1167.

Brady, K., Casto, S., & Lydiard, R.B. (1991). Substance abuse in an inpatient psychiatric sample. *American Journal of Drug and Alcohol Abuse, 17,* 389–397.

Breakey, W. R., Goodell, H., Lorenz, P. C., & McHugh, P. R. (1974). Hallucinogenic drugs as precipitants of schizophrenia. *Psychological Medicine, 4,* 255–261.

Buckley, P., Thompson. P. A.; Way, L. & Meltzer, H Y. (1994a). Substance abuse among, patients with treatment-resistant schizophrenia: Characteristics and implications for clozapine therapy, *American Journal of Psychiatry, 151*(l), 385–389.

Buckley, P.; Thompson, P. A.; Way, L., & Meltzer, H. Y. (1994b). Substance abuse and clozapine treatment. *Journal of Clinical Psychiatry, 55,* 114–116.

Caskey. N. R., Jarvik, M. E., & Wirshing, W. C. (In press). The effects of dopaninergic D, stimulation and blockade on smoking behavior. *Experimental and Clinical Psychopharmacology.*

Childress, A R., Ehrman, R., Rohsenow, D. J., Robbins, S. J., & O'Brien, C. P. (1992). Classically conditioned factors in drug dependence. In J. H. Lowinson, P. Ruiz, & R. B. Millman (Eds.). *Substance abuse: A comprehensive textbook.* Baltimore, MD: Williams and Wilkins Company, pp. 56–69.

Derogatis, L., Lipman, R.; & Covi, L. (1973). SCL-90: An outpatient psychiatric rating scale—Preliminary report. *Psychopharmacology Bulletin, 9*(1), 13–17.

Dixon, L., Haas, 0., Weiden. P. J., Sweeney, J., & Frances, A. J. (1991). Drug abuse in schizophrenic patients: Clinical correlates and reasons for use. *American Journal of Psychiatry, 148*(2), 224–230.

Dixon. L., Weiden, P. J.; Haas, G., Sweeney, J., & Frances, A. J. (1992). Increased tardive dyskinesia in alcohol abusing schizophrenic patients. *Comprehensive Psychiatry, 33*(2), 121–122.

Endicott, J., Spitzer, R. L., Fleiss, J. L., & Cohen. J. (1976). The Global Assessment Scale—A procedure for measuring overall severity of psychiatric disturbance. *Archives of General Psychiatry, 33,* 766–771.

Flaum, M., & Schultz, S. (1996). When does amphetamine induced psychosis become schizophrenia? *American Journal of Psychiatry, 153*(6), 812–815.

Freed, E. X. (1975). Alcoholism and schizophrenia: The search for perspectives: A review. *Journal of Studies on Alcohol, 36*(7), 853–881.

Fulton, M. K., Kramer, G; Moeller, F. G., Chae, Y., Isbell, P. G., & Petty, F. (1995). Low plasma homovanillic acid levels in recently abstinent alcoholic men. *American Journal of Psychiatry, 152*(12), 1819–1820.

Galanter, M., Castaneda. R., & Ferman. J. (1998). Substance abuse among general psychiatric patients: Place of presentation, diagnosis, and treatment. *American Journal of Drug and Alcohol Abuse, 14*(2), 211–235.

Garcia. L. C. (1991). Dependencia a anticolinergicos en esquizofrenicos: Iatrogenia o automedication? (Anticholinergic dependence in schizophrenics: Iatrogenic or automedication?). *Actas Luso-Espanolas de Neurologia, Psiquiatria y Ciencias Afines, 19*(6), 298–303.

Gawin, F. H. (1986). Neurcleptic reduction of cocaine-induced paranoia but not euphoria? *Psychopharmacology, 90,* 142–143.

Gawin, F. H., Allen, D., & Humblestone, B. (1989). Outpatient treatment of "crack" cocaine smoking with flupenthixol decanoate. *Archives of General Psychiatry, 46,* 322–325.

Gawin. F. K., & Ellinwood, E. H. (1988). Cocaine and other stimulants: Actions, abuse, and treatment. *New England Journal of Medicine, 318,* 1173–1182.

Gawin. F. H., & Kleber, H. D. (1986). Abstinence symptomatology and psychiatric diagnosis in chronic cocaine abusers. *Archives of General Psychiatry, 43,* 107–113.

Goff, D. C., Guochuan, T.,. Manoach. D. S., & Coyle, J. T. (1995). Dose-finding trial of D-cyclosenne added to neuroleptics for negative symptoms in schizophrenia. *American Journal of Psychiatry, 152*(8), 1213–1215.

Goff, D. C., Henderson, D. C., & Amico, E. (1992). Cigarette smoking in schizophrenia: Relationship to psychopathology and medication side effects. *American Journal of Psychiatry, 149*(9), 1189–1194.

Greden, J. F., & Walters, A. (1992). Caffeine. In J. H. Lowinson, P. Ruiz, R. B. Millman, & J. G. Langrod, (Eds.). *Substance abuse: A comprehensive textbook, 2nd ed.* Baltimore, MD: Williams and Wilkins Company, pp. 357–370.

Griffiths, R. R., Bigelow. G. E., & Liebson, I. A. (1986). Human coffee drinking: Reinforcing and physical dependence producing effects of caffeine. *Journal of Pharmacology and Experimental Therapeutics. 239*(2), 416–425.

Gritz, E. R., Stapleton, J. M., Hill, M. A., & Jarvik, M. E. (1985). Prevalence of cigarette smoking in medical and psychiatric hospitals. *Bulletin of the Society of Psychologists in Addictive Behaviors, 4*(3), 151–165.

Guy, W. (Ed.). (1976). *ECDEU assessment manual for psychopharmacology, revised.* Rockville, MD: National Institute of Mental Health, DHEW Publication No. (ADM)76–338.

Hagan, R. M., Kilpatrick, G. J., & Tyers. M. B. (1993). Interactions between 5-HT$_3$ receptors and cerebral dopamine function: Implications for the treatment of schizophrenia and psychoactive substance abuse, *Psychopharmucology, 112*(Suppl.), 68–75.

Hamilton, M. (1959). The assessment of anxiety states by rating. *British Journal of Medical Psychology, 32,* 50–55.

Hartman, N., Leong, G.B., Glynn, S.M., Wilkins, J.N., & Jarvik, M.E. (1991). Transdermal nicotine and smoking behavior in psychiatric patients. *American Journal of Psychiatry, 148,* 374–375.

Haywood, T.A., Kravitz, H.M., Grossman, L.S., Cavanaugh, J.L., Davis, J.M., & Lewis, D.A. (1995). Predicting the "revolving door" phenomenon among patients with schizophrenic, schizoaffective, and affective disorders. *American Journal of Psychiatry, 152*(6), 856–861.

Higgins, S.T., Budney, A.J., Bickel, W.K., Foerg, F.E., Donham, R., & Badger, G.J. (1994). Incentives improve outcome in outpatient behavioral treatment of cocaine dependence. *Archives of General Psychiatry, 51,* 568–576.

Hogarty, G.E., McEvoy, J.P., Ulrich, R.F., DiBarry, A.L., Bartone, P., Cooley, S., Hammill, K., Carter, M., Munetz, M.R., & Perel, J. (1995). Pharmacotherapy of impaired affect in recovering schizophrenic patients. *Archives of General Psychiatry, 52,* 29–41.

Hyde, A.P. (1990). Response to "Effects of caffeine on behavior of schizophrenic inpatients." *Schizophrenia Bulletin, 16*(3), 371–372.

Kapur, S. & Remington, G. (1996). Serotonin-dopamine interaction and its relevance to schizophrenia. *American Journal of Psychiatry, 153*(4), 466–476.

Kingsbury, S.J. & Salzman, C. (1990). Disulfiram in the treatment of alcoholic patients with schizophrenia. *Hospital and Community Psychiatry, 41*(2), 133–134.

Knudsen, P. & Vilmar, T. (1984). Cannabis and neuroleptic agents in schizophrenia. *Acta Psychiatrica Scandinavica, 69,* 162–170.

Kofoed, L., Kania, J., Walsh, T., & Atkinson, R. (1986). Outpatient treatment of patients with substance abuse and coexisting psychiatric disorders. *American Journal of Psychiatry, 143*(7), 867–872.

Kosten, T.R. (1992). Pharmacotherapies. In: T.R. Kosten & H.D. Kleber (Eds.), *Clinician's guide to cocaine addiction.* New York, NY: Guilford Press, pp. 273–289.

Kosten, T.R., Morgan, C,.M., Falcione, M.A., & Schottenfeld, R.S. (1992). Pharmacotherapy for cocaine-abusing methadone-maintained patients using amantadine or desipramine. *Archives of General Psychiatry, 49,* 894–898.

LeDuc, P.A. & Mitfleman, G. (1995). Schizophrenia and psychostimulant abuse: A review and re-analysis of clinical evidence. *Psychopharmacology, 121*(4), 407–427.

Leon, J.D., Dadvand, M., Canuso, C., White, A.O., Stanilla, J.K., & Simpson, G.M. (1995). Schizophrenia and smoking: An epidemiological survey in a State hospital. *American Journal of Psychiatry, 152*(3), 453–455.

Levin, F.R., Evans, S.M., Coomaraswarnmy, S., Collins, E.D., Regent, N., & Kleber, H.D. *Flupenthixol treatment for cocaine abusers with schizophrenia: A pilot study.* Submitted for publication.

Liberman, R.P. & Corrigan, P.W. (1993). Designing new psychosocial treatments for schizophrenia. *Psychiatry, 56*, 236–249.

Liberman, R.P., DeRisi, W.J., & Mueser, R. (1989). *Social training for psychiatric patients.* New York, NY: Pergamon Press.

Liddon, S. & Satran, R. (1967). Disulfiram (Antabuse) psychosis. *American Journal of Psychiatry, 123*, 1284–1289.

Ling, W. & Shoptaw, S. (In press). Research in pharmacotherapy for substance abuse: Where are we? Where are we going? *Journal of Addiction Medicine.*

Linszen, D.H., Dingemans, P.M., & Lenior, M.E (1994). Cannabis abuse and the course of recent-onset schizophrenic disorders. *Archives of General Psychiatry, 51*, 273–279.

Marchesi, G.F., Santone, G., Cotani, P., Giordano, A., & Chelli, F. (1992). Naltrexone in chronic negative schizophrenia [Abstract]. *Clinical Neuropharmacology, 15*, 56–57.

McLellan, A.T., Luborsky, L., Woody, G.E., & O'Brien, C.P. (1980). An improved diagnostic evaluation instrument for substance abuse patients: The addiction severity index. *Journal of Nervous and Mental Disease, 168*, 26–33.

Miller, F. & Tanenbaum, J. (1989). Drug abuse in schizophrenia. *Hospital and Community Psychiatry, 40*(8), 847–849.

Mueser, K.T., Yarnold, P.R., Levinson, H.S., Singh, H., Bellack, A.S., Kee, K., Morrison, R.L., & Yadalam, K.G. (1990). Prevalence of substance abuse in schizophrenia: Demographics and clinical correlates. *Schizophrenia Bulletin, 16*(1), 31–51.

Negrete, J.C., Knapp, W.P., Douglas, D.E., & Smith, B. (1986). Cannabis affects the severity of schizophrenic symptoms: Results of a clinical survey. *Psychological Medicine, 16*, 515–520.

Nordstrom, A., Farde, L., Nyberg, S., Karlsson, P., Halldin, C., & Sedvall, G. (1995). D_1, D_2, and 5-HT_2 receptor occupancy in relation to clozapine serum concentration: A PET study of schizophrenic patients. *American Journal of Psychiatry, 152*(10), 1444–1449.

Olivera, A.A., Kiefer, M.W., & Manley, N.K. (1990). Tardive dyskinesia in psychiatric patients with substance abuse disorders. *American Journal of Drug and Alcohol Abuse, 16*, 57–66.

O'Malley, S., Jaffe, A., & Chang, G. (1992). Naltrexone and coping skill therapy for alcohol dependence. *Archives of General Psychiatry, 49*, 881-887.

Overall, J.E. & Gorham, D.R. (1962). The Brief Psychiatric Rating Scale. *Psychological Reports, 10*, 799–812.

Peralta, V. & Cuesta, M.J. (1995). Negative symptoms in schizophrenia: A confirmatory factor analysis of competing models. *American Journal of Psychiatry, 152*(10), 1450–1457.

Schneier, F.R. & Siris, S.G. (1987). A review of psychoactive substance use and abuse in schizophrenia: Patterns of drug choice. *Journal of Nervous and Mental Disease, 175,* 641–652.

Self, D.W., Barnhart, W.J., Lehman, D.A., & Nestler, E.J. (1996). Opposite modulation of cocaine-seeking behavior by D_1- and D_2-like dopamine receptor agonists. *Science, 271*(52), 1586–1589.

Serper, M.R., Alpert, M., Richardson, N.A., Dickson, S., Allen, M.H., & Werner, A. (1995). Clinical effects of recent cocaine use on patients with acute schizophrenia. *American Journal of Psychiatry, 152*(10), 1464–1469.

Sevy, S., Kay, S.R., Opler, L.A., & Praag, H.M. (1990). Significance of cocaine history in schizophrenia. *Journal of Nervous and Mental Disease, 178,* 642–648.

Shaner, A., Khalsa, H., Roberts, L.J., Wilkins, J.N., Anglin, D., & Hsieh, S.C. (1993). Unrecognized cocaine using among schizophrenic patients. *American Journal of Psychiatry, 150*(5), 758–762.

Shaner, A., Mintz, J., Eckman, T.A., Roberts, L.J., Wilkins, J.N., Tucker, D.E., & Tsuang, J. (1995). Disability income, cocaine use and repeated hospitalizations among schizophrenic cocaine abusers: A government-sponsored revolving door? *New England Journal of Medicine, 333,* 777-783.

Shaner, A., Roberts, L.J., Eckman, T.A., Wilkins, J.N., & Mintz, J. (In press). Monetary reinforcement of cocaine abstinence in cocaine dependent schizophrenic patients. *Psychiatric Services.*

Siris, S.G., Kane, J.M., Frechen, K., Sellew, A.P., Mandell, J., & Fasano-Dube, B. (1988a). Histories of substance abuse in patients with post-psychotic depressions. *Comprehensive Psychiatry, 29,* 550-557.

Siris, S.G., Mason, S.E., Bermanzohn, P.C., Shuwall, M.A., & Aseniero, M.A. (1993). Dual-diagnosis/psychiatric comorbidity of drug dependence: Epidemiology and treatment. *Psychopharmacology Bulletin, 29*(1), 127-132.

Siris, S.G., Sellew, A.P., Frechen, K., Cooper, T.B., Mandell, J., & Casey, E. (1988b). Antidepressants in the treatment of post-psychotic depression in schizophrenia: Drug interactions and other considerations. *Clinical Chemistry, 34*(5), 837-840.

Soyka, M. & Sand, P. (1995). Successful treatment with flupenthixol decanoate of a patient with both schizophrenia and alcoholism. *Pharmacopsychiatry, 28*(2), 64-65.

Spitzer, R.L., Williams, J.B.W., Gibbon, M., & First, M.B. (1988). Structured Clinical Interview for DSM-III-R-Patient Version. New York, NY: Biometrics Research Department, New York State Psychiatric Institute.

Tandon, R. & DeQuardo, J.R. (1995). Treatment of schizophrenia with anticholinergic medications. [Letter] *American Journal of Psychiatry, 152*(5), 814-815.

Treffert, D.A. (1978). Marijuana use in schizophrenia: A clear hazard. *American Journal of Psychiatry, 135*(10), 1213–1215.

van Kammen, D.P. & Boronow, J.J. (1988). Dextroamphetamine diminished negative symptoms in schizophrenia. *International Clinical Journal of Psychopharmacology, 3,* 111–121.

Volpicelli, J., Alterman, A., Hayashida, M., & O'Brien, C. (1992). Naltrexone in the treatment of alcohol dependence. *Archives of General Psychiatry, 49,* 876-880.

Welch, E.B. & Thompson, D.F. (1994). Opiate antagonists for the treatment of schizophrenia. *Journal of Clinical Pharmacy and Therapeutics, 19,* 279-283.

Weller, R.A. & Weller, E.B. (1986). Tricyclic antidepressants in prepubertal depressed children: Review of the literature. *Hillside Journal of Clinical Psychiatry, 8*(1), 46-55.

Wilkins, J.N., Gorelick, D.A., Levine, D., Gold, J., von Raffay, V., Tucker, D.E., Roberts, L.J., Eckman, T.A., Racenstein, M., Shaner, A.L., Ashofteh, A., Jerger, D., & Li, S.-H. (1996). Double-blind trial of desipramine for treatment of cocaine-abusing schizophrenics. In L.S. Harris (Ed.), *Problems of Drug Dependence,* 1995: Proceedings of the 57th Annual Scientific Meeting. Rockville, MD: U.S. Department of Health and Human Services, National Institutes of Health, National Institute on Drug Abuse, p.325.

Wilkins, J.N., Gorelick, D.A., Shaner, A.L., Setoda, D.Y., von Raffay, V., & Tucker, D.E. (1993). Cocaine and marijuana effects in schizophrenia: In: *New Research Program and Abstracts*: Proceedings of the 144th Meeting of the American Psychiatric Association. Washington, DC: American Psychiatric Association, p. 165.

Wilkins, J.N., Shaner, A.L., Patterson, C.M., Setoda, D., & Gorelick, D.A. (1991). Discrepancies between patient report, clinical assessment, and urine analysis in psychiatric patients during inpatient admission. *Psychopharmacology Bulletin, 27*(2), 149-154.

Wolkowitz, O.M. & Pickar, D. (1991). Benzodiazepines in the treatment of schizophrenia: A review and reappraisal. *American Journal of Psychiatry, 148*(6), 714–726.

Zaretsky, A., Rector, N.A., Seeman, M.V., & Fornazzari, X. (1993). Current cannabis use and tardive dyskinesia. *Schizophrenia Research, 11,* 3–8.

Ziedonis, D.M., Fisher, W., Harris, P., Trudeau, K., Rao, S., & Kosten, T.R. (1996). Adjunctive selegiline in the treatment of cocaine-abusing schizophrenics. In L.S. Harris (Ed.), *Problems of Drug Dependence,* 1995: Proceedings of the 57th Annual Scientific Meeting. Rockville, MD: U.S. Department of Health and Human Services, National Institutes of Health, National Institute on Drug Abuse, p.325.

Ziedonis, D.M. & George, T.P. (1997). Schizophrenia and nicotine use: Report of a pilot smoking cessation program and review of neurobiological and clinical issues. *Schizophrenia Bulletin, 23*(3), 247–254.

Ziedonis, D.M., Kosten, T.R., Glazer, W.M., & Frances, R.J. (1994). Nicotine dependence and schizophrenia. *Hospital and Community Psychiatry, 45*(3), 204–206.

Ziedonis, D.M., Richardson, T., Lee, E., Petrakis, I., & Kosten, T.R. (1992). Adjunctive desipramine in the treatment of cocaine abusing schizophrenics. *Psychopharmacology Bulletin, 28*(3), 309–314.

Zweben, J.E. & O'Connell, K. (1992). Strategies for breaking marijuana dependence. *Journal of Psychoactive Drugs, 24*(2), 165–171.

Determinants of Medication Compliance in Schizophrenia: Empirical and Clinical Findings

Wayne S. Fenton, Crystal R. Blyler & Robert K. Heinssen

This article originally appeared in the *Schizophrenia Bulletin,* 1997, 23(4), 637–651, and is reprinted with permission.

Wayne S. Fenton, M.D., is Medical Director, Chestnut Lodge Hospital, and Director, Chestnut Lodge Research Institute; Crystal R. Blyler, Ph.D., is Research Psychologist, Chestnut Lodge Research Institute; and Robert K. Heinssen, Ph.D., is Director, Partial Hospitalization and Psychiatric Rehabilitation for Schizophrenia, Chestnut Lodge Hospital, Rockville, MD.

Advances in psychopharmacology have produced medications with substantial efficacy in the treatment of positive and negative symptoms of schizophrenia and the prevention of relapse or symptom exacerbation after an acute episode. In the clinical setting, the individual patient's acceptance or rejection of prescribed pharmacological regimens is often the single greatest determinant of these treatments' effectiveness. For this reason, an understanding of factors that impede and promote patient collaboration with prescribed acute and maintenance treatment should inform both pharmacological and psychosocial treatment planning. We review the substantive literature on medication adherence in schizophrenia and describe a modified health belief model within which empirical findings can be understood. In addition to factors intrinsic to schizophrenia psychopathology, medication-related factors, available social support, substance abuse comorbidity, and the quality of the therapeutic alliance each affect adherence and offer potential points of intervention to improve the likelihood of collaboration. Because noncompliance as a clinical problem is multidetermined, an individualized approach to assessment and treatment, which is often best developed in the context of an ongoing physician-patient relationship, is optimal. The differential diagnosis of noncompliance should lead to interventions that target specific causal factors thought to be operative in the individual patient.

Although advances in psychopharmacology have vastly improved the range of treatment options for schizophrenia, outcome variance explained by the choice of medication is likely small compared with that accounted for by how and if the patient takes what is prescribed.

Compliance is defined as "the extent to which a person's behavior coincides with medical or health advice" (Haynes, 1979, p. 2). The term has been criticized for over 20 years as a reflection of an outmoded and paternalistic conception of the physician-patient relationship (Holm, 1993; Stimson, 1974). Nonetheless, compliance is a word often used in clinical settings where for clinicians, patients, and families it remains one of the most vexing challenges in psychopharmacology.

Compliance is difficult to quantify and study for several reasons. Clinicians' ability to identify which patients do not take medicine is limited (McClellan & Cowan, 1970; Norell, 1981). Other measures of adherence include patient or relative self-report, prescription renewals and pill counts, saliva and urine screens, or steady-state serum determinations. Concordance across different measures of compliance is often low, although self-reported noncompliance is corroborated more often than is self-reported adherence (Boczkowski et al., 1985; Gordis, 1976; Rickels & Briscoe, 1970). Measurement is further complicated because compliance is rarely an all-or-none phenomenon, but may include errors of omission, mistakes in dosage and timing, and taking medications that are not prescribed (Blackwell, 1976).

A 1986 review of 26 studies using a variety of definitions and detection methods to assess medication use among outpatients with schizophrenia reported a median default rate of 41% (range, 10 to 76%) with oral medications and 25% (range, 14 to 36%) with depot injections over time periods up to 1 year (Young et al., 1986). Fifteen subsequent studies using varying definitions of noncompliance and many mixing patients taking oral and depot medications reported a median 1-month to 2-year noncompliance rate of 55% (range, 24% to 88%) (Adams & Howe, 1993; Ayers et al., 1984; Boczkowski et al., 1985; Buchanan, 1992; Carman et al., 1984; Frank & Gunderson, 1990; Gaebel & Pietzcker, 1985; Hogan et al., 1983; Kelly & Scott, 1990; Macpherson et al., 1996a, 1996b; Munetz & Roth, 1985; Owen et al., 1996; Parker & Hadzi-Pavlovic, 1995; Pristach & Smith, 1990; Razali & Yahya, 1995).

The belief that noncompliance is a direct result of disease processes in schizophrenia dominates the clinical perception of noncompliance for these patients. Reported noncompliance rates for schizophrenia, however, are in the middle range of those reported for other common medical disorders. Medication noncompliance rates of 55 to 71% have been reported for patients with arthritis (Berg et al., 1993), 54 to 82% for patients with seizure disorders (Shope, 1988), 20 to 57% for patients with bipolar affective disorder (Elixhauser et al., 1990), and 19 to 80% for patients with diabetes (Friedman, 1988). Half of patients with hypertension drop out of care within 1 year, and only two-thirds of those who remain take adequate medication (Eraker et al., 1984).

A review of compliance with maintenance regimens—rheumatic fever prophylaxis, glaucoma, isoniazid for tuberculosis, and self-administered insulin—found a mean noncompliance rate for these long-term illnesses of 54% (Sacket, 1976). Compliance is lowest when the condition is prolonged, treatment is prophylactic or suppressive, and the consequences of stopping treatment are delayed. In disorders sharing these features, adherence declines with time (Blackwell, 1973).

Through 1994 at least 14,000 English-language articles have addressed compliance-related issues in medical care (Donovan, 1995). Recent reviews converge in concluding that noncompliance is far better documented than understood and that a focus on the patient's decision-making process is often a key missing ingredient in extant research (Donovan, 1995; Morris & Schulz, 1993; Trostle, 1988). Health belief (Becker & Maiman, 1975; Kirscht & Rosenstock, 1979) or health decision (Eraker et al., 1984) models that emphasize a patient's subjective assessment of the risks and benefits of treatment in the context of personal values and goals are advanced as best integrating available data on compliance research. Although these models may require modification in disorders like schizophrenia in which cognition and motivation are affected directly by illness processes (Babiker, 1986; Bebbington, 1995), they do facilitate a shift in perspective: rather than viewing noncompliance as the patient's problem, it is redefined as an indication that the therapeutic regimen is not assisting the individual patient to achieve his or her goals.

In this article, we review the substantive literature on medication compliance in schizophrenia with an emphasis on empirical studies that (1) identify current or predictive correlates of adherence and noncompliance and (2) assess interventions targeted to improve adherence. These findings provide an empirical basis for the differential diagnosis and understanding of noncompliance within a modified health belief or health decision model.

Methods

This review is limited to studies of medication adherence in schizophrenia: studies focused on psychiatric patients without specifying diagnosis and those focused on adherence to other aspects of treatment, such as aftercare appointments, were not included. Clinical correlates of compliance that have been studied include patient sociodemographic features; illness characteristics, including comorbidity and insight; medication features, including side effects and route and frequency of administration; family and social support; and treatment system characteristics, including quality of the physician-patient relationship. Interventions studied include reinforcement, education, skills training, and memory enhancement.

Potentially relevant English-language articles were identified from the English language psychiatric and psychological literature with the aid of computer searches using such key words as compliance, adherence, psychopharmacology, and schizophrenia. Bibliographies from primary sources and reviews were then reviewed to identify earlier relevant works. In addition to empirical studies (those including some measure of compliance or intention to comply), clinical reports were included for review if they presented useful perspectives on social or psychodynamic issues that would generally be inaccessible to empirical study. In selecting studies for review, reliability testing and corroboration of patient self-report were not required criteria; had they been, very few studies would be left for review.

Correlates of Adherence and Noncompliance

Patient-Related Factors

Patient demographic characteristics. As in other medical disorders, demographic variables are not consistently associated with compliance in schizophrenia. Eleven studies assessed the relationship between one or more patient demographic characteristics and compliance (Buchanan, 1992; Draine & Solomon, 1994; Hoffman et al., 1974; Hogan et al., 1983; Leff & Wing, 1971; Owen et al., 1996; Pan & Tantam, 1989; Parker & Hadzi-Pavlovic, 1995; Razali & Yahya, 1995; Sellwood & Tarrier, 1994; Soskis, 1978). Eight of ten found no association with age, six of nine found no association with gender, four of five found no association with ethnicity, and four of four no association with education or income. In contrast, two studies found noncompliance associated with youth, three with male gender, one with single marital status, and one with African-Caribbean ethnicity.

Illness Characteristics

Illness history. Studies have failed to reveal an association between compliance and age at onset and duration of illness (Buchanan, 1992), age at first hospitalization (McEvoy et al., 1984), and premorbid functioning (Adams & Howe 1993). Data relating the number of prior hospitalizations to compliance are contradictory: Three studies indicated more prior hospitalizations (Nelson et al., 1975; Pan & Tantam, 1989; Sellwood & Tarrier, 1994); two studies, fewer prior hospitalizations (McEvoy et al., 1984; Reilly et al., 1967); and one study, no difference in prior hospitalizations (Hogan et al., 1983) among patients judged to be noncompliant at an index assessment. Although these data do not strongly support the contention that patients learn to adhere to medications after repeated relapses, hospitalization may improve compliance in the period immediately after discharge: Two studies assessing compliance among patients before and after an index admission showed significant decreases in noncompliance rates at followup (Christensen, 1974; Owen et al., 1996).

The association between compliance and future hospitalization risk is far less equivocal: Seven studies indicated that patients rated as noncompliant have a 6-month to 2-year risk of relapse that is an average of 3.7 times greater than patients rated as compliant (Gaebel & Pietzcker, 1985; Kashner et al., 1991; Leff & Wing, 1971; Linn et al., 1982; McFarlane et al., 1995; Munetz & Roth, 1985; Parker & Hadzi-Pavlovic, 1995). Two additional studies did not allow calculation of relative risk, but identified irregular medication adherence as a significant predictor of relapse (Falloon et al., 1978; Verghese et al., 1989). The magnitude of elevated risk associated with noncompliance seems comparable with that conveyed by randomization to placebo in maintenance trials (Baldessarini et al., 1990). Consistent with these data is the finding of recent medication noncompliance in the history of 38 to 68% of relapsed patients (Christensen, 1974; del Campo et al., 1983; Herz & Melville, 1980; Owen et al., 1996; Parker & Hadzi-Pavlovic, 1995; Reilly et al., 1967). Because relapse typically occurs weeks to months after the discontinuation of medication, however, patients only rarely attribute it to noncompliance (Chien, 1975; Herz & Melville, 1980).

Although the association between noncompliance and relapse is robust, causality is likely bidirectional: Crawford and Forrest (1974) found erratic pill-taking associated with worsening symptoms for patients taking placebo tablets while maintained on depot phenothiazine injections. Likewise, in a study that randomized schizophrenia patients to drug or placebo groups 2 months after hospital discharge, Hogarty et al. (1973) found that about 50% of the relapsers from either group were noncompliant compared with only 15% of patients from either group who had not relapsed within 6 months.

Illness severity and subtype. Both inpatient drug refusal and outpatient noncompliance are consistently associated with more severe ratings of psychopathology. Eight studies assessed the relationship between symptom severity or global functioning and inpatient medication refusal, future outpatient medication compliance, or attitude toward medication. Marder et al. (1983) found more severe psychopathology, including disorganization, hostility, and suspiciousness, associated with inpatient drug refusal. Five investigations reported a positive association between symptom severity at or after discharge and poor outpatient compliance (Kelly et al., 1987; Pan & Tantam, 1989; Renton et al., 1963; Van Putten et al., 1976) or poor attitude toward compliance (Draine & Solomon, 1994). One study found only the Brief Psychiatric Rating Scale (Overall & Gorham, 1962) grandiosity score to be associated with poor compliance (Bartko et al., 1988), and one study reported no relationship between symptom severity at discharge and future outpatient compliance (Ayers et al., 1984).

Seven studies investigating the relationship between paranoid suspiciousness, persecutory delusions, or schizophrenia subtype and medication adherence yielded mixed results. Two studies reported that noncompliance preceding a hospitalization is more common among patients with paranoid schizophrenia subtype (Pristach & Smith, 1990; Reilly et al., 1967). An additional investigation reported greater noncompliance as measured with urine screens among inpatients with paranoid delusions (Wilson & Enoch, 1967). In contrast, one investigation found no association between paranoid schizophrenia subtype and the expressed willingness to take medications (Soskis, 1978), one study found no association between subtype and self-reported outpatient compliance (Hoffman et al., 1974), and another study reported no association between paranoid ratings and missed depot appointments (Bartko et al.,

1988). In a study that may reconcile these discrepant findings, Van Putten et al. (1976) found no association between compliance and paranoid schizophrenia subtype, but noted that 85% of paranoid schizophrenia patients with delusions of persecution or influence habitually complied with medications, whereas 92% of paranoid patients with grandiose delusions habitually refused medications.

Cognition/memory. Neither overall intelligence (Adams & Howe, 1993), discharge Mini-Mental State Exam score (Buchanan, 1992; Folstein et al., 1975), nor Neurobehavioral Cognitive Status Exam results (Cuffel et al., 1996; Northern California Neurobehavioral Group, 1988) has been associated with compliance. The potential association between specific neuropsychological deficits and compliance has not been explored. A significant percentage of outpatients, however, attribute noncompliance to forgetting (Hoffman et al., 1974) or indicate that they believe reminders to take their medicine would be helpful (Serban & Thomas, 1974).

Insight. The concept of insight has undergone considerable elaboration in recent years, coincident with a shift in explanatory focus from psychological to neurologically based formulations of self-awareness deficits (Amador et al., 1993, 1994). A review emphasized the multidimensional nature of insight and its relative independence from symptom severity (Amador et al., 1991). Using a variety of self-report measures of illness awareness, nine studies assessed the relationship between insight and adherence with prescribed pharmacological regimens. Poor insight was consistently associated with noncompliance. Three studies reported an association between poor insight assessed at admission or during hospitalization and medication noncompliance among inpatients (Lin et al., 1979; Marder et al., 1983; McEvoy et al., 1989). Four studies reported an association between a lack of insight at hospital admission, discharge, or post discharge assessment and poor outpatient compliance (Bartko et al., 1988; Macpherson et al., 1996a, 1996b; Nelson et al., 1975; Van Putten et al., 1976). Perhaps reflecting the fact that both insight and compliance can fluctuate with clinical state, one study found that an awareness of illness and medication compliance were related only when measured concurrently (Cuffel et al., 1996). One study reported an association between involuntary admission status (an indirect index of insight) and poor 2-year post discharge medication compliance, but no association between ratings from attitude questionnaires and compliance

(Buchanan, 1992). Although a statistical relationship between insight and adherence has been replicated in a variety of settings, several investigators noted that a sizable subgroup of patients who do not believe they are ill or require medication nonetheless are regularly compliant.

Other Health Beliefs

Except for the consistent relationship between awareness of the presence of a psychiatric illness and medication compliance, the association between specific health beliefs and medication compliance among patients with schizophrenia is more ambiguous. Kelly et al. (1987) found that greater perceived susceptibility to rehospitalization was associated with increased compliance among a population made up largely of patients with schizophrenia. Hogan et al. (1983) also found that schizophrenia outpatients rated by their therapists as generally compliant with medication were more likely than noncompliant patients to believe that staying on medication would prevent relapse. Noncompliant patients were more likely to believe that medication should only be taken when one feels sick, that it would harm them physically, and that it is unnatural to take medication. In contrast, Pan and Tantam (1989) found no difference in beliefs about the possibility of relapse if maintenance treatment were stopped between regular attenders and outpatients who had missed two or more appointments over 12 months at a depot neuroleptic clinic. Buchanan (1992) found no association between compliance and self-appraisal of the likelihood of becoming ill again. Serban and Thomas (1974) found that most hospitalized schizophrenia patients who reported that they did not use prescribed medications between hospitalizations failed to do so despite their expressed belief that regular medication would be helpful. It should be noted that this disjunction between health beliefs and behaviors is by no means unique to schizophrenia.

Subjective Well-Being

Perceived immediate benefit and a subjective sense of well-being derived from medications seem to be associated more consistently with compliance than are expressed beliefs concerning susceptibility to relapse. Patients who do not comply are likely to feel that their medications do not help, are of no benefit, or are ineffective and unnecessary (Herz & Melville, 1980; Lin et al., 1979; Nelson et al., 1975; Soskis, 1978). Patients who consent to and comply with neuroleptics are more likely to report feeling better (Marder et al., 1983), getting help (Buchanan, 1992), and endorsing a direct (Hogan et al., 1983; Razali & Yahya, 1995) or indirect (Adams & Howe, 1993) beneficial effect of medication on their well-being. After resolution of an acute episode, however, some patients stop medications because they feel well and therefore no longer in need of treatment (Hoffman et al., 1974; Reilly et al., 1967). As described below in the section on side effects, to the extent that subjective well-being is associated with initial and long-term adherence, subjective discomfort is associated with medication refusal or noncompliance.

Co-Occurring Alcohol and Drug Use

Comorbid alcohol or other substance abuse is common among individuals with schizophrenia (Regier et al., 1990) and is a strong predictor of neuroleptic noncompliance. Drake et al. (1989) studied 115 outpatients with schizophrenia and found that 45% were occasional and 23% heavy alcohol users. More severe alcohol use and abuse were associated with medication noncompliance, psychosocial problems (including homelessness), disorganized and hostile behavior, medical problems, and frequent rehospitalizations over a 1-year followup. In a second group of outpatients, Kashner et al. (1991) found that substance-abusing patients with schizophrenia were 13 times more likely than non-substance-abusing patients to be noncompliant with antipsychotic medication. In a group of schizophrenia inpatients with a rate of self-reported noncompliance (72%) before admission that was too high to find an overall association with their substance abuse history, Pristach and Smith (1990) reported that 62% stopped taking medications while drinking. Patients often cited their physicians' advice not to mix medicine and alcohol as a reason for intermittent noncompliance. Among inpatients assessed for substance abuse and followed after discharge for 6 months, Owen et al. (1996) reported that substance abuse in the 30 days before index assessment was the strongest predictor of noncompliance at followup assessment. Substance abuse increased the risk of noncompliance eightfold and seemed to interact with decreased outpatient contact to result in poor clinical outcome. Of potential relevance to compliance are reports that tardive dyskinesia and akathisia may be more prevalent among patients who abuse alcohol (Dixon et al., 1992; Lutz, 1976; Olivera et al., 1990).

Medication-Related Factors

Side effects. Neuroleptic side effects that may be particularly unpleasant include sedation, anticholinergic effects, cognitive blunting, depression, sexual dysfunction, and extrapyramidal syndromes—dystonia, akinesia, Parkinsonian effects, akathisia, and tardive dyskinesia (Weiden et al., 1986). Between one-quarter and two-thirds of patients who unilaterally discontinue prescribed neuroleptic medicines cite side effects as their primary reason for noncompliance (del Campo et al., 1983; Hoffman et al., 1974; Reilly et al., 1967; Renton et al., 1963). Among outpatients, both self (Falloon et al., 1978; Hogan et al., 1983; Kelly et al., 1987) and physician (Buchanan, 1992; Nelson et al., 1975; Pan & Tantam, 1989) ratings of side effects are associated with or predictive of noncompliance.

Although side effects are consistently associated with poor maintenance adherence among outpatients, inpatients may not reliably report a history of side effects. Pristach and Smith (1990) did not find self-reported history of neuroleptic side effects to be related to noncompliance among inpatients before admission. Marder et al. (1983) found no overall association between the self-reported history of side effects and inpatient drug refusal: Inpatient drug refusers were described as including a subgroup of patients with severe side effects and a second group in whom illness-related factors, such as denial, hostility, and grandiosity, were major determinants of refusal. Fleischhacker et al. (1994) attributed their failure to find an association between side effects during the first 4 weeks of treatment and subsequent compliance among patients on haloperidol and clozapine to an aggressive approach to detect and treat adverse effects by changing medications, lowering dosages, and prescribing concomitant medications.

In an important series of studies based on the observation that normnal volunteers differed in their reactions to a test dose of phenothiazines (Heninger et al., 1965), Van Putten et al. (1974) described a subgroup of schizophrenia patients who experienced a dysphoric response to a variety of conventional neuroleptics available at that time. These patients felt miserable on neuroleptics, complained about drug effects, and pleaded to have their medications stopped or dosages reduced. In contrast, nondysphoric responders reported that they "liked" medications and "felt better" on them. Akathisia was found to be the most significant factor underlying a dysphoric neuroleptic response and was highly associated with medication refusal or outpatient noncompliance or both. In some patients, akathisia was experienced as a catastrophic sense of terror and impending annihilation that was phenomenologically similar to an exacerbation of psychosis (Van Putten, 1974). More frequently, patients reported a subtle inner restlessness, anxiety, and inability to feel comfortable in any position, a phenomenon that was incompatible with any productive activities and could not be tolerated for any period of time. However, much of the akathisia responsible for outpatient noncompliance was described as sufficiently mild as to remain undetected by an observer who lacked a close and continuous relationship with the patient (Van Putten, 1974). Two subsequent studies replicated the finding of a significant association between an initial dysphoric response to a test dose of thiothixene or haloperidol, akathisia, and subsequent medication noncompliance (Van Putten et al., 1981, 1984). In a third independent sample, a greater proportion of patients with a dysphoric than a syntonic response to a chlorpromazine test dose were noncompliant over a 9-month followup period (Ayers et al., 1984). Together, these results point to a strong association among a dysphoric response to medication, akathisia, and medication refusal or noncompliance or both.

Dosage and agent. Higher (Pan & Tantam, 1989), lower (Nelson et al., 1975), and no different (Hogan et al., 1983) neuroleptic dosages have been reported among outpatients rated as less compliant with maintenance treatment. A curvilinear relationship between dosage and compliance, with very low doses associated with lack of efficacy and very high doses with excessive side effects, seems likely. However, few data are available that assess differential compliance rates to different agents. Carman et al. (1984) found noncompliance rates as measured by serum and urine assays to be significantly higher among patients taking high-potency compared with low-potency agents (65% vs. 13%). Among outpatients receiving phenothiazine injections, Carney and Sheffield (1976) reported a higher noncompliance rate (43%) among those receiving fluphenazine enanthate than among patients receiving fluphenazine decanoate or flupenthixol decanoate (23%). The difference was attributed to a higher rate of extrapyramidal side effects among those prescribed fluphenazine enanthate. We were unable to locate any randomized controlled study assessing compliance with different agents.

The correlation between greater psychopathology at index assessment and noncompliance likely reflects an association between the efficacy of prescribed treatment and compliance. The finding that noncompliance rates for chlorpromazine were substantially higher than those for imipramine among depressed (70% vs. 44%) but not schizophrenia (32% vs. 25%) outpatients provides additional support for a relationship between efficacy and compliance (Willcox et al., 1965).

Route. A 1986 review of 26 studies reporting noncompliance rates indicated a lower mean default rate (25%) in studies of depot compared with oral (41%) neuroleptics (Young et al., 1986). Based on the hypothesized advantage of depot preparations in improving compliance, six controlled studies comparing relapse rates among patients randomized to oral versus depot neuroleptics were reviewed more recently (Davis et al., 1993). These studies suggest a modest advantage for the depot route in reducing relapse rates that may be greater in nonresearch samples (Dixon et al., 1995). Changing patients to depot preparations does not, however, seem to be an effective global strategy to eliminate noncompliance: Van Putten et al. (1976) found that 83% of habitually noncompliant schizophrenia outpatients who were switched to decanoate did not return with any regularity for bimonthly injections. Likewise, Falloon et al. (1978) reported that 73% of schizophrenia patients returned to the community after hospital treatment who were irregular in their tablet taking also missed at least one injection in 12 months. Buchanan (1992) found no difference in compliance rates over 2 years post discharge for patients taking oral and depot neuroleptics.

Although long-acting phenothiazine injections do not ensure medication compliance because they must be administered by a treatment provider, noncompliance with this type of treatment can be detected quickly and with certainty. Such noncompliance allows an assessment of clinical impact for the individual patient and may trigger assertive interventions. For this reason, the major advantage of depot neuroleptics may be the ability to eliminate covert noncompliance as a cause of clinical decompensation (Schooler & Keith, 1993).

Complexity of regimen. Although the complexity of a medication regimen is associated with compliance across a broad range of medical disorders (Haynes, 1976), only one (Razali & Yahya, 1995) of four empirical studies that focused exclusively on schizophrenia identified a statistically significant association between complexity of regimen and compliance. Hoffman et al. (1974), Hogan et al. (1983), and Buchanan (1992) found no such association.

Environmental Factors

Family and social support. Social support, in general, and the availability of family or friends to assist or supervise medications, in particular, are consistently associated with outpatient adherence. Eight studies indicated that patients living with relatives or whose medications are supervised by relatives are more likely than those lacking such support to maintain adherence to prescribed antipsychotic medication (Buchanan, 1992; Hoffman et al., 1974; Nelson et al., 1975; Parkes et al., 1962; Razali & Yahya, 1995; Reilly et al., 1967; Renton et al., 1963; Van Putten et al., 1976). An additional study found a nonsignificant association between stability of living arrangements and compliance (Owen et al., 1996). Causality is likely bidirectional in determining the association between family or social support and compliance. In a group of mostly schizophrenia outpatients, Draine and Solomon (1994) found that better social functioning and more extensive social networks were related to positive attitudes toward medication compliance. In addition, negative or stressful social interactions may counteract the positive effect on compliance of living with others (Reilly et al., 1967).

Practical barriers. In one investigation, 28% of patients who had reduced or stopped taking medications before an inpatient admission cited financial burden as the principal reason for discontinuation (Reilly et al., 1967). Sullivan et al. (1995) found that family informants reported that 7% of previously hospitalized patients lacked money for medication and 19% had missed medication because of a lack of transportation to the pharmacy. Practical barriers or lack of access to care may be particularly salient for homeless individuals, who are often viewed as noncompliant (Interagency Council on the Homeless, 1992).

Physician-patient relationship. The clinical supposition that a positive therapeutic alliance facilitates medication compliance finds empirical support in three studies. Nelson et al. (1975) found that the single best predictor of medication compliance among discharged schizophrenia patients was the patient's perception of the physician's interest in him or her as a person. Marder et al. (1983) found that, compared with patients who refused medications, schizophrenia inpatients who consented to neuroleptic treatment rated themselves as more satisfied with ward staff and their own physicians and felt that their physicians understood them, had their best interests in mind, and had explained the reasons for taking medications and their potential side effects. Illness severity or treatment response may partially explain these associations. Frank and Gunderson (1990) found that 74% of patients with fair or poor therapeutic alliances (rated at 6 months) failed to comply fully with prescribed medication regimens during the next year and a half. In contrast, only 26% of schizophrenia patients with a good alliance with their therapist (rated at 6 months) were noncompliant. In this study, the association between therapeutic alliance and medication compliance was independent of the patient's severity of psychopathology, type or dosage of medication, or inpatient/outpatient status.

Attitude of staff. Irwin et al. (1971) reported a nonsignificantly higher noncompliance rate as determined by urine screen (39% vs. 25%) among outpatients treated by physicians who viewed medication as having questionable value, compared with patients of physicians who viewed medication as an essential aspect of treatment.

Interventions

Psychosocial treatments for schizophrenia often include promotion of medication compliance as an implicit or explicit goal. Data bearing on the efficacy of individual psychotherapy, social skills training, case management, family psychoeducation, and assertive community treatment programs have been reviewed recently (Lehman et al., 1995). Here we review a more narrow set of interventions that specifically target medication compliance: reinforcement, education, and memory enhancement.

Reinforcement. When characterized by institutional surroundings, long waits, and impersonal or bureaucratic treatment, mental health clinics can be uninviting in a way that discourages attendance and compliance (Chen, 1991; Dencker & Liberman, 1995; Talbott et al., 1986). Making the setting more appealing by providing reinforcement has improved adherence. Liberman and Davis (1975) designed a program to reinforce compliance by serving lunch at a monthly medication clinic and allowing patients who tested positive for neuroleptics to select among several rewards, including toiletries and personal items. Compared with patients randomly assigned to a control medication group, the experimental group showed better attendance, higher compliance levels, and more positive attitudes toward medication. Cassino et al. (1987) successfully increased attendance among schizophrenia patients at a decanoate clinic from 58 to 76% over a 17-week period by offering brunch at morning sessions of the clinic. Offering lunch-type food at an afternoon session, however, had little effect on attendance.

Education. Circumscribed educational interventions aimed at providing information about schizophrenia and its treatment have been ineffective at increasing compliance. Boczkowski et al. (1985) found no difference in compliance between an experimental group of outpatients provided a 30- to 50-minute information session and a control group for whom no specific attempt to focus on medication or diagnosis was made. Macpherson et al. (1996a) randomly assigned patients to one of three groups: one receiving three educational sessions at weekly intervals, one receiving a single educational session, and one having no educational intervention. Although participants in the group receiving the three sessions did have fewer knowledge errors at 1-month followup, their scores on a medication compliance scale did not change. Similarly, Brown et al. (1987) documented an increase in knowledge among schizophrenia outpatients who received two instructional sessions 1 month apart, but noted that instruction did not affect independently rated compliance.

Skills training in areas related to medication seems to be more effective than providing factual information. Eckman et al. (1990) designed a medication management module that trained patients in four skill areas: obtaining information about medications, administering medication and evaluating its benefits, identifying side effects, and negotiating medication with health care providers. The module was delivered to patients in a variety of settings for 3 hours per week over 15 to 20 weeks. Upon completion of the module and over a 3-month followup, knowledge about medication, skill utilization, and compliance improved over baseline. Compliance assessed by the patients' psychiatrists increased from 67% before training to 82% after training, and compliance assessed by designated caregivers increased from 60 to 79%.

Based on a randomized trial of individual and family education, Kelly and Scott (1990) described two circumscribed interventions that each reduced noncompliance at 6-month followup. The individual intervention was delivered by a health educator before the first two post discharge aftercare appointments and focused on increasing the patient's ability to communicate with providers by expressing concerns and asking questions. The family intervention included up to three home visits that focused on the development of an individualized behaviorally oriented compliance plan that, if necessary, included family involvement in aftercare. The authors believed that the critical ingredients in each of these effective interventions were frequent repetition and behavioral modeling, rather than appealing to attitudes and beliefs. Skills training of this sort was described as least effective for patients with comorbid alcoholism, who frequently dropped out of treatment. Nelson et al. (1975) reported that a basic form of skills-training—allowing schizophrenia patients to self-administer medications while hospitalized—increased outpatient compliance over a 6- to 24-week followup. The intervention was effective, however, only for patients who, based on Rorschach test data, accepted that they were psychiatrically disturbed.

In a study of the impact of psychoeducationally oriented family therapy on medication compliance, Strang et al. (1981) randomly assigned to individual supportive or family therapy recently discharged schizophrenia patients living with a relative who exhibited high expressed emotion. Patients receiving family therapy that included specific behavioral compliance strategies worked out between patient and family (Falloon et al., 1984) were more likely to take their prescribed tablets, less likely to require a change to depot neuroleptics, and showed higher and more stable neuroleptic plasma levels, despite identical mean daily doses for the two groups.

Memory enhancement. Boczkowski et al. (1985) described a "behavioral tailoring" intervention that included identifying a highly visible location for storing medication, pairing medication intake with specific routine behaviors, and prescribing a self-monitoring calendar with tear-off slips. In a randomized trial, behavioral training participants were more compliant at 1 and 3-month followup than patients receiving a didactic educational session or control intervention.

Psychodynamic Considerations

Data concerning the role of psychodynamic factors in medication compliance derive from the observations of clinicians prescribing medication to patients with schizophrenia over time. Three areas are consistently identified as pertinent: the psychological meaning of medication to the individual patient, the role of psychotic symptoms in maintaining self-esteem or personality organization, and issues related to transference and countertransference.

Psychological meaning. Clinicians have reported a wide range of psychological meanings ascribed to medications. Patients who are preoccupied with issues of authority and control may be particularly prone to engage in struggles over medication (Amdur 1979). In view of the significant loss of personal control associated with psychosis, Diamond (1984) described noncompliance as an effort to regain control over one's life and feel better. Gutheil (1977) noted that individual patients may concretely equate medication with sickness ("If I need drugs I must be sick. The higher the dose the sicker I am. I'll stop being sick if I stop taking drugs"). Book (1987) described several dynamic issues affecting compliance: paranoid patients' experience of being controlled, poisoned, or invaded by medication; the painful reminder of a defective, "about to fall apart" self among patients who make extensive use of denial; and the possibility that patients' attitudes toward medication are influenced by identification with relatives who received similar medication and experienced poor outcomes, such as suicide.

While viewing compliance primarily as a learned behavioral response, Falloon (1984) noted that some patients fear that prolonged medication may lead to dependence and addiction or equate the need for medication with having a weak character. Taking medication may also be equated with physical or psychological weakness so that the recovering patient who feels strong enough will stop taking medicine (Amdur 1979). Noncompliance in this context may be a test or gamble designed to determine if the illness is still present (Morris & Schulz, 1993).

Medication may be an area around which family or interpersonal conflicts are enacted, so patients stop medication to express anger toward a relative or mental health professional (Kane, 1983). Similarly, patients may discontinue medications in the face of increased pressure to improve functioning or on the verge of hospital discharge or beginning a new job, school, or rehabilitation program. In these circumstances noncompliance can be understood as an unconscious expression of the fear of autonomy or as a communication that expectations have been set too high (Fenton & McGlashan, 1995).

Psychological homeostasis. Psychotic symptoms may be syntonic or serve to support an individual against further personality disintegration or the collapse of self-esteem. Grandiose delusions cast the self as powerful, and persecutory delusions mark the sufferer as worthy of special persecution. When psychosis provides a more positive self-image than can be provided by reality, patients will cling tenaciously to delusions and resist efforts to ameliorate them (Corrigan et al., 1990; Van Putten et al., 1976). Under these circumstances a frontal attack on psychotic symptoms is rarely effective and may precipitate a catastrophic collapse in self-esteem that leads to self-destructive behavior (Drake & Sederer, 1986). Some patients, particularly young men, who organize a sense of self-cohesion around body well-being and activity may experience the physical effect of neuroleptics as a threat to self-organization (Heninger et al., 1965). Other patients may adapt to impending personality disorganization by globally organizing in opposition to the will of others and may resist medications as part of an overall effort to maintain a tenuous sense of effectiveness or control.

Transference/countertransference. Clinicians have noted that patients' views of medications arise in relation to their attitude toward the prescriber and may be distorted by these attitudes. In the context of a relationship perceived as authoritarian, the physical effects of medication may be perceived as rejecting, hostile, or threatening (Sarwer-Foner, 1960) or as a bodily attack or invasion (Gutheil, 1977). Other interpretations may cast the prescription as a negative dismissal of the patient, or the patient may fear that the reduction of symptoms will be accompanied by a parallel reduction in the physician's interest and attention. Positive transference toward the prescriber may spill over to the medication, which can be viewed as a "relationship equivalent" or gift (Gutheil, 1978).

Countertransference, or feelings and attitudes evoked in the physician by the patient, has also been described as potentially undermining pharmacotherapy. Hopelessness and frustration in the face of patient noncompliance and a desire to see the patient taught a lesson by suffering a relapse have been described as common countertransference reactions (Book, 1987; Weiden et al., 1986). The urge to abandon or humiliate the noncompliant patient may also be felt. In this respect, allowing the noncompliant patient who leaves treatment against medical advice to do so with dignity can at least set the stage for more collaborative interactions should the patient return in the future (Diamond, 1983; Frances & Weiden, 1987).

Discussion

Major difficulties in empirical studies of noncompliance include both ascertainment and the fact that the most severely noncompliant individuals leave treatment altogether. Those who remain are the "curiously ambivalent" individuals who continue in care, but do not adhere

Table 1

Empirical correlates of noncompliance in schizophrenia

Patient-related factors	Greater illness symptom severity or grandiosity or both
	Lack of insight
	Substance abuse comorbidity
Medication-related factors	Dysphoric medication side effects
	Subtherapeutic or excessively high dosages
Environmental factors	Inadequate support or supervision
	Practical barriers, such as lack of money or transportation
Clinician-related factors	Poor therapeutic alliance

to prescriptions (Blackwell, 1972). In view of these limitations it is perhaps surprising that available empirical studies yield a relatively consistent set of correlates of noncompliance in schizophrenia, as outlined in table 1.

In evaluating these findings, it is important to note that data suggest multiple possible causes of noncompliance. Because noncompliance can have many causes, its statistical association with any single factor is diluted by the presence of patients in the sample for whom other factors are causal. Similarly, the potential impact of interventions that focus on a single cause of noncompliance—inadequate knowledge or skills, for example—is limited to those in the sample whose noncompliance derives from that cause.

Based on the empirical and clinical literature reviewed here, a general set of treatment recommendations to maximize the likelihood of compliance are outlined in table 2. Given noncompliance in an individual patient, however, a process of differential diagnosis should lead to specific hypotheses regarding underlying causes that allow the design of focal and targeted clinical interventions.

Health Belief Model and Differential Diagnosis of Noncompliance

The health belief model posits that health behavior is a product of an implicit and subjective assessment of the relative costs and benefits of compliance in relation to personal goals and the constraints of everyday life. Elements of this model include (1) individual goals and priorities; (2) an evaluation of the perceived adverse effects of illness and the personal risk of suffering these effects; (3) the individual's perception of the

Table 2
General interventions to maximize the likelihood of compliance

- Conduct an assessment of compliance history and risk factors, including substance abuse and financial or other practical barriers, as part of the evaluation of every patient.

- Allow sufficient time to know the patient as a person and to understand his or her personal goals, concerns, and psychodynamic issues. Place assisting the patient in meeting self-defined goals at the center of treatment.

- Use a negotiated approach to medication. Create a therapeutic environment where deviation from recommendations can be discussed openly, rather than concealed. Show an interest in medication by asking in a nonauthoritarian manner how much is being taken and the effects. Involve the patient in medication treatment by allowing self-regulation of dosage, if possible.

- Maximize efficacy and minimize side effects in choosing agents and dosages. Attend seriously to all side effects and actively elicit and respond to concerns.

- Educate patient and family regarding the biological underpinnings of illness, relapse prevention, and medication side effects.

- Enlist support in the community, including family, friends, and employers. If needed, arrange for supervised medication administration.

- Employ cognitive and memory-enhancing strategies if disorganization or forgetfulness is a problem.

- When the patient is rendered incompetent because of illness, be prepared to recommend judicial intervention.

- If the patient will not comply and is competent, manage countertransference to allow for a continued relationship and the possibility of future treatment.

- Promote the patient's participation in activities that can compete with psychosis as sources of gratification and self-esteem.

advocated health behavior's likely effectiveness and feasibility (the patient's subjective assessment of benefits weighed against the costs of treatment, including physical, psychological, and practical disadvantages and barriers to action); and (4) the availability of internal or external cues to action that trigger health behavior (Bebbington, 1995; Becker & Maiman, 1975). Because schizophrenia may disrupt illness perception and the capacity to plan and act, consideration of the cognitive and motivational resources available to assess risk and formulate action should be an additional element of a health belief model applicable to schizophrenia.

Elements of this modified health belief model outline areas of assessment pertinent to the differential diagnosis of noncompliance. A structured interview that explores many of these areas has been developed to facilitate patient evaluation (Weiden et al., 1994).

Noncompliance may signal that patient and physician goals and priorities differ (Weiden et al., 1986). Maintaining sexual functioning, avoiding obesity, or not missing work for a doctor's appointment, for example, may be of primary importance to the patient, whereas relapse reduction is the physician's priority. An assessment of patient goals forms the basis of a negotiated approach to prescription that is likely to enhance compliance (Eisenthal et al., 1979; Wilson, 1995).

Since pursuing strategies designed to remedy inadvertent noncompliance will fail when noncompliance is purposeful, the differential diagnosis should attempt to separate intentional from inadvertent noncompliance. Empirical studies suggest that from the patient's perspective an immediate subjective dysphoria or other side effects are the most significant costs of compliance. Psychological reports suggest that stigma, loss of the sick role, or disturbed psychic homeostasis may be less discernible costs. These costs may weigh heavily, particularly when accompanied by a low perceived benefit of medication that derives from a lack of knowledge, poor insight, denial, or grandiosity. Interventions under such circumstances should target potentially modifiable elements thought to be operative for the individual patient. Neuroleptic dosage reductions, use of adjunctive agents, or a change to an atypical neuroleptic with fewer side effects may reduce the cost side of the equation. Promoting participation in self-esteem-enhancing activities may diminish the need to maintain delusional sources of self-esteem. Change to an agent with greater efficacy may reduce denial and grandiosity and create the potential for greater insight and perceived medication benefits.

Inadvertent noncompliance is associated with severe psychopathology, including cognitive disorganization, memory impairment, or motivational deficits. The chaotic life circumstances associated with substance abuse comorbidity, as well as such practical considerations as finances and transportation, may also be operative. Here behavioral skill and memory-enhancing interventions, assertive outreach efforts, and recruiting the assistance of family or other supports to supervise medication are major treatment considerations.

New Neuroleptics Versus Depot Preparations

Because of their reduced extrapyramidal side effects and greater efficacy against positive and negative symptoms, new neuroleptics, such as clozapine, risperidone, olanzapine, and sertindole, should provide greater patient benefits at a reduced perceived cost. Depot preparations have the advantage of eliminating covert noncompliance and maximizing the likelihood of steady-state neuroleptic blood levels in patients with cognitive disorganization, memory disturbance, or motivational deficits. Although an empirical basis for choosing among these two pharmacological interventions is not available, the full range of factors associated with noncompliance might be considered clinically relevant. Patients with good insight and a good therapeutic alliance but who report intolerable side effects are likely the best candidates for a trial of a new agent. Patients with poor insight, grandiosity, or other psychotic symptoms or those with memory, motivational, or cognitive deficits might also benefit from a trial of a new agent in the absence of comorbid substance abuse and the presence of either a good therapeutic alliance or adequate family or other supervision to ensure regular adherence. Poor insight and severe psychopathology in the absence of sufficient supervision favor the use of depot agents. Weiden (1995) has suggested that family factors may also have a bearing on the decision between atypical depot agents: Family concern over akinesia or other side effects favors a trial of a new agent, whereas chronic family conflict over taking oral medications favors depot preparations.

It is useful to reassess the decision between depot and new neuroleptics periodically. Some patients, for example, may require a considerable period of depot treatment to attain a level of clinical stability, therapeutic alliance, and insight sufficient to render a trial of a new agent feasible.

Conclusion

The prevention and treatment of noncompliance are of major importance in the care of patients with schizophrenia. Although noncompliance has multiple causes, the empirical literature identifies a circumscribed set of factors that alone or in varying combinations are likely to be operative in individual cases. Exploring each of these factors within a modified health belief model should allow for differential diagnosis and an individualized approach to reducing noncompliance. A comprehensive understanding and integration of patient, illness, treatment, and environmental factors are needed to manage noncompliance (Kane 1986). This integrated approach can best be accomplished within an ongoing physician-patient relationship that allows sufficient time for doctor and patient to know each other and maintain a collaborative therapeutic association over time (Fenton & McGlashan, 1995).

References

Adams, S.G., Jr., & Howe, J.T. (1993). Predicting medication compliance in a psychotic population. *Journal of Nervous and Mental Disease, 181*(9), 558–560.

Amador, X.F., Andreasen, N.C., Flaum, M., Strauss, D.H., Yale, S.A., Clark, S., & Gorman, J.M. (1994). Awareness of illness in schizophrenia, schizoaffective and mood disorders. *Archives of General Psychiatry, 51,* 826–836.

Amador, X.F., Strauss, D.H., Yale, S.A., Flaum, M.M., Endicott, J., & Gorman, J.M. (1993). Assessment of insight in psychosis. *American Journal of Psychiatry, 150,* 873–879.

Amador, X.F., Strauss, D.H., Yale, S.A., & Gorman, J.M. (1991). Awareness of illness in schizophrenia. *Schizophrenia Bulletin, 17*(1), 113–132.

Amdur, M.A. (1979). Medication compliance in outpatient psychiatry. *Comprehensive Psychiatry, 20,* 339–346.

Ayers, T., Liberman, R.P., & Wallace, C.J. (1984). Subjective response to antipsychotic drugs: Failure to replicate predictions of outcome. *Journal of Clinical Psychopharmacology, 4*(2), 89–93.

Babiker, I.E. (1986). Noncompliance in schizophrenia. *Psychiatric Developments, 4,* 329–337.

Baldessarini, R.J., Cohen, B.M., & Teicher, M. (1990). Pharmacological treatment. In S.T. Levy & P.T. Ninan, Eds., *Schizophrenia: Treatment of acute episodes.* Washington, DC: American Psychiatric Press, pp. 61–118.

Bartko, G., Herczeg, I., & Zador, G. (1988). Clinical symptomatology and drug compliance in schizophrenic patients. *Acta Psychiatrica Scandinavica, 77,* 74–76.

Bebbington, P.E. (1995). The content and context of compliance. *International Clinical Psychopharmacology, 9(Suppl. 5),* 41–50.

Becker, M.H. & Maiman, L.A. (1975). Sociobehavioral determinants of compliance with health and medical care recommendations. *Medical Care, 13,* 10–24.

Berg, J.S., Dischler, J., Wagner, D.J., Raia, J.J., & Palmer-Shevlin, N. (1993). Medication compliance: A healthcare problem. *Annals of Pharmacotherapy, 27(Suppl.),* 5–24.

Blackwell, B. (1972). The drug defaulter. *Clinical Pharmacology and Therapeutics, 13*(6), 841–848.

Blackwell, B. (1973). Patient compliance. *New England Journal of Medicine, 289,* 249–252.

Blackwell, B. (1976). Treatment adherence. *British Journal of Psychiatry, 129,* 513–531.

Boczkowski, J.A., Zeichner, A., and DeSanto, N. (1985). Neuroleptic compliance among chronic schizophrenic outpatients: An intervention outcome report. *Journal of Consulting and Clinical Psychiatry, 53*(5), 666–671.

Book, H.E. (1987). Some psychodynamics of non-compliance. *Canadian Journal of Psychiatry, 32,* 115–117.

Brown, C.S., Wright, R.G., & Christensen, D.B. (1987). Association between type of medication instruction and patients' knowledge, side effects, and compliance. *Hospital and Community Psychiatry, 38,* 55–60.

Buchanan, A. (1992). A two-year prospective study of treatment compliance in patients with schizophrenia. *Psychological Medicine, 22,* 787–797.

Carman, J.S., Wyatt, E.S., Fleck, R., Martin, D., & Gold, M. (1984). Neuroleptic compliance in schizophrenic outpatients. *Psychiatric Hospital, 15*(4), 173–178.

Carney, M.W.P. & Sheffield, B.F. (1976). Comparison of antipsychotic depot injections in the maintenance treatment of schizophrenia. *British Journal of Psychiatry, 129,* 476–481.

Cassino, T, Spellman, N., Heiman, J., Shupe, J., & Sklebar, H.T. (1987). Invitation to compliance: The prolixin brunch. *Journal of Psychosocial Nursing, 25*(10), 15–16.

Chen, A. (1991). Noncompliance in community psychiatry: A review of clinical interventions. *Hospital and Community Psychiatry, 42,* 282-287.

Chien, C.P. (1975). Drugs and rehabilitation in schizophrenia. In M. Greenblatt, Ed., *Drugs in combination with other therapies.* New York, NY: Grune & Stratton, pp. 13–34.

Christensen, J.K. (1974). A 5-year follow-up study of male schizophrenics: Evaluation of factors influencing success and failure in the community. *Acta Psychiatrica Scandinavica, 50,* 60–72.

Corrigan, P.W., Liberman, R.P., & Engle, J.D. (1990). From noncompliance to collaboration in the treatment of schizophrenia. *Hospital and Community Psychiatry, 41* 1203–1211.

Crawford, R. & Forrest, A. (1974). Controlled trial of depot fluphenazine in out-patient schizophrenics. *British Journal of Psychiatry, 124,* 385–391.

Cuffel, B.J., Alford, J., Fischer, E.P., & Owen, R.R. (1996). Awareness of illness in schizophrenia and outpatient treatment adherence. *Journal of Nervous and Mental Disease, 184,* 653–659.

Davis, J.M., Janicak, P.G., Singla, A., & Sharma, R.P. (1993). Maintenance antipsychotic medication. In T.R.E. Barnes, Ed., *Antipsychotic drugs and their side effects.* New York, NY: Academic Press, pp. 183–203.

del Campo, E.J., Carr, C.F., & Correa, E. (1983). Rehospitalized schizophrenics: What they report about illness, treatment and compliance. *Journal of Psychosocial Nursing and Mental Health Services, 21*(6), 29–33.

Dencker, S.J. & Liberman, R.P. (1995). From compliance to collaboration in the treatment of schizophrenia. *International Clinical Psychopharmacology, 9*(Suppl. 5), 75–78.

Diamond, R.J. (1983). Enhancing medication use in schizophrenic patients. *Journal of Clinical Psychiatry, 44*(Sect. 2), 7–14.

Diamond, R.J. (1984). Increasing medication compliance in young adult chronic psychiatric patients. In B. Pepper & R. Ryglewicz, Eds. Advances in treating the young adult chronic patient *(New Directions for Mental Health Services. No. 21).* San Francisco, CA: Jossey-Bass, pp. 59–69.

Dixon, L.B., Lehman, A.F., & Levine, J. (1995). Conventional antipsychotic medications for schizophrenia. *Schizophrenia Bulletin, 21*(4), 567–577.

Dixon, L.B., Weiden, P., Haas, G., Sweeney, J., & Frances, A. (1992). Increased tardive dyskinesia in alcohol abusing schizophrenic patients. *Comprehensive Psychiatry, 33,* 121–122.

Donovan, J.L. (1995). Patient decision making: The missing ingredient in compliance research. *International Journal of Technology Assessment in Health Care, 11,* 443–455.

Draine, J. & Solomon, P. (1994). Explaining attitudes toward medication compliance among a seriously mentally ill population. *Journal of Nervous and Mental Disease, 182*(1), 50–54.

Drake, R.E., Osher, F.C., & Wallach, M.A. (1989). Alcohol use and abuse in schizophrenia. *Journal of Nervous and Mental Disease, 177,* 408–414.

Drake, R.E. & Sederer, L.I. (1986). The adverse effects of intensive treatment of chronic schizophrenia. *Comprehensive Psychiatry, 27,* 313–326.

Eckman, T.A., Liberman, R.P., Phipps, C.C., & Blair, K.E. (1990). Teaching medication management skills to schizophrenic patients. *Journal of Clinical Psychopharmacology,* 10(1), 33–38.

Eisenthal, S., Emery, R., Lazare, A., & Udin, H. (1979). "Adherence" and the negotiated approach to patienthood. *Archives of General Psychiatry, 36,* 393–398.

Elixhauser, A., Eisen, S.A., Romeis, J.C., & Homan, S.M. (1990). The effects of monitoring and feedback on compliance. *Medical Care, 28,* 883–893.

Eraker, S.A., Kirscht, J.P., & Becker, M.H. (1984). Understanding and improving patient compliance. *Annals of Internal Medicine, 100,* 258–268.

Falloon, I.R.H. (1984). Developing and maintaining adherence to long-term drug-taking regimens. *Schizophrenia Bulletin, 10*(3), 412–417.

Falloon, I.R.H., Boyd, J.L., & McGill, C.W. (1984). *Family care of schizophrenia: A problem-solving approach to the treatment of mental illness.* New York, NY: Guilford Press.

Falloon, I.R.H., Watt, D.C., & Shepherd, M. (1978). A comparative controlled trial of pimozide and fluphenazine decanoate in the continuation therapy of schizophrenia. *Psychological Medicine, 8,* 59–70.

Fenton, W.S. & McGlashan, T.H. (1995). Schizophrenia: Individual psychotherapy. In H.I. Kaplan & B.J. Sadock, Eds., *Comprehensive textbook of psychiatry. Vol 1, 6th ed.* Baltimore, MD: Williams & Wilkins Company, pp.1007–1018.

Fleischhacker, W.W., Meise, U., Gunther, V., & Kurz, M. (1994). Compliance with antipsychotic drug treatment: Influence of side effects. *Acta Psychiatrica Scandinavica, 89,* 11–15.

Folstein, M., Folstein, S., & McHugh, P. (1975). "Mini-mental state." A practical method for grading the cognitive state of patients for the clinician. *Journal of Psychiatric Research, 12,* 189–198.

Frances, A. & Weiden, P. (1987). Promoting compliance with outpatient drug treatment. *Hospital and Community Psychiatry, 38,* 1158–1160.

Frank, A.F. & Gunderson, J.G. (1990). The role of the therapeutic alliance in the treatment of schizophrenia: Relationship to course and outcome. *Archives of General Psychiatry, 47,* 228–236.

Friedman, M. (1988). Compliance with chronic disease regimens: Diabetes. *Journal of Diabetic Complications, 2,* 140–144.

Gaebel, W. & Pietzcker, A. (1985). One-year outcome of schizophrenic patients: The interaction of chronicity and neuroleptic treatment. *Pharmacopsychiatry, 18,* 235–239.

Gordis, L. (1976). Methodologic issues in measurement of patient compliance. In D.L. Sacket & R.B. Haynes, Eds., *Compliance with therapeutic regimens.* Baltimore, MD: Johns Hopkins University Press, pp. 51–66.

Gutheil, T.G. (1977). Improving patient compliance: Psychodynamics in drug prescribing. *Drug Therapy, 7,* 82–95.

Gutheil, T.G. (1978). Drug therapy: Alliance and compliance. *Psychosomatics, 19,* 219–225.

Haynes, R.B. (1976). A critical review of the "determinants" of patient compliance with therapeutic regimens. In D.L. Sacket & R.B. Haynes, Eds., *Compliance with therapeutic regimens.* Baltimore, MD: Johns Hopkins University Press, pp. 26–39.

Haynes, R.B. (1979). Introduction. In R.B. Haynes, D.L. Sacket, & D.W. Taylor, Eds., *Compliance in health care.* Baltimore, MD: Johns Hopkins University Press, pp. 1–10.

Heninger, G., Dimascio, A., & Klerman, G.L. (1965). Personality factors in variability of response to phenothiazines. *American Journal of Psychiatry, 121,* 1091–1094.

Herz, M.I. & Melville, C. (1980). Relapse in schizophrenia. *American Journal of Psychiatry, 137*(7), 801–805.

Hoffman, R.P., Moore, W.E., & O'Dea, L.F. (1974). A potential role for the pharmacist: Medication problems confronted by the schizophrenic outpatient. *Journal of the American Pharmaceutical Association, NS14*(5), 252–265.

Hogan, T.P., Awad, A.G., & Eastwood, R. (1983). A self-report scale predictive of drug compliance in schizophrenics: Reliability and discriminative validity. *Psychological Medicine, 13,* 177–183.

Hogarty, G.E., Goldberg, S.C., & the Collaborative Study Group. (1973). Drug and sociotherapy in the aftercare of schizophrenic patients. *Archives of General Psychiatry, 28,* 54–64.

Holm, S. (1993). What is wrong with compliance? *Journal of Medical Ethics, 19,* 108–110.

Interagency Council on the Homeless. (1992). *Outcasts on Main Street: Report of the federal task force on homelessness and severe mental illness.* Washington, DC: The Council.

Irwin, D.S., Weitzel, W.D., & Morgan, D.W. (1971). Phenothiazine intake and staff attitudes. *American Journal of Psychiatry, 127*(12), 67–71.

Kane, J.M. (1983). Problems of compliance in outpatient treatment of schizophrenia. *Journal of Clinical Psychiatry, 44*(Sect. 2), 3–6.

Kane, J.M. (1986). Prevention and treatment of neuroleptic noncompliance. *Psychiatric Annals, 16,* 576–579.

Kashner, T.M., Rader, L.E., Rodell, D.E., Beck, C.M., Rodell, L.R., & Muller, K. (1991). Family characteristics, substance abuse, and hospitalization patterns of patients with schizophrenia. *Hospital and Community Psychiatry, 42*(2), 195–197.

Kelly, G.R., Mamon, J.A., & Scott, J.E. (1987). Utility of the health belief model in examining medication compliance among psychiatric outpatients. *Social Science Medicine, 25*(11), 1205–1211.

Kelly, G.R. & Scott, J.E. (1990). Medication compliance and health education among outpatients with chronic mental disorders. *Medical Care, 28*(12), 1181–1197.

Kirscht, J.P. & Rosenstock, I.M. (1979). Patients' problems in following recommendations of health experts. In G.C. Stone, N.E. Adler, & F. Cohen, Eds., *Health psychology handbook: Theories, applications, and challenges of a psychological approach to the health care system.* San Francisco, CA: Jossey-Bass, pp. 189–215.

Leff, J.P. & Wing, J.K. (1971). Trial of maintenance therapy in schizophrenia. *British Medical Journal, 3,* 599–604.

Lehman, A.F., Carpenter, W.T., Jr., Goldman, H.H., & Steinwachs, D.M. (1995). Treatment outcomes in schizophrenia: Implications for practice, policy, and research. *Schizophrenia Bulletin, 21*(4), 669–675.

Liberman, R.P., & Davis, J. (1975). Drugs and behavior analysis. *Progress in Behavior Modification, 1,* 307–330.

Lin, I.F., Spiga, R., & Fortsch, W. (1979). Insight and adherence to medication in chronic schizophrenics. *Journal of Clinical Psychiatry, 40,* 430–432.

Linn, M.W., Klett, C.J., & Caffey, E.M. (1982). Relapse of psychiatric patients in foster care. *American Journal of Psychiatry, 139,* 778–783.

Lutz, E.G. (1976). Neuroleptic-induced akathisia and dystonia triggered by alcohol. *Journal of the American Medical Association, 236*(21), 2422–2423.

Macpherson, R., Jerrom, B., & Hughes, A. (1996a). A controlled study of education about drug treatment in schizophrenia. *British Journal of Psychiatry, 168,* 709–717.

Macpherson, R., Jerrom, B., & Hughes, A. (1996b). Relationship between insight, educational background, and cognition in schizophrenia. British *Journal of Psychiatry, 168,* 718–122.

Marder, S.R., Mebane, A., Chien, C.-P., Winslade, W.J., Swann, E., & Van Putten, T. (1983). A comparison of patients who refuse and consent to neuroleptic treatment. *American Journal of Psychiatry, 140*(4), 470–472.

McClellan, TA. & Cowan, G. (1970). Use of antipsychotic and antidepressant drugs by chronically ill patients. *American Journal of Psychiatry, 126*(12), 113–115.

McEvoy, J.P., Apperson, L.J., Apelbaum, P.S., Ortlip, P., Brecosky, J., & Hammill, K. (1989). Insight in schizophrenia: Its relation to acute psychopathology. *Journal of Nervous and Mental Disease, 177,* 43–47.

McEvoy, J.P., Howe, A.C., & Hogarty, G.E. (1984). Differences in the nature of relapse and subsequent inpatient course between medication-compliant and noncompliant schizophrenic patients. *Journal of Nervous and Mental Disease, 172*(7), 412–416.

McFarlane, W.R., Lukens, E., Link, B., Dushay, R., Deakins, S.A., Newmark, M., Dunne, E.J., Horen, B., & Toran, J. (1995). Multiple-family groups and psychoeducation in the treatment of schizophrenia. *Archives of General Psychiatry, 52,* 679–687.

Morris, L.S. & Schulz, R.M. (1993). Medication compliance: The patient's perspective. *Clinical Therapeutics, 15,* 593–606.

Munetz, M.R. & Roth, L.H. (1985). Informing patients about tardive dyskinesia. *Archives of General Psychiatry, 42,* 866–871.

Nelson, A.A., Gold, B.H., Huchinson, R.A., & Benezra, E. (1975). Drug default among schizophrenic patients. *American Journal of Hospital Pharmacy, 32,* 1237–1242.

Norell, S.E. (1981). Accuracy of patient interviews and estimates by clinical staff in determining medication compliance. *Social Science and Medicine, 15,* 57–61.

Northern California Neurobehavioral Group, Inc. (1988). *Manual for the neurobehavioral cognitive status examination.* Fairfax, CA: The Group.

Olivera, A.A., Kiefer, M.W., & Manley, N.K. (1990). Tardive dyskinesia in patients with substance use disorders. *American Journal of Drug and Alcohol Abuse, 16,* 57–66.

Overall, J.E. & Gorham, D.R. (1962). The Brief Psychiatric Rating Scale. *Psychological Reports, 10,* 799–812.

Owen, R.R., Fischer, E.P., Booth, B.M., & Cuffel, B.J. (1996). Medication noncompliance and substance abuse among patients with schizophrenia. *Psychiatric Services, 47*(8), 853–858.

Pan, P.C. & Tantam, D. (1989). Clinical characteristics, health beliefs and compliance with maintenance treatment: A comparison between regular and irregular attenders at a depot clinic. *Acta Psychiatrica Scandinavica, 79,* 564–570.

Parker, G. & Hadzi-Pavlovic, D. (1995). The capacity of a measure of disability (the LSP) to predict hospital readmission in those with schizophrenia. *Psychological Medicine, 25,* 157–163.

Parkes, C.M., Brown, G.W., & Monck, E.M. (1962). The general practitioner and the schizophrenic patient. *British Medical Journal, 1,* 972–976.

Pristach, C.A. & Smith, C.M. (1990). Medication compliance and substance abuse among schizophrenic patients. *Hospital and Community Psychiatry, 41*(12), 1345–1348.

Razali, M.S. & Yahya, H. (1995). Compliance with treatment in schizophrenia: A drug intervention program in a developing program. *Acta Psychiatrica Scandinavica, 91,* 331–335.

Regier, D.A., Farmer, M.E., & Rae, D.S. (1990). Comorbidity of mental disorders with alcohol and other drug abuse. *Journal of the American Medical Association, 264*(25) 2511–2518.

Reilly, E.L., Wilson, W.P., & McClinton, H.K. (1967). Clinical characteristics and medication history of schizophrenics readmitted to the hospital. *International Journal of Neuropsychiatry, 39,* 85–90.

Renton, C.A., Affleck, J.W., Carstairs, G.M., & Forrest, A.D. (1963). A follow-up of schizophrenic patients in Edinburgh. *Acta Psychiatrica Scandinavica, 39,* 548–600.

Rickels, K. & Briscoe, E. (1970). Assessment of dosage deviation in outpatient drug research. *Journal of Clinical Psychopharmacology and the Journal of New Drugs, 10*(3), 153–160.

Sacket, D.L. (1976). The magnitude of compliance and noncompliance. In D.L. Sacket & R.B. Haynes, Eds., *Compliance with therapeutic regimens.* Baltimore, MD: Johns Hopkins University Press, pp. 9–25.

Sarwer-Foner, G.J. (1960). The role of neuroleptic medication in psychotherapeutic interaction. *Comprehensive Psychiatry, 1,* 291–300.

Schooler, N.R. & Keith, S.J. (1993). The clinical research base for the treatment of schizophrenia. *Psychopharmacology Bulletin, 29*(4), 431–446.

Sellwood, W. & Tarrier, N. (1994). Demographic factors associated with extreme non-compliance in schizophrenia. *Social Psychiatry and Psychiatric Epidemiology, 29,* 172–177.

Serban, G. & Thomas, A. (1974). Attitudes and behaviors of acute and chronic schizophrenic patients regarding ambulatory treatment. *American Journal of Psychiatry, 131*(9), 991–995.

Shope, J.T. (1988). Compliance in children and adults: A review of studies. In D. Schmidt & I.E. Leppik, Eds., *Compliance in epilepsy (epilepsy research supplement 1).* New York, NY: Elsevier Science Publishers. pp. 23–47.

Soskis, D.A. (1978). Schizophrenic and medical inpatients as informed drug consumers. *Archives of General Psychiatry, 35,* 645–647.

Stimson, G.V. (1974). Obeying doctors orders: A view from the other side. *Social Science and Medicine, 8,* 97–194.

Strang, J.S., Falloon, I.R.H., Moss, H.B., Razani, J., & Boyd, J.L. (1981). The effects of family therapy on treatment compliance in schizophrenia. *Psychopharmacology Bulletin, 17*(3), 87–88.

Sullivan, G., Wells, K.B., Morgenstern, H., & Leake, B. (1995). Identifying modifiable risk factors for rehospitalization: A case-control study of seriously mentally ill persons in Mississippi. *American Journal of Psychiatry, 152*(12), 1749–1756.

Talbott, J.A., Bachrach, L., & Ross, L. (1986). Noncompliance and mental health systems. *Psychiatric Annals, 16,* 586–599.

Trostle, J.A. (1988). Medical compliance as an ideology. *Social Science and Medicine, 27,* 1299–1308.

Van Putten, T. (1974). Why do schizophrenic patients refuse to take their drugs? *Archives of General Psychiatry, 31,* 67–72.

Van Putten, T., Crumpton, E., & Yale, C. (1976). Drug refusal in schizophrenia and the wish to be crazy. *Archives of General Psychiatry, 33,* 1443–1446.

Van Putten, T., May, P.R.A., & Marder, S.R. (1984). Response to antipsychotic medication: The doctor's and the consumer's view. *American Journal of Psychiatry, 141*(1), 16–19.

Van Putten, T., May, P.R.A., Marder, S.R., & Wittmann, L.A. (1981). Subjective response to antipsychotic drugs. *Archives of General Psychiatry, 38,* 187–190.

Van Putten, T., Mutalipassi, L.R., & Malkin, M.D. (1974). Phenothiazine-induced decompensation. *Archives of General Psychiatry, 30,* 102–105.

Verghese, A., John, J.K., Rajkurnar, S., Richard, J., Sethi, B.B., & Trivedi, J.K. (1989). Factors associated with the course and outcome of schizophrenia in India: Results of a two-year multicentre follow-up study. *British Journal of Psychiatry, 154,* 499–503.

Weiden, P.J. (1995). Antipsychotic therapy, Patient preference and compliance. *Current Approaches to Psychosis, 4,* 1–7.

Weiden, P.J., Rapkin, B., Mott, T., Zygmunt, A., Goldman, D., Horvitz-Lennon, M., & Frances, A. (1994). Rating of medication influences (ROMI) scale in schizophrenia. *Schizophrenia Bulletin, 20*(2), 297–310.

Weiden, P.J., Shaw, E., & Mann, J. (1986). Causes of neuroleptic noncompliance. *Psychiatric Annals, 16,* 571–575.

Willcox, D.R.C., Gillan, R., & Hare, E.H. (1965). Do psychiatric out-patients take their drugs? *British Medical Journal, 2,* 790–792.

Wilson, B.M. (1995). Promoting compliance: The patient provider partnership. *Advances in Renal Replacement Therapy, 3,* 199–206.

Wilson, J.D., and Enoch, M.D. (1967). Estimation of drug rejection by schizophrenic in-patients, with analysis of clinical factors. *British Journal of Psychiatry, 113,* 209–211.

Young, J.L., Zonana, H.V., and Shepler, L. (1986). Medication noncompliance in schizophrenia: Codification and update. *Bulletin of the American Academy of Psychiatry and the Law, 14,* 105–122.

Chapter Six: Role Recovery

Recovery from Mental Illness: The Guiding Vision of the Mental Health Service System in the 1990s

William A. Anthony

This article originally appeared in *Psychosocial Rehabilitation Journal,* (1993) 16 (4), 11–24, and is reprinted with permission.

William A. Anthony, Ph.D., is Executive Director of the Center for Psychiatric Rehabilitation at Boston University, Boston, MA.

The implementation of deinstitutionalization in the 1960s and 1970s, and the increasing ascendance of the community support system concept and the practice of psychiatric rehabilitation in the 1980s, have laid the foundation for a new 1990s vision of service delivery for people who have mental illness. Recovery from mental illness is the vision that will guide the mental health system in this decade. This article outlines the fundamental services and assumptions of a recovery-oriented mental health system. As the recovery concept becomes better understood, it could have major implications for how future mental health systems are designed.

The seeds of the recovery vision were sown in the aftermath of the era of deinstitutionalization. The failures in the implementation of the policy of deinstitutionalization confronted us with the fact that a person with severe mental illness wants and needs more than just symptom relief. People with severe mental illnesses may have multiple residential, vocational, educational, and social needs and wants. Deinstitutionalization radically changed how the service system attempts to meet these wants and needs. No longer does the state hospital attempt to meet these multiple wants and needs; a great number of alternative community-based settings and alternative inpatient settings have sprung up since deinstitutionalization. This diversity has required new conceptualizations both of how services for people with severe mental illnesses should be organized and delivered, and of the wants and needs of people with severe mental illness. This new way of thinking about services and about the people served has laid the foundation for the gradual emergence of the recovery vision in the 1990s.

As a prelude to a discussion of the recovery vision, the present paper briefly describes the community support system (CSS) concept and the basic services integral to a comprehensive community support system. Next, the more thorough understanding of the total impact of severe mental illness, as conceptualized in the rehabilitation model, is succinctly overviewed. With the CSS service configuration and the rehabilitation model providing the historical and conceptual base, the recovery concept, as we currently understand it, is then presented.

The Community Support System

In the mid-1970s, a series of meetings at the National Institute of Mental Health (NIMH) gave birth to the idea of a community support system (CSS), a concept of how services should be provided to help persons with long-term psychiatric disabilities (Turner & TenHoor, 1978). Recognizing that post-deinstitutionalization services were unacceptable, the CSS described the array of services that the mental health system needed for persons with severe psychiatric disabilities (Stroul, 1989). The CSS filled the conceptual vacuum resulting from the aftermath of deinstitutionalization (Test, 1984). The CSS was defined (Turner & Schifren, 1979, p. 2) as "a network of caring and responsible people committed to assisting a vulnerable population meet their needs and develop their potentials without being unnecessarily isolated or excluded from the community." The CSS concept identifies the essential components needed by a community to provide adequate services and support to persons who are psychiatrically disabled.

The essential components of a CSS have been demonstrated and evaluated since its inception. Test (1984) concluded from her review that programs providing more CSS functions seem to be more effective (with fewer rehospitalizations and improved social adjustment in some cases) than programs that provide fewer CSS functions. More recently, Anthony and Blanch (1989) reviewed data relevant to CSS and concluded that research in the 1980s documented the need for the array of services and supports originally posited by the CSS concept. It appears that the need for the component services of CSS has a base in empiricism as well as in logic. Most comprehensive mental health system initiatives in the 1980s can be traced to the CSS conceptualization (National Institute of Mental Health, 1987).

Based on the CSS framework, the Center for Psychiatric Rehabilitation has refined and defined the services fundamental to meeting the wants and needs of persons with long-term mental illness. Table 1 presents these essential client services.

Table 1

Essential Client Services in a Caring System

Service Category	Description	Consumer Outcome
Treatment	Alleviating symptoms and distress	Symptom relief
Crisis intervention	Controlling and resolving critical or dangerous problems	Personal safety assured
Case management	Obtaining the services client needs and wants	Services accessed
Rehabilitation	Developing clients' skills and supports related to clients' goals	Role functioning
Enrichment	Engaging clients in fulfilling and satisfying activities	Self-development
Rights protection	Advocating to uphold one's rights	Equal opportunity
Basic support	Providing the people, places, and things client needs to survive (e.g., shelter, meals, health care)	Personal survival assured
Self-help	Exercising a voice and a choice in one's life	Empowerment

Adapted from: Cohen, M., Cohen, B., Nemec, P., Farkas, M. & Forbess, R. (1988). *Training technology: Case management.* Boston, MA: Center for Psychiatric Rehabilitation.

The Impact of Severe Mental Illness

This new understanding of the importance of a comprehensive, community-based service system is based on a more thorough and clear understanding of that system's clients. The field of psychiatric rehabilitation, with its emphasis on treating the consequences of the illness rather than just the illness per se, has helped bring to this new service system configuration a more complete understanding of the total impact of severe mental illness. The psychiatric rehabilitation field relied on the World Health Organization's 1980 classification of the consequences of disease to provide the conceptual framework for describing the impact of severe mental illness (Frey, 1984).

In the 1980s, proponents of psychiatric rehabilitation emphasized that mental illness not only causes mental impairments or symptoms but also causes the person significant functional limitations, disabilities, and handicaps (Anthony, 1982; Anthony & Liberman, 1986; Anthony, Cohen, & Farkas, 1990; Cohen & Anthony, 1984). The World Health Organization (Wood, 1980), unlike mental health policymakers, had already developed a model of illness which incorporated not only the illness or impairment but also the consequences of the illness (disability and handicap). As depicted in table 2, these terms can be reconfigured as impairment, dysfunction, disability, and disadvantage. This conceptualization of the impact of severe mental illness has come to be known as the rehabilitation model (Anthony, Cohen, & Farkas, 1990).

The development of the concept of a comprehensive community support system, combined with the rehabilitation model's more comprehensive understanding of the impact of severe mental illness, has laid the conceptual groundwork for a new vision for the mental health service system of the 1990s. Based on the insights of the 1970s and 1980s, service delivery programs and systems will be guided by a vision of promoting recovery from mental illness (Anthony, 1991).

Recovery: The Concept

The concept of recovery, while quite common in the field of physical illness and disability (Wright, 1983), has heretofore received little attention in both practice and research with people who have a severe and persistent mental illness (Spaniol, 1991). The concept of recovery from physical illness and disability does not mean that the suffering has disappeared, all the symptoms removed, and/or the functioning completely restored (Harrison, 1984). For example, a person with paraplegia can recover even though the spinal cord has not. Similarly, a person with mental illness can recover even though the illness is not "cured."

In the mental health field, the emerging concept of recovery has been introduced and is most often discussed in the writings of consumers/survivors/clients (Anonymous, 1989; Deegan, 1988; Houghton, 1982; Leete, 1989; McDermott, 1990; Unzicker, 1989). Recovery is described as a deeply personal, unique process of changing one's attitudes, values, feelings, goals, skills, and/or roles. It is a way of living a satisfying, hopeful, and contributing life even with limitations caused by illness. Recovery involves the development of new meaning and purpose in one's life as one grows beyond the catastrophic effects of mental illness.

Recovery from mental illness involves much more than recovery from the illness itself. People with mental illness may have to recover from the stigma they have incorporated into their very being; from the iatrogenic effects of treatment settings; from lack of recent opportunities for self-determination; from the negative side effects of unemployment;

Table 2
The Negative Impact of Severe Mental Illness

Stages	I. Impairment	II. Dysfunction	III. Disability	IV. Disadvantage
Definitions	Any loss or abnormality of psychological, physiological, or anatomical structure or function	Any restriction or lack of ability to perform an activity or task in the manner or within the range considered normal for a human being	Any restriction or lack of ability to perform a role in the manner or within the range considered normal for a human being	A lack of opportunity for an individual that limits or prevents the performance of an activity or the fulfillment of a role that is normal (depending on age, sex, social, cultural factors) for that individual
Examples	Hallucinations, delusions, depression	Lack of work adjustment skills, social skills, ADL skills	Unemployment, homelessness	Discrimination and poverty

Adapted from: Anthony, W. A., Cohen, M. R., & Farkas, M. D. (1990). Psychiatric rehabilitation. Boston: MA, Center for Psychiatric Rehabilitation.

and from crushed dreams. Recovery is often a complex, time-consuming process.

Recovery is what people with disabilities do. Treatment, case management, and rehabilitation are what helpers do to facilitate recovery (Anthony, 1991). Interestingly, the recovery experience is not an experience that is foreign to services personnel. Recovery transcends illness and the disability field itself. Recovery is a truly unifying human experience. Because all people (helpers included) experience the catastrophes of life (death of a loved one, divorce, the threat of severe physical illness, and disability), the challenge of recovery must be faced. Successful recovery from a catastrophe does not change the fact that the experience has occurred, that the effects are still present, and that one's life has changed forever. Successful recovery does mean that the person has changed, and that the meaning of these facts to the person has therefore changed. They are no longer the primary focus of one's life. The person moves on to other interests and activities.

Recovery: The Outcome

Recovery may seem like an illusory concept. We still know very little about what this process is like for people with severe mental illness. Yet many recent intervention studies have in fact measured elements of recovery, even though the recovery process went unmentioned. Recovery is a multi-dimensional concept: there is no single measure of recovery, but many different measures that estimate various aspects of it. The recovery vision expands our concept of service outcome to include such dimensions as self-esteem, adjustment to disability, empowerment, and self-determination. However, it is the concept of recovery, and not the many ways to measure it, that ties the various components of the field into a single vision. For service providers, recovery from mental illness is a vision commensurate with researchers' vision of curing and preventing mental illness. Recovery is a simple yet powerful vision (Anthony, 1991).

A Recovery-Oriented Mental Health System

A mental health services system that is guided by the recovery vision incorporates the critical services of a community support system organized around the rehabilitation model's description of the impact of severe mental illness—all under the umbrella of the recovery vision. In a recovery-oriented mental health system, each essential service is analyzed with respect to its capacity to ameliorate people's impairment, dysfunction, disability, and disadvantage (see table 3).

Table 3 provides an overview of the major consumer outcome focus of the essential community support system of services. The services mainly directed at the impairment are the traditional "clinical" services, which in a recovery-oriented system deal with only a part of the impact of severe mental illness (i.e., the symptoms). Major recovery may occur without complete symptom relief. That is, a person may still experience major episodes of symptom exacerbation, yet have significantly restored task and role performance and/or removed significant opportunity barriers. From a recovery perspective, those successful outcomes may have led to the growth of new meaning and purpose in the person's life.

Recovery-oriented system planners see the mental health system as greater than the sum of its parts. There is the possibility that efforts to affect the impact of severe mental illness positively can do more than leave the person less impaired, less dysfunctional, less disabled, and less disadvantaged. These interventions can leave a person not only with "less," but with "more"—more meaning, more purpose, more success, and more satisfaction with one's life. The possibility exists that the outcomes can be more than the specific service outcomes of, for example, symptom management and relief, role functioning, services accessed, entitlements assured, etc. While these outcomes are the raison d'être of each service, each may also contribute in unknown ways to recovery from mental illness. A provider of specific services recognizes, for example, that symptoms are alleviated not only to reduce discomfort, but also because symptoms may inhibit recovery; that crises are controlled not only to assure personal safety, but also because crises may destroy opportunities for recovery; that rights protection not only assures legal entitlements, but also that entitlements can support recovery. As mentioned previously, recovery outcomes include more subjective outcomes such as self-esteem, empowerment, and self-determination.

Basic Assumptions of a Recovery-Focused Mental Health System

The process of recovery has not been researched. The vagaries of recovery make it a mysterious process, a mostly subjective process begging to be attended to and understood. People with severe disabilities (including psychiatric disabilities) have helped us glimpse the process

Table 3

Focus of Mental Health Services

Recovery: Development of new meaning and purpose as one grows beyond the catastrophic effects of mental illness.

Mental Health Services (and Outcomes)	Impact of Severe Mental Illness			
	Impairment (Disorder in Thought, Feelings, and Behavior)	Dysfunction (Task Performance Limited)	Disability (Role Performance Limited)	Disadvantage (Opportunity Restrictions)
Treatment (Symptom Relief)	X			
Crisis Intervention (Safety)	X			
Case Management (Access)	X	X	X	X
Rehabilitation (Role Functioning)		X	X	X
Enrichment (Self-Development)		X	X	X
Rights Protection (Equal Opportunity)				X
Basic Support (Survival)				X
Self-Help (Empowerment)			X	X

through their words and actions (Weisburd, 1992). In addition, all of us have directly experienced the recovery process in reaction to life's catastrophes. Based on information gained from the above, a series of assumptions about recovery can be identified.

1. Recovery can occur without professional intervention. Professionals do not hold the key to recovery; consumers do. The task of professionals is to facilitate recovery; the task of consumers is to recover. Recovery may be facilitated by the consumer's natural support system. After all, if recovery is a common human condition experienced by us all, then people who are in touch with their own recovery can help others through the process. Self-help groups, families, and friends are the best examples of this phenomenon.

It is important for mental health providers to recognize that what promotes recovery is not simply the array of mental health services. Also essential to recovery are non-mental health activities and organizations, e.g., sports, clubs, adult education, and churches. There are many paths to recovery, including choosing not to be involved in the mental health system.

2. A common denominator of recovery is the presence of people who believe in and stand by the person in need of recovery. Seemingly universal in the recovery concept is the notion that critical to one's recovery is a person or persons in whom one can trust to "be there" in times of need. People who are recovering talk about the people who believed in them when they did not even believe in themselves, who encouraged their recovery but did not force it, who tried to listen and understand when nothing seemed to be making sense. Recovery is a deeply human experience, facilitated by the deeply human responses of others. Recovery can be facilitated by any one person. Recovery can be everybody's business.

3. A recovery vision is not a function of one's theory about the causes of mental illness. Whether the causes of mental illness are viewed as biological and/or psychosocial generates considerable controversy among professionals, advocates, and consumers. Adopting a recovery vision does not commit one to either position on this debate, nor on the use or nonuse of medical interventions. Recovery may occur whether one views the illness as biological or not. People with adverse physical abnormalities (e.g., blindness, quadriplegia) can recover even though the physical nature of the illness is unchanged or even worsens.

4. Recovery can occur even though symptoms reoccur. The episodic nature of severe mental illness does not prevent recovery. People with other illnesses that might be episodic (e.g., rheumatoid arthritis, multiple sclerosis) can still recover. Individuals who experience intense psychiatric symptoms episodically can also recover.

5. Recovery changes the frequency and duration of symptoms. People who are recovering and experience symptom exacerbation may have a level of symptom intensity as bad as or even worse than previously experienced. As one recovers, the symptom frequency and duration appear to have been changed for the better. That is, symptoms interfere with functioning less often and for briefer periods of time. More of one's life is lived symptom-free. Symptom recurrence becomes less of a threat to one's recovery, and return to previous function occurs more quickly after exacerbation.

6. Recovery does not feel like a linear process. Recovery involves growth and setbacks, periods of rapid change and little change. While the overall trend may be upward, the moment-to-moment experience does not feel so "directionful." Intense feelings may overwhelm one unexpectedly. Periods of insight or growth happen unexpectedly. The recovery process feels anything but systematic and planned.

7. Recovery from the consequences of the illness is sometimes more difficult than recovering from the illness itself. Issues of dysfunction, disability, and disadvantage are often more difficult than impairment issues. An inability to perform valued tasks and roles, and the resultant loss of self-esteem, are significant barriers to recovery. The barriers brought about by being placed in the category of "mentally ill" can be overwhelming. These disadvantages include loss of rights and equal opportunities, and discrimination in employment and housing, as well as barriers created by the system's attempts at helping—e.g., lack of opportunities for self-determination, disempowering treatment practices. These disabilities and disadvantages can combine to limit a person's recovery even though one has become predominantly asymptomatic.

8. Recovery from mental illness does not mean that one was not "really mentally ill." At times people who have successfully recovered from severe mental illness have been discounted as not "really" mentally ill. Their successful recovery is not seen as a model, as a beacon of hope for those beginning the recovery process, but rather as an aberration, or worse yet as a fraud. It is as if we said that someone who has quadriplegia but recovered did not "really" have a damaged spinal cord! People who have or are recovering from mental illness are sources of knowledge about the recovery process and how people can be helpful to those who are recovering.

Implications for the Design of Mental Health Systems

Recovery as a concept is by no means fully understood. Much research, both qualitative and quantitative, still needs to be done. Paramount to the recovery concept are the attempts to understand the experience of recovery from mental illness from those who are experiencing it themselves. Qualitative research would seem particularly important in this regard.

However, it is not too early for system planners to begin to incorporate what we currently think we know about recovery. For example, most first-person accounts of recovery from catastrophe (including mental illness) recount the critical nature of personal support (recovery assumption #2). The questions of system planners are: Should personal support be provided by the mental health system? And if so, how can this personal support be provided? Should intensive care managers fill this role? What about self-help organizations? Should they be expanded and asked to perform even more of this function?

If personal support is characterized as support that is trusting and empathic, do human resource development staff members need to train helpers in the interpersonal skills necessary to facilitate this personal relationship? Quality assurance personnel would need to understand the time it takes to develop such a relationship and figure out ways to assess and document this process.

Recovery, as we currently understand it, involves the development of new meaning and purposes in one's life as one grows beyond the catastrophic effects of mental illness. Does the mental health system help in the search for this new meaning? Does it actively seek to provide opportunities that might trigger the development of new life purposes? Is this the type of service professionals and survivors talk about when the value of "supportive psychotherapy" is mentioned? Is there the support of therapists trained to help persons with mental illness control their lives once again—even without fully controlling their mental illness?

There are a number of possible stimulants to recovery. These may include other consumers who are recovering effectively. Books, films, and groups may cause serendipitous insights to occur about possible life options. Visiting new places and talking to various people are other ways in which the recovery process might be triggered. Critical to recovery is regaining the belief that there are options from which one can choose— a belief perhaps even more important to recovery than the particular option one initially chooses.

Recovery-oriented mental health systems must structure their settings so that recovery "triggers" are present. Boring day treatment programs and inactive inpatient programs are characterized by a dearth of recovery stimulants. The mental health system must help sow and nurture the seeds of recovery through creative programming. There is an important caveat to this notion of recovery triggers. At times the information provided through people, places, things, and activities can be overwhelming. Different amounts of information are useful at different times in one's recovery. At times denial is needed when a recovering person perceives the information as too overwhelming. At particular points in one's recovery, denial of information prevents the person from becoming overwhelmed. Information can be perceived as a bomb or a blanket—harsh and hostile or warm and welcome. Helpers in the mental health system must allow for this variation in the time frame of information they are providing—and not routinely and simply characterize denial as non-functional.

Similarly, the range of emotions one experiences as one recovers cannot simply be diagnosed as abnormal or pathological. All recovering people, whether mentally ill or not, experience strong emotions and a wide range of emotions. Such emotions include depression, guilt, isolation, suspiciousness, and anger. For many persons who are recovering from catastrophes other than mental illness, these intense emotions are seen as a normal part of the recovery process. For persons recovering from mental illness, these emotions are too quickly and routinely considered a part of the illness rather than a part of the recovery. The mental health system must allow these emotions to be experienced in a non-stigmatizing and understanding environment. Helpers must have a better understanding of the recovery concept in order for this recovery-facilitating environment to occur.

Concluding Comments

Many new questions and new issues are stimulated for system planners by a recovery-oriented perspective. While we are nowhere near understanding the recovery concept nor routinely able to help people achieve it, a recovery vision for the 1990s is extremely valuable.

A vision pulls the field of services into the future. A vision is not reflective of what we are currently achieving, but of what we hope for and dream of achieving. Visionary thinking does not raise unrealistic expectations. A vision begets not false promises but a passion for what we are doing (Anthony, Cohen, & Farkas, 1990).

Previous "visions" that guided the mental health system were not consumer based. They did not describe how the consumer would ultimately benefit. For example, the deinstitutionalization "vision" described how buildings would function and not how service recipients would function. Similarly, the CSS "vision" described how the service system would function and not the functioning of the service recipients. In contrast, a recovery vision speaks to how the recipients of services would function. Changes in buildings and services are seen in the context of how they might benefit the recovery vision.

In contrast to the field of services, biomedical and neuroscience researchers have a vision. They speak regularly of curing and preventing severe mental illness. They have helped to declare the 1990s "the decade of the brain." Recovery from mental illness is a similarly potent vision. It speaks to the heretofore unmentioned and perhaps heretical belief that any person with severe mental illness can grow beyond the limits imposed by his or her illness. Recovery is a concept that can open our eyes to new possibilities for those we serve and how we can go about serving them. The 1990s might also turn out to be the "decade of recovery."

References

Anonymous (1989). How I've managed chronic mental illness. *Schizophrenia Bulletin, 15,* 635–640.

Anthony, W. A. (1982). Explaining "psychiatric rehabilitation" by an analogy to "physical rehabilitation." *Psychosocial Rehabilitation Journal, 5*(1), 61–65.

Anthony, W. A. (1991). Recovery from mental illness: The new vision of services researchers. *Innovations and Research, 1*(1), 13–14.

Anthony, W. A., & Blanch, A. K. (1989). Research on community support services: What have we learned? *Psychosocial Rehabilitation Journal, 12*(3), 55–81.

Anthony, W. A., Cohen, M. R., & Farkas, M. D. (1990). *Psychiatric rehabilitation.* Boston: Boston University, Center for Psychiatric Rehabilitation.

Anthony, W. A., & Liberman, R. P. (1986). The practice of psychiatric rehabilitation: Historical, conceptual, and research base. *Schizophrenia Bulletin, 12,* 542–559.

Cohen, B. F., & Anthony, W. A. (1984). Functional assessment in psychiatric rehabilitation. In A. S. Halpern & M. J. Fuhrer (Eds.), *Functional assessment in rehabilitation* (pp. 79–100). Baltimore: Paul Brookes.

Cohen, M. R., Cohen, B., Nemec, P. B., Farkas, M. D., & Forbess, R. (1988). *Psychiatric rehabilitation training technology: Case management (trainer package).* Boston: Boston University, Center for Psychiatric Rehabilitation.

Deegan, P. E. (1988). Recovery: The lived experience of rehabilitation. *Psychosocial Rehabilitation Journal, 11*(4), 11–19.

Frey, W. D. Functional assessment in the '80s: A conceptual enigma, a technical challenge. In A. S. Halpern & M. J. Fuhrer (Eds.), *Functional assessment in rehabilitation* (pp. 11–43). Baltimore: Paul Brookes.

Harrison, V. (1984). A biologist's view of pain, suffering and marginal life. In F. Dougherty (Ed.), *The depraved, the disabled and the fullness of life.* Delaware: Michael Glazier.

Houghton, J. F. (1982). Maintaining mental health in a turbulent world. *Schizophrenia Bulletin, 8,* 548–552.

Leete, E. (1989). How I perceive and manage my illness. *Schizophrenia Bulletin, 15,* 197–200.

McDermott, B. (1990). Transforming depression. *The Journal, 1*(4), 13–14.

National Institute of Mental Health. (1987). *Toward a model plan for a comprehensive, community-based mental health system.* Rockville, MD: Division of Education and Service Systems Liaison.

Spaniol, L. (1991). Editorial. *Psychosocial Rehabilitation Journal, 14*(4), 1.

Stroul, B. (1989). Community support systems for persons with long-term mental illness: A conceptual framework. *Psychosocial Rehabilitation Journal, 12,* 9–26.

Test, M. A. (1984). Community support programs. In A. S. Bellack (Ed.), *Schizophrenia treatment, management and rehabilitation* (pp. 347–373). Orlando, FL: Grune & Stratton.

Turner, J. E., & Shifren, I. (1979). Community support systems: How comprehensive? *New Directions for Mental Health Services, 2,* 1–23.

Turner, J. E., & TenHoor, W. J. (1978). The NIMH Community Support Program: Pilot approach to a needed social reform. *Schizophrenia Bulletin, 4,* 319–348.

Unzicker, R. (1989). On my own: A personal journey through madness & re-emergence. *Psychosocial Rehabilitation Journal, 13*(1), 71–77.

Weisburd, D. (Ed.) (1992). *The Journal, 3, 2* (entire issue).

Wood, P. H. (1980). Appreciating the consequence of disease: The classification of impairments, disability, and handicaps. *The WHO Chronicle, 34,* 376–380.

Wright, B. (1983). *Physical disability — A psychosocial approach.* New York: Harper & Row.

Fidelity to Assertive Community Treatment and Client Outcomes in the New Hampshire Dual Disorders Study

Gregory J. McHugo, Robert E. Drake, Gregory B. Teague & Haiyi Xie

B. This article originally appeared in *Psychiatric Services*, 1999, 50(6), 818–824 and is reprinted with permission.

Gregory J. McHugo, Ph.D. and Haiyi Xie, Ph.D., are research assistant professors of community and family medicine and Robert E. Drake, M.D., Ph.D., is professor of psychiatry at Dartmouth Medical School in Hanover, New Hampshire. Gregory B. Teague, Ph.D. is associate professor of community mental health at Louis de la Parte Florida Mental Health Institute at the University of South Florida in Tampa.

This research was supported by grants MH-00839, MH-46072, and MH-47567 from the National Institute of Mental Health and by grant AA-08341 from the National Institute on Alcohol Abuse and Alcoholism.

The study examined the association between fidelity of programs to the assertive community treatment model and client outcomes in dual disorders programs. Methods: Assertive community treatment programs in the New Hampshire dual disorders study were classified as low-fidelity programs (3 programs) or high-fidelity programs (4 programs) based on extensive longitudinal process data. The study included 87 clients with a dual diagnosis of severe mental illness and a comorbid substance use disorder. Sixty-one clients were in the high-fidelity programs, and 26 were in the low-fidelity programs. Client outcomes were examined in the domains of substance abuse, housing, psychiatric symptoms, functional status, and quality of life, based on interviews conducted every 6 months for 3 years. Results: Clients in the high-fidelity assertive community treatment programs showed greater reductions in alcohol and drug use and attained higher rates of remission from substance use disorders than clients in the low-fidelity programs. Clients in high-fidelity programs had higher rates of retention in treatment and fewer hospital admissions than those in low-fidelity programs. No differences between groups were found in length of hospital stays and other residential measures, psychiatric symptoms, family and social relations, satisfaction with services, and overall life satisfaction. Conclusions: Faithful implementation of, and adherence to, the assertive community treatment model for persons with dual disorders was associated with superior outcomes in the substance use domain. The findings underscore the value of measures of model fidelity, and they suggest that local modifications of the assertive community treatment model or failure to comply with it may jeopardize program success.

Assertive community treatment is the most widely tested model of community care for persons with severe mental illness (Burns & Santos, 1995; Mueser, Bond, Drake, et al., 1998). Yet until recently, the model has not been defined operationally in a manual, and its critical components have not been identified and evaluated. The recent appearance of two manuals on assertive community treatment (Allness & Knoedler, 1998; Stein & Santos, 1998) and of studies of its critical components (McGrew, Bond, & Dietzen, 1994), coupled with the development of a scale to evaluate critical components (Teague, Bond, & Drake, 1998), have fundamentally changed the potential for research on assertive community treatment.

Together these research tools should permit model-guided implementation, comprehensive and consistent process analysis, and theory-driven outcome studies. For clinicians and program directors, clear guidelines and measurement tools make it easier to shape program performance in formative stages. For researchers, a fidelity measure enables not only studies of process but also studies of the relationships between model fidelity and outcomes and between program components and outcomes (Scott & Sechrest, 1989).

In a number of areas, studies have shown that program fidelity is associated with participant outcomes. For example, Blakely and associates (Blakely, Mayer, Gottschalk, et al., 1987) studied criminal justice and education projects and found that high-fidelity programs produced better outcomes in a variety of areas than low-fidelity programs. Similarly, McDonnell and colleagues (McDonnell, Nofs, Hardman, et al., 1989) found that standardization of procedures in supported employment programs was associated with better employment outcomes.

More specific to assertive community treatment, McGrew and co-workers (McGrew et al., 1994) found that programs with higher fidelity, defined in terms of identified critical ingredients, were more effective in reducing hospital use. Finally, in treating persons with dual disorders, Jerrell and Ridgely (Jerrell & Ridgely, 1999) reported that when either behavioral skills training or intensive case management programs included their respective core elements, participants had significantly higher psychosocial functioning and lower costs for services, compared with participants in programs that did not include all the core elements.

Despite findings that the quality of implementation is related to outcomes, debate continues about implementation of model programs.

At the theoretical level, the debate involves arguments between supporters of the classic research, development, and diffusion model and those who advocate local adaptation (Blakely et al., 1987). For example, within the community mental health field, assertive community treatment advocates have argued strongly for faithful implementation (Allness & Knoedler, 1998), while others have argued that model programs cannot be transferred to other sites without local adaptation (Bachrach, 1998; Mowbray, Plum, & Masterton, 1998).

Essential to resolving this debate is the reliable and valid measurement of program implementation and fidelity to the model. Measurement begins with a thorough listing of a program's critical components and their operational definitions, accompanied by suggested sources of data from which to rate a program's performance on each component. Teague and colleagues (Teague et al., 1998) have described the development of an assertive community treatment fidelity scale, which profiles a program across numerous critical components and thereby enables comparison with other programs, with the same program at other points in time, and with a priori fidelity criteria. Thus classifying an assertive community treatment program as having high fidelity or low fidelity can be either relative or absolute, depending on the goals and design of a given study.

The purpose of this study was to examine the relationship between fidelity of assertive community treatment programs and outcomes of participants in a 3-year study of treatment for persons with dual disorders of severe mental illness and substance abuse or dependence. One key issue was how to determine whether a study participant was exposed to a high-fidelity or low-fidelity assertive community treatment program. In general, data from multiple sources can be used to classify programs or to quantify the involvement of each participant (McHugo, Hargreaves, Drake, et al., 1998). For the study reported here, we classified seven assertive community treatment programs as either high or low fidelity, based on extensive quantitative and qualitative information gathered at the program and client levels and analyzed for several years before the analysis of outcomes (Teague, Drake, & Ackerson, 1995).

In addition, we included only participants who had the opportunity for exposure to the programs over the 3-year course of the study. That is, analysis of client outcomes relative to program fidelity used only participants who remained engaged in treatment, even if minimally, for at least 1 year. A previous report of data from this 3-year study focused on the outcomes of the randomized clinical trials and used an intent-to-treat approach (Drake, McHugo, Clark et al., 1998), which included patients who were assigned to the assertive community treatment programs but who were not actually exposed to this treatment because of attrition, refusal, or prolonged institutionalization. The approach used in the current report thus shifts the focus from effectiveness toward efficacy.

Methods

Overview of the Main Study

The New Hampshire dual disorders study was a three-year randomized clinical trial of the effectiveness of assertive community treatment versus standard case management for persons with both severe mental illness and a substance use disorder. Seven community mental health centers (CMHCs) throughout New Hampshire provided both programs, and 223 persons with dual disorders were assigned randomly, within CMHCs, to receive treatment.

Diagnostic interviews were conducted before randomization, and research interviews were administered at intake and every 6 months for 3 years (1989 to 1995). The interviews included assessment of psychiatric symptoms, quality of life, alcohol and drug use, residential history, involvement in the legal system, medical status, and service utilization. Additional data were collected from case managers, CMHC management information systems, Medicaid records, hospital and legal system records, and participants' families. The methods and outcomes of the clinical trial have been reported elsewhere in fuller detail (Clark, Teague, Ricketts, et al., 1998; Drake et al., 1998).

Participants

Of the 240 eligible referrals to the New Hampshire dual disorders study, 223 completed intake assessments and entered the clinical trial. During the 3 years of the study, 20 of the original 223 participants (9%) were lost from the study due to refusal to participate, relocation without contact, or death. Of the 203 participants who completed the study, 30 had less than 1 year of exposure to treatment for a variety of reasons, including relocation, long-term institutionalization, transfer to another program, or treatment refusal. Thus 173 participants constituted the group exposed to treatment. Of these participants, 87 were exposed to

Table 1

Nine essential components of assertive community treatment and four essential components of dual disorder programs in the New Hampshire dual disorders study

Program type and components

Essential components of assertive community treatment programs

- Community locus: services are provided in the community; community living skills are developed in vivo rather than in the office
- Assertive engagement: intensive outreach is used via visits to community settings; legal mechanisms are used for engagement such as representative payees
- High intensity: case management and other services are provided as often as needed
- Small caseload: the client-clinician ratio is maintained at low levels (a ratio of ten to one)
- Continuous responsibility: the team has 24-hour responsibility for a discrete group of clients, handles crises, and is involved in hospital discharges and admissions
- Staff continuity: the team is composed of the same staff over time
- Team approach: a group of providers functions as a team, rather than as individual clinicians; team members know and work with all clients assigned to them
- Multidisciplinary staff: the team includes at least a psychiatrist, a nurse, a substance abuse treatment specialist, and another clinician with experience treating persons with severe mental illness
- Work closely with support system: the team provides the interface with the support network, including family members, landlords, employers, and other service providers, and develops clients' skills for using the network

Essential components of dual disorders programs

- Individualized substance abuse treatment: one or more team members provide direct substance abuse treatment; substance use is monitored closely
- Dual disorders model: the team uses a multistep motivational model of recovery, without demand for immediate abstinence; the treatment approach is nonconfrontational and follows behavioral principles; and the treatment considers the interaction of mental illness and substance abuse
- Dual disorders treatment groups: the team leads treatment groups appropriate to each stage—persuasion, active treatment, and relapse prevention—and assertively engages clients in the groups
- Dual disorders focus: the treatment program emphasis within the caseload is on clients with dual disorders

assertive community treatment programs, and they form the study group for these analyses.

The study group contained 68 men (78%) and 85 Caucasians (98%). The mean ± SD age of the group members was 35 ± 8.1 years.

Sixty participants were diagnosed as having schizophrenia or schizoaffective disorder (69%); the remainder had bipolar disorder. All participants had one or more substance use disorders; 62 (71%) had an alcohol use disorder, and 38 (44%) had a drug use disorder, most commonly involving cannabis or cocaine.

Outcome Measures

The client interview included the Time-Line Follow-Back (Sobell, Maisto, Sobell, et al., 1980) to assess days of alcohol and drug use during the previous six months and a detailed chronological assessment of residential history, using a self-report follow-back calendar, which was supplemented by outpatient and hospital records (Clark, Ricketts, & McHugo, 1996). The interview also assessed objective and subjective quality of life using Lehman's Quality of Life Interview (QOLI) (Lehman, 1988), current psychiatric symptoms using the 24-item Brief Psychiatric Rating Scale (BPRS) (Lukoff & Nuechterlein, 1986), and overall functional status using the Global Assessment Scale (GAS) (Endicott, Spitzer, Fleiss, et al., 1976).

Self-reports of substance use from persons with severe mental illness are suspect for a variety of reasons (Drake, Alterman, & Rosenberg, 1993). Therefore, to obtain valid ratings of substance use, a team of researchers evaluated all available data for each participant—from client self-reports, clinician ratings, and urine drug screens. They used this information to establish consensus ratings on the Alcohol Use Scale (AUS), Drug Use Scale (DUS), and Substance Abuse Treatment Scale (SATS) at intake and every 6 months for 3 years (Drake, Mueser, & McHugo, 1996).

The AUS and DUS are 5-point scales based on *DSM-III-R* criteria for rating substance abuse status during the previous six months. A rating of 1 indicates abstinence; 2, use without impairment; 3, abuse; 4, dependence; and 5, severe dependence. The SATS is an 8-point scale based on a motivational model of substance abuse recovery in a series of stages. A rating of 1-2 indicates the engagement stage; 3-4, persuasion; 5-6, active treatment; and 7-8, relapse prevention and recovering.

Assessment of Model Fidelity

Assertive community treatment programs for persons with dual disorders were implemented in seven CMHCs in New Hampshire through a grant from the Robert Wood Johnson Foundation in 1988

(Drake, Teague, & Warren, 1990). Implementation criteria for the programs included nine essential components of assertive community treatment and four additional components that focused on dual disorders. The components are listed in table 1. Ratings on these program components were made throughout the study period by research staff, using information drawn from interviews with clinical and administrative staff, activity logs kept by case managers, clinical records, and direct observation. The details of the fidelity scale and the rating process used in the New Hampshire dual disorders study are presented elsewhere (Teague et al., 1995).

Using factor analysis, ratings on the 13 components were found to coalesce into two higher-order factors, one capturing program components related to structure and community treatment (staff continuity, multidisciplinary staff, community locus, assertive engagement, continuous responsibility, dual disorders treatment groups, and dual disorders model) and one capturing program components related to the team mandate and the integration of services (team approach, small caseload, high intensity, collaboration with support system, individualized substance abuse treatment, and focus on dual disorders). Each factor contains general assertive community treatment components and specific dual disorders components.

Little variation was found among the ratings of the seven assertive community treatment programs on the second factor, but substantial variation on the first factor was noted. Thus, based on the composite scores on the first factor, four programs form the high-fidelity group; their scores on the 5-point scale were 4.9, 4.1, 4, and 3.9. Three programs form the low-fidelity group; their scores were 2.9, 2.8, and 2.2.

Data Analysis

In the study group of 87 participants, 61 were exposed to high-fidelity programs, and 26 were exposed to low-fidelity programs. Thus the group sizes are relatively small, and the analyses lack statistical power, especially when they involve a subset of the study group (for example, drug users).

In response to this limitation, we report effect sizes, so that the difference between the high-fidelity and low-fidelity groups can be judged apart from statistical significance. As used here, effect sizes depict the mean difference between groups, in standard deviation units, and thus they express the magnitude of the group effect. The effect size has a pos-

Table 2

Differences between assertive community treatment programs with high fidelity and low fidelity to the model during the third year of the New Hampshire dual disorders study

Variable	High-fidelity programs (N=4)		Low-fidelity programs (N=3)		Test statistic	df	p<	Effect size
	Mean	SD	Mean	SD				
Alcohol Use Scale score[1,2]	2.53	1.00	3.05	1.03	F= 3.57	1,60	.10	.53
N days of alcohol use[1]	35.40	42.85	79.2	59.62	F= 15.51	1,60	.01	.90
Drug Use Scale score[1,2]	2.42	1.19	3.09	1.09	F= 3.18	1,34	.10	.58
N days of drug use[1]	27.59	35.41	60.18	60.05	F= 5.51	1,34	.05	.71
Substance Abuse Treatment								
Scale score	5.48	1.78	4.12	1.44	F= 8.94	1,84	.01	.81
N hospital admissions[3]	2.87	3.40	4.69	5.19	F= 5.02	1,84	.05	.45
N hospital days[3]	47.60	67.21	49.46	83.43	F= .19	1,83	ns	.03
Proportion of days in the community	.93	.15	.97	.06	F= .77	1,84	ns	-.25
N residential moves	5.31	5.00	4.31	4.73	F= .60	1,84	ns	-.20
Satisfaction scores[4]								
Overall life	4.65	1.12	4.59	1.01	F= .01	1,84	ns	.05
Medical services[5]	5.14	.92	4.78	.88	t= 1.73	85	.10	.40
Substance abuse services[5]	5.15	1.16	4.94	.85	t= .81	85	ns	.19
Social relations	4.58	.82	4.54	1.00	F= .30	1,82	ns	.04
Family relations	4.64	1.22	4.81	1.01	F= .90	1,79	ns	-.15

(continued)

Table 2 (*continued*)

Variable	High-fidelity programs (N=4)		Low-fidelity programs (N=3)		Test statistic	df	p<	Effect size
	Mean	SD	Mean	SD				
Social contact[6]	2.83	.82	2.65	.83	F= .43	1,84	ns	.22
Family contact[6]	3.25	.98	3.55	1.05	F= .23	1,58	ns	-.30
Global Assessment Scale score[7]	49.74	9.95	44.9	7.82	F= 2.85	1,82	.10	.52
Brief Psychiatric Rating Scale total score[8]	40.34	10.05	39.69	7.36	F= .65	1,74	ns	-.07

1 Cell sizes are reduced because the analyses included only persons with alcohol or drug problems.

2 Possible scores range from 1 to 5, with higher scores indicating greater dependence.

3 Hospital data were cumulated over the entire three-year study period.

4 From Lehman's Quality of Life Interview (Lehman, 1988); possible scores range from 1 to 7, with higher scores indicating greater satisfaction.

5 Endpoint data were analyzed alone, because baseline data were incomplete.

6 From Lehman's Quality of Life Interview (Lehman, 1988); possible scores range from 1 to 5, with higher scores indicating more frequent contact.

7 Possible scores range from 1 to 100, with higher scores indicating higher functional status.

8 Possible scores range from 24 to 168, with higher scores indicating greater symptom severity.

itive sign when the group difference favors the high-fidelity assertive community treatment group and a negative sign when it favors the low-fidelity group. By convention, group-difference effect sizes of .20, .50, and .80 represent small, medium, and large effects, respectively (Cohen, 1988; Lipsey, 1990).

We examined group equivalence at baseline, using t tests and chi square tests on a set of demographic, illness related, and outcome variables. Differences in outcome between fidelity groups were based primarily on data gathered in the third year of the study. Thus the outcome variables were often formed by averaging scores, or cumulating totals, from the 30-month and the 36-month assessment points. Analysis of covariance was used to compare group means in the third year, which were adjusted for baseline levels.

Results

Attrition and Baseline Equivalence

At the beginning of the study, the low-fidelity programs had 37 participants and the high-fidelity programs had 72 participants. Due to study attrition and to lack of exposure to treatment, both groups lost 11 participants, reducing the final group sizes to 26 in the low-fidelity programs and 61 in the high-fidelity programs (30% attrition for low-fidelity programs and 15% for high-fidelity programs; $\chi^2 = 3.17$, $df = 1$, $p = .08$).

We examined 21 baseline variables for differences between the high-fidelity and low-fidelity groups; data for participants lost to attrition were not included. Only one difference was significant ($p < .05$). Participants in the high-fidelity programs began the study at a somewhat higher mean stage of substance abuse treatment, although both groups were between the engagement and early persuasion stages. The absence of differences indicates that the two fidelity groups were equivalent at the beginning of the study.

Outcome Differences

Table 2 presents the results of tests for differences between the two fidelity groups during the third year of the study. Primary outcomes were from the domains of substance use and housing, which includes hospitalization. Substance use and housing are the outcomes that were targeted most directly by the assertive community treatment programs and for which conventional criteria were used to judge statistical signif-

Figure 1

Percentage of participants in the New Hampshire dual disorders study whose substance use disorder remained in stable remission, by participation in programs that showed high or low fidelity to the assertive community treatment model

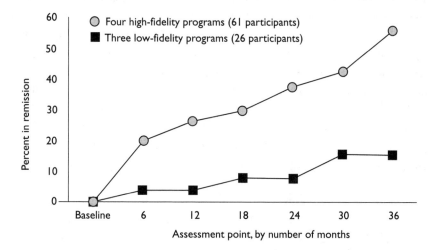

icance ($p < .05$). Secondary outcomes were from the domains of psychiatric symptoms, functional status, and quality of life, and they were judged as statistically significant after the analysis adjusted for multiple tests. These important outcomes would be expected to differ between assertive community treatment programs and standard case management. However, few differences in these outcomes were expected to be found between the high-fidelity and low-fidelity dual disorders assertive community treatment programs, because the outcome variables were not the explicit focus of treatment.

Participants from high-fidelity programs reported significantly fewer days of alcohol and drug use than those in low-fidelity programs. These differences are complemented by differences in scores on the AUS and DUS; on average the high-fidelity group was in the remission range on both scales, with scores less than 3, whereas the low-fidelity group was in the abuse range, with scores of 3 or higher. In addition, the mean Substance Abuse Treatment Scale score for the high-fidelity group was in the active treatment stage, whereas the low-fidelity group was closer to the persuasion stage. The effect sizes indicate that substantial differences existed between groups during the third year of the study for each outcome variable related to substance use, although small group sizes precluded highly significant statistical results for some variables.

We also examined remission from alcohol and drug use as an important and clinically meaningful outcome. An individual was considered in remission during the third year of the study if both the 30- and 36-month AUS scores were less than 3 and both DUS scores were less than 3. The remission rate in the high-fidelity programs during the third year was 43.3%, whereas it was 15.4% in the low-fidelity programs ($\chi^2 = 6.24$, $df = 1$, $p = .01$).

As a final step, we defined a participant as being in stable remission if the AUS and DUS scores were less than 3 at a given assessment point and at all subsequent points. Figure 1 shows the longitudinal rates of stable remission for the two fidelity groups. The Fisher's exact test for differences in proportions approached significance at the 6-month follow-tip ($p = .10$) and was significant ($p < .05$) at each subsequent assessment point.

The findings were mixed in the housing domain. To reduce the number of zeros and enable the use of parametric statistical tests, the hospital data were cumulated over the entire 3-year period. The mean number of hospital admissions during the 3 years of the study was significantly lower for patients in the high-fidelity programs, although no difference between the two groups was found in the mean number of days spent in the hospital. Regarding residential status more generally, the two groups did not differ in the number of residential moves or in community tenure in the third year.

No substantial differences between clients in the high-fidelity and low-fidelity programs were found for the secondary outcomes. The groups did not differ on general life satisfaction or on scales from the Quality of Life Interview measuring social and family contact and satisfaction with social and family relations. The two groups also did not differ in their satisfaction with substance abuse treatment, although a marginal difference was noted in their satisfaction with medical care overall—that is, physical health, emotional health, and substance use combined. Both groups showed improvement over time in symptom severity as measured by the BPRS total score and functional status as rated on the GAS, but no significant differences between groups were found at the endpoint of the study.

Discussion

The results of this study indicate that the fidelity of the implementation of the dual disorders assertive community treatment model is related to client outcomes. However, the outcome differences noted in this study were confined primarily to those domains that were most proximal to the treatment provided. That is, clients in high-fidelity programs had better substance use outcomes than those in low-fidelity programs. In addition, consistent with the general assertive community treatment model, high-fidelity programs had higher client retention rates, and they also reduced hospital admissions during the 3-year study period, although no differences on other residential measures were found.

Other outcomes, more distal from dual disorders treatment, such as psychiatric symptoms, functional status, and quality of life, were not associated systematically with fidelity to the assertive community treatment model. Clients in both fidelity groups improved over time on many of these outcomes.

These gains may have resulted from non-specific factors associated with engagement with the treatment system and with participation in assertive community treatment programs. As is typical of persons with dual disorders, numerous participants at the time of study had not been recently connected with the mental health treatment system, or that connection had been ineffective. Reaching out to them and providing competent and broad-based clinical services over a 3-year period enabled gains in many areas and in diffuse ways. Some of these gains at the group level were probably due to regression to the mean, and some were likely due to engagement with the assertive community treatment programs.

The differential gains found for participants in this study emerged despite the relatively minor differences between high-fidelity and low-fidelity assertive community treatment programs. The implementation ratings that were used to classify the seven assertive community treatment programs revealed as much similarity as dissimilarity among them. All seven programs faithfully implemented many components of the assertive community treatment model, and it was only on one cluster of program components that they differed. Thus labels like "high fidelity" and "low fidelity" may lead to a distorted view of what actually happened in the programs and must be understood as encoding only relative differences.

Nevertheless, the cluster of implementation criteria on which the two groups differed contained components related to the adoption of the dual diagnosis model and the provision of dual disorders treatment groups, which may explain why outcomes in the substance use domain were affected most prominently. In addition, this cluster contained items related to the extent of community outreach and assertive engagement, which are factors that may be associated with the difference in rate of hospitalization and retention in treatment. It is uncertain whether the correspondence between the differences in program components and the differences in client outcomes is as tight as suggested, but the plausibility of this strong relationship strengthens the case for attention to model fidelity and specific program components.

The results of this study must be interpreted in light of its limitations. Participants were not assigned randomly to high-fidelity and low-fidelity assertive community treatment programs; this distinction among the programs arose during the study period. Although self-selection is not a threat to validity because the programs were dispersed geographically, it is still possible that important unobserved differences existed among clients at the seven sites. Our analysis of baseline characteristics indicated equivalence of the two groups, but this study is a quasi-experimental evaluation and must be interpreted as a correlational study.

In addition, the external validity of the study is constrained by its sample size and constitution. The study group was small, and it was composed primarily of white males with schizophrenia-spectrum disorders and alcohol abuse. Similar research from diverse settings is needed to understand the influence of study group characteristics on program fidelity effects.

Another limitation is the small number of assertive community treatment programs. Not enough programs were included to design the study as a multilevel evaluation that used hierarchical statistical models to examine variation at the client level and at the program level. To the extent that dependency exists within the data due to the clustering of participants within single programs, unknown bias may be present in our results.

An additional consequence of the small number of programs is an alternative explanation of the findings, which is related to the small number of case managers involved. If more competent clinicians are better able to grasp the importance of model fidelity and to embrace the assertive community treatment philosophy, then their programs would score more highly on fidelity measures and their clients may have better outcomes. Consequently, it is difficult with a small number of programs to distinguish between the effectiveness of individual clinicians and the effectiveness of the assertive community treatment model per se.

Overall, these findings speak loudly of an association between program fidelity and participant outcomes, but they are silent about causal mechanisms. As noted, differences between participants and clinicians across sites are possible explanations, but so are the many ways in which faithfully implemented assertive community treatment programs differ from less competent, or locally modified, versions of the assertive community treatment model.

Despite its shortcomings, this study provides evidence that more complete and more faithful implementation of the model components of assertive community treatment is associated with better client outcomes. The importance of this finding cannot be overstated in this era of widespread proliferation of assertive community treatment programs. As variations of the model arise in practice due to philosophical differences, treatment focus, or local conditions, the link between model fidelity and client outcomes must not get lost. That is, to the extent that program effectiveness depends on fidelity to a particular model, modifications of program components may jeopardize positive client outcomes.

Each of the low-fidelity programs in this study justified their deviations from the assertive community treatment model with arguments about necessary modifications to fit local circumstances. That the assertive community treatment programs at these sites were associated with poorer outcomes leads one to question the wisdom of their decisions. Until systematic research identifies the critical components of the assertive community treatment model, there is risk in disassembling the model and reconfiguring its components unless careful attention is paid to both process and outcome evaluation.

References

Allness, D. J., & Knoedler, W. H. (1998). *The pact model of community-based treatment for persons with severe and persistent mental illnesses: A manual for PACT start-up.* Alexandria, VA: National Alliance for the Mentally Ill, Anti-Stigma Foundation.

Bachrach, L. L. (1998). The chronic patient: On exporting and importing model programs. *Hospital and Community Psychiatry, 39,* 1257–1258.

Blakely, C. H., Mayer, J. P., Gottschalk, R. G., et al. (1987). The fidelity-adaptation debate: Implications for the implementation of public sector social programs. *American Journal of Community Psychology, 15,* 253–268.

Burns, B. J. & Santos, A. B. (1995). Assertive community treatment: An update of randomized trials. *Psychiatric Services, 46,* 669–675.

Clark, R. E., Ricketts, S. K., & McHugo, G. J. (1996). Measuring hospital use without claims: A comparison of patient and provider reports. *Health Services Research, 31,* 153–169.

Clark, R. E., Teague, G. B., Ricketts, S. J., et al. (1998). Cost-effectiveness of assertive community treatment versus standard case management for persons with co-occurring severe mental illness and substance use disorders. *Health Service Research, 33,* 1285–1308.

Cohen, J. (1988). *Statistical power analysis for the behavioral sciences (2nd ed.).* Hillsdale, NJ: Erlbaum.

Drake, R. E., Alterman, A. I., & Rosenberg, S. R. (1993). Detection of substance use disorders in severely mentally ill patients. *Community Mental Health Journal, 29,* 175–192.

Drake, R. E., McHugo, G. J., Clark, R. E., et al. (1998). Assertive community treatment for patients with co-occurring severe mental illness and substance use disorder: A clinical trial. *American Journal of Orthopsychiatry, 68,* 201–215.

Drake, R. E., Mueser, K. T., & McHugo, G. J. (1996). Using clinician rating scales to assess substance use among persons with severe mental illness. In L. I. Sederer & B. Dickey (Eds.), *Outcomes assessment in clinical practice.* Baltimore, MD: Williams & Wilkins.

Drake, R. E., Teague, G. B., & Warren, R. S. (1990). New Hampshire's dual diagnosis programs for people with severe mental illness and substance abuse. *Addiction and Recovery, 10,* 35–39.

Endicott, J., Spitzer, R. L., Fleiss, F. L., et al. (1976). The global assessment scale. *Archives of General Psychiatry, 33,* 766–771.

Jerrell, J. M. & Ridgely, M. S. (1999). Impact of robustness of program implementation on outcomes of clients in dual diagnosis programs. *Psychiatric Services, 50,* 109–112.

Lehman, A. F. (1988). A quality of life interview for the chronically mentally ill. *Evaluation and Program Planning, 11,* 51–62.

Lipsey, M. W. (1990). *Design sensitivity: Statistical power analysis for experimental research.* Newbury Park, CA: Sage.

Lukoff, D., Nuechterlein, K. H., & Ventura, J. (1986). Ventura manual for the expanded Brief Psychiatric Rating Scale (BPRS). *Schizophrenia Bulletin, 12,* 594–602.

McDonnell, J., Nofs, D., Hardman, M., et al. (1989). An analysis of the procedural components of supported employment programs associated with employment outcomes. *Journal of Applied Behavior Analysis, 22,* 417–428.

McGrew, J. H., Bond, G. R., & Dietzen, L. L. (1994). Measuring the fidelity of implementation of a mental health program model. *Journal of Consulting and Clinical Psychology, 62,* 670–678.

McHugo, G. J., Hargreaves, W., Drake, R. E., et al. (1998). Methodological issues in assertive community treatment studies. *American Journal of Orthopsychiatry, 68,* 246–260.

Mowbray, C. T., Plum, T. B., & Masterton, T. (1998). Harbinger II: Deployment and evolution of assertive community treatment in Michigan. *Administration and Policy in Mental Health, 25,* 125–139.

Mueser, K. T., Bond, G. R., Drake, R. E., et al. (1998). Models of community care for severe mental illness: A review of research on case management. *Schizophrenia Bulletin, 24,* 37–74.

Scott, A. G. & Sechrest, L. (1989). Strength of theory and theory of strength. *Evaluation and Program Planning, 12,* 329–336.

Sobell, M. B., Maisto, S. A., Sobell, L. C., et al. (1980). Developing a prototype for evaluating alcohol treatment effectiveness. In L. C. Sobell, M. B. Sobell & E. Ward (Eds.), *Evaluating alcohol and drug abuse treatment effectiveness.* New York: Pergamon.

Stein, L. I. & Santos, A. B. (1998). *Assertive community treatment of persons with severe mental illness.* New York: Norton.

Teague, G. B., Bond, G. R., & Drake, R. E. (1998). Program fidelity in assertive community treatment: Development and use of a measure. *American Journal of Orthopsychiatry, 68,* 216–232.

Teague, G. B., Drake, R. E., & Ackerson, T. H. (1995). Evaluating use of continuous treatment teams for persons with mental illness and substance abuse. *Psychiatric Services, 46,* 689–695.

Housing for Persons with Co-Occurring Mental and Addictive Disorders

Fred C. Osher & Lisa B. Dixon

This article originally appeared in *New Directions for Mental Health Services,* (1996) 70 (Summer), 53–63, and is reprinted with permission.

Fred Osher, M.D., is associate professor of psychiatry and director of community psychiatry at the School of Medicine, University of Maryland. Lisa Dixon, M.D., is associate professor of psychiatry and research psychiatrist at the Center for Mental Health Services, School of Medicine, University of Maryland.

Homelessness is a far too common outcome for persons with dual diagnoses. This article discusses existing housing barriers and suggests housing, treatment, and support services responsive to population need.

Case Example

Ms. B is a 35-year-old Caucasian woman with a long history of frequent psychiatric hospitalization beginning at age 17. She has a diagnosis of schizophrenia (paranoid type) and at referral met criteria for binge-pattern alcohol dependence. Her drinking was associated with impulsive outbursts of violence, both toward herself and others. When not drinking, she was childlike and friendly although persistently paranoid about the efforts of others to "poison her." She had been living in the streets and in the shelter system of a large urban city for 10 years prior to referral to an assertive community treatment (ACT) team that targeted homeless persons with severe mental illnesses. After a 6-month period of outreach and regular meetings at a local diner, she seemed increasingly comfortable with several members of the case management team and agreed to a low dose of antipsychotic medication that she took irregularly. She initially refused to discuss her alcohol use, stating "it's none of your business." Over the 6 months, she acknowledged that she drank but vehemently denied that this alcohol use created any problems for her. At this point, she agreed to live in a transitional shelter that prohibited any substance use and provided on-site AA and NA group meetings. The ACT team was able to convince the shelter staff to waive their program requirement that all residents attend daily self-help meetings for Ms. B because of her behavior in groups. The team assured the shelter staff that alcohol abuse would be addressed in individual meetings with Ms. B. She did not drink for almost 3 months while living at this shelter. During this time, the ACT team assisted her in obtaining social security disability benefits; the team was named as the representative payee for this income support. She was assisted in finding her own apartment and being sober enabled her to gain access to housing subsidies. Although the team ensured that Ms. B's rent and bills were paid, she would sometimes use the leftover funds to buy alcohol, which induced bizarre behavior. When her landlord threatened eviction because of a behavioral disturbance, the ACT team would intervene by coming into the apartment to provide crisis counseling. These binging episodes became less frequent. Ms. B slowly became willing to acknowledge that alcohol use was not in her best interest and agreed to try group educational meetings about alcohol. She became increasingly attached to her apartment and stated that she did not want to do anything that might lead to her becoming homeless again. The team used this information to gently persuade her to examine the likely consequences of ongoing alcohol abuse and over time her drinking episodes disappeared entirely Ms. B's compliance with medication improved somewhat but she remains suspicious and slightly paranoid.

Dual Diagnosis and Unstable Housing

Access to appropriate housing is a critical component of care for persons with co-occurring mental and addictive disorders. Homelessness and housing instability can exacerbate addiction and mental illness, creating a malignant cycle of increased symptomatology, disability, and exposure to harsh living environments. Studies focusing on persons with dual diagnoses have shown that they are disproportionately at risk for housing instability and homelessness (Drake, Osher, & Wallach, 1991). Epidemiologic studies have revealed that roughly 10 to 20% of homeless persons suffer from severe mental illnesses and co-occurring addictions (Belcher, 1989; Drake, Osher et al., 1991; Tessler & Dennis, 1989). Furthermore, the majority of persons with co-occurring disorders never receive any mental or addictive treatment services (Kessler et al., 1994).

An aftercare study of patients of an urban state hospital revealed that over one-fourth of all patients and over one-half of patients with dual diagnoses had unstable housing and were at least temporarily homeless during the 6 months following discharge (Drake, Wallach, & Hoffman, 1989). Another study of discharged state hospital patients found that 36% of patients experienced homelessness within 6 months of their discharge (Belcher, 1989) and patients who used alcohol or other drugs were more likely to be in the homeless group. When homeless men with mental illness were followed from shelters to community housing, 44% returned to homelessness within 18 months and co-occurring substance use disorders significantly increased the risk for homelessness (Caton, Wyatt, Felix, Grunberg, & Dominquez, 1993). Drake and others (1991) found that this phenomenon is not restricted to urban locations (Drake, Wallach et al., 1991). They studied housing instability of patients with schizophrenia in a rural area where patients had extensive family supports and low-cost housing was available. Their study found that co-occurring disorders were strongly correlated with housing instability and that the majority of patients with schizophrenia and alcohol problems experienced housing instability during a 6-month period.

Thus alcohol and drug abuse by persons with severe mental illness must be considered a high-risk behavior for homelessness. In fact, a cohort of five investigators funded under the Stewart B. McKinney Homeless Assistance Act cited co-occurring substance use disorder as the major clinical factor associated with prolonged and repeated homeless episodes among homeless persons with severe mental illnesses (Center for Mental Health Services, 1994). Effective treatment of co-occurring disorders is critical to enabling an individual to escape cycles of homelessness. Conversely, effective interventions should reduce the risk of homelessness for those dually diagnosed persons currently in housing.

Reasons for Dual Diagnosis–Homeless Relationship

Consideration of systemic, legal, and clinical perspectives facilitates understanding of why persons with dual diagnoses are at risk for housing instability and homelessness. Although research on all aspects of these issues has not been conducted, these issues merit consideration in developing residential and treatment services for dually diagnosed individuals.

Systemic Issues
Systemic barriers to services for persons with dual diagnoses have been well documented. Lack of a common administrative structure for alcohol, drug, and mental health services at the federal, state, and local levels; insufficient resources; historic distrust and philosophical conflicts between providers of addiction services and mental health services; and separate funding streams for treatment of both disorders have contributed to these barriers (Ridgely, Goldman, & Willenbring, 1990). Rapidly evolving health care reform initiatives that limit access to or funding for psychiatric or substance abuse services are likely to com-

pound these barriers by failing to recognize, or respond to, the complex service needs of dually diagnosed individuals.

As a result of administrative divisions, many residential treatment programs for persons with mental illness specifically bar patients with co-occurring substance abuse problems. If they admit them, they may evict them after an episode of use. Residential addiction programs similarly bar patients with co-occurring mental illnesses, often identified as those who use prescribed psychopharmacologic medications. Clients encountering these bureaucratic barriers may experience frustration and anger or may accept the inaccessibility of the system as further justification for continued maladaptive behavior and hopelessness. The locus of responsibility for providing housing and clinical services to homeless persons with dual diagnoses is unclear and variable in different communities. The lack of clarity about whether mental health providers, substance abuse providers, or providers of housing services are responsible for assuring access to housing perpetuates the existence of housing gaps.

Legal Issues

Legal issues present obstacles to housing for persons with dual diagnoses. The Fair Housing Amendments Act of 1988 extended protection of federal fair housing legislation to persons with disabilities, including persons with mental illness. The full impact of this act in protecting against discriminatory housing practices remains to be seen (Petrila, 1995). In practice, however, persons with dual diagnoses face discriminatory treatment. Individuals with histories of drug dependence are not eligible for public housing programs unless they are receiving addiction treatment (Rubenstein, 1989) that is often in short supply with long waiting lists. Thus persons with mental illnesses may be shut out of the housing programs established for their care because of disabilities associated with drug or alcohol use. In addition, potential landlords may reject persons involved with illicit drugs because of perceived liability issues (Drake, Osher et al., 1991).

Criminal records and sometimes even contact with the criminal justice system can be a barrier to housing access. Homeless persons with dual diagnoses have been shown to have greater histories of arrest when compared to homeless persons without dual diagnoses. These arrests are frequently for misdemeanors caused by bizarre symptoms and erratic behavior, publicly displayed because of their lack of shelter (Abram & Teplin, 1991). Once they have an arrest record, it may be more difficult for persons with dual diagnoses to obtain housing of any kind.

In 1994 Congress passed legislation that limits the duration of income supports and entitlements to anyone whose disability is related to a substance use disorder to 36 months. Although it is too early to measure the effects of this legislation, one can hypothesize that increasing numbers of persons with addictive disorders, including those with dual diagnoses, will be unable to afford even the cheapest of accommodations. These legal issues serve as examples of how housing instability of persons with dual diagnoses can be an epiphenomenon of social policy rather than a clinical correlate.

Clinical Issues

Persons with dual diagnoses have been found to have greater rates of psychiatric symptoms (Negrete, Knapp, Douglas, & Smith, 1986), noncompliance with treatment (Osher et al., 1994), psychiatric hospitalizations and use of emergency services (Bartels et al., 1993; Safer, 1987), and violent, disruptive behavior (Abram & Teplin, 1991; Safer, 1987)— including suicide (Bartels, Drake, & McHugo, 1992; Dassori, Mezzich, & Keshavan, 1990; Drake, Osher, & Wallach, 1989)—than persons with mental illnesses only. It is not surprising, then, that individuals with this clinical profile have trouble accessing housing and are at risk for losing housing.

Families already under stress from years of coping with mental illness may be unable to tolerate the additional disruption—and perhaps danger—associated with co-occurring substance abuse, resulting in eviction from the family home (Robinson, Dixon, Stewart, Harold, & Lehman, 1993). Providers in other residential settings such as board and care homes or public housing settings may also evict persons with dual diagnoses because they are unable to tolerate their erratic behaviors, their disturbance of other tenants, or their unreliable rental payments. Frequent or prolonged hospitalizations may result in loss of housing placement, particularly in locations where affordable housing is scarce and waiting lists are common.

Another important consideration is that persons with dual diagnoses may be unable to manage income or benefits, particularly if such funds are diverted to support a drug or alcohol habit. Consequently when no money for rent and other bills is available, streets, hospitals, or prisons become the only other shelter alternatives. The use of a representative payee, which can ameliorate this problem, is currently required for persons disabled as a result of a substance use disorder receiving social security income. Unfortunately, even if the need for a representative payee is obvious, it can be extremely difficult to find persons willing to serve as payees for these dually diagnosed individuals.

Clinical Strategies That Facilitate Stable Housing

In order to treat dually diagnosed persons who are homeless or who are at risk for homelessness, clinicians must have an adequate understanding of the basic principles of treating persons with dual diagnoses. The heterogeneity of the dually diagnosed population with regard to both disabilities associated with their mental and addictive disorders and to their demographic, socioeconomic, and cultural backgrounds makes it incumbent on clinicians to design individualized treatment strategies. Distinguishing between substance abuse and dependence in persons with serious mental illnesses, for example, may govern the intensity of early treatment interventions (Bartels, Drake, & Wallach, 1995). Others have suggested that tailoring interventions to the unique needs of dually diagnosed women should be considered (Alexander, 1996).

As discussed by Carey (1996), an integrated treatment program for dually diagnosed individuals organized around treatment phases—engagement, persuasion, active treatment, and relapse prevention (Osher & Kofoed, 1989)—has gained widespread acceptance. Successful programs have recognized the need to attend to both disorders, persisting through multiple crises and relapses, utilizing educational and supportive groups, and in many cases providing comprehensive case management services (Drake & Noordsy, 1994). Integrating motivational interventions matched to these stages is currently being investigated (Ziedonis & Fisher, 1994). Specific effects of these and other model interventions on housing stability remain to be studied. Clinical strategies to stabilize housing for persons with dual diagnoses will be discussed in terms of the treatment phases mentioned above.

Engagement

Housing instability and homelessness complicate the already difficult engagement phase in the treatment of individuals with co-occurring mental and addictive disorders. Assertive and prolonged outreach is essential because clients in this phase generally do not come to the program office or keep appointments. Lack of money for transportation, the daily demands of obtaining food and shelter, psychiatric symptoms, ongoing substance use, and associated organic deficits may cause clients to miss appointments. This can be a critical problem in efforts to secure limited housing resources such as Section 8 certificates (Dixon, Krauss,

Myers, & Lehman, 1994). Because clients often have limited access to phones and mail, tracking clients requires tenacity as well as extensive contacts with providers in the community.

Providing for basic needs such as clothes, showers, and food may be helpful in the engagement process. Provision of badly needed material resources can help to draw clients into a trusting relationship in which staff can persuade them to enter treatment for substance abuse or mental illness and help them identify other long-term goals. The promise of safe, clean housing may motivate clients to enter the treatment system (Gaffney & Dixon, 1995). A treatment team must be able to access diverse housing or shelter options on an acute basis. Because housing instability persists even after housing is obtained, provision of on-site support is usually required. The capacity for crisis intervention for persons with dual diagnoses is critical. Crises, whether they are psychiatric, medical, or housing-related, may provide important opportunities to engage clients by addressing their acute needs.

Assessment of homeless individuals with dual diagnoses must begin in the engagement phase and continue longitudinally. Homeless persons with co-occurring disorders frequently avoid treatment; they may be suspicious of providers and unwilling to provide much personal information. They may also try to hide their substance use pattern for fear that disclosure may restrict their access to housing (Goldfinger et al., in press).

Persuasion

Persuasion involves reducing a patient's denial about a mental illness or substance abuse problem. Progress can be measured by a patient's acknowledgment that a problem exists and by the commitment to pursue active treatment. In addition to the persuasion strategies for dually diagnosed clients mentioned elsewhere in this volume, the link between housing opportunities and abstinence should be emphasized. How substance use has influenced housing arrangements in the past should be examined and, if appropriate, how access to current housing options is limited by ongoing drug use should be pointed out. Developing a discrepancy between the housing that the client hopes to obtain or maintain and the obstacles to this goal created by their ongoing drug abuse can be a key to persuading the individual to consider abstinence.

The use of representative payeeship assumes special importance in working with dually diagnosed homeless persons in the persuasion phase. Implicit in the condition of homelessness is that the client's basic needs are not being met. Although there may be a multitude of reasons for this (for example, the absence of decent affordable housing), the only way to stop the cycle of homelessness and drug use may be for the program, family, or some other individual to assume the responsibility of managing the person's finances. Stable housing requires stable finances. If a patient relapses and requires hospitalization and detoxification or simply spends some time on the streets, there can at least be a home to which he or she can return if the rent is paid. The implementation of a representative payee system fits well with the goals of the persuasion phase; it may alienate individuals during the engagement phase and may be a necessary condition for active treatment to proceed.

Related to the use of a representative payee is the use of other strategies that patients may perceive as coercive. The frequent legal entanglements of dually diagnosed persons offer opportunities for clinicians to use the requirement for court-ordered treatment. The clinician's attitude and approach in using coercion are critical. There is clearly an obligation to honor court-ordered requirements; additionally, concrete contingencies with direct consequences for failure to meet these conditions may be an important way to persuade people to begin treatment. Coercive approaches are *not* substitutes for treatment but may be an important component of an overall treatment strategy. Future research may reveal the extent to which structure and rules are themselves therapeutic at different phases of treating persons with dual diagnoses.

Active Treatment

In the active treatment phase, patients develop the skills and relationships necessary to achieve and maintain sobriety and minimize disabilities associated with their mental illness. The basic strategies useful in this phase include individual and group therapies, education, and psychosocial rehabilitation (Carey, 1996). During this phase, the client's housing status should be reviewed and environmental or situational threats (living in a heavy drug trafficking zone, for example) to attaining abstinence should be identified.

Relapse Prevention

Both addictions and mental illnesses tend to be relapsing disorders. The relapse prevention phase focuses on minimizing the extent of and damage caused by a patient relapse. The lack of social and family supports of the homeless individual with dual diagnoses may lead to increased fragility and greater vulnerability to relapse, both in terms of addiction and mental illness. Unanticipated relapses can lead to another episode of homelessness. It is thus especially important for programs and clinicians to plan contingencies if relapses occur to minimize the risk of repeated homelessness.

Housing Strategies To Facilitate Recovery

Housing strategies for homeless or marginally-housed persons with dual diagnoses must be developed in tandem with clinical strategies. Development of housing strategies requires consideration of types of housing, associated support, organization, and funding. Newman (1992) describes two different philosophies that have been organizing principles of housing programs for severely and persistently mentally ill persons. The first, more traditional program uses a *level of care,* or *continuum* approach. The varying needs of the heterogeneous mentally ill population are addressed by offering several settings, each with different levels of service and supervision as well as restrictiveness. In this model, treatment and housing are linked. A second model has been called the *supported housing* model. In this model, the intensity of supported services varies with client need and the residential site remains the same (Harp, 1990; Ridgeway & Zipple, 1990).

Although some view these models as mutually exclusive, the authors and others believe that supported housing is simply another important part of the continuum of residential housing. The objective of housing diversity is to optimize choice, maintain community tenure, and ultimately to improve effectiveness (Fields, 1990; Kline, Harris, Bebout, & Drake, 1991). For persons with dual diagnoses, housing choice will be determined by community alternatives. This selection should be made by an assessment of the clinical needs and personal preferences of the individual. Housing selection may vary depending on what phase of treatment the person is in and what support needs exist. In addition to factors important to the housing choice of any citizen such as location, costs, and convenience, housing for dually diagnosed individuals requires the following special considerations.

Residential Tolerance

A critical question for persons with dual diagnoses is whether treatment can or should be separated from housing. Residential options must include settings that will tolerate the lengthy adjustment process required to feel safe and simultaneously struggle to control two disabling disorders. Kline et al. (1991) argue that "transitions necessitated by administrative factors such as arbitrary time constraints, rather than by clinical needs, should be avoided."

The arguments to separate housing from treatment can lead to practical clinical problems. So-called *wet housing*, or housing in which the use of drugs and alcohol is tolerated, may be the only housing choice acceptable to the client in the early phases of engagement and treatment. Yet some clinicians believe that allowing substance use in housing sustains or enables use and is countertherapeutic. At the same time, the achievement and maintenance of sobriety may be unlikely, if not impossible, without adequate housing (Drake, Osher et al., 1991). Some patients may be motivated to stop using drugs if they are aware that their housing depends on their sobriety. Other patients will continue to use despite prohibitions, will get evicted, and will wind up on the streets in circumstances that are not conducive to pursuing sobriety. The solution to this dilemma is vexing and will require experimentation with different models and client choices.

At the, present time, most housing options sponsored by mental health or substance abuse providers are *dry housing*, or housing in which alcohol and drug use is prohibited. Perhaps a housing continuum should provide for degrees of dryness, including *damp housing*, where there is an expectation of abstinence on the premises but clients are not required to agree to be abstinent off-site. At one end of the housing continuum could be shelters and other safe havens that are very tolerant of use, whereas toward the other end of the continuum there could be stronger expectations and limits. In a housing demonstration in which homeless persons were empowered to make house rules, alcohol was initially allowed on-site but later banned by the residents as they became aware of its destabilizing influence (Center for Mental Health Services, 1994).

The engagement phase might require flexible housing regulations while intensive and assertive support services are provided. High levels of structure and supervision may be unacceptable to persons during engagement. Once engagement is achieved, however, clients might tolerate a greater degree of structure and supervision during the persuasion and active treatment phases when peer interaction and clear limits may be therapeutic. Less structure and supervision consistent with supported housing models may be more appropriate during later phases of treatment such as the relapse prevention phase. The duration of on-site residential care remains a critical question for future investigations.

Safety

As mentioned above, homeless individuals are frequently victims of crime, and life on the streets is wrought with danger. Consideration of this fact is essential in planning housing for persons with mental illness who have drug addiction problems. Housing must be safe, whether it is a transitional shelter with a time-limited stay, a group home with other residents with mental illness, or an independent apartment fully integrated into the community.

Client Preference

In making choices about housing, programs must balance housing availability, client preferences, and client needs. Schutt and Goldfinger (1996) have found that although most people prefer independent housing, they do not always succeed at this choice (Schutt & Goldfinger, 1996). Clients with active addiction problems may prefer independent living but may have previous experience that suggests that they need more structure and supervision. Dixon, Krauss, Myers, and Lehman (1994) have shown that it was possible to honor the housing preferences of the majority of homeless mentally ill patients treated in their program that had a limited number of Section 8 certificates.

Shelterization

Unique to the long-term homeless individual is the phenomenon of *shelterization*. This refers to a process of acculturation and adaptation that homeless persons who use shelters may experience (Gounis & Susser, 1990; Grunberg & Eagle, 1990). Although it helps homeless persons cope with their surroundings in the short term, this process may impede the process of moving out of the shelter system that becomes a social community with familiar social rules. Some formerly homeless clients may experience loneliness when they make the transition from the noisy, busy shelter system to independent housing. There is some evidence that more intensive support during the transition from shelter to housing may result in increased residential stability (Center for Mental Health Services, 1994). If programs attend to these issues as well as clinical needs, housing stability should be enhanced.

Cooperative Agreements Between Providers and Housers

Given the complex and varied requirements of providing housing and clinical care as well as the historic administrative and economic separation of housing and treatment services, mental health, substance abuse, and housing providers should all agree prospectively to work together. Otherwise there is considerable danger that patients will fall between the cracks, receiving housing without mental health and addiction services or vice versa. Cooperative agreements should outline the respective roles and responsibilities of housing providers, mental health providers, and substance abuse providers. The specific details of such an agreement will need to reflect community resources. The common goal will be to maintain individuals with dual diagnoses in the community.

Conclusion

Hypotheses about the optimal degree of structure, supervision, and support in housing for dually diagnosed persons await future research. Evaluators of the Robert Wood Johnson Foundation HUD Demonstration Program on Chronic Mental Illness noted, "It is particularly difficult to serve active substance abusers and those with recent histories of destructive behaviors using an independent housing strategy" (Newman, 1992). Inclusiveness has been advocated (Kline et al., 1991) as a principle of program development in which the goal is to provide services to as diverse a set of people as possible.

Although models for providing housing to individuals with co-occurring disorders have not been fully explicated and evaluated, reducing the morbidity and mortality associated with homelessness for these persons is critical. Dually diagnosed persons who are homeless or at risk for homelessness have special needs and characteristics that must be considered in treatment planning. Common principles must guide approaches to this population until empirical data are available. These include the following guidelines: individualized housing and treatment planning must be derived from thorough assessments, flexibility and creativity must outweigh intolerance and categorical programs, and ongoing therapeutic relationships must be established over time.

References

Abram, K. M., & Teplin, L. A. (1991). Co-occurring disorders among mentally ill jail detainees. *American Psychologist, 46*, 1036–1045.

Alexander, M. J. (1996). Women with co-occurring addictive and mental disorders: An emerging profile of vulnerability. *American Journal of Orthopsychiatry, 66*(1), 61–70.

Bartels, S. J., Drake, R. E., & McHugo, G. J. (1992). Alcohol use, depression and suicide in schizophrenia. *American Journal of Psychiatry, 149*, 394–395.

Bartels, S. J., Drake, R. E., & Wallach, M. A. (1995). Long-term course of substance use disorders among patients with severe mental illness. *Psychiatric Services, 46*(3), 248–251.

Bartels, S. J., Teague, G. B., Drake, R. E., Clark, R. E., Bush, P., & Noordsy, D. L. (1993). Substance use in schizophrenia: Service utilization and costs. *Journal of Nervous and Mental Disease, 181*, 227–232.

Belcher, J. R. (1989). On becoming homeless: A study of chronically mentally ill persons. *Journal of Community Psychology, 17*, 173–185.

Carey, (1996). Chapter 2 in *New Directions for Mental Health Services, No. 70.* San Francisco: Jossey-Bass.

Caton, C. L., Wyatt, R., Felix, A., Grunberg, J., & Dominquez, B. (1993). Follow-up of chronically homeless mentally ill men. *American Journal of Psychiatry, 150*(11), 1639–1642.

Center for Mental Health Services. (1994). *Making a difference: Interim status report of the McKinney Research Demonstration Program for Homeless Mentally Ill Adults.* Rockville, MD: Center for Mental Health Services, Substance Abuse and Mental Health Services Administration.

Dassori, A. M., Mezzich, J. E., & Keshavan, M. (1990). Suicidal indicators in schizophrenia. *Acta Psychiatrica Scandinavica, 81,* 409–413.

Dixon, L., Krauss, N., Myers, P., & Lehman, A. L. (1994). Clinical and treatment correlates of access to section 8 certificates for homeless mentally ill persons. *Psychiatric Services, 45,* 1196–1200.

Drake, R. E., & Noordsy, D. L. (1994). Case management for people with coexisting severe mental disorder and substance use disorder. *Psychiatric Annals, 24,* 427–431.

Drake, R. E., Osher, F. C., & Wallach, M. A. (1989). Alcohol use and abuse in schizophrenia: A prospective community study. *Journal of Nervous and Mental Disease, 177,* 408–414.

Drake, R. E., Osher, F. C., & Wallach, M. A. (1991). Homelessness and dual diagnosis. *American Psychologist, 46,* 1149–1158.

Drake, R. E., Wallach, M. A., & Hoffman, J. S. (1989). Housing instability and homelessness among aftercare patients of an urban state hospital. *Hospital and Community Psychiatry, 40,* 46–51.

Drake, R. E., Wallach, M. A., Teague, G. B., Freeman, D. H., Paskus, T. S., & Clark, T. A. (1991). Housing instability and homelessness among rural schizophrenic patients. *American Journal of Psychiatry, 148,* 330–336.

Fields, S. (1990). The relationship between residential treatment and supported housing in a community system of services. *Psychosocial Rehabilitation Journal, 13,* 105–113.

Gaffney, L., & Dixon, L. (1995). Engagement of homeless persons in treatment. Miami, FL: 148th Annual Meeting of the American Psychiatric Association. Abstract published in *New Research Program and Abstracts,* 95–96.

Goldfinger, S. M., Schutt, R. K., Seidman, L. M., Turner, W., Penk, W. E., & Tolomiczenko, G. (In press). Alternative measures of substance abuse among homeless mentally ill persons in cross-section and over time. *Journal of Nervous and Mental Disease.*

Gounis, K., & Susser, E. (1990). Shelterization and its implications for mental health services. In N. Cohen (Ed.), *Psychiatry takes to the streets: Outreach and crisis intervention for the mentally ill.* New York: Guilford Press.

Grunberg, J., & Eagle, P. F. (1990). Shelterization: How the homeless adapt to shelter living. *Hospital and Community Psychiatry, 41,* 521–525.

Harp, H. (1990). Independent living with support services: The goal and future for mental health consumers. *Psychosocial Rehabilitation Journal, 13*(4), 85–89.

Kessler, R. C., McGonagle, K. A., Zhao, S., Nelson, C. B., Hughes, M., Eshleman, S., Wittchen, H., & Kendler, K. S. (1994). Lifetime and twelve-month prevalence of *DSM-III-R* pßsychiatric disorders in the United States. *Archives of General Psychiatry, 51,* 8–19.

Kline, J., Harris, M., Bebout, R. E., & Drake, R. E. (1991). Contrasting integrated and linkage models of treatment for homeless, dually diagnosed adults. In K. Minkoff & R. E. Drake (Eds.), Dual diagnosis of major mental illness and substance use disorder. *New Directions for Mental Health Services, No. 50.* San Francisco: Jossey-Bass.

Negrete, J. C., Knapp, W. P., Douglas, D. E., & Smith, W. B. (1986). Cannabis affects the severity of schizophrenic symptoms: Results of a clinical survey. *Psychological Medicine, 16,* 515–520.

Newman, S. E. (1992). *The severely mentally ill homeless: Housing needs and housing policy.* Baltimore, MD: John Hopkins University Institute for Policy Studies, Occasional Paper No. 12.

Osher, F. C., & Kofoed, L. I. (1989). Treatment of patients with psychiatric and psychoactive substance abuse disorders. *Hospital and Community Psychiatry, 40,* 1025–1030.

Osher, F. C., Drake, R., Noordsy, D., Teague, G. E., Hurlbut, S. C., Biesanz, S. C., & Beaudett, M. S. (1994). Correlates of outcomes of alcohol use disorder among rural schizophrenic outpatients. *Journal of Clinical Psychiatry, 55,* 109–113.

Petrila, J. (1995). The Supreme Court's ruling in Edmonds v Oxford House: Implications for group homes *Psychiatric Services, 46,* 1011–1012.

Ridgely, M. S., Goldman, H. H., & Willenbring, M (1990). Barriers to the care of persons with dual diagnoses: Organizational and financing issues. *Schizophrenia Bulletin, 16,* 123–132.

Ridgway, P., & Zipple, A. M. (1990). The paradigm shift in residential services: From the linear continuum to supported housing approaches. *Psychosocial Rehabilitation Journal, 13,* 11–31.

Robinson, C. T., Dixon, L., Stewart, B., Harold, J., Lehman, A. F. (1993). *Family connections of the homeless mentally ill.* Poster Session. 146th annual meeting of the American Psychiatric Association, San Francisco, California.

Rubinstein, L. (1989). *The impact of the fair housing amendments on land-use regulations affecting people with disabilities.* Washington, D.C.: Mental Health Law Project.

Safer, D. (1987). Substance abuse by young adult chronic patients. *Hospital and Community Psychiatry, 38,* 511–514.

Schutt, R. K., & Goldfinger, S. M. (1996). Housing preferences and perceptions of health and functioning among homeless mentally ill persons. *Psychiatric Services, 47,* 381–386.

Tessler, R. C., & Dennis. D. L. (1989). *A synthesis of NIMH-funded research concerning persons who are homeless and mentally ill.* Rockville, MD: National Institute of Mental Health.

Ziedonis, D. M., & Fisher, W. (1994). Assessment and treatment of comorbid substance abuse in individuals with schizophrenia. *Psychiatric Annals, 24,* 477–483.

An Overview of the Research: Current Realities

William Anthony, Mikal Cohen, Marianne Farkas & Cheryl Gagne

This article originally appeared in *Psychiatric Rehabilitation, 2nd Edition* (2002), and is reprinted with permission.

William A. Anthony, Ph.D., Mikal Cohen, Ph.D., Marianne Farkas, Sc.D. & Cheryl Gagne, M.S., Center for Psychiatric Rehabilitation at Boston University, Boston, MA.

Although early research helped dispel the myths of psychiatric rehabilitation, more recent research has helped define the current realities and future promise of psychiatric rehabilitation. The literature overviewed in this chapter focuses on the persons served, outcomes, and types of interventions that characterize the field of psychiatric rehabilitation. This overview sets the context for a discussion of current and future research issues.

Psychiatric Rehabilitation Research

The persons served by psychiatric rehabilitation are those persons who have become disabled due to severe psychiatric illness. There are various definitions of psychiatric disability. Psychiatric rehabilitation research studies are focused on persons whose characteristics are consistent with the definition used by the National Institute of Mental Health's Community Support Program (CSP), the Rehabilitation Services Administration (RSA), and Goldman (Goldman et al., 1981).

The outcomes of psychiatric rehabilitation are fairly unique and specific relative to other mental health service interventions. Psychiatric rehabilitation ultimately attempts to improve role performance or status in people's living, learning, working, or social environments. While there might be important ancillary outcomes (such as symptom reduction, increased skill performance, changes in service utilization) the goals of psychiatric rehabilitation services are changes in role performance.

The role performance outcomes identified with psychiatric rehabilitation can be distinguished from other service outcomes. As conceptualized initially by Cohen, Nemec, Farkas & Forbess (1988), the outcomes achieved by other service system components are as follows: treatment = symptom relief; crisis intervention = personal safety assured; case management = services accessed; enrichment = self-development; rights protection = equal opportunity; basic support = personal survival assured; self-help = empowerment; wellness/prevention = health status improved. Each unique intervention also can impact outcomes that are the specific targeted outcomes of other interventions (e.g., psychiatric rehabilitation may have important ancillary outcomes such as satisfaction with leisure activities) (Holzner, Kemmler & Meise, 1998), but it is important to distinguish the unique outcomes of each service in order to keep track of the contributions of each service component. In research studies, it is absolutely necessary to differentiate the outcomes that each service is expected to achieve.

Another important distinction with respect to psychiatric rehabilitation outcomes is the difference between skill performance and role performance. In psychiatric rehabilitation, skill performance includes such dimensions as job interviewing skills, punctuality skills, interpersonal skills, etc. These measures of skill performance are in actuality process measures. Skill development occurs *so that* individuals will be more successful and satisfied in their chosen role. For several reasons, improvements in skill performance cannot be a proxy measure for role performance—which is the fundamental rehabilitation outcome. First of all, role performance can be impacted without skill improvements (for example, by simply making the environment more supportive or accommodating). Secondly, skills can improve but not to a level that impacts role performance, or perhaps the targeted skills were not most relevant to role performance. In essence, changes in skill and changes in role are two very different types of measures, and it is role performance that is the quintessential rehabilitation outcome (Anthony, 1992).

The *interventions* of psychiatric rehabilitation emphasize changing a person's skills, changing a person's environmental supports, or both. The assumption of psychiatric rehabilitation is that through positive changes in the person's skills and/or environmental supports, role performance benefits will accrue. Studies involving skill development and support development interventions are considered to be psychiatric rehabilitation studies, whether or not the author specifically labeled the intervention a psychiatric rehabilitation intervention.

In summary, this article discusses individual studies and reviews of studies that meet the inclusion criteria of focusing on people with psychiatric disabilities, using rehabilitation outcome measures, and rehabilitation intervention techniques. That is, the people studied had to be comprised of persons with psychiatric disabilities; the outcomes had to include improved role functioning; and the intervention techniques had to be designed to develop an individual's skills and/or environmental supports.

Major Intervention Studies Not Included in This Overview

Several types of studies of skill development and support development interventions are not discussed, in particular, studies of 1) social skills training (SST); and 2) family psychoeducation. These areas are excluded because they represent a somewhat discrete focus of inquiry in which periodic reviews have been published (Benton & Schroeder, 1990; Dilk & Bond, 1996; Penn & Mueser, 1996). The findings from these types of interventions have been incorporated into the general psychiatric rehabilitation literature (Anthony, 1979, 1998; Anthony, Cohen & Cohen, 1984).

Social Skills Training

With respect to Social Skills Training, SST holds most promise as a specifically targeted component of a comprehensive rehabilitation program. The methodology of SST can be integrated with the skills teaching component of a psychiatric rehabilitation intervention. In general, sophisticated, rigorous research studies of SST (e.g., Kopelowicz et al., 1997; Liberman et al., 1998; Marder et al., 1996) focus on changes in skill performance rather than rehabilitation outcome, i.e., changes in role performance.

Family Interventions

With respect to family psychoeducation approaches, rehabilitation philosophy historically has emphasized including the family in a comprehensive rehabilitation approach (Power & Dell Orto, 1980; Agnetti, Barbato & Young, 1993). Rehabilitation practitioners around the world, who work with persons with physical disabilities or developmental disabilities, use the family as a valuable resource in rehabilitation. This is particularly evident in countries where professionals are less available and the family is still considered to be the central social unit (Pearson & Phillips, 1994; Nagaswami, 1995; El Islam, 1982). In contrast, mental health practitioners who work with persons with psychiatric disabilities in industrialized countries have been much slower in perceiving the family as a resource (Spaniol, Zipple & Fitzgerald, 1984). The development of structured family interventions (e.g., North et al., 1998) has expanded the possibilities for involving the family as a resource in the rehabilitation of persons with psychiatric disabilities.

Residential, Educational, and Vocational Status of Persons with Psychiatric Disabilities

Before focusing on the impact of psychiatric rehabilitation interventions on rehabilitation outcomes for persons with long-term psychiatric disabilities, the typical residential, educational, and vocational status of persons with psychiatric disabilities must be considered. That is, in the absence of a rehabilitation intervention targeted at that particular outcome, what is the base rate of functioning in that particular environment.

Residential Status

Historically, the residential status of persons with psychiatric disabilities was assessed in two ways: recidivism rates and place of residence. Hospital recidivism figures continue to be used routinely even though their use has been repeatedly critiqued over the years on the grounds of their susceptibility to a variety of influences other than the persons' adjustment to their living situation (Anthony et al., 1972, 1978; Bachrach, 1976a; Lyons et al., 1997). Factors such as the course of the psychiatric disability, admission policies of the hospital or managed care firm and/or the quality of community services can affect recidivism (Lyons et al., 1997). Comprehensive reviews of the literature indicate a gradually increasing rate of recidivism as the follow-up period lengthens. Early studies of rehabilitation outcome reported an inpatient recidivism rate at 6 months of approximately 30 to 40%; at 12 months, 35 to 50%; and at 5 years, 65 to 75% (Anthony et al., 1972, 1978). Later research (Hafemeister & Banks, 1996) has shown significant variation between hospitals, but in a range similar to the early base rate figures (6 months = 22–50%, 1 year = 32–57%, 2 years = 43–64%).

With respect to the place of residence, unfortunately most of the residential data cannot be compared across studies. Each study defines types of residences (e.g., group homes, transitional homes, foster homes) differently. Thus, there are no accurate estimates of the typical degree of independent living status of persons with severe psychiatric disabilities. An early multistate sample of people attending community support programs indicates that 40% lived in a private home or apartment, 12% in board and care settings, 10% in family foster care placements, and the rest in other residential categories with less than 10% each (Tessler & Goldman, 1982). A later survey of a similar sample reported that 57% were living in private homes and apartments, with a significantly lower percentage in structured community settings (Mulkern & Manderscheid,

1989). The National Plan for the Chronically Mentally Ill (U.S. Department of Health and Human Services, 1980) estimated that of those persons residing in the community, 38 to 50% lived in board-and-care settings and 19 to 21% lived with families. Estimates of the number of people who were homeless and had a severe mental illness were that approximately one third of individuals who are homeless have psychiatric disabilities (Dennis et al., 1991). The first nationwide survey of family members of persons with severe psychiatric disabilities, who also were members of the National Alliance for the Mentally Ill (NAMI), reported that approximately 30% lived at home with family, 15% in a community residence, and 18% in hospitals (Spaniol et al., 1984). It is clear from these studies that the type and definition of residential categories varied from study to study, thus precluding national estimates of the degree of independent living.

The social life of individuals with disabilities living in the community is significantly restricted (Champney & Dzurec, 1992; Kaye, 1998). With respect to housing preference, most people with psychiatric disabilities, just like most every one else, prefer to live in their own apartments or houses, while the preference of family members and staff often is that people with psychiatric disabilities live in more supervised settings (Holley, Hodges & Jeffers, 1998; Minsky, Riesser & Duffy, 1995; Rogers, Danley, Anthony, Martin & Walsh, 1994).

Educational Status

The educational status of persons with severe psychiatric disabilities has received scant attention in the literature until the 1980s. However, the available data do point to the advanced educational status of many persons with severe psychiatric disabilities. Depending on the particular sample taken, between 52 to 92% of persons with severe psychiatric disabilities are high school graduates, and 15 to 60% of these high school graduates have attended college. For a specific example, the NAMI survey data (Spaniol et al., 1984) indicated that of the total sample, 92% graduated from high school, 59% also attended college, and 17% graduated from college. Admittedly, the NAMI survey sampled middle to upper-middle income families, thus accounting for the relatively high educational levels. Data from a study of persons attending the Transitional Employment Program (TEP) at Fountain House in New York City indicated that approximately 70% were high school graduates, 48% also attended college, and 14% were college graduates

(Fountain House, 1985). These figures were the same as the figures for the general population of New York City. A more recent study of TEP members at Fountain House reported that 47% had some type of post-high school education (Macias, Kinney & Rodican, 1995). A study of 505 persons with long-term psychiatric disabilities discharged from hospitals in Toronto, Canada, reported that 72% were high school graduates and 16% also attended college (Goering, Wasylenki, Lancee & Freeman, 1984). Two studies of Community Support Program individuals reported 53 to 55% high school graduates and 19 to 23% with post-high school education (Mulkern & Manderscheid, 1989; Tessler & Goldman, 1982). We estimate that approximately 70% of individuals choosing to attend a vocational program will be high school graduates.

Concern over educational status has increased as people with psychiatric disabilities become more apt to pursue professional and managerial careers (Russinova, Ellison & Foster, 1999). People with psychiatric disabilities have the requisite desire and intellectual ability to achieve higher educational goals, yet a significant number drop out. In addition to the complications brought about by mental health problems, some of the barriers to higher education include lack of financial aid, a lack of understanding of mental illness by faculty and peers, and mandatory psychiatric withdrawal policies. Mowbray and Megivern (1992) have reported on the experiences of a sample of individuals who enrolled in post-secondary education. When asked to identify what assistance would help them stay in school they reported in decreasing order of importance the following needs: financial support, tutoring services, special classes, transportation, having a note-taker, and help with registration.

Vocational Status

Studies containing data on the competitive employment rate of persons discharged from psychiatric hospitals have been surveyed periodically by Anthony and associates in the 1970s and 1980s (Anthony et al., 1972, 1978; Anthony, Howell & Danley, 1984) and others in the 1990s (Bond & McDonel, 1991; OMH Quarterly, 1998). The data have been fairly consistent, suggesting a full-time competitive employment figure of 20 to 30% for all persons discharged from psychiatric hospitals. However, if just persons with long-term psychiatric disabilities are studied, the full- and part-time competitive employment figure drops to approximately 15% and below. For example, the NAMI survey of well educated persons with long-term psychiatric disabilities from middle- to upper-income families reported a full-time employment rate of about 5% (Spaniol et al., 1984). Farkas, Rogers, and Thurer (1987) followed up 54 long-term state hospital inpatients who had been targeted for deinstitutionalization in 1979. Over a 5-year period, 0% obtained competitive employment. Tessler and Goldman (1982) reported an 11% full- and part-time competitive employment for Community Support Program individuals. A later survey by Mulkern and Manderscheid (1989) of persons served by CSP reported a competitive employment rate of slightly less than 10%. Wasylenki et al. (1985) reported that 11% of their hospitalized sample in Canada were employed prior to admission. Dion, Tohen, Anthony, and Waternaux (1988) followed people hospitalized with bipolar disorder and found evidence of the impact of severity on vocational outcome. At 6-month follow-up, 64% of first admission patients were employed at some level of competitive employment versus 33% of persons with one or more prior hospitalizations. Interestingly, only 20% of the total sample were functioning at their expected level of employment, that is, at the occupational level expected on the basis of previous work history and education. Compared to individuals with other types of disabilities whose unemployment rate is around 67%, the unemployment rate for people with psychiatric disabilities in the United States is 85 to 92% (New York State Office of Mental Health, 1998).

An Overview of the Psychiatric Rehabilitation Research Field

Examples of individual empirical studies that meet the aforementioned inclusion criteria have been organized around the key dimensions of location, outcome measures, types of intervention, research design, and outcomes. Every effort was made to include examples of the relevant psychiatric rehabilitation research studies and research reviews that appear in all the various mental health and rehabilitation journals. Of course, some relevant studies were unavailable because they were either in press, being prepared for journal submission, or had just been received by the granting agency that supported the research. Computer searches were conducted of several databases; current, not-yet-indexed journal issues were read, and major funding sources of psychiatric rehabilitation research (NIMH, CMHS, NIDRR) were contacted for information about recently completed studies. Most of the individual studies and reviews occurred within the last 30 years because few databased evaluations of psychiatric rehabilitation existed before the 1970s.

Other Relevant Literature Reviews

Early reviews of the literature that met the inclusion criteria of person served, intervention, and outcome were done by Anthony and his colleagues in the following chronological order (Anthony, Buell, Sharratt & Althoff, 1972; Anthony & Margules, 1974; Anthony, 1977; Anthony, Cohen & Vitalo, 1978; Anthony, 1979; Anthony, 1980; Anthony & Nemec, 1984). Because of the paucity of psychiatric rehabilitation research funding in the 1960s and 1970s, these early reviews included pre-post and quasi-experimental studies almost exclusively. However, in spite of the design deficiencies, these first reviews did report significant improvement over base rate for groups of individuals participating in psychiatric rehabilitation interventions. It is these less rigorous research methodologies that up until the 1990s have been the greatest source of psychiatric rehabilitation knowledge (Anthony, 1998).

A number of reviews of the psychiatric rehabilitation field occurred in the 1990s, and these reviews were able to incorporate more experimental studies (Barton, 1999; Bond, Drake, Becker & Mueser, 1999; Cook, Pickett, Razzano, Fitzgibbon, Jonikas & Cohler, 1996; Farkas, 1999; Mueser, Drake & Bond, 1997). Universal in their request for more and better research, the reviewers arrive at fairly similar conclusions. In general, research reviews of the psychiatric rehabilitation field suggest that skills and support development interventions focused on improving functioning produce significantly better outcomes than the conditions to which they have been compared.

For example, "Recent research has continued to show that psychiatric rehabilitation, when added to standard psychopharmacological treatment, can enhance many aspects of functional status and quality of life for patients with serious mental illness" (Mueser, Drake & Bond, 1997, p. 130). "...The research on the effectiveness of supported employment was consistently positive" (Bond, Drake, Becker & Mueser, 1999, p.18). "The continuation of these treatments (rehabilitation and psychopharmacology) appears to be effective in restoring the individual to a higher level of functioning" (Cook et al., 1996, p. 101). "...Longitudinal and outcomes research strongly supports the effectiveness and efficacy of psychosocial rehabilitation, but further research is needed to further refine intervention strategies" (Barton, 1999, p. 530).

Location

Psychiatric rehabilitation studies have been conducted in a variety of settings, including psychosocial rehabilitation centers, hospitals, community mental health centers and offices of state divisions of vocational rehabilitation. A number of early studies have investigated the delivery of psychiatric rehabilitation interventions in more than one setting: hospital/community linkages (Paul & Lentz, 1977; Wasylenki et al., 1985) and mental health—vocational rehabilitation collaborative programming (Dellario, 1985; Rogers, Anthony & Danley, 1989). Many of the single settings (e.g., psychosocial rehabilitation centers) use places outside the setting's physical location, such as employment sites (Fountain House, 1985). The frequent disjointing of rehabilitation intervention settings is illustrative of the need for a comprehensive and coordinated approach to planning service delivery.

As would be expected, much of the psychiatric rehabilitation research literature focuses on the vocational environment. In part, this is because the term *rehabilitation* emerged in a vocational context, that is, the vocational rehabilitation of persons with physical disabilities. However, within the mental health field, rehabilitation focuses on the residential environment as well; residential success and satisfaction is a factor closely related to the amelioration and aggravation of the psychiatric condition. This fact is reflected in the early and routine collection of recidivism data (Anthony et al., 1972; 1978). The research investigations reviewed are characteristic of the field's interest in both vocational and residential environments. In contrast, as evidenced by the types of outcome measures used, until the mid-1980s, investigations of the educational and social environments have been more rare (Center for Psychiatric Rehabilitation, 1989; Unger & Anthony, 1984; Unger, Danley, Kohn & Hutchinson, 1987).

Outcome Measures

The field has moved far beyond a simple reliance on recidivism and employment figures as outcome measures. In the first comprehensive review of the psychiatric rehabilitation field, Anthony, et al. (1972) had to rely exclusively on studies that reported recidivism and employment outcomes, the only types of data routinely collected. Yet, even these early studies suggested a lack of relationships between outcome measures across environments (in this instance, recidivism and employment) and the need for more refined measures in all the different outcomes of interest (Anthony et al., 1972).

In an early comprehensive review of outcome measures used in psychiatric rehabilitation, Anthony and Farkas (1982) concluded that:

1. Change on a single measure of outcome does not indicate that seemingly related measures of change have been affected (e.g., change in vocational functioning may not be correlated with change in psychosocial functioning).

2. A positive effect on one outcome measure may have an associated negative effect on another (e.g., an increase in skills associated with an increase in anxiety).

Thus, from the 1980s on, researchers in psychiatric rehabilitation were being challenged to study the impact of their interventions on a wider range of outcomes (e.g., Saraceno, 1995) and to make no assumptions about an intervention's impact on outcomes not specifically studied. In general, the recent research literature seems compatible with these guidelines.

Psychiatric rehabilitation outcome studies are somewhat atypical in the mental health field in that many of the intended outcomes are specific, observable, understandable, and valued by the general public. In the 1970s and 1980s, various methods of skill development and/or support interventions were found to have an impact on such seemingly straightforward outcome criteria as days in the community (Cannady, 1982; Paul & Lentz, 1977), earnings (Bond, 1984), reduction in disability pensions (Jensen, Spangaard, Juel-Neilsen & Voag, 1978), and employment (Turkat & Buzzell, 1983).

The types of outcomes currently used indicate increasing sophistication of outcome measures. In terms of vocational status, simple yes/no measures of employment have been complemented by measures of types of employment, for example, pre-vocational, transitional, supported, part-time, and full-time (Fountain House, 1985), satisfaction with income (Drake et al., 1999), self-esteem (Ellison, Danley, Bromberg & Palmer-Erbs, 1999), satisfaction with work (National Institute of Handicapped Research, 1980), productivity (Hoffman, 1980), job tenure (Chandler, Levin & Barry, 1999), and instrumental role functioning (Goering, Farkas, Wasylenki, Lancee & Ballantyne, 1988). With respect to residential status, simple recidivism measures have been all but replaced by measures of total days in the community (e.g., Cannady, 1982), time spent in various types of housing (Brown, Ridgway, Anthony & Rogers, 1991), social adjustment (e.g., Linn, Caffey, Klett, Hogart & Lamb, 1979), number of friends and activities (e.g., National Institute of Handicapped Research, 1980; Vitalo, 1979), loneliness (Stein et al., 1999), degree of independent living (e.g., Mosher & Menn, 1978), satisfaction with community adjustment (e.g., Katz-Garris, McCue, Garris & Herring, 1983), quality of life (Shern et al., 2000), psychosocial functioning (Brekke et al., 1999), and social skills (e.g., Aveni & Upper, 1976; Jerrell, 1999).

As outcome measurements in psychiatric rehabilitation studies have become more refined, i.e., measuring degrees of improvement over time rather than yes/no categorical measures at one point in time, the findings with respect to psychiatric rehabilitation interventions have become more targeted and specific. For example, studies that have not shown change on recidivism have reported positive results on measures of community tenure (Beard et al., 1978) and instrumental role functioning (Goering et al., 1988). In several studies, the longer the follow-up period, the more dramatic the findings. For example, differences in instrumental role functioning and social adjustment increased from the 6-month to the 2-year follow-up (Goering et al., 1988); differences in employment not apparent at 9 months appeared at 15 months (Bond & Dincin, 1986); and the longer the follow-up after the transitional employment placement, the greater the vocational outcome (Fountain House, 1985).

Few early studies in psychiatric rehabilitation investigated educational status, yet many academically capable young adults have had their educational progress interrupted by a psychiatric disability (Spaniol et al., 1984; Unger & Anthony, 1984). The outcome of rehabilitation interventions designed to improve functioning in the educational area can be assessed by using such educational status outcome measures as degree programs entered, degree programs completed, courses completed, professional/educational certificate programs completed, academic skills learned, course grades, achievement test scores, as well as measures of employment status (Mowbray, Brown, Sullivan Soydan & Furlong-Norman, in press).

The increased interest in outcome measurement has stimulated several other developments relevant to psychiatric rehabilitation. Consistent with psychiatric rehabilitation's emphasis on an individual's direction and choice, studies have confirmed that the person with a psychiatric disability can be a primary and direct source of outcome information (Boothroyd, Skinner, Shern & Steinwachs, 1998). Many outcome measures and methods now use the person with a disability as a major source of information about the effectiveness of the program. Secondly, new outcome instruments continue to be developed (Cuffel, Fischer, Owen & Smith, 1997) in such areas as empowerment (Rogers, Chamberlin, Ellison & Crean, 1997), quality of life (Greenley, Greenberg & Brown, 1997; Van Nieuwenhuizen, Schene, Boevink & Wolf, 1997), and community functioning (Dickerson, 1997).

Due to the proliferation of instrumentation a number of researchers have attempted to organize the types of outcome instruments into a small number of outcome domains. Docherty and Streeter (1996) identified seven dimensions of outcome: symptomatology, social/interpersonal functioning, work functioning, satisfaction, treatment utilization, health state, and health-related quality of life. Dickerson (1997) identified 11 outcome categories just within the community functions domain: activities of daily living, social skills, ability to manage money, social supports, work skills, life satisfaction, family relationships, burden to family members, use of leisure time, physical health care, and personal safety. Srebnik et al. (1997) grouped outcome measures most parsimoniously into just four domains, which seem to encompass other categorizations—satisfaction, functioning, quality of life, and clinical status. Outcome categories give both the researcher and program developer a better conceptual understanding of the targets of the intervention.

Principles for outcome measurement have been advanced (Smith, Manderscheid, Flynn & Steinwachs, 1997). Blankertz and Cook (1998) have provided a set of useful principles for choosing and using outcome measures in psychiatric rehabilitation:

- Outcomes should measure changes in "real world" behaviors.

- Outcome measures of change should represent the longitudinal basis of the psychiatric rehabilitation process.

- Outcome measures used should be comparable to others in use.

- Outcome measures should collect information from the person served.

- Outcome measures should reflect the consequences of mental illness and rehabilitation in many areas of a person's life.

- Outcome measures should reflect the main focus of an agency's activities.

- Outcome measurement should proceed only after support has been gained from all stakeholders (including staff, people served, and family members).

Type of Intervention

In order to be considered psychiatric rehabilitation research, the intervention under study has to provide either skill development, increased support, or both. However, several obvious limitations must be noted in how psychiatric rehabilitation interventions have been studied. First, many of the interventions are not described in sufficient detail to permit replication, either in future research studies or in clinical practice. Simply knowing the setting of the intervention provides little information about the specific intervention. Limitations imposed by journal space no doubt account for some of this brevity, but even the references accompanying most articles do not indicate the existence of any materials (e.g., manuals or videotapes) that might facilitate replication. Exceptions are studies of psychiatric rehabilitation (Anthony, Cohen & Farkas, 1990) using technology developed by Cohen and colleagues at Boston University (see for example, Anthony, Cohen & Pierce, 1980; Goering, Wasylenki et al., 1988; Lamberti, Melburg & Madi, 1998; National Institute of Handicapped Research, 1980; Shern et al., 1997); the Fountain House transitional employment approach (Fountain House, 1985; Macias, Kinney & Rodican, 1995); Liberman's social skills training (Liberman, Mueser & Wallace, 1986; Liberman et al., 1998); Paul's social learning approach (Paul & Lentz, 1977; Paul, Stuve & Cross, 1997); Azrin's job seeking skills program (Jacobs et al., 1984); Stein & Test's ACT program (Santos, Henggelar, Burns, Arana, et al., 1995; Stein & Test, 1978); and Drake's IPS vocational model (Drake, Becker, Clark & Mueser, 1999; Drake, McHugo, Becker, Anthony & Clark, 1996).

A second problem is the difficulty in separating the unique contributions to rehabilitation outcome of skill development versus support interventions. Support interventions typically mean supportive programs that accommodate the persons' deficits (e.g., supported living) or supportive persons that help the person with a psychiatric disability to meet the demands of nonsupportive environments (e.g., these supportive persons provide personal counseling, companionship, advocacy, and practical advice). Some of these supportive programs and people also provide opportunities for persons with psychiatric disabilities to learn skills. Some programs may promote skill development by providing an environment that facilitates learning; other programs provide a more structured, formalized skill teaching program. From a research perspective, skill development and support interventions have been inextricably linked. Investigations have lacked either the methodology or the intent to study the relative merits of the two types of interventions. The research currently suggests that the interventions that provide the client with an opportunity both to learn skills and to receive support remain the preferred rehabilitation interventions.

Research Design

Just as the types of outcomes studied have become more refined, the research designs have become more rigorous—albeit more slowly. Studies already exist, and are being done more frequently, that use random assignments to experimental and control groups (e.g., Atkinson et al., 1996; Bell & Lysaker, 1997; Blankertz & Robinson, 1996; Bond, 1984; Bond & Dincin, 1986; Chandler et al., 1996; Dincin & Witheridge, 1982; Drake et al., 1996; Drake et al., 1999; Paul & Lentz, 1977; Ryan & Bell, 1985; Shern et al., 1997; Wolkon, Karmen & Tanaka, 1971) or matched experimental and control groups (Beard, Malamud & Rossman, 1978; Goering, Wasylenki, et al., 1988; Hoffman, 1980; Matthews, 1979; Mosher & Menn, 1978; Vitalo, 1979; Wasylenki et al., 1985). An examination of those experimental studies suggests that the positive outcomes of these better controlled studies seem in no way different from the outcomes generated by quasi-experimental designs.

However, the design deficiencies in most psychiatric rehabilitation research literature are readily apparent. Still too few studies have designs that permit reasonable, causal inferences to be made. Also, many designs are plagued by inadequate sample size, incomplete descriptions of the sample, lack of specificity and replicability of treatment approach, and lack of outcome measures appropriate to the interventions used. In addition, the vast majority of studies use one group and posttest only designs.

Yet these nonexperimental studies do have value. They have provided the empirical and conceptual foundation for the experimental studies that have begun to appear. They have seized the available data and used the results to fashion more specific interventions that can now be researched experimentally. Much of this previous research can be considered exploratory, examining the practical significance of interventions before the experimental test. When viewed from this perspective, the psychiatric rehabilitation field is prepared for the additional, critical, experimental studies that will be undertaken in the coming decades.

Outcomes

Any discussion of outcomes is, of course, limited by the previously discussed design deficiencies. However, as a group the research studies suggest that rehabilitation interventions produce improved rehabilitation outcomes in the persons served. These studies can be grouped by the specific types of rehabilitation programs that were evaluated.

Some of the very first rehabilitation studies reported positive outcomes through joint programming between two different settings or agencies. These coordinated programs included cooperative hospital and community programming (Becker & Bayer, 1975; Jacobs & Trick, 1974; Paul & Lentz, 1977; Wasylenki et al., 1985) and collaborative mental health and vocational rehabilitation programs (Dellario, 1985; Rogers, Anthony & Danley, 1989). That collaborative interventions initiated from a hospital base can produce rehabilitation outcome in the community is particularly noteworthy. Dellario and Anthony (1981), based on their own literature review, as well as on reviews by Kiesler (1982) and Test and Stein (1978), concluded that hospital care and community-based care should not be compared with one another but rather to the stated mission of the agency, no matter what its location. This, of course, presumes a statement of mission that articulates the intended outcomes for each facility—a condition that may not exist in many settings (Farkas, Cohen & Nemec, 1988). Nevertheless, replacing hospital care with community care requires a commitment to provide rehabilitation programming without arbitrary time limits. The critical determinant of the effectiveness of services provided within a particular setting could be the relationship of that setting to an overall system of long-term community support. Even though use of public psychiatric hospitals continues to decline, and the policy of public mental health systems continues to emphasize community-based services, psychiatric hospitalization per se remains a significant part of most public mental health systems. The most dramatic changes have been in the increased use of the general hospital setting and the growth of private psychiatric hospitals. These trends present potential problems in providing relevant services, given the often limited experience of these new settings with long-term psychiatric disabilities, the psychiatric rehabilitation approach, and community support systems.

While policy debates over the specific role of the hospital in mental health systems continue, change to a rehabilitation orientation in at least some hospital settings is promising. The technology of changing a traditional hospital program to a psychiatric rehabilitation program is available (Anthony, Cohen & Farkas, 1987; Farkas, Cohen & Nemec, 1988; Hart, 1997). The research studies suggest that a rehabilitation approach providing integrated development of skills and supports within the variety of settings in which people are served (inpatient and community) may be the most effective approach.

The positive vocational outcomes associated with collaborative mental health and vocational rehabilitation interventions suggest the benefits of better coordination among existing services. In an era of cost containment, such data give impetus to increasing the effectiveness of those service components already in place. More efficient service delivery need not sacrifice improved client outcome—indeed, it may improve it. However, another way to overcome the difficulties of interagency coordination is to bring both services into one agency. By bringing mental health and vocational programming under one roof, Drake has reported improved vocational outcome beyond that provided through interagency programming (Drake, McHugo, Becker, Anthony & Clark, 1996).

With the continued development of psychosocial rehabilitation centers, research conducted at these centers takes on increasing importance. Several studies conducted at psychosocial rehabilitation centers are studies of a Transitional Employment Program (TEP). TEP is a vocational training innovation currently in use in many psychosocial rehabilitation agencies around the country (Fountain House, 1985). In a traditional TEP, a member (client) of the psychosocial rehabilitation center is placed in an entry-level job in a normal place of business. All placements are temporary (3–9 months), typically half-time, and are supervised by the psychosocial rehabilitation center (Beard et al., 1982).

A TEP is designed to develop the self-confidence, job references, and work habits necessary to secure permanent employment.

Until the 1980s, there was little research studying the effectiveness of TEPs. Typically, studies have examined the vocational outcomes of persons served by a psychosocial rehabilitation center, whose services included a TEP. In a very early study, Beard, Pitt, Fisher, and Goertzel (1963) reported no significant differences in employment between experimental and comparison subjects. In a randomized control group design, Dincin and Witheridge (1982) found no differences in employment at the 9-month follow-up.

Another follow-up study of Fountain House members who spent at least 1 day in a TEP has been reported (Fountain House, 1985). The results for 527 individuals who participated in a TEP indicated that employment outcome increased as a function of the time since the initial TEP. For members whose initial TEP was at least 42 months ago, 36% were competitively employed. At 12 months and 24 months, the employment rates were 11% and 19%, respectively.

Thresholds, a psychosocial rehabilitation center, conducted another study of two different types of TEPs, an accelerated TEP and a traditional TEP. Persons in the traditional TEP were required to remain in pre-vocational settings a minimum of 4 months longer than persons in the accelerated TEP condition. At the 15-month follow-up, the 20% and 7% employment rates in the accelerated and traditional TEP conditions approximate Fountain House's employment figure for the same time period (Bond & Dincin, 1986).

The results of TEP research conducted by Fountain House suggest that TEPs have a significant impact on employment as the follow-up period increases, and that those members who spent more time in Fountain House before beginning a TEP worked more days on their first TEP (Macias, Kinney & Rodican, 1995). However, the research conducted by Thresholds suggests that for a person with prior work experience, the entrance into a TEP could be accelerated and the time needed to obtain employment shortened.

Long-term programmatic research of particular approaches to psychiatric rehabilitation have tended to use interventions (mentioned in the previous section on types of interventions) that are more replicable—due to training and/or procedures manuals. Included in this group are: rehabilitation interventions, such as the Choose-Get-Keep program model (Danley & Anthony, 1987) that is based on the psychiatric rehabilitation practitioner training technology developed at Boston University (Anthony, Cohen & Pierce, 1980; Cohen, Danley & Nemec, 1985; Cohen, Farkas & Cohen, 1986; Cohen et al., 1988; Cohen, Farkas, Cohen & Unger, 1991); the social learning program developed by Paul (Paul & Lentz, 1977; Paul, Stuve & Cross, 1997); and the ACT program model originally developed by Stein and Test (1978). Becker and Drake's Individual Placement and Support model (Becker & Drake, 1993) is a relatively more recent, yet replicable, psychiatric rehabilitation intervention. Chapter 9 gives examples of some of the better known program models and the research underpinning these program models. In general, it appears that the program models which emphasize vocational outcomes can triple the employment outcomes (30–55% employed). These program models that focus on the living and social areas can reduce the re-hospitalization rate by two-thirds (0–15% a year). All program models can positively impact other measures, such as quality of life, self-esteem, and satisfaction.

Conclusions

Within the obvious limitations of the measurement, design, and description of the intervention, current research studies and reviews of many studies suggest that a psychiatric rehabilitation approach does affect rehabilitation outcome positively. Almost all of the studies combine different elements of skill development and support, making it impossible at this time to unravel the unique contributions of the different elements to outcome. As early as 1974, Anthony and Margules (1974) conducted a review of the literature and tentatively concluded that persons with severe psychiatric disabilities can learn important skills despite their symptomatology, and that these skills, when combined with appropriate community supports, can have an impact on rehabilitation outcome. Two and one half decades later the same conclusion can be drawn, based on additional data, relatively more sophisticated research designs, and more comprehensive reviews.

Current and Future Research Issues

Monumental problems still exist in psychiatric rehabilitation research. The most critical problem is the continued need for experimental research on replicable, rehabilitation interventions. Over two decades ago Mosher and Keith (1979), Goldberg (1980), Meyerson and

Herman (1983), and Keith and Matthews (1984) all called for well-controlled process and outcome studies of a psychiatric rehabilitation approach. While more such studies have since been conducted, especially recently, studies with sophisticated and rigorous research designs are still very much needed.

Further research of psychiatric rehabilitation is critical because community mental health centers, and new managed care entities, are expanding their services in a renewed attempt to treat persons with long-term psychiatric disabilities in the community. A NIMH-sponsored study by Larsen (1987) indicated that the community mental health services experiencing greatest growth in the 1980s were those primarily directed toward people with long-term mental illness residing in the community—that is, those persons most apt to receive a psychiatric rehabilitation approach. In the 1990s, managed care approaches expanded in this same direction (Cummings, 1998; Shaffer, 1997). The high percentage of treatment dollars used to serve persons with long-term psychiatric disabilities has been well documented, and more and more mental health authorities are developing psychiatric rehabilitation services for this group of individuals.

One of the most difficult problems to overcome in future psychiatric rehabilitation outcome research is the development of practical, meaningful, reliable, and valid outcome measures. Because of the limited space in professional journals, new instruments developed for the study are not often described in sufficient detail. Consequently, replicating the measurement can seem as difficult as replicating the rehabilitation interventions, which are also incompletely described. Many early studies do not even reference the instruments that were used, making it more difficult to identify the potential standardized measures.

Another problem that must be corrected in future research studies is that reliability and validity measures of instruments often are not reported. Reliability tends to be more frequently reported than validity—perhaps reflecting the problems in establishing convergent or concurrent validity for a vaguely defined set of complex behaviors. Indeed, the question of the validity of behavioral measures rarely has been considered (Wallace et al., 1980). In the past, many instruments used in outcome research were developed for the assessment of the acute population and were applied to the long-term population, for lack of a population-specific instrument. When the researcher moved beyond direct measurements of change (e.g., number of days attending a workshop) and applied assessment techniques standardized on other populations, problems with reliability and validity arose.

Researchers are unanimous in calling for future research measures designed to assess the generalization of skill development interventions. However, in addition to assessing whether the skills learned in training are applied in the targeted environment, there is a pressing need for the development of skill measures that positively correlate with concrete measures of rehabilitation outcomes. Skill measures developed many years ago by Paul and Lentz (1977) and by Griffiths (1973) are models in this regard. Predictive validity based on measures of inpatient behaviors has been reported by Power (1979) and Redfield (1979), using the Clinical Frequencies Recording System and the Time Sample Behavior Checklist, respectively. Both instruments were developed and standardized in the decade-long investigation conducted by Paul and his associates. Predischarge scores on these instruments can significantly predict the discharged person's role performance in the community (Paul, 1984).

Designed to measure vocational behaviors of persons with psychiatric disabilities, the Standardized Assessment of Work Behavior (Griffiths, 1973, 1974; Watts, 1978) assesses a broad range of behaviors (e.g., uses tools/equipment, communicates spontaneously, grasps instructions quickly). Items are rated on a continuum from a strength (e.g., looks for more work) to a deficit (e.g., waits to be given work). Impressive reliability and predictive validity data are available for this scale. More recently the Work Behavior Index has been shown to predict future work success with respect to hours worked and earnings (Bryson, Bell, Greig & Kaplan, 1999).

Interest has increased in outcome measures of overall level of skill functioning, compatible with the increased use of functional assessment in psychiatric rehabilitation practice in the 1980s and 1990s (Slaton & Westphal, 1999). However, these assessments of skill function are inherently flawed as measures of outcome because of the previously mentioned fact that skill performance is a process measure, not an outcome. No matter how thorough and comprehensive the skill assessment is, it is not the same as a status measure. Although these instruments do represent a first step in grappling with the problems of measuring changes during the psychiatric rehabilitation process, they are, nevertheless, still crude. Both Ridgway (1988), who reviewed over 200 levels of functioning instruments with respect to residential needs, and Anthony and Farkas (1982), who reviewed the major functional assessment instruments across domains, previously pointed out the lack of specificity in the items and their lack of relevancy to a person's preferred housing and work environments as major deficits in the validity and meaningfulness of these standardized instruments.

The field of outcome measurement for people with psychiatric disabilities has been stimulated by the entrance into the policy arena of two different constituencies: people with psychiatric disabilities and behavioral managed care organizations. Now more than ever, outcome measurement is seen by departments of mental health, people with psychiatric disabilities, providers, and taxpayers as one way to help assure and improve quality, to evaluate outcomes, and to demonstrate the value of services, including psychiatric rehabilitation.

Influence of People with Psychiatric Disabilities

People with psychiatric disabilities have increased their own interest in research and, at the same time, their influence in all aspects of behavioral health, including research, has become the policy of the U.S. Federal Government (SAMHSA, 1993). At the level of implementation, Participatory Action Research (PAR) is a methodology developed to include people who are the focus of the research as full members of the research team (Nelson et al., 1998; Rogers & Palmer-Erbs, 1994). People with psychiatric disabilities have taken a leadership role in the development of all aspects of research, from the research questions to outcome instruments. An example of an instrument constructed with a PAR methodology is the Empowerment Scale (Corrigan, Faber, Rashid & Leary, 1999; Rogers, Chamberlin, Ellison & Crean, 1997; Wowra & McCarter, 1999).

A recent development has been the involvement of people with psychiatric disabilities in identifying a core outcome data set that can be used to monitor, evaluate, and research interventions from the perspective of people with psychiatric disabilities. Campbell (1998) has summarized some of the outcome domains identified by various workgroups and taskforces. These outcome indicators include:

* Self-help outcomes—the effects of self-help approaches in terms of benefits and costs;

- Well-being and personhood outcomes—quality of life, freedom, safety, privacy and the like;

- Empowerment outcomes—self-esteem and self-efficacy;

- Recovery outcomes—maximization of one's life and the minimization of one's illness;

- Iatrogenic effects and negative outcomes—undesired consequences or side effects of services; and

- Satisfaction and dissatisfaction outcomes—the view of people with psychiatric disabilities about services and their results.

Campbell (1998) also identifies other outcomes for consideration, such as the context in which people live (poverty, discrimination); diversity of recipients; opportunities for choice; and the relationship between the helper and person served. It is obvious that the perspective of people with psychiatric disabilities with respect to outcome indicators, while congruent with the values and principles of psychiatric rehabilitation, brings to the outcome table a different emphasis and view of what's important. The field of psychiatric rehabilitation needs to be directed in its identification of outcome domains by the perspective of the people the field is trying to help.

Managed Care Influence

Outcome measurement is required now in most behavioral managed care contracts. Psychiatric rehabilitation services, like all other services for people with psychiatric disabilities, must be able to demonstrate its impact on outcome. The entrance of managed care approaches into the public behavioral health arena has stimulated outcome researchers to identify what are called "evidence-based" services. In essence, evidence-based services are those services which a number of experimentally designed studies have shown to be effective in achieving certain outcomes. Hughes (1999) has described what this concept means for the field of psychiatric rehabilitation. In psychiatric rehabilitation, like all fields of practice, most early evidence is descriptive or anecdotal. It was this type of "evidence" which nurtured the early growth of the field of psychiatric rehabilitation. Next came a number of program evaluation studies, survey research, correlational research, and quasi-experimental studies, which reported positive outcomes for psychiatric rehabilitation. Until the 1990s there was almost no experimental research supporting the field of psychiatric rehabilitation (Anthony, 1998), yet the field continued to grow because of people's demand for these services.

In order to be considered an "evidence-based" service, a number of studies using an experimental design must be conducted, which essentially means:

- A random assignment to control and experimental groups;

- Assessment of outcomes in which the assessor does not know group membership;

- A clear description and delivery of the intervention;

- Clear criteria for inclusion and exclusion of participants; and

- Sufficient number of participants to justify the statistical analyses.

Interestingly, only 20% of all medical treatments meet the level of "evidence-based" treatments, when the requirement is a body of studies using rigorous experimental designs (Hughes, 1999). At present, psychiatric rehabilitation has shown its value, but not through a body of well controlled experimental studies. Until that time, decisions to fund psychiatric rehabilitation services must be based on the research that currently exists, as well as other factors, such as: "Does the intervention address the needs of the people targeted for the service? Do we value the goals and potential outcomes of the service? Is there evidence of any negative effects of the service? What is the strength of the scientific evidence? What is the financial impact of these services over the short term and over the long term?" (Hughes, 1999, p. 12). And lastly, is there more compelling scientific evidence to achieve these valued outcomes in a different way? The empirical answer to the last question is a resounding no.

Managed care approaches also have stimulated renewed interest in the cost of an intervention. Unfortunately, outcome studies using measures of cost are most unusual (Bond, Clark & Drake, 1995; Clark & Bond, 1995). The vocational outcome area has been the outcome most often investigated with respect to cost (Rogers, Sciarappa, MacDonald-Wilson & Danley, 1995).

Rogers (1997) has reviewed cost-benefit studies of vocational interventions, i.e., whether the benefits that accrue to the person served, taxpayers, and/or society exceed the expenditures. Unlike cost effectiveness studies, cost-benefit studies examine the perspective from which one is determining both costs and benefits. As an example, what one might consider a benefit to a program participant (e.g., the receipt of entitlements), is a cost to society. Rogers (1997) also outlines a series of basic steps involved in implementing cost-benefit studies, which highlights the difficulties in drawing conclusions from studies to date. However, Rogers (1997) does conclude that, with respect to cost, supported employment programs do increase participant wages and decrease the use of alternative services.

With the increased interest in outcome measures during the 1990s, a variety of outcome measurement systems have been proposed by organizations, such as advocacy groups, accreditation organizations, trade associations, and the government. In behavioral health care, a number of organizations, such as the Center for Mental Health Services, the National Alliance for the Mentally Ill, and the American Behavioral Healthcare Association are developing "report cards" to assess the impact of services from the perspective of a number of different stakeholders. The combined suggestions for possible outcome indicators have been multitudinous.

One intriguing effort is that of the American College of Mental Health Administration (ACMHA). Their intent is to identify a few essential indicators that would be included in all measurement systems. ACMHA has convened several meetings of representatives from the major accrediting organizations in behavioral health care, including CARF (the Rehabilitation Accreditation Commission), the Council on Accreditation, the Joint Commission on the Accreditation of Healthcare Organizations, the National Committee on Quality Assurance, and the Council. These accrediting organizations, often in competition with one another, are in a unique position to influence the development and use of such measures (Mental Health Weekly, 1998).

The accrediting bodies, under ACMHA's sponsorship, have agreed on three domains of measurement: 1) outcomes (services are effective), 2) process (services are appropriate to the needs of the person served), and 3) access (persons served can receive the services they need).

Each of these domains has several indicators, such as work and school (persons served are productively involved in work and/or school), experience of care (persons served perceive and experience service providers as responsive and sensitive), and services are convenient (persons served perceive and experience services as convenient, i. e., available services are well located, offered at convenient hours, etc.) (American College of Mental Health Administration, 1997). While agreement on the factors to be included in the taxonomy of indicators has been possible, the most difficult task of identifying specific measuring instruments and benchmarks for each indictor awaits consensus.

There are many possible benefits in having a core set of indicators and measures that should be included in all measurement systems (Eddy, 1998). A core set of indicators will encourage the feasibility of the measurement process itself, empower decision making about services, and lead to more informed choice. From a psychiatric rehabilitation perspective, it will focus providers on certain meaningful targets, and permit comparisons across programs for the purpose of program improvement.

Summary

Large-scale experimental studies of psychiatric rehabilitation are not only needed, they also are increasingly feasible. Issues of measurement and design are being addressed. Currently, a number of psychiatric rehabilitation interventions can be described at a level of detail that permits their implementation to be observed and monitored reliably. Thus, the researchers can collect data as to the degree to which the intervention under investigation was implemented. The intervention is now sufficiently described so that, if the results are promising, it can be replicated in service settings and clinical research programs.

Well designed psychiatric rehabilitation outcome studies also are critical because of the recent influence of people with psychiatric disabilities and behavioral managed care organizations. People with psychiatric disabilities, payers, and administrators want to know the outcomes of psychiatric rehabilitation and its cost. Unfortunately, outcome studies using measures of cost are most unusual. The vocational outcome area has been the outcome most often investigated with respect to cost.

It is important to raise a caution, however, should the psychiatric rehabilitation field's pursuit of research-based services become all encompassing. At the beginning of the 1990s Anthony (1991) raised the question as to whether or not everything in the psychiatric rehabilitation field was researchable. Currently, what is not researchable is whether or not rehabilitation services should be offered to people with psychiatric disabilities. Either we as a people value and believe in the opportunity for rehabilitation for people with psychiatric disabilities, or we do not.

That is a question of humanism and not empiricism, and does not contradict the argument that research in psychiatric rehabilitation is extremely important. Once we have committed ourselves to the value of psychiatric rehabilitation, the critical research questions become how can we do rehabilitation most effectively and efficiently, and not whether or not we should provide the opportunity for rehabilitation. The opportunity for people with psychiatric disabilities to avail themselves of rehabilitation has been long in coming relative to the opportunities for rehabilitation for people with physical disabilities. The concept of psychiatric rehabilitation has arrived, and it is not because of research data. Like the framers of the Declaration of Independence, people believe that this basic belief in the opportunity for psychiatric rehabilitation is "self-evident."

In summary, the reviewed research on innovative rehabilitation programs has illustrated that experimental studies of replicable, measurable psychiatric rehabilitation interventions are not only possible but are in fact happening with increasing regularity. As would be expected, the psychiatric rehabilitation field is becoming more empirically based with each passing decade.

References

Agnetti, G., Barbato, A., & Young, J. (1993). A systems view of family interventions in residential psychosocial rehabilitation programs. *International Journal of Mental Health, 22*(3), 73–82.

American College of Mental Health Administration. (1997). *The Santa Fe Summit on Behavioral Health.* Pittsburgh, PA: Author.

Anthony, W. A. (1972). Societal rehabilitation: Changing society's attitudes toward the physically and mentally disabled. *Rehabilitation Psychology, 19,* 117–126.

Anthony, W. A. (1977). Psychological rehabilitation: A concept in need of a method. *American Psychologist, 32,* 658–662.

Anthony, W. A. (1979). *The principles of psychiatric rehabilitation.* Baltimore, MD: University Park Press.

Anthony, W. A. (1980). Rehabilitating the person with a psychiatric disability: The state of the art [Special Issue]. *Rehabilitation Counseling Bulletin, 24.*

Anthony, W. A. (1992). Psychiatric rehabilitation: Key issues and future policy. *Health Affairs, 11*(3), 164–171.

Anthony, W. A. (1998). Psychiatric rehabilitation technology: Operationalizing the "black box" of the psychiatric rehabilitation process. In P. W. Corrigan & F. Giffort (Eds.), Building teams for effective psychiatric rehabilitation (pp. 79–87, *New Directions for Mental Health Services, No. 79*). San Francisco: Jossey-Bass.

Anthony, W. A., Buell, G. J., Sharratt, S., & Althoff, M. E. (1972). Efficacy of psychiatric rehabilitation. *Psychological Bulletin, 78,* 447–456.

Anthony, W. A., Cohen, M. R., & Cohen, B. F. (1984). Psychiatric rehabilitation. In A. Talbott (Ed.), *The chronic mental patient: Five years later* (pp. 137–157). Orlando: Grune & Stratton.

Anthony, W. A., Cohen, M. R., & Farkas, M. D. (1987). Training and technical assistance in psychiatric rehabilitation. In A. T. Meyerson & T. Fine (Eds.), *Psychiatric disability: Clinical, legal, and administrative dimensions* (pp. 251–269). Washington, D. C.: American Psychiatric Press.

Anthony, W. A., Cohen, M. R., & Farkas, M. D. (1990). *Psychiatric rehabilitation.* Boston, MA: Boston University, Center for Psychiatric Rehabilitation.

Anthony, W. A., Cohen, M. R., & Pierce, R. M. (1980). *Instructors' guide to the psychiatric rehabilitation practice series.* Baltimore: University Park Press.

Anthony, W. A., Cohen, M. R., & Vitalo, R. L. (1978). The measurement of rehabilitation outcome. *Schizophrenia Bulletin, 4,* 365–383.

Anthony, W. A., & Farkas, M. D. (1982). A client outcome planning model for assessing psychiatric rehabilitation interventions. *Schizophrenia Bulletin, 8,* 13–38.

Anthony, W. A., Howell, J., & Danley, K. S. (1984). Vocational rehabilitation of the psychiatric disabled. In M. Mirabi (Ed.), *The chronically mentally ill: Research and services* (pp. 215–237). Jamaica, NY: Spectrum Publications.

Anthony, W. A., & Margules, A. (1974). Toward improving the efficacy of psychiatric rehabilitation: A skills training approach. *Rehabilitation Psychology, 21,* 101–105.

Anthony, W. A., & Nemec, P. B. (1984). Psychiatric rehabilitation. In A. S. Bellack (Ed.), *Schizophrenic treatment, management, and rehabilitation* (pp. 375–413). Orlando: Grune & Stratton.

Atkinson, J. M., Coia, D. A., Gilmour, W. H., & Harper, J. P. (1996). The impact of education groups for people with schizophrenia on social functioning and quality of life. *British Journal of Psychiatry, 168*(2), 199–204.

Aveni, C. A., & Upper, D. (1976). *Training psychiatric patients for community living.* Paper presented at the meeting of the Midwestern Association of Behavior Analysis, Chicago.

Bachrach, L. L. (1976a). *Deinstitutionalization: An analytical review and sociological perspective.* Rockville, MD: National Institute of Mental Health.

Bachrach, L. L. (1976b). A note on some recent studies of released mental hospital patients in the community. *American Journal of Psychiatry, 133*(1), 73–75.

Barton, R. (1999). Psychosocial rehabilitation services in community support systems: A review of outcomes and policy recommendations. *Psychiatric Services, 50*(4), 525–534.

Beard, J. H., Malamud, T. J., & Rossman, E. (1978). Psychiatric rehabilitation and long-term rehospitalization rates: The findings of two research studies. *Schizophrenia Bulletin, 4*(4), 622–635.

Beard, J. H., Pitt, R. B., Fisher, S. H., & Goertzel, V. (1963). Evaluating the effectiveness of a psychiatric rehabilitation program. *American Journal of Orthopsychiatry, 33*(4), 701–712.

Beard, J. H., Propst, R. N., & Malamud, T. J. (1982). The Fountain House model of psychiatric rehabilitation. *Psychosocial Rehabilitation Journal, 5*(1), 47–53.

Becker, D. R., & Drake, R. E. (1993). *A working life: The individual placement and support (IPS) program.* Concord, NH: Dartmouth Psychiatric Research Center.

Becker, P., & Bayer, C. (1975). Preparing chronic patients for community placement: A four-stage treatment program. *Hospital and Community Psychiatry, 26*(7), 448–450.

Bell, M., & Lysaker, P. (1997). Clinical benefits of paid work activity in schizophrenia: 1-year follow-up. *Schizophrenia Bulletin, 23*(2), 317–328.

Benton, M. K., & Schroeder, H. E. (1990). Social skills training with schizophrenics: A meta-analytic evaluation. *Journal of Consulting and Clinical Psychology, 58*(6), 741–747.

Blankertz, L., & Cook, J. A. (1998). Choosing and using outcome measures. *Psychiatric Rehabilitation Journal, 22*(2), 167–174.

Blankertz, L., & Robinson, S. (1996). Adding a vocational focus to mental health rehabilitation. *Psychiatric Services, 47*(11), 1216–1222.

Bond, G. R. (1984). An economic analysis of psychosocial rehabilitation. *Hospital and Community Psychiatry, 35*(4), 356–362.

Bond, G. R., Clark, R. E., & Drake, R. E. (1995). Cost-effectiveness of rehabilitation. *Psychotherapy and Rehabilitation Research Bulletin, 4*, 26–31.

Bond, G. R., & Dincin, J. (1986). Accelerating entry into transitional employment in a psychosocial rehabilitation agency. *Rehabilitation Psychology, 31*(3), 143–155.

Bond, G. R., Drake, R. E., Becker, D. R., & Mueser, K. T. (1999). Effectiveness of psychiatric rehabilitation approaches for employment of people with severe mental illness. *Journal of Disability Policy Studies, 10*(1), 18–52.

Bond, G. R., & McDonel, E. C. (1991). Vocational rehabilitation outcomes for persons with psychiatric disabilities: An update. *Journal of Vocational Rehabilitation, 1*(3), 9–20.

Boothroyd, R., Skinner, E., Shern, D., & Steinwachs, D. (1998). Feasibility of consumer-based outcome monitoring: A report from the national outcomes reountable. In R. W. Manderscheid & M. J. Henderson (Eds.), *DHHS Pub. No. (SMA) 99-3285.* Washington, D. C.: Supt. of Docs., U. S. Govt. Print. Office.

Brekke, J. S., Ansel, M., Long, J., Slade, E., & Weinstein, M. (1999). Intensity and continuity of services and functional outcomes in the rehabilitation of persons with schizophrenia. *Psychiatric Services, 50*(2), 248–256.

Brekke, J. S., Ansel, M., Long, J., Slade, E., & Weinstein, M. (1999). Intensity and continuity of services and functional outcomes in the rehabilitation of persons with schizophrenia. *Psychiatric Services, 50*(2), 248–256.

Brown, M. A., Ridgway, P., Anthony, W. A., & Rogers, E. S. (1991). A comparison of supported housing for voluntary and involuntary clients. *Hospital and Community Psychiatry, 42*(11), 1150–1153.

Bryson, G., Bell, M., Greig, T., & Kaplan, E. (1999). The work behavior inventory: Prediction of future work success of people with schizophrenia. *Psychiatric Rehabilitation Journal, 23*(2), 113–117.

Campbell, J. (1998). Assesment of outcomes. In R. W. Manderscheid & M. J. Henderson (Eds.), *DHHS Pub. No. (SMA) 99-3285.* Washington, D. C.: Supt. of Docs., U. S. Govt. Print. Office.

Cannady, D. (1982). Chronics and cleaning ladies. *Psychosocial Rehabilitation Journal, 5*(1), 13–16.

Center for Psychiatric Rehabilitation. (1989a). Refocusing on locus. *Hospital and Community Psychiatry, 40,* 418.

Center for Psychiatric Rehabilitation. (1989b). *Research and training center final report (1984–1989).* Boston: Boston University.

Champney, T. F., & Dzurec, L. C. (1992). Involvement in productive activities and satisfaction with living situation among severely mentally disabled adults. *Hospital and Community Psychiatry, 43*(9), 899–903.

Chandler, D., Levin, S., & Barry, P. (1999). The menu approach to employment services: Philosophy and five-year outcomes. *Psychiatric Rehabilitation Journal, 23*(1), 24–33.

Chandler, D., Meisel, J., Hu, T. w., McGowen, M., & Madison, K. (1996). Client outcomes in a three-year controlled study of an integrated service agency model. *Psychiatric Services, 47*(12), 1337–1343.

Chandler, D., Spicer, G., Wagner, M., & Hargreaves, W. (1999). Cost-effectiveness of a capitated assertive community treatment program. *Psychiatric Rehabilitation Journal, 22*(4), 327–336.

Clark, R. E., & Bond, G. R. (1995). Costs and benefits of vocational programs for people with serious mental illness. In Moscarelli & Santorius (Eds.), *The economics of schizophrenia* (pp. 1–42). Sussex, England: John Wiley & Sons.

Cohen, M. R., Danley, K. S., & Nemec, P. B. (1985). *Psychiatric rehabilitation training technology: Direct skills teaching* (Trainer package). Boston: Boston University, Center for Psychiatric Rehabilitation.

Cohen, M. R., Farkas, M. D., & Cohen, B. F. (1986). *Psychiatric rehabilitation training technology: Functional assessment* (Trainer package). Boston: Boston University, Center for Psychiatric Rehabilitation.

Cohen, M. R., Farkas, M. D., Cohen, B. F., & Unger, K. V. (1991). *Psychiatric rehabilitation traning technology: Setting an overall rehabilitation goal* (Trainer package). Boston: Boston University, Center for Psychiaric Rehabilitation.

Cohen, M. R., Nemec, P. B., Farkas, M. D., & Forbess, R. (1988). *Psychiatric rehabilitation training technology: Case management* (Trainer package). Boston: Boston University, Center for Psychiatric Rehabilitation.

Cook, J. A., Pickett, S. A., Razzano, L., Fitzgibbon, G., Jonikas, J. A., & Cohler, J. J. (1996). Rehabilitation services for persons with schizophrenia. *Psychiatric Annals, 26*(2), 97–104.

Corrigan, P. W., Faber, D., Rashid, F., & Leary, M. (1999). The construct validity of empowerment among consumers of mental health services. *Schizophrenia Research, 38*(1), 77–84.

Cuffel, B. J., Fischer, E. P., Owen, R. R., Jr., & Smith, G. R., Jr. (1997). An instrument for measurement of outcomes of care for schizophrenia: Issues in development and implementation. *Evaluation and the Health Professions, 20*(1), 96–108.

Cummings, N. A. (1998). Spectacular accomplishments and disappointing mistakes: The first decade of managed behavioral care. *Behavioral Healthcare Tomorrow, 7*(4), 61–63.

Danley, K. S., & Anthony, W. A. (1987). The choose-get-keep model: Serving severely psychiatrically disabled people. *American Rehabilitation, 13*(4), 6–9, 27–29.

Dellario, D. J. (1985). The relationship between mental health, vocational rehabilitation interagency functioning, and outcome of psychiatrically disabled persons. *Rehabilitation Counseling Bulletin, 28*(3), 167–170.

Dellario, D. J., & Anthony, W. A. (1981). On the relative effectiveness of institutional and alternative placement for the psychiatrically disabled. *Journal of Social Issues, 37*(3), 21–33.

Dennis, D. L., Buckner, J. C., Lipton, F. R., & Levine, I. S. (1991). A decade of research and services for homeless mentally ill persons: Where do we stand? *American Psychologist, 46*(11), 1129–1138.

Dickerson, F. B. (1997). Assessing clinical outcomes: The community functioning of persons with serious mental illness. *Psychiatric Services, 48*(7), 897–902.

Dilk, M. N., & Bond, G. R. (1996). Meta-analytic evaluation of skills training research for individuals with severe mental illness. *Journal of Consulting and Clinical Psychology, 64*(6), 1337–1346.

Dincin, J., & Witheridge, T. F. (1982). Psychiatric rehabilitation as a deterrent to recidivism. *Hospital and Community Psychiatry, 33*(8), 645–650.

Dion, G. L., Tohen, M., Anthony, W. A., & Waternaux, C. S. (1988). Symptoms and functioning of patients with bipolar disorder six months after hospitalization. *Hospital and Community Psychiatry, 39*, 652–657.

Docherty, J. P., & Streeter, M. J. (1996). Measuring outcomes. In L. I. Sederer & B. Dickey (Eds.), *Outcome assessment in clinical practice* (pp. 8–18). Baltimore, MD: Williams & Wilkins.

Drake, R. E., Becker, D. R., Biesanz, J. C., & Wyzik, P. F. (1996). Day treatment versus supported employment for persons with severe mental illness: A replication study. *Psychiatric Services, 47*(10), 1125–1127.

Drake, R. E., Becker, D. R., Clark, R. E., & Mueser, K. T. (1999). Research on the individual placement and support model of supported employment. *Psychiatric Quarterly, 70*, 289–301.

Drake, R. E., McHugo, G., Becker, D. R., Anthony, W. A., & Clark, R. E. (1996). The New Hampshire study of supported employment for people with severe mental illness. *Journal of Consulting and Clinical Psychology, 64*(2), 391–399.

Eddy, D. M. (1998). Performance measurement: Problems and solutions. *Health Affairs, 17*(4), 7–25.

El Islam, M. F. (1982). Rehabilitation of schizophrenics by the extended family. *Acta Psychiatrica Scandinavica, 65*(2), 112–119.

Ellison, M. L., Anthony, W. A., Sheets, J., Dodds, W., Yamin, Z., & Barker, W. (2001). *The integration of psychiatric rehabilitation services into managed behavioral health care structures: A state example.* Submitted for publication.

Ellison, M. L., Danley, K. S., Bromberg, C., & Palmer-Erbs, V. K. (1999). Longitudinal outcome of young adults who participated in a psychiatric vocational rehabilitation program. *Psychiatric Rehabilitation Journal, 22*(4), 337–341.

Farkas, M. (1999). *"Where have rehabilitation values and research led us?" An update on the field.* Lecture, Nova University, Ft. Lauderdale, FL, November 6–8, 1999.

Farkas, M. D., Cohen, M. R., & Nemec, P. B. (1988). Psychiatric rehabilitation programs: Putting concepts into practice? *Community Mental Health Journal, 24*(1), 7–21.

Farkas, M.D., O'Brien, W.F., Cohen, M.R., & Anthony, W.A. (1994). Assessment and planning in psychiatric rehabilitation. In J.R. Bedell (Ed.), *Psychological assessment and treatment of persons with severe mental disorders* (pp. 3–30). Washington, DC: Taylor & Francis.

Farkas, M. D., O' Brien, W. F., & Nemec, P. B. (1988). A graduate level curriculum in psychiatric rehabilitation: Filling a need. *Psychosocial Rehabilitation Journal, 12*(2), 53–66.

Farkas, M. D., Rogers, E. S., & Thurer, S. (1987). Rehabilitation outcome of long-term hospital patients left behind by deinstitutionalization. *Hospital and Community Psychiatry, 38,* 864–870.

Farkas, M. D., & Vallee, C. (1996). De la réapprobation au pouvoir dagir: La dimension discrete d'une reelle réadaption. *Santé Mentale au Quebec, XXI*(2), 21–32.

Farr, R. K. (1984). The Los Angeles Skid Row Mental Health Project. *Psychosocial Rehabilitation Journal, 8*(2), 64–76.

Fekete, D. M., Bond, G. R., McDonel, E. C., Salyers, M., Chen, A., & Miller, L. (1998). Rural assertive community treatment: A field experiment. *Psychiatric Rehabilitation Journal, 21*(4), 371–379.

Felix, R. H. (1967). *Mental illness: Progress and prospect.* New York: Columbia University Press.

Felton, C. J., Stastny, P., Shern, D. L., Blanch, A., & et al. (1995). Consumers as peer specialists on intensive case management teams: Impact on client outcomes. *Psychiatric Services, 46*(10), 1037–1044.

Fenton, W. S., Blyler, C. R., & Heinssen, R. K. (1997). Determinants of medication compliance in schizophrenia: Empirical and clinical findings. *Schizophrenia Bulletin, 23*(4), 637–651.

Fergus, E. O. (1980). Maintaining and advancing the lodge effort. In G. W. Fairweather (Ed.), The Fairweather Lodge: A twenty-five year retrospective *(New Directions for Mental Health service, No. 7,* pp. 46–56). San Francisco: Jossey-Bass.

Field, G., Allness, D., & Knoedler, W. (1980). Application of the Training in Community Living program to rural areas. *Journal of Community Psychology, 8*(1), 9–15.

Field, G., & Yegge, L. (1982). A client outcome study of a community support demonstration project. *Psychosocial Rehabilitation Journal, 6*(2), 15–22.

Fishbein, S. (1991). *Psychosocial academic linkage.* National Institute of Mental Health, Human Resource Development Program grant application.

Fishbein, S. M. (1988). Partial care as a vehicle for rehabilitation of individuals with severe psychiatric disability. *Rehabilitation Psychology, 33*(1), 57–64.

Fishbein, S. M., & Cassidy, K. (1989). A system perspective on psychiatric rehabilitation: New Jersey. In M. D. Farkas & W. A. Anthony (Eds.), *Psychiatric rehabilitation programs: Putting theory into practice* (pp. 179–188). Baltimore: Johns Hopkins University Press.

Fisher, D., & Ahern, L. (1999). People can recover from mental illness. *National Empowerment Center Newsletter*, 8–9.

Fisher, D. B. (1994). Health care reform based on an empowerment model of recovery by people with psychiatric disabilities. *Hospital and Community Psychiatry, 45*(9), 913–915.

Fisher, D. B. (1998). Comments on the article, "The right to refuse medication: Navigating the ambiguity." *Psychiatric Rehabilitation Journal, 21*(3), 250–251.

Fisher, G., Landis, D., & Clark, K. (1988). Case management service provision and client change. *Community Mental Health Journal, 24*(2), 134–142.

Fiske, D. W. (1983). The meta-analytic revolution in outcome research. *Journal of Consulting and Clinical Psychology, 51*(1), 65–75.

Fitz, D., & Evenson, R. (1999). Recommending client residence: A comparison of the St. Louis Inventory of community living skills and global assessment. *Psychiatric Rehabilitation Journal, 23*(2), 107–112.

Forbess, R., & Kennard, W. (1997). *Components, functions, and process of a Role Recovery Operating System.* Marlborough, MA: BCPR.

Foreyt, J. P., & Felton, G. S. (1970). Change in behavior of hospitalized psychiatric patients in a milieu therapy setting. *Psychotherapy: Theory, Research and Practice, 7*(3), 139–141.

Forsyth, R. P., & Fairweather, G. W. (1961). Psychotherapeutic and other hospital treatment criteria: The dilemma. *Journal of Abnormal and Social Psychology, 62*, 598–604.

Fortune, J. R., & Eldredge, G. M. (1982). Predictive validation of the McCarron-Dial Evaluation System for psychiatrically disabled sheltered workshop workers. *Vocational Evaluation and Work Adjustment Bulletin, 15*(4), 136–141.

Fountain House (1976). *Rehabilitation of the mental patient in the community.* Grant #5T24MH14471. Rockville, MD: National Institue of Mental Health.

Fountain House. (1985). *Evaluation of clubhouse model community-based psychiatric rehabilitation: Final report for the National Institute of Handicapped Research* (Contract No. 300-84-0124). Washington, DC: National Institute of Handicapped Research.

Foy, D. W. (1984). Chronic alcoholism: Broad-spectrum clinical programming. In M. Mirabi (Ed.), *The chronically mentally ill: Research and services* (pp. 273–280). Jamaica, NY: Spectrum Publications.

Frank, J. D. (1981). Reply to Telch. *Journal of Consulting and Clinical Psychology, 49*(3), 476–477.

Frankie, P. A., Levine, P., Mowbray, C. T., Shriner, W., & et al. (1996). Supported education for persons with psychiatric disabilities: Implementation in an urban setting. *Journal of Mental Health Administration, 23*(4), 406–417.

Franklin, J. L., Solovitz, B., Mason, M., Clemons, J. R., & Miller, G. E. (1987). An evaluation of case management. *American Journal of Public Health, 77*, 674–678.

Franz, M., Lis, S., Plueddemann, K., & Gallhofer, B. (1997). Conventional versus atypical neuroleptics: Subjective quality of life in schizophrenic patients. *British Journal of Psychiatry, 170*, 422–425.

Fraser, M. W., Fraser, M. E., & Delewski, C. H. (1985). The community treatment of the chronically mentally ill: An exploratory social network analysis. *Psychosocial Rehabilitation Journal, 9*(2), 35–41.

Freeman, H. E., & Simmons, O. G. (1963). *The mental patient comes home.* NY, John Wiley. (1963).

Frese, F. (1997). The mental health service consumer's perspective on mandatory treatment. *New Directions for Mental Health Services, 75,* 17–26.

Frey, W. D. (1984). Functional assessment in the 80s: A conceptual enigma, a technical challenge. In A. S. Halpern & M. J. Fuhrer (Eds.), *Functional assessment in rehabilitation* (pp. 11–43). Baltimore: Paul Brookes.

Friday, J. C. (1987). *What's available in psychosocial rehabilitation training?* Atlanta, GA: Southern Regional Education Board.

Goering, P. N., Farkas, M. D., Wasylenki, D. A., Lancee, W. J., & Ballantyne, R. (1988). Improved functioning for case management clients. *Psychosocial Rehabilitation Journal, 12*(1), 3–17.

Goering, P. N., Wasylenki, D. A., Farkas, M. D., Lancee, W. J., & Ballantyne, R. (1988). What difference does case management make? *Hospital and Community Psychiatry, 39,* 272–276.

Goering, P. N., Wasylenki, D. A., Lancee, W. J., & Freeman, S. J. (1984). From hospital to community: Six-month and two-year outcomes for 505 patients. *Journal of Nervous and Mental Disease, 172,* 667–673.

Goldberg, S. C. (1980). Drug and psychosocial therapy in schizophrenia: Current status and research needs. *Schizophrenia Bulletin, 6*(1), 117–121.

Goldman, H. H., Gattozzi, A. A., & Taube, C. A. (1981). Defining and counting the chronically mentally ill. *Hospital and Community Psychiatry, 32,* 21–27.

Greenley, J. R., Greenberg, J. S., & Brown, R. (1997). Measuring quality of life: A new and practical survey instrument. *Social Work, 42*(3), 244–254.

Griffiths, R. (1974). Rehabilitation of chronic psychotic patients. *Psychological Medicine, 4,* 316–325.

Griffiths, R. D. (1973). A standardized assessment of the work behaviour of psychiatric patients. *British Journal of Psychiatry, 123*(575), 403–408.

Hafemeister, T. L., & Banks, S. M. (1996). Methodological advances in the use of recidivism rates to assess mental health treatment programs. *Journal of Mental Health Administration, 23*(2), 190–206.

Hart, R. V. (1997). *Final report for the Psychiatric Rehabilitation Task Force for Systems Reform.* Montgomery, AL: Alabama Department of Mental Health and Mental Retardation.

Hoffman, D. A. (1980). *The differential effects of self-monitoring, self-reinforcement and performance standards on the production output, job satisfaction and attendance of vocational rehabilitation clients.* Catholic U of America.

Holley, H. L., Hodges, P., & Jeffers, B. (1998). Moving psychiatric patients from hospital to community: Views of patients, providers, and families. *Psychiatric Services, 49*(4), 513–517.

Holzner, B., Kemmler, G., & Meise, U. (1998). The impact of work-related rehabilitation on the quality of life of patients with schizophrenia. *Social Psychiatry and Psychiatric Epidemiology, 33*(12), 624–631.

Hughes, R. (1999). The meaning of "evidence based" services in PSR. *PSR Connection Newsletter, 2*(1), 10–12.

Jacobs, H. E., & et al. (1984). A skills-oriented model for facilitating employment among psychiatrically disabled persons. *Rehabilitation Counseling Bulletin, 28*(2), 87–96.

Jacobs, M., & Trick, O. (1974). Successful psychiatric rehabilitation using an inpatient teaching laboratory: A one-year follow-up study. *American Journal of Psychiatry, 131,* 145–148.

Jensen, K., Spangaard, P., Juel-Neilsen, N., & Voag, V. H. (1978). Experimental psychiatric rehabilitation unity. *International Journal of Social Psychiatry, 24,* 53–57.

Jerrell, J. M. (1999). Skill, symptom and satisfaction changes in three service models for people with psychiatric disability. *Psychiatric Rehabilitation Journal, 22*(4), 342–348.

Katz Garris, L., McCue, M., Garris, R. P., & Herring, J. (1983). Psychiatric rehabilitation: An outcome study. *Rehabilitation Counseling Bulletin, 26*(5), 329–335.

Kaye, H. S. (1998). Is the status of people with disabilities improving? *Disability Statistics Abstract, 21,* 1–4.

Keith, S. J., & Matthews, S. M. (1984). Research overview. In J. A. Talbott (Ed.), *The chronic mental patient: Five years later* (pp. 7–13). Orlando, FL: Grune & Stratton.

Kiesler, C. A. (1982). Mental hospitals and alternative care: Noninstitutionalization as potential public policy for mental patients. *American Psychologist, 37*(4), 349–360.

Kopelowicz, A., Liberman, R. P., Mintz, J., & Zarate, R. (1997). Comparison of efficacy of social skills training for deficit and nondeficit negative symptoms in schizophrenia. *American Journal of Psychiatry, 154*(3), 424–425.

Lamberti, J. S., Melburg, V., & Madi, N. (1998). Intensive psychiatric rehabilitation treatment (IPRT): An overview of a new program. *Psychiatric Quarterly, 69*(3), 211–234.

Larsen, J. K. (1987). Community mental health services in transition. *Community Mental Health Journal, 23*(4), 250–259.

Liberman, R. P., Mueser, K. T., & Wallace, C. J. (1986). Social skills training for schizophrenic individuals at risk for relapse. *American Journal of Psychiatry, 143*(4), 523–526.

Liberman, R. P., Wallace, C. J., Blackwell, G., Kopelowicz, A., Vaccaro, J. V., & Mintz, J. (1998). Skills training versus psychosocial occupational therapy for persons with persistent schizophrenia. *American Journal of Psychiatry, 155*(8), 1087–1091.

Lieberman, J. A., Sheitman, B., Chakos, M., Robinson, D., Schooler, N., & Keith, S. (1998). The development of treatment resistance in patients with schizophrenia: A clinical and pathophysiologic perspective. *Journal of Clinical Psychopharmacology, 18*(2, Suppl 1), 20s–24s.

Linn, M. W., & Caffey, Klette, Hogart, & Lamb. (1979). Day treatment and psy-chotropic drugs in the aftercare of schizophrenic patients: A veterans admin-istration cooperative study. *Archives of General Psychiatry, 36*(10), 1055–1066.

Lyons, J. S., O' Mahoney, M. T., Miller, S. I., Neme, J., & et al. (1997). Predicting readmission to the psychiatric hospital in a managed care environment: Implications for quality indicators. *American Journal of Psychiatry, 154*(3), 337–340.

Macias, C., Kinney, R., & Rodican, C. (1995). Transitional employment: An evalua-tive desciption of Fountain House practice. *Journal of Vocational Rehabilitation, 5*(2), 151–157.

Marder, S. R., Wirshing, W. C., Mintz, J., & McKenzie, J. (1996). Two-year out-come of social skills training and group psychotherapy for outpatients with schizophrenia. *American Journal of Psychiatry, 153*(12), 1585–1592.

Matthews, W. C. (1979). Effects of a work activity program on the self-concept of chronic schizophrenics. *Dissertations Abstracts International, 41,* 358B. (University Microfilms No. 8816281, 98).

Mental Health Policy Resource Center. (1988). A typology for mental health case management for persons with severe mental illness. In *Report on the state-of-the-art of case management programs.* Washington, DC: Author.

Meyerson, A. T., & Herman, G. S. (1983). What's new in aftercare? A review of recent literature. *Hospital and Community Psychiatry, 34*(4), 333–342.

Minsky, S., Reisser, G. G., & Duffy, M. (1995). The eye of the beholder: Housing preferences of inpatients and their treatment teams. *Psychiatric Services, 46*(2), 173–176.

Mosher, L. R., & Keith, S. J. (1979). Research on the psychosocial treatment of schizophrenia: A summary report. *American Journal of Psychiatry, 136*(5), 623–631.

Mosher, L. R., & Menn, A. Z. (1978). Community residential treatment for schizo-phrenia: Two-year follow-up. *Hospital and Community Psychiatry, 29*(11), 715–723.

Mowbray, C., Brown, K. S., Sullivan Soydan, A., & Furlong-Norman, K. (In press). *Supported education and psychiatric rehabilitation: Models and methods.* Columbia, MD: International Association of Psychosocial Rehabilitation Services.

Mowbray, C. & Megivern, D. (1992). Higher education and rehabilitation for peo-ple with psychiatric disabilities. *Journal of Rehabilitation, 65*(4), 31–38.

Mueser, K. T., Drake, R. E., & Bond, G. R. (1997). Recent advances in psychiatric rehabilitation for patients with severe mental illness. *Harvard Review of Psychiatry, 5*(3), 123–137.

Mulkern, V. M., & Manderscheid, R. W. (1989). Characteristics of community sup-port program clients in 1980 and 1984. *Hospital and Community Psychiatry, 40*(2), 165–172.

Nagaswami, V. (1995). Psychosocial rehabilitation: The other side of the mountain. *International Journal of Mental Health, 24*(1), 70–81.

National Institute of Handicapped Research. (1980). A skills training approach in psychiatric rehabilitation. *Rehabilitation Research Brief, 4*(1). Washington, DC.

Nelson, G., Ochocka, J., Griffin, K., & Lord, J. (1998). "Nothing about me, without me": Participatory action research with self-help/mutual aid organizations for psychiatric consumer/survivors. *American Journal of Community Psychology, 26*(6), 881–912.

New York State Office of Mental Health. (1998). Jobs: People should not face "40 years of unemployment." *OMH Quarterly, 4*(1), 3.

North, C. S., Pollio, D. E., Sachar, B., Hong, B., Isenberg, K., & Bufe, G. (1998). The family as caregiver: A group psychoeducation model for schizophrenia. *American Journal of Orthopsychiatry, 68*(1), 39–46.

OMH Quarterly. (June 1998). People should not face 40 years of unemployment., *4*(1).

Paul, G. L. (1984). Residential treatment programs and aftercare for the chronically institutionalized. In M. Mirabi (Ed.), *The chronically mentally ill: Research and services* (pp. 239–269). Jamaica, NY: Spectrum Publications.

Paul, G. L., & Lentz, R. J. (1977). *Psychosocial treatment of chronic mental patients: Milieu versus social-learning programs.* Cambridge, MA: Harvard University Press.

Paul, G. L., Stuve, P., & Cross, J. V. (1997). Real-world inpatient programs: Shedding some light—A critique. *Applied and Preventive Psychology, 6*(4), 193–204.

Pearson, V., & Phillips. M. R. (1994). The social context of psychiatric rehabilitation in China. *British Journal of Psychiatry, 165 (Suppl 24),* 11–18.

Penn, D. L., & Mueser, K. T. (1996). Research update on the psychosocial treatment of schizophrenia. *American Journal of Psychiatry, 153*(5), 607–617.

Power, C. (1979). The time-sample behavior checklist: Observational assessment of patient functioning. *Journal of Behavioral Assessment, 1*(3), 199–210.

Power, P. W., & Dell Orto, A. E. (Eds.). (1980). *The role of the family in the rehabilitation of the physically disabled.* Austin, TX: PRO-ED.

Redfield, J. (1979). Clinical frequencies recording systems: Standardizing staff observations by event recording. *Journal of Behavioral Assessment, 1*(3), 199–210.

Ridgway, P. (1988). *The voice of consumers in mental health systems: A call for change.* Unpublished manuscript, Boston University, Center for Psychiatric Rehabilitation, Boston.

Rogers, E. S. (1997). Cost-benefit studies in vocational services. *Psychiatric Rehabilitation Journal, 20*(3), 35–32.

Rogers, E. S., Anthony, W. A., & Danley, K. S. (1989). The impact of interagency collaboration on system and client outcome. *Rehabilitation Counseling Bulletin, 33*(2), 100–109.

Rogers, E. S., Chamberlin, J., Ellison, M. L., & Crean, T. (1997). A consumer-constructed scale to measure empowerment among users of mental health services. *Psychiatric Services, 48*(8), 1042–1047.

Rogers, E. S., Danley, K. S., Anthony, W. A., Martin, R., & Walsh, D. (1994). The residential needs and prefernces of persons with serious mental illness: A comparison of consumers and family members. *Journal of Mental Health Administration, 21*(1), 42–51.

Rogers, E. S., & Palmer-Erbs, V. K. (1994). Participatory action research: Implications for research and evaluation in psychiatric rehabilitation. *Psychosocial Rehabilitation Journal, 18*(2), 3–12.

Rogers, E. S., Sciarappa, K., MacDonald-Wilson, K., & Danley, K. (1995). A benefit cost analysis of a supported employment model for persons with psychiatric disabilities. *Evaluation and Program Planning, 18*(2), 105–115.

Russinova, Z., Ellison, M., & Foster, R. (1999). *Survey of professionals and managers with psychiatric disabilities.* Presentation at IAPSRS 24th annual conference. Minneapolis, MN, May 10–14.

Ryan, E. R., & Bell, M. D. (1985). *Rehabilitation of chronic psychiatric patients: A randomized clinical study.* Paper presented at the meeting of the American Psychiatric Association, Los Angeles.

SAMHSA. (1993). *SAMHSA strategic plan.* Washington, DC: DHHS.

Santos, A. B., Henggeler, S. W., Burns, B. J., & Arana, G. W. (1995). Research on field-based services: Models for reform in the delivery of mental health care to populations with complex clinical problems. *American Journal of Psychiatry, 152*(8), 1111–1123.

Saraceno, B. (1995). *La fine dell intrattenimento.* Milano: Etas Libri.

Shaffer, I. A. (1997). Treatment outcomes: Economic and ethical considerations. *Psychiatric Annals, 27*(2), 104–107.

Shern, D. L., Tsemberis, S., Anthony, W. A., Lovell, A.M., Richmond, L., Felton, V. J., Winarski, J. & Cohen, M. (2000). Serving street dwelling individuals with psychiatric disabilities: Outcomes of a psychiatric rehabilitation clinical trial. *American Journal of Public Health, 90,* 1873–1878.

Shern, D. L., Tsemberis, S. Winarski, J., Cope, N., Cohen, M. R., & Anthony,W.A. (1997). The effectiveness of psychiatric rehabilitation for persons who are street dwelling with serious disability related to mental illness. In W.R. Breakey and J.W. Thompson (Eds), *Mentally ill and homeless: Special programs for special needs.* Amsterdam, Netherlands: Harwood Academic.

Slaton, G., & Westphal. (1999). The Slaton-Westphal Functional Assessment Inventory for Adults with Psychiatric Disability: Development of an instrument to measure functional status and psychiatric rehabilitation outcome. *Psychiatric Rehabilitation Journal, 23*(2).

Smith, G. R., Manderscheid, R. W., Flynn, L. M., & Steinwachs, D. M. (1997). Principles for assessment of patient outcomes in mental health care. *Psychiatric Services, 48*(8), 1033–1036.

Spaniol, L. J., Zipple, A. M., & Fitzgerald, S. (1984). How professionald can share power with families: Practical approaches to working with famililies of the mentally ill. *Psychosocial Rehabilitation Journal, 8*(2), 77–84.

Srebnik, D., Hendryx, M., Stevenson, J., Caverly, S., & et al. (1997). Development of outcome indicators for monitoring the quality of public mental health care. *Psychiatric Services, 48*(7), 903–909.

Stein, L. I., Barry, K. L., Van Dien, G., Hollingsworth, E. J., & Sweeney, J. K. (1999). Work and social support: A comparison of consumers who have achieved stability in ACT and clubhouse programs. *Community Mental Health Journal, 35*(2), 193–204.

Stein, L. I., & Test, M. A. (1980). Alternative to mental hospital treatment: I. Conceptual model, treatment program, and clinical evaluation. *Archives of General Psychiatry, 37*(4), 392–397.

Stein, L. I., & Test, M. A. (Eds.). (1978). *Alternatives to mental hospital treatment.* New York: Plenum Press.

Tessler, R. C. (1987). Continuity of care and client outcome. *Psychosocial Rehabilitation Journal, 1*(1), 39–53.

Tessler, R. C., & Manderscheid, R. W. (1982). *The chronically mentally ill: Assessing community support programs.* Cambridge, MA: Ballinger Press.

Test, M. A. & Stein, L. I. (1978). Community treatment of the chronic patient: Research overview. *Schizophrenia Bulletin, 4,* 350–364.

Turkat, D., & Buzzell, V. M. (1983). Recidivism and employment rates among psychosocial rehabilitation clients. *Hospital and Community Psychiatry, 34*(8), 741–742.

Unger, K. V., & Anthony, W. A. (1984). Are families satisfied with services to young adult chronic patients? A recent survey and a proposed alternative. In B. Pepper & H. Ryglewicz (Eds.), Advances in treating the young adult chronic patient *(New Directions for Mental Health Services, No. 21,* pp. 91–97). San Francisco: Jossey-Bass.

Unger, K. V., Danley, K. S., Kohn, L., & Hutchinson, D. (1987). Rehabilitation through education: A university-based continuing education program for young adults with psychiatric disabilities on a university campus. *Psychosocial Rehabilitation Journal, 10*(3), 35–49.

United States Department of Health and Human Services. (1980). *Toward a national plan for the chronically mentally ill.* Report to the Secretary by the Department of Health and Human Services Steering Committee on the Chronically Mentally Ill. Washington, DC: U. S. Government Printing Office.

van Nieuwenhuizen, C., Schene, A. H., Boevink, W. A., & Wolf, J. R. L. M. (1997). Measuring the quality of life of clients with severe mental illness: A review of instruments. *Psychiatric Rehabilitation Journal, 20*(4), 33–41.

Vitalo, R. L. (1979). An application in an aftercare setting. In W. A. Anthony (Ed.), *The principles of psychiatric rehabilitation* (pp. 193–202). Baltimore: University Park Press.

Wallace, C. J., & et al. (1980). A review and critique of social skills training with schizophrenic patients. *Schizophrenia Bulletin, 6*(1), 42–63.

Wasylenki, D., & et al. (1985). Psychiatric aftercare in a metropolitan setting. *Canadian Journal of Psychiatry, 30*(5), 329–336.

Watts, F. N. (1978). A study of work behaviour in a psychiatric rehabilitation unit. *British Journal of Social and Clinical Psychology, 17*(1), 85–92.

Wolkon, G. H., Karmen, M., & Tanaka, H. T. (1971). Evaluation of a social rehabilitation program for recently released psychiatric patients. *Community Mental Health Journal, 7*(4), 312–322.

Wowra, S. A., & McCarter, R. (1999). Validation of the Empowerment Scale with an outpatient mental health population. *Psychiatric Services, 50*(7), 959–961.

Serving Street-Dwelling Individuals with Psychiatric Disabilities: Outcomes of a Psychiatric Rehabilitation Clinical Trial

David L. Shern, Sam Tsemberis, William Anthony, Anne M. Lovell,
Linda Richmond, Chip J. Felton, Jim Winarski & Mikal Cohen

This article originally appeared in the *American Journal of Public Health*, 2000, 90(12), 1873–1878, and is reprinted with permission.

At the time of the study, David L. Shern, Anne M. Lovell, and Linda Richmond were with the New York State Office of Mental Health, Albany. Sam Tsemberis is with Pathways to Housing, New York, NY. William Anthony is with the Center for Psychiatric Rehabilitation, Boston University, Boston, MA. Chip J. Felton is with the New York State Office of Mental Health, Albany. At the time of the study, Jim Winarski and Mikal Cohen were with the Center for Psychiatric Rehabilitation, Boston University, Boston, MA.

This study was supported by a grant (MH–48215) from the National Institute of Mental Health and the Center for Mental Health Services.

Objectives: This study tested a psychiatric rehabilitation approach for organizing and delivering services to street-dwelling persons with severe mental illness. Methods: Street-dwelling persons with severe mental illness were randomly assigned to the experimental program (called Choices) or to standard treatment in New York City. We assessed study participants at baseline and at 6-month intervals over 24 months, using measures of service use, quality of life, health, mental health, and social psychological status. The average deviation from baseline summary statistic was employed to assess change. Results: Compared with persons in standard treatment ($n = 77$), members of the experimental group ($n = 91$) were more likely to attend a day program (53% vs 27%), had less difficulty in meeting their basic needs, spent less time on the streets (55% vs 28% reduction), and spent more time in community housing (21% vs 9% increase). They showed greater improvement in life satisfaction and experienced a greater reduction in psychiatric symptoms. Conclusions: With an appropriate service model, it is possible to engage disaffiliated populations, expand their use of human services, and improve their housing conditions, quality of life, and mental health status.

Homelessness continues to be a serious public health problem in the United States. In addition to their poverty and housing needs, homeless individuals have multiple health and mental health problems (Wright, 1990; Brickner, Filardo, Iseman, Green, Conanan, & Elvy, 1984) Best estimates indicate that approximately one third of homeless individuals have severe mental illness (Dennis, Buckner, Lipton, & Levine, 1991; Fisher, & Breakey, 1991) with about one half comorbid for alcohol and substance abuse disorders (Drake, Osher, & Wallach; 1991) and at least one half comorbid for health problems (Burt & Cohen, 1989). Homeless individuals with mental illness also have greater problems with social and family relationships, employment, and the criminal justice system than do homeless individuals without mental illness (Dennis, Buckner, Lipton, & Levine, 1991).

These health, mental health, and social service problems require access to multiple human service systems, each with a unique set of eligibility requirements for participation (Bachrach, 1984). While homeless persons with mental illness have been characterized as resistant to treatment because they often reject help offered by mental-health and other providers, we now believe that these individuals will use services when the services address their self-defined needs and are delivered in ways that facilitate rather than frustrate access (Freddolino & Moxley, 1992; Susser, Goldfinger, & White, 1990; Morse, Calsyn, Miller, Rosenberg, West, & Gilliland, 1996). Designing effective engagement strategies and minimizing barriers to access, however, continue to be major challenges for human service systems, which are typically characterized by limited resources, rigidly controlled eligibility requirements, and highly fragmented structures (Rowe, Hoge, & Fisk, 1996).

This study tested an alternative approach for organizing and delivering services to street-dwelling persons with severe mental illness. The experimental approach was specifically designed to overcome access barriers and any dissonance between offered services and subject-defined needs (Lovell & Cohn, 1998).

We hypothesized that owing to the individualized engagement strategies and rehabilitation techniques practiced at the experimental program, experimental subjects would obtain greater access to the full range of resources needed for successful community living. This would be evidenced by increased use of community services by experimental subjects compared with individuals in the standard treatment condition. Next, we predicted that individuals in the experimental condition would experience greater improvements in their housing status, evidenced by less time living on the streets and more in shelters and community housing. We thought that, given an improved housing status and better access to treatment and support resources, individuals in the experimental group would report higher quality of life than would control group participants. Improved access to treatment also suggested that experimental subjects would report a greater reduction in psychiatric symptoms. Finally, since a major focus of psychiatric rehabilitation is on achievement of individually defined goals, we expected that experimental subjects would report higher self-esteem and greater feelings of mastery.

On the basis of technology developed at the Boston University Center for Psychiatric Rehabilitation (Anthony, Cohen, & Farkas, 1990) an approach was crafted to address key structural and functional New York City service system deficits. As in most systems, the New York City homelessness treatment and support system is structurally segmented and transitionally oriented, requiring engagement with multiple programs and caregivers to negotiate a pathway out of homelessness. Functionally, the system has a strong normative orientation in which set pathways in and out of services are prescribed and adherence to behavioral norms are mandated for successfully obtaining and maintaining housing (e.g., remaining sober as prerequisite for entry into a community reintegration program) (Lovell, Richmond, & Shern, 1993. In contrast, the experimental program, called Choices, was designed to be structurally continuous and idiographic in orientation, with caregiver behavior directed by client-defined choices about engaging in rehabilitative treatment and defining their needs and goals (Anthony, 1992).

Methods

Experimental and Standard Treatment Conditions

Street-dwelling individuals with severe mental illness who provided informed consent were randomly offered participation in the experimental Choices program or information about "standard treatment"—that is, the existing array of homelessness and specialty mental health services in New York City. To ensure replicable research findings, we chose the well-codified technology developed by the Center for Psychiatric Rehabilitation as the basis for the program intervention (Anthony, Cohen, & Farkas, 1990). This technology and its underlying values emphasize individual choice, continuity in relationships, and skills development and support to foster achievement of personal goals. This technology has been demonstrated as effective in numerous experimental and quasi-experimental studies (Dion & Anthony, 1987).

Choices had the following 4 major features:

1. Outreach and engagement, designed to foster the development of rudimentary relationships between Choices staff and homeless individuals.

2. Invitation to attend and join the Choices Center, a low-demand environment where desirable resources (e.g., showers, food) were available for only the experimental study participants from 7AM to 7PM daily. Participation in structured group activities was not required, but assistance was available to anyone requesting help in obtaining health, mental health, dental, and social services and in developing and implementing individual rehabilitation plans. Additionally, the center provided an opportunity for members to meet new friends and socialize.

3. Respite housing in 10-bed, informal church-based shelters or in blocks of YMCA rooms rented by the program and overseen by program staff.

4. In-community and on-site rehabilitation services to assist individuals in finding and maintaining community-based housing.

The Choices program was similar in structure to an intensive case management program (Surles, Blanch, Shern, & Donahue, 1992; Mueser, Bond, Drake, & Resnick, 1998), with a client-to-staff ratio of about 13:1. Choices was staffed by 6 rehabilitation specialists who received extensive training and ongoing supervision from Boston University personnel and respite staff who oversaw the respite housing and operated the center on weekends and holidays. Many respite staff had themselves been homeless and many were in recovery from alcohol or substance abuse; their presence added experiential knowledge to the program's available resources. A psychiatrist visited the program weekly for informal consultations, and a public health nurse was also on staff 8 hours per week. A more detailed description of the Choices program is presented in Shern et al., 1997. The Choices program was found to faithfully represent the key components of the psychiatric rehabilitation model through both quantitative (Shern, Trochim, & LaComb, 1995) and ethnographic assessments (Lovell & Cohn, 1998).

We conducted a detailed study of standard treatment in New York City to understand the services available to individuals in the control condition (Lovell, Richmond, & Shern, 1993). Standard treatment involved a range of programs for homeless individuals and specialty programs for homeless persons with mental illness. These included outreach services, drop-in centers, case management programs, mental health and health services, soup kitchens, municipal and private shelters, and specialized municipal shelters for persons with psychiatric disabilities. Approximately 2,700 units of specialty housing for persons with mental illness were developed through a joint city/state program. This housing, which varied from structured community residences to independent apartments, was available to experimental and control subjects. Owing to problems in gaining access to this housing, Choices developed special relationships with housing providers and eventually its own housing program to help ensure access for difficult-to-place clients.

Study Sample

Research participants were recruited directly from the streets of midtown and downtown Manhattan through direct observation by highly trained research interviewers (56%) or referral by outreach teams (44%). Most referrals came from a collaborating mobile emergency and outreach team, Project HELP (Tsemberis, Cohen, & Jones, 1993). A structured screening instrument, which operationalized the required eligibility criteria for research participation, was completed for each potential subject. The criteria included (1) having spent at least 7 of the last 14 nights homeless (i.e., sleeping in any space not designed for overnight accommodation); (2) meeting New York State's definition of serious and persistent mental illness, a definition that is generally consistent with those used throughout the country (Schinnar, Rothbard, Kanter, & Jung, 1990) and one that includes evidence of mental illness (individuals with an exclusive diagnosis of chemical abuse/dependence or mental retardation would not be included) combined with serious disability resulting from mental illness; (3) being 18 years or older; and (4) being judged not to be dangerous to themselves or others. Only 3 subjects were rejected for the dangerousness criterion.

The screening protocol employed scales from the Psychiatric Epidemiology Research Instrument (Dohrenwend, Krasnoff, Askenasy, & Dohrenwend, 1978), which have been shown to be predictive of psychiatric diagnosis (Susser & Struening, 1990), and gate questions from the Diagnostic Interview Schedule (Robins, Helzer, Croughan, & Ratcliff, 1981) for major affective disorders. The gate questions have been successfully used with other homeless populations. Both self-report and observational data were used to complete the screening.

Of approximately 400 individuals recruited on the basis of inter-viewer observation or referral information, 308 remained eligible after screening. Of these, 168 (55%) agreed to participate and completed the baseline interview. Random assignment procedures resulted in 91 indi-viduals being assigned to the Choices experimental program and 77 to the standard treatment control condition ($\chi^2 = 1.16$; not significant). Individuals in the control group were provided information by the research interviewers about local homelessness service programs. For persons assigned to the Choices program, interviewers attempted to coordinate first meetings with Choices program staff.

Few differences distinguished the individuals who participated ($n = 168$) from those who did not ($n = 140$). Individuals of Hispanic origin consented at a higher rate (81% vs 52% than non-Hispanic individuals; $\chi^2_1 = 6.46$, $P < .05$). Clinically, study participants were more likely to report a prior hospitalization (62% vs 38%; $\chi^2 = 6.49$, $P < .05$).

Of the 168 research participants, no differences were found between the experimental and control groups on any of the sociodemo-graphic or clinical (symptoms, prior hospitalizations) variables included in the screening instrument. The typical subject was non-Hispanic (90%), Black (61%), male (76%), single (88%), and aged approximately 40 years (mean = 39.97, range = 21–66). Most were unemployed (98%), with 73% having not held a job in over 1 year. Almost half (46%) had not completed high school. The sample was characterized by chronic homelessness. Nearly half (48%) reported more than 1 episode of home-lessness, and 61% of the remaining subjects who reported only 1 episode had been homeless for 4 or more years.

The Structured Clinical Interview for the *Diagnostic and Statistical Manual of Mental Disorders, Revised Third Edition (DSM-III-R)* (Spitzer, Williams, Gibbon, & First, 1992) was used with a random sub-sample of 57 participants to verify the accuracy of the street-screening procedures for assessing severe mental illness. Data showed that only 9% ($n = 5$) were found to have no major mental illness diagnosis and 54% ($n = 31$) received a lifetime alcohol or substance abuse disorder diagnosis, yielding a dual-diagnosis rate of 47%.

The potential for high rates of sample attrition was a major risk for this study, given the homelessness and system disaffiliation characteristic of our participants. We remained in contact with 69% of all subjects throughout the 24 months of follow-up. However, differential attrition occurred between the experimental and control conditions, with fewer experimental subjects lost to follow-up. High mortality also characterized this sample: 9 deaths occurred over the 24 months, a 2.5% mortality rate per year. Individuals with whom we remained in contact over the course of the study did not differ from those lost to follow-up on any demographic, clinical, or homelessness history characteristic as measured at baseline. We chose analytic techniques that allowed us to include all observations from each subject, including all available observations for individuals who ultimately left the study.

Measures

Research participants were followed intensively for 24 months by research interviewers specially trained in locating and contacting homeless individuals. Additionally, state and municipal computer databases were searched routinely to help locate missing subjects. To assess participant outcomes, 2 face-to-face interview protocols were used. Data from both protocols were employed to assess the major hypothesized outcomes associated with participation in the experimental program.

With the first protocol, interviewers attempted to contact subjects biweekly to complete a brief service use and housing status questionnaire. A structured recall method was employed to account for where the respondent slept each of the last 14 nights; it included a systematic review of human services use, documenting formal and informal resources used by the respondent to meet basic survival, health, mental health, chemical abuse, and social service needs. Many of the service use measures were adapted from those employed by Barrow et al., (1990; 1984; 1985) in their homelessness research. The questionnaire included questions asking subjects to report, using a 4-point frequency scale (i.e., always to never), the degree of difficulty that they experienced in obtaining needed services, as well as questions related to specific use of services (e.g., number of emergency room visits, arrests).

The second protocol was a lengthy structured interview completed at baseline and reattempted at 4 successive 6-month follow-up points. The interview gathered detailed information regarding quality of life, health, mental health, and social psychological status, employing scales that had been developed for and in some cases successfully used with individuals with severe mental illness (Felton, Stastny, Shern, et al.,

1995). Instruments included Lehman's Quality of Life Scales (Lehman, 1988), the Colorado Symptom Index (Shern, Wilson, Coen, et al., 1994), Rosenberg's Self-Esteem Scale (Rosenberg, 1979), and Pearlin and Schooler's Mastery Scale (Pearlin & Schooler, 1978). The average α reliability coefficient for all scales was .87.

Optimally, the interview schedule would have resulted in biweekly contacts with all subjects. However, given the difficulties of following extremely mobile street-dwelling individuals, we never anticipated obtaining complete data for all subjects. In reality, we succeeded in conducting a housing status/service use protocol about every 7 weeks per subject (median = 7.4 weeks, range = 87.7 weeks). The total number of observations over 24 months varied between 1 and 55 (median = 12 observations). Eighty-two percent (n = 138) of respondents completed at least 1 of the more lengthy 6-month follow-up interviews, with 44% (n = 74) of the subjects completing all 4.

Analysis

Analyses of change in this study were complicated by missing observations on most subjects. Missing data precluded our use of conventional repeated-measures analysis of variance techniques. Because such models require complete data for every subject, many of our cases would have been dropped from analysis. Fortunately, alternative techniques now exist that can accommodate missing observations and thus allow use of all available data, including random regression (Gibbons, Hedecker, Elkin, et al., 1993) and the summary statistics approach advanced by Dawson and Lagakos (Dawson & Lagakos, 1993). Examples of the use of univariate summary statistics in the analysis of repeated-measures designs may be found in Di Bisceglie et al. (1989) and Dawson (1998).

The summary statistic method adopted as our analytic strategy modeled change by using the average deviation from baseline (ADB), a simpler version of the area under the curve statistic used by Di Bisceglie et al., (DiBisceglie et al., 1989; Banks, Shern, & Felton, 2000). An ADB for a given measure is formed by averaging an individual's available follow-up observations and subtracting the baseline observation from that average. The ADB represented the average change experienced over the course of the 24-month intervention, adjusted to account for baseline scores. Between-group comparisons were then conducted by an independent-samples t test.

We compared outcomes for the 2 groups across 5 domains: unmet needs, housing status, quality of life, psychological status, and service use. Multiple comparisons were conducted within each domain. To account for this, we employed a modified Bonferroni procedure (Simes, 1986) within each domain to correct for the higher probability of significant findings when there are multiple tests.

The summary statistic approach facilitated examining for potential biases associated with sample attrition. We carried out comparisons for cohorts that varied in the length of study participation on all outcome measures. In no instance were between-group results for subjects who left the study early at odds with the findings for all subjects. We therefore feel confident that our summary statistic approach fairly represents study findings.

Results

Unmet Needs

Table 1 presents information regarding individuals' ability to meet their basic food, clothing, shelter, and personal care needs. Compared with control subjects, individuals in the experimental group reported significantly less difficulty getting food ($t = 2.99$, $P < .01$), finding a place to sleep ($t = 3.02$, $P < .01$), and keeping clean ($t = 3.07$, $P < .01$). (All of the reported t tests involve approximately 167 degrees of freedom and are 2-tailed.)

Housing Status

Table 1 also summarizes the changes in living situation experienced by both groups over the 24-month intervention. While both groups showed substantial decreases in the time spent on the streets, the rate of decline was approximately twice as great for the experimental group as for the control group ($t = 4.18$, $P < .001$). Consistent with their street-dwelling status at baseline, individuals in the control group continued not to use shelters. However, individuals assigned to the Choices condition reported a 23% increase in the proportion of time spent in shelters, using the Choices-provided respite housing almost exclusively ($t = -5.73$, $P < .001$).

The community housing category encompassed the full range of community housing options, from transitional settings (e.g., hotel rooms, community residences) to long-term settings (e.g., apartments).

Table 1

Changes From Baseline in Street-Dwelling Individuals' Unmet Needs, Housing Status, Quality of Life, and Psychological Status: New York City, 1991–1994

| Measure | Change From Baseline | | | | | |
| | Experimental Group (n = 91) | | Control Group (n = 77) | | | |
	Mean	SD	Mean	SD	t	P
Unmet needs (change in difficulty meeting basic needs)						
Getting food	−0.84	1.13	−0.31	1.11	2.99	.003a
Having a place to sleep	−1.06	1.10	−0.48	1.31	3.02	.003a
Getting clothing	−0.80	1.29	−0.47	1.38	1.61	.109a
Keeping clean	−0.95	1.14	−0.34	1.41	3.07	.003a
Finding a bathroom	−0.70	1.15	−0.46	1.15	1.36	.175
Keeping possessions	−0.85	1.08	−0.72	1.20	0.71	.48
Housing status (change in proportion of time spent in residential setting)						
Streets	−54.93	36.92	−28.22	44.49	4.18	.001a
Shelters	23.08	29.27	2.79	15.23	−5.73	.001a
Community living	21.01	30.39	9.94	32.34	−2.27	.025a
Institutions	13.53	22.28	15.86	32.81	0.53	.599
Quality of life (change in satisfaction in life area)						
Overall	1.19	1.99	−0.02	1.65	−4.21	.001a
Leisure	0.72	1.72	0.18	1.31	−2.23	.027a
Financial	1.06	1.79	−0.12	1.67	−4.33	.001a
Safety	1.12	1.95	0.36	1.35	−2.85	.005a
Health	0.70	1.57	0.09	1.19	−2.78	.006a
Family	0.94	1.97	0.14	1.29	−2.86	.005a
Social	0.45	1.75	−0.05	1.18	−1.93	.56
Psychological status (change in psychiatric symptoms, self-esteem, mastery)						
Symptoms (anxiety, depression, thought disturbance)	−0.28	0.69	0.04	0.72	2.74	.007a
Self-esteem	0.05	0.37	−0.02	0.41	1.11	.268
Mastery	0.06	0.45	0.02	0.35	0.58	.563

Note. All means reflect the average deviation from baseline scores. A 4-point scale was used.

a. Significant after modified Bonferroni adjustment.

Over the course of the study, experimental clients increased their amount of time in community housing at twice the rate of persons assigned to standard treatment ($t = 2.27$, $P < .05$). A comparison of where subjects were living at the end of the study shows the result of this differential trend: at their final follow-up data collection point, 38% of experimental subjects were residing in community settings, as contrasted with 24% of control-group participants.

Interestingly, time spent in institutional settings, which included psychiatric, medical, and forensic inpatient facilities, increased by about 13% to 16% for both groups. This change probably reflects simply a regression to mean levels of institutionalization for this population.

Quality of Life

Table 1 includes a summary of between-group differences in life satisfaction across 7 life areas (Felton, et al., 1995). Individuals in the experimental condition reported consistently greater improvement in life satisfaction than their peers in the control group in 6 of the 7 life areas. In most areas, gains reported by individuals in the experimental group were substantial, often 0.5 standard deviation greater than changes reported by individuals in the control group.

Psychological Status

This domain included assessments of psychiatric symptoms, self-esteem, and mastery. As shown in table 1, the experimental subjects reported significantly greater reductions in anxiety, depression, and thought disturbances than did control group participants ($t = 2.41$, $P < .001$). Between-group differences were not significant for either mastery or self-esteem, with ratings for both groups on these measures remaining stable over time.

Service Use

Service use data are presented in table 2. The summary statistic used here is not the ADB (the absence of this set of variables from the baseline interview precluded using the ADB) but rather the percentage of individuals using the service at least once in a given 6-month follow-up period, averaged over all available follow-ups. Experimental subjects were much more likely to attend a day program, attending at twice the rate of control subjects ($t = 4.39$, $P < .01$). This difference largely reflects attendance at the Choices Center. Although between-group differences

Table 2

Use of Services Among Street-Dwelling People as a Percentage of Subjects Receiving the Service at Least Once During a 6-Month Follow-Up Period: New York City, 1991–1994

| | Percent Receiving Service | | | | | |
| | Experimental Group(n = 91) | | Control Group (n = 77) | | | |
Measure	Mean	SD	Mean	SD	t	P^a
Service						
Any help	74.01	28.11	72.07	33.52	0.37	.710
Cash entitlement	46.69	31.75	33.72	32.91	2.44	.016
Health insurance	34.18	30.29	21.34	28.56	2.65	.009
Alcohol/drug	27.25	31.95	16.08	24.83	2.41	.017
Emergency department	21.97	30.47	24.63	31.89	0.52	.606
Psychiatric medications	43.80	43.70	26.19	37.90	2.52	.013
Outpatient care	35.86	32.75	27.33	33.01	1.58	.118
Inpatient care	20.26	27.50	17.38	30.86	0.59	.554
Day program	52.73	37.62	27.30	33.32	4.39	.001*
Outreach	45.41	36.33	40.87	38.55	0.73	.465
Self-help	31.29	33.50	21.16	32.12	1.88	.062
Inpatient alcohol/drug	6.31	15.43	3.62	14.92	1.08	.283
Outpatient alcohol/drug	6.03	15.62	4.07	14.61	0.79	.431
Dentist	15.47	26.22	9.02	20.18	1.71	.089
Police contact	26.78	28.44	41.02	38.85	2.49	.014
Jail	7.43	17.23	7.77	21.65	1.10	.918
Court	19.48	28.08	15.50	24.88	0.92	.360
Other help	36.70	35.34	31.69	36.91	0.84	.403

Note. All means reflect the percentage of subjects using the service at least once in a 6-month period.

a P value was significant after the modified Bonferroni adjustment was applied.

in the use of other services did not reach statistical significance, absolute rates of service use were generally higher for the experimental group.

Discussion

In the aggregate, these results indicate that the experimental program was more successful in serving and housing individuals with severe mental illness who lived on the streets than was the standard treatment system in Manhattan. At a minimum, the results indicate that with an appropriate service model, it is possible to engage disaffiliated populations, expand their use of human services, and improve their housing conditions, quality of life, and mental health status.

This project may have important implications for the design of human services, particularly as we continue to debate health care reform strategies and consider their implications for the most vulnerable and disaffiliated populations. Perhaps most important is the need to systematically assess barriers to the receipt of needed services for populations that choose not to or are unable to gain access to services through usual channels. Not surprisingly, given the Boston University philosophy and technology in which the Choices staff had been trained, several participants reported that the Choices program was unlike any other they had encountered because the staff genuinely attempted to help them realize their own self-defined goals (Lovell & Cohn, 1998). Choices clients reported that most other programs would prescribe both the appropriate goal (e.g., psychiatric treatment, sobriety) and the required steps to achieve it.

Our analysis of the standard treatment condition was consistent with their reports (Lovell, Richmond, & Shern, 1993). While such programs are surely well-intentioned, the prescription of both means and ends and restriction of services and resources to clients who are compliant with these prescriptions may frustrate access for underserved populations. It is important to underscore that such provider practices usually are not grounded on systematic investigations of service effectiveness but more typically on scattered data from self-selecting caseloads as well as beliefs derived from dominant treatment paradigms.

It is interesting to note that Choices participants did not use general medical or mental health treatment resources (table 1) at any greater rate than control group participants. It was our observation that most of the generic services and supports available in the community were not used by clients in the experimental group at any greater rate than by clients in the control group. In fact, we noted that both experimental and control participants used emergency and inpatient services at approximately equivalent rates, which we may not have expected because programs like Choices are often associated with decreased inpatient and emergency use (Surles, Blanch, Shern, & Donahue, 1992). We found that, even with strong advocacy, individuals in the Choices program preferred to receive most services solely through Choices.

Access to housing resources, even specialty housing for homeless persons, proved very difficult to obtain. To gain access to needed housing for this street-dwelling population, we developed close relations with a supported apartment program and ultimately were forced to initiate our own supported apartment program (Simes, 1986; Shern, Tsemberis, Winarski, Cope, Cohen, & Anthony, 1997). We therefore found it necessary to control the full spectrum of resources to meet the needs of our clientele. It would have been preferable to gain better access to generic resources, thereby integrating Choices clients into the surrounding community rather than continuing to segregate them.

These results raise further empirical questions. What is the most effective program model for providing services to homeless individuals who have severe psychiatric disabilities and comorbid substance abuse and physical health problems? Is it a model that strives to simulate an integrated system through advocacy and referrals to various providers, or is it a model in which a multidisciplinary team provides services directly?

The study also has several important limitations. First, although we have ethnographically (Lovell & Cohn, 1998) and quantitatively described important characteristics of the experimental program and standard treatment control (Lovell et al., 1993), the design does not permit us to rigorously test the varying components of the experimental model to determine its most important elements. We also have not explicated the characteristics of individuals for whom the intervention may be particularly effective; instead, we have restricted our analyses to "intent to treat." While we could not identify any important differences between individuals whom we successfully followed and those who were lost to follow-up, attrition is always an important consideration in generalizing these results to the overall population of homeless persons. Similarly, persons who refused to participate in the research may also represent an important component of the homeless population with mental illness to whom we cannot generalize. Finally, individuals who were not competent to give informed consent could not participate in the research. Although very few individuals consistently were judged to be incompetent, a few gravely ill individuals could not participate in the trial.

Conclusion

As we continue to debate the structure and functions of a more efficient mental health care system, it is critically important to assess systematically the assumptions upon which such a system is designed. In this project, we purposely selected a population of individuals who were not being well served by the existing system. These individuals in effect provided a window through which we observed the functioning of that system. By carefully following this cohort, we documented both the effectiveness of a psychiatric rehabilitation approach and some of the assumptions and operating procedures of the existing "standard treatment" system that may underlie poorer client outcomes. It is only by conducting such careful examination, documenting both processes and outcomes of system structure and functioning, that we will be successful in developing a health care system that works even for those most disaffiliated.

References

Anthony, W.A. (1992). Psychiatric rehabilitation: Key issues and future policy. *Health Affairs, 11*, 165–171.

Anthony, W.A., Cohen M.R., Farkas M. (1990). *Psychiatric rehabilitation.* Boston, MA: Center for Psychiatric Rehabilitation.

Bachrach, L.L. Interpreting research on the homeless mentally ill: some caveats. (1984). *Hospital and Community Psychiatry, 35*, 914–917.

Banks, S.M., Shern, D.L., & Felton, C.J. (2000). *Estimating power in a repeated measures design.* Tampa: University of South Florida.

Barrow, S.M., Cordova, P.,& Struening, E.L. (1990). *Evaluation of a project to link up services. A-plus Baseline Interview.* New York, NY: New York State Psychiatric Institute, Epidemiology of Mental Disorders Research Department.

Barrow, S.M., Hellman, F., Lovell, A.M., Plapinger, J.D., & Struening, E.L. (1985). *Personal History Follow-Up Form.* New York, NY. New York State Psychiatric Institute, Community Support Systems Program, Epidemiology of Mental Disorders Research Department.

Barrow, S.M., Hellman, F., Lovell, A.M., Plapinger, J.D., Robinson, D.R., & Struening, E.L. (1984). *Personal History Form.* New York, NY: New York State Psychiatric Institute, Community Support Systems Program, Epidemiology of Mental Disorders Research Department.

Brickner, P.W., Filardo, T., Iseman, M., Green, R., Conanan, B., & Elvy, A. (1984). Medical aspects of homelessness. In H. R. Lamb (Ed.), *The homeless mentally ill.* Washington, DC: American Psychiatric Association Press, 243–259.

Burt, M.R., & Cohen, B.E. (1998). Differences among homeless single women, women with children and single men. *Social Problems, 36*, 508–524.

Dawson, J.D. (1985). Sample size calculations based on slopes and other summary statistics. *Biometrics, 54*, 323–330.

Dawson, J.D., & Lagakos, S.W. (1993). Size and power of two-sample tests of repeated measures data. *Biometrics, 49*, 1022–1032.

Dennis, D., Buckner, J.C., Lipton, F.R., & Levine, I.S. (1991). A decade of research and services for homeless mentally ill persons: Where do we stand? *American Psychologist, 46,* 1129–1138.

Di Bisceglie, A.M., Martin, P., Kassianides, C., et al. (1989). Recombinant interferon alpha for chronic hepatitis C. A randomized, double-blind, placebo-controlled trial. *New England Journal of Medicine, 321,* 1506–1510.

Dion, G.L., & Anthony, W.A. (1987). Research in psychiatric rehabilitation: A review of experimental and quasi-experimental studies. *Rehabilitation Counseling Bulletin, 30,* 177–203.

Dohrenwend, B.S., Krasnoff, L., Askenasy, A., & Dohrenwend, B.P. (1978) Exemplification of a method for scaling life events: The PERI Life Events Scale. *Journal of Health and Social Behavior; 19,* 220–229.

Drake, R.E., Osher, F.C., & Wallach, M.A. (1991) Homelessness and dual diagnosis. *American Psychologist, 46,* 1149–1158.

Felton, C.F., Stastny, P., Shern, D.L., et al. (1995). Consumers as peer specialists on intensive case management teams: Impact on client outcomes. *Psychiatric Services, 46,* 1037–1044.

Fisher, P.J., & Breakey, W.R. (1991). The epidemiology of alcohol, drug and mental disorders among homeless persons. *American Psychologist, 46,* 1115–1128.

Freddolino, P.P., & Moxley, D.P. (1992). Refining an advocacy model for homeless people coping with psychiatric disabilities. *Community Mental Health Journal, 28,* 337–352.

Gibbons, R.D., Hedecker, D., Elkin, I., et al. (1993). Some conceptual and statistical issues in analysis of longitudinal psychiatric data. *Archives of General Psychiatry, 50,* 739–750.

Lehman, A.F. (1988). A quality of life interview for the chronically mentally ill. *Evaluation and Program Planning, 11,* 51–62.

Lovell, A.M, & Cohn, S. (1998). The elaboration of choice in a program for homeless persons labeled psychiatrically disabled. *Hum Organ, 57,* 8–20.

Lovell, A., Richmond L., & Shern, D. (1993) *Measuring standard treatment in a complex environment: An illustration from a study of psychiatric rehabilitation for homeless "street people."* Albany: New York State Office of Mental Health.

Morse, G.A., Calsyn, R.J., Miller, J., Rosenberg, P., West, L., & Gilliland, J. (1996). Outreach to homeless mentally ill people: Conceptual and clinical considerations. *Community Mental Health Journal, 32,* 261–274.

Mueser, K.T., Bond, G.R., Drake, R.E., Resnick, S. (1998). Models of community care for severe mental illness: a review of research on case management. *Schizophrenia Bulletin, 24,* 37–74.

Pearlin, L.I., & Schooler, C. (1978). The structure of coping. *Journal of Health and Social Behavior, 19,* 2–21.

Robins, L.N., Helzer, J.E., Croughan, J., & Ratcliff, K.S. (1981). National Institute of Mental Health Diagnostic Interview Schedule: Its history, characteristics and validity. *Archives of General Psychiatry, 38,* 381–389.

Rosenberg, M. (1979). *Concerning the self.* New York, NY: Basic Books.

Rowe, M, Hoge, M.A., & Fisk, D. (1996). Critical issues in serving people who are homeless and mentally ill. *Administration and Policy in Mental Health, 23,* 555–565.

Schinnar, A.R., Rothbard, A.B., Kanter, R., & Jung, Y.S. (1990). An empirical literature review of definitions of severe and persistent mental illness. *American Journal of Psychiatry, 147,* 1602–1608.

Shern, D.L., Felton, C.J., Hough, R., et al. (1997). Housing outcomes for homeless adults with mental illness: Results from the second-round McKinney program. *Psychiatric Services, 48,* 239–241.

Shern, D.L., Tsemberis, S., Winarski, J., Cope, N., Cohen, M., & Anthony, W.A. (1997). A psychiatric rehabilitation demonstration for individuals who are street dwelling and seriously disabled. In: W. Breakey & J. Thompson (Eds.), *Mentally ill and homeless: Special programs for special needs.* Amsterdam, the Netherlands: Harwood Academic Publishers; 119–147.

Shern, D., Trochim, W., & LaComb, C. (1995). The use of concept mapping for assessing fidelity of model transfer: An example from psychiatric rehabilitation. *Evaluation and Program Planning, 18,* 143–153.

Shern, D.L., Wilson, N.Z., Coen, A.S., et al. (1994). Client outcomes, II: Longitudinal client data from the Colorado treatment outcome study. *Milbank Quarterly, 72,* 123–148.

Simes, R.J. (1986). An improved Bonferroni procedure for multiple tests of significance. *Biometrika, 73,* 751–754.

Spitzer, R.L., Williams, J.B., Gibbon, M., & First, M.B. (1992). The Structured Clinical Interview for *DSM-III-R* (SCID), I: History, rationale, and description. *Archives of General Psychiatry, 49,* 624–629.

Surles, R.C., Blanch, A.K., Shern, D.L., & Donahue, S.A. (1992). Case management as a strategy for systems change. *Health Affairs, 11,* 151–163.

Susser, E.S., & Struening, E.L. (1990). Diagnosis and screening for psychotic disorders in a study of the homeless. *Schizophrenia Bulletin, 16,* 133–145.

Susser, E., Goldfinger, S., & White, A. (1990). Some clinical approaches to the homeless mentally ill. *Community Mental Health Journal, 26,* 463–480.

Tsemberis, S., Cohen, N.L., & Jones, R. (1993). Conducting emergency psychiatric evaluation on the street. In: S. Katz, D. Nardacci, & A. Sabatini (Eds.), *Intensive treatment of the homeless mentally ill.* Washington, DC: American Psychiatric Press; 71–89.

Wright, J.D. (1990). Poor people, poor health: the health status of the homeless. *Journal of Social Issues, 46,* 49–64.

Family Support for Persons with Dual Disorders

Robin E. Clark

This article originally appeared in Dual Diagnosis of Major Mental Illness and Substance Abuse, Volume 2: Recent Research and Clinical Implications. *New Directions for Mental Health Services,* 1996, Summer, No. 70, 65–78, and is reprinted with permission.

Robin E. Clark, Ph.D., is assistant professor in psychiatry at the Dartmouth Medical School, research associate at the New Hampshire-Dartmouth Psychiatric Research Center, and director of the cost-effectiveness laboratory at Dartmouth Medical School.

Michael was 20 years old when he was diagnosed with schizophrenia. His family had noticed that he was spending more time alone in his room and that he increasingly voiced thoughts that they found bizarre or frightening. Still, they were surprised when his boss called one day to say that he had begun shouting at co-workers, accusing them of trying to poison him. After 3 months in a private hospital, a psychiatrist confirmed Michael's diagnosis and prescribed antipsychotic medication. Insurance covered only a portion of the medical bills, so his family took out a second mortgage on their home to pay the additional hospital charges.

In the ensuing years, Michael was rehospitalized a number of times. A local mental health center arranged for him to live in a group home, but he had difficulty complying with the rules and eventually left to live in a rented room downtown. Complaining that it made him feel like "a crash-test dummy" and that he really did not need it, he went for long periods without taking his medication. Michael, who had been a moderate drinker in high school, began getting into minor scrapes with the police when he drank. Sometimes he disappeared for long periods of time. Eventually his family received a call from a distant hospital, police department, or shelter asking them to come take him home.

Relations with his family, which had been tense since his teens, have become even more strained since Michael, now 38, began to suspect that his parents are conspiring with the FBI to implant "thought amplifiers" in his brain. Fearful of a widening conspiracy, Michael tells his case manager that his family hates him and that he rarely sees them. In spite of their difficulties, Michael's mother continues to call him and often takes him out for lunch and on shopping trips during which she buys him clothes or furnishings for his room. Michael periodically runs out of money toward the end of the month and his parents give him money for food or help him pay his rent. When he gets in trouble with the police or is hospitalized away from home, it is almost always his father who comes to post bail or to take him home.

Michael's father is now in his mid-seventies and is becoming increasingly immobile from arthritis and heart disease. His mother, who spends most of her time looking after Michael and his father, feels isolated and worries about what will happen when she and her husband are no longer able to give Michael the help he needs. Michael worries, too.

Benefits and Burdens of Family Support

Like Michael, most persons with severe mental illness and substance disorders rely heavily on others to assist them with the basics of daily living. Families are the primary source of much of this help. Recent research suggests that they play a central role in the survival and well-being of their relatives with dual disorders, supplying large amounts of direct care and financial support (Carpentier et al., 1992; Clark & Drake, 1994; Franks, 1990; Tausig, Fisher, & Tessler, 1992). Still, we know relatively little about how families cope with these added demands, how treatment affects clients and families, and how family support—or the lack of it—influences a person's recovery from mental illness and substance disorders. As a consequence of our lack of understanding, treatment providers often underestimate the importance of families in the lives of their clients with dual disorders.

Persons with severe mental illness who also abuse alcohol or other drugs have difficulty managing tasks of daily living and have higher rates of unemployment than do persons with mental illness alone (Drake & Wallach, 1989, Kay, Kalathara, & Meinzer, 1989). Because of these problems they often depend on families or friends for assistance in securing the basic necessities of life. Although families make many other important contributions to their relatives, the basic assistance they give is, for many persons with dual disorders, a primary means of survival and the foundation on which formal treatment and rehabilitative services are built. Without first satisfying these primary needs, persons with dual disorders are unlikely to participate in or respond fully to treatment interventions.

Having a relative with dual disorders clearly places significant additional demands on families. A study of New Hampshire parents with adult children revealed that when a son or daughter had a dual disorder they spent over twice as much time giving direct care and contributed significantly more financial support than when their children were free of chronic illnesses (Clark, 1994). Parents of persons with dual disorders spent a good deal more time providing general care, for example, cooking and cleaning. They also spent more time giving rides, intervening in crises, and creating structured leisure activities for their relatives. A comparable amount of service provided by formal caregivers—case managers or home health aides, for example—would have cost almost $14,000 per year in 1992 dollars. Economic support given by parents in the dual disorder group totaled almost 16% of their annual income, whereas comparison families contributed an amount equal to about 6% of their annual income.

Family support may also have different long-term results for recipients. Financial assistance for adult children without dual disorders tends to be for purposes that could be considered investments, such as college tuition or a down payment on a car or house. Economic support for persons with dual disorders is most often for basic necessities like food, clothing, or shelter. For persons without dual disorders, family assistance may provide a boost to economic status or earning potential. For those with dual disorders, family assistance has the far more immediate consequence of ensuring adequate nutrition and a place to stay. Losing this support could have serious consequences.

Homelessness is a potential result of lost family support. Although being homeless is stressful in itself, it also increases the risk that one will acquire AIDS, or be assaulted, robbed, or incarcerated (Fisher & Breakey, 1991; Torres, Mani, Altholz, & Brickner, 1990). Evidence for a connection between lack of family support and homelessness comes from separate studies of men and women with schizophrenia in the New York area conducted by Caton and others (1994, 1995). Matching one hundred men with schizophrenia currently living in a homeless shelter with one hundred who were similar in other characteristics but who had never been homeless, Caton and her colleagues found that a lack of adequate current family support was more strongly associated with homelessness than any of the other variables they considered. Positive psychiatric symptoms, drug abuse, antisocial personality, and treatment engagement were also important in explaining differences between the two groups, but less so than current family assistance in the form of money, shelter, food, clothing, advice, and companionship. A second study of homeless women produced very similar results: inadequate current family support was again the factor most strongly associated with homelessness (Caton et al., 1995).

In a separate study Tessler and others (1992) found that persons with mental illness who had been homeless during the previous year were more dissatisfied with and had less faith in their families than those who had not been homeless. Families of the homeless group reported less involvement, gave less care, and had more negative attitudes toward them than families of the never homeless group. When combined with other patient characteristics such as gender, deficits in daily living, work, and incarceration history, however, family variables were not significantly associated with previous homelessness.

Although family support may benefit persons with dual disorders it can also be a burden to families. Intuitively it seems likely that substance abuse would add to the burden that families of persons with severe mental illness feel, but current research does not allow us to confirm or refute this supposition or to say how much more burden substance abuse might add.

Typically family burden is seen as a combination of objective (how much families do) and subjective (how they feel about what they do) factors (Hoenig & Hamilton, 1966; Thompson & Doll, 1982). Family caregivers may perform certain types of tasks frequently, such as preparing meals, but may not feel especially burdened by them. Other tasks, like restraining an intoxicated or angry relative, occur less often but are experienced as more burdensome.

Tessler and Gamache (1994) have further refined tasks assisted by families according to whether they are related to care (routine support) or control (behavioral problems). Care items mentioned frequently include providing transportation, time and money management, and preparing meals. Control items include attention seeking, night disturbances, embarrassing behavior, substance abuse, and a range of other troublesome behaviors (Tessler & Gamache, 1994). Some studies indicate that family members experience the care tasks as more burdensome; this finding may be influenced, however, by specific characteristics of the groups studied or by the relative infrequency of control tasks (Maurin & Boyd, 1990). Logically one would expect that persons with dual disorders would require more family efforts to control behaviors than persons with mental illness alone. It is less clear how dual disorders might affect the amount of general supportive care required.

Factors That Influence Family Support

The sheer burden of caring for a relative with multiple problems might seem enough to discourage families, but the New York study of homeless men did not find differences in the level of burden reported by families of homeless and domiciled men (Caton et al., 1994). The two groups did score differently on an index of family disorganization. Men in the homeless group were over four times more likely to come from families that were inconsistent in nurturing, had unstable housing, inadequate income, and relied on public assistance. Parents of men in this group were more likely to have a history of criminal involvement, mental illness, and substance abuse. Family history does not appear to be strongly associated with homelessness among women with schizophrenia (Caton et al., 1995).

It is not entirely clear from this study why traditional patterns of family support break down. Low family support could be the result rather than the cause of homelessness, but the combination of differences between the two groups in reported family histories of disorganization and similarities in levels of current family burden suggests that the seeds of lower support are sown before the men become homeless. Families beset by extreme poverty, illness, and a range of other problems are likely to have fewer resources to give to their relatives than do others. It is important to note that not all of the study subjects came from impoverished, disorganized families, and that current behaviors like psychiatric symptoms and substance abuse are also associated with homelessness.

Although poor family support and substance abuse are both associated with homelessness, this does not necessarily mean that families of persons with dual disorders are unwilling or unable to help. Most give substantial amounts of economic and direct care support to their relatives despite active substance use. As substance abuse becomes more severe, the amount of economic support that families give decreases, but the amount of direct care appears to be unaffected (Clark & Drake, 1994).

When it comes to living together, drug and alcohol use seem to exert a more complex influence on family decisions. In an unpublished statewide survey of over 2,000 people receiving publicly funded treatment for severe mental illness in New Hampshire, clients who used alcohol were significantly less likely to live with their families. This could be interpreted as evidence that families are less willing to house a substance-abusing relative. However, there are other explanations for the finding. For example, people who do not live with their families may have less supervision and are therefore more likely to abuse drugs or alcohol; substance abusers initially may be more socially competent and therefore may be more likely to form relationships outside the home; different living situations may reflect different levels of psychiatric impairment that may be related in turn to substance abuse.

Another study of persons enrolled in specialized treatment for dual disorders suggests that parents are more willing than other relatives to house someone who is actively abusing substances (Clark & Drake, 1994). Persons who abuse drugs or alcohol more severely are less likely to live with relatives in general. When they do live with family, they are more likely to live with parents than with siblings or other relatives. This somewhat confusing picture may be explained by thinking of parents as service or housing providers of last resort.

Substance abuse decreases the range of available living options. The New Hampshire study indicates that substance abuse is associated with more stress and less appropriate housing wherever the person lives. This is generally consistent with other data that show that persons with dual disorders tend to live in less desirable housing (Uehara, 1994). When their adult children with dual disorders leave or are asked to leave their present accommodations, parents may, with some reluctance, be their only housing option. In one survey of family caregivers for persons with schizophrenia, over two-thirds of whom were parents, practical concerns like "being able to keep an eye on the patient's drinking" were the benefits of living together that caregivers cited most frequently (Winefield & Harvey, 1994). Filial relationships seem to be a critical buffer against homelessness for persons with dual disorders.

Housing a relative with dual disorders is not purely a burden; relatives with mental illness often contribute positively to their families, both financially and otherwise (Greenberg, Greenley & Benedict, 1994). Still, living together is not without its risks. Increased contact is associated with more family stress, particularly for spouses and parents (Anderson & Lynch, 1984; Winefield & Harvey, 1994). Living together increases the risk that parents or spouses will be assaulted (Gondolf, Mulvey, & Lidz, 1990; Straznickas, McNiel, & Binder, 1993). Substance abuse seems to increase further the likelihood that the relative with mental illness will threaten or attack a family member (Monahan, 1992; Swan & Lavitt, 1988). Families who house a relative with a dual disorder are thus particularly in need of support.

Cohabitation may also be difficult for the person with a dual disorder. About one-fourth of persons with severe mental illness say they prefer to live with their families (Massey & Wu, 1993). It is not clear if substance abuse alters these preferences. In most cases persons with mental illness and their families agree on the decision to live together, but substance abuse may reduce consensus. Disagreement about the desirability of living together leads to conflict and dissatisfaction. Stressful family atmospheres are associated with increased relapse rates (Kashner et al., 1991; Kavanagh, 1992), and persons with dual disorders report more dissatisfaction with family relations and a greater desire for family treatment than do persons with mental illness alone (Dixon, McNary, & Lehman, 1995). Moreover, evidence linking parental substance abuse to current substance abuse by adult offspring means that in some cases the family environment may not be conducive to controlling substance abuse (Gershon et al., 1988; Noordsy, Drake, Biesanz, & McHugo, 1994).

Even though increased contact, behavioral problems, and greater demands for direct care add to family burden, there is no clear relationship between these stressors and a family's decision to terminate support for a relative with dual disorders. Evidence from studies of family caregivers for elderly relatives who are frail or have Alzheimer's disease suggests that the decision is influenced by a combination of the ill relative's behavior, the family's financial resources, and their attitudes toward care-giving. One study found that family caregivers were more likely to place their relatives with Alzheimer's disease in a nursing home when they felt frustrated or trapped by the caregiving role (Aneshensel, Pearlin, & Schuler, 1993). Other factors such as more severe functional impairment, caregiver stress, and having enough money to pay for out-of-home care were also associated, albeit more weakly, with the decision to place.

Help and emotional support from other family members almost certainly make the difficult aspects of caregiving more bearable. Single caregivers report more stress than married ones (Carpentier et al., 1992). Family cohesiveness and support appear to be particularly important in reducing the frustration that family caregivers feel (Greenberg, Seltzer, & Greenley, 1993). The extent to which burden can be reduced or to which family ties can be maintained by formal services is still unknown.

Many families continue providing direct and financial support in the face of great demands and stress. Why some families continue and others distance themselves from their relatives with dual disorders is a puzzle whose answer has important implications for relatives, treatment providers, and families. Preserving family support has obvious benefits for persons with dual disorders and probably for their families as well. Knowing what factors lead to family estrangement would enable more appropriately focused interventions to prevent family breakup.

Treatment and Family Relationships

Because there are few longitudinal studies of family support, we know almost nothing about how treatment of persons with dual disorders affects family support or what roles families play in recovery. Evidence from the mental health literature provides some clues. For example, it seems logical to conclude that treatment that reduces hospitalization will increase family contact and will thereby lead to greater family burden (see, for example, Goldman, 1982), but there is little recent documentation to support this notion. Most studies find no relationship between amount of hospitalization and measures of objective or subjective family burden (Maurin & Boyd, 1990). One study reported that families of persons who received intensive community services and less hospital care than customary actually preferred the community intervention (Reynolds & Hoult, 1984).

There appears to be little difference in the impact of various client-focused treatments on families, but interventions that target families (primarily families of persons with schizophrenia) have specifically shown significant changes in patterns of family interaction and in-patient relapse rates (Bellack & Mueser, 1993).

Two studies illustrate these findings. Falloon and others (1982) compared in-home family therapy to individual treatment for a small group of patients with schizophrenia who were receiving psychotropic medication. Over a 9-month period, patients in the family therapy group had significantly fewer relapses and lower levels of psychiatric symptoms than those who participated only in individual treatment. In a larger study, Hogarty and others (1986) compared the effects of a family-focused intervention to those of individual treatment for patients with schizophrenia who came from high *expressed emotion* households. Expressed emotion covers a range of strong negative affects in family interactions, particularly criticism and emotional overinvolvement. After 1 year of treatment, patients whose families participated in a psychoeducational intervention designed to "lower the emotional climate of the home while maintaining reasonable expectations for patient performance" had significantly fewer relapses than persons whose families did not participate. No patients relapsed in families who successfully changed from high to low expressed emotion status. Although neither of the studies discussed above focused specifically on persons with dual disorders, the high levels of dissatisfaction with family relations among persons with dual disorders suggest that family-focused interventions may prove beneficial for them as well.

Interventions that attempt to improve family interactions have sometimes been criticized for focusing only on the family's response to the identified relative's behavior rather than on the behavior of both parties (Kanter, Lamb, & Loeper, 1987). Evidence suggests that the combination of difficult behaviors presented by the person with mental illness and his or her family's reactions contribute to the phenomenon known as expressed emotion (Kavanagh, 1992). Approaches that blame either party for relationship difficulties are likely to be less effective than those that view expressed emotion as an interactive phenomenon. Although recent theories posit a more complex interaction between persons with mental illness and their families (Maurin & Boyd, 1990; Mueser & Glynn, 1990), it is not clear that those ideas have been widely incorporated into treatment practice.

We do not know whether there is any association between the criticism and emotional overinvolvement that characterize high expressed emotion situations and the amounts of direct caregiving and economic assistance that families provide. This is an area in which further research may help. For now we should be careful not to confuse the amount of objective family support with the emotional content of family interactions. We cannot assume that emotional overinvolvement means that the family is giving too much direct support or that families who are giving a great deal of support are doing so inappropriately.

A limitation of virtually all treatment studies that include measures of family burden is that they tend to be relatively brief, often lasting for a year or less. Recent work by Tessler and Gamache (1994) suggests that continuity of service rather than the type or intensity of treatment a person receives may be a critical factor in reducing the burden that a person's family experiences. In their analysis of data from three sites in Ohio, Tessler and Gamache found a significant relationship between the continuity of a relative's treatment and aspects of family burden for families with whom the client lived. They defined continuity as having a case manager or other formal caregiver who "helped them plan and obtain the services they needed" at each of three points over a 2-year period. Continuity did not have the same benefits for families who lived separately from study participants. Consistent with other studies, being a parent and sharing a residence were associated with higher levels of family burden.

Family services specifically designed for persons with dual disorders, a relatively new phenomenon, are often incorporated into integrated treatment programs (Fox, Fox, & Drake, 1992; Sciacca, 1991). Most take a group psychoeducational approach that provides information about the effects of substance use for persons with mental illness and discusses strategies for behavior management (Clark & Drake, 1992). Typical psychoeducational groups are shorter in duration than the groups for families of persons with schizophrenia mentioned earlier; information on substance abuse can easily be incorporated into long-term family groups, however (Ryglewicz, 1991).

As yet there is little information about the effectiveness of family interventions specifically targeted for relatives of persons with dual disorders. Additional research could help determine the effectiveness of these approaches for persons with psychiatric diagnoses other than schizophrenia. Existing research and clinical opinion suggest that a "one size fits all" approach may not be appropriate for family services (Pfeiffer & Mostek, 1991). Not only may different psychiatric diagnoses present different problems, but family members may experience them differently depending on their relationship to the person with a dual disorder. Spouses, who often drop out of family groups composed primarily of parents, are more likely to remain engaged in a group of their peers (Mannion, Mueser, & Solomon, 1994). Evidence also shows that siblings have views of their brothers and sisters with mental illness that are substantially different from those of their parents (Horwitz, Tessler, Fisher, & Gamache, 1992). Services must be tailored to fit differing needs of family members.

One area of potential conflict between persons with dual disorders and their families is money management. Persons with dual disorders may have a particularly difficult time managing their funds (Drake & Wallach, 1989). Families often become involved as informal money managers or more formally as payees for government programs like supplemental security income or social security disability insurance. Although money management is a frequent subject of disagreement within families, it can be an effective way of reducing substance abuse and relapse rates (Spittle, 1991). Whether or not families are the most appropriate money managers is currently debated, but the fact is that many family members find themselves in that role. Given its potential importance, this issue should be addressed explicitly in psychoeducational interventions for families.

Although research shows that substance abuse has negative consequences for families as well as for persons with dual disorders, families often do not make the connection between substance abuse and these difficulties. In one survey of preferences for additional education, families whose relatives had schizophrenia ranked information on drug and alcohol abuse last on a list of 45 topics; families whose relatives had a major affective disorder ranked the topic slightly higher at 32 out of 45 (Mueser et al., 1992). Other studies show that families often do not see incidents of drug or alcohol abuse as particularly disturbing (Gubman, Tessler, & Willis, 1987; Hatfield, 1978). In contrast, families usually do report behaviors that are associated with substance abuse—such as temper tantrums, violence, or symptom exacerbations—as disturbing or stressful. Thus families' apparent lack of interest in substance abuse problems could stem from their attribution of behavioral problems to the mental disorder rather than to substance abuse.

Just as persons with dual disorders go through progressive phases of treatment readiness, from engagement to persuasion to active treatment (Drake et al., 1993), families may also need to be convinced that the formal treatment system has something helpful to offer them. Many families feel frustrated or disappointed about their relationships with the providers who serve their relatives and may be wary of offers to help (Hanson & Rapp, 1992). An unknown percentage of families have little or no contact with their relatives and therefore may be particularly difficult to engage (Wasow, 1994). A cooperative approach to working with families, one that recognizes and appreciates their knowledge and skills, is needed to establish a trusting, working relationship with families. This does not mean that treatment providers should wait for families to make the first move. An assertive but respectful approach to establishing a relationship with families is likely to be most effective.

Clinical Implications of Family Support

The goals of provider-family relationships are multifaceted. Providers may be able to reduce some of the stress or burden on families by providing timely crisis response and training in management of substance abuse and other behavioral problems. As emphasized in earlier schizophrenia studies, support and education for families can benefit clients by reducing relapse rates and perhaps improving symptoms. Providers can also learn a great deal from families that will help them anticipate crises and generally improve treatment effectiveness. Better provider-family relationships are likely to benefit all parties.

Maintaining family ties is a critically important goal of treatment and rehabilitation that has largely been ignored. Recent research documents the potential life-saving benefits of the basic support that families give. Although the strains that dual disorders place on family relations can cause providers, families, or their relatives with dual disorders to conclude that a respite is needed, the value of maintaining strong family ties should not be discounted.

Informal discussions with treatment providers suggest that they are often unaware of the substantial amounts of direct care and economic support that families give their clients. The reasons for this are not clear. Perhaps their clients prefer to keep such matters private, or perhaps providers do not ask about family support. In either case, the result is that providers may not fully appreciate the vital role that families play in the lives of their clients. Studies indicate that although the amount of family support varies widely, the percentage of families who give direct or financial support is impressive (Clark, 1994; Franks, 1990). Current clinical assessment techniques focus on problems in family relations but are not adequate for documenting family support. Providers may need to make a special effort to understand the extent to which a family gives concrete support to a client. This often means talking directly with the family about the kinds of support they extend in a typical month (see Clark, 1994 or Clark & Drake, 1994 for examples of support categories).

Although the intensity of conflict may lead providers and family members to conclude that a temporary separation is necessary, the potential negative impact of emotional conflict should be weighed against possible loss of family support that can be caused by separation. Indeed, preservation and enhancement of family support systems should be considered an important measure of treatment effectiveness.

Conclusion

Despite the stresses imposed by severe mental illness and substance abuse, families play a critical role in the lives of most persons with dual disorders. That role is broader than the one traditionally afforded them by treatment providers. Family concerns include not only their effect on clinical outcomes and the inevitable difficulties they encounter in caring for a relative with a severe, chronic illness, but also the effects of the direct support they give in the form of time, money, and in-kind gifts.

Although community mental health and psychosocial rehabilitation programs place a high premium on helping persons with severe mental illness to live independently, independence cannot be achieved at the expense of informal social support from family and friends. Improved functioning may reduce reliance on these systems, but evidence from surveys of the general population shows that mutual support among family members throughout the lifespan is overwhelmingly the norm rather than the exception (MacDonald, 1989; Marks, 1993). Perhaps a more fitting goal than independence, one that reflects more accurately the experience of most people, is *effective interdependence.* Such a goal suggests that optimal functioning, or, to use a term from psychosocial rehabilitation, recovery, is not something a person achieves independently but rather in the context of a supportive system. Research suggests that this system is particularly important for the survival of persons with dual disorders. This view has yet to be fully integrated into current treatment interventions for persons with dual disorders. Incorporating services that strengthen family relationships is a challenge that clinicians and policy makers must learn to meet.

References

Anderson, E. A., & Lynch, M. M. (1984). A family impact analysis: The deinstitutionalization of the mentally ill. *Family Relations, 33,* 41-46.

Aneshensel, C. S., Pearlin, L. I., & Schuler, R. H. (1993). Stress, role captivity, and the cessation of caregiving. *Journal of Health and Social Behavior, 34,* 54–70.

Bellack, A. S., & Mueser, K. T. (1993). Psychosocial treatment for schizophrenia. *Schizophrenia Bulletin, 19,* 317–336.

Carpentier, N., Lesage, A., Goulet, J., Lalonde, P., & Renaud, M. (1992). Burden of care of families not living with young schizophrenic relatives. *Hospital and Community Psychiatry, 43*(1), 38–43.

Caton, C. L. M., Shrout, P. E., Dominguez, B., Eagle, P. F., Opler, L. A., & Cournos, F. (1995). Risk factors for homelessness among women with schizophrenia. *American Journal of Public Health, 85*(8), 1153–1156.

Caton, C. L. M., Shrout, P. E., Eagle, P. F., Opler, L. A., Felix, A., & Dominguez, B. (1994). Risk factors for homelessness among schizophrenic men: A case-control study. *American Journal of Public Health, 84*(2), 265–270.

Clark, R. E. (1994). Family costs associated with severe mental illness and substance use. *Hospital and Community Psychiatry, 45*(8), 808–813.

Clark, R. E., & Drake, R. E. (1992). Substance abuse and mental illness: What families need to know. *Innovations and Research, 1*(4), 3–8.

Clark, R. E., & Drake, R. E. (1994). Expenditures of time and money by families of people with severe mental illness and substance use disorders. *Community Mental Health Journal, 30*(2), 145–163.

Dixon, L., McNary, S., & Lehman, A. (1995). Substance abuse and family relationships of persons with severe mental illness. *American Journal of Psychiatry, 152*(3), 456–458.

Drake, R. E., Bartels, S. J., Teague, G. B., Noordsy, D. L., & Clark, R. E. (1993). Treatment of substance abuse in severely mentally ill patients. *Journal of Nervous and Mental Disease, 181*(10), 606–610.

Drake, R. E. & Wallach, M. A. (1989). Substance abuse among the chronic mentally ill. *Hospital and Community Psychiatry, 40*(10), 1041–1046.

Falloon, I. R. H., Boyd, J. L., McGill, C. W., Razani, J., Moss, H. B., & Gilderman, A. M. (1982). Family management in the prevention of exacerbations of schizophrenia: A controlled study. *New England Journal of Medicine, 306*(24), 1437–1440.

Fisher, P. J. & Breakey, W. R. (1991). The epidemiology of alcohol, drug, and mental disorders among homeless persons. *American Psychologist, 46*(11), 1115–1128.

Fox, T., Fox, L. & Drake, R. E. (1992). Developing a statewide service system for people with co-occurring mental illness and substance use disorders. *Innovations and Research, 1*(4), 9–14.

Franks, D. D. (1990). Economic contribution of families caring for persons with severe and persistent mental illness. *Administration and Policy in Mental Health, 18*(1), 9–18.

Gershon, E. S., Delisi, L. E., Hamovit, J., Nurnberger, J. I., Maxwell, M. E., Schreiber, J., Dauphinais, D., Dingman, C. W., & Guroff, J. J. (1988). A controlled family study of chronic psychoses: schizophrenia and schizoaffective disorder. *Archives of General Psychiatry, 45*, 328–336.

Goldman, H. H. (1982). Mental illness and family burden: a public health perspective. *Hospital and Community Psychiatry, 33*(7), 557–560.

Gondolf, E. W., Mulvey, E. P., & Lidz, G. W. (1990). Characteristics of perpetrators of family and nonfamily assaults. *Hospital and Community Psychiatry, 41*(2), 191–193.

Greenberg, J. S., Greenley, J. R., & Benedict, P. (1994). Contributions of persons with serious mental illness to their families. *Hospital and Community Psychiatry, 45*(5), 475–480.

Greenberg, J. S., Seltzer, M. M., & Greenley, J. R. (1993). Aging parents of adults with disabilities: The gratifications and frustrations of later-life caregiving. *Gerontologist, 33*(4), 542–550.

Gubman, G. D., Tessler, R. C., & Willis, G. (1987). Living with the mentally ill: Factors affecting household complaints. *Schizophrenia Bulletin, 13*(4), 727–736.

Hanson, J. G. & Rapp, C. A. (1992). Families' perceptions of community mental health programs for their relatives with a severe mental illness. *Community Mental Health Journal, 28*(3), 181–197.

Hatfield, A. B. (1978). Psychological costs of schizophrenia to the family. *Social Work, 23*, 355–359.

Hoenig, J. & Hamilton, M. W. (1966). The schizophrenic patient in the community and his effect on the household. *International Journal of Social Psychiatry, 12*(3), 165–176.

Hogarty, G. E., Anderson, C. M., Reiss, D. J., Kornblith, S. J., Greenwald, D. P., Javna, C. D., & Madonia, M. J. (1986). Family psychoeducation, social skills training, and maintenance chemotherapy in the aftercare treatment of schizophrenia. *Archives of General Psychiatry, 43*, 633–642.

Horwitz, A., Tessler, R., Fisher, G., & Gamache, G. (1992). The role of adult siblings in providing social support to the seriously mentally ill. *Journal of Marriage and the Family, 54*, 233–241.

Kanter, J., Lamb, H. R., & Loeper, C. (1987). Expressed emotion in families: A critical review. *Hospital and Community Psychiatry, 38*(4), 374–380.

Kashner, T. M., Rader, L. E., Rodell, D. E., Beck, C. M., Rodell, L. R., & Muller, K. (1991). Family characteristics, substance abuse, and hospitalization patterns of patients with schizophrenia. *Hospital and Community Psychiatry, 42*(2), 195–197.

Kavanagh, D. J. (1992). Recent developments in expressed emotion and schizophrenia. *British Journal of Psychiatry, 160*, 601–620.

Kay, S. R., Kalathara, M., & Meinzer, A. E. (1989). Diagnostic and behavioral characteristics of psychiatric patients who abuse substances. *Hospital and Community Psychiatry, 40*(10), 1061–1064.

MacDonald, M. M. (1989). Family background, the life cycle, and inter-household transfers. *National survey of families and households, Working paper no. 13.* Madison, WI: Center for Demography and Ecology, University of Wisconsin, Madison.

Mannion, E., Mueser, K., & Solomon, P. (1994). Designing psychoeducational services for spouses of persons with serious mental illness. *Community Mental Health Journal, 30*(2), 177–190.

Marks, N. F. (1993). Caregiving across the lifespan: A new national profile. *National survey of families and households, Working paper no. 55.* Madison, WI: Center for Demography and Ecology, University of Wisconsin, Madison.

Massey, O. T. & Wu, L. (1993). Service delivery and community housing: perspectives of consumers, family members, and case managers. *Innovations and Research, 2*(3), 9–15.

Maurin, J. T. & Boyd, C. B. (1990). Burden of mental illness on the family: A critical review. *Archives of Psychiatric Nursing, 4*(2), 99–107.

Monahan, J. (1992). Mental disorder and violent behavior: Perceptions and evidence. *American Psychologist, 47*(4), 511–521.

Mueser, K. T. & Glynn, S. M. (1990). Behavioral family therapy for schizophrenia. In M. Hersen, R. M. Eisler & P. M. Miller (eds.), *Progress in behavior modification. Vol. 16.* Newbury Park, CA: Sage Publications.

Mueser, K. T., Bellack, A. S., Wade, J. H., Sayers, S. L., & Rosenthal, C. K. (1992). An assessment of the educational needs of chronic psychiatric patients and their relatives. *British Journal of Psychiatry, 160,* 674–680.

Noordsy, D. L, Drake, R. E., Biesanz, J. C., & McHugo, G. J. (1994). Family history of alcoholism in schizophrenia. *Journal of Nervous and Mental Disease, 182*(11), 651–655.

Pfeiffer, E. J. & Mostek, M. Services for families of people with mental illness. (1991). *Hospital and Community Psychiatry, 42*(3), 262–264.

Reynolds, I. & Hoult, J. E. (1984). The relatives of the mentally ill: A comparative trial of community-oriented and hospital-oriented psychiatric care. *Journal of Nervous and Mental Disease, 172*(8), 480–489.

Ryglewicz, H. (1991). Psychoeducation for clients and families: A way in, out, and through in working with people with dual disorders. *Psychosocial Rehabilitation Journal, 15*(2), 79–89.

Sciacca, K. (1991). An integrated treatment approach for severely mentally ill individuals with substance disorders. In K. Minkoff & R. Drake (eds.), *Dual diagnosis of major mental illness and substance disorder. New Directions for Mental Health Services, no. 50.* San Francisco: Jossey-Bass.

Spittle, B. (1991). The effect of financial management on alcohol-related hospitalization. *American Journal of Psychiatry, 148*(2), 221–223.

Straznickas, K. A., McNiel, D. E., & Binder, R. L. (1993). Violence toward family caregivers by mentally ill relatives. *Hospital and Community Psychiatry, 44*(4), 385–387.

Swan, R. W. & Lavitt, M. (1988). Patterns of adjustment to violence in families of the mentally ill. *Journal of Interpersonal Violence, 3*(1), 42–54.

Tausig, M., Fisher, G. A., & Tessler, R. C. (1992). Informal systems of care for the chronically mentally ill. *Community Mental Health Journal, 28*(5), 413–425.

Tessler, R. & Gamache, G. (1994). Continuity of care, residence, and family burden in Ohio. *Milbank Quarterly, 72*(1), 149–169.

Tessler, R. C., Gamache, G. M., Rossi, P. H., Lehman, A. F., & Goldman, H. H. (1992). The kindred bonds of mentally ill homeless persons. *New England Journal of Public Policy, 8,* 265–280.

Thompson, E. H., Jr. & Doll, W. (1982). The burden of families coping with the mentally ill: An invisible crisis. *Family Relations, 31,* 379–388.

Torres, R. A., Mani, S., Altholz, J., & Brickner, P. W. (1990). Human immunodeficiency virus infection among homeless men in a New York City shelter. *Archives of Internal Medicine, 150*(10), 2030–2036.

Uehara, E. S. (1994). Race, gender, and housing inequality: An exploration of the correlates of low-quality housing among clients diagnosed with severe and persistent mental illness. *Journal of Health and Social Behavior, 35,* 309–321.

Wasow, M. (1994). A missing group in family research: Parents not in contact with their mentally ill children. *Hospital and Community Psychiatry, 45*(7), 720–721.

Winefield, H. R. & Harvey, E. J. (1994). Needs of family caregivers in chronic schizophrenia. *Schizophrenia Bulletin, 20*(3), 557–566.

Substance Abuse and Family Relationships of Persons with Severe Mental Illness

Lisa Dixon, Scot McNary & Anthony Lehman

This article originally appeared in the *American Journal of Psychiatry*, 1995, 152(3) 456–458, and is reprinted with permission.

Lisa Dixon, M.D., M.P.H., Scot McNary, M.A., and Anthony F. Lehman, M.D., M.S.P.H.

Dr. Dixon is at the Department of Psychiatry, University of Maryland, Baltimore, Maryland.

Supported by National Institute on Drug Abuse grant DA-05114.

Objective: The authors sought to determine how substance abuse affects family relationships of persons with severe mental illness. Method: Patient reports of family relationships were compared between 101 psychiatric inpatients with a concurrent substance use disorder and 78 subjects with severe mental illness only. Results: Patients with comorbid substance abuse reported significantly lower family satisfaction and a greater desire for family treatment. Objective indicators of frequency of family contact did not differ. Conclusions: Substance abuse is associated with low levels of satisfaction with family relationships among persons with severe mental illness. Family interventions would meet the stated needs of persons with mental illness and a comorbid substance use disorder and might help to engage them in treatment.

Research has revealed the high prevalence and adverse sequelae of comorbid substance use disorders in persons with severe mental illness (Polcin, 1992). In spite of greater recognition of the value of involving families in the care of family members with severe mental illness (Lam, 1991; Lefley, 1987), little is known about how substance abuse influences the family relationships of persons with severe mental illness.

Clinician assessments of families of mentally ill subjects with a comorbid substance use disorder are inconsistent. Family problems were reported by nurses for over half of 25 inpatients with schizophrenia who abused alcohol (Alterman, Erdlen, McLellan, & Mann, 1980). Substance abuse was significantly associated with clinician ratings of disturbed family affect in 121 persons with schizophrenia (Kashner et al., 1991). Clinicians reported no differences in family relationships between 19 outpatients with schizophrenia and alcohol use disorders and 56 outpatients with schizophrenia alone (Osher et al., 1994).

Studies of the family perspective have been limited. A survey by the National Alliance for the Mentally Ill found that only 18% of respondents reported that drugs or alcohol were problematic (Clark & Drake, 1994). Families of 169 mentally ill patients with a comorbid substance use disorder in New Hampshire spent over $300 monthly on their relative (Skinner, Steinwachs, & Kasper, 1992).

We sought to determine whether individuals with severe mental illness alone differ in their family contact and feelings about their family relationships from individuals with comorbid substance abuse. We expected that persons with a comorbid substance use disorder would report poorer family relationships and less family contact.

Method

The subjects for this study, described in detail elsewhere (Lehman, Myers, Thompson, & Corty, 1993), were drawn from a prospective study of consecutive admissions to two urban psychiatric hospitals—one state operated and the other university operated—from April 1988 to December 1990. Eligible subjects resided in the hospital catchment area, were 18–65 years of age, spoke English, and gave informed consent. The diagnostic assessment used the Structured Clinical Interview for *DSM-III-R* (Spitzer, Williams, & Gibbon, 1987), administered in a face-to-face interview with the patient, and subsequent clinical chart review (kappa=0.81). Questions on the Addiction Severity Index (McLellan, Luborsky, Woody, & O'Brien, 1980) and Lehman Quality of Life Interview (Lehman, 1988), conducted in person by trained interviewers, provided patient perceptions of family relationships. Two types of family questions were considered. The first included patients' reports of *objective* indicators of family relationships such as frequency of contact. The second included patients' *subjective* feelings about their family relationships and the importance they placed on family treatment.

A *DSM-III-R* axis I current primary mental disorder was found in 198 subjects. Complete family data were available for 179 patients, of whom 101 had an additional current psychoactive substance use disorder. Any diagnosis of alcohol or drug abuse or dependence was considered a psychoactive substance use disorder. Group differences between patients with and without a comorbid substance use disorder on subjective and objective family indicators were determined by using analysis of variance. Gender, race, age, education, marital status, diagnosis (schizophrenia versus affective disorder), and a Gender by Drug Group interaction were entered into the equations as covariates. The Bonferroni adjustment required p values lower than 0.02 and 0.008 for objective and subjective indicators, respectively.

There were no demographic differences between the groups except for the higher percentage of men in the comorbid substance use disorder group (65% versus 42% for the group with no comorbid substance use disorder) ($\chi2 = 10.05$, $df = 1$, $p < 0.05$). Sixty-one percent ($N = 110$) of patients were African American, and 59% ($N = 106$) were never married. The mean age of the group was 33.8 years ($SD = 9.9$), and mean number of years of schooling was 10.6 (SD = 2.3). Major depression ($N = 59$), schizophrenia ($N = 48$), bipolar disorder ($N = 41$) and schizoaffective disorder ($N = 19$) were the most common psychiatric diagnoses.

Results

Table 1 shows that patients with a comorbid substance use disorder reported feeling significantly worse about their families and believed obtaining family treatment was more important than did patients with severe mental illness alone. All other subjective indicators of family satisfaction consistently tended to show less family satisfaction among persons with a comorbid substance use disorder, although these variables did not reach statistical significance. Objective family indicators showed no group differences.

Discussion

This study provides empirical evidence that inner-city mentally ill inpatients with a comorbid substance use disorder perceive lower levels of family satisfaction than comparable patients with severe mental illness only. That family treatment was significantly more important to patients with a comorbid substance use disorder suggests that family interventions may help to engage these individuals in substance abuse and mental health treatment. Of note, patients with a comorbid substance use disorder did not report less frequent family contacts, which made their family potentially no less available.

Unfortunately, patients with a comorbid substance use disorder have had limited access to treatments offered to other persons with severe mental illness (Minkoff & Drake, 1991). Recently, the Treatment Strategies in Schizophrenia study (Schooler, personal communication)

Table 1

Objective and Subjective Family Variables for Patients with *DSM-III-R* Axis I Primary Mental Disorders with and without Psychoactive Substance Use Disorders

Family Variable	Patients with Comorbid Psychoactive Substance Use Disorder (N=101)		Patients with Primary Mental Disorder Alone (N=78)		Analysis		
	Mean[a]	SD	Mean[a]	SD	t	df[b]	p
Objective							
Days in conflict with family in last month	2.81	7.78	2.14	7.79	0.59	177	0.55
How often do you talk to your family?[c]	3.80	1.25	4.03	1.25	-1.27	176	0.21
How often do you see your family?[c]	3.74	1.32	3.98	1.31	-1.23	176	0.22
Subjective							
How bothered are you by your family?[d]	1.59	1.72	1.00	1.71	2.42	178	0.02
How important is family treatment?[d]	1.48	1.71	0.82	1.71	2.71	177	0.008
How do you feel about your family?[e]	4.28	1.93	5.10	1.94	-2.97	177	0.003
How do you feel about the frequency of family contact?[e]	4.31	1.90	4.85	1.90	-1.99	176	0.05
How do you feel about family interaction?[e]	3.89	1.98	4.60	1.98	-2.52	176	0.01
How do you feel about your family in general?[e]	4.06	2.05	4.74	2.04	-2.35	176	0.02

a. Means adjusted for gender, race, education, marital status, diagnosis, and Gender by Diagnosis interaction.
b. Ns differ slightly because of missing observations.
c.. 1 = not at all, 5 = daily; scale refers to previous year.
d. 1 = not at all, 5 = extremely; scale refers to previous month.
e. 1 = terrible, 7 = delighted; scale refers to previous year.

and New York Family Psychoeducation Project (McFarlane, personal communication) have offered psychoeducational and supportive family interventions to persons with schizophrenia, which included many patients who abused substances. Sciacca developed MICAA-NON, a substance abuse program analogous to Al-Anon for families who have members who are mentally ill (Sciacca, 1989). Although these groups focus on the family rather than the patient, their role deserves more attention.

The greater rates of substance abuse found in families of persons with mental illness and substance use disorders (Gershon et al., 1988) might present obstacles to family treatment. These families might be more difficult to locate and engage in family interventions. Nevertheless, the identification of family problems and desire for family treatment reported by patients with a comorbid substance use disorder suggest the urgent need to provide such interventions.

References

Alterman, A. I., Erdlen, F. R., McLellan, A. T., & Mann, S. C. (1980). Problem drinking in hospitalized schizophrenic patients. *Addictive Behaviors, 5,* 273–276.

Clark, R. K., & Drake, R. E. (1994). Expenditures of time and money by families of people with severe mental illness and substance use disorders. *Community Mental Health Journal, 30,* 145–163.

Gershon, E. S., DeLisi, L. E., Hamovit, J., Nurnberger Jr., J. I., Maxwell, M. E., Schreiber, J., Dauphinais, D., Dingman II, C. W., & Guroff, J. J. (1988). A controlled family study of chronic psychoses: Schizophrenia and schizoaffective disorder. *Archives of General Psychiatry, 45,* 328–336.

Kashner, T. M., Rader, L. E., Rodell, D. E., Beck, C. M., Rodell, L. R., & Muller, K. (1991). Family characteristics, substance abuse and hospitalization patterns of patients with schizophrenia. *Hospital and Community Psychiatry, 42,* 195–197.

Lam, D. H. (1991). Psychosocial family interventions in schizophrenia: A review of empirical studies. *Psychological Medicine, 21,* 423–441.

Lefley, H. P. (1987). The family's response to mental illness in a relative. In A. B. Hatfield (Ed.), Families of the mentally ill: Meeting the challenges, *New Directions for Mental Health Services, 34.* San Francisco, CA: Jossey-Bass.

Lehman, A. F. (1988). A quality of life interview for the chronically mentally ill. *Evaluation and Program Planning, 11,* 51–62.

Lehman, A. F., Myers, C. P., Thompson, J. W., & Corty, E. (1993). Implications of mental and substance use disorders: A comparison of single and dual diagnosis patients. *Journal of Nervous Mental Disease, 181,* 365–370.

McLellan, A. T., Luborsky, L., Woody, G. E., & O'Brien, C. (1980). An improved evaluation instrument for substance abuse patients: The addiction severity index. *Journal of Nervous and Mental Disease, 168,* 26–33.

Minkoff, K., & Drake, R. E. (1991). *Dual diagnosis of major mental illness and substance disorder.* San Francisco, CA: Jossey-Bass.

Osher, F. C., Drake, R. E., Noordsy, D. L., Teague, G. B., Hurlbut, S. C., Biesanz, J. C., & Beaudett, M. S. (1994). Correlates and outcomes of alcohol use disorder among rural outpatients with schizophrenia. *Journal of Clinical Psychiatry, 55,* 109–113.

Polcin, D. L. (1992). Issues in the treatment of dual diagnosis clients who have chronic mental illness. *Professional Psychology: Research and Practice, 23,* 30–37.

Sciacca, K. (1989). MICAA-NON, working with families, friends and advocates of mentally ill chemical abusers and addicted (MICAA). *TIE Lines, 6,* 6–7.

Skinner, E. A., Steinwachs, D. M., & Kasper, J. A. (1992). Family perspectives on the service needs of people with serious and persistent mental illness, part 1: Characteristics of families and consumers. *Innovations & Research, 1,* 23–30.

Spitzer, R. L., Williams, J. B. W., & Gibbon, M. (1987). *Structured clinical interview for DSM-III-R–patient version (SCID-P).* New York, NY: New York State Psychiatric Institute, Biometrics Research.

The Role of Self-Help Programs in the Rehabilitation of Persons with Severe Mental Illness and Substance Use Disorders

Douglas L. Noordsy, Brenda Schwab, Lindy Fox & Robert E. Drake

This article originally appeared in the *Community Mental Health Journal*, 1996, 32(1), 71–81, and is reprinted with permission.

Douglas L. Noordsy, MD, is Assistant Professor of Psychiatry at Dartmouth Medical School and Research Associate at New Hampshire–Dartmouth Psychiatric Research Center. Brenda Schwab, PhD, is Research Associate at New Hampshire–Dartmouth Psychiatric Research Center and Research Assistant Professor of Community and Family Medicine, Dartmouth Medical School. Lindy Fox, MA is Clinical Interviewer and Trainer at New Hampshire–Dartmouth Psychiatric Research Center. Robert Drake is director of New Hampshire–Dartmouth Psychiatric Research Center and Andrew Thomson Professor of Psychiatry and Community and Family Medicine, Dartmouth Medical School.

Substance abuse treatment programs in the United States frequently incorporate self-help approaches, but little is known about the use of self-help groups by individuals with dual disorders. This paper brings together several current studies on the role of self-help programs in treating substance use disorders among individuals with severe mental illness. These studies indicate that only a minority of individuals with dual disorders become closely linked to self-help. Psychiatric diagnosis and possibly social skills are correlates of participation. Dually disordered consumers often experience the use of 12-step philosophy and jargon by mental health professionals as alienating and unempathic. The authors propose suggestions for incorporating self-help approaches into the comprehensive community care of individuals with dual disorders.

The high prevalence of co-occurring substance use disorders among individuals with severe mental illness is now widely recognized (Minkoff & Drake, 1991). As patients with dual disorders have poor short-term outcomes in traditional mental health programs and do not readily fit into traditional substance abuse treatment programs (Ridgely et al., 1990), models that integrate mental health and substance abuse treatments have been developed (Drake et al., 1991a, 1993a; Hellerstein & Meehan, 1987; Kofoed et al., 1986; Lehman et al., 1993; Minkoff, 1989). Linkage with Alcoholics Anonymous (AA) and other self-help groups for people with substance abuse has been included in many of these models. However, little information is available about how individuals with severe mental illness use these self-help groups.

The purpose of this paper is to report (a) findings from several studies on the use of AA and other self-help groups by patients who have coexisting severe mental illness and substance use disorder, and (b) our clinical observations regarding the use of self-help groups, based on working for several years in dual-disorder programs. The context for these studies and observations is New Hampshire's statewide service program for people with coexisting severe mental illness and substance use disorder (Drake et al., 1990b, 1991a; Noordsy & Fox, 1991).

Research Studies

Treatment of Alcoholism Among Schizophrenic Outpatients

Based on a pilot sample of outpatients with schizophrenia, we have previously reported the rate and correlates of alcohol use disorders (Drake et al., 1990a, 1991b; Noordsy et al., 1991; Osher et al., 1994), and the rate of recovery from alcohol use disorders over a 4-year follow-up period (Drake et al., 1993b). We will present here previously unreported findings on the use of self-help in this study group.

The 18 patients with alcoholism and schizophrenia were treated continuously between 1987 and 1991 in a community mental health center-based dual-disorder program that included intensive case management, substance abuse treatment groups, and linkage with self-help groups in the community. Linkage to self-help was promoted through work on development of motivation to attend meetings, education about the content and format of meetings, transportation, and a "Double Trouble" AA meeting specifically for people with dual disorders held at the mental health center after hours. Patients were reevaluated approximately 4 years after their original evaluation. Alcohol use and street drug use were assessed through a combination of hospital records, mental health center records, psychiatric interviews, case manager ratings, and intensive case reviews to resolve disagreements. Use of self-help programs was assessed by case managers based on client reports, behavioral observations in the community and collateral information from families, community contacts, and other caregivers.

The 11 people who attained full remission from alcohol use disorders as defined in *DSM-III-R* (Remission group) were compared with the 7 people who did not (Active Abuse group). The two groups did not differ significantly at baseline in age, sex, diagnosis, marital status, or the number of months of prior hospitalization. There was a trend towards higher average MAST scores (29.3 vs. 20.6, t (16)= -1.31, p = .21) in the Active Abuse group at baseline.

Of the 18 patients, five (28%) attended self-help meetings during the 4-year follow-up interval, and only one (5.6%) attended regularly (at least once a month). In contrast, 13 (72%) attended specialized dual-disorder treatment groups in the mental health center, and six (33%) attended these groups regularly (most attended nearly weekly). There was a weak trend towards patients being more likely to attend clinician-led groups than self-help groups during the interval (Fisher's exact test, p = .150).

The five individuals with schizophrenia who had attended self-help meetings were all diagnosed with alcohol dependence syndrome and two had co-occurring drug abuse. They had an average MAST score of 28.8. They all attended clinician-led dual-disorders treatment groups in addition to self-help meetings. Four of them were in the Active Abuse group at follow-up. Members of the Active Abuse group were more likely to use self-help during the study interval than were members of the Remission group (Fisher's exact test, p = .047).

An Ethnographic Study of Dual Disorders Treatment

This study reports on the ethnographic component of a randomized clinical trial of standard and intensive case management for persons with co-occurring severe mental illness and substance use disorders (Schwab, 1991). For 2 years, two ethnographers conducted participant observation and qualitative interviews with clients and case managers in both community and treatment settings, including self-help meetings (see Schwab, 1991 and Schwab et al., 1991 for a description of the ethnographic procedures). We will summarize findings on clinicians' efforts to promote self-help attendance, not on the use of twelve-step groups by consumers.

Several clients in this study found self-help programs helpful and were committed to participation. However, many reacted negatively to the use of twelve-step philosophy and jargon by clinicians. Consumers perceived this approach as minimizing the considerable problems they faced in living with their disabilities. One of the central precepts that seemed to contribute to misunderstandings and impasses in treatment was the attempt to challenge denial. Case managers used jargon such as "stinkin' thinkin'" to confront explanations for substance use. Clients were told, "It's your disease talking," to signify that an explanation for behavior was not coming from a client him- or herself; or the phrase, "people, places, and things," was used to refer to a person's blaming other persons or situations for his/her drug use rather than blaming the drug use for causing these problems (Schwab et al., 1991).

One consequence of using these standard responses was that case managers often missed opportunities to explore meanings from the client's perspective and, in some instances, used the concept of denial to discount clients' complaints about aspects of treatment. Clients perceived case managers' use of jargon, particularly in reference to the concept of denial, as a negation of their reasoning. Applying the concept of denial to clients' explanations and statements thus gave many clients the impression that case managers were ignoring their experience and their suffering (cf. Kleinman et al., 1992). Another consequence was that clients would admit to alcohol use and declare their intention to attend AA meetings in order to avoid discussion about their cocaine or other drug use and lack of participation in other aspects of treatment.

Resistance to self-help was seen by some case managers as noncompliance with treatment or failure to accept therapeutic goals and strategies (cf. Estroff, 1991; Kaljee & Beardsley, 1992). Use of standard phrases or statements about self-help participation became a kind of currency used between clients and case managers to negotiate treatment. In such discussions, self-help meeting attendance was treated as if it was a major goal of treatment, rather than a means to an end.

A significant limitation of this study was that the suitability of the model could not be separated from idiosyncrasies in staff characteristics. During the first year of this study, some staff with little addictions treatment training were acquiring experience and expertise on the job. Over time they became more sophisticated at integrating 12-step approaches with other treatment strategies. The ethnographic methods had the power to distinguish one fairly clear finding despite the limitations: when attempting to promote self-help among individuals with dual diagnoses, case managers' use of a monolithic, inflexible approach was experienced as alienating by many clients.

Our observations are consistent with other anthropological findings in a variety of clinical settings. Impasses in treatment occur when clinicians do not explore or share the explanations or meanings patients attribute to their problems (Good & Good, 1981; Katon & Kleinman, 1981; Kleinman, 1981, 1988). Research shows that consumers of psychiatric services have ideas about their illnesses and medications that affect their behavior (Estroff, 1991; Kaljee & Beardsley, 1992; Rhodes, 1984). A more meaning-centered approach (Good & Good, 1981) to the treatment of substance abuse among mental health clients would emphasize listening to clients' explanatory models of their distress, rather than trying to impose a specific model of addiction on them.

Preliminary Findings from Other Studies

This section surveys preliminary findings of two studies that are in preparation. One is a survey of self-help use among a group of individuals with dual disorders treated by case management teams in the community (Noordsy et al., in preparation), and the other is a follow-up of attendees of a residential dual-diagnosis program to evaluate outcomes including self-help use (Bartels, 1992; Bartels & Thomas, 1991).

Preliminary evaluations of these studies show some consistent themes. First, both studies show that few individuals use self-help groups consistently over time, despite the fact that the programs were successful in getting the majority of individuals to attend self-help meetings at some point. Second, diagnosis appears to be associated with intensity of self-help use in these study groups. Regular attendance at self-help programs seems to be more common among individuals with affective disorders than among those with schizophrenic disorders. Third, better social ability appeared to be associated with use of self-help programs.

We expect that these studies will demonstrate that self-help programs can be used by some clients with dual-disorders, although they do not usually participate fully. Social impairment may be an intervening variable between diagnosis and difficulty using self-help intensively, and deserves further study.

Clinical Observations

We have frequently heard from individuals with severe mental illness about their experiences attempting to use self-help groups in the recovery process. Several recurring themes are described here.

Many individuals reported avoiding initial attendance at self-help meetings because of a fear of large crowds and the feeling that everyone would be watching them. Symptoms of mental illness, medication use, and associated side-effects made them feel different from others. Some consumers reported that other self-help members encouraged them to discontinue psychiatric medications because all they needed were meetings.

Individuals who attempted to use self-help programs reported dropping out or finding it hard to make a regular commitment for several reasons. Some stated that once at a meeting they had difficulty sitting still, but felt uncomfortable getting up and leaving. If they were able to listen, many found the stories increased their desire to use substances. They often were unable to relate to the negative side of the stories they heard, as they hadn't experienced the same losses. They usually hadn't had a spouse, job, or car to lose because of substance abuse. Other individuals had difficulty distinguishing the spiritual recovery of 12-step programs from religious themes. Talk of spiritual awakening and advice to "let go and let God" became laden with delusional significance.

Although encouraged to attend self-help in order to develop a sober peer group, many individuals had difficulty finding people whom they felt similar to there. They often reported an inability to relate to others at meetings, and intimidation by the expectations that sponsorship would have placed on them. Their negative symptoms, suspiciousness, and social deficits were often misunderstood and responded to with confrontation. Some consumers who had trouble affiliating with self-help groups in the early stages of treatment attended more regularly in the later stages when they had established an abstinence goal.

Those people with dual diagnoses who were successful in linking to community self-help groups for management of their addiction generally described them as extremely helpful. Some obtained sponsors and got a list of members' phone numbers. They pointed to the network of support, broad availability, and flexibility to speak or just listen. In some instances they were able to talk about not only drug and alcohol problems, but also problems in living and coping on a daily basis. They liked feeling that they were not alone.

The religious aspects of 12-step meetings were very appealing to some clients who had strong religious backgrounds. Some found that the "one day at a time" approach worked for them and liked the routine and structure the meetings brought to their lives. A self-help meeting in one part of town had many of the same elements as a meeting anywhere.

Some of these consumers had accompanied their peers to self-help meetings or helped start special self-help meetings for people with dual disorders. They described being able to help a fellow addict or alcoholic as a very empowering experience.

Discussion

Our data and observations suggest that self-help has an important but limited role in the treatment of substance use disorders among individuals with severe mental illness. We found evidence in several settings that only a small proportion of individuals with severe mental illness attend self-help programs regularly, despite extensive efforts at linkage by their treatment providers. We also found a trend towards greater use of clinician-led dual-diagnosis groups than self-help groups in one study. This supports the view that offering multiple treatment options for substance use disorders is important to comprehensive care for individuals with dual diagnoses (Drake & Noordsy, 1994).

The finding that vigorous attempts to promote self-help as the treatment of choice frequently alienated clients suggests the importance of using client preferences to guide treatment planning. Some clients who refuse self-help group membership initially may join at later treatment stages, which suggests that clients' receptiveness to self-help promotion efforts may vary over time. The finding that active abusers in the first study were more likely to attend self-help suggests that linkage could occur over time for those dually diagnosed individuals who are still struggling with substance use.

Linkage to self-help appears to be related to diagnosis and possibly to social skills, which are also related to diagnosis (Samson et al., 1988). People with affective disorders may have different service needs and preferences than people with schizophrenia, and treatment should be tailored accordingly. Social ability deserves further study as a potential predictor of likelihood to affiliate with self-help groups.

The fact that some consumers affiliated strongly with self-help groups and found them helpful in their recovery indicates that self-help approaches remain a viable treatment option for people with dual-diagnoses. As difficulty fitting-in was a problem cited by many consumers in these studies, self-help groups specific to dual disorders may have some advantage (Bricker, 1994). Double Trouble groups, for example, are self-help meetings based on AA specifically for individuals with dual disorders (Hendrickson & Schmal, 1994). Such groups were available in the mental health centers during these studies on a once weekly basis, but were not otherwise broadly available. The trend towards higher rates of affiliation with clinician-led groups than with self-help in general could reflect the greater presence of peers with dual disorders in the former groups.

Those consumers who did affiliate with self-help cited the importance of a network of support, structure, wide availability, and the option to just listen. Assuming that self-help is not optimal treatment for all consumers, there may be value in investigating the incorporation of these factors into clinician-provided treatment.

It is not clear how the intensity of self-help affiliation found here would compare to a sample without mental illness. Less intensive use of self-help may be optimal for some individuals. Individuals with serious mental illness may be self-selecting a comfortable level of involvement with self-help programs that does not include establishing a sponsor or frequent attendance.

These findings were generated under conditions of considerable support and assistance in using self-help and the simultaneous availability of extensive case management and other substance abuse treatment services. As these studies took place in the context of assertive treatment in residential and community settings in rural and small urban environments, the applicability of these findings to other treatment settings is unknown. The context of treatment initiation in these studies was also different from most substance abuse treatment settings, although typical of work with individuals with severe mental illness. Clients were identified by clinicians and research instruments as having substance abuse problems, often well before they identified such problems themselves.

Clinical Guidelines

These studies suggest that without careful attention to clients' explanatory models and tolerance for intensity of intervention we may have difficulty developing plans for treatment of substance abuse that clients can comfortably participate in. The approach we have developed provides an array of addictions treatment services, including self-help promotion, brought to the individual with mental illness in their natural environment and fit to their needs. Basic needs such as housing (Drake et al., 1991b) and vocational rehabilitation (Becker & Drake, 1994) are attended to in a fashion that supports engagement around substance use issues. Multiple addictions treatment models are tried, with their relative effectiveness guiding further application for each individual. We feel that self-help programs have their greatest potential when chosen by individuals in this context. Suggested guidelines are as follows:

1. Introduce self-help programs as one treatment option that is helpful for many people, and make other treatment options available.

2. Help clients to sample self-help by offering to accompany them to meetings. Help them overcome the social barriers by introducing them to people at the meeting and translating the meeting during and afterwards.

3. Treat the mental illness, addiction and underlying social skills deficits aggressively to increase clients' ability to function independently in self-help.

4. If the client doesn't like self-help, back off. Don't pair yourself so tightly with self-help that the client has to reject you to reject self-help. Use other treatment approaches to help the client make progress and gain trust in you. At later treatment stages gently introduce self-help options again.

5. Encourage attendance at Double Trouble or similar groups when possible to improve member-group fit. Recovering individuals with dual disorders can be helpful in facilitating the affiliation process as well.

Conclusions

We have compiled several perspectives on the role of self-help interventions from our work on the treatment of substance use disorders among individuals with severe mental illness. Collectively these suggest that a minority of consumers with dual diagnoses affiliate closely with self-help programs, that diagnosis and possibly social function are associated with successful linkage, that most achieve remission without using self-help, and that emphasizing a 12-step model with those who don't gravitate to it can be counter-productive. Our clinical experience suggests that self-help programs are experienced as most helpful by consumers when the program philosophy is consistent with their own explanatory models and chosen voluntarily.

References

Bartels, S.J. (1992). *Programming for mentally ill substance abusers.* Washington: Presented at the 145th American Psychiatric Association annual meeting. May 4th.

Bartels, S.J. & Thomas, W. (1991). Lessons from a residential program for people with dual diagnoses of severe mental illness and substance use disorder. *Psychosocial Rehabilitation Journal, 15,* 19–30.

Becker, D.R. & Drake, R.E. (1994). Individual placement and support: A community mental health center approach to vocational rehabilitation. *Community Mental Health Journal, 30,* 193–206.

Bricker, M. (1994). The evolution of mutual help groups for dual recovery. *Tie Lines, 11,* 1–4.

Drake, R.E., Antosca, L., Noordsy, D.L., Bartels, S.J. & Osher, F.C. (1991a). New Hampshire's specialized services for the dually diagnosed. In K. Minkoff & R.E. Drake (Eds.), *Dual diagnosis of major mental illness and substance disorder.* San Francisco: Jossey-Bass.

Drake, R.E., Bartels, S.J., Teague, G.B., Noordsy, D.L. & Clark, R.E. (1993a). Treatment of substance abuse in severely mentally ill patients. *Journal of Nervous & Mental Disease, 181,* 606–611.

Drake, R.E., McHugo, G.J. & Noordsy, D.L. (1993b). Treatment of alcoholism among schizophrenic outpatients: Four-year outcomes. *American Journal of Psychiatry, 150,* 328–329.

Drake, R.E. & Noordsy, D.L. (1994). Case management for people with coexisting severe mental disorder and substance use disorder. *Psychiatric Annals, 24,* 427–431.

Drake, R.E., Osher, F.C., Noordsy, D.L., Hurlbut, S.C., Teague, G.B. & Beaudett, M.S. (1990a). Diagnosis of alcohol use disorders in schizophrenia. *Schizophrenia Bulletin, 16,* 57–67.

Drake, R.E., Teague, G.B. & Warren, R.S. (1990b). New Hampshire's dual diagnosis program for people with severe mental illness and substance use disorder. *Addiction Recovery, 10,* 35–39.

Drake, R.E., Wallach, M.A., Teague, G.B., Freeman, D.H., Paskus, T.S. & Clark, T.A. (1991b). Housing instability and homelessness among rural schizophrenic outpatients. *American Journal of Psychiatry, 148,* 330–336.

Estroff, S.E. (1991). Everybody's got a little mental illness: Accounts of self among people with severe, persistent mental illness. *Medical Anthropology Quarterly, 5,* 331–369.

Good, B.J. & Delvecchio-Good, M.J. (1981). The meaning of symptoms: A cultural hermeneutics model for clinical practice. In L. Eisenberg & A. Kleinman (Eds), *The relevance of social science for medicine.* Boston: |D. Reidel Publishing.

Hellerstein, D.J. & Meehan, B. (1987). Outpatient group therapy for schizophrenic substance abusers. *American Journal of Psychiatry, 144,* 1337–39.

Hendrickson, E. & Schmal, M. (1994). Dual disorder. *Tie Lines, 11,* 10–11.

Kaljee, L.M. & Beardsley, R. (1992). Psychotropic drugs and concepts of compliance in a rural mental health clinic. *Medical Anthropology Quarterly, 6,* 271–287.

Katon, W. & Kleinman, A. (1981). Doctor-patient negotiation and other social science strategies in patient care. In L. Eisenberg & A. Kleinman (Eds.), *The relevance of social science for medicine.* Boston: D. Reidel Publishing.

Kleinman, A. (1981). On illness meanings and clinical interpretation. *Culture, Medicine and Psychiatry, 5,* 373–377.

Kleinman, A. (1988). *The illness narratives: Suffering, healing and the human condition.* New York: Basic Books.

Kleinman, A., Brodwin, P.E., Good, B.J. & Good, M.J. DelVecchio (1992). Pain as human experience: An introduction. In M.J.D. Good, P.E. Good, B.J. Good, A. Kleinman (Eds.), *Pain as human experience: an anthropological perspective.* Berkeley: University of California Press.

Kofoed, L., Kania, J., Walsh, T. & Atkinson, R. (1986). Outpatient treatment of patients with substance abuse and coexisting psychiatric disorders. *American Journal of Psychiatry, 143,* 867–872.

Lehman, A.F., Herron, J.D. & Schwartz, R.P. (1993). Rehabilitation for young adults with severe mental illness and substance use disorders: A clinical trial. *Journal of Nervous & Mental Disease, 181,* 86–90.

Minkoff, K. (1989). An integrated treatment model for dual diagnosis of psychosis and addiction. *Hospital & Community Psychiatry, 40,* 1031–1036.

Minkoff, K. & Drake, R.E. (Eds.) (1991). *Dual diagnosis of major mental illness and substance disorder.* San Francisco: Jossey-Bass.

Noordsy, D.L., Drake, R.E., Teague, G.B., Osher, F.C., Hurlbut, S.C., Beaudett, M.S., Paskus, T.S. (1991). Subjective experiences related to alcohol use among schizophrenics. *Journal of Nervous & Mental Disease, 179,* 410–414.

Noordsy, D.L. & Fox, L. (1991). Group intervention techniques for people with dual diagnoses. *Psychosocial Rehabilitation Journal, 15,* 67–78.

Noordsy, D.L., Kremzner, S.A., Parker J. & Drake, R.E. (in preparation). *Self-help use among dually diagnosed individuals in treatment.*

Osher, F.C., Drake, R.E., Noordsy, D.L., Teague, G.B., Hurlbut, S.C., Paskus, T.S. & Beaudett, M.S. (1994). Correlates and outcomes of alcohol use disorder among rural schizophrenic outpatients. *Journal of Clinical Psychiatry, 55,* 109–113.

Rhodes, L.A. (1984). "This will clear your mind": The use of metaphors for medication in psychiatric settings. *Culture, Medicine and Psychiatry, 8,* 49–70.

Ridgely, M.S., Goldman, H.H. & Willenbring, M. (1990). Barriers to the care of persons with dual diagnoses: Organizational and financing issues. *Schizophrenia Bulletin, 16,* 123–132.

Samson, J.A., Simpson, J.C. & Tsuang, M.T. (1988). Outcome studies of schizoaffective disorders. *Schizophrenia Bulletin, 14,* 543–554.

Schwab, B. (1991). *Explanatory models in conflict: Substance abuse treatment for persons with chronic mental illness.* Chicago: Presented at the American Anthropological Association annual meeting, November 2nd.

Schwab, B., Clark, R.E. & Drake, R.E. (1991). An ethnographic note on clients as parents. *Psychosocial Rehabilitation Journal, 15,* 95–99.

Addictions Services: Support, Mutual Aid, and Recovery from Dual Diagnosis

Alexandre B. Laudet, Stephen Magura, Howard S. Vogel
& Edward Knight

This article originally appeared in *Community Mental Health Journal,* Vol. 36, No. 5, October 2000, and is reprinted with permission.

Alexandre B. Laudet, Ph.D., is Project Director, Co-Investigator, National Development and Research Institutes. Stephen Magura, Ph.D., is Institute Director, Institute for Treatment and Services Research, at the National Development and Research Institutes, Inc. Howard S. Vogel, C.S.W., is Deputy Director, the Mental Health Empowerment Project, Inc. Edward Knight, Ph.D., is Chief Executive Officer, the Mental Health Empowerment Project, Inc.

The work reported here was supported by National Institute on Drug Abuse Grant R01 DA11240-01.

Recovery from substance abuse and mental health disorders (dual diagnosis) requires time, hard work and a broad array of coping skills. Empirical evidence has demonstrated the buffering role of social support in stressful situations. This paper investigates the associations among social support (including dual-recovery mutual aid), recovery status and personal well-being in dually-diagnosed individuals ($N = 310$) using cross-sectional self-report data. Persons with higher levels of support and greater participation in dual-recovery mutual aid reported less substance use and mental health distress and higher levels of well-being. Participation in mutual aid was indirectly associated with recovery through perceived levels of support. The association between mutual aid and recovery held for dual-recovery groups but not for traditional, single focus self-help groups. The important role of specialized mutual aid groups in the dual recovery process is discussed.

Introduction

The rate of co-occurring substance abuse and mental health disorders in the United States ranges between 29% and 59% (Kessler, 1995; Regier et al., 1990). Such comorbidity is associated with poor prognosis and with "revolving door" treatment admissions (Haywood et al., 1995). Recovering from dual diagnosis requires more than abstaining from illicit substances and complying with mental health treatment, although these two steps may be considered necessary. Recovery is a long-term, gradual process that requires time, hard work and commitment; it also requires skills and strategies to cope with novel, sometimes stressful, situations and with painful feelings about the past, such as grief and loss (Baxter & Diehl, 1998). For dually-diagnosed persons, the stress of change may be compounded by many other obstacles including stigma, discrimination, low self-esteem, inadequate education, limited vocational skills, housing and financial resources, as well as possible cognitive impairment, emotional lability and side-effects from prescribed medications. Yet individuals do recover from dual diagnosis, not only maintaining abstinence and emotional stability, but also living independently, being employed and actively involved in the community. Dually-diagnosed individuals need to develop inner strengths and learn new coping skills to negotiate the recovery process successfully.

Social Support

The importance of social support in influencing behavior has been shown in a large number of different contexts. Social relationships have been extensively studied as resources for coping with stress. A considerable body of literature has elucidated the mechanisms through which social support promotes physical and mental health and buffers psychological stresses (Greenblatt, Becerra, & Serafetinides, 1982; Taylor & Aspinwall, 1996; for a review, see Taylor, 1995). Empirical evidence has linked social support to increased health, happiness and longevity (Berkman, 1985; Lin, 1986). In particular, research has shown the positive influence of social support networks on the course of mental illness (Beard, 1992; Goering, 1992; Kelly et al., 1993; Viinamaeki, Niskanen, Jaeaeskelaeinen & Antikainen, 1996). In a sample of clients suffering from clinical depression, higher levels of social support at baseline were found to predict all but the first episode of depression (Brugha, Bebbington, Stretch & MacCarthy, 1997).

Levels and types of social support are also correlates of alcohol and drug use, treatment outcomes and relapses (e.g., Gordon & Zrull, 1991; Mermelstein, Cohen, Lichtenstein, Baer, & Karmack, 1986; for review, see El-Bassel, Duang-Rung, & Cooper, 1998). Social support has been linked to better quality of life, both among substance users and individuals with a mental disorder (e.g., Nelson, 1992; Brennan & Moos, 1990). However, few studies have investigated the effect of social support in the course of dual diagnosis. A pilot study conducted among dually-diagnosed clients reported that combining peer social support with intensive case management was associated with positive outcomes including fewer crisis events and hospitalizations, perceived improvements in quality of life, and physical and emotional well-being (Klein, Caanan, & Whitecraft, 1998; for a review, see also O'Reilly, 1998).

Self-Help/Mutual Aid

The self-help/mutual aid movement, beginning with Alcoholics Anonymous (AA) in 1935, has grown to encompass a wide spectrum of addictions. Self-help groups are based on the premise that individuals who share a common behavior they identify as undesirable can collectively support each other and eliminate that behavior and its consequences. They learn to accept their problem and to share their experiences, strengths and hopes. The only requirement for attending such a group is the desire to abstain from the problem behavior (Alcoholics Anonymous, 1976). Mutual, honest sharing affords participants a forum where often-stigmatized habits can be discussed in an accepting, trusting environment. It also provides a source of strategies to cope with the behavior and an opportunity for more advanced members to become role models to others (White & Madara, 1998). An essential aspect of mutual aid, in contrast to other, more traditional forms of treatment for addictions and/or mental health, is the absence of "professional" involvement; this is experienced by members as encouraging a more active, creative role in their own recoveries (Carpinello & Knight, 1991).

Many, although not all, self-help groups follow some version of the AA 12-step program of recovery emphasizing personal and spiritual growth. Participation in self-help groups in the U.S. is estimated at six million at any one time, with AA participation at 1.6 million (Moos, Finney, & Maude-Griffin, 1993); for chemical addictions, Narcotics Anonymous and Cocaine Anonymous are the two largest self-help organizations (Peyrot, 1985). Self-help groups addressing psychiatric disabilities are growing rapidly (Markowitz et al., 1996); Recovery Anonymous and Schizophrenic Anonymous are the best known (Chamberlin, 1990).

Current evidence suggests that involvement in a self-help group has a positive effect on recovery (e.g., Devine, Brody, & Wright; Humphreys, Huebsch, Finney, & Moos, 1999; McCrady & Miller, 1993; Moos et al., 1999; Timko & Moos, 1997). For example, decreased drinking was associated with AA participation over time (e.g., Emerick, Tonigan, Montgomery, & Little, 1993); increased involvement in 12-step oriented self-help groups was associated with higher proportion of abstinence from drugs and alcohol, less severe distress and psychiatric symptoms, and with higher likelihood of being employed at 1-year follow-up (Moos et al., 1999). The latter findings held for dually-diagnosed clients as well as for those with only substance abuse disorders. Involvement in Recovery, Inc., a mental health peer group, increased general well-being and decreased neurotic distress (Galanter, 1988). Participation in self-help was associated with better self-concept and improved interpersonal quality of life (Markowitz et al., 1996). Longitudinal studies of alcoholics found no difference in outcomes between clients choosing professional treatment versus AA participation, noting a significantly lower cost of treatment for the AA participants (Humphreys & Moos, 1996; Walsh, Hingson, & Merrigan, 1991). For individuals with mental disorders, peer group attendance increased self-confidence and social skills, helped maintain employment, and decreased drugs and alcohol use (New York State Office of Mental Health, 1993).

This article investigates the associations among support (including mutual aid), recovery status, and personal well-being in a sample of dually-diagnosed persons. Based on the empirical evidence reviewed above, the study hypothesized that higher levels of perceived support and longer, more frequent attendance in mutual aid groups would be associated with fewer mental health symptoms and less substance use, as well as with higher levels of personal well-being.

Method

Subjects and Setting

Study participants were recruited from individuals attending Double Trouble in Recovery (DTR) meetings throughout New York City. DTR is a mutual aid fellowship adapted from the 12-step AA program of recovery, specifically embracing those who have a dual diagnosis of substance dependency and mental disorder. DTR was started in New York State in 1989 and currently has over 100 groups meeting in the US. New DTR groups are being started continually, some initiated by consumers, others by professionals who believe that mutual help fellowships are a useful addition to formal treatment, especially for the hard-to-engage dually-diagnosed population. DTR, Inc., a small nonprofit organization, supports this growth by training consumers to start and conduct groups and by providing ongoing support to existing groups. DTR developed as a grassroots initiative and functions today with minimal involvement from the professional community. Groups meet in community-based organizations, psychosocial clubs, day treatment programs for mental health, substance abuse and dual diagnosis, and hospital inpatient units. All DTR groups are led by recovering individuals (for a more detailed discussion on DTR, see Vogel, Knight, Laudet & Magura, 1998).

Procedures

Prospective study participants were recruited at 24 DTR groups meetings held in community-based organizations and day treatment programs throughout New York City. All DTR members who had been attending for 1 month or more were eligible to participate in the study. Groups were visited approximately three times each during baseline data collection. An estimated 14% of group members declined to participate; the main reasons cited for declining to be interviewed were a concern about confidentiality (especially in groups held in a treatment facility), length of the interview (ranging from 2.5 to 3 hrs), and scheduling conflicts (for some individuals attending intensive day treatment programs). [According to group facilitators, DTR members who declined to participate were not newer to the groups or less involved than were those who participated; no mention of concerns about potential breach of anonymity were made either to the researchers or DTR groups leaders.] A total of 310 interviews were completed between January and December 1999. Client participation was voluntary based on informed consent; administration of the baseline instrument took about 2.5 hours; and participants were given a $35 cash incentive.

Measures

The baseline interview is a semi-structured instrument covering sociodemographics and background, mental health status and history, mental health treatment history (including medications), substance use status and history, substance use treatment history, and history of participation in DTR and other 12-step fellowships.

The following measures were used to assess support in the recovery process:

Social support for recovery. After determining through social science database searches that no existing instrument measured adequately the specific social support construct of interest, an instrument was developed to assess support during the recovery process. Scale development is presented in the Results section.

Steady partner support. "Are you currently in a steady relationship and if so with whom? (if more than one steady partner, answer about the one with whom you spend the most time)." Response categories: Legal spouse/common law-marriage; steady male partner; steady female partner; no steady partner. Responses were dichotomized: partner vs. no partner.

Spiritual support. This construct was assessed using an abbreviated, adapted version of the Spiritual Well-Being scale (Ellison, 1983). The 12 most relevant items of the original 20-item scale were retained and scored on a 4 point Likert-type index: 1 = strongly disagree, 2 = disagree, 3 = agree, 4 = strongly agree. Sample items: "my relationship with my Higher Power contributes to my sense of well-being," "I don't have a personally satisfying relationship with my Higher Power." Cronbach Alpha = .85. Higher scores = higher spiritual support.

DTR participation. (a) Length of attendance: "When did you first attend a DTR meeting?" Responses: 1 to 3 months ago; 4 to 6 months ago; 7 months to 1 year ago; 1 to 2 years ago; 2 to 3 years ago; 3 to 5 years ago; over 5 years ago; (b) Frequency of attendance: "How often are you currently attending DTR?" Responses: Less than once a month, once a month, every other week, 2 to 5 times a week, 6 to 7 times a week.

DTR networking. "Do you ever speak to other DTR members about your issues?" Resulting dichotomy: networks with other DTR members vs. does not network with other members.

Attendance at 12-step fellowships other than DTR. "Do you regularly attend meetings at a fellowship or self-help group (such as AA, NA) other than DTR?" List of fellowships: Alcoholics Anonymous, Narcotics Anonymous, Cocaine Anonymous, Al-Anon, Sex Anonymous, Emotions Anonymous, Codependence Anonymous, Gamblers Anonymous, Overeaters Anonymous, Recoveries Anonymous, Other Anonymous (specify).

Involvement with 12-step fellowships other than DTR: An index of other 12-step involvement was created using (a) frequency of attendance for each fellowship attended, (b) frequency of sharing at meetings "(How often do you usually share at meetings?" Never, rarely, sometimes, often, always), and (c) "Do you have a sponsor at (each fellowship attended)." For this index, a higher score represents higher involvement. Although a similar question was asked for DTR, the variable was not entered into the analyses because only 1% of DTR members reported having a DTR sponsor. DTR is a relatively new fellowship, and sponsorship has not been formalized at this time. As more DTR members progress further in their recoveries over time, it is expected that one-on-one AA-style sponsorship will become more frequent.

The following indicators of recovery and well-being were used:

Mental health. (1) Past year—report of mental health symptoms in the past year was obtained from a checklist of 13 items (e.g., "felt nervous, tense, worried frustrated or afraid," "heard voices, heard or saw things that other people don't think are there," and "felt like seriously hurting someone else"); (b) Past month—severity of mental health symptoms in the past month: "Overall, how troubled have you been by mental health or emotional problems in the past month (30 days)?" Responses: 1 = Not at all, 2 = somewhat, 3 = moderately, 4 = very. For both mental health indices, a higher score represents higher mental health distress.

Substance use. (a) Past year: "In the past year, did you use (name of drug)?" (b) Past month: "[For drugs used past year] In the last 30 days, how many times did you use (name of drug)?" For both substance use indices, a higher score represents higher level of substance use.

Personal well-being. This construct was measured using the Personal Feelings of Well-Being subscale of the Quality of Life Enjoyment and Satisfaction Scale (Endicott, Nee, Harrison & Blumenthal, 1993) adapted in language for the present study. The scale consisted of 14 items following the question: "Thinking now about your feelings, in the past month (30 days), how often have you felt (item)." Items were rated using five response categories (never, rarely, sometimes, often/most of the time, all the time). Internal reliability for the resulting scale was high ($\alpha = .93$).

Analytic Procedures

A principal-components factor analysis with Varimax rotation was used for the construction of the "social support for recovery" scale. A three-phase procedure was employed to test the hypothesized associations among support, recovery status and well-being. First, the predictor and outcome variables were included in a bivariate correlation matrix. Next, multiple regression analyses with simultaneous entry were conducted entering as predictors only the variables significantly associated with each of the recovery and well-being indices. Finally, each of the support variables that were significantly associated with recovery and well-being indices in the second stage of the analysis were used as dependent variables in multiple regressions, entering as predictors the other support variables. One-tailed tests of statistical significance are used throughout because directional hypotheses are being tested.

Results

Sociodemographics and Background

The study participants were male (72%) and African-American (58%), Hispanic (16%), non-Hispanic white (25%). Ages ranged from 20 to 63 years of age (median = 39 years). Over one-half (59%) finished high school or obtained a GED. Almost all (95%) reported government assistance as their primary income.

Over one-half (52%) lived in a community residence or apartment program; 21% lived in their own apartment or house; 11% with friends/relatives, 10% in a Single Room Occupancy Residence (SRO) and 6% in a homeless shelter. They were single (62%), separated, divorced or widowed (30%), married or in a common law marriage (8%); and 32% reported currently having a steady partner. Most (91%) had no current involvement with the criminal justice system; 7% were on probation or parole; 2% had a case pending. Six percent reported being HIV-positive.

Drug and Alcohol Use

DTR members' experience with substance use was extensive, starting with their first use at a median age of 14 years. Overall, crack/cocaine has been the primary substance for 42% of members; 34% cited alcohol as primary, 11% heroin, 10% marijuana, 2% "pills" and 1% other drugs. Nearly one-half (47%) reported having used drugs and/or alcohol in the 12 months preceding the interview; 9% reported using drugs and/or alcohol in the past month. (While self-reported drug use was low, there are reasons to believe that it was not generally being under-reported. Participants were in treatment programs where urine samples are collected and many lived in residences with varying degree of supervision. Further, they were members of a 12-step program that places the utmost emphasis on honesty. All these factors were identified as yielding "highly valid" self-reported substance abuse among non-psychotic dually-diagnosed individuals [Weiss, Najavits, Greenfield, Soto, Shaw, & Wyner, 1998].)

Table 1
Support Items and Recovery Indices: Descriptives

Support Items

DTR networking	80%	
Other 12-step fellowship attendance	73%	
Steady partner support	32%	
Length of DTR attendance (months)	Mean = 26	SD = 26
Frequency of DTR attendance	Mean = 2.7*	SD = 6.3
Other 12-step fellowship involvement		
Full sample (N = 310)	Mean = 4.0	SD = 2.9
Fellowship attendees (N = 226)	Mean = 5.2	SD = 2.2
Spiritual support	Mean = 48	SD = 5.3

Recovery Indices

Any substance use past year	47%	
Any substance use past month	9%	
Mental health symptoms past year	Mean = 8.25	SD = 3.5
Severity mental health symptoms past month	Mean = 2.26	SD = .93
Personal well-being	Mean = 3.73	SD = .72

* 2-5 times per week.

Mental Health

DTR members have a long history of mental health symptoms, reporting their first episode in adolescence (median age = 18 years). Almost all (96%) have been diagnosed with a mental health disorder; median age when first diagnosed was 30 years. The most prevalent diagnoses were schizophrenia (43%), bipolar disorder (25%), major depression (26%), schizoaffective (7%), and post-traumatic stress disorder (5%).

Self-Help Participation

Length of DTR attendance among study participants ranged from 1 month to 5 years or more; two-thirds (68%) have been attending for 1 year or more (table 1). The majority of members attend regularly: 37% more than once a week, 60% once a week.

Three-quarters (75%) also attended traditional 12-step meetings: 73% were to AA and 64% to NA. Among those who attended such meetings, level of involvement was low to moderate, averaging (mean) 5.2 on a possible range of 0 to 11. One-half (49%) only reported discussing mental health issues at these meetings. Those who did not attend traditional 12-step groups said that they felt uncomfortable, judged, or not accepted because of mental health issues or medications, or that

Table 2

Social Support Scale: Item Descriptives, Factor Structure and Item Loadings
(N = 310)

	Individual Items		Factor Loadings	
	Mean*	SD	Factor I*	Factor 2**
Factor I: Extent of Support and Understanding in Recovery				
The people in my life are no help at all	1.9	0.7	.79	.12
I'm on my own in my recovery, I don't get any support	1.9	0.7	.71	.03
The people in my life go out of their way to show me support	3.1	0.8	.67	.00
No one in my life really understands me	2.1	0.8	.63	.12
My friends and relatives don't bother with me much	2.2	0.8	.62	.04
The people in my life understand that I am working on myself	3.4	0.7	.59	.18
Service providers do not understand my recovery needs	2.1	0.8	.52	-.07
I get a lot of support from everyone I know	2.9	0.8	.46	.09
Factor II: Sources of Support and Encouragement in Recovery				
Other DTR members are encouraging and supporting me in my recovery efforts	3.7	0.6	.19	.68
Service providers are encouraging/ supporting me	3.7	0.8	.09	.65
Members at fellowships other than DTR are encouraging/supporting me	2.7	1.6	-.10	.62
My roommates/housemates are encouraging/supporting me	2.8	1.6	-.15	.56
My friends are encouraging/supporting me	3.4	1.1	.17	.55
My relatives are encouraging/supporting me	3.1	1.3	.25	.49

*   Cronbach α= .87;
** α = .66.

DTR met their needs; many were not having any problem with drugs or alcohol, such as cravings or slips.

Social Support for Recovery Scale Construction

Support items were developed in collaboration with DTR members consulting on this study, from members' answers to open-ended questions in qualitative interviews reported elsewhere (Vogel et al., 1998) and from what members have been heard to share at open meetings. Principal components factor analysis with Varimax rotation produced

Table 3

Correlations Between Support and Recovery Indices

	Mental Health		Substance Use		
	Past Year	Past Month	Past Year	Past Month	Personal Well-Being
Extent of support and understanding	−.19**	−.15**	−.10*	−.12*	.29**
Sources of support	.20**	−.04	−.12*	−.25**	.09
Length of DTR attendance	−.12*	−.03	−.23**	−.12*	.05
Frequency of DTR attendance	.05	.02	.10*	−.04	.15**
DTR networking	.10*	.06	−.11*	−.07	.00
Other 12-step fellowship attendance	.09	.00	−.07	−.07	−.12*
Other 12-step fellowship involvement	−.03	−.06	−.08	−.05	.05
Steady partner support	.00	−.02	−.08	−.04	.13*
Spiritual support	.02	−.07	−.06	−.03	.18**

*p <.05; **p <.01. All one-tailed.

two interpretable factors accounting for 25.7% and 14.0% of the variance, respectively. The individual item descriptives and factor loadings are presented in table 2. The first factor was labeled "Extent of Support and Understanding of Recovery" and the second factor "Sources of Support in Recovery." Internal consistency was high for the first factor (Cronbach α = .87) and moderate for the second (α = .66); the latter result is not surprising as degree of support may vary considerably across sources (e.g., family, service providers and roommates).

Additional Support Indices

Descriptive findings for individual support variables are presented in tables 1 and 2. DTR involvement (length and frequency of attendance and networking with other members) was high, as was perceived spiritual support (table 1). Members generally reported high levels of social support; in particular, they reported receiving the highest level of support from service providers and from other DTR members (table 2).

Recovey Indices

Findings for recovery indices (table 1) indicated that while drug/alcohol use was relatively low, mental health symptoms were moderately elevated, both in the past year and in the past month. Well-being was generally high.

Association Among Recovery Indices

The correlation coefficients among recovery indices ranged from r = -.02 and r = .41. The indices of substance use and mental health symptoms were moderately correlated within domains (r = .33 and r = .41 respectively) but coefficients across domains were low (ranging from r = .07 to r = -.08). Personal well-being was significantly correlated with the mental health indices (r = -.31 for past year and r = -.33 for past year) and substance use in the past year (r = -.12) but not in the past month.

Associations Among Support, Mutual Aid and Mental Health

Bivariate correlations indicated that greater extent of support was associated with less mental health distress in the past year and past month (table 3). Having more sources of support was associated with mental health in the past year (although not in the expected direction) but not in the past month. Longer attendance at DTR was also associated with less mental health distress in the past year, but not in the past month. Multivariate analyses confirmed the association of both extent (B = .65, p = .002) and sources of support (B = -.65, p = .01) with mental health in the past year; only extent of perceived support was associated with mental health in the past month (B = -.11, p = .05).

Associations Among Support, Mutual Aid and Substance Use

There were significant correlations between social support and substance use (Table 3) such that subjects who perceived high levels of support and more sources of support were less likely to report having used drugs and/or alcohol in the past year and past month. Longer, more frequent attendance at DTR, as well as networking with other DTR members were significantly associated with less substance use in the past year. In multivariate analyses, sources of support and length of DTR attendance were associated with substance use in the past year (B = -.07, p = .02 and B = -.06, p = .03 respectively). Sources of support and length of DTR attendance were also associated with substance use in the past month (B = -.07, p = .00 and B = -.02, p = .03 respectively), as was extent of support (B = -.03, p = .03).

Associations Among Support, Mutual Aid and Well-Being

The extent of support participants reported getting from the people in their lives was the strongest correlate of personal well-being (Table 3). Spiritual support and frequency of DTR attendance were also associated with well-being such that those with higher spiritual support and who attended DTR more frequently were more likely to report higher well-being. There was also a modest correlation between well-being and having a steady relationship. Attending meetings at 12-step fellowships other than DTR was associated with lower reported well-being. In the multiple regression analysis, higher levels of well-being had four significant correlates: greater spiritual support ($B = .04$, $p = .00$), less attendance at other 12-step fellowships ($B = -.29$, $p = .00$), more frequent attendance at DTR ($B = -14$, $p = .02$), and having a steady relationship ($B = -.17$, $p = .04$).

Association Among Support Variables

The Social Support scales (Extent of Support and Understanding and Multiple Sources of Support) were found to be associated with both mental health and substance use. To elucidate the relationship between the social support scales and the other support indices, each of these two support scales was entered as the dependent variable in multiple regression analyses, using the other support variables as predictors. (Other support variables that were significantly associated with recovery indices in Table 3 were included). Greater frequency of attendance at DTR was significantly associated with higher levels of perceived support and understanding ($B = .20$, $p = .02$), while higher networking with DTR members was associated with more perceived sources of support ($B = .46$, $p = .00$).

Discussion

In sum, it was hypothesized that higher levels of perceived support and more participation in 12-step mutual aid groups would be associated with more successful recovery (less mental health symptoms and substance use) and with higher levels of personal well-being. The hypothesized associations among support, dual recovery and well-being were confirmed. The hypothesized associations between participation in 12-step mutual aid and dual recovery were confirmed for dual recovery groups (DTR) but not for traditional 12-step groups. Participation in specialized mutual aid was associated with recovery status indirectly by contributing to perceived levels of support. Personal well-being was directly associated with participation in DTR, and spiritual and steady partner support. The associations were generally moderate, perhaps, in part, because of the skewed distribution of some of the variables (e.g., substance use past month). However, these results are encouraging.

Participants generally reported high levels of support from various sources; in particular, they reported receiving the highest levels of support from both DTR peers and treatment providers. Increases in the number of supportive relationships have been shown to improve quality of life in individuals with mental health disorders (Rosenfield & Wenzel, 1997). In the present study, the various sources of support could intervene at different levels, forming a protective network around participants. For example, DTR peers could share their experiences and coping strategies while treatment providers could offer clinical interventions (such as individual counseling or medication).

Participants' reports of multiple supportive relationships also offered an interpretation for the finding that having a greater number of supportive people was associated with more mental health distress in the past year. While this association seems counterintuitive, an explanation can be proposed for this sample. The majority of study participants lived in settings where various supportive resources are available (community residence, treatment programs, self-help groups). It may be that the number of people offering support increased when the individual was showing signs of mental health distress. According to this interpretation, participants would receive support from several people or sources in their everyday lives, and the number of supports would increase when participants were not feeling well. For example, treatment providers and peers would perceive that more support was needed and would rally around the individual through the crisis and for some time afterwards. The number of sources of support could thus follow rather than precede the crisis. This interpretation is strengthened by the fact that the association between number of supportive people and mental health disappeared when the time frame for mental health symptoms was the past month. Moreover, this interpretation does not contradict or negate the authors' overall conclusion that support enhances the likelihood of recovery; rather, it suggests that recovery from mental health may be associated with having a supportive network that is sensitive to one's need for support at a given moment in time.

The study findings indicate that extent of support is associated with better mental health. Perceived extent of support can be thought of as answering the question: "Am I getting the support that I need?" allowing for the fact that need for support varies. While perceived extent is not the equivalent of satisfaction with levels of support, it can reasonably be interpreted as a measure of the match between need for support and support received. (A large discrepancy between support needed and support received would likely result in low perceived extent of support.) Thus, taken together, the findings suggest that extent of support, that is, support received that matches need, is associated with better mental health.

The association between support and substance use was more straightforward: higher levels of support derived from a greater number of people or sources were associated with less substance use. That support was differently associated with recovery from mental health disorders and addiction suggests that the processes underlying the two recoveries and the role of support networks in each may also be different. It may be that in the case of mental disorders, an imminent crisis is preceded by visible warning signs (e.g., isolation, reported by many DTR members as preceding the recurrence of symptoms) that allow members of one's support group to rally around the individual and "cushion the fall"; in the case of addiction, perhaps because of the strong role of denial, a slip or relapse is not preceded by signs that can be as easily interpreted by members of the support network because the nature of addiction is such that the individual will conceal urges, at least in the early stages of recovery. Empirical investigation of these questions can contribute greatly to understanding the course of the two disorders, particularly in treating dually-diagnosed individuals.

The association between importance of spiritual support and well-being underscores the role of spirituality in the recovery process and calls attention to the need to incorporate spirituality in addiction treatment (for discussion, see Goldfarb, Galanter, McDowell, Lifshutz & Dermatis, 1996). A previous study reported that dually-diagnosed clients view spirituality as crucial to their recovery, and that staff underestimated both clients' level of spirituality and the importance they placed on such issues (McDowell, Galanter, Goldfarb, & Lifshutz, 1996). In the present sample, levels of perceived spiritual support were generally high, which may be expected for individuals who attend 12-step fellowship meetings where spirituality is viewed as the path to recovery.

The results indicate that participating in DTR contributes to dual recovery directly, in the case of substance use, and indirectly, in the case of mental health, by increasing the sources and extent of perceived support. While DTR participation was associated with less substance use, participation in other 12-step fellowships was not, but instead had a negative association with well-being, such that those who attended other 12-step fellowships had *lower* levels of well-being. One possible interpretation of this result comes from participants' reported reasons for attending or not attending such meetings. Reasons to attend traditional 12-step meetings generally centered around drugs and alcohol issues, while one of reasons for not attending was that no group other than DTR was necessary since participants were "not currently having cravings or slips." Traditional 12-step fellowships are single problem-focused and members typically attend such meetings to deal with that specific issue. Thus it appears that DTR participants, many who feel uncomfortable at other 12-step fellowship meetings (Vogel et al., 1998), attend these groups only when they are struggling with drug and alcohol issues and need to focus on that. According to this interpretation, decreased well-being and increased attendance at traditional 12-step groups would not be causally related, but rather would occur simultaneously as a result of a current struggle with addiction.

Vaillant (1983) has described the conditions necessary to the process of recovery as abstinence, substitute dependencies, behavioral and medical consequences, enhanced hope and self-esteem, and social support in the form of unambivalent relationships. These factors may be even more crucial to recovery from co-occurring disorders than for overcoming "simple" addiction or mental disorder alone. As noted, dually-diagnosed individuals are faced not only with a double recovery challenge but may also lack some of the support resources available to those striving to recover from single disorders. The isolation and ostracism associated with having a mental disorder may be compounded by low self-esteem and inadequate social skills, so that a dually-diagnosed person may not be able to reach out for support-indeed, may not feel worthy of it. This is consistent with the finding that two-thirds of DTR members reported starting to use drugs and alcohol in adolescence to fit in with and be accepted by peers, many adding that using substances made them feel normal for the first time (Vogel et al., 1998).

A recent study of the issues challenging dually-diagnosed individuals in recovery found that dealing with emotions and feelings was reported as "very difficult" by the majority of subjects (Laudet, Magura, Vogel, & Knight, 2000). The difficulty of dealing with feelings is understandable for individuals whose addiction is aggravated by mental disorders in which inappropriate affect regulation plays a large role. Dealing with feelings that may have been previously masked by active addiction and addressing feelings associated with entering recovery are crucial issues to work on in recovery. The importance of emotion management is heightened by the fact that how individuals deal with their feelings about the past (e.g., anger, shame, guilt, regret, sadness), the present (e.g., confusion, pain, isolation) and the future (e.g., fear, hopelessness) bears on their sobriety. In qualitative interviews, most subjects asked about slips and relapses to drug use mentioned an emotional cause: loneliness, isolation, and in particular, anger. To cope with these painful, sometimes new, and often confusing feelings, individuals need to explore and express their emotions. Clients with mental disorders function better in treatment climates that are supportive and encourage personal expression (Timko & Moos, 1998). Personal disclosure, the sharing of one's story, is one of the techniques used in group therapy offered at most treatment programs, as well as the hallmark of mutual aid groups. Personal disclosure is difficult and can only be therapeutic in a highly supportive environment where the individual feels that he/she will be accepted and loved, rather than judged, no matter what is disclosed. Unconditional acceptance and understanding are two of the key ingredients members find in self-help groups: personal disclosure among people who share your experience, understand it, and thus will accept you as one of their own.

Involvement in self-help has many recognized benefits, including validating one another's experience, providing a structure for a new sense of self, and helping move from isolation and loneliness to empowerment and reconnection with ordinary life (Baxter & Diehl, 1998). Further, self-help groups based on the 12-step program of recovery, such as DTR, go beyond "simple support" for achieving and maintaining abstinence, offering a forum for members to share information, coping strategies and life skills. For dually-diagnosed persons, the traditional "one-disease-one recovery" 12-step self-help group falls short of meeting their needs because it cannot afford them these benefits. Only a minority of the dually-diagnosed participate in substance use self-help groups, finding them alienating and unempathic (Noordsy, Schwab, Fox, & Drake, 1996). This is also the experience of a substantial minority of participants in this study and present findings show no beneficial association between traditional 12-step attendance and dual recovery. In most cases, many of the critical ingredients of mutual aid, including identifying, bonding, and sharing coping strategies, are not available to dually-diagnosed persons in a traditional 12-step group (for discussion,

Vogel et al., 1998). In the cross-sectional analyses reported here, participation in DTR, a mutual aid group of dually-diagnosed individuals, is associated with recovery from both mental health disorders and substance use through members' perceptions of support. Networking with other DTR members is correlated with greater perceived number of sources of support, and greater frequency of attendance is correlated with greater perceived extent of support.

All data presented here were based on self-report. Further, the findings were based on cross-sectional data; it is thus not possible to establish causation. Alternative interpretations (e.g., that individuals with less severe symptoms and/or substance addiction feel better, go to more meetings and thus receive more support) cannot presently be rejected. Later in the study, however, the analyses will be repeated using baseline data as predictors of 1-year follow-up recovery status and personal well-being. Overall, the fact that the present findings are consistent with those of previous empirical studies of support and mutual aid is encouraging.

References

Alcoholics Anonymous (1976). *Alcoholics anonymous: the story of how many thousands of men and women have recovered from alcoholism. (3rd ed.).* NY: Alcoholics Anonymous World Services Inc.

Baxter, E. & Diehl, S. (1998) Emotional stages: Consumers and family members recovering from the trauma of mental illness. *Psychiatric Rehabilitation Journal, 21*(4), 349–355.

Beard, M. L. (1992). Social networks. *Psychosocial Rehabilitation Journal, 16,* 111-116.

Berkman, L. F. (1985) The relationship of social networks and social support to morbidity and mortality. In S. Cohen and S. Syme (Eds.) *Social support and health.* Orlando, FL: Academic Press, pp. 241–262.

Brennan, P. L. & Moos, R. H. (1990). Life stressors, social resources, and late-life problem drinking. *Psychology and Aging, 5,* 491–501.

Brugha, T. S., Bebbington, P. E., Stretch, D., & MacCarthy, B. (1997). Predicting the short-term outcome of first episodes and recurrences of clinical depression: A prospective study of life events, difficulties and social support networks. *Journal of Clinical Psychiatry, 58*(7), 298–306.

Carpinello, S. E. & Knight, E. L. (1991) *A qualitative study of the perceptions of the meaning of self-help by self-help group leaders, members, and significant others.* New York State Office of Mental Health Bureau of Evaluation and Services Research.

Chamberlin, J. (1990). The ex-patients movement: Where we've been and where we're going. *Journal of Mind and Behavior, 11,* 323–336.

Cobb, S. (1976). Social support as a moderator of life stress. *Psychosomatic Medicine, 38*(5), 300–314.

Devine, J., Brody, C., & Wright, J. Evaluating and alcohol and drug program for the homeless: An econometric approach. *Evaluation and Program Planning, 20,* 205–215.

El-Bassel, N., Duan-Rung, C. & Cooper, D. (1998) Social support and social network profiles among women in methadone. *Social Service Review,* 379–401.

Ellison, C. W. (1983) Spiritual well-being. Conceptualization and measurement. *Journal of Psychology and Theology, 11*(4), 330–340.

Emrick, C. D., Tonigan, J.S., Montgomery, H., & Little, L. (1993). Alcoholics Anonymous: What is currently known? In B. McCrady & W. R. Miller (Eds.), *Research on Alcoholics Anonymous: Opportunities and alternatives,* pp. 41–78.

Endicott, J., Nee, J., Harrison, W., & Blumenthal, R. (1993). Quality of Life Enjoyment and Satisfaction Questionnaire: A new measure. *Psychopharmacology Bulletin, 29,* 321–326.

Flaherty, J. A., Gaviria, F. M., Black, E. M., Altman, E., & Mitchell, T. (1983) The role of social support in the functioning of patients with unipolar depression. *Amercian Journal of Psychiatry, 140,* 473–476.

Galanter, M. (1988). Zealous self-help groups as adjuncts to psychiatric treatment: A study of Recovery, Inc. *American Journal of Psychiatry, 145,* 1248–1272.

Goering, P., Durbing, J., Foster, R., Boyles S., Babiak, T., & Lancee, B. (1992). Social networks of residents in supportive housing. *Community Mental Health Journal, 28*(3), 199–214.

Goldfarb, L., Galanter, M., McDowell, D., Lifshutz, H., & Dermatis, H. (1996). Medical students' and patients' attitudes toward religion and spirituality in the recovery process. *American Journal of Drug and Alcohol Abuse, 22*(4), 549–561.

Gordon, A. & Zrull, M. (1991). Social networks and recovery: One year after inpatient treatment. *Journal of Substance Abuse Treatment, 8,* 141–152.

Greenblatt, M., Becerra, R. M., & Serafetinides, E. (1982). Social networks and mental health: An overview. *Amercian Journal of Psychiatry, 139,* 977–984.

Hawkins, J. & Fraser, M. (1987). The social network of drug abusers before and after treatment. *International Journal of the Addictions, 22*(4), 343–355.

Haywood, T.W., Kravitz, H., Grossman, L., Cavanaugh, J.L., Davis, J. M., & Lewis, D. A. (1995). Predicting the "revolving door" phenomenon among patients with schizophrenic, schizoaffective and affective disorders. *American Journal of Psychiatry, 152,* 856–861.

Hoffman, N. G., Harrison, P. A., & Belile, C. A. (1983). Alcoholics Anonymous after treatment: Attendance and abstinence. *International Journal of the Addictions, 18,* 311–318.

Humphreys, K. & Moos, R. (1996). Reduced substance abuse-related health care costs among voluntary participants of Alcoholics Anonymous. *Psychiatric Services, 47,* 709–713.

Humphreys, K., Huebsch, P., Finney, J., & Moos, R. (1999) A comparative evaluation of substance abuse treatment: V. Substance abuse treatment can enhance the effectiveness of self-help groups. *Alcoholism: Clinical and Experimental Research, 23*(3), 558–563.

Kelly, J., Murphy, G., Bahr, G., Kalichman, M., Morgan, M., Stevenson, L., Koob, J., Brasfield, T., & Bernstein, B. (1993). Outcome of cognitive-behavioral and support group brief therapies for depressed, HIV infected persons. *American Journal of Psychiatry, 150,* 1679–1686.

Kessler, R. C. (1995) The national comorbidity survey: Preliminary results and future directions. *International Journal of Methods in Psychiatric Research, 5,* 139–151.

Khantzian, E. J. & Mack, J. E. (1994). How AA works and why it's important for clinicians to understand. *Journal of Substance Abuse Treatment, 11*(2), 77–92.

Kyrouz, E. & Humphreys, K. (1997). *A review of research on the effectiveness of self-help mutual aid groups.* The Mental Health Network.

Laudet, A., Magura, S., Vogel, H., & Knight, E. (in press). Recovery challenges among dually diagnosed individuals. *Journal of Substance Abuse Treatment.*

Lin, N. Conceptualizing social support. In N. Lin, A. Dean and W. Ensel (Eds.) *Social support, life events and depression.* New York: Academic Press, pp. 17–30.

Markowitz, F., DeMasi, M., Carpinello, S., Knight, E.,Videka-Sherman, L., & Sofka, C. (1996). *The role of self help in the recovery process.* Paper presented at the 6th Annual National Conference on State Mental Health Agency Services Research and Program Evaluation, Arlington, VA.

McCrady, B. S. & Miller, W. R. (1993). *Research on Alcoholics Anonymous.* Alcohol Research Documentation, Inc.

McDowell, D., Galanter, M., Goldfarb, L., & Lifshutz, H. (1996). Spirituality and the treatment of the dually-diagnosed: An investigation of patient and staff attitudes. *Journal of Addictive Diseases, 15*(2), 55–68.

Mein, A., Cnaan, R., & Whitecraft, J. (1998). Significance of peer social support with dually-diagnosed clients: Findings from a pilot study. *Research on Social Work Practice, 8*(5), 529–551.

Mermelstein, R., Cohen, S., Lichentenstein, E., Baer, J., & Karmack, T. (1986). Social support and smoking cessation and maintenance. *Journal of Consulting and Clinical Psychology, 54,* 447–453.

Moos, R., Finney, J., Ouimette, P. C. and Suchinsky, R. (1999). A comparative evaluation of substance abuse treatment: I. treatment orientation, amount of care, and 1-year outcomes. *Alcoholism: Clinical and Experimental Research, 23*(3), 529–536.

Moos, R. H., Finney, J., & Maude-Griffin, P. (1993). The social climate of self-help and mutual support groups: assessing group implementation, process, and outcome. In B. McCrady & W. R. Miller (Eds.), *Research on Alcoholics Anonymous: Opportunities and alternatives,* pp.251–276.

Nelson, G., Hall, G. B., Squire, D., & Walsh-Bowers, R. (1992). Social network transactions of psychiatric patients. *Social Science and Medicine, 34,* pp. 433–445.

New York State Office of Mental Health (1993). *Commissioner's report.*

Noordsy, D., Schwab, B., Fox, L., & Drake, R. (1996). The role of self-help programs in the rehabilitation process of persons with severe mental illness and substance use disorders. *Community Mental Health Journal, 32*(l), 71–81.

O'Reilly, P. (1998). Methodological issues in social support and social network research. *Social Science and Medicine, 26*(8), 863–873.

Peyrot, M. (1985). Narcotics Anonymous: Its history, structure, and approach. International Journal of Addiction, 20(10), 1509–1522.

Regier, D. A., Farmer, M. E., Rae, D. S., Locke, B. Z., Keith, S. J., Judd, L. L., & Goodwin, F. K. (1990) Comorbidity of mental disorders with alcohol and other drug abuse. *JAMA, 264,* 2511–2518.

Rosenfield, A. & Wenzel, S. (1997) Social networks and chronic mental illness: A test of four perspectives. *Social Problems, 44*(2), 200–216.

Taylor, S. E. & Aspinwall, L. G. (1996) Mediating and moderating processes in psychosocial stress. In: Kaplan, H.B. (Ed.) *Psychosocial stress.* Academic Press, New York, pp. 71–110.

Timko, C. & Moos, R. H. (1998). Outcomes of the treatment climate in psychiatric and substance abuse program. *Journal of Clinical Psychology, 54*(8), 1137–1150.

Timko, C., Finney, J., Moos, R., & Moos, B. (1995). Short-term treatment careers and outcome of previously untreated alcoholics. *Journal of Studies on Alcoholism, 56,* 597–610.

Vaillant, G. E. (1983). *The natural history of alcoholism.* Cambridge, MA: Harvard University.

Viinamaeki, H., Niskanen, L., Jaeaeskelaeinen, J., & Antikainen, R. (1996). Factors predicting psychosocial recovery in psychiatric patients. *Acta Psychiatrica Scandinavica,* 94(5), 365–371.

Vogel, H. S., Knight, E., Laudet, A. B., & Magura, S. (1998). Double Trouble in Recovery: Self help for the dually-diagnosed. *Psychiatric Rehabilitation Journal, 21*(4), 356–364.

Walsh, D., Hingson, R., & Merrigan, D. (1991). A randomized trial of treatment options for alcohol-abusing workers. *The New England Journal of Medicine, 325*(11), 775–782.

Weiss, R., Najavits, L., Greenfield, S., Soto, J., Shaw, S., & Wyner, D. (1998). Validity of substance use self-reports in dually-diagnosed outpatients. *American Journal of Psychiatry, 155*(1), 127–128.

White, B. J., & Madara, E. J. (1998). *Self-help sourcebook online.* American Self-Help Clearing House. Mental Health Net.

Double Trouble in Recovery: Self-Help for People with Dual Diagnoses

Howard S. Vogel, Edward Knight, Alexandre B. Laudet & Stephen Magura

This article originally appeared in *Psychiatric Rehabilitation Journal*, 1998, 21(4), and is reprinted with permission.

Howard S. Vogel, C.S.W., C.A.S.A.C., is with the Mental Health Empowerment Project, Albany, New York. Edward Knight, Ph.D, is with the Mental Health Empowerment Project, Albany, New York. Alexandre B. Laudet, Ph.D., is with the National Development And Research Institutes, Inc., New York, New York. Stephen Magura, Ph.D., is with the National Development And Research Institutes, Inc., New York, NY.

Self-help is gaining increased acceptance among treatment professionals as the advent of managed care warrants the use of cost-effective modalities. Traditional "one disease-one recovery" self-help groups cannot serve adequately the needs of the dually diagnosed. This article discusses Double Trouble in Recovery (DTR), a 12-step self-help group designed to meet the special needs of those diagnosed with both a psychiatric disability and a chemical addiction. DTR differs from traditional self-help groups by offering people a safe forum to discuss their psychiatric disabilities, medication, and substance abuse. Preliminary data collected at four DTR sites in NYC indicate that DTR members have a long history of psychiatric disabilities and of substance abuse, and extensive experience with treatment programs in both areas. They are actively working on their recovery, as evidenced by their fairly intensive attendance at DTR. Recent substance use is limited, suggesting that participation in DTR (in conjunction with formal treatment when needed) is having a positive effect. Most members require medication to control their psychiatric disabilities, and that alone may make attendance at "conventional" 12-step groups uncomfortable. Ratings of statements comparing DTR to other 12-step meetings suggest that DTR is a setting where members can feel comfortable and safe discussing their dual recovery needs.

Introduction

There is a high prevalence of persons diagnosed with both a psychiatric disability and a chemical dependency in the United States, as evidenced by both epidemiological data and studies of treatment-seekers in substance abuse and mental health programs (Dixon, Haas, Weiden, Sweeney & Frances, 1991; Gawin & Kleber, 1985; Greenfield, Weiss & Tohen, 1995; Hesselbrock, Meyer & Keener, 1985; Kleinman, Miller & Millman, 1990; Marlowe et al., 1995; Mirin, Weiss & Michael, 1988; Rounseville, Anton & Carroll, 1991; Rounseville, Kosten, Weissman & Kleber, 1986; Rounseville, Weissman, Kleber & Wilber, 1982; Weiss et al., 1986). There is also evidence that those with lifetime comorbidity are more likely than those with a single disorder to experience major impairments in economic roles (e.g., unemployment, financial problems) and social roles (e.g., social isolation, interpersonal conflicts; see Kessler, 1995).

Formal treatment and traditional self-help groups have fallen short of meeting the special needs of the dually diagnosed. In this paper, we discuss Double Trouble in Recovery (DTR), an innovative 12-step self-help program designed specially to meet the needs of persons in dual recovery. Preliminary findings about DTR are presented and discussed.

Formal Services and Their Limitations

Comorbidity has many far-reaching treatment implications. There is evidence that comorbid disorders are more severe and chronic than single, "pure" psychiatric disorders (Hagnell & Grasbeck, 1990; Hirschfeld, Hasin, Keller, Endicott & Wunder, 1990; Kessler, 1995; Murphy, 1990). Comorbidity is a predictor of negative treatment outcomes among substance abusers (Brooner et al., 1990; McLellan, Luborsky, Woody, O'Brien & Druley, 1983; Rounseville et al., 1986; Rutherford, Cacciola & Alterman, 1994; Walker, Donovan, Kiivahan & O'Leary, 1983). Among mental health clients, particularly persons with schizophrenia, a comorbid addiction is associated with a variety of negative consequences including noncompliance with mental health treatment and medication, higher rehospitalization and emergency room visits, the need for higher dosages of neuroleptics, housing problems and homelessness, criminality and violence, suicide attempts, and increased fluctuation and severity of psychiatric symptoms (Bartels et al., 1993; Bergman & Harris, 1985; Mueser, Bellack & Blanchard, 1992; Osher & Kofoed, 1989; Osher et al., 1994; Westermeyer & Walzer, 1975). Another crucial consideration in servicing the dually diagnosed is the interaction between street drugs and medication (for a review, see Ziedonis & Fisher, 1994). The dually diagnosed thus present a greater challenge to service providers than do singly-diagnosed individuals. Consequently, perhaps, many dually diagnosed clients are excluded from services because the providing agency does not know how to deal with such cases: It is not rare to see psychiatric disabilities among the exclusion criteria for admission in a substance abuse treatment program; similarly, many mental health providers may not serve clients with an addictive disorder.

Both clinical observation and formal research have shown the complexity of the relationships between substance abuse and psychiatric disabilities (Drake, 1995; Lehman, Myers & Corty, 1989, Lehman, Myers, Dixon & Johnson, 1994; Meyer, 1988; Nunes & Deliyannides, 1993). Although the reasons for initial onset of substance use or psychiatric symptoms may vary, careful investigations have found that in some cases substance abuse and mental disorders begin to reinforce each other, while in other cases they describe a relatively autonomous course (Hein, Zimberg, Weissman, First & Ackerman, 1993; Lehman, et al., 1994). Thus, remediating either the substance use or mental disorder will often not automatically resolve the other. Recent research indicates that two thirds of dually diagnosed persons appear to have dual primary diagnoses, that these disorders interact, and that the goal of recovery in these cases is synonymous with dual recovery (Hein et al., 1993). Mental health providers are becoming more aware of the need to address dual recovery issues holistically (for a review, see Rosenthal, Hellerstein & Miner, 1992). However, recovery is a lifelong process and clients need long-term continuing care beyond program completion. Community-based self-help groups are often included in aftercare planning for discharge from an inpatient treatment program, and used as a complement to formal treatment for clients attending outpatient (day) treatment programs.

Self-Help Programs

The self-help movement, beginning with Alcoholics Anonymous (AA) in 1935, has grown to encompass a wide spectrum of addictions. Participation in self-help groups in the U.S. is estimated at six million at any one time, with AA participation at 1.6 million (Moos, Finney & Maude-Griffin, 1993); for chemical addictions, Narcotics Anonymous and Cocaine Anonymous are the two largest self-help organizations (Peyrot, 1985). Although relatively new, self-help groups addressing psychiatric disabilities are growing rapidly (Markowitz et al., 1996);

Recovery Anonymous and Schizophrenic Anonymous are the best known (Chamberlin, 1990).

Self-help groups are based on the premise that a group of individuals who share a common behavior they identify as undesirable can collectively support each other and eliminate that behavior. They learn to accept their problem, and share their experiences, strengths, and hopes. The only requirement for attending a given self-help group is the desire to abstain from the problem behavior. This mutual, honest sharing affords participants a forum where often stigmatized habits can be discussed in an accepting, trusting environment. It also provides a source of strategies to cope with the behavior and an opportunity to help others by sharing experiences and becoming a helper and a role model to others. Most self-help groups follow some version of the 12-step model originally developed by the founders of AA. One of the essential aspects of self-help, in contrast to other, more traditional forms of treatment for addictions, is the absence of "professional" involvement. Individuals come together to share with one another and to help one another—an active, self-enhancing role—instead of being viewed as service recipients, a passive and often demeaning role in our society.

There is little research on self-help; the anonymity of participants makes formal study difficult and little is known about the "effectiveness" of self-help (noted exceptions include Khantzian & Mack, 1994; McCrady & Miller, 1993; Ogborne, 1993). Most research studies have been conducted with AA groups, and have been limited in scope and plagued with methodological shortcomings; overall, empirical research in the area is sparse and inconclusive (Watson, Hamcock, Gearhart, Mendez, Malovrh & Raden, 1997). The recent changes in the health care system and the advent of managed care are converging to make self-help increasingly attractive to service providers who are beginning to recognize it as a potentially cost-effective treatment modality, especially when combined with formal treatment or as aftercare. Despite the paucity of formal effectiveness studies, there is evidence that involvement in a self-help group has a positive effect on recovery: Decreased drinking is associated with AA participation over time (see Emrick, Tonigan, Montgomery & Little, 1993, Hoffman, Harrison & Belile, 1983; Pettinati, Sugerman, DiDonato & Maurer, 1982); increased general well-being and decreased neurotic distress are associated with involvement in Recovery, Inc., a mental health group (Galanter, 1988); further, participation in self-help is associated with better self-concept and improved interpersonal quality of life (Markowitz et al., 1996). There seems little doubt that self-help (especially AA, the acknowledged parent of 12-step) has directly and indirectly set millions of individuals worldwide on the path to recovery.

Limitations of Traditional Self-Help for the Dually-Diagnosed

Traditional self-help groups are based on the premise of one disease, one recovery. This specialization allows group participants to feel understood and accepted. For individuals dealing with more than one illness, however, particularly individuals dually diagnosed with a psychiatric disability and a chemical addiction, such groups often fall short of meeting their needs. This is especially true as it relates to social/emotional support and learning/skills development, two crucial ingredients in self-help. Identifying and bonding with other members is difficult because the experiences associated with dual diagnosis are not shared experiences. Direction and personal guidance from others cannot be obtained, or may be uninformed or misguided. Dually diagnosed members have difficulty following the essential, highly valued norms of openness and honesty about themselves: there is a danger of eventually minimizing, denying, or ignoring the "other half" of their recovery needs. The societal stigma associated with dual diagnosis may become reinforced in the group and internalized. Dually diagnosed persons who are newcomers to 12-step meetings often find them bewildering, anxiety-provoking experiences, leading these persons to discontinue their participation (Vogel, 1993).

Another area where traditional 12-step groups do not meet adequately the recovery needs of the dually diagnosed is that of prescribed medications. Dually diagnosed members report receiving misguided advice about psychiatric illness and the use of medication in 12-step substance abuse groups (Hazelden, 1993). Although AA as an organization neither endorses nor prohibits use of psychiatric medications, the Alcoholics Anonymous World Service has been quite open about the limitations of AA. Many individual traditional 12-step groups and members have taken an anti-medication stance and believe that those taking medications should not speak at meetings or otherwise participate fully. This view has resulted in members stopping their medication, with consequent psychiatric breaks as well as guilt and shame in being "dependent" on medication (Alcoholics Anonymous World Services, 1984;

Bean-Bayog, 1993). An analogous situation occurs in mental health recovery groups, where the "secondary shame" of substance abuse often is insufficiently recognized and addressed (Zaslav, 1993).

In sum, when self-help is a part of the treatment plan for the dually diagnosed, traditional 12-step meetings are often not fully adequate as their benefits for members may be offset by inner conflict. Dual recovery does not fall into their primary goals, and it has become clear that dual disorders cannot be divided into simple and separate parts; a holistic approach is required to deal with two or more linked, interacting recovery needs. Recognizing these limitations, self-help groups for dually diagnosed persons have been emerging in the past decade and are intended to overcome the problems encountered in traditional single-purpose groups. In contrast to the approach in substance abuse groups, in groups for dually diagnosed persons the issues of mental disorders, medication, psychiatric hospitalizations and experiences with the mental health system can be dealt with openly. In contrast to the approach in many mental health groups, in groups for dually diagnosed persons the issues of drug and alcohol dependence can be discussed without shame (Zaslav, 1993). These specialized self-help groups generally follow the AA 12-step process and are intended to be led by a recovering individual. As put forth by Caldwell and White (1991), the groups follow one of three models ranging from traditional self-help recovery group to support/engagement model with staff participation.

Double Trouble in Recovery

Double Trouble in Recovery (DTR) is a mutual aid program adapted from the 12-step method of AA, which specifically embraces those who have a dual diagnosis of substance abuse/dependency and psychiatric disability. The fellowship was spearheaded in New York State by the first author in 1989 out of his own experiences in dual recovery. Having attended traditional 12-step meetings for his addictions, he found that existing groups were not suitable for those with added psychiatric disabilities who have problems unaddressed and often stigmatized in traditional 12-step programs (e.g., psychiatric symptoms, taking medications, dealing with medication side effects). DTR developed as a grassroots initiative, from one individual to one group and growing; over the years and throughout its growth, it has kept and promises to keep this grassroots bend with which consumers feel at ease, thus reinforcing (or perhaps contributing to) the benefits of the fellowship. DTR was developed and functions today with minimal involvement from the professional community. All DTR groups are led by recovering individuals, even where groups are held in institutional settings.

From the first group formed in New York City in 1989, DTR has grown and spread nationwide by word of mouth, and recommendations from social workers and therapists, as well as through conferences and workshops. Currently, there are over 100 DTR groups in the US (47 in New York City). New DTR groups are being started constantly, some as a consumers' initiative, others at the behest of professionals who feel that mutual help fellowships are a useful addition to formal treatment, especially for the hard-to-engage population of the dually diagnosed. In the last 3 years, there has been on average at least one new DTR group started each month. This rate of expansion promises to continue or even increase, particularly since large managed-care companies nationwide are expressing interest in adding a self-help component to the menu of services offered to their client companies. DTR, Inc., a small nonprofit organization, supports this growth by training consumers as group facilitators on how to start a DTR group, and by providing ongoing support to existing groups.

DTR is not the only self-help dual-recovery program; other organizations with similar goals include Dual Recovery Anonymous (DRA) and Dual Disorders Anonymous. At this writing however, the authors have been unable to locate an organization with ongoing group meetings in the New York area (where the need is so great) other than DTR. Experience tells us that it is difficult to maintain such specialized fellowships, perhaps more so than for those with a single diagnosis focus; mundane issues such as funding and organization must be addressed and can become insurmountable obstacles for a fellowship of individuals whose own existence is often at risk, dealing not only with psychiatric disabilities and chemical dependency but also with community residence living, entitlements and so on. There are also a few dual-diagnosis meetings conducted under the auspices of Alcoholics Anonymous, most often in halfway houses, according to AA (Alcoholics Anonymous General Services, March 25, 1997, personal communication), these meetings are not considered "groups" and are excluded from the meeting list, as their purpose is perceived to depart from AA's primary goal of sobriety; some states do include such meetings on their list however. As to empirical findings on the effectiveness of self-help for the dually diagnosed, a literature search of the social sciences databases proved fruitless.

While no outcome data on DTR are yet available, two preliminary studies were conducted in preparation for a full-scale evaluation. (A 3¹/₂-year, NIDA-funded longitudinal study began in early 1998.)

Preliminary Findings

Study One

This study was designed to obtain background information about DTR members, including sociodemographics, psychiatric and substance use history, and treatment experiences. The instrument was a two-page anonymous, structured, self-administered questionnaire. A sample (N = 52) was obtained by recruiting participants at four DTR meetings in New York City in June–September 1996. Three were established 5, 3, and 2.5 years ago; the fourth had started 1 month previously. The four sites, in the aggregate, were designated as approximately representative of the overall DTR membership by DTR's executive director. By observation, 90% or more of the attendees at each group completed the questionnaire, suggesting that this sample was representative of the population from which it was drawn.

Sociodemographics. DTR members are predominantly male (73%) and ethnically diverse: African American (45%), Hispanic (22%), non-Hispanic white (33%). Members' ages range from 22 to 67 (median = 42). Sixteen percent of the sample graduated from college, 28% attended college but did not graduate, 22% graduated high school or the equivalent, while 34% did not. Forty-four percent are currently employed (22% full-time, 22% part-time), 16% are disabled, and 37% are not employed.

Substance use.

1. Ever used: DTR's members' experience with drugs is extensive: 58% have used cocaine, 50% crack, 31% heroin, 81% alcohol, 37% non-prescribed pills to get high, 31% methamphetamines, 65% marijuana, 13% street methadone; 17% have been IV drug users.

2. Past year use: Recent use is very limited; in the past year, 6% have used cocaine, 2% crack, 4% heroin, 10% alcohol, 2% non-prescribed pills to get high, 2% methamphetamines, 2% smoked marijuana, 4% street methadone, and 2% injection. 3) Treatment history: 46% have been in alcohol treatment or detox, 33% in drug detox (7 days or less),

31% in drug rehab (short-term), 46% in a drug-free outpatient program, 15% in a methadone maintenance program, 37% in a residential or therapeutic community; 54% have attended traditional 12-step meetings. Currently, 2% are attending a drug-free outpatient program and 2% are in methadone maintenance.

Mental health.

1. Diagnosis: All DTR members surveyed reported at least one psychiatric diagnosis: 44% have a diagnosis of schizophrenia, 46% unipolar depression, 21% bipolar disorder, 10% anxiety disorder/phobia, and 6% post-traumatic stress (nearly half of members have multiple diagnoses).

2. Medications: 76% are currently taking prescribed medication for their psychiatric illness.

3. Treatment history: 63% have been in an inpatient psychiatric treatment program, 56% in an outpatient program, 60% in individual counseling or therapy; 48% have attended group counseling or therapy. Currently, 12% are attending an outpatient psychiatric treatment program, 13% are receiving individual counseling, and 13% are in group counseling.

About DTR.

1. Attendance: DTR attendance among study participants ranges from less than 1 month to over 2 years (median=18 months): 10% have been attending less than 1 month, 16% 1 to 3 months, 12% 4 to 6 months, 10% 7 months to 1 year, 33% 1 to 2 years, and 18% over 2 years. The majority of members attend very regularly: 43% more than once a week, 43% once a week, 4% once every other week, 10% once a month or less. Of those attending for a year or more, 90% are attending a meeting at least once a week. The data suggest an association between DTR attendance and medication status: of those not currently taking medication, 83% attend at least one DTR meeting a week and 73% have been coming for a year or more. The most common routes to DTR are through a therapist or social worker (49%) or a friend or associate (31%); 12% of participants heard about DTR in the community, and 8% at another 12-step meeting—70% of members surveyed attend a traditional 12-step meeting (AA or NA) at least once a week.

2. Members' views about DTR: participants were asked to express their degree of agreement with 13 statements designed to assess their experience with DTR as well as with other 12-step groups (see table 1).

Table I

Members' Opinions about DTR and Other 12-Step Programs

	Strongly/ Slightly Agree %	Strongly/ Slightly Disagree %
The meetings help me deal better with stress.	98	0
Meetings help me when I get the urge to pick up.	98	2
I feel more comfortable here than at other 12-step meetings.	86	0
I get along with people better since I started coming.	93	2
I feel more in control since I started coming.	95	2
I really like other 12-step meetings better.	27	59
I am drinking less alcohol since coming to meetings.	87	10
I am using less drugs since coming.	97	3
Coming to meetings helps me focus on my goals.	93	2
I can relate to people better here than at other 12-step meetings.	81	9
I take my meds more regularly since I started coming.	81	14
I have learned more about mental illness and addiction.	98	2
I feel better about myself since I started coming.	95	2

Study Two

The second study was qualitative and designed to supplement and elucidate the information obtained in Study One. It consisted of a semi-structured ethnographic interview focusing on members' experiences with DTR including what was happening in their lives when they first attended a DTR meeting, comparisons with other 12-step groups they may attend, what they derive from DTR attendance, and a history of their psychiatric disabilities and substance use from initiation to present.

Eight DTR members were interviewed: six men and two women, all minority members, ranging in age from 29 to 42 years. This is a convenience sample of volunteers obtained at one meeting. While the details vary, all recounted similar histories, which we have organized by common themes:

"I had no childhood." Members recount growing up in a neglectful, dysfunctional family, often with one alcoholic parent or guardian; most report first experimenting with alcohol and drugs (from marijuana

to heroin) often because of peer and parental pressure (alcoholic parent forcing child to drink) and experiencing psychiatric symptoms (ranging from hearing voices to major depression and suicidal ideations) in early adolescence. About half underwent psychiatric care including medications, although medication was usually discontinued almost immediately due to unpleasant side effects and to the feeling that medications were not necessary and that drugs were better.

"I felt normal for the first time." The result of using drugs and/or alcohol was a feeling of confidence and "belonging" which led to increased substance use, often of multiple substances such as marijuana and alcohol, LSD and alcohol, or heroin and cocaine or crack. That in turn brought about increased psychiatric symptoms that were disregarded, as individuals were by then caught up in a drug lifestyle including crime, incarcerations, and homelessness. While some members have an extensive history of drug abuse treatment going back to adolescence, the majority of those interviewed did not come to formal treatment until "hitting bottom" (i.e., experiencing some turning point such as having drug-induced seizures, passing out and being robbed in the middle of winter, or attempting suicide). Death felt close at hand, and the individual grasped at treatment as the last hope.

"My new life." It is no coincidence that many DTR members refer to the date they "turned around" as their birth date. Most of those interviewed had their turning point about 3 years ago, on the heels of some 20 or more years of substance use and psychiatric disabilities going unchecked. Treatment usually began in a hospital inpatient psychiatric program, from where comorbidity often directed members to a program for substance abusers with a mental health disorder (MICA). For two members, treatment started in a substance abuse program; while they had experienced psychiatric symptoms since early adolescence, no psychiatric diagnosis had ever been made until recently.

Fellowship as "safety net." It is at that point that those interviewed came to hear about DTR and began attending—some while still in an inpatient unit, others after having moved on to an outpatient program. Most had had superficial experience with AA and/or NA but typically did not feel connected and thus did not share, or shared only about their substance use, which bothered them. Coming to DTR, members felt relieved and exhilarated by being with others who had had the same experiences with drugs, psychiatric symptoms, and medication, and could freely discuss it in a nonjudgmental, supportive atmosphere. For the first time, they report, they feel they can be themselves, be accepted, and trust others; this is in the context of a history where they felt no one could be trusted, be it psychiatrist, drug counselor or peers at 12-step meetings. These members report that DTR allows them to feel more comfortable seeking help for both their addiction and their psychiatric illness; it gives them a more positive attitude toward medication and provides them with a safety net: "When you're walking a tight rope, if you know there is a safety net under you, you don't think about falling; DTR is my safety net."

"My rock of Gibraltar." Because DTR is a true mutual-help group, members are invited early on to take an active role in the group, be it by "qualifying" (being the main speaker at a meeting and speaking of one's experiences in front of the entire group), by making a presentation about DTR at another facility, or by becoming a group facilitator ("chairman" in AA parlance, that is, leading the group protocol, opening, closing, etc.). As described by members, the combination of sharing with others who have had similar experiences (mutual support), seeing those who are further along in their recovery (role models), and becoming a helper to other newer members (as opposed to being a stigmatized service recipient) brings about a new feeling of self-confidence and empowerment (self-efficacy), which facilitates the struggle for staying clean and taking one's medications. Thus, DTR members credit DTR for giving them the ability to stay on the path of their double recovery: "If it was not for DTR, I would be back in the hospital or using; it's my rock of Gibraltar."

Discussion

Taken together, findings from these two preliminary studies yield a profile of DTR members and give some indication of how DTR fits into members' lives and into their recovery. The first study suggests that DTR members are mostly male, African-American, or Hispanic, with a long history of psychiatric illness and substance abuse as well as extensive experience with treatment programs in both areas. They are actively working on their recovery, as evidenced by their fairly intensive attendance at DTR and sometimes other 12-step meetings. Recent substance use is limited, suggesting that participation in DTR (in conjunction with formal treatment when needed) may have a positive effect. The relatively low level of substance use is supported by the observations of group facilitators, who are familiar with the membership. Most members require medication to control their psychiatric disabilities, and that fact alone may make attendance at "conventional" 12-step groups uncomfortable, as such groups often tacitly equate medications with "drugs." When that is the case, clients are less likely to attend and thus jeopardize the fragile processes involved in recovery, especially as it applies to the dually diagnosed.

DTR members' ratings of statements comparing DTR to other 12-step meetings indicate that DTR seems to be a setting where they can feel comfortable and safe discussing not only their addiction but also their psychiatric disabilities, hence increasing the likelihood that recovery will proceed. DTR participation also enables the majority of members to attend other 12-step groups as well, because they do not need to depend on the latter for their entire support network for recovery. Findings from Study Two buttress and elucidate these data: the majority of those interviewed have progressed from a precarious existence to independent living and economic independence. They attend a DTR meeting at least once a week and some now also attend AA and/or NA, where they discuss their substance use issues only. DTR members voice future goals centering on staying in recovery, decreasing their medication, enrolling in college, and entering a profession where they can help other dually diagnosed individuals. One member said it best: "DTR gives me a tomorrow."

Study Limitations

Although encouraging, these data have several limitations. First, the sample was one of convenience and, while every effort was made to collect data at sites deemed representative of the DTR fellowship, resulting findings cannot automatically be generalized to all DTR members, numbering in the thousands. Second, the absence of random assignment and of a control group further limits generalizability and precludes causal analyses. Finally, while in excess of 90% of DTR attendees completed surveys, speaking to the representativeness of the sample, one needs acknowledge that the 10% who did not may differ significantly from their peers. Thus, the authors caution the reader that the present findings are an encouraging but preliminary step in assessing effectiveness of DTR among the dually diagnosed. A full-scale longitudinal evaluation study is scheduled to begin later this year.

Conclusion

Interest in self-help is growing rapidly in the context of managed care health service delivery. The single focus (one disease, one recovery) of traditional self-help groups is an important part of their appeal to members. However, those suffering from more than one disease (such as addiction and psychiatric disability) may feel isolated and even stigmatized in traditional meetings because of their multiple recovery needs. Preliminary findings suggest that self-help groups designed to embrace the dually diagnosed, such as DTR, provide a safe forum where members feel accepted and are able to discuss both their addictions and their psychiatric disabilities. This in turn allows members to realize the recognized benefits of self-help: honesty, trust, acceptance, and mutual sharing of experiences, strengths, and hopes.

References

Alcoholics Anonymous General Services (1997). Personal communication.

Alcoholics Anonymous World Services (1984). *The AA member: Medications and other drugs.*

Bartels, S. J., Teague, G. B., Drake, R. E., Clark, R. E., Bush, P. W., & Noordsy, D. L. (1993). Substance abuse in schizophrenia: Service utilization and costs. *Journal of Nervous and Mental Disease, 181,* 227–232.

Bean-Bayog, M. (1993). AA processes and change: How does it work? In B. McCrady & W. R. Miller (Eds.), *Research on Alcoholics Anonymous: Opportunities and alternatives* (pp. 99–112). New Brunswick, NJ: Rutgers Center on Alcohol Studies.

Bergman, H. C., & Harris, M. (1985). Substance abuse among young adult chronic patients. *Psychosocial Rehabilitation Journal, 9,* 49–54.

Brooner, R. K., Bigelow, G. E., Strain, E. & Schmidt, C. W. (1990) Intravenous drug abusers with antisocial personality disorder: Increased HIV risk behavior. *Drug and Alcohol Dependence, 26,* 39–44.

Caldwell, S., & White, K. K. (1991). Co-creating a self-help recovery movement. *Psychosocial Rehabilitation Journal, 15,* 3–9.

Chamberlin, J. (1990). The ex-patients movement: Where we've been and where we're going. *Journal of Mind and Behavior, 11,* 323–336.

Dixon, L., Haas, G., Weiden, P. J., Sweeney, J., & Frances, A. J. (1991). Drug abuse in schizophrenic patients: Clinical correlates and reasons for use. *American Journal of Psychiatry, 148,* 224–230.

Drake, R. E. (1995). *Substance abuse and mental illness.* Arlington, VA: National Alliance for the Mentally Ill.

Emrick, C. D., Tonigan, J. S., Montgomery, H., & Little, L. (1993). Alcoholics anonymous: What is currently known? In B. McCrady & W. R. Miller (Eds.), *Research on Alcoholics Anonymous: Opportunities and alternatives* (pp. 41–78). New Brunswick, NJ: Rutgers Center on Alcohol Studies.

Galanter, M. (1988). Zealous self-help groups as adjuncts to psychiatric treatment: A study of recovery, Inc. *American Journal of Psychiatry, 145,* 1248–1272.

Gawin, F. H., & Kleber, H. D. (1985). Cocaine abuse in treatment population: Patterns and diagnostic distractions. In E. H. Adams & N. J. Kozel (Eds.), *Cocaine use in America: Epidemiologic and clinical perspectives.* (pp. 182–192). Washington, DC: NIDA Research Monograph Series, 61.

Greenfield, S. F., Weiss, R. D., & Tohen, M. (1995). Substance abuse and the chronically mentally ill: A description of dual diagnosis treatment services in a psychiatric hospital. *Community Mental Health Journal, 31*(3), 265–277.

Hagnell, O., & Grasbeck, A. (1990). Comorbidity of anxiety and depression in the Lunby 25-year prospective study: The pattern of subsequent episodes. In J. D. Maser & C. R. Cloninger (Eds.), *Comorbidity of mood and anxiety disorders* (pp. 139–152). Washington, DC: American Psychiatric Press.

Hazelden (1993). *The dual diagnosis recovery book.* Hazelden Foundation.

Hesselbrock, M. N., Meyer, R. E., & Keener, J. J. (1985). Psychopathology in hospitalized alcoholics. *Archives of General Psychiatry, 42,* 1050–1055.

Hien, D., Zimberg, S., Weissman, S., First, M., & Ackerman, S. (1993). *Dual diagnosis subtypes in urban substance abuse and mental health clinics.* Presented in part at the American Psychiatric Association 148th Annual Meeting, San Francisco.

Hirschfeld, R. M. A., Hasin, D., Keller, M. B., Endicott, J., & Wunder, J. (1990). Depression and alcoholism: Comorbidity in a longitudinal study. In J. D. Maser & C. R. Cloninger (Eds.), *Comorbidity of mood and anxiety disorders* (pp. 293–304). Washington, DC: American Psychiatric Press.

Hoffman, N. G., Harrison, P. A., & Belile, C. A. (1983). Alcoholics anonymous aftertreatment: Attendance and abstinence. *International Journal of the Addictions, 18,* 311–318.

Kessler, R. C. (1995). The national comorbidity survey: Preliminary results and future directions. *International Journal of Methods in Psychiatric Research, 5,* 139–151.

Khantzian, E. J., & Mack, J. E. (1994). How AA works and why it's important for clinicians to understand. *Journal of Substance Abuse Treatment, 11* (2), 77–92.

Kleinman, P. H., Miller, A. B., & Millman, R. B. (1990). Psychopathology among cocaine abusers entering treatment. *Journal of Nervous and Mental Disease, 178,* 442–447.

Lehman, A. F., Myers, C. P., & Corty, E. (1989). Assessment and classification of patients with psychiatric and substance abuse syndromes. *Hospital and Community Psychiatry, 40* (10), 1019–1025.

Lehman, A. F., Myers, C. P., Dixon, L. B., & Johnson, J. L. (1994). Defining subgroups of dual diagnosis patients for service planning. *Hospital and Community Psychiatry, 45* (6), 556–561.

Markowitz, F. E., DeMasi, M. E., Carpinelli, S. E., Knight, E. L., Videka-Sherman, L., & Sofka, C. (1996). *The role of self-help in recovery process.* Paper presented at the 6th Annual National Conference on State Mental Health Agency Services. Research and Program Evaluation, Arlington, VA, February.

Marlowe, D. B., Husband, S. D., Lamb, R. J., Kirby, K. C., Iguchi, M. Y., & Platt, J. J. (1995). Psychiatric comorbidity in cocaine dependence. *American Journal on Addictions, 4,* 70–81.

McCrady, B. S., & Miller, W. R. (1993). *Research on alcoholics anonymous.* Alcohol Research Documentation, Inc.

McLellan, A. T., Luborsky, L., Woody, G. E., O'Brien, C. P., & Druley, K. (1983). Predicting response to alcohol and drug abuse treatments: Role of psychiatric severity. *Archives of General Psychiatry, 40,* 620–625.

Meyer, R. E. (1988). Conditioning phenomena and the problem of relapse in opioid addicts and alcoholics (pp. 161–179). Washington, DC: *NIDA Research Monograph, 84.*

Mirin, S. M., Weiss, R. D., & Michael, J. (1988). Psychopathology in substance abusers: Diagnosis and treatment. *American Journal of Drug and Alcohol Abuse, 14,* 139–157.

Moos, R. H., Finney, J., & Maude-Griffin, P. (1993). The social climate of self-help and mutual support groups: Assessing group implementation, process, and outcome. In B. McCrady & W. R. Miller (Eds.), *Research on Alcoholics Anonymous: Opportunities and alternatives* (pp. 251–276). New Brunswick, NJ: Rutgers Center on Alcohol Studies.

Mueser, K. T., Bellack, A. S., & Blanchard, J. J. (1992). Comorbidity of schizophrenia and substance abuse: Implications for treatment. *Journal of Consulting and Clinical Psychology, 60,* 845–856.

Murphy, J. M., (1990). Diagnostic comorbidity and symptom co-occurence: The Stirling County study. In J. D. Maser & C. R. Cloninger (Eds.), *Comorbidity of mood and anxiety disorders* (pp. 153–176). Washington, DC: American Psychiatric Press.

Nunes, E. V., & Deliyannides, D. A. (1993). Research issues in dual diagnosis. In J. Solomon, S. Zimber, & E. Sholler, *Dual diagnosis* (pp. 287–309). Plenum Publishing Corporation, New York.

Ogborne, A. C. (1993). Assessing the effectiveness of alcoholics anonymous in the community: Meeting the challenges. In B. McCrady & W. R. Miller (Eds.), *Research on Alcoholics Anonymous: Opportunities and alternatives* (pp. 339–356). New Brunswick, NJ: Rutgers Center on Alcohol Studies.

Osher, F. C., & Kofoed, L. L. (1989). Treatment of patients with psychiatric and psychoactive substance use disorders. *Hospital and Community Psychiatry, 40* (10), 1025–1030.

Osher, F. C., Drake, R. E., Noordsy, D. L., Teague, G. B., Hurlbut, S. C., Biesamz, J.C., et al. (1994). Correlates and outcomes of alcohol use disorder among rural outpatients with schizophrenia. *Journal of Clinical Psychiatry, 55,* 109–113.

Pettinati, H. M., Sugerman, A., DiDonato, N., & Maurer, H. S. (1982). Natural history of alcoholism over four years of treatment. *Journal of Studies on Alcohol, 43,* 201–215.

Peyrot, M. (1985). Narcotics anonymous: Its history, structure, and approach. *International Journal of Addiction, 20* (10), 1509–1522.

Rosenthal, R. N., Hellerstein, D. J., & Miner, C. R. (1992). A model of integrated services for outpatient treatment of patients with comorbid schizophrenia and addictive disorders. *The American Journal of the Addictions, 1*(4), 339–348.

Rounseville, B. J., Anton, S. F., & Carroll, K. (1991). Psychiatric diagnoses of treatment-seeking cocaine abusers. *Archives of General Psychiatry, 48,* 43–51.

Rounseville, B. J., Kosten, T. R., Weissman, M. M., & Kleber, H. D. (1986). Prognostic significance of Psychopathology in treated opiate addicts. *Archives of General Psychiatry, 43,* 739–745.

Rounseville, B. J., Weissman, M. M., Kleber, H. D., & Wilber, C. (1982). Heterogeneity of psychiatric diagnosis in treated opiate addicts. *Archives of General Psychiatry, 39,* 161–166.

Rutherford, M. J., Cacciola, J. S., & Alterman, A. I. (1994). Relationships of personality disorders with problem severity in methadone patients. *Drug and Alcohol Dependence, 35* (pp. 69–76).

Vogel, H. (1993). *Double trouble in recovery.* Albany, NY: Mental Health Empowerment Project.

Walker, R. D., Donovan, D. M., Kiivahan, D. R., & O'Leary, M. R. (1983). Length of stay, neuropsychological performance, and aftercare: Influences on alcohol treatment outcome. *Journal of Consulting and Clinical Psychologist, 51,* 900–911.

Watson, C. G., Hamcock, M., Gearhart, L. P., Mendez, C. M., Malovrh, P. & Raden, M. (1997). A comparative outcome study of frequent, moderate, occasional and nonattenders of Alcoholics Anonymous. *Journal of Clinical Psychology, 53* (3), 209–214.

Weiss, R. D., Mirin, S. M., & Griffin, M. L., et al. (1986). Psychopathology in chronic cocaine abusers. *American Journal of Drug and Alcohol Abuse, 12,* 17–29.

Westermeyer, J., & Walzer, V. (1985). Sociopathology and drug abuse in a young psychiatric population. *Diseases of the Nervous System, 36,* 673–677.

Zaslav, P. (1993). The role of self-help groups in the treatment of the dual diagnosis patient. In J. Solomon, S. Zimber, S., & E. Sholler, *Dual diagnosis,* (pp. 105–126). New York: Plenum Publishing Corporation.

Ziedonis, D. M., & Fisher, W. (1994). Assessment and treatment of comorbid substance abuse in individuals with schizophrenia. *Psychiatric Annals, 24* (9), 477–483.

First Person Account: Living in a Nightmare

Alyce Kagigebi

This article originally appeared in the *Schizophrenia Bulletin*, 1995, 21(1), 155–159.

Alyce Kagigebi is employed at North West Passage, a residential treatment center located in Northern Wisconsin.

"You little …! I thought parents were supposed to help their kids. I'm going to get a restraining order so you can't call me or come near me." My son said this to me when I told him he couldn't come home to live. I was real surprised that he called me a name because he has never called me names. My first reaction was that it was funny, but deep down it hurt. I know he said those things because of his mental illness, but it can still hurt.

My son, Burt, is 24 years old, and 2 years ago he was diagnosed with schizophrenia. This is when the first living nightmares began.

Burt had always been an easy child with no unusual problems. But when Burt was 16, my husband, Dan, and I started having behavioral problems with him. It was as if Burt's personality changed overnight. He started drinking and running with a wild crowd. I thought Burt was chemically dependent. Dan is his stepfather, and Burt's biological father is an alcoholic and uses drugs. I joined Al-Anon, went to therapy, and eventually learned about "Tough Love." Burt became emotionally distant with Dan and me. He used drugs and alcohol and missed a lot of school. He also had a job at a grocery store and had plans of becoming manager some day.

In Burt's last year of high school we realized he wouldn't graduate because he had missed too much school. That same year he only lived with us part of the time. Each time Burt came home we had him sign a contract as to the rules to follow while living in our home. We asked Burt to leave twice that year because he had broken two serious rules. Once he was smoking pot in his room, and the other time he was selling drugs from our house. It was very hard and painful for me to follow through with these consequences, but Burt had to know that I meant business and he couldn't walk all over us.

It nearly killed me when Burt didn't graduate. I still feel sad about it. Now I realize that Burt was probably using drugs and alcohol to ease the sound of the voices he was hearing and to ease the imaginary things he was seeing. How hard it must have been for him when all this was going on. How could you tell anyone that you were seeing and hearing things that no one else was? They would have thought you were nuts. He must have been scared to death.

When I was going through these troubled times I thought, "This must be a living nightmare." Little did I know that the real living nightmare would come later. This was just openers.

At age 19, Burt was living in his car. He lost his job because he couldn't make it to work due to too much partying. He had run out of places to stay. With no money to pay rent, no one wanted him. He came home to visit one night and wanted to move back in with us. By this time we couldn't handle him or trust him to follow through with anything he said. It was so hard not to take him in and take care of him. I love him so much. Dan and I told Burt that if he went to treatment for drugs and alcohol we would let him come home. I lied to him and I didn't feel very good about myself for it. I had no intentions of having him come home. After treatment I wanted him to go to a halfway house. If he could prove to me that he was serious about changing his life, then I would let him come back home. It was very hard for me to follow through with what I said. Burt agreed to go to treatment. While he was in treatment I told him I changed my mind and he couldn't come home. That was one of the hardest things I have ever done. He looked like I had stabbed him with a knife. His counselors helped him through the pain he was in. He never brought up the fact that I lied to him, but months later I wrote him a letter asking for his forgiveness. Burt never replied. I don't think he could.

After treatment Burt went to a halfway house in Minneapolis. He stayed there until he was 23 years old. I knew he wasn't growing emotionally and I couldn't figure out why. I didn't think he was drinking or using drugs, but he was emotionally distant. Dan and I visited Burt once a month and wrote often. He never wanted to come home, but I wasn't sure why.

On one monthly visit we picked Burt up and went to shop and lunch. Burt was very strange. He looked like he was on drugs. His body language was odd, and his motor movements seemed slow and different. He talked about lifting weights and said a bar fell on his head. I felt panicky. I was worried about brain damage, and I still wondered if he was on drugs. After our visit, I called him that evening. He seemed distant but OK. He wanted to come home for a weekend. I was surprised and said we would be happy to have him come home, but I was still feeling frightened about his behavior. Burt came home the following weekend. I took one look at him when he got off the bus and knew he wasn't on drugs. I knew he had a mental illness. I felt so scared. I didn't know what to do. I knew I had to get him to a doctor but I also knew he wouldn't go. I felt so helpless.

When Burt got off the bus he was holding a Styrofoam cup and he carried it with him all weekend. He also had a tube of toothpaste in his pocket, and he ate toothpaste and spit it into the cup constantly. I couldn't believe it! I went up to him and I nearly started yelling at him. I wanted to say, "Put that darn cup away. Don't you know how crazy you look?" Something stopped me and instead I talked gently to him and asked him why he was doing that. He said, "Because it tastes good. You know?" He was in pretty bad shape. That evening he became frantic and said his heart was pounding and he was in pain. I was working. He woke up everyone in the house and said he needed to go to the hospital. Dan called me and I dropped everything and drove home. I was scared. I decided to call an ambulance because I was afraid Burt might jump out of the car on the way to the hospital. (We live 40 miles from the nearest psychiatric hospital.) I called the ambulance and waited for them to come. I tried to explain to the police what was going on. When the ambulance arrived I was afraid to tell Burt because I thought he might get angry and they would have to force him to go, but he went very willingly. Dan and I followed in our car. Burt was going to the hospital for the pain in his chest, and I was going to see if I could get him committed. Dan and I had never been through anything like this in our lives.

I couldn't believe what was happening. I was in shock. I didn't know what to think. Could Burt have gotten some bad drugs that had damaged his brain? Could the bar that fell on his head have damaged his brain? Did a bar really fall on his head? The big question was, when was he going to be normal again?

First Burt saw a general practitioner who thought that Burt's chest pain was not a physical pain but a mental pain. Burt then saw a psychiatric doctor who wanted him to stay at the hospital for observation. Burt wouldn't stay, and the hospital couldn't force him to stay because he wasn't a danger to himself or to others. We all tried so hard to talk him into staying, but he wouldn't budge. It was so hard. It was a nightmare.

We took him home. I was exhausted. We had been at the hospital for 5 hours and both Dan and I were drained of emotions.

The next day I was to drive Burt to the halfway house, which was 100 miles away. But he agreed instead to go to a hospital in Minneapolis where he lived. Again, Burt was going to the doctor for the pain in his chest, and I was taking him for the pain in his head. I felt that a hospital in Minnesota was worth trying because one of the doctors in Wisconsin (where we live) said that the laws in Minnesota were more liberal, and we would have a better chance of getting help for Burt. The doctor was mistaken. The laws are the same, and we went through 7 hours of hell only to find out nothing. The hospital couldn't hold Burt unless he was a danger to himself or someone else. I was devastated and exhausted. I was hitting a dead end. I still didn't know any answers to why Burt was acting so strange. Inside I was asking, "What does a person have to do around here to get some help?" All the medical people agreed that there was something drastically wrong with Burt. I wonder if any of them thought their hands were tied because of the laws.

I had to give Burt a ride back to his halfway house. I dreaded the ride because we were in the inner city and I wasn't used to driving with all the traffic. I was tired and also very angry with Burt for not cooperating. Actually, I was feeling so many emotions I didn't know which end was up. I just wanted to go home and get away from Burt. He asked me if we could stop at a fast food restaurant and get something to eat. I told him no because I had to get home. I felt instant guilt for not taking the time to have dinner with him.

After I dropped Burt off, I drove to the nearest grocery store and bought a sandwich and a pack of cigarettes. I had quit smoking 2 years before, but I started smoking again that day. I smoked five cigarettes before I got home. I needed some comforting, and my familiar friend cigarettes helped. That was 2 years ago and I'm not sorry I started smoking that day. A lot of people can't understand that. I wish I didn't smoke but I'm not sorry.

The following day I called the halfway house and talked to their psychologist. Her name is Lori and she has been a great source of strength to me. She has also become a close friend. Lori said that she thought Burt had schizophrenia. That was the first time I had heard the name schizophrenia in reference to my son. She explained that schizophrenia was a virus in the brain and that to her knowledge it is a biological disease. She also told me that this type of mental illness strikes teenagers and young adults. I felt as if I had been knocked off my feet. I was feeling all kinds of feelings at once—shock, fear, helplessness, and frustration.

Lori also informed me that Burt had been demonstrating bizarre behavior. He had been wearing strings to "hold up his arms." She also mentioned Burt's toothpaste routine. On several occasions, Burt said the radio was talking to him and for some reason he tried to put his bed on his dresser. I didn't know what to think about all this. My mind was spinning. Lori was in the process of trying to place Burt in a board and care facility because the halfway house wasn't equipped to handle his illness. She was having a hard time placing him because he had to see a doctor first, and he wouldn't see a doctor because he didn't think anything was wrong with him.

When I got off the phone I looked up schizophrenia in our medical book. After reading their information I didn't see much hope for Burt. I felt depressed. I blamed myself. It had to be someone's fault. Maybe I shouldn't have smoked when I was pregnant. Then, I remembered I had quit at that time. Maybe I never should have married my ex-husband because he was an alcoholic and verbally abusive. Maybe I shouldn't have been watching my weight so closely when I was pregnant. I was driving myself crazy. I called friends and they were very supportive. I sent for books on schizophrenia, and they have helped me more than anything. The books told me it wasn't my fault and talked about what I was feeling. Most important, the books talked about what other families had gone through. This helped me feel that I wasn't alone.

Several months after I talked to Lori, Burt was placed in a board and care facility. The day he entered the facility I remember thinking that his friends are going to college and my son is going to a mental institution. It was heartbreaking. I looked at the other patients there and wondered how my son could be going here. I felt a lot of pain. I cried all the way home.

Burt was at the board and care home for a year. He refused to take medication and wouldn't participate in any of their activities. He ate junk food and the nurses had a hard time getting him to clean up his room. Finally his doctor said he was a nonpatient and he was discharged. The caseworker at the board and care home said that Burt would have to go to the shelter because there were no other facilities that would take him because he refused medications. I panicked! I had heard terrible stories about shelters, and Lori had said, "Whatever you do, don't let Burt go to a shelter." I had all kinds of frightening thoughts going through my head. I was afraid he might get raped, murdered, or beat up. I was afraid his belongings would get stolen from him. I was afraid that he would use drugs and alcohol. I was afraid he would get AIDS. These thoughts were very real for me.

I was told that Burt's doctor had suggested that he go to the shelter. I called his doctor and asked him if he thought the shelter was the best place for Burt. He hesitated for a long time and then said, "I don't know." That said a lot to me. I feel that Burt's doctor didn't know what to do with him or how to help him, so he just threw him away to the shelter. He also said that when Burt got tired of living at the shelter he would ask for help. I can't believe an educated person would say something like this about a person who is delusional. I believed that when Burt got tired of living at the shelter he would be living in a cardboard box and telling me, "This isn't so bad, Mom."

At this time my husband and I considered having Burt come home to live with us. We had gone over and over this subject. The bottom line is we can't handle Burt. He has not lived with us for 3 years and he isn't the same person he was when he left home. I would end up smothering him to death. He wouldn't have to do anything for himself. We would all go mad. I feel that I have a responsibility to help him, and I feel guilty because he can't live with us. The hardest thing I ever had to do is tell Burt that he couldn't come home to live. Think about telling your adult child that he can't come home to stay.

I hate schizophrenia. I hate it! Schizophrenia robs its victims of everything that is important in life. It's ugly, selfish, and takes away simple joys in life such as laughing, holding down a job, and being able to have a conversation with anyone. Schizophrenia causes enormous emotional pain, fear, anger, frustration, resentment, and disappointment to the families and the person with schizophrenia.

One of the things that Burt misses is working. He worked from age 14 through age 20, and he doesn't understand why he can't work now. He thinks if he "kicks back and rests for awhile" that he will be able to work. But he has been kicking back and resting for 3 years now.

What must Burt be going through? I ask him if he is happy and he says he is. But what is happiness to him now? He listens to his headphones and watches TV most of the day. He also goes to the store and buys pop and candy. He smokes but not a lot, and at times smoking bothers him.

Sometimes he eats in the dining area and sometimes he doesn't. He says the meat looks rotten to him. He used to go to the movies once a month, but he doesn't do that anymore. He doesn't wear strings on his arms anymore, and he doesn't eat toothpaste. He stopped doing those things after he moved into the board and care home. I think that is a big accomplishment. Of course, he takes no medications, and he looks depressed. Once in a while we will see his real laugh. We count how many times he laughs when he is with us. Once we counted four real laughs from him. It makes our family feel good to see him laugh. It is important to us.

Then there is the crazy laughter—when Burt's face twists and he laughs at something only he sees or hears. When I first heard that crazy laughter come out of him, I couldn't stand it. I wanted to say, "Stop that stupid laughing. Don't you know how dumb you look?" It embarrassed me. But I didn't say anything and afterward I felt compassion.

If you don't have a close family member who has schizophrenia, you don't really know what it's like. I don't care if you are a doctor, nurse, or case manager and have had thousands of patients or clients with the disease. You can't feel the gut-wrenching grief that a mother, father, or siblings feel from losing a son, daughter, brother, or sister to schizophrenia. It's as if that person has died and here stands a different person who is your loved one but who looks and acts like a crazy person. You love them but you wonder where your old loved one has gone, and you long for his or her return. I miss the old Burt. I miss his companionship, his laughter, and the Mother's Day and birthday cards he used to remember. But most of all I miss his love and his hugs. Right now, he doesn't want anyone to touch him. I cry for the old Burt and remember the good times. It seems long ago.

I have had to force myself to get to know the mentally ill Burt. As you can see it is hard. Sometimes he's OK and we can do things together, but it still isn't the same. Sometimes his hair is dirty and his clothes look like he slept in them. On one occasion, we were standing in line at a fast food place. The lady standing behind Burt looked at his dirty hair and the rest of his appearance and stepped back from him and whispered something about Burt to her companion. I fought back tears because that really hurt me. To think that someone thought my son was too gross to even stand behind.

But I can't help but think that I might have done the same to someone's daughter or son given the same situation. You never know.

As I am writing this story, Burt is going to a shelter. I am turning Burt over to God. I have written letters and made numerous phone calls to find a safe place for him to live, but I have gotten nowhere. God will have to take care of Burt. I am at a dead end.

I will manage. I will not desert my son no matter how painful it is for me. I know if I had schizophrenia the old Burt would stand by me. I don't see much hope for Burt's future. I understand and can accept the way he wants to live his life. People tell me there is always hope, but I ask them how you can have hope when things have just gotten worse for years. I would rather accept the present than have false hope. I can have some peace with that. I don't believe I will ever have my old son back and anything else isn't enough. It just isn't. It's OK and I can handle it and I will be grateful for any progress Burt makes, but it will never be enough.

I hope my words will give insight to the effects that schizophrenia has on patients and their families. This is the end of this essay but it is not the end of Burt's story.

The nightmare goes on and on and on!

Violence and Severe Mental Illness: The Effects of Substance Abuse and Nonadherence to Medication

Marvin S. Swartz, Jeffrey W. Swanson, Virginia A. Hiday,
Randy Borum, H. Ryan Wagner & Barbara J. Burns

This article appeared in the *American Journal of Psychiatry*, 1998; 155, 226–231, and is reprinted with permission.

Marvin S. Swartz, M.D., Jeffrey W. Swanson, Ph.D., Virginia A. Hiday, Ph.D., Randy Borum, Psy.D., H. Ryan Wagner, Ph.D., & Barbara J. Burns, Ph.D, Services Effectiveness Research Program, Department of Psychiatry and Behavioral Sciences, Duke University Medical Center, and the Department of Sociology and Anthropology, North Carolina State University, Raleigh.

Supported by NIMH grant MH-48103 and by the University of North Carolina-Chapel Hill/Duke Program on Services Research for People with Severe Mental Disorders (NIMH grant MH-51410).

Objective: Violent behavior among individuals with severe mental illness has become an important focus in community-based care. This study examines the joint effect of substance abuse and medication noncompliance on the greater risk of serious violence among persons with severe mental illness. Method: Involuntarily admitted inpatients with severe mental illness who were awaiting a period of outpatient commitment were enrolled in a longitudinal outcome study. At baseline, 331 subjects underwent an extensive face-to-face interview. Complementary data were gathered by a review of hospital records and a telephone interview with a family member or other informant. These data included subjects' sociodemographic characteristics, illness history, clinical status, medication adherence, substance abuse, insight into illness, and violent behavior during the 4 months that preceded hospitalization. Associations between serious violent acts and a range of individual characteristics and problems were analyzed by using multivariable logistic regression. Results: The combination of medication noncompliance and alcohol or substance abuse problems was significantly associated with serious violent acts in the community, after sociodemographic and clinical characteristics were controlled. Conclusions: Alcohol or other drug abuse problems combined with poor adherence to medication may signal a higher risk of violent behavior among persons with severe mental illness. Reduction of such risk may require carefully targeted community interventions, including integrated mental health and substance abuse treatment.

Introduction

Violence committed by individuals with severe mental illness living in the community has become an increasing focus of concern among clinicians, policy makers, and the general public—often as the result of tragic, albeit uncommon events (Monahan & Steadman, 1994; Mulvey, 1994; Torrey, 1994). In the current era of cost containment, in which the use of hospitalization is increasingly limited, there is a renewed priority on developing strategies for managing violence risk in the community. Such strategies may include formalized risk assessment procedures (Borum, Swartz, & Swanson, 1996), closer monitoring of outpatient treatment, greater attention to substance abuse comorbidity, and efforts to improve treatment retention and compliance through intensive case management (Dvoskin & Steadman, 1994). Legal interventions such as court-mandated, community-based treatment or involuntary outpatient commitment are also being cited as promising methods of improving treatment adherence (Geller, 1990; Hiday & Scheid-Cook, 1991; Swanson, Swartz et al., 1997; Swartz et al., 1995) and thereby reducing violence (Buchanan & David, 1994; Torrey, 1994).

As risk management strategies per se, a number of these approaches are being advocated on the strength of general clinical assumptions about what may cause mentally ill individuals to commit violent acts, but they lack the benefit of a solid research base that demonstrates the specific and interacting effects of major risk factors for violent behavior as they actually operate in the severely mentally ill population. Such effects are shaped not only by the features of major psychiatric disorder but by the social environments in which people with severe mental illness often live. The present article takes a step toward providing a better empirical understanding of violent behavior in individuals with severe mental illness by specifying the magnitude of violence risk represented by two key problems—substance abuse and medication noncompliance—and showing how these risk factors operate together in a group of 331 recently hospitalized severely mentally ill individuals.

A number of studies have linked medication noncompliance to decompensation and hospital readmission. Substance abuse comorbidity has also been associated with generally poor clinical outcomes among severely mentally ill individuals in the community (Bartels, Drake, & Wallach, 1995; Bartels et al., 1993; Casper & Regan, 1993; Drake, Bartels, Teague, Noordsy, & Clark, 1993; Drake & Wallach, 1992; Drake et al.,

1991; Haywood et al., 1995; Osher & Drake, 1996; Pristach & Smith, 1990). Haywood and co-workers (Haywood et al., 1995) found high rates of alcohol or other drug abuse and medication noncompliance among a subgroup of state mental hospital patients who exhibited a pattern of multiple readmissions. Other studies of severely mentally ill individuals in the community have shown that substance abuse comorbidity is associated with medication and aftercare noncompliance (Osher & Drake, 1996; Owen, Fischer, Booth, & Cuffel, 1996) as well as with violent behavior (Cuffel, Shumway, Chouljian, & MacDonald, 1994; Salloum, Daley, Cornelius, Kirisci, & Thase, 1996; Smith & Hucker, 1994; Swanson, 1994; Swanson, Borum, Swartz, & Monahan, 1996).

A new analysis by Swanson and colleagues (Swanson et al., 1997) suggests that substance abuse, psychotic symptoms, and lack of contact with specialty mental health services in the community all are associated with greater risk of adult-lifetime violence among persons with severe mental illness. In a state forensic hospital population, Smith (Smith, 1989) found a significant relationship between medication noncompliance and violent acts in the community. Similarly, Bartels and colleagues (Bartels, Drake, Wallach, & Freeman, 1991) reported a relationship among noncompliance, hostility, and violence in a group of 133 outpatients with schizophrenia. Consistent with the findings of Bartels and colleagues, a new analysis from the same study presented here shows that both violent behavior and the combination of substance use with medication noncompliance are significant statistical predictors of police encounters for people with severe mental illness (Borum, Swanson, Swartz, & Hiday, 1997).

Taken together, these findings suggest that medication noncompliance may exert an effect on violence by means of a preexisting or concomitant relationship with alcohol or other drug abuse. Both of these variables—substance abuse and medication nonadherence—may combine to increase the risk of violence, or perhaps a third variable, such as poor insight into illness (Amador et al., 1993; David, 1990; Markova & Berrios, 1995; McEvoy, Appelbaum, Apperson, Geller, & Freter, 1989; McEvoy et al., 1989), may lead both to substance abuse and noncompliance and thus increase the risk of violence and institutional recidivism.

Lack of awareness of illness and need for treatment—termed poor insight into illness—has been associated with noncompliance, illness relapse, and recidivism (McEvoy, Appelbaum et al., 1989; McEvoy et al.,

1989; McEvoy et al., 1989), but systematic research has not linked poor insight with violence per se. For that matter, limited empirical evidence to date has implicated noncompliance as a direct risk factor for violent acts among severely mentally ill individuals or has documented its potential interaction with substance abuse while holding constant demographic and social-contextual variables (Buchanan & David, 1994; Pristach & Smith, 1990).

Identifying the relative and combined impact of specific risk factors is a necessary first step in designing more effective ways to prevent the violent and threatening behavior that often attends relapse and hospital recidivism in this population. Hence, the current study seeks to examine the effects of selected predictors of recent community violence in a multivariable analysis of 331 hospitalized individuals with severe mental illness.

Method

Data for this article are drawn from a randomized clinical trial (Swartz et al., 1995) that examined the effectiveness of involuntary outpatient commitment and case management in reducing noncompliance with psychiatric treatment and preventing relapse, rehospitalization, reduced functioning, and other poor outcomes among people with severe mental illness. Because the present article will include only the baseline data of the 331 severely mentally ill subjects from the longitudinal study, the random assignment of subjects after their baseline interview will not be an issue here; hence, all the baseline data will be analyzed as one study group.

Involuntarily admitted patients were recruited from the admissions unit of a regional state psychiatric hospital and three other inpatient facilities that serve the catchment area in which the participating area mental health programs are located. Because involuntary admission is used extensively in public-sector psychiatric institutions in North Carolina (accounting for about 90% of admissions to the state mental hospitals), patients admitted to inpatient treatment under this status are quite representative of the population of persons with severe and persistent mental disorders—particularly the subgroup of repeatedly admitted ("revolving door") patients in the public mental health system. Eligible patients were approached for informed consent to participate and included individuals with a primary diagnosis of a severe and persistent psychiatric disorder who were awaiting a period of court-ordered outpatient commitment. Of 374 identified eligible patients, about 11.5% (N = 43) refused.

An extensive face-to-face interview was conducted with each respondent and by telephone with a designated family member or other informant who knew the respondent well. Interviews covered a wide variety of personal historical information, sociodemographic and clinical characteristics, and specific information about violent behavior and its surrounding context. In addition, a systematic review of the hospital record was conducted, including clinical assessments, treatment progress notes, and the legal section of the chart in which involuntary commitment petitions and criminal charges were noted.

In the direct interviews, subjects were asked specifically whether they had gotten into trouble with the law or had been arrested for physical or sexual assault. Each respondent was also asked specifically about getting into physical fights in the past 4 months in which someone was "hit, slapped, kicked, grabbed, shoved, bitten, hurt with a knife or gun, or had something thrown at them." Subjects were also asked a series of questions about engaging in threatening behavior, defined as "saying or doing anything that makes a person afraid of being harmed by you—like saying you are going to hit them, demanding money, raising a fist, pointing a weapon, trying to pick a fight, following or chasing or stalking someone, or anything like that." Family members or other collateral informants were asked similar questions about the subject's behavior.

For the present study, we used combined data from subjects, family members, and hospital records to adopt a severity threshold for serious violent events that included any assaultive act in which the respondent used a weapon against another person or made a threat with a weapon or that resulted in an injury to another person. This operational definition of serious violent behavior corresponds to level 1 violence as measured specifically in the MacArthur Research Network on Mental Health and the Law (Steadman et al., 1994). A more detailed examination of the prevalence and characteristics of violent events in this study group is in preparation (unpublished 1997 study of J.W. Swanson et al.).

Medication noncompliance was measured by the subject's self-report or the report of a family member or collateral informant. Informants were asked (1) whether there had been prescription medications or shots (for mental or emotional health problems) that the subject was supposed to take but did not, or (2) whether the subject had never or almost never taken the shots or oral medications as prescribed. Insight into illness was assessed with the Insight and Treatment Attitudes Questionnaire (McEvoy et al., 1989), an 11-item scale that measures recognition of mental illness and the need for treatment. Low scores on the Insight and Treatment Attitudes Questionnaire have been shown to be predictive of poor treatment compliance and higher rates of hospital readmission (McEvoy et al., 1989).

Overall, 17.8% of the study group ($N = 59$) had engaged in serious violent acts that involved weapons or caused injury. Characteristics of the subjects are presented in table 1. Respondents in the group were predominantly male, younger, of lower educational level, and neither married nor cohabiting. The racial distribution of the cohort was about two-thirds African American and one-third white. This racial and sociodemographic composition is quite representative of the severely mentally ill population in these public hospitals and closely matches the sociodemographic composition of study subjects screened for the study. While a majority of respondents were city residents, a substantial proportion lived in rural areas and small towns.

The study group was made up predominantly of persons with psychotic disorders (schizophrenia, schizoaffective disorder, or other psychotic disorders). An additional 26.9% ($N = 89$) had discharge diagnoses of bipolar disorder, and only a small minority—5.1% ($N = 17$)—were diagnosed with major depression. While the current analysis used discharge diagnoses that incorporated chart review data, approximately one-third of the group were administered the Structured Clinical Interview for *DSM-III-R* (SCID) (Spitzer, Williams, Gibbon, & First, 1990). These interviews showed a very high level of agreement with chart review diagnoses, which used all sources of available data; hence, the SCID assessments were discontinued.

The study interview elicited extensive data on lifetime and recent use of alcohol and illicit substances, including sedatives, cocaine, cannabis, stimulants, opioids, hallucinogens, inhalants, and other substances. It was found that 33.8% of the subjects ($N = 112$) had used at least one type of illicit substance, 53.2% ($N = 176$) had used alcohol, and 58.9% ($N = 195$) had used either (or both) at least once a month during the 4 months before hospitalization. These rates reflect data combined from three sources: respondent's self-report, interview with family members or collateral informants, and hospital record review. In addition, 57.4% (N = 112) of the users (33.8% of the total cohort) had "problems" related to alcohol or substance abuse according to one or more sources (e.g., problems with family, friends, job, or police or physical health problems due to drinking) or had a co-occurring diagnosis of substance use disorder at discharge. Since research suggests that use of alcohol or illicit drugs below a diagnostic abuse threshold by persons with major psychiatric disorders can lead to trouble and complicates treatment (Drake, Alterman, & Rosenburg, 1993; Drake et al., 1993), the present study uses co-occurring alcohol or drug use problems in the previous 4 months as the key severity threshold.

Results

Table 1 shows selected characteristics of study subjects and the percent in each category who committed serious violent acts in the 4 months before admission. In all subsequent analyses, any serious violent act (i.e., assault or threat with a weapon or causing injury to another person) was used as the dependent variable. While most of these sample characteristics showed no significant bivariate relationship to violence, it can be seen that serious violent acts were more likely to be committed by subjects who were male, African American, or victims of crime in the previous 4 months and by those with co-occurring substance abuse problems. We used Fisher's exact test, an appropriate alternative statistic, to demonstrate significance for adjusted chi-square values that were close to significance. Victimization was used in this and subsequent analyses as a proxy contextual measure of exposure to crime and violence in the surrounding social environment (unpublished 1997 study of Hiday et al.), since victimized subjects are likely to feel more threatened and may engage in violent acts at least partly in self-protection. Preliminary data suggested that much of the bivariate association of race and violence could be explained by higher rates of criminal victimization in the particular communities of these African American subjects.

Surprisingly, urban residence in and of itself was not associated with serious violent acts nor was medication noncompliance or low insight into illness, as measured by the Insight and Treatment Attitudes Questionnaire. Also surprising was the lack of relationship of serious violent acts with the clinical characteristics of diagnosis and score on the Global Assessment of Functioning Scale.

Table 1

Characteristics of 331 Involuntarily Admitted Inpatients with Severe Mental Illness and Relation to Prevalence of Serious Violence in the 4 Months Before Admission

Characteristic	N	%	Committed Violent Act in Previous 4 Months N	Committed Violent Act in Previous 4 Months %	Analysis[a] Adjusted χ^2	df	p
Age (years)					2.89	2	n.s.
18-29	60	18.13	15	25.00			
30-44	168	50.76	29	17.26			
≥45	103	31.12	15	14.56			
Sex[b]					3.81	1	<0.06
Female	153	46.22	20	13.07			
Male	178	53.78	39	21.91			
Education[c]					1.53	2	n.s.
Less than high school	114	34.44	23	20.18			
High school	186	56.19	33	17.74			
College	29	8.76	3	10.34			
Marital status					0.84	1	n.s.
Married or cohabiting	67	20.24	15	22.39			
Not married or cohabiting	264	79.76	44	16.67			
Place of residence					0.51	1	n.s.
Rural	124	37.46	25	20.16			
Urban	207	62.54	34	16.43			
Race					3.85	1	0.05
White	112	33.84	13	11.61			
African American	219	66.16	46	21.00			
Victimization history[b]					4.34	1	<0.05
Crime victim in past 4 months	90	27.19	23	25.56			
Not a crime victim	241	72.81	36	14.94			
Discharge diagnosis					0.41	2	n.s.
Schizophrenia or schizoaffective disorder	198	59.82	35	17.68			
Other psychotic disorder	27	8.16	6	22.22			
Affective disorder	106	32.02	18	16.98			
Alcohol or drug problem					8.38	1	<0.01
No	219	66.16	29	13.24			
Yes	112	33.84	30	26.79			
Score for insight into illness[d]					0.88	1	n.s.
Low (below median)	164	49.55	33	20.12			
High (above median)	167	50.45	26	15.57			

(continued)

Table I *(continued)*

Characteristic	N	%	N	%	χ^2	df	p
			Committed Violent Act in Previous 4 Months		**Analysis**[a]		
					Adjusted		
Global functioning score[e]					0.01	1	n.s.
Low (lowest quartile)	69	20.85	12	17.39			
Other (upper quartiles)	262	79.15	47	17.94			
Medication noncompliance					0.68	1	n.s.
No	96	29.00	14	14.58			
Yes	235	71.00	45	19.15			

a. For two-level categorical variables, Yates's correction is used; for three-level variables, adjusted likelihood chi-square is used.
b. $p = 0.04$, Fisher's exact test.
c. Data missing for two subjects.
d. Score on the Insight and Treatment Attitudes Questionnaire (McEvoy et al., 1989); median = 14.00 (mean=13.10, SD = 5.74).
e. Score on the Global Assessment of Functioning Scale; median=47.00 (mean = 48.82, SD = 7.94); lowest quartile = 25-45.

Since some bivariate associations with violence were confounded by relationships among predictors, we next conducted multivariable logistic regression analyses that used demographic characteristics, diagnosis, victimization, alcohol or drug problems, insight into illness, and medication noncompliance as predictor variables. The dependent variable in these models was, again, a dichotomous measure of any serious violent acts in the previous 4 months, as determined from any one of three sources of information.

Variables were entered into the regression equations in three stages: (1) demographic variables (age, gender, education, marital status, urban residence, race, and victimization); (2) clinical variables (diagnosis, insight into illness, Global Assessment of Functioning Scale score, medication noncompliance, and alcohol or drug problems); and (3) terms that showed the single and combined effects of noncompliance and substance abuse problems on violence. Results are shown in table 2.

In stage 1, the combination of being African American and a crime victim was the only predictor of violence that emerged as statistically significant. Race and victimization were coded together in the manner shown because race was not of interest as an intrinsic individual risk fac-

Table 2

Logistic Regression Analysis of Predictors of Serious Violence by 331 Involuntarily Admitted Inpatients with Severe Mental Illness

Predictor	Stage 1 (demographic variables)[a]		Stage 2 (stage 1 plus clinical variables)[b]		Stage 3 (stage 2 plus noncompliance and substance problems)[c]	
	Odds Ratio	95% Confidence Interval	Odds Ratio	95% Confidence Interval	Odds Ratio	95% Confidence Interval
Age	0.74	0.48–1.16	0.75	0.48–1.19	0.81	0.51–1.28
Male	1.77	0.95–3.30	1.59	0.81–3.11	1.64	0.84–3.23
Education	0.89	0.67–1.17	0.87	0.66–1.15	0.86	0.66–1.14
Married or cohabiting	1.84	0.90–3.75	1.72	0.83–3.59	1.79	0.85–3.76
Urban versus rural	0.71	0.39–1.31	0.62	0.33–1.17	0.62	0.33–1.19
African American and not crime victim	1.69	0.76–3.76	1.55	0.67–3.56	1.58	0.69–3.65
Crime victim and not African American	1.04	0.26–4.20	0.99	0.24–4.10	0.99	0.24–4.13
African American and crime victim	3.92**	1.63–9.42	3.87**	1.56–9.63	3.96**	1.59–9.86
Schizophrenia			0.96	0.47–1.95	0.93	0.46–1.91
Other psychotic disorder			1.36	0.44–4.21	1.28	0.41–4.01
Insight into illness			1.68	0.91–3.12	1.71	0.91–3.21
Low global functioning score			0.63	0.29–1.35	0.63	0.29–1.35
Noncompliant with medications			1.39	0.67–2.87		
Alcohol or drug problems			2.00*	1.03–3.86		
Compliant and has substance problems					0.24	0.03–2.10
Noncompliant but no substance problems					0.77	0.33–1.79
Noncompliant and has substance problems					2.29*	1.01–5.21

a. Observed/predicted ratio = 0.69, χ^2 = 20.92, df = 8, p = 0.007.
b. Observed/predicted ratio = 0.74, χ^2 = 29.47, df = 14, p = 0.009.
c. Observed/predicted ratio = 0.75, χ^2 = 36.43, df = 15, p = 0.002.
*p<0.05, **p<0.01.

tor but rather as a social designation that may correlate with environmental precipitants of violence. As shown by Hiday and colleagues (unpublished 1997 study) in related analyses of these data, African Americans were no more likely than whites to commit violent acts *unless* they also reported recent victimization. Similarly, the current analysis shows that African American crime victims were roughly twice as likely as African American nonvictims to have committed violent acts. Rates of violence among these African American nonvictims were not significantly higher than those of their white counterparts. This suggests that the apparent race effect is largely explained by social-environmental strains.

In stage 2, diagnosis, insight into illness, and noncompliance were not significant as main effects, while patients with substance abuse problems were twice as likely to have engaged in violent behavior. In stage 3, we followed the lead of prior studies, which, taken together, suggested a complex linkage among noncompliance, substance abuse, assaultiveness, and poor clinical outcomes. Specifically, we explored the potential for a combined effect of substance abuse and medication noncompliance on the risk of serious violent acts by creating a new dummy variable for subjects with both substance abuse *and* noncompliance to compare to subjects without one of these two attributes. It should be noted that these dummy variables are subcategories of subjects with these co-occurring attributes and not interaction terms as are often used in multivariable regression analyses.

These results suggest that the co-occurrence of substance abuse with medication noncompliance may explain much of the observed relationship of comorbidity with violence among the severely mentally ill. Specifically, it can be seen that those respondents with *both* noncompliance and substance abuse problems were more than twice as likely to commit violent acts, while those individuals with either of these problems alone had no greater risk of violence. Thus, compliant, substance-abusing, or non-substance-abusing and noncompliant severely mentally ill individuals were no more likely to commit violent acts than other individuals in the study.

A final model (not shown here) examined the risk of violence among respondents who, in addition to medication nonadherence and substance abuse, also manifested low insight into illness, as measured by the Insight and Treatment Attitudes Questionnaire score. This analysis also showed a high risk of violence in the group with all three of these risk factors, but the paucity of subjects in certain comparison groups (e.g., subjects with noncompliance, substance abuse, and *high* insight) makes this model less reliable.

Discussion

In this study we examined a number of risk factors for violent behavior in a study group of recently hospitalized severely mentally ill individuals. In a multivariable model, the combination of substance abuse problems *and* medication noncompliance was found to be significantly associated with serious violent behavior that occurred in the 4-month period before hospitalization after key sociodemographic and clinical characteristics were controlled. Greater risk for violence was also likely associated with the combination of substance problems, medication noncompliance, and low levels of insight into illness, but we have less confidence in results that incorporate insight because low insight was highly correlated with these other variables.

Among the sociodemographic variables examined, only the combined effect of being victimized and African American was significant, while urban residence was not. One way to interpret this result is that the living environments in which many severely mentally ill African Americans find themselves—high-crime areas experienced as dangerous and threatening—explains much of the violence risk that might otherwise be statistically attributable to race per se.

These findings suggest generally that substance abuse problems, medication noncompliance, and low insight into illness operate together to increase violence risk. However, the study is limited in several ways. In these cross-sectional, retrospective analyses, the sequencing of pathways to violence among these risk factors is not possible. Future analyses will examine such causal relationships and pathways by using longitudinal data currently being collected in this study.

The findings presented here may not be generalizable to all persons with severe mental illness. Subjects in this study were involuntarily admitted and outpatient committed patients—individuals who exhibited "dangerous" or "gravely disabled" behavior and who were also judged to be at risk for poor outcomes in community treatment. However, while the subjects were arguably more severely impaired than many severely mentally ill patients, there is nothing to suggest that the relationship between violence and the predictors shown here would be different for less severely ill individuals. For example, controlling for level of functional impairment did not change these relationships.

Various interpretations of our findings are plausible. Noncompliance and substance abuse may be mutually reinforcing problems in that substance impairment may impede medication adherence while noncompliance, in turn, may lead to self-medicating with alcohol or illicit drugs (Pristach & Smith, 1996). However, it is also possible that both variables—noncompliance and substance abuse—result from some other latent factor such as general disaffiliation from treatment or unspecified personality traits, although we have no evidence of these factors at present. We did not administer a personality inventory, which is another limitation to this study.

In sum, these findings shed light on a particular set of problems experienced by persons with severe mental disorders—specifically those who may fall into a self-perpetuating cycle of resistance to treatment, illness exacerbation, substance abuse, violent behavior, and institutional recidivism (Hiday, 1995; Mulvey, 1994; Osher & Drake, 1996; Torrey, 1994). Adverse side effects and complicated dosing regimens can make it especially difficult for patients to take neuroleptic medications as prescribed. In turn, untreated psychopathology and distress may lead to alcohol and other drug abuse (Pristach & Smith, 1996). Risk of violence may then increase as well because of substance use, exacerbation of psychiatric symptoms, or the influence of criminal environments in which illicit drugs are procured. Finally, violent behavior may further erode supportive social and therapeutic relationships and may precipitate involuntary commitment or incarceration (Borum et al., 1997). As these problems compound one another, conventional separate-track mental health and substance abuse treatment is unlikely to succeed (Osher & Drake, 1996; Owen et al., 1996; Swanson et al., 1997).

Our data also suggest that effective community treatment for this population requires careful attention to medication adherence and the availability of integrated substance abuse and mental health treatment (Drake et al., 1993; Osher & Drake, 1996). Specialized outpatient services focused on people with dually diagnosed severe mental illness are in short supply in many publicly funded mental health systems but may be crucial for effective management of violence risk in the era of cost containment.

References

Amador, X. F., Strauss, D. H., Yale, S. A., Flaum, M. M., Endicott, J., & Gorman, J. M. (1993). Assessment of insight in psychosis. *American Journal of Psychiatry, 150,* 873–879.

Bartels, S. J., Drake, R. E., & Wallach, M. A. (1995). Long-term course of substance use disorders among patients with severe mental illness. *Psychiatric Services, 46,* 248–251.

Bartels, S. J., Drake, R. E., Wallach, M. A., & Freeman, D. H. (1991). Characteristic hostility in schizophrenic outpatients. *Schizophrenia Bulletin, 17,* 163–171.

Bartels, S. J., Teague, G. B., Drake, R. E., Clark, R. E., Bush, P. W., & Noordsy, D. L. (1993). Substance abuse in schizophrenia: Service utilization and costs. *Journal of Nervous and Mental Disease, 181,* 227–232.

Borum, R., Swanson, J. W., Swartz, M. S., & Hiday, V. A. (1997). Substance abuse, violent behavior and police encounters among persons with severe mental disorders. *Journal of Contemporary Criminal Justice, 13,* 236–249.

Borum, R., Swartz, M. S., & Swanson, J. W. (1996). Assessing and managing violence risk in clinical practice. *Journal of Practical Psychiatry and Behavioral Health, 2,* 205–215.

Buchanan, A., & David, A. (1994). Compliance and the reduction of dangerousness. *Journal of Mental Health, 3,* 427–429.

Casper, E. S., & Regan, J. R. (1993). Reasons for admission among six profile subgroups of recidivists of inpatient services. *Canadian Journal of Psychiatry, 38,* 657–661.

Cuffel, B. J., Shumway, M., Chouljian, T. L., & MacDonald, T. (1994). A longitudinal study of substance use and community violence in schizophrenia. *Journal of Nervous and Mental Disease, 182,* 704–708.

David, A. S. (1990). Insight and psychosis. *British Journal of Psychiatry, 156,* 798–808.

Drake, R. E., Alterman, A. I., & Rosenberg, S. R. (1993). Detection of substance use disorders in severely mentally ill patients. *Community Mental Health Journal, 29,* 175–192.

Drake, R. E., Bartels, S. J., Teague, G. B., Noordsy, D. L., & Clark, R. E. (1993). Treatment of substance abuse in severely mentally ill patients. *Journal of Nervous and Mental Disease, 181,* 606–611.

Drake, R. E., & Wallach, M. A. (1992). Mental patients' attraction to the hospital: Correlates of living preference. *Community Mental Health Journal, 28,* 5–12.

Drake, R. E., Wallach, M. A., Teague, G. B., Freeman, D. H., Paskus, T. S., & Clark, T. A. (1991). Housing instability and homelessness among rural schizophrenic patients. *American Journal of Psychiatry, 148,* 330–336.

Dvoskin, J. A., & Steadman, H. J. (1994). Using intensive care management to reduce violence by mentally ill persons in the community. *Hospital and Community Psychiatry, 45,* 679–684.

Geller, J. L. (1990). Clinical guidelines for the use of involuntary outpatient treatment. *Hospital and Community Psychiatry, 41,* 749–755.

Haywood, T. W., Kravitz, H. M., Grossman, L. S., Cavanaugh Jr., J. L., Davis, J. M., & Lewis, D. A. (1995). Predicting the "revolving door" phenomenon among patients with schizophrenic, schizoaffective, and affective disorders. *American Journal of Psychiatry, 152,* 856–861.

Hiday, V. A. (1995). The social context of mental illness and violence. *Journal of Health and Social Behavior, 36,* 122–137.

Hiday, V. A., & Scheid-Cook, T. L. (1991). Outpatient commitment for "revolving door" patients: Compliance and treatment. *Journal of Nervous and Mental Disease, 179,* 83–88.

Markova, I. S., & Berrios, G. E. (1995). Insight in clinical psychiatry revisited. *Comprehensive Psychiatry, 36,* 367–376.

McEvoy, J. P., Appelbaum, P. S., Apperson, L. J., Geller, J. L., & Freter, S. (1989). Why must some schizophrenic patients be involuntarily committed? The role of insight. *Comprehensive Psychiatry, 30,* 13–17.

McEvoy, J. P., Apperson, L. J., Appelbaum, P. S., Ortlip, P., Brecosky, J., Hammill, K., Geller, J. L., & Roth, L. H. (1989). Insight in schizophrenia: Its relationship to acute psychopathology. *Journal of Nervous and Mental Disease, 177,* 43–47.

McEvoy, J. P., Freter, S., Everett, G., Geller, J. L., Appelbaum, P. S., Apperson, L. J., & Roth, L. H. (1989). Insight and the clinical outcome of schizophrenic patients. *Journal of Nervous and Mental Disease, 177,* 48–51.

Monahan, J., & Steadman, H. J. (1994). Violence and mental disorder: *Developments in risk assessment.* Chicago, IL: University of Chicago Press.

Mulvey, E. V. (1994). Assessing the evidence of a link between mental illness and violence. *Hospital and Community Psychiatry, 45,* 663–668.

Osher, F. C., & Drake, R. E. (1996). Reversing a history of unmet needs: Approaches to care for persons with co-occurring addictive and mental disorders. *American Journal of Orthopsychiatry, 66,* 4–11.

Owen, R. R., Fischer, E. P., Booth, B. B., & Cuffel, B. J. (1996). Medication noncompliance and substance abuse among patients with schizophrenia. *Psychiatric Services, 47,* 853–858.

Pristach, C. A., & Smith, C. M. (1990). Medication compliance and substance abuse among schizophrenic patients. *Hospital and Community Psychiatry, 41,* 1345–1348.

Pristach, C. A., & Smith, C. M. (1996). Self-reported effects of alcohol use on symptoms of schizophrenia. *Psychiatric Services, 47,* 421–423.

Salloum, I. M., Daley, D. C., Cornelius, J. R., Kirisci, L., & Thase, M. E. (1996). Disproportionate lethality in psychiatric patients with concurrent alcohol and cocaine abuse. *American Journal of Psychiatry, 153,* 953–955.

Smith, J., & Hucker, S. (1994). Schizophrenia and substance abuse. *British Journal of Psychiatry, 165,* 13–21.

Smith, L. D. (1989). Medication refusal and the rehospitalized mentally ill inmate. *Hospital and Community Psychiatry, 40,* 491–496.

Spitzer, R. L., Williams, J. B. W., Gibbon, M., & First, M. B. (1990). *User's guide for the structured clinical interview for DSM-III-R (SCID).* Washington, DC: American Psychiatric Press.

Steadman, H. J., Monahan, J., Appelbaum, P. S., Grisso, T., Mulvey, E. P., Roth, L. H., Robbins, P. C., & Klassen, D. (1994). Designing a new generation of risk assessment research. In J. Monahan & H. J. Steadman (Eds.), *Violence and mental disorder: Developments in risk assessment* (pp. 287–318) Chicago, IL: University of Chicago Press.

Swanson, J. W. (1994). Mental disorder, substance abuse, and community violence: An epidemiological approach. In J. Monahan & H. J. Steadman (Eds.), *Violence and mental disorder: Developments in risk assessment* (pp. 101–136). Chicago, IL: University of Chicago Press.

Swanson, J. W., Borum, R., Swartz, M. S., & Monahan, J. (1996). Psychotic symptoms and disorders and the risk of violent behavior in the community. *Criminal Behavior and Mental Health, 6,* 309–329.

Swanson, J. W., Estroff, S. E., Swartz, M. S., Borum, R., Lachicotte, W., Zimmer, C., & Wagner, H. R. (1997). Violence and severe mental disorder in clinical and community populations: The effects of psychotic symptoms, comorbidity, and lack of treatment. *Psychiatry, 60,* 1–22.

Swanson, J. W., Swartz, M. S., George, L. K., Burns, B. J., Hiday, V. A., Borum, R., & Wagner, H. R. (1997). Interpreting the effectiveness of involuntary outpatient commitment: A conceptual model. *Journal of American Academic Psychiatry Law, 25,* 5–16.

Swartz, M. S., Burns, B. J., Hiday, V. A., George, L. K., Swanson, J. W., & Wagner, H. R. (1995). New directions in research on involuntary outpatient commitment. *Psychiatric Services, 46,* 381–385.

Torrey, E. F. (1994). Violent behavior by individuals with serious mental illness. *Hospital and Community Psychiatry, 45,* 653–662.

Legal System Involvement and Costs for Persons in Treatment for Severe Mental Illness and Substance Use Disorders

Robin E. Clark, Susan K. Ricketts & Gregory J. McHugo

This article originally appeared in *Psychiatric Services*, 1999, 50(5) and is reprinted with permission.

Robin E. Clark, Ph.D., Susan K. Ricketts, B.S., & Gregory J. McHugo, Ph.D., Hampshire-Dartmouth Psychiatric Research Center and Dartmouth Medical School.

This project was supported by grants MH-00839, MH-46072, and MH-47567 from the National Institute of Mental Health, by grant AA-08341 from the National Institute on Alcohol Abuse and Alcoholism, and by the New Hampshire Division of Mental Health and Developmental Services.

Objective: Persons with co-occurring severe mental illness and-substance use disorders were followed for 3 years to better understand how they are involved with the legal system and to identify factors associated with different kinds of involvement. Methods: Data came from a 3-year study of 203 persons enrolled in specialized treatment for dual disorders. Cost and utilization data were collected from multiple data sources, including police, sheriffs and deputies, officers of the court, public defenders, prosecutors, private attorneys, local and county, jails, state prisons, and paid legal guardians. Results: Over 3 years 169 participants (83%) had contact with the legal system, and 90 (44%) were arrested at least once. Participants were four times more likely to have encounters with the legal system that did not result in arrest than they were to be arrested. Costs associated with nonarrest encounters were significantly less than costs associated with arrests. Mean costs per person associated with an arrest were $2,295, and mean costs associated with a nonarrest encounter were $385. Combined 3-year costs averaged $2,680 per person. Arrests and incarcerations declined over time. Continued substance use and unstable housing were associated with a greater likelihood of arrest. Poor treatment engagement was associated with multiple arrests. Men were more likely to be arrested, and women were more likely to be the victims of crime. Conclusions: Effective treatment of substance use among persons with mental illness appears to reduce arrests and incarcerations but not the frequency of nonarrest encounters. Stable housing may also reduce the likelihood and number of arrests.

Persons with severe mental illnesses, such as schizophrenia and bipolar disorder, are at greater risk for arrest and incarceration than the general population (McFarland, Faulkner, Bloom, et al., 1989; Teplin, 1984). Abuse of alcohol or other drugs further increases the likelihood of involvement in the legal system (Abram & Teplin, 1991; Holcomb & Ahr, 1988).

Despite the more frequent contact with criminal justice authorities by persons with mental illness, research does not support the widely held notion that this group represents a significant threat to others. Most offenses are minor, and the association between violence and mental illness is weak (Fischer, 1988; Teplin, 1985). However, a recent study suggests that substance abuse increases the likelihood of violent behavior among persons with mental illness (Stedman, Mulvey, Monahan, et al., 1998). Some studies indicate that increased vulnerability and stigma may contribute significantly to higher arrest rates in this group (Robertson, 1988; Teplin, 1984).

Contact between persons with serious mental illness and the legal system extends beyond activities related to illegal behavior. It is increasingly recognized that persons with serious mental illness have high rates of physical and sexual victimization (Carmen, Rieker, & Mills, 1984; Jacobson & Richardson, 1987). In some locations, jails and prisons substitute for distant or overburdened mental health facilities. Much has been written about persons with mental illness who go untreated in urban correctional facilities (Belcher, 1988; Lamb & Grant, 1982), but the problem is not limited to cities. Sullivan and Spritzer (Sullivan & Spritzer, 1997) documented systematic use of jails as temporary holding facilities for persons with serious mental illness in rural areas. Legal processes associated with involuntary commitment and guardianship, police assistance in psychiatric emergencies, and the role of law enforcement officials in transporting persons with serious mental illness to treatment facilities may also contribute to costs incurred by the legal system (Clark, Teague, Ricketts, et al., 1994).

Despite the extensive contact that persons with serious mental illness have with police, courts, corrections facilities, probation and parole officers and legal advocates, the costs of such contact have been difficult to measure, and factors contributing to such costs remain poorly understood. Better information about contacts and costs would help identify problems and might suggest policy interventions that could improve the lives of persons with serious mental illness and the legal system's efficiency.

In this study, we used data from a more comprehensive cost-effectiveness study that examined social costs incurred by patients with co-occurring serious mental illness and substance use disorders who were in assertive community treatment and standard case management. The study reported here examined costs of involvement in the legal system by this group and explored factors associated with arrests and other types of encounters with the legal system.

Previous studies have identified several correlates of police encounters among persons with serious mental illness. Both substance abuse and homelessness are associated with high arrest and incarceration rates (Martell, Rosner, & Harmon, 1995; Solomon, Draine, Marcenko, et al., 1992). Men are more likely than women to be arrested (Fischer, 1988); young adults have higher arrest rates than older adults (Holcomb & Ahr, 1988). Persons with serious mental illness who live in urban areas appear to be at greater risk of arrest and incarceration than those in rural areas (Holcomb & Ahr, 1988) and may also be at greater risk of victimization (Sampson & Castellano, 1982). The contribution to arrest or incarceration made by clinical factors, such as diagnosis, symptoms, and aggressiveness, is not well established.

Because most studies have focused on arrest and incarceration rates or on criminal behavior, relatively little is known about the frequency and cost of encounters not resulting in arrest. Some empirical evidence suggests that encounters that do not result in arrest are much more frequent than those that do (Wolff, Diamond, & Helminiak, 1997). Police often note that because of the frequency of these encounters, they absorb significant amounts of time. Furthermore, despite the relative frequency of civil actions, such as lawsuits, guardianship activities, and involuntary hospitalizations, costs associated with civil actions have been ignored by most researchers.

The impact of treatment on the involvement of persons with mental illness with the legal system is ambiguous. Contact with the legal system is often seen as a result of inadequate treatment. Interventions such as assertive community treatment, which provide services to clients in natural settings, would seem to reduce encounters by substituting treatment providers for police in crisis response situations and by reducing the frequency of behaviors that lead to legal intervention, such as public disturbances. However, Wolff and associates (Wolff et al., 1997) found a high 1-year rate of involvement in the legal system among a sample of persons with serious mental illness who were receiving assertive community treatment. Some investigators have suggested that assertive community treatment reduces encounters with the legal system (Bond, Witheridge, Dincin, et al., 1990), some have found no effect (Solomon, Draine, & Meyerson, 1994), and others have observed increases in encounters (McGrew, Bond, Dietzen, et al., 1995).

Attempts to measure the frequency and cost of legal system encounters by persons with serious mental illness have been hampered by several problems. Many studies have relied on self-reported encounters, which may underestimate involvement. Few studies have measured the cost of services provided by all elements of the legal system, raising questions about the accuracy of total cost estimates. There are almost no data on the involvement in the legal system of persons with mental illness for a period longer than 1 year. Finally, most studies have been conducted in cities. Although crime may be more common there, it is also important to understand the characteristics of persons with serious mental illness involved with the legal system in rural areas.

In this study we went beyond these limitations by using an extensive, multisource system for tracking encounters for 3½ years and by carefully measuring the costs of each legal system component during the final 3 years of this period.

Our goals were to present a more complete picture of how persons with dual disorders are involved with the legal system, to identify factors associated with varieties of involvement, and to clarify the implications of these findings for mental health policy.

Methods

Data used in this analysis are from the New Hampshire dual disorder treatment study. Clinical and functional outcomes, as well as a cost-effectiveness analysis, are reported elsewhere (Clark, Teague, Ricketts, et al., 1998; Drake, McHugo, Clark, et al., 1998). The cost-effectiveness analysis reported only total legal costs. This paper examines legal system involvement and its correlates in greater detail.

Sample

Study participants were selected from seven of New Hampshire's ten mental health catchment areas. Two of these areas were urban, centered around cities with populations between 100,000 and 150,000; the remaining five were predominantly rural, with towns of 25,000 persons or less. Participants were eligible for the study if they had a *DSM-III-R* diagnosis of schizophrenia, schizoaffective disorder, or bipolar disorder and a *DSM-III-R* diagnosis of an active substance use disorder within the past 6 months, with no additional severe medical conditions or mental retardation. Participants had to be between the ages of 18 and 60 years and be willing to provide written informed consent to participate in the study.

Of the 306 persons who were initially screened, 223 were enrolled in the study and randomly assigned to assertive community treatment or standard case management. Both programs provided enhanced community-based treatment in the context of a highly rated public mental health system (Torrey, Erdman, Wolfe, et al., 1990). A total of 166 participants (74%) were male, and 215 (96%) were from white nonminority groups. A total of 136 participants (61%) had never been married, 140 (63%) had at least a high school education, and 183 (82%) were unemployed. The mean $\pm SD$ age at study entry was 34±8.5 years.

A total of 120 participants (54%) were diagnosed as having schizophrenia. Fifty (23%) had a diagnosis of schizoaffective disorder, and the remainder (53 participants, or 24%) met criteria for bipolar disorder. All participants had a substance use disorder; 163 (73%) had an alcohol use disorder, and 94 (42%) had a drug use disorder, primarily cannabis or cocaine.

Over the study period (1989 to 1993), 20 participants were lost to follow-up. Of these, 11 refused to continue the study, 7 died, and 2 moved to other states and could not be located for subsequent interviews. Among the remaining 203 participants, those enrolled in standard case management and assertive community treatment did not differ significantly in the number of legal system encounters during the 6 months before study entry or on any criteria for study entry. A more detailed description of sample selection has been published elsewhere (Drake et al., 1998).

Legal system encounters were tracked for $3^{1}/2$ years, beginning 6 months before participants were randomly assigned to the treatment groups and continuing for 3 years afterward. Costs were computed only for the 3 years after randomization. We were unable to collect comprehensive treatment cost data on ten of the 203 participants who completed the study (five participants from each treatment group). These participants received significant amounts of treatment from an out-of-state provider for one or more of the 6-month measurement periods, preventing us from accurately assessing mental health treatment costs.

Measurement Procedures

We measured all legal system costs associated with the study participants. The costs of receiving a report, investigating, adjudicating, and carrying out the sentence associated with a crime were included; however, personal costs associated with criminal victimization, such as the value of items stolen or income lost due to an injury, were excluded. All services provided by police, sheriffs and deputies, officers of the court, public defenders, prosecutors, private attorneys, local and county jails, state prisons, and paid legal guardians were included in our analysis. Medical records at the state psychiatric hospital were used to document involuntary commitment hearings in probate court because we were denied access to records. Lack of access to probate court records also prevented accurate measurement of divorce and child custody proceedings.

With each participant's written consent, data were collected from a statewide registry of arrests and from records maintained by local police, courts, jails, probation and parole offices, public guardians, state hospitals, and prisons. Reports from participants, family members, and case managers were also used to identify possible encounters with the legal system that occurred outside the state or that were not identified through initial record reviews. We then attempted to verify these self-reports with additional record reviews.

To determine unit costs, we examined expenditures and management information of representative police departments, courts, jails, prisons, an office of public guardianship, public prosecutors and defenders, private attorneys, and probation and parole offices. Time estimates for various types of court appearances were based on a combination of court records and interviews with court personnel. Police time was measured from police activity logs. Costs were determined for appropriate production units such as cost per hour of direct police service, cost per day of incarceration, cost per month of parole supervision at each of three levels of intensity, and so forth. When appropriate, expenditures were adjusted to include costs of operation, such as depreciated building space or vehicles purchased through another department.

We used an episode approach to allocate costs to time periods. All legal costs were associated with a triggering event, such as an arrest; costs were attributed to the period in which that event occurred. For example, for a person convicted because of an event occurring in the 6 months before the study period, all costs associated with that event (court appearances, legal representation, and imprisonment) were attributed to the baseline period. If a participant was arrested near the end of the study, all subsequent costs (discounted by 3% because they were incurred at a later time) were included in the study period.

Analytic approach

We calculated total legal system encounters and costs. Costs related to arrests and to encounters that did not result in arrests were examined separately because they represent qualitatively different events. Little is known about costs of encounters not resulting in arrest because they are seldom included in cost analyses.

Episode counts and cost distributions were bimodal, with several participants having no episodes and several having large numbers of encounters. We used both parametric statistics (t tests with log-transformed data) and nonparametric statistics (Mann-Whitney U tests) to compare participants who received assertive community treatment and standard case management. Analyses were repeated with data for patients with extremely high scores excluded from the analysis.

To explore factors related to legal system encounters over the 3 years after participants were randomly assigned to a treatment group, we used three logistic regression models with similar independent variables and with three dichotomous dependent variables: ever arrested versus never arrested, arrested more than once versus arrested once or never arrested, and having three or more encounters not leading to arrest versus having fewer than three. These classifications were adopted after examining distributional patterns of the continuous variables from which they were derived. In their continuous form, arrests and nonarrest encounters were skewed, making a categorical transformation appropriate. A different grouping was used for multiple nonarrest encounters (more than three encounters) than for arrest encounters (more than one arrest) to reflect the relatively greater frequency of nonarrest encounters than encounters that ended in arrest.

The models included variables that have been associated in the literature with legal system involvement or that were of theoretical importance (for example, housing instability). Independent variables included age, gender, diagnosis (schizophrenia spectrum versus bipolar disorder), urban or rural residence, treatment assignment (assertive community treatment versus standard case management), stage of substance abuse treatment at the beginning of the study (McHugo, Drake, Burton, et al., 1996), a cumulative measure of time spent in various stages of substance abuse treatment over the course of the study (stage of treatment multiplied by the amount of time spent in that stage), 3-year inpatient and outpatient treatment costs, a variable indicating the number of 6-month periods in which the participant reported physically attacking someone, the number of residential moves (excluding hospitalizations) over 3 years, and a variable indicating that the participant lived in unsupervised housing for more than 1 year.

Results

Contact with the legal system was common among the 203 study participants. A total of 169 of the persons enrolled in the study (83%) had an encounter with the legal system during the 3-year period after they were randomly assigned to a treatment group. More than half of these persons were arrested at least once.

As Table 1 shows, the 3-year cost of all legal system encounters by the study sample was $543,950, approximately 2% of the total social costs of $23,353, 274 associated with the study participants (Clark et al., 1998). Participants were almost four times more likely to have an encounter not resulting in arrest than to be arrested, but arrests were far more costly, accounting for 85.6% of total legal system costs.

Participants in assertive community treatment and those in standard case management did not differ significantly in costs or encounters. None of the Mann-Whitney U test comparisons for arrests, arrest costs, nonarrest encounters, and costs for nonarrest encounters indicated a significant difference. T tests with log-transformed variables and with outliers removed also failed to detect significant differences between participants in assertive community treatment and those receiving standard case management.

A wide variety of types of encounters with the legal system occurred. Table 2 shows the number of encounters and the number of participants with encounters in 11 arrest categories and seven categories of encounters not resulting in arrest, plus the average costs associated with each. Nonarrest encounters were particularly diverse, which led to a rather large miscellaneous category.

Costs associated with specific types of arrest and nonarrest encounters varied. Sexual offenses, such as rape or public exposure, were

Table I

Legal system costs incurred over 3 years by persons with dual disorders assigned to assertive community treatment or standard case management[1]

Type of encounter	Total sample (N = 203)	Standard case management (N = 98)	Assertive community treatment (N = 105)
Arrest			
Total costs	$465,897	$237,053	$228,844
N of arrests	207	84	123
N of clients arrested	90	43	47
Mean ±SD cost per client	$2,295 ± $6,467	$2,419 ± $7,174	$2,179 ± $5,762
Encounter not resulting in arrest			
Total costs	$78,053	$36,280	$41,773
N of nonarrest encounters	803	334	469
N of clients with a nonarrest encounter	155	74	81
Mean ±SD cost per client	$385 ± $620	$370 ± $574	$398 ± $663
Total for arrests and nonarrest encounters			
Total costs	$543,950	$273,333	$270,617
N of clients with an arrest or a nonarrest encounter	169	80	89
Mean ±SD cost per client	$2,680 ± $6,487	$2,789 ± $7,180	$2,577 ± $5,798

1 All costs are reported in 1995 dollars.

Table 2

Costs associated with legal system involvement over 3 years by 169 persons with dual disorders who had contact with the legal system, by category of arrest or encounter[1]

Category	N arrests or encounters	N of clients	% of total sample	Cost per arrest or encounter	
				Mean	SD
Arrest					
Shoplifting, theft, or robbery	40	28	14	$2,395	$4,229
Substance abuse related charge	36	30	15	1,787	3,285
Disorderly conduct, criminal mischief	35	25	12	1,072	771
Assault, criminal threatening	28	23	11	1,353	1,169
Domestic violence petition (perpetrator)	23	18	9	395	204
Criminal trespass	16	12	6	2,160	2,622
Minor or miscellaneous charge	10	8	4	2,367	4,148
Sexual offense	9	7	3	16,589	19,330
Miscellaneous motor vehicle charge	5	5	2	874	154
Prostitution	4	3	2	2,007	2,167
Weapon possession	1	1	1	1,376	na
Encounter not resulting in arrest					
Mental health or medical assistance	190	76	37	$51	$56
Complaint by client	176	52	26	20	43
Involuntary commitment or guardian	127	57	28	390	274
Miscellaneous contact	126	61	30	33	75
Victimization	113	58	29	52	68
Complaint against client	62	36	18	41	67
Civil suit	9	8	4	287	156

1. The total sample included 203 dually diagnosed persons. All costs are reported in 1995 dollars.

Figure 1

Arrests, encounters with the legal system not resulting in arrests, and incarceration among 203 persons with dual disorders 6 months before the study and in 6-month periods over 3 years

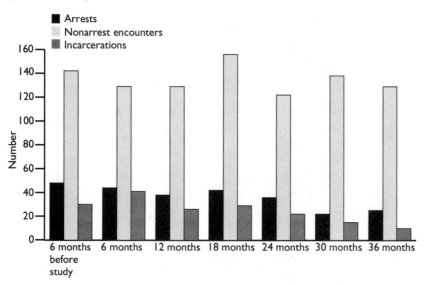

infrequent but costly, due primarily to lengthy prison sentences. Although more frequent than arrests, encounters that did not result in arrest, such as complaints filed by or against study participants and medical assistance received, were the least costly.

As shown in figure 1, repeated-measures analysis of variance indicated that the number of arrests in each 6-month period declined over the study period, dropping from 48 arrests for the entire sample in the 6 months before study entry to 25 arrests in the final 6-month period ($F = 2.40$, $df = 6,196$, $p = .029$). The number of incarcerations also declined, from 23 during the baseline period to eight in the final period ($F = 3.50$, $df = 6,196$, $p = .003$). A total of 142 encounters not resulting in arrest were recorded for the baseline period, and 129 encounters were recorded in the last period, not a statistically significant decrease.

Table 3 outlines sources of legal system costs for persons who had contacts with the legal system. Although relatively infrequent, jailings and imprisonments accounted for more than half of arrest costs (55%). Courts and police accounted for the largest proportion of costs for nonarrest encounters—43% and 36%, respectively. Cost for legal episodes varied widely between individuals.

Table 3

Costs associated with legal system involvement over 3 years by 169 persons with dual disorders who had contact with the legal system[1]

Type of encounter	% of sample	Ratio of arrests or encounters to clients	Cost per client by service category													
			Police		Court		Attorney		Jail		Probation and parole		Sheriff transport		Total	
			Mean	SD	Mean	SD	Mean	SD	Mean	SD	Mean	SD	Mean	SD	Mean	SD
Arrest	44	2.30	$209	$250	$868	$752	$905	$809	$2,821	$7,819	$332	$1,773	$41	$90	$5,177	$8,935
Nonarrest encounter	76	5.21	182	291	217	449	64	146	7	24	0	—	35	86	507	$667
Arrests and nonarrest encounters	83	5.98	278	389	661	925	541	856	1,509	6,450	177	1,169	54	115	3,219	6,989

1 All costs are reported in 1995 dollars.

Table 4

Odds ratios for variables associated with being arrested, being arrested more than once, and having multiple encounters with the legal system that did not end in arrest (nonarrest encounters) among 203 persons with dual disorders[1]

Variable	Odds of being arrested	Odds of being arrested more than once	Odds of having three or more nonarrest encounters
Age	.999	1.016	.979
Bipolar disorder	1.683	.845	.926
Assertive community treatment	.894	1.173	.992
Female	.259***	.280**	2.966***
Stage of substance abuse treatment at study entry	.815	.877	.939
Stage of substance abuse treatment during the study	.856***	.924	.985
Costs of nonarrest encounters above $1,000	4.761***	3.071**	—
Costs of arrests above $1,000	—	—	1.010
Costs of inpatient treatment above $1,000	.993	.998	1.019***
Costs of outpatient treatment above $1,000	.991	.978***	.997
Number of arrests in 6 months before study entry	1.591*	1.826**	—
Number of nonarrest encounters in 6 months before study entry	—	—	1.360**
Number of 6-month periods participant reported attacking someone	1.192	1.530*	1.784**
Urban area	1.191	1.049	1.827
Number of residential moves	1.639*	2.570***	1.350
Residence in unsupervised housing for 1 year or more	1.272	1.336	4.070**
% of cases classified correctly by the model	68.9	84.5	77.7

1. 44% of clients were arrested, 24% were arrested more than once, and 42% had more than three nonarrest encounters. The -2 log likelihood values for being arrested, being arrested more than once, and having three or more nonarrest encounters were 202.889, 146.612, and 200.001, respectively.

*$p < .10$, **$p < .05$, ***$p < .01$

Factors contributing to the likelihood of any arrest, of multiple arrests, or of multiple nonarrest contacts are shown in Table 4. The odds of being arrested were higher for men, for persons in the earlier stages of substance abuse recovery, for those who had higher legal costs associated with nonarrest encounters, and for persons who changed residences more frequently. A trend toward a greater likelihood of arrest for those with more arrests during the 6 months before study entry was also noted ($p = .08$).

Gender and costs for nonarrest encounters were also significant predictors of multiple arrests. Arrests in the baseline period and number of residential moves were stronger predictors of multiple arrests than of the probability of any arrest. Lower outpatient treatment costs and more frequent physical attacks on others were significant predictors of multiple arrests but not of the likelihood of any arrest.

In the third logistic regression model, which assessed factors associated with multiple nonarrest encounters, gender effects were reversed. Women more likely than men to be involved in multiple nonarrest contacts. This finding appears to have been due to women's greater likelihood of being victimized compared with men ($\chi^2 = 8.40$, $df = 1$, $p = .004$). Higher inpatient treatment costs, more nonarrest contacts during the 6 months before study entry, and more frequent attacks on others were associated with greater odds of having multiple nonarrest contacts. Persons who lived in unsupervised housing for a year or more were four times more likely to have multiple nonarrest contacts with the legal system than were those who spent less time in such settings.

Although the urban-rural distinction was not associated with being arrested or with having multiple nonarrest encounters, it seemed to be associated with the type of encounter. Persons in urban areas were more likely to file a complaint with police ($\chi^2 = 10.14$, $df = 1$, $p = .002$) and to be victims of crimes ($\chi^2 = 9.66$, $df = 1$, $p = .002$) than those in less densely populated areas. Persons living in rural areas were more likely to have complaints filed against them than their urban-dwelling counterparts ($\chi^2 = 3.91$, $df = 1$, $p = .05$).

Discussion

Even among participants enrolled in state-of-the-art treatment programs, arrests and other encounters with the legal system are regular occurrences for persons with dual disorders. This study found that the cost of these encounters varied widely by type of encounter. Informal encounters that do not end in arrest, by far the most frequent category of involvement, were usually inexpensive. Most costly were the small number of cases in which participants were convicted of a serious offense such as rape or aggravated assault and given a lengthy prison sentence.

Study participants who were arrested fit a profile different from those with multiple encounters not resulting in arrest. Persons with many nonarrest encounters had a history of such contacts, were likely to be women, and tended to live in unsupervised housing. Compared with those who had few contacts with the legal system, they received more inpatient treatment and reported being violent more often. The greater frequency of nonarrest encounters among women appeared to result from their greater likelihood of being crime victims compared with men. Unlike men, whose legal system involvement appeared to follow the pattern observed in homeless populations—frequent arrests, substance abuse, housing, instability, and tenuous engagement in treatment— women with multiple encounters with the legal system appeared to be relatively well engaged in treatment and living independently in unsupervised housing.

Our findings support the contention that effective treatment of persons with co-occurring serious mental illness and substance use disorders can reduce some legal system costs. Both arrests and incarcerations declined over time. Given the brief period for which data were available before participants entered the study (6 months) and the absence of an untreated control group, we cannot reject with complete confidence the hypothesis that the decline of arrests and incarcerations was due to a natural regression to more typical levels from an elevated level of involvement in the legal system at study entry. However, the association between lower outpatient costs, which we interpret as an indicator of poor treatment engagement, and multiple arrests suggests a more direct connection between treatment and arrests. Interestingly, this relationship did not hold for encounters that did not end in arrest.

We believe these data are among the most comprehensive and valid available on legal system costs for persons with dual disorders. They capture the majority of legal system activity associated with the study participants. However, the data probably underestimate the frequency of domestic violence perpetrated by participants, and therefore the costs to the legal system. The underestimation is due to the fact that such reports are typically filed under the victim's name rather than the assailant's, which hampered case identification. We suspect that this inability to identify some cases had only a small impact on our cost estimates overall.

A standard, but nonetheless important, caveat is that law enforcement and civil commitment practices in New Hampshire may differ from those in other areas. However, we were unable to identify specific examples of any practices that were unique to the state.

Conclusions

For individuals who have serious mental illness, stable supervised housing and effective treatment of substance abuse appear to reduce their involvement in the legal system and thus the associated costs. Given the relatively high cost of treatment and the comparatively low cost of involvement in the legal system, lowering legal system costs is not a sufficient rationale for undertaking intensive integrated treatment for dual disorders. Rather, reducing involvement in the legal system by persons with serious mental illness is an important by-product of the improved quality of life that persons with dual disorders experience when they are able to reduce or eliminate substance use, which benefits both these individuals and society.

Mental health treatment providers can reduce arrests by making substance abuse an important focus of treatment and by increasing their efforts to engage reluctant clients in treatment. Working with law enforcement officials and with clients to reduce the likelihood of victimization and treat its consequences, particularly among women, should also be a high priority.

The question of which costs should reasonably be included in a cost-effectiveness analysis is particularly difficult for persons with conditions such as comorbid serious mental illness and a substance use disorder because these conditions are often associated with social costs in addition to treatment. This study suggests that although costs associated with legal system involvement of persons with dual disorders represent a small portion of total social costs, measurement and analysis of legal system costs can provide useful information for treatment and policy planning. However, the relatively small proportion of costs associated with encounters not resulting in arrests may not justify the investment of substantial research resources in the precise measurement of such costs.

This study provides further evidence that persons with mental disorders, even those receiving high-quality treatment and those living in predominately rural areas, have a great deal of contact with law enforcement officials. Previous studies suggest that some of this contact is related to stigma and thus is inappropriate. Although this may be true in some cases, in many instances, such as serious criminal behavior or criminal victimization, the legal system is probably the appropriate point of first contact. However, police and others in the legal system must be equipped to work effectively with persons who have dual disorders and with their treatment providers.

References

Abram, K. M., & Teplin, L. A. (1991). Co-occurring disorders among mentally ill jail detainees. *American Psychologist, 46,* 1036–1045.

Belcher, J. R. (1988). Are jails replacing the mental health system for the homeless mentally ill? *Community Mental Health Journal, 24,* 185–195.

Bond, G. R., Witheridge, T. F., Dincin, J., et al. (1990). Assertive community treatment for frequent users of psychiatric hospitals in a large city: A controlled study. *American Journal of Community Psychology, 18,* 865–891.

Carmen, E. H., Rieker, P. P., & Mills, T. (1984). Victims of violence and psychiatric illness. *American Journal of Psychiatry, 141,* 378–383.

Clark, R. E., Teague, G. B., Ricketts, S. K., et al. (1994). Measuring resource use in economic evaluations: Determining the social costs of mental illness. *Journal of Mental Health Administration, 21,* 32–41.

Clark, R. E., Teague, G. B., Ricketts, S. K., et al. (1998). Cost-effectiveness of assertive community treatment versus standard case management for persons with co-occurring severe mental illness and substance use disorders. *Health Services Research, 33,* 1283–1306.

Drake, R. E., McHugo, G. J., Clark, H. E., et al. (1998). A clinical trial of assertive community treatment for patients with co-occurring severe mental illness and substance use disorder. *American Journal of Orthopsychiatry, 64,* 201–215.

Fischer, P. J. (1988). Criminal activity among the homeless: A study of arrests in Baltimore. *Hospital and Community Psychiatry, 39,* 46–51.

Holcomb, W. R., & Ahr, P. R. (1988). Arrest rates among young adult psychiatric patients treated in inpatient and outpatient settings. *Hospital and Community Psychiatry, 39,* 52–57.

Jacobson, A., & Richardson, B. (1987). Assault experiences of 100 psychiatric inpatients: Evidence of the need for routine inquiry. *American Journal of Psychiatry, 144,* 908–913.

Lamb, H. R., & Grant, R. W. (1982). The mentally ill in an urban county jail. *Archives of General Psychiatry, 39,* 17–22.

Martell, D. A., Rosner, R., & Harmon, R. B. (1995). Base-rate estimates of criminal behavior by homeless mentally ill persons in New York City. *Psychiatric Services, 46,* 596–600.

McFarland, B. H., Faulkner, L. R., Bloom, J. D., et al. (1989). Chronic mental illness and the criminal justice system. *Hospital and Community Psychiatry, 40,* 718–723.

McGrew, J. H., Bond, G. R., Dietzen, L., et al. (1995). A multisite study of client outcomes in assertive community treatment. *Psychiatric Services, 46,* 696–701.

McHugo, G. J., Drake, R. E., Burton, H. L., et al. (1996). A scale for assessing the stage of substance abuse treatment in persons with severe mental illness. *Journal of Nervous and Mental Disease, 183,* 762–767.

Robertson, G. (1988). Arrest patterns among mentally disordered offenders. *British Journal of Psychiatry, 153,* 313–316.

Sampson, R. J., & Castellano, T. C. (1982). Economic inequality and personal victimisation: An area perspective. *British Journal of Criminology, 22,* 363–385.

Solomon, P. L., Draine, J. N., Marcenko, M. O., et al. (1992). Homelessness in a mentally ill urban jail population. *Hospital and Community Psychiatry, 43,* 169–171.

Solomon, P. L., Draine, J. N., & Meyerson, A. (1994). Jail recidivism and receipt of community mental health services. *Hospital and Community Psychiatry, 45,* 793–797.

Stedman, H. J., Mulvey, E. P., Monahan, J., et al. (1998). Violence by people discharged from acute psychiatric inpatient facilities and by others in the same neighborhoods. *Archives of General Psychiatry, 55,* 393–404.

Sullivan, G., & Spritzer, K. (1997). The criminalization of persons with serious mental illness living in rural areas. *Journal of Rural Health, 13,* 6–13.

Teplin, L. A. (1984). Criminalizing mental disorder: The comparative arrest rate of the mentally ill. *American Psychologist, 39,* 794–803.

Teplin, L. A. (1985). The criminality of the mentally ill: A dangerous misconception. *American Journal of Psychiatry, 142,* 593–599.

Torrey, E. F., Erdman, K., Wolfe, S. M., & et al. (1990). *Care of the seriously mentally ill: A rating of state programs.* Washington, DC: Public Citizen Health Research Group and the National Alliance for the Mentally Ill.

Wolff, N., Diamond, R. J., & Helminiak, T. W. (1997). A new look at an old issue: People with mental illness and the law enforcement system. *Journal of Mental Health Administration, 24,* 152–165.

Physical and Sexual Assault History in Women with Serious Mental Illness: Prevalence, Correlates, Treatment, and Future Research Directions

Lisa A. Goodman, Stanley D. Rosenberg, Kim T. Mueser &
Robert E. Drake

This article appeared in the *Schizophrenia Bulletin*, 23(4), 1997, 685–696, and is reprinted with permission.

Lisa A. Goodman, Ph.D., is Assistant Professor, Department of Psychology, University of Maryland, College Park, MD. Stanley D. Rosenberg, Ph.D., is Professor of Psychiatry; Kim T. Mueser, Ph.D., is Associate Professor of Psychiatry and Community and Family Medicine; and Robert E. Drake, M.D., Ph.D., is Professor of Psychiatry, Dartmouth Medical School, Hanover, NH, and New Hampshire-Dartmouth Psychiatric Research Center, Hanover, NH.

An emerging body of research on the physical and sexual abuse of seriously mentally ill (SMI) women documents a high incidence and prevalence of victimization within this population. While causal links are not well understood, there is convergent evidence that victimization of SMI women is associated with increased symptom levels, HIV-related risk behaviors, and such comorbid conditions as homelessness and substance abuse. These abuse correlates may influence chronicity, service utilization patterns, and treatment alliance. This article reviews the research literature on the prevalence, symptomatic and behavioral correlates, and treatment of abuse among SMI women, particularly women with schizophrenia. Within each topic, we discuss relevant research findings, limitations of available studies, and key questions that remain unanswered. We also discuss mechanisms that may underlie the relationship between trauma and schizophrenia spectrum disorders. We conclude by outlining directions for future research in this area.

Over the past decade, a large body of empirical evidence has documented the high prevalence and devastating psychological effects of physical and sexual abuse of women. Only recently, however, have researchers investigated violent victimization of seriously mentally ill (SMI) women. This article reviews the emerging body of research literature on the prevalence, correlates, and treatment of physical and sexual assault among women with schizophrenia and other types of major mental illness. Under each of these topics, we will summarize current research findings on abuse in the female population as a whole, since this more general trauma literature provides a context for interpreting findings on SMI women. We also review within each topic the most relevant findings on abuse of women with severe mental illness, discussing the limitations of available studies and key questions that remain unanswered, and discuss mechanisms that may underlie the relationship between trauma and schizophrenia-spectrum disorders. Finally, we suggest directions for future research in this area.

This article is based on a complete review of those studies in which most respondents were diagnosed with an Axis I disorder and at least a significant portion were diagnosed with schizophrenia. We were unable to limit our review to studies of women with schizophrenia because too few published studies report exclusively on this group. The review excludes studies using outpatient samples that were not identified explicitly as severely or chronically mentally ill.

Our purposes are (1) to alert researchers and service providers to what is now known about the role of trauma in the lives of women who have schizophrenia and other serious mental illnesses and (2) to develop a research strategy for illuminating the relationship between trauma, the course of illness, and treatment of schizophrenia in women.

Prevalence of Physical and Sexual Victimization

Definitions

Throughout this article, *physical abuse* is defined as an act intended to produce severe pain or injury, including repeated slapping, kicking, biting, choking, burning, beating, or threatening with or using a weapon. *Sexual abuse* is defined as forcible touching of breasts or genitals or forcible intercourse, including anal, oral, or vaginal sex. Investigators generally define events occurring before either the 16th or the 18th birthday as *child abuse*.

Problems of Self-Report and Disclosure

As research on the prevalence of victimization becomes more sophisticated, two methodological concerns have been identified: overreporting and underreporting. Overreporting may be related to suggestion or possible secondary gain (Briere, 1992). With regard to underreporting, female victims of rape and domestic abuse often do not report such experiences because they feel ashamed, guilty, or fearful; because they wish to protect their perpetrators, with whom they may have ongoing relationships (Della Femina, Yaeger, & Lewis, 1990); because they are reluctant to raise or discuss unpleasant memories (Dill, Chu, & Grob, 1991); or because they fear such responses as horror, disbelief, denial, or outright rejection (Symonds, 1979). Additionally, many victims report periods of amnesia for assaults occurring in childhood (Briere & Conte, 1993; Feldman-Summers & Pope, 1994). Finally, victims may not label physical or sexual assaults as "abusive" (Berger, Knutson, Mehm, & Perkins, 1988; Cascardi, Mueser, DeGirolomo, & Murrin, 1996) and therefore fail to report them in response to questions about abuse per se.

Especially relevant to SMI women, accurate recall of events may be complicated by delusions or hallucinations, pharmacotherapy, or severe substance abuse, all of which affect memory, language, and cognition to varying degrees. With particular regard to schizophrenia, although a variety of cognitive deficits are characteristic of the disorder, memory impairments are among the most common (Goldman-Rakic, 1994; Saykin et al., 1991) and may result in the underreporting of traumatic events, even under specific questioning. Thus, assessing the abuse histories of SMI women, and those with schizophrenia in particular, may be especially difficult.

Prevalence of Violent Victimization in Community Samples of Women

In addition to the problems of overreporting and underreporting, accurate prevalence estimates of physical and sexual abuse of women in the general population are somewhat difficult to obtain because of a lack of comprehensive studies and of uniform definitions of physical and sexual assault or abuse (Koss et al., 1994). Nevertheless, data from the largest and most detailed community studies conducted to date suggest that rates of lifetime violent victimization of women are high. Among women, reported rates of adult physical abuse by an intimate range from 21% to 34% (Russell, 1982, 1986; Straus & Gelles, 1992; White & Koss, 1991). Reported rates of adult sexual abuse range from 14 to 25% (Kilpatrick, Saunders, Veronen, Best, & Von, 1987; National Victims Center, 1992; Russell, 1986; Sorenson, Stein, Siegel, Golding, & Burnam, 1987; Wyatt, 1992). Similarly, reported rates of child sexual abuse in the general female population range from 15 to 33% (Finkelhor, Hotaling, Lewis, & Smith, 1990; Russell, 1986; Saunders, Villeponteaux, Lipovsky, Kilpatrick, & Veronen, 1992; Wyatt, 1985). Finally, one of the few studies to document child physical abuse in a mixed-gender general community sample reported an incidence rate of 11% for parent-to-child abuse in the United States (Straus & Gelles, 1992; Wauchope & Straus, 1992).

Prevalence of Violent Victimization Among Women with SMI

Table 1 summarizes the findings of studies reporting on the prevalence of physical and sexual abuse among SMI women. In those studies that asked about lifetime abuse, between 51 and 97% of women report some form of physical or sexual abuse. In addition, a significant proportion of respondents were multiply traumatized. Cole (1988), using therapist reports, found that 12% of her inpatient sample disclosed having experienced three or more forms of abuse. Jacobson and Richardson (1987), relying on interviews, found that 18% of their inpatient sample reported three or more forms; and Goodman et al. (1995), also using interviews, found that 75% of their outpatient, episodically homeless sample had experienced at least three forms of abuse (Goodman, Dutton, & Harris, 1995; Jacobson & Richardson, 1987).

A number of substantive and methodological factors help explain the variation in these rates. First, definitions of abuse were not consistent across studies. Second, despite extensive research documenting that detailed and behaviorally specific questions are necessary to elicit accurate abuse information (Koss et al., 1994), in most of these studies, only a few general questions were asked about each type of abuse; in some, client records were the sole source of data. With the exception of one study (Bell, Taylor-Crawford, Jenkins, & Chalmers, 1988), those that interviewed respondents reported significantly higher rates than those that used charts or therapist ratings. Third, respondents in each of these studies were a heterogeneous group with regard to ethnicity, social class, age, and diagnosis—factors that may influence the epidemiology of violent victimization. For example, the two studies reporting the highest rates of each form of abuse (Davies-Netzley, Hurlburt, & Hough, 1996; Goodman et al., 1995) were based on samples of low-income, episodically homeless SMI women.

Despite the variations in definitions, methodologies, and study samples, some patterns do emerge from these data. First, those studies that asked more detailed questions tended to report higher prevalence rates. Second, these rates suggest that a majority of SMI women have experienced violent victimization at some point in the course of their lives. And third, it appears that a large proportion of women with a seri-

Table 1

Victimization prevalence among samples of seriously mentally ill women

Study characteristics			Study results						
Study	Sample	Methods	Overall abuse (%)	Child sexual abuse (%)	Child physical abuse (%)	Adult sexual abuse (%)	Adult physical abuse (%)	Child both (%)	Adult both (%)
Carmen et al. (1984)	122 female inpatients at discharge from university teaching hospital (sample included adolescents) [1] Diagnoses for male and female subjects (%): 51 affective disorder 18 psychoses 13 personality disorder 18 other	Chart review	53	—	—	—	—	—	—
Beck and van der Kolk (1987)	26 inpatient women, hospitalized at State hospital for ≥1 yr Diagnoses: 100% psychoses	Record review, staff interviews	—	46 (incest history)	—	—	—	—	—
Bryer et al. (1987)	66 female inpatients in private psychiatric hospital Diagnoses: not noted	Interview	72	44	38	34	44	59	58
Jacobson and Richardson (1987)	50 female inpatients at university-affiliated county hospital[1] Diagnoses for male and female subjects (%): 32 affective disorder 29 psychoses 29 personality or substance use disorder 10 other	Interview	81[2]	54	44	38	64	57[2]	67

(continued)

Table 1 (continued)

Study	Study characteristics		Study results						
	Sample	Methods	Overall abuse (%)	Child sexual abuse (%)	Child physical abuse (%)	Adult sexual abuse (%)	Adult physical abuse (%)	Child both (%)	Adult both (%)
Bell et al. (1988)	220 female outpatient or day-treatment clients at public community mental health center Diagnoses: not noted	Interview	51	—	—	—	—	—	—
Cole (1988)	254 female inpatients at discharge from university teaching hospital (sample included adolescents)[1] Diagnoses: not noted	Therapist report	62	26.3 (incest history)	36	21 (marital rape)	42	—	—
Craine et al. (1988)	105 female inpatients from 9 State hospitals Diagnoses (%): 41 schizophrenia 22 affective disorder 14 personality disorder 23 other	Interview	—	51	35	—	—	—	—
Rose et al. (1991)	39 female intensive case management clients at public community health center[1] Diagnoses: not noted	Interview	—	41 (incest history)	—	—	—	—	—

(continued)

Table 1 (continued)

Study	Sample	Methods	Study results						
			Overall abuse (%)	Child sexual abuse (%)	Child physical abuse (%)	Adult sexual abuse (%)	Adult physical abuse (%)	Child both (%)	Adult both (%)
Muenzenmaier et al. (1993)	78 outpatient women in State hospital-affiliated outpatient clinic Diagnoses (%): 57 schizophrenia or schizoaffective disorder 27 affective disorder 8 personality disorder 8 other	Interview	–	45	51	32	–	74	–
Goodman et al. (1995)	99 episodically homeless intensive case management clients at public community mental health center Diagnoses (%): 59 schizophrenia or schizoaffective disorder 16 personality disorder 14 affective disorder 11 other	Interview	97	65	87	76	87	92	92
Cascardi et al. (1996)	34 female inpatients who had at least 3-mo contact with relative or partner within the last year[l] Diagnoses: 100% Axis I	Interview	–	–	–	–	79.4 (within last year by partner or relative)	–	–

Table I (continued)

Study	Sample	Methods	Study results						
			Overall abuse (%)	Child sexual abuse (%)	Child physical abuse (%)	Adult sexual abuse (%)	Adult physical abuse (%)	Child both (%)	Adult both (%)
Cloitre et al. (1996)	409 female inpatients at urban private university psychiatric hospital Diagnoses: not noted	Interview	–	31	34	22	–	45	–
Davies-Netzley et al. (1996)	105 homeless women with severe mental illness living on the street or in shelters Diagnoses (%): 47 schizophrenia 22 bipolar disorder 31 major depression	Interview	–	55	60	–	–	77	–

1. Although male and female subjects were included in the sample, we have reported data obtained from female respondents only. Where we could not distinguish between male and female respondents, we did not report the statistic.

2. Although these statistics are for male and female subjects combined, the authors reported no significant differences in reported rates of abuse in these categories for male and female subjects.

ous mental disorder are victimized repeatedly in the course of their lives. What remains unclear, however, is whether serious mental illness itself is related to the elevated prevalence rates found in these studies, or whether such factors as poverty and substance abuse—conditions that often accompany severe mental illness—are responsible for the high rates of abuse reported.

Correlates of Physical and Sexual Victimization

Psychiatric Correlates of Abuse in Community Samples
Studies of community samples report a diffuse and overlapping set of symptoms and self-harming behaviors in women with trauma histories. Exposure to physical and sexual violence has been associated with posttraumatic stress disorder (PTSD) (Kemp, Green, Hovanitz, & Rawlings, 1995; National Victims Center, 1992), anxiety (Follingstad, Brennan, Hause, Polek, & Rutledge, 1991; Wirtz & Harrell, 1987), depression (Saunders, Hamberger, & Hovey, 1993; Sorenson & Golding, 1990), psychotic symptoms (Butler, Mueser, Sprock, & Braff, 1996; Mueser & Butler, 1987), personality disorders (Heard & Linehan, 1994; Herman, Perry, & van der Kolk, 1989), and dissociation (Briere & Runtz, 1988; Cole & Putnam, 1992). Commonly reported behavioral correlates include suicidal tendencies (Briere, 1992; Hilberman, 1980), risky sex and drug practices (Cunningham, Stiffman, Dore, & Earls, 1994; Zierler et al., 1991), and substance use disorders (Briere & Zaidi, 1989; Pribor & Dinwiddie, 1992). For a recent review of the literature on child sexual abuse, see Polusny and Follette (1995); for a review of the literature on the sequelae of adult abuse, see Koss et al. (1994) (Koss et al., 1994; Polusny & Follette, 1995).

The PTSD diagnosis—which includes symptoms involving reexperiencing of the trauma, arousal, and avoidance of stimuli related to the trauma—may be the most commonly reported and discussed consequence of a wide range of victimization experiences. It provides a broad framework within which many seemingly disparate symptoms can be incorporated, and it enables researchers and service providers to borrow from the rich body of literature on psychological trauma in general to understand and help women who have been physically or sexually abused. Recent modifications to the PTSD model have been proposed (see, e.g., Herman 1992) to account for the complex set of cognitions, affects, and symptoms that have been reported by victims of ongoing abuse, as opposed to those reported by victims of a single assault (Herman, 1992).

Symptomatic Correlates of Abuse in SMI Women

The few studies that have examined the relationship between abuse and symptoms among SMI women present a fairly consistent, though incomplete, picture. With two exceptions (Cascardi et al., 1996; Goodman, Dutton, & Harris, 1997), all published studies have focused on the symptomatic correlates of childhood rather than adult abuse. Beck and van der Kolk (1987) found that inpatient women with a history of childhood incest were significantly more likely than those without such a history to have sexual delusions, depressive symptoms, and major medical problems (Beck & van der Kolk, 1987). Similarly, Muenzenmaier et al. (1993) found that SMI female outpatients with a self-reported history of abuse in childhood had higher levels of both depressive and psychotic symptoms than those without such a history (Muenzenmaier, Meyer, Struening, & Ferber, 1993). Bryer et al. (1987) found that among a sample of female inpatients, reported sexual or physical abuse in childhood was significantly associated with somatization, interpersonal sensitivity, depression, anxiety, paranoid ideology, and psychoticism (Bryer, Nelson, Miller, & Krol, 1987). Also, those with both physical and sexual abuse in childhood reported higher levels of symptoms than those with just one type of abuse. Finally, Craine et al. (1988) found that 66% of a State hospital sample of women who reported being sexually abused as children met diagnostic criteria for PTSD, although none had received that diagnosis (Craine, Henson, Colliver, & MacLean, 1988). By contrast, however, Davies-Netzley et al. (1996) did not find a significant relationship between childhood physical or sexual abuse and PTSD (Davies-Netzley et al., 1996).

Finally, only one study (Ross et al. 1994) has investigated the relationship between reported child abuse (both physical and sexual) and types of symptoms within a sample of respondents (men and women, inpatient and outpatient) specifically diagnosed with schizophrenia (Ross, Anderson, & Clark, 1994). According to this study, respondents who reported a history of child abuse were also significantly more likely to report positive symptoms of schizophrenia, including ideas of reference, commenting voices, paranoid ideation, thought insertion, and visual hallucinations.

With regard to adult abuse, Cascardi et al. (1996) found that 40% of female inpatients met the criteria for PTSD in response to physical abuse experienced over the past year (Cascardi et al., 1996). Goodman et al. (1997) investigated the impact of dimensions of victimization across the lifespan, as opposed to child or adult abuse alone (Goodman et al., 1997). Their study found that frequency of violence across the lifespan, recency, and the addition of child sexual abuse to child physical abuse were associated with a broad range of psychiatric symptoms—including levels of depression, hostility, anxiety, dissociation, somatization, and PTSD.

While these studies provide important information and raise interesting questions for further work in this area, they are too few, too disparate, and too atheoretical to provide a well-grounded understanding of the relationship between trauma and symptoms among mentally ill women. More specifically, almost all of these studies, with the exceptions of Cascardi et al. (1996) and Goodman et al. (1997), focused primarily on the impact of child abuse, rather than on both child and adult abuse; thus, the differential impact of abuse during childhood and adulthood is unknown (Cascardi et al., 1996; Goodman et al., 1997). Second, most studies did not examine some of the mental health disturbances most commonly associated with trauma, such as dissociation and PTSD. With regard to PTSD in particular, although three studies showed a relationship between prior trauma and symptoms of PTSD, only two (Cascardi et al., 1996; Davies-Netzley et al., 1996) used complete enough measures to make definitive PTSD diagnoses. Third, with the exception of Ross et al. (1994), none of these studies addressed the question of whether and how trauma history is related to the exacerbation of diagnosis-specific symptoms, such as hallucinations or delusions (Ross et al., 1994). Despite these limitations, the results of these studies indicate that among SMI women, exposure to violence is associated with more severe symptoms overall.

Behavioral Correlates of Abuse in SMI Women

Few researchers have examined the relationship between physical and sexual assault and current behavioral disturbances in SMI women. One early exception was a study of inpatient men and women (Carmen, Rieker, & Mills, 1984), which found that compared with their nonabused counterparts, female inpatients with histories of child or adult abuse (either physical or sexual) were more likely to remain in the hospital longer, to direct their anger inwardly in a self-destructive fashion, and to have a past history of suicide attempts. Similarly, both Bryer et al. (1987) and Davies-Netzley et al. (1996) found that inpatients with histories of suicidal ideation, gestures, or attempts were more likely to have been abused in childhood (Bryer et al., 1987; Davies-Netzley et al., 1996). In particular, Davies-Netzley et al. (1996) found that women who had experienced physical and sexual abuse in childhood were just over 5 times more likely to have thoughts about suicide and 5.6 times more likely to have attempted suicide than women with no abuse histories (Davies-Netzley et al., 1996).

With regard to substance abuse, Beck and van der Kolk (1987) found that among women hospitalized for 1 year or longer, those with incest histories were significantly more likely to be substance abusers (Beck & van der Kolk, 1987). Similarly, Craine et al. (1988) found that among a sample of inpatients, child sexual abuse was generally associated with chemical dependence; and Goodman and Fallot (in press) found that among a sample of episodically homeless, mentally ill women, both child sexual abuse and child physical abuse were related to adult abuse of alcohol and cocaine (Craine et al., 1988; Goodman & Fallot, in press). Although these studies suggest that earlier trauma may be a risk factor for substance abuse in SMI women, the association between trauma and substance abuse in women with schizophrenia remains unclear. This would be an important area for future research, however, given the high rate of substance use disorders in people with schizophrenia (Cuffel, 1996; Regier et al., 1990).

Finally, two studies have examined the relationship between victimization and HIV-related risk behavior among SMI women. Although not focusing on risky behaviors, Craine et al. (1988) found that among inpatient women, child sexual abuse was associated with compulsive sexual behavior (Craine et al., 1988). Goodman and Fallot (in press) found that among homeless, mentally ill women, child sexual abuse was strongly associated with prostitution and marginally associated with knowingly having sexual relations with risky (i.e., HIV-positive or intravenous-drug using) partners (Goodman & Fallot, in press). While these latter data are quite preliminary, HIV-related risk behaviors are sufficiently common in women with serious mental disorders (Knox, Boaz, Friedrich, & Dow, 1994) that this issue should be investigated further.

Treatment of Trauma Correlates

General Treatment Models

In recent years, a wide variety of treatment strategies have been proposed to address PTSD and other syndromes related to trauma. Unfortunately, few have been subjected to rigorous outcome research. The few well-evaluated treatment protocols for survivors of violent victimization that do exist (e.g., Foa et al., 1994; Foa, Rothbaum, Riggs, & Murdock, 1991; Resick & Schnicke, 1992) emphasize cognitive-behavioral treatment strategies and encourage clients to expose themselves to memories and stimuli related to the traumatic event or events in order to decrease anxiety and related symptoms. However, researchers have generally excluded psychotic or substance-abusing women from participation in these protocols, so the suitability of these methods for an SMI population is untested.

Treatment of Trauma in SMI Women

There is currently a paucity of well-articulated and validated treatments for trauma effects in SMI women. However, some writers have suggested the need for such interventions, especially in light of the possible relationship between trauma and current difficulties accepting treatment. Past physical or sexual assault, particularly by a caregiver or partner, may lead to extreme distrust of service providers or even the belief that a supposed "helper" may actually be a potential assailant (Jacobson & Richardson, 1987). Additionally, current abuse may lead to an inability to keep appointments or engage in programs because of shame, fear of discovery, or the tight control of an abusive partner.

The association between trauma history and ability to form a therapeutic relationship in women with schizophrenia may be especially important considering the difficulties these women frequently experience with interpersonal relationships. It is possible that early trauma in women who develop schizophrenia interferes with the development of social adjustment, a potent predictor of outcome in schizophrenia (Mueser, Bellack, Morrison, & Wixted, 1990; Zigler & Glick, 1986). Following the onset of schizophrenia, poor relationship skills may contribute to a worse course of illness by interfering with both the ability to form therapeutic relationships with treatment providers and the development of social support networks among nonproviders which, in turn, may serve to buffer the psychological effects of stress (Alloway & Bebbington, 1987).

It is unclear., whether traditional, exposure-based trauma treatment interventions can be used or adapted for women with schizophrenia. Some women might experience substantial stress associated with recalling and focusing on disturbing memories. Such stress might lead to cognitive disorganization, thought disorder, and linguistic failure (Barch & Berenbaum, 1996; Haddock, Wolfenden, Lowens, Tarrier, & Bentall, 1995; Harvey & Serper, 1990), thus interfering with habituation to the feared stimuli. Furthermore, if unchecked, high stress could precipitate symptom relapse. A more graduated approach to extinguishing anxiety might be less stressful for women with schizophrenia, even if it is more time consuming.

Although some women with schizophrenia may benefit from a more gradual form of traditional exposure-based treatment, as with other groups of trauma survivors (Frueh, Mirabella, & Turner, 1995), some portion of this group either will be deemed too fragile to benefit from such treatment or will decline to participate. Thus, alternative interventions should be designed to meet the specific needs of women with schizophrenia. One potentially fruitful approach builds on accumulating research data that support the efficacy of social-learning approaches for individuals with schizophrenia (Penn & Mueser, 1996). Applied to trauma, such an approach might involve training women in specific skill areas related to interpersonal relationships.

For example, Harris (1996, 1997) has developed a weekly, 9- to 12-month psychosocial group intervention and accompanying treatment manual for physically or sexually victimized, SMI women (Harris, 1996, 1997). The intervention builds on a social skills training model to address difficulties in three domains likely to be affected by physical and sexual victimization: (1) intrapersonal skills, including self-knowledge, self-soothing, self-esteem, and self-trust; (2) interpersonal skills, including self-expression, social perception and labeling, self-protection, self-assertion, and relational mutuality; and (3) global skills, including identity formation, initiative taking, and problem solving (Harris & Fallot, 1996).

Hypothesized Relationships Between Traumatic Victimization and Schizophrenia

It is likely that trauma and symptoms in women diagnosed with schizophrenia are related in complex and reciprocal ways. To sort out causal patterns would require research using highly refined longitudinal designs, close observation, and careful measurement. However, the correlational studies that exist offer several hypotheses about causal relationships among key variables. First, given the high rates of trauma seen in SMI women, we hypothesize that schizophrenia is a risk factor for adult abuse. It seems likely that common cognitive and behavioral manifestations of schizophrenia—such as limited reality testing, impaired judgment, planning difficulties, and difficulty with social relationships—increase an individual's vulnerability to physical abuse or to coercive or exploitative sexual relationships (Fetter & Larson, 1990; Kelly et al., 1992).

Second and conversely, abuse may be viewed as a "stressor" that could either precipitate the onset of schizophrenia in vulnerable individuals or trigger relapses in women already diagnosed with schizophrenia. This hypothesis is compatible with the stress-vulnerability model of schizophrenia (Norman & Malla, 1993; Ventura, Nuechterlein, Lukoff, & Hardesty, 1989), which specifies that stressful life events exert a moderate effect on increasing schizophrenia patients' vulnerability to relapse. Physical and sexual assault are extremely stressful experiences. However studies of the link between stressful life events and schizophrenic relapse have yet to assess victimization history with adequate instruments and procedures.

Third, in some cases, abuse survivors may be misdiagnosed as having a schizophrenia-spectrum disorder, when a diagnosis of PTSD or a dissociative disorder may be more appropriate. This hypothesis has yet to be tested systematically. However, it is consistent with findings that the more extreme correlates of trauma reported in victimized women include paranoid or other delusions (Oruc & Bell, 1995) and that individuals with PTSD can present with both acute and chronic psychotic symptoms, including hallucinations, delusions, and bizarre behavior (Butler et al., 1996; Mueser & Butler, 1987; Waldfogel & Mueser, 1988). Furthermore, Carmen (1994) has observed that even in the absence of distinct hallucinations or delusions, the amnesia and dissociation that sometimes stem from early abuse may be mistaken for psychosis and may therefore be misdiagnosed and incorrectly treated (Carmen, 1994).

Finally, it is clear that traumatic abuse is also a major risk factor for several of the more severe comorbidities of schizophrenia: homelessness (Browne, 1993; Feitel, Margetson, Chamas, & Lipton, 1992), substance use disorder (Burnam et al., 1988), and HIV infection (Cunningham et al., 1994; Goodman & Fallot, in press). Thus, even if trauma does not directly exacerbate schizophrenia symptoms, it may well affect the course of the illness through these other routes.

Research Directions

Our emergent awareness of the scope and significance of the victimization of SMI women raises many questions and challenges for services researchers. Fully understanding and addressing the problems raised in this review require epidemiological studies, clinical research, and services research.

First, the extent and nature of victimization in this population require further investigation. To address this goal, measures will have to be developed that are reliable and valid for this particular population. This task will be complex because of the cognitive deficits common among SMI women. The reliability of these measures could be established with test-retest procedures to determine the extent to which self-reports vary with the mental status of the respondent. Assessment of a measure's validity will be much more difficult and may ultimately require researchers to seek some form of external corroboration (Krinsley, Gallagher, & Weathers, 1996).

New measures may need to be developed that better reflect the language and cultural constructions of violence held by those SMI women who are unable to take advantage of available educational opportunities and may be excluded from mainstream culture. To help potentially delusional respondents to attend and comprehend the questions, measures should be kept simple and concrete and should be administered by an interviewer rather than as paper-and-pencil questionnaires. Additionally, standard definitions and assessment procedures should be developed, and measures should ask about multiple forms of abuse within a particular sample in order to place one type of abuse within the context of lifespan victimization.

To tease out some of the confounds associated with both serious mental illness *and* victimization, prevalence studies should systematically examine differences among women based on ethnic group, class, geographic region, residential status (homeless or not), diagnoses, and levels of functioning.

Second, more thorough investigation of abuse correlates in women with schizophrenia is clearly needed. Studies should use comprehensive past and current trauma assessments and reliable, valid methods of diagnosis. Careful assessment will be needed to identify possible comorbid disorders, such as PTSD, in a population that may have overlapping and potentially masking symptoms associated with their primary psychiatric disorder.

Third, as with research on prevalence, such potential confounds as poverty, substance abuse, homelessness, and stigma—phenomena that co-occur with both victimization and serious mental illness—should be considered among theoretical formulations and choices of comparison groups or covariates to examine. Additionally, because so many SMI women appear to have suffered multiple types of trauma across their lifespan and because most have complex psychiatric histories, cross-sectional or retrospective research may be unable to detect the links between specific types of trauma and specific types of psychological effects. Prospective research could begin to identify such links, as well as some of the mechanisms by which traumatic events affect this population.

Fourth, trauma treatment models are needed to address the special needs of this population. Two approaches should be considered. First, the effectiveness of existing protocols could be evaluated for their usefulness for a population of SMI women. Second, new treatment models specifically designed for SMI women should be developed and tested. It is important to note, however, that specific treatment protocols are only one part of the picture. As Harris (1996) and Redner and Herder (1992) point out, program planners and clinicians must go beyond a single intervention to modify all aspects of an SMI client's milieu, if they are to address the multiple and complex consequences of abuse (Harris, 1996; Redner & Herder, 1992).

In conclusion, current research suggests an extremely high incidence and prevalence of violent victimization among women with schizophrenia and other major mental illnesses. While causal links are not well understood, there is convergent evidence that victimization of women with schizophrenia and other serious mental illnesses is related to symptom levels, risky behavior, and such comorbid conditions as homelessness and substance abuse. Left untreated, these abuse correlates may influence chronicity, service utilization patterns, and treatment alliance. Mental health providers should identify clients' abuse experiences and acknowledge the potentially complex relationships among abuse, symptom severity, and self-harming behaviors. Systematic empirical inquiry is also crucial for disentangling the causes and effects of abuse in this population, as well as for evaluating effective interventions.

References

Alloway, R., & Bebbington, P. (1987). The buffer theory of social support: A review of the literature. *Psychological Medicine, 17,* 91–108.

Barch, D. M., & Berenbaum, H. (1996). Language production and thought disorder in schizophrenia. *Journal of Abnormal Psychology, 105,* 81–88.

Beck, J. C., & van der Kolk, B. A. (1987). Reports of childhood incest and current behavior of chronically hospitalized psychotic women. *American Journal of Psychiatry, 144,* 1474–1476.

Bell, C. C., Taylor-Crawford, K., Jenkins, E. J., & Chalmers, D. (1988). Need for victimization screening in a black psychiatric population. *Journal of the National Medical Association, 80*(1), 41–48.

Berger, A., Knutson, J., Mehm, J., & Perkins, K. (1988). The self-report of punitive childhood experiences of young adults and adolescents. *Child Abuse and Neglect, 12,* 251–262.

Briere, J. (1992). *Child abuse trauma: Theory and treatment of the lasting effects.* Newbury Park, CA: Sage Publications.

Briere, J., & Conte, J. R. (1993). Self-reported amnesia for abuse in adults molested as children. *Journal of Traumatic Stress, 6*(1), 2212–2231.

Briere, J., & Runtz, M. (1988). Symptomatology associated with childhood sexual victimization in a nonclinical sample. *Child Abuse and Neglect, 12,* 51–59.

Briere, J., & Zaidi, L. (1989). Sexual abuse histories and sequelae in female psychiatric emergency room patients. *American Journal of Psychiatry, 146,* 1602–1606.

Browne, A. (1993). Family violence and homelessness: The relevance of trauma histories in the lives of homeless women. *American Journal of Orthopsychiatry, 63,* 370–384.

Bryer, J. B., Nelson, B. A., Miller, J. B., & Krol, P. A. (1987). Childhood sexual and physical abuse as factors in adult psychiatric illness. *American Journal of Psychiatry, 144*(11), 1426–1430.

Burnam, M. A., Stein, J. A., Golding, J. M., Siegel, J. M., Sorenson, S. B., Forsythe, A. B., & Telles, C. A. (1988). Sexual assault and mental disorders in a community population. *Journal of Consulting and Clinical Psychology, 56,* 843–850.

Butler, R. W., Mueser, K. T., Sprock, J., & Braff, D. L. (1996). Positive symptoms of psychosis in posttraumatic stress disorder. *Biological Psychiatry, 39*(10), 839–844.

Carmen, E. (1994). *Victim-to-patient-survivor process: Clinical perspectives.* Boston, MA: Presented at the Conference on Dare to Vision: Shaping the National Agenda for Women, Abuse, and Mental Health Services.

Carmen, E., Rieker, P. P., & Mills, T. (1984). Victims of violence and psychiatric illness. *American Journal of Psychiatry, 141*(3), 378–383.

Cascardi, M., Mueser, K. T., DeGirolomo, J., & Murrin, M. (1996). Physical aggression against psychiatric inpatients by family members and partners: A descriptive study. *Psychiatric Services, 47*(5), 531–533.

Cloitre, M., Tardiff. K., Marzuk, P., Leon, A., & Portera, L. (1996). Childhood abuse and subsequent sexual assault among female patients. *Journal of Traumatic Stress, 9*(3), 473–482.

Cole, C. (1988). Routine comprehensive inquiry for abuse: A justifiable clinical assessment procedure. *Clinical Social Work Journal, 16*, 33–42.

Cole, C., & Putnam, F. (1992). Effect on incest on self and social functioning: A developmental psychopathology perspective. *Journal of Consulting and Clinical Psychology, 60*, 174–184.

Craine, L. S., Henson, C. E., Colliver, J. A., & MacLean, D. G. (1988). Prevalence of a history of sexual abuse among female psychiatric patients in a state hospital system. *Hospital and Community Psychiatry, 39*(3), 300–304.

Cuffel, B. J. (1996). Comorbid substance use disorder: Prevalence, patterns of use, and course. In R. E. Drake & K. T. Mueser (Eds.), *Dual diagnosis of major mental illness and substance abuse: Recent research and implications* (pp. 93–105). San Francisco, CA: Jossey-Bass.

Cunningham, R. M., Stiffman, A. R., Dore, P., & Earls, F. (1994). The association of physical and sexual abuse with HIV risk behaviors in adolescence and young adulthood: Implications for public health. *Child Abuse and Neglect, 18*(3), 233–245.

Davies-Netzley, S., Hurlburt, M. S., & Hough, R. (1996). Childhood abuse as a precursor to homelessness for homeless women with severe mental illness. *Violence and Victims, 11*(2), 129–142.

Della Femina, D., Yaeger, D., & Lewis, D. (1990). Child abuse: Adolescent records vs. adult recall. *Child Abuse and Neglect, 14*(2), 227–231.

Dill, D., Chu, J., & Grob, M. (1991). The reliability of abuse history reports: A comparison of two inquiry formats. *Comprehensive Psychiatry, 32*(2), 166–169.

Feitel, B., Margetson, N., Chamas, J., & Lipton, C. (1992). Psychosocial background and behavioral and emotional disorders of homeless and runaway youth. *Hospital and Community Psychiatry, 43*, 155–159.

Feldman-Summers, S., & Pope, K. S. (1994). The experience of "forgetting" childhood abuse: A national survey of psychologists. *Journal of Consulting and Clinical Psychology, 62*(3), 636–639.

Fetter, M. S., & Larson, E. (1990). Preventing and treating human immunodeficiency virus infection in the homeless. *Archives of Psychiatric Nursing, 6,* 379–383.

Finkelhor, D., Hotaling, G., Lewis, I. A., & Smith, C. (1990). Sexual abuse in a national survey of adult men and women: Prevalence, characteristics, and risk factors. *Child Abuse and Neglect, 14,* 19–28.

Foa, E. B., Freund, B. F., Hembrec, E., Dancu, C. V., Franklin, M. E., Perry, K. J., Riggs, D. S., & Minar, C. (1994). *Efficacy of short-term behavioral treatment of PTSD in sexual and nonsexual assault victims.* Paper presented at the Annual Meeting of the Association for the Advancement of Behavioral Treatment, San Diego, CA.

Foa, E. B., Rothbaum, B. O., Riggs, D. S., & Murdock, T. B. (1991). Treatment of post-traumatic stress disorder in rape victims: A comparison between cognitive-behavioral procedures and counseling. *Journal of Consulting and Clinical Psychology, 59,* 715–723.

Follingstad, D. R., Brennan, A. F., Hause, E. S., Polek, D. S., & Rutledge, L. L. (1991). Factors moderating physical and psychological symptoms of battered women. *Journal of Family Violence, 6*(1), 81–95.

Frueh, B. C., Mirabella, R. F., & Turner, S. M. (1995). Exposure therapy for combat-related PTSD: Some practical considerations regarding patient exclusion. *Behavior Therapist, 18,* 190–191.

Goldman-Rakic, P. S. (1994). Working memory dysfunction in schizophrenia. *Journal of Neuropsychiatry and Clinical Neurosciences, 6,* 348–357.

Goodman, L. A., Dutton, M. A., & Harris, M. (1995). Physical and sexual assault prevalence among episodically homeless women with serious mental illness. *American Journal of Orthopsychiatry, 65*(4), 468–478.

Goodman, L. A., Dutton, M. A., & Harris, M. (1997). The relationship between dimensions of violent victimization and symptom severity among episodically homeless, mentally ill women. *Journal of Traumatic Stress, 10*(1), 51–70.

Goodman, L. A., & Fallot, R. (in press). The association of physical and sexual abuse with HIV risk behaviors and revictimization in episodically homeless, mentally ill women. *American Journal of Orthopsychiatry.*

Haddock, G., Wolfenden, M., Lowens, I., Tarrier, N., & Bentall, R. P. (1995). Effect of emotional salience on thought disorder inpatients with schizophrenia. *British Journal of Psychiatry, 167,* 618–620.

Harris, M. (1996). Treating sexual abuse trauma with dually diagnosed homeless women. *Community Mental Health Journal, 32*(4), 371–385.

Harris, M. (1997). *Trauma recovery skills development and enhancement.* Washington, DC: Unpublished manuscript, Community Connections.

Harris, M., & Fallot, R. (1996). *Domains of trauma recovery skills development and enhancement.* Washington, DC: Unpublished manuscript, Community Connections.

Harvey, P. D., & Serper, M. R. (1990). Linguistic and cognitive failures in schizophrenia: A multivariate analysis. *Journal of Nervous and Mental Disease, 178*, 487–493.

Heard, H. L., & Linehan, M. M. (1994). Dialectical behavior therapy: An integrated approach to the treatment of borderline personality disorder. *Journal of Psychotherapy Integration, 4*(1), 55–82.

Herman, J. L. (1992). *Trauma and recovery.* New York, NY: Basic Books.

Herman, J. L., Perry, J. C., & van der Kolk, B. A. (1989). Childhood trauma in borderline personality disorder. *American Journal of Psychiatry, 146,* 490–495.

Hilberman, E. (1980). Overview: The "wife-beater's wife" reconsidered. *American Journal of Psychiatry, 137,* 1336–1347.

Jacobson, A., & Richardson, B. (1987). Assault experiences of 100 psychiatric inpatients: Evidence of the need for routine inquiry. *American Journal of Psychiatry, 144,* 908–913.

Kelly, J. A., Murphy, D. A., Bahr, G. R., Brasfield, T. L., Davis, D. R., Hauth, A. C., Morgan, M. G., Stevenson, L. Y., & Eilers, M. K. (1992). AIDS/HIV risk behavior among the chronic mentally ill. *American Journal of Psychiatry, 149*(7), 886–889.

Kemp, A., Green, B. L., Hovanitz, C., & Rawlings, E. I. (1995). Incidence and correlates of posttraumatic stress disorder in battered women: Shelter and community samples. *Journal of Interpersonal Violence, 10*(1), 43–55.

Kilpatrick, D. G., Saunders, B. E., Veronen, L. J., Best, C. L., & Von, J. M. (1987). Criminal victimization: Lifetime prevalence, reporting to police, and psychological impact. *Crime and Delinquency, 33,* 479–489.

Knox, M. D., Boaz, T. L., Friedrich, M. A., & Dow, M. G. (1994). HIV risk factors for persons with serious mental illness. *Community Mental Health Journal, 30*(6), 551–564.

Koss, M. P., Goodman, L. A., Browne, A., Fitzgerald, L. F., Keita, G. P., & Russo, N. F. (1994). *No safe haven: Male violence against women at home, at work, and in the community.* Washington, DC: American Psychological Association Press.

Krinsley, K. E., Gallagher, J. G., & Weathers, F. W. (1996). *The development of a trauma history protocol: Defining and assessing reliability and validity.* Jerusalem, Israel: Paper presented at the Second World Conference of the International Society for Traumatic Stress Studies.

Muenzenmaier, K., Meyer, I., Struening, E., & Ferber, J. (1993). Childhood abuse and neglect among women outpatients with chronic mental illness. *Hospital and Community Psychiatry, 44*(7), 666–670.

Mueser, K. T., Bellack, A. S., Morrison, R. L., & Wixted, J. T. (1990). Social competence in schizophrenia: Premorbid adjustment, social skill, and domain of functioning. *Journal of Psychiatric Research, 24,* 51–63.

Mueser, K. T., & Butler, R. W. (1987). Auditory hallucinations in chronic combat-related posttraumatic stress disorder. *American Journal of Psychiatry, 144,* 299–302.

National Victims Center. (1992). *Rape in America: A report to the nation.* Arlington, VA: The Center.

Norman, R. M. G., & Malla, A. K. (1993). Stressful life events and schizophrenia: I. A review of the research. *British Journal of Psychiatry, 162,* 161–166.

Oruc, L., & Bell, P. (1995). Multiple rape trauma followed by delusional pasitosis: A case report from the Bosnian war. *Schizophrenia Research, 16,* 173–174.

Penn, D. L., & Mueser, K. T. (1996). Research update on psychosocial treatment of schizophrenia. *American Journal of Psychiatry, 153,* 607–617.

Polusny, M., & Follette, V. (1995). Long-term correlates of child sexual abuse: Theory and review of the empirical literature. *Applied and Preventive Psychology,* 143–166.

Pribor, E. F., & Dinwiddie, S. H. (1992). Psychiatric correlates of incest in childhood. *American Journal of Psychiatry, 149*(1), 52–56.

Redner, L. L., & Herder, D. D. (1992). Case management's role in effecting appropriate treatment for persons with histories of childhood sexual trauma. *Psychosocial Rehabilitation Journal, 15*(3), 37–45.

Regier, D. A., Farmer, M. E., Rae, D. S., Locke, B. Z., Keith, S. J., Judd, L. L., & Goodwin, F. K. (1990). Comorbidity of mental disorders with alcohol and other drug abuse. *Journal of the American Medical Association, 264,* 2511–2518.

Resick, P. A., & Schnicke, M. K. (1992). Cognitive processing therapy for sexual assault victims. *Journal of Consulting and Clinical Psychology, 60,* 748–756.

Rose, S. M., Peabody, C. G., & Stratigeas, B. (1991). Undetected abuse among intensive case management clients. *Hospital and Community Psychiatry, 42*(5), 499–503.

Ross, C. A., Anderson, G., & Clark, P. (1994). Childhood abuse and the positive symptoms of schizophrenia. *Hospital and Community Psychiatry, 45*(5), 489–491.

Russell, D. E. H. (1982). The prevalence and incidence of forcible rape and attempted rape of females. *Victimology: An International Journal, 7,* 81–93.

Russell, D. E. H. (1986). *The secret trauma: Incest in the lives of girls and women.* New York, NY: Basic Books.

Saunders, B. E., Villeponteaux, L. A., Lipovsky, J. A., Kilpatrick, D. G., & Veronen, L. J. (1992). Child sexual assault as a risk factor for mental health disorders among women: A community sample. *Journal of Interpersonal Violence, 7,* 189–204.

Saunders, D. G., Hamberger, L. K., & Hovey, M. (1993). Indicators of woman abuse based on a chart review at a family practice center. *Archives of Family Medicine, 2,* 537–543.

Saykin, A. J., Gur, R. C., Gur, R. E., Mozley, P. D., Mozley, L. H., Resick, S. M., Kester, D. B., & Stafiniak, P. (1991). Neuropsychological functioning in schizophrenia: Selective impairment in memory and learning. *Archives of General Psychiatry, 48,* 618–624.

Sorenson, S. B., & Golding, J. M. (1990). Depressive sequelae of recent criminal victimization. *Journal of Traumatic Stress, 3,* 337–350.

Sorenson, S. B., Stein, J. A., Siegel, J. M., Golding, J. M., & Burnam, M. A. (1987). Prevalence of adult sexual assault: The Los Angeles epidemiologic catchment area study. *American Journal of Epidemiology, 126,* 1154–1164.

Straus, M. A., & Gelles, R. J. (1992). How violent are American families? Estimates from the National Family Violence Resurvey and other studies. In M. A. Straus & R. J. Gelles (Eds.), *Physical violence in American families: Risk factors and adaptations to violence in 8,145 families* (pp. 95–127). New Brunswick, NJ: Transaction Publishers.

Symonds, A. (1979). Violence against women: The myth of masochism. *American Journal of Psychotherapy, 33*(2), 161–173.

Ventura, J., Nuechterlein, K. H., Lukoff, D., & Hardesty, J. P. (1989). A prospective study of stressful life events and schizophrenic relapse. *Journal of Abnormal Psychology, 98,* 407–411.

Waldfogel, S., & Mueser, K. T. (1988). Another case of chronic PTSD with auditory hallucinations. *American Journal of Psychiatry, 145,* 1314.

Wauchope, B. A., & Straus, M. A. (1992). Physical punishment and physical abuse of American children: Incidence rates by age, gender, and occupational class. In M. A. Straus & R. J. Gelles (Eds.), *Physical violence in American families: Risk factors and adaptations to violence in 8,145 families* (pp. 133–143). New Brunswick, NJ: Transaction Publishers.

White, J. W., & Koss, M. P. (1991). Courtship violence: Incidence in a national sample of higher education students. *Violence and Victims, 6,* 247–256.

Wirtz, P. W., & Harrell, A. V. (1987). Assaultive versus nonassaultive victimization: A profile analysis of psychological response. *Journal of Interpersonal Violence, 2,* 264–277.

Wyatt, G. E. (1985). The sexual abuse of Afro-American and White-American women in childhood. *Child Abuse and Neglect, 9,* 507–519.

Wyatt, G. E. (1992). The sociocultural context of African American and White American women's rape. *Journal of Social Issues, 48,* 77–92.

Zierler, S., Feingold, L., Laufer, D., Velentgas, P., Krantrowitz-Gordon, I., & Mayer, K. (1991). Adult survivors of childhood sexual abuse and subsequent risk of HIV infection. *American Journal of Public Health, 81,* 572–575.

Substance Misuse, Psychiatric Disorder, and Violent and Disturbed Behaviour

Michael Soyka

This article was originally published in the *British Journal of Psychiatry*, (2000), 176, 345–350 and is reprinted with permission.

Michael Soyka, M.D., Psychiatric Hospital, University of Munich, NuBbaumstrasse 7, 80336 Munich, Germany.

Background: Epidemiological studies suggest schizophrenia and substance misuse to be associated with a higher rate of violence and crime. Aims: The literature was evaluated to assess whether people with schizophrenia who use substances have an increased risk for violence and disturbed behaviour. Method: A detailed Medline analysis was performed and relevant studies were reviewed. Results: A large number of studies have linked substance misuse in schizophrenia with male gender, high incidence of homelessness, more pronounced psychotic symptoms, non-adherence with medication, poor prognosis, violence and aggression. The latter has been proved by clinical, epidemiological and longitudinal prospective studies of unselected birth cohorts. The increased risk for aggression and violent acts cannot be interpreted only as a result of poor social integration. Male gender, more severe psychopathology, a primary antisocial personality, repeated intoxications and non-adherence with treatment are important confounding variables. Conclusion: Substance misuse has been shown consistently to be a significant risk factor for violence and disturbed behaviour. Future research should try to evaluate possible pharmacological and psychosocial treatment approaches.

Epidemiological studies repeatedly have shown elevated rates of violence in people with mental disorder (Steuve & Link, 1997; Swanson et al., 1990). This is especially true for individuals who had been treated as psychiatric inpatients when they were adolescents (Kjelsberg & Dahl, 1998). Violent and aggressive acts committed by psychiatric patients have attracted psychiatric and public attention for a long time. Over the past decades a number of prominent individuals have been attacked or killed by people with a psychosis or other mental disorders, including ex-Beatle John Lennon, former US president Reagan and the German top politicians Oscar Lafontaine and Wolfgang Schaueble who were both seriously wounded in the early 1990s. Although these cases may be spectacular, violence and aggression displayed by the mentally ill is usually directed against partners or family members, rather than others (Danielson et al., 1998). There is little evidence of an increasing number of violent acts made by patients with psychosis over time (Taylor & Gunn, 1999), but the literature suggests that patients with major mental disorders have an increased risk for committing such acts compared with the general population (Coid, 1996; Modestin & Ammann, 1996); this is especially the case for schizophrenia. Wallace et al. (1998) reported that 7.2% of men convicted of homicide had been treated for schizophrenia before, and similar findings of 5 to 11% have been found in other studies (Eronen et al., 1996a,b; Häfner & Böker, 1992; Taylor & Gunn, 1984). As Wallace et al. (1998) stated, this means that the present data indicate that men with schizophrenia have a risk that is 5-18 times higher than that of the general population. This cannot only be attributed to social factors. The increased risk, especially for psychotic illness, is diminished but persists when demographic factors are taken into account (Marzuk, 1996). Psychiatric and forensic research at present tries to identify not only high-risk groups for committing violent acts but also individual variables and symptoms that can be linked to violence and aggression and may be considered for prevention. One of these covariables might be substance use. There is increasing evidence for substance misuse being a major risk factor for violence and disturbed behaviour per se (Pernanen, 1991) but also in individuals with major psychiatric disorders, especially schizophrenia (Mullen, 1997; Scott et al., 1998; Smith & Hucker, 1994; Soyka et al., 1993; Wessely, 1997). The major studies conducted to elucidate the inter-relationship between substance misuse and major mental disorders will be discussed here.

Substance Misuse in Schizophrenia

Clinical Studies
The comorbidity of schizophrenia and substance misuse has attracted considerable attention in recent years (Mueser et al., 1992a; Soyka et al., 1993; Smith & Hucker, 1994). A review of Mueser et al. (1990) on 32 studies published so far showed lifetime prevalence esti-

mates of: 12.3 to 50% for alcohol misuse and/or dependence; 12.5 to 35.8% for cannabis misuse; 11.3 to 31% for misuse/dependence of stimulants; 5.7 to 15.2% for hallucinogens; 3.5 to 11.3% for sedatives; and 2 to 9% for opioids. The latter phenomenon, which is a comparatively low rate of opioid dependence compared with other substances of misuse, has been reported consistently in the literature. More recent studies have shown even higher prevalence estimates for substance misuse in schizophrenia (Cuffel, 1992). High prevalence estimates for substance misuse have been reported not only in North America but also in Europe (Soyka et al., 1993) and Australia, for which Fowler et al. (1998) reported 6-month and lifetime prevalences of 26.8% and 59.8%, respectively, for substance use in schizophrenia.

Is Substance Misuse in Schizophrenia Increasing?

It is a matter of debate whether substance abuse in schizophrenia is really increasing over time (Cuffel, 1992). A recent study of Boutros et al. (1998) has linked a rapid increase in new admissions with schizophrenia to Connecticut State Hospitals to an increase in drug-related admissions. For first-episode psychosis, prevalence rates with schizophrenia and alcohol dependency was 9.5-fold. One-fifth of male subjects with schizophrenia were already dependent on alcohol ($n = 11$) before the age of 27 years and they were seven times more likely to commit a violent crime than other patients with schizophrenia. The authors pointed out that these findings greatly exceed other figures reported in the literature (Eronen et al., 1996a; Lindquist & Allebeck, 1989; Swanson et al., 1990).

Reasons for Violence

The reasons for violence and aggression, especially among dual-diagnosis patients, are a matter of debate because male gender, more severe psychopathology, early onset of psychosis, a primary antisocial personality, social class, employment status, poor insight and non-adherence to treatment are possible important confounding variables, among others. Also, Swartz et al. (1998), Smith (1989) and Bartels et al. (1991) had already demonstrated a significant relationship between medication nonadherence and violent acts. Interestingly, demographic factors have not been found to be reliable in identifying high-risk individuals in clinical practice (Taylor & Monahan, 1996). Persecutory delusions seem to be of special relevance for violence in schizophrenia (Nestor et al., 1995). Psychostimulants and cocaine especially were found to provoke or worsen psychotic symptomatology (Dixon et al., 1991). Also, poor neuroleptic response in patients with a history of psychogenetic drug use has been postulated. Junginger et al. (1998) stated that although delusional motivation of violence is rare, a moderate risk exists that delusions will motivate violence at some time during the course of a violent patient's illness. The role of intoxication should also be emphasized (Häfner & Böker, 1992).

Discussion

Identifying Patients at Risk

There is substantial evidence for substance misuse being a major risk factor for violence and aggression in patients with major mental disorder, especially schizophrenia. Even so, it is frequently overlooked or poorly documented. Research should move on now to predominantly longitudinal studies to identify risk factors that could have clinical utility for anticipating violent behaviour (Smith & Hucker, 1994; Steadman et al., 1998). Antisocial personality traits, the importance of intoxication, exacerbation of psychotic symptoms, social factors and treatment non-adherence may be among them.

The next step will be the development of risk management strategies and the evaluation of treatment in people with dual-diagnosis schizophrenia and violent offenders. As stated above, most authors agree that substance misuse in schizophrenia is associated not only with violence, but also with a number of other problems, including poor treatment adherence, an increased suicide risk and increased rates of hospital admissions and HIV infection.

Treatment Perspectives

Pharmacological interventions. Possible pharmacotherapeutic approaches in dual-diagnosis schizophrenia have been discussed in detail elsewhere (Soyka, 1996). Key problems are choice of neuroleptic agent and dosage, drug interactions, management of side effects, possible role of atypical neuroleptics, antidepressant treatment and relapse prevention. Although few studies have been conducted on this topic, any strategy to reduce psychotic relapse and minimize the risk for side effects of antipsychotic treatment, including the use of atypical neuroleptics, should be advocated. Alcohol dependency in particular, but also cannabis, were linked to increased rates of tardive dyskinesia. Some authors feel that substance misuse may be explained as a form of self-medication to improve psychopathology (depression, anhedonia, negative symptoms) or to ameliorate the side effects of neuroleptic treatment. Pharmacological interactions may also be of importance. Serum levels of neuroleptics (fluphenazine) were found to be decreased in those suffering from schizophrenia and alcohol misuse. A relative neuroleptic refractoriness and a cannabis-neuroleptic antagonism were postulated. Although the antipsychotic dose given to dual-diagnosis patients did not differ from that used for patients with simple schizophrenia, the topic deserves specific attention (for a review, see Soyka, 1996). Little is known about the effect of new anticraving drugs such as acamprosate or naltrexone in dual-diagnosis schizophrenia but they should be looked at in more detail.

Psychosocial interventions. In which facilities should patients with dual-diagnosis schizophrenia be treated—more in the psychiatry or the addiction section of psychiatry, or both? Scott et al. (1998) suggested strengthening links between general adult and addiction services, or introducing special services for dual-diagnosis patients (Johnson, 1997) may be a possible strategy. A number of both inpatient and outpatient treatment models for dual-diagnosis schizophrenia have been proposed (Evans & Sullivan, 1990) but there is little catamnestic evidence for the efficacy of special treatment models. Even so, this is where the future for these patients lies.

References

Allebeck, P., Adamsson, C., Engström, A., et al. (1993). Cannabis and schizophrenia: a longitudinal study of cases treated in Stockholm County. *Acta Psychiatrica Scandinavica, 88,* 21–24.

Andréasson, S., Allebeck, P., Engström, A., et al. (1987). Cannabis and schizophrenia: a longitudinal study of Swedish conscripts. *Lancet, ii,* 1483–1486.

Andréasson, S., Allebeck, P., & Rydberg, U. (1989) Schizophrenia in users and nonusers of cannabis: a longitudinal study in Stockholm County. *Acta Psychiatrica Scandinavica, 79,* 505–510.

Arndt, S., Tyrell, G., Flaum, M., et al. (1992).. Comorbidity of substance abuse and schizophrenia: the role of pre-morbid adjustment. *Psychological Medicine, 22,* 379–388.

Bartels, S. S. J., Drake, R. E., Wallach, M. A., et al. (1991). Characteristic hostility in schizophrenic Outpatients. *Schizophrenia Bulletin, 17,* 163–171.

Berkson, J. (1949) Limitations of the application of four-fold tables to hospital data. *Biological Bulletin, 2,* 47–53.

Boutros, M. N., Bowers, M. B. & Quinlan, D. (1998). Chronological association between increases in drug abuse and psychosis in Connecticut State Hospitals. *Journal of Neuropsychiatry and Clinical Neuroscience, 10,* 48–54.

Cantwell, R., Brewin, J., Glazebrook, C., et al. (1999). Prevalence of substance misuse in first-episode psychosis. *British Journal of Psychiatry 174,* 150–153.

Coid, J.W (1996). Dangerous patients with mental illness: increased risks warrant new policies, adequate resources, and appropriate legislation. *British Medical Journal, 312,* 965–966.

Cuffel, B. J. (1992). Prevalence estimates of substance abuse in schizophrenia and their correlates. *Journal of Nervous and Mental Disease, 180,* 589–592.

Cuffel, B. J., Shumway, M., Chouljian,T. L., et al. (1994). A longitudinal study of substance use and community violence in schizophrenia. *Journal of Nervous and Mental Disease, 182,* 704–708.

Danielson, K. K., Moffit, T. E., Caspi, A., et al. (1998). Comorbidity between abuse of and adult and *DSM-III-R* mental disorders: evidence from an epidemiological study. *American Journal of Psychiatry, 155,* 131–133.

DeQuardo, J. R., Carpenter, C. F. & Tandon, R. (1994). Patterns of substance abuse in schizophrenia: nature and significance. *Journal of Psychiatric Research, 28,* 267–275.

Dixon, I., Haas, G., Weiden, P. J., et al. (1991). Drug abuse in schizophrenic patients: clinical correlates and reasons for use. *American Journal of Psychiatry, 148,* 224–230

Endicott, J., Spitzer, R., Fleiss, J., et al. (1976). The global assessment scale: a procedure for measuring; overall severity of psychiatric disturbances. *Archives of General Psychiatry, 33,* 766–771.

Eronen, M., Tiihonen, J. & Hakola, P. (1996a). Schizophrenia and homicidal behaviour. *Schizophrenia Bulletin, 22,* 83–89.

Eronen, M., Hakola, P. & Tiihonen, J. (1996b). Mental disorders and homicidal behaviour in Finland. *Archives of General Psychiatry, 53,* 497–501.

Evans, K. & Sullivan, J. M. (1990). *Dual diagnosis—Counseling the mentally ill substance abuser.* New York: Guilford.

Fowler, I. L., Carr, V. C., Carter, N.T., et al. (1998). Patterns of current and lifetime substance use in schizophrenia. *Schizophrenia Bulletin, 24,* 443–455.

Häfner, H. & Böker, W. (1992). *Crimes of violence by mentally abnormal offenders.* Cambridge: Cambridge University Press.

Hambrecht, M. & Häfner, H. (1996). Substance abuse and the onset of schizophrenia. *Biological Psychiatry, 40,* 1155–1163.

Hodgins, S. (1992). Mental disorder, intellectual deficiency, and crime: evidence from a birth cohort. *Archives of General Psychiatry, 49,* 476–483.

Hodgins, S., Mednick, S. A., Brennan, P. A., et al. (1996). Mental disorder and crime: evidence from a Danish cohort. *Archives of General Psychiatry 53,* 489–496.

Janowsky, D. S., El.-Yousef, M. K., Davis, J. M., et al. (1973). Provocation of schizophrenic symptoms by intravenous administration of methylphenidate. *Archives of General Psychiatry, 28*, 185–191.

Johnson, S. (1997). Dual diagnosis of severe mental illness and substance misuse: a case for specialist services? *British Journal of Psychiatry, 171*, 205–208.

Junginger, J., Parks-Levy, J. & McGuire, L. (1998). Delusions and symptom-consistent violence. *Psychiatric Services, 49*, 218–220.

Kirkpatrick, B., Amador, X. F., Flaunn, M., et al. (1996) The deficit syndrome in the *DSM–IV* field trial: alcohol and other drug abuse. *Schizophrenia Research, 20*, 69–77.

Kjelsberg, E. & Dahl, A. A. (1998). High delinquency, disability and mortality— A register study of former adolescent psychiatric in-patients. *Acta Psychiatrica Scandinavica, 98*, 34–40.

Liberman, R. P., Mueser, K. T., Wallace, C. J., et al. (1986). Training skills in the psychiatrically disabled: learning coping and competence. *Schizophrenia Bulletin, 12*, 631–647.

Lieberman, J. A., Kane, J. M. & Alvir, J. (1987). Provocative tests with psycho stimulant drugs in schizophrenia. *Psychopharmacology, 91*, 415–433.

Lindquist, P. & Allebeck, P. (1989) Schizophrenia and assaultive behavior: the role of alcohol and drug abuse. *Acta Psychiatrica Scandinavica, 82*, 191–195.

Linszen, D. H., Dingemans, P. M. & Lenior, M. E. (1994). Cannabis abuse and the course of recent-onset schizophrenic disorders. *Archives of General Psychiatry, 51*, 273–279.

Marzuk, P. M. (1996). Violence, crime and mental illness: how strong a link? *Archives of General Psychiatry, 53*, 481–486.

Modestin, J. & Ammann, R. (1996). Mental disorder and criminality: male schiz-ophrenia. *Schizophrenia Bulletin, 22*, 69–82.

Mueser, K. T., Yarnold, P. R., Levinson, D. F., et al. (1990). Prevalence of sub-stance abuse in schizophrenia: demographic and clinical correlates. *Schizophrenia Bulletin, 16*, 31–56.

Mueser, K. T., Bellack, A. S. & Blanchard, J. J. (1992a). Comorbidity of schizo-phrenia and substance abuse: implications for treatment. *Journal of Consulting and Clinical Psychology, 60*, 845–856.

Mueser, K. T., Drake, R. E. & Wallach, M. A. (1998) Dual diagnosis: a review of etiological theories. *Addictive Behaviors, 23*, 717–734.

Mullen, P. E. (1997). A reassessment of the link between mental disorder and violent behavior, and its implications for clinical practice. *Australian and New Zealand Journal of Psychiatry, 31*, 3–11.

Nestor, P. G., Haycock, J., Doiron, S., et al. (1995). Lethal violence and psy-chosis: a clinical profile. *Bulletin of American Academy of Psychiatry and the Law, 23*, 331–334.

Pernanen, K. (1991). *Alcohol in human violence.* New York: Guilford Press.

Räsänen, P., Tiihonen, J., Isohanni, M., et al. (1998). Schizophrenia, alcohol abuse, and violent behavior: a 26-year followup study of an unselected birth cohort. *Schizophrenia Bulletin, 24,* 437–441.

Regier, D. A., Farmer, M. E., Rae, D. S., et al. (1990). Comorbidity of mental disorders with alcohol and other drug abuse: results from the epidemiologic catchment area (ECA) study. *Journal of the American Medical Association, 264,* 2511–2518.

Rice, M. E. & Harris, T. (1995). Psychopathy, schizophrenia, alcohol abuse, and violent recidivism. *International Journal of Law and Psychiatry, 18,* 333–342.

Scheller-Gilkey, G., Lewine, R. R. J., Caudle, J., et al. (1999). Schizophrenia, substance use, and brain morphology. *Schizophrenia Research, 35,* 113–120.

Scott, H., Johnson, S., Menezes, R, et al. (1998). Substance misuse and risk of aggression and offending among the severely mentally ill. *British Journal of Psychiatry, 172,* 345–350.

Serper, M. R., Alpert, M., Richardson, N. A., et al. (1995). Clinical effects of recent cocaine use on patients with acute schizophrenia. *American Journal of Psychiatry, 152,*1464–1469.

Smith, J. & Hucker, S. (1994). Schizophrenia and substance abuse. *British Journal of Psychiatry, 165,* 13–21.

Smith, L. D. (1989). Medication refusal and the rehospitalized mentally ill inmate. *Hospital and Community Psychiatry, 40,* 491–496.

Soyka, M. (1994). Substance abuse and dependency as a risk factor for delinquency and violent behavior in schizophrenic patients—how strong is the evidence? *Journal of Clinical and Forensic Medicine, 1,* 3–7.

Soyka, M. (1996). Dual diagnosis in patients with schizophrenia: issues in pharmacological treatment. *CNS Drugs, 6,* 414–425.

Soyka, M., Albus, M., Finelli, A., et al. (1993). Prevalence of alcohol and drug abuse in schizophrenic inpatients. *European Archives of Psychiatry and Clinical Neuroscience, 242,* 362–372.

Steadman, H. J., Mulvey, E. P., Monahan, J., et al. (1998). Violence by people discharged from acute psychiatric inpatient facilities and by others in the same neighborhoods. *Archives of General Psychiatry, 55,* 393–401.

Strakowski, S. M., Tohen, M., Stoll, A. L., et al. (1993). Comorbidity in psychosis at first hospitalization. *American Journal of Psychiatry, 150,* 752–757.

Steuve, A. & Link, B. (1997). Violence and psychiatric disorders: Results from an epidemiologic study in Israel. *Psychiatry Quarterly, 68,* 327–342.

Swanson, J., Holtzer, C., Ganju, V., et al. (1990). Violence and psychiatric disorder in the community. Evidence from the Epidemological Catchment Area Surveys. *Hospital and Community Psychiatry, 41,* 761-770.

Swartz, M. S. Swanson, J. W., Hiday, V. A., et al. (1998). Violence and severe mental illness. The effects of substance abuse and nonadherence to medication. *American Journal of Psychiatry, 155,* 226–231.

Taylor, P. J., & Gunn, J. (1984). Violence and psychosis: I. The risk of violence among psychotic men. *British Medical Journal, 288,* 1945–1949.

Taylor, P. J., & Gunn, J. (1999). Homicides by people with mental illness: Myth and reality. *British Journal of Psychiatry, 174,* 9–14.

Taylor, P. J., & Monahan, J. (1996). Dangerous patients or dangerous diseases? *British Medical Journal, 312,* 967–969.

Wallace, C., Mullen, P., Burgess, P., et al. (1998). Serious criminal offending and mental disorders. *British Journal of Psychiatry, 172,* 477–484.

Wessely, S. (1997). The epidemiology of crime, violence, and schizophrenia. *British Journal of Psychiatry, 170 (suppl 32),* 8–11.